Colombia

San Andrés & Providencia p169

Caribbean Coast p119

Boyacá, Santander & Norte de Santander p81

Pacific Coast p259

Medellín & Zona Cafetera p183

Bogotá p39

Los Llanos p273

Cali & Southwest Colombia p227

Amazon Basin p281

Jade Bremner, Alex Egerton, Anna Kaminski,
Tom Masters, Kevin Raub, Brendan Sainsbury

PLAN YOUR TRIP

Welcome to Colombia ... 4
Highlights Map ... 6
Colombia's Top Experiences ... 8
Need to Know ... 18
Month by Month ... 20
Itineraries ... 22
Colombia Outdoors ... 28
Regions at a Glance ... 34

JESSE KRAFT / EYEEM/GETTY IMAGES ©

CARTAGENA P122

ALLEN CRAIG SCHLOSSMAN/LONELY PLANET IMAGES ©

FERIA DE LAS FLORES P190

ON THE ROAD

BOGOTÁ ... 39
Around Bogotá ... 77

BOYACÁ, SANTANDER & NORTE DE SANTANDER ... 81
Boyacá ... 83
Villa de Leyva ... 83
Around Villa de Leyva ... 89
Santuario de Iguaque ... 91
Sogamoso ... 92
Monguí ... 92
Sierra Nevada del Cocuy ... 94
Santander ... 100
San Gil ... 100
Barichara ... 104
Guane ... 107
Cañon del Chicamocha ... 108
Bucaramanga ... 108
Guadalupe ... 112
Norte de Santander ... 114
Pamplona ... 114
Playa de Belén ... 116

CARIBBEAN COAST ... 119
Cartagena & Around ... 122
Cartagena ... 122
Islas del Rosario ... 136
Playa Blanca ... 138
Volcán de Lodo El Totumo ... 138
Northeast of Cartagena ... 138
Santa Marta ... 139
Minca ... 144
Taganga ... 147
Parque Nacional Natural Tayrona ... 148
Palomino ... 150
Ciudad Perdida ... 152
La Guajira Peninsula ... 155
Riohacha ... 156
Cabo de la Vela ... 157
Punta Gallinas ... 159
Valledupar ... 159
Mompós ... 160
Southwest of Cartagena ... 163
Tolú ... 163
Islas de San Bernardo ... 164
Capurganá & Sapzurro ... 165

SAN ANDRÉS & PROVIDENCIA ... 169
San Andrés ... 170
Providencia ... 176

MEDELLÍN & ZONA CAFETERA ... 183
Medellín ... 186
Around Medellín ... 199
Guatapé ... 199
Piedra del Peñol ... 200
Santa Fe de Antioquia ... 201
Jardín ... 203
Río Claro ... 205
Zona Cafetera ... 205
Manizales ... 205
Around Manizales ... 210
Parque Nacional Natural Los Nevados ... 212
Pereira ... 215
Termales de Santa Rosa ... 217
Termales San Vicente ... 217
Santuario Otún Quimbaya ... 218

Contents

Parque Ucumarí........218
Armenia................219
Around Armenia........220
Salento................222
Filandia...............224
Valle de Cocora.........225

CALI & SOUTHWEST COLOMBIA....... 227

Cali.................229
Around Cali..........235
Pance.................236
Lago Calima...........236
Darién.................237
Cauca & Huila........238
Popayán...............238
Coconuco..............243
San Agustín............243
Tierradentro...........248
Desierto de la Tatacoa..........251
Villavieja..............252
Nariño...............252
Pasto.................252
Laguna de la Cocha.....255
Ipiales.................256
Santuario de Las Lajas..............257

PACIFIC COAST ... 259

Chocó................260
Bahía Solano...........260
Around Bahía Solano....263
El Valle................264
Parque Nacional Natural Ensenada de Utría......265
Nuquí.................266
Around Nuquí..........267
South Coast.........270
Parque Nacional Natural Isla Gorgona.... 271

LOS LLANOS...... 273

Villavicencio...........274
San José del Guaviare...........276
Caño Cristales.........277
Parque Nacional Natural El Tuparro......279

AMAZON BASIN... 281

Leticia.................282
Parque Nacional Natural Amacayacu.....289
Puerto Nariño..........289
Río Yavarí..............291

UNDERSTAND

History...............294
Life in Colombia......304
The Arts..............306
The Natural World....309

SURVIVAL GUIDE

Safe Travel............316
Directory A–Z.........319
Transportation.......329
Language.............336
Glossary.............341

COVID-19

We have re-checked every business in this book before publication to ensure that it is still open after the COVID-19 outbreak. However, the economic and social impacts of COVID-19 will continue to be felt long after the outbreak has been contained, and many businesses, services and events referenced in this guide may experience ongoing restrictions. Some businesses may be temporarily closed, have changed their opening hours and services, or require bookings; some unfortunately could have closed permanently. We suggest you check with venues before visiting for the latest information.

SPECIAL FEATURES

Colombia Outdoors.... 28
Life in Colombia......304
The Arts.............306
The Natural World....309
Safe Travel........... 316

Right: San Andrés (p170)

DC_COLOMBIA/GETTY IMAGES ©

WELCOME TO

Colombia

It's not a destination for the faint of heart – Colombia is all about adventure by the truckload. However you like to get your highs, this diverse destination delivers. Its untamed natural landscape is a biodiversity jackpot, with cloudforested mountains, glorious beaches, calm deserts and lush Amazon jungle to explore. Combine all this with a tumultuously rich history, pulsating cities with excellent museums, friendly locals, and fierce Latin energy – there's nowhere quite like it on earth.

By Jade Bremner, Writer
@jadebremner jadeob
For more about our writers, see p352

Colombia

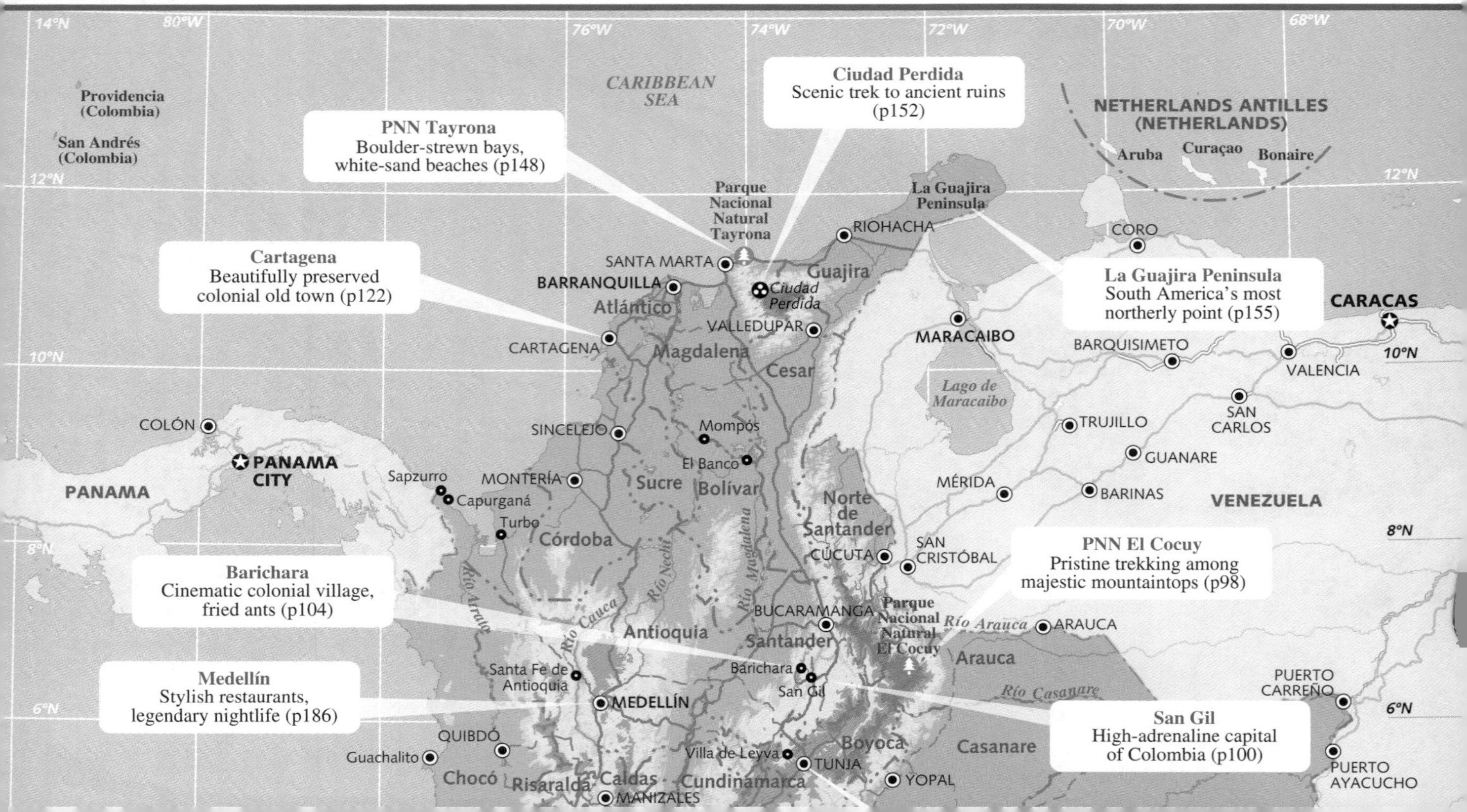

0 — 200 km
0 — 100 miles

Ciudad Perdida
Scenic trek to ancient ruins (p152)

PNN Tayrona
Boulder-strewn bays, white-sand beaches (p148)

Cartagena
Beautifully preserved colonial old town (p122)

La Guajira Peninsula
South America's most northerly point (p155)

PNN El Cocuy
Pristine trekking among majestic mountaintops (p98)

Barichara
Cinematic colonial village, fried ants (p104)

Medellín
Stylish restaurants, legendary nightlife (p186)

San Gil
High-adrenaline capital of Colombia (p100)

14°N
12°N
10°N
8°N
6°N
80°W
76°W
74°W
72°W
70°W
68°W
CARIBBEAN SEA
Providencia (Colombia)
San Andrés (Colombia)
NETHERLANDS ANTILLES (NETHERLANDS)
Aruba
Curaçao
Bonaire
Parque Nacional Natural Tayrona
La Guajira Peninsula
RIOHACHA
CORO
SANTA MARTA
BARRANQUILLA
Guajira
Ciudad Perdida
Atlántico
CARTAGENA
VALLEDUPAR
MARACAIBO
CARACAS
Magdalena
Cesar
BARQUISIMETO
VALENCIA
Lago de Maracaibo
COLÓN
SINCELEJO
Mompós
TRUJILLO
SAN CARLOS
PANAMA CITY
El Banco
GUANARE
PANAMA
Sapzurro
MONTERÍA
Capurganá
Sucre
Bolívar
Norte de Santander
MÉRIDA
BARINAS
VENEZUELA
Turbo
Córdoba
Río Nechí
Río Magdalena
CÚCUTA
SAN CRISTÓBAL
Río Atrato
Río Cauca
BUCARAMANGA
Parque Nacional Natural El Cocuy
Río Arauca
ARAUCA
Antioquia
Santander
Arauca
Santa Fe de Antioquia
Barichara
San Gil
Río Casanare
PUERTO CARREÑO
MEDELLÍN
QUIBDÓ
Guachalito
Villa de Leyva
TUNJA
Boyacá
Casanare
YOPAL
PUERTO AYACUCHO
Chocó
Risaralda
Caldas
Cundinamarca
MANIZALES

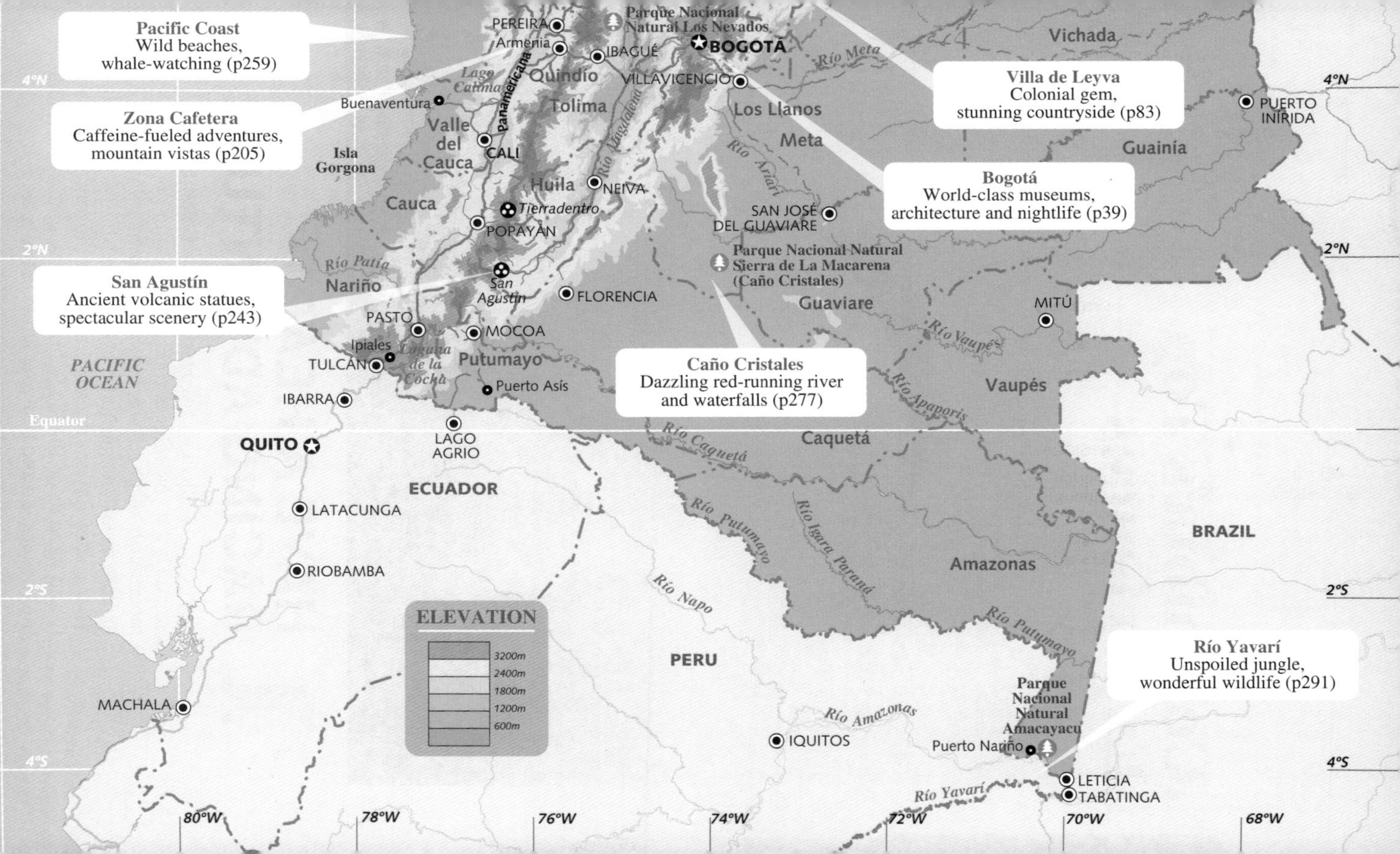
Pacific Coast
Wild beaches, whale-watching (p259)
Zona Cafetera
Caffeine-fueled adventures, mountain vistas (p205)
San Agustín
Ancient volcanic statues, spectacular scenery (p243)
Caño Cristales
Dazzling red-running river and waterfalls (p277)
Villa de Leyva
Colonial gem, stunning countryside (p83)
Bogotá
World-class museums, architecture and nightlife (p39)
Río Yavarí
Unspoiled jungle, wonderful wildlife (p291)
Parque Nacional Natural Los Nevados
PEREIRA
Armenia
IBAGUÉ
BOGOTÁ
VILLAVICENCIO
Vichada
Río Meta
Lago Calima
Quindío
Tolima
Panamericana
Buenaventura
Valle del Cauca
CALI
Los Llanos
Meta
Guainía
PUERTO INÍRIDA
Isla Gorgona
Río Magdalena
Río Ariari
Huila
NEIVA
Cauca
Tierradentro
POPAYÁN
SAN JOSÉ DEL GUAVIARE
Parque Nacional Natural Sierra de La Macarena (Caño Cristales)
Río Patía
Nariño
San Agustín
FLORENCIA
Guaviare
MITÚ
PASTO
MOCOA
Ipiales
Laguna de la Cocha
Putumayo
TULCÁN
Puerto Asís
PACIFIC OCEAN
Río Vaupés
Río Apaporis
Vaupés
IBARRA
Equator
LAGO AGRIO
QUITO
Río Caquetá
Caquetá
ECUADOR
LATACUNGA
Río Putumayo
Río Igara Paraná
BRAZIL
RIOBAMBA
Amazonas
Río Napo
ELEVATION
3200m
2400m
1800m
1200m
600m
PERU
Parque Nacional Natural Amacayacu
MACHALA
Río Amazonas
IQUITOS
Puerto Nariño
LETICIA
TABATINGA
Río Yavarí
4°N
2°N
2°S
4°S
80°W
78°W
76°W
74°W
72°W
70°W
68°W

Colombia's Top Experiences

1 HAVE A HEART-RACING ADVENTURE

High-octane activities are everywhere in Colombia. And San Gil is the epicenter of thrill. Choose your poison: mountain bike, paddle rapids, rappel down a waterfall, explore caves, bungee jump or soar like a bird attached to a paraglider. Rafters flock to San Gil for the famous Class IV and V rapids on the Río Suárez. Face your fears, and feel the exhilaration and test your limits to the max.

ROBERTHARDING/ALAMY ©

PABLO ANDRES DELGADO/SHUTTERSTOCK ©

Rappel a Waterfall

Take a day trip to a spectacular 180m-high waterfall where you can swim in its natural pool or relax on the rocks. Adventure junkies can rappel the sheer face of the falls. p100

Right: Cascadas de Juan Curi

REISEGRAF.CH/SHUTTERSTOCK ©

VW PICS/GETTY IMAGES ©

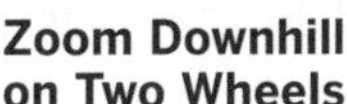

Zoom Downhill on Two Wheels

On this 50km downhill extravaganza through the Cañón del Río Suárez you'll take in absolutely epic country-side with the wind in your hair and your heart beating out of your chest. Book with Colombian Bike Junkies. p102

Catapult Yourself into an Abyss

For high-thrills, two 300m-long zip-lines cross the mountain and go high above the town on the road to Barich-ara. There's also a massive extreme swing that catapults participants into the sky. Book with Peñon Guane. p102

2 CULTURE CRAWL IN BOGOTÁ

Long-lost buried treasure awaits discovery at Bogotá's museums, where astonishing exhibits impress with their epic proportions. There are plenty of left-field attractions too – everything from cocaine-kingpin firearms and presidential helicopters to Bolívarian swords and exquisitely tiled bathrooms.

Hunt for Gold

Containing more than 55,000 pieces of gold and other materials from all of Colombia's major pre-Hispanic cultures, Bogotá's most famous museum is one of the most fascinating in South America. Collections are laid out in logical, thematic rooms over three floors at the Museo del Oro (pictured below). p46

KRIS DAVIDSON/LONELY PLANET IMAGES ©

MIROSLAW SKORKA/SHUTTERSTOCK ©

MATYAS REHAK/SHUTTERSTOCK ©

Book a Gang Tour

Discover the insalubrious parts of the city with former gang members, who swapped their lives of crime for cultural tourism. Tours will take you though 'no-go zones' unless under the guides' protection, where you'll learn the history of organized crime. p51

Above left: Alleyway in Bogotá

View Modern Colombian Art

See more than 100 pieces by the father of Boterismo and Colombia's most famous living artist – Fernando Botero – who depicts figures in exaggerated volumes, in the Museo Botero (pictured above right). Characters include dodgy dictators, fleet-footed dancers, dogs and birds. p42

3 WANDER OLD COLORFUL STREETS

The hands of the clock on the Puerta del Reloj wind back 400 years in an instant as visitors enter the walled old town of Cartagena. These streets offer one of the finest examples of preserved colonial architecture in the Americas, the pastel-toned balconies pour with bougainvillea and the streets are abuzz with food stalls around magnificent Spanish-built churches, squares and historic mansions.

Eat Tapas in Style

One of Cartagena's most interesting restaurants, the Lobo de Mar sports water features and a very cool gin bar. The gourmet tapas menu is bursting with flavors, and is particularly strong on seafood, and veggie choices. p133

JESS KRAFT/SHUTTERSTOCK ©

Sample Tangy Ceviche

Try hot and cold ceviche at El Boliche, an intimate six-table spot, offering raw fish laced with bold and adventurous ingredients such as tamarind, coconut milk and mango. Wash it down with a tangy mojitos. p132

4 PADDLE IN KALEIDO-SCOPIC RIVERS

The multihued rivers and streams of Caño Cristales delight all who visit. You could be mistaken for thinking that food dye has been tipped into the rivers to create this wondrous effect, but it's actually created by an eruption of kaleidoscopic plants that grow on its shallow bed. This natural phenomenon occurs for a few months between July and November. Trekking between waterfalls and natural swimming pools is a fabulous experience.

Camp in the Wild

Go on an immersive and atmospheric overnight nature-watching trip with Doris Mora, who runs overnight tours to the colorful rivers of Caño Cristales (pictured) in the national park, so you can wake up to the sounds of the lush forest. Cristales Macarena p278

Take a Dip

Swim in the main watering holes, Piscina del Turista, Piscina de Carol Cristal, Cascada del Aguila, Cascada de Piedra Negra and Caño la Virgen; all can be reached via guided access inside Parque Nacional Natural Sierra de La Macarena. p277

5 LAZE ON PRISTINE BEACHES

Among the country's most beautiful and clean beaches are those at Parque Nacional Natural Tayrona near Santa Marta on the Caribbean coast (pictured top left). The picturesque white-sand beaches are flanked by palm trees and a backdrop of jungle that sweeps like a leafy avalanche down from the soaring Sierra Nevada de Santa Marta. The landscape is dotted with mighty boulders, some cleaved in half, as if a giant has had a geological temper tantrum.

MICHA WEBER/SHUTTERSTOCK ©

DC_COLOMBIA/GETTY IMAGES ©

Fall Asleep by the Ocean

Cabo San Juan del Guía (pictured bottom left) is a beautiful cape with a knockout beach. The area has a restaurant and a campsite, with hammocks and cabins, in a spectacular lookout on a rock in the middle of the beach. It's very atmospheric at night. Swimming is also possible most of the time. p148

Boat to a Secret Playa

Once a ceremonial site for the indigenous community, where they buried their dead, the gorgeous boat-in beach Playa Cristal used to be known as Playa del Muerto (Beach of the Dead; pictured above right). This mysterious place has crystal clear waters and shacks serving freshly caught fish and cold beers. p148

6 DANCE SALSA IN CALI

JSANCHEZFOTOS/SHUTTERSTOCK ©

KIKE CALVO/ALAMY ©

ZAID DIAZ/SHUTTERSTOCK ©

Attend a Dance Fest

If you want to see how it is really done, catch the amazing dancers of all ages from Cali and around the world take to the stage in colorful costumes during this hugely competitive annual salsa event in September. Finals take place in the Plaza de Toros. p232

Learn the Moves

Shake your hips to the rhythms of bachata and merengue at one of Colombia's largest dance schools, Sabor Manicero, which offers cheap group salsa classes for all ability levels. p229

Cali didn't invent the salsa, but wow it knows how to dance it. Salsa unites *Caleños* in this sprawling city. From the tiny barrio bars with oversized sound systems to the mega salsatecas (salsa dance clubs) of Juanchito, this is the place to experience Latin energy.

7 WALK ON THE WILD SIDE

Colombia is home the largest glacier zone in South America, plus dunes and deserts, snow-covered peaks and majestic tropical jungle scenery – all ripe for an expedition. Keen hikers can summit mountains, discover an ancient lost city, after crossing surging rivers pumping faster than your pulse, and spot endless nature as they silently cross varied landscapes.

Climb a Glacier

Burnt-auburn sunrises bounce off craggy peaks, and the tough páramo ecosystem of icy valleys in El Cocuy, with its bare mountain plains, high-altitude lakes and rare vegetation (pictured top right). On clear days, entire swaths of Los Llanos can be seen before you from any number of surrounding 5000m-peak viewpoints. p98

CHRISTIAN KOBER/GETTY IMAGES ©

Wander the Colombian Andes

The snow-covered peaks of Parque Nacional Natural Los Nevados have long been revered by indigenous cultures and visitors alike. The southern reaches offer awesome trekking through diverse ecosystems. p212

Discover a Lost City

One of Colombia's best multiday hikes is to the ancient Ciudad Perdida. The thrilling walk goes through majestic tropical jungle scenery and ends at a mysterious city 'discovered' by grave robbers and gold-digging bandits. p152

8 DRINK SERIOUSLY GOOD COFFEE

In Zona Cafetera coffee connoisseurs can strap on a basket and head into the plantation to pick their own beans right from the source. Then, head back to a traditional *finca* house and enjoy the stunning vistas with a perfectly prepared cup of arabica, while listening to the sounds of flowing rivers and birdsong. Much of the best coffee is exported but the are many places to try excellent Colombian coffee, if you know where to look.

Try a Local Favorite

Pergamino in Medellin serves pure farm-to-cup coffee. Its En Kioto cold brew is served strong in an espresso cup, with a slightly salty kick, while the punchy Urrao roast is made from beans grown at 2000 meters. p195

Visit a Shrine to Coffee

No caffeine aficionado should miss a stop at Cafe Quindio in Armenia, dotted with baby coffee plants and serving highland coffee from the surrounding region every which way: drip coffee, French press and Chemex. p220

Need to Know

For more information, see Survival Guide (p315)

Currency
Colombian peso (COP$)

Language
Spanish (and English in San Andrés & Providencia)

Visas
Nationals of many countries, including Western Europe, the Americas, Japan, Australia, New Zealand and South Africa, don't need a visa. Otherwise, expect a nominal fee.

Money
ATMs are widely available. Credit cards are common.

Cell Phones
Cell (mobile) phone and mobile data coverage is excellent. Most unlocked cell phones will work with a local SIM card.

Time
GMT/UTC minus five hours. There is no daylight savings.

When to Go

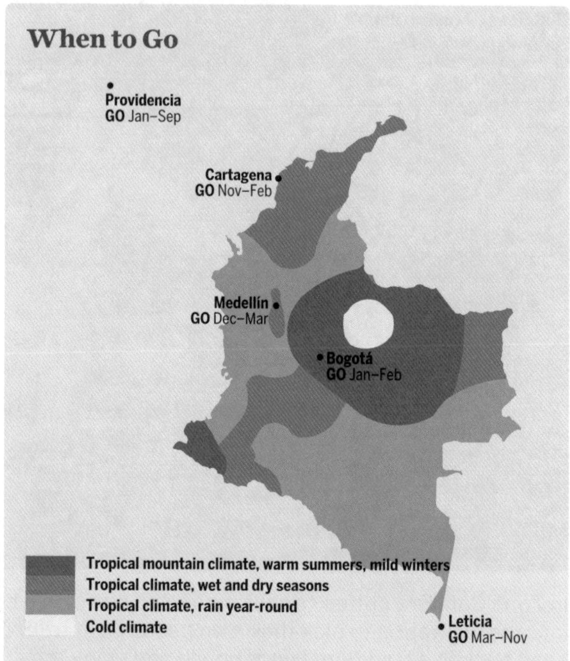

High Season (Dec–Feb)

- Sunny skies and warmish days throughout the Andes.
- Dry everywhere but the Amazon.
- San Andrés and Providencia are gorgeous.
- Prices countrywide are at their highest.

Shoulder (Mar–Sep)

- Bogotá, Medellín and Cali suffer a secondary rainy season in April/May.
- Best whale-watching is July to October on the Pacific coast.
- Cartagena shines through April; hard rains begin in May.

Low Season (Oct–Nov)

- Flash floods often wash out roads in the Andean region.
- Cartagena and the Caribbean coast is disproportionally wet in October.
- Low water levels in the Amazon means excellent hiking and white-sand beaches.
- Prices everywhere are at their lowest.

Useful Websites

This is Colombia (www.colombia.co/en) A superb website aimed at promoting Colombia to the world.

Proexport Colombia (www.colombia.travel/en) The official government tourism portal.

Colombia Reports (www.colombiareports.co) Top English-language news source.

BBC News (www.bbc.com/news/world/latin_america) The Beeb has excellent South American coverage.

Parques Nacionales Naturales de Colombia (www.parquesnacionales.gov.co) Detailed parks information.

Lonely Planet (www.lonelyplanet.com/colombia) Destination information, hotel reviews, traveler forum and more.

Important Numbers

Colombia's country code	☎+57
International access code	☎00
Directory assistance	☎113
Ambulance, fire & police	☎123

Exchange Rates

Australia	A$1	COP$2840
Brazil	R$1	COP$759
Canada	C$1	COP$3040
Eurozone	€1	COP$4467
Japan	¥100	COP$3380
New Zealand	NZ$1	COP$2642
UK	£1	COP$5208
USA	US$1	COP$3744

For current exchange rates, see www.xe.com

Daily Costs

Budget: Less than COP$60,000

➡ Dorm bed: COP$20,000–40,000

➡ *Comida corriente* (set meal): COP$6000–12,000

➡ Bus ticket Bogotá–Villa de Leyva: COP$27,000

Midrange: COP$100,000–200,000

➡ Double room in midrange hotel: COP$80,000–120,000

➡ Main in decent local restaurant: COP$20,000–30,000

Top end: More than COP$200,000

➡ Double room in a top-end hotel: from COP$160,000

➡ Multicourse meal with wine: from COP$50,000

Opening Hours

Banks 9am to 4pm Monday to Friday, 9am to noon Saturday

Bars 6pm to around 3am

Cafes 8am to 10pm

Nightclubs 9pm until very late Thursday to Saturday

Restaurants Breakfast from 8am, lunch from noon, dinner until 9pm or 10pm

Shops 9am to 5pm Monday to Friday, 9am to noon or 5pm Saturday; some shops close for lunch

Arriving in Colombia

Aeropuerto Internacional El Dorado (Bogotá) Buses (COP$2200) run every 10 minutes from 4:30am to 10:45pm; a taxi (COP$35,000) takes 45 minutes to the center.

Aeropuerto Internacional José María Córdoba (Medellín) Buses (COP$9500) leave every 15 minutes 24 hours a day; a taxi (COP$65,000) takes 45 minutes to the city.

Aeropuerto Internacional Rafael Núñez (Cartagena) Buses (COP$1500) run every 15 minutes from 6:50am to 11:45pm; taxis (COP$13,000) take 15 minutes to the old town.

Getting Around

Air Domestic flights in Colombia are the best way to travel longer distances.

Boat The only way to get around in most of the Amazon and Pacific coast, boat travel is far more expensive than a comparable trip in a bus.

Bus There are frequent bus connections between all major cities in Colombia. Long-distance services tend to be large comfortable buses while shorter runs are often covered with less roomy vans and even sedans.

For much more on **getting around**, see p331

Month by Month

TOP EVENTS

Carnaval de Barranquilla, February

Feria de las Flores, August

Semana Santa in Popayán, March or April

Festival de Música del Pacífico Petronio Álvarez, August

Carnaval de Blancos y Negros, January

January

Colombia's equatorial position means temperatures fluctuate by altitude, not season, so almost anytime is a good time to visit. January could be considered ideal for dissipating holiday crowds coupled with lingering festivals and parties.

Carnaval de Blancos y Negros

Pasto's uproarious post-Christmas bash, originating during slavery times, sees drunken crowds throwing grease, talcum powder, flour and chalk on each other until everyone is coughing up powdery mucus and doused in gunk. Leave the haute couture at the hotel. (p254)

February

The Andean region remains pleasant and Cartagena almost drought-stricken, making February a great time to beach-hop along the Caribbean coast. With kids back in school and domestic merrymakers returned to the grind, Colombia is *tranquila*.

Fiesta de Nuestra Señora de la Candelaria

A solemn procession is held in Cartagena on 2 February to honor the town's patron saint. Celebrations begin nine days earlier, the Novenas, when pilgrims flock to the convent. (p129)

Carnaval de Barranquilla

Held 40 days before Easter, Barranquilla's Carnaval is the continent's second-biggest after Rio de Janeiro. A spectacular four-day bash of drinking, dancing, parades, costumes and Colombian music concludes on Mardi Gras with the symbolic burial of 'festival icon' Joselito Carnaval. (p306)

March

Easter is big business. Whether it falls in March or April, the country is seriously tuned in. Expect crowds, high prices and changeable weather.

Semana Santa in Popayán

Colombia's most famous Semana Santa (Holy Week) celebration is held in Popayán, with nighttime processions on Monday, Thursday and Good Friday. Thousands of the faithful and tourists take part in this religious ceremony and the accompanying festival of religious music. (p239)

Festival Iberoamericano de Teatro de Bogotá

Held during Semana Santa, this biennial festival of Latin American theater takes place in even-numbered years, and is considered the largest performing-arts festival in the world. (p53)

June

After a respite in April and May, storm clouds once again loom. Bogotá is at its driest, though, and humpback whales begin arriving on the Pacific coast. Prices rise for summer school vacations.

A Whalin' Good Time

June marks the beginning of the spectacular whale-watching season on Colombia's Pacific coast, when hundreds of humpback whales arrive from Antarctica, some 8500km away, to give birth and raise their young in Colombia's tropical waters. (p265)

August

Relatively mild August can be drizzly, but excellent festivals more than make up for impending rains. Bogotá, Cali and Medellín all soak up the end-of-summer atmosphere with a bonanza of music and culture.

Festival de Música del Pacífico Petronio Álvarez

This Cali festival celebrates the music of the Pacific coast, which is heavily influenced by African rhythms introduced to Colombia by the slaves who originally populated the region.

Feria de las Flores

This week-long feria is Medellín's most spectacular event. The highlight is the Desfile de Silleteros, when up to 400 *campesinos* (peasants) come down from the mountains and parade along the streets carrying flowers on their backs. (p193)

September

Showers hit most of the country, but Amazonian river levels are low, making it an excellent time for wildlife viewing, hiking or just kicking back on a sandy river beach.

Festival Mundial de Salsa

Don't miss this classic Cali festival. Despite the name, it's not really a worldwide festival, but you'll see some amazing dancers and there are often free salsa shows. (p232)

Festival Internacional de Teatro

Held since 1968, Manizales' theater festival is Colombia's second-most important (after Festival Iberoamericano de Teatro de Bogotá). It features free shows in Plaza de Bolívar. (p191)

Mompox Jazz Festival

This relatively new festival began in 2012 and has helped attract visitors to Mompós, a beautiful but very remote colonial town in northern Colombia. Its program includes international jazz performers; the festival even attracted the Colombian president in 2014. (p162)

October

On average, October is one of Colombia's wettest months, along with November. Bogotá, Cali, Medellín and Cartagena are all at the mercy of the weather.

Rock al Parque

Three days of rock, metal, pop, funk and reggae bands rocking out at Parque Simón Bolívar in Bogotá. Rock al Parque is free and swarming with fans – it's now Colombia's biggest music festival. (p53)

November

November is wet, wet, wet throughout Colombia. Your best refuge from the deluge is Bogotá, but you'll still be breaking out the umbrella on a regular basis.

Reinado Nacional de Belleza

Also known as the Carnaval de Cartagena or Fiestas del 11 de Noviembre, this beauty pageant and festival, Cartagena's most important annual bash, celebrates the city's independence day and the crowning of Miss Colombia. Festivities include street dancing, music and fancy-dress parades.

December

The rains begin to recede and the country is awash instead in holiday festivals, spectacular light displays and spur-of-the-moment partying. Expect crowds throughout Colombia.

Let There Be Light!

Every Christmas, Colombian cities compete in the annual Alumbrado Navideño, or Christmas Lighting, to see who can put up the most elaborate lighting display along their respective rivers – Medellín's colorful display is well worth a detour.

Feria de Cali

Commerce pretty much grinds to a halt during Cali's annual bash. Instead, parties spill into the streets, food and beer pavilions magically appear, spontaneous dancing commences, and the Río Cali is illuminated in a spectacular display of lights.

Itineraries

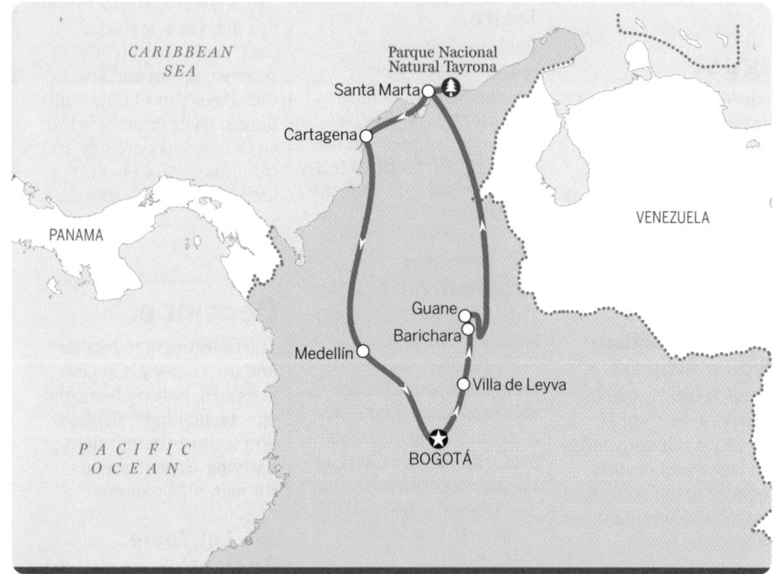

Bogotá to Bogotá

Welcome to Colombia! Cosmopolitan cities, looming mountains, colonial villages, verdant jungles and Caribbean beaches await. Pulling off this itinerary requires fifth gear and copious amounts of caffeine – good thing you're in the land of coffee!

Spend a day or two in **Bogotá**, admiring La Candelaria (its colonial center), the best of myriad museums and world-class food and nightlife. Shake off the hangover a few hours north in the calming colonial villages of **Villa de Leyva** and **Barichara**, both miraculously preserved and picturesque. Take a day to walk the historic El Camino Real to **Guane**. Bus to San Gil to pick up the long bus ride to **Santa Marta**, from where you can access **Parque Nacional Natural (PNN) Tayrona** – linger on the park's otherworldly beaches for a few days. Continue southwest along the Caribbean coast to **Cartagena**, Colombia's crown jewel – a postcard-perfect old city chock-full of colonial romance. It's another long bus ride (or a quicker flight) to **Medellín**, where again you're faced with Colombia in overdrive: culture, cuisine and Pilsen, *paisa*-style. Raise a toast to El Dorado and exit via Bogotá, bowled-over by Colombia's hospitality.

The See (Almost) Everything Route

The beauty of Colombia's diverse landscapes is that you can choose to fully immerse yourself in just one – Caribbean beaches, wildlife-rich jungle or soaring Andean highlands – or you can go for the Full Monty!

Hit the ground running with three or four days in **Bogotá**, Colombia's Gotham; don't miss Museo del Oro, one of the continent's most fascinating museums, or the city's atmospheric colonial center, La Candelaria. From there head north to **Villa de Leyva**. Explore its cobbled streets and enjoy some colonial charm for a day or two, then visit **San Gil** for hiking and rafting, making time for nearby historic **Barichara**. Pass through Bucaramanga to catch a long-haul bus to **Santa Marta**. It's worth moving quicker than normal up to this point in order to free up some time for the sweaty, multiday trek to **Ciudad Perdida** or blissing-out for a day or two in the beach-riddled **Parque Nacional Natural (PNN) Tayrona**, Colombia's most popular national park. Next stop, **Cartagena** – you'll need a few days to indulge this exquisite colonial city.

Take a bus or fly south to spend a week exploring **Medellín** and the Zona Cafetera. Enjoy some time in the nature reserves around **Manizales** before testing your fitness among the spectacular peaks of **PNN Los Nevados**. Next stop, the breathtaking **Valle de Cocora** outside Salento. Visit a coffee *finca* (farm) near Armenia and stock up on single-origin coffee beans direct from the source.

Spend the night in **Cali** to experience the city's hopping salsa joints. Travel down through colonial **Popayán** to the archaeological ruins at **San Agustín** and **Tierradentro**, two of the country's most important pre-Columbian sites and worthy of a few days. Return to Bogotá via the startling **Desierto de la Tatacoa** and catch a flight to **Leticia**, where a wildly different Colombia exists. Spend a few days exploring the three Amazonian ecosystems: *terra firme* (dry), *várzea* (semiflooded) and *igapó* (flooded) along the **Río Yavarí**, the best spot in Amazonia to observe wildlife undisturbed in its natural habitat. Fly back to Bogotá or, from Tabatinga across the Brazilian border from Leticia, head deeper into the Amazon via river-boat rides to Manaus (Brazil) or Iquitos (Peru).

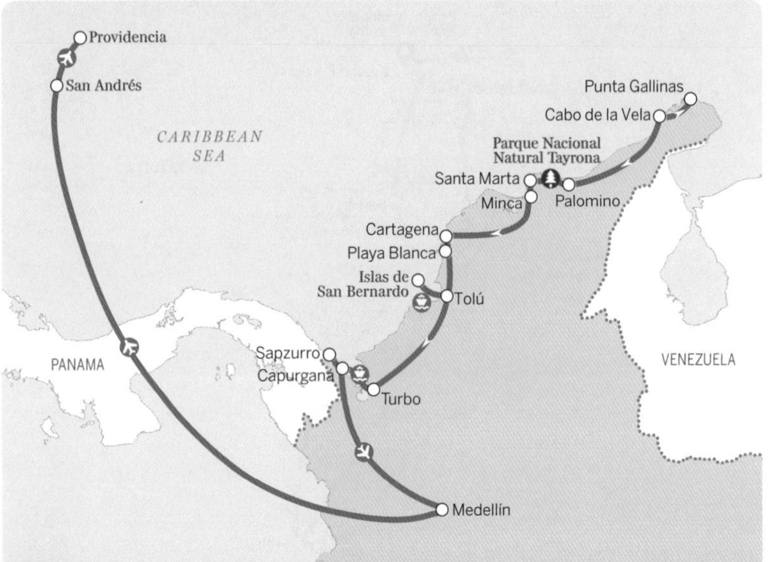

Complete Caribbean

This is the ultimate beach adventure; Colombia's northern coast and islands serve up slices of luminous Caribbean waters backed by an astonishing variety of landscapes.

Start out east of Santa Marta with a few days at **Cabo de la Vela** on La Guajira Peninsula, a striking panorama where the desert meets the sea at the top of the continent. Don't skip South America's northernmost tip, **Punta Gallinas**, where you can sleep in a hammock and feast on local lobster near towering dunes somersaulting into remote beaches.

Heading southwest, make your way to lovely **Palomino**, where you'll find a crystal-clear river running down from the majestic Sierra Nevada to a wild palm-studded beach. A short drive away is **Parque Nacional Natural (PNN) Tayrona**, very popular among aspiring beach bums and fancier travelers alike. Giant boulders frame pretty coves and you can ride horses through the jungle and climb up to the ruins of a pre-Hispanic settlement in the foothills. Spend a couple of days, then pass through **Santa Marta** and take a break from the heat with a short side-trip to the charming mountain town of **Minca**.

Next spend a leisurely couple of days exploring the colonial splendor of **Cartagena** before getting your tanning plans back on track with a trip to **Playa Blanca**. Hit the road again and make your way to **Tolú**, where you can take a trip in the mangroves before boarding a boat to the **Islas de San Bernardo** for three days of white sands, crystalline waters and tiny fishing communities.

Suitably relaxed, make the fairly arduous journey southwest to spend a few days in **Capurganá** and **Sapzurro**, two wonderfully remote beachside neighbors offering excellent diving and surrounded by jungle right on the border with Panama.

If you're hungry for more, take a flight via **Medellín** to quirky **San Andrés** to experience Raizal culture with its British-Caribbean roots. The next day, take the tiny plane or bumpy catamaran to truly remote **Providencia** to soak up the tranquillity as well as a few coco locos, while reclining beside some of Colombia's most idyllic stretches of sand.

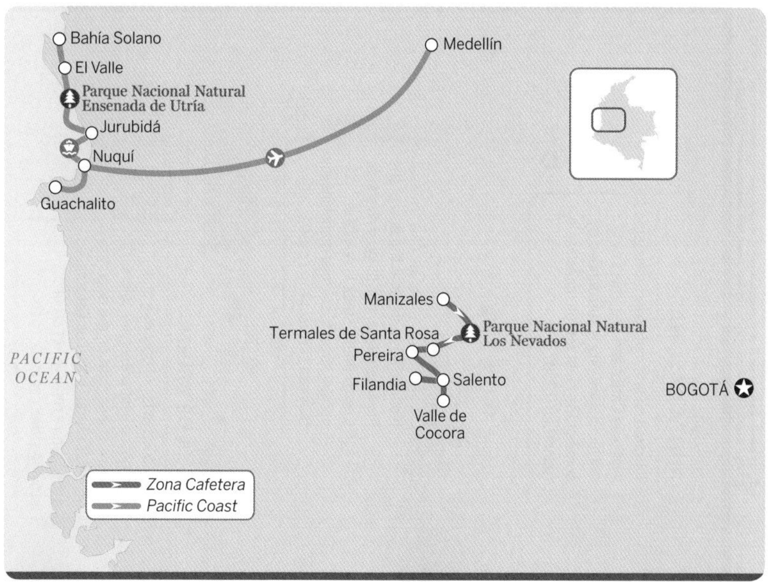

Zona Cafetera

In this arabica-fueled region, hearts are pumped by caffeine as much as blood. Start by spending a few days in the nature parks around **Manizales** – Los Yarumos, Recinto del Pensamiento and Reserva Ecológica Río Blanco. Indulge in a coffee tour just outside town at Hacienda Venecia, which offers an excellent overview of all things coffee.

Return to Manizales to organize a hiking trip among snow-covered volcanic peaks in **Parque Nacional Natural (PNN) Los Nevados**. Spend a night in the *páramo* beside the mystical Laguna de Otún before heading down the mountain to **Termales de Santa Rosa** to reinvigorate tired muscles. Suitably revitalized, pass through **Pereira** to spend four days in coffee-crazy **Salento**, full of quaint charm and typical *bahareque* (adobe and reed) architecture. Take a classic jeep up to the impressive **Valle de Cocora**, one of Colombia's most beautiful half-day hikes. Finally, make the short trip across the highway for a couple of days in slow-paced **Filandia** and toast your tour from its towering *mirador* (lookout), which offers some of the best views in coffee country.

Pacific Coast

Colombia's ultimate off-the-beaten-path destination boasts tropical jungle, diving, whale-watching, world-class sportfishing and black-sand beaches.

Start by flying in for a couple of days at **Bahía Solano**, where you can get used to the pace of El Chocó while lounging in a hammock at Punta Huína. After a spot of diving or a jungle trek, take a taxi south for a night in **El Valle**, where in nesting season you can observe turtles laying eggs and swim beneath a thundering waterfall. Hike south to **Parque Nacional Natural (PNN) Ensenada de Utría** and take a row boat to the visitor center, where you can spend the night. During whale season you can spot the magnificent mammals playing in the inlet.

Next hire a boat to take you to the friendly village of **Jurubidá** and visit the thermal pools hidden in the jungle. Yet another boat will take you to **Nuquí** for an overnight stay. From here you can pick up transport to **Guachalito**, a top-class beach with several comfortable eco-lodges. After three days, return to Nuquí to take a quick flight back to **Medellín**.

Colombia: Off the Beaten Track

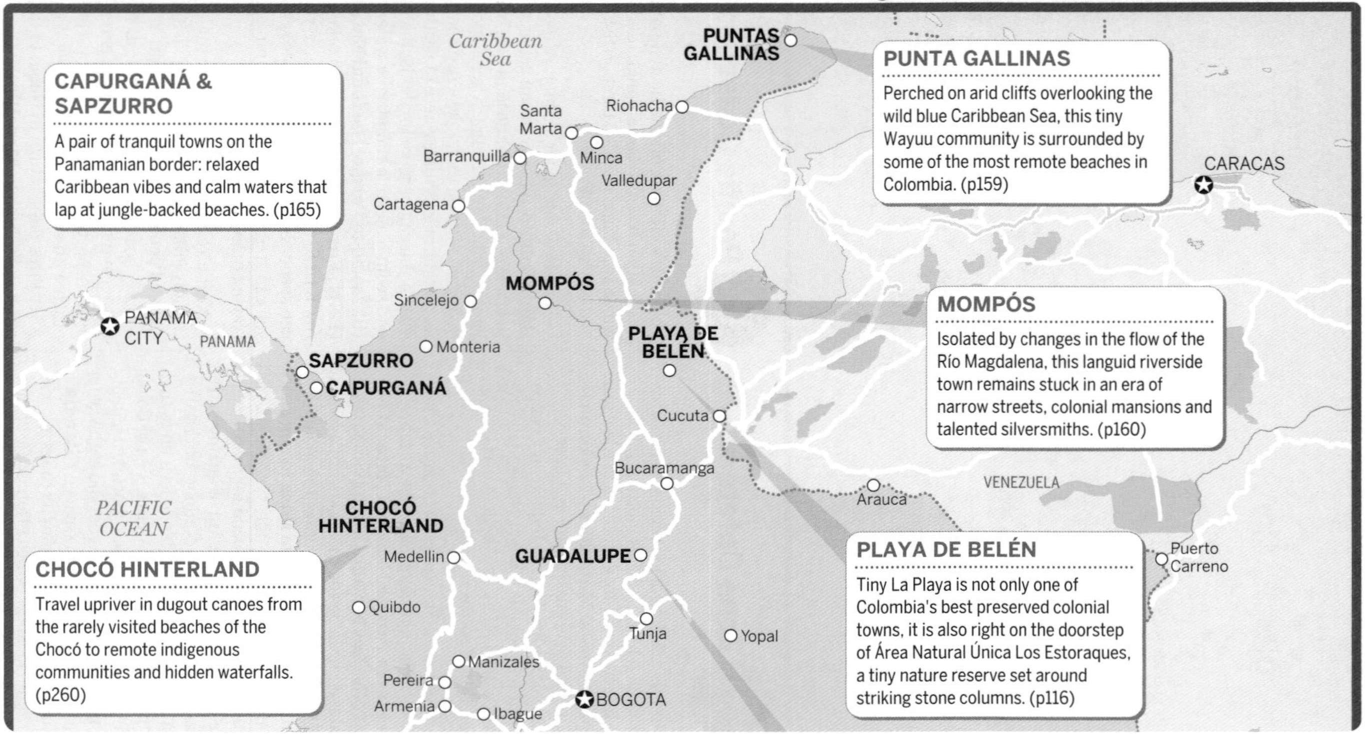

0 — 500 km
0 — 250 miles

Caribbean Sea
PUNTAS GALLINAS
Riohacha
Santa Marta
Minca
Barranquilla
Valledupar
Cartagena
CARACAS
MOMPÓS
Sincelejo
PANAMA CITY
PANAMA
Monteria
PLAYA DE BELÉN
SAPZURRO
CAPURGANÁ
Cucuta
Bucaramanga
Arauca
VENEZUELA
PACIFIC OCEAN
CHOCÓ HINTERLAND
Medellin
GUADALUPE
Puerto Carreno
Quibdo
Tunja
Yopal
Manizales
Pereira
Armenia
Ibague
BOGOTA

CAPURGANÁ & SAPZURRO

A pair of tranquil towns on the Panamanian border: relaxed Caribbean vibes and calm waters that lap at jungle-backed beaches. (p165)

CHOCÓ HINTERLAND

Travel upriver in dugout canoes from the rarely visited beaches of the Chocó to remote indigenous communities and hidden waterfalls. (p260)

PUNTA GALLINAS

Perched on arid cliffs overlooking the wild blue Caribbean Sea, this tiny Wayuu community is surrounded by some of the most remote beaches in Colombia. (p159)

MOMPÓS

Isolated by changes in the flow of the Río Magdalena, this languid riverside town remains stuck in an era of narrow streets, colonial mansions and talented silversmiths. (p160)

PLAYA DE BELÉN

Tiny La Playa is not only one of Colombia's best preserved colonial towns, it is also right on the doorstep of Área Natural Única Los Estoraques, a tiny nature reserve set around striking stone columns. (p116)

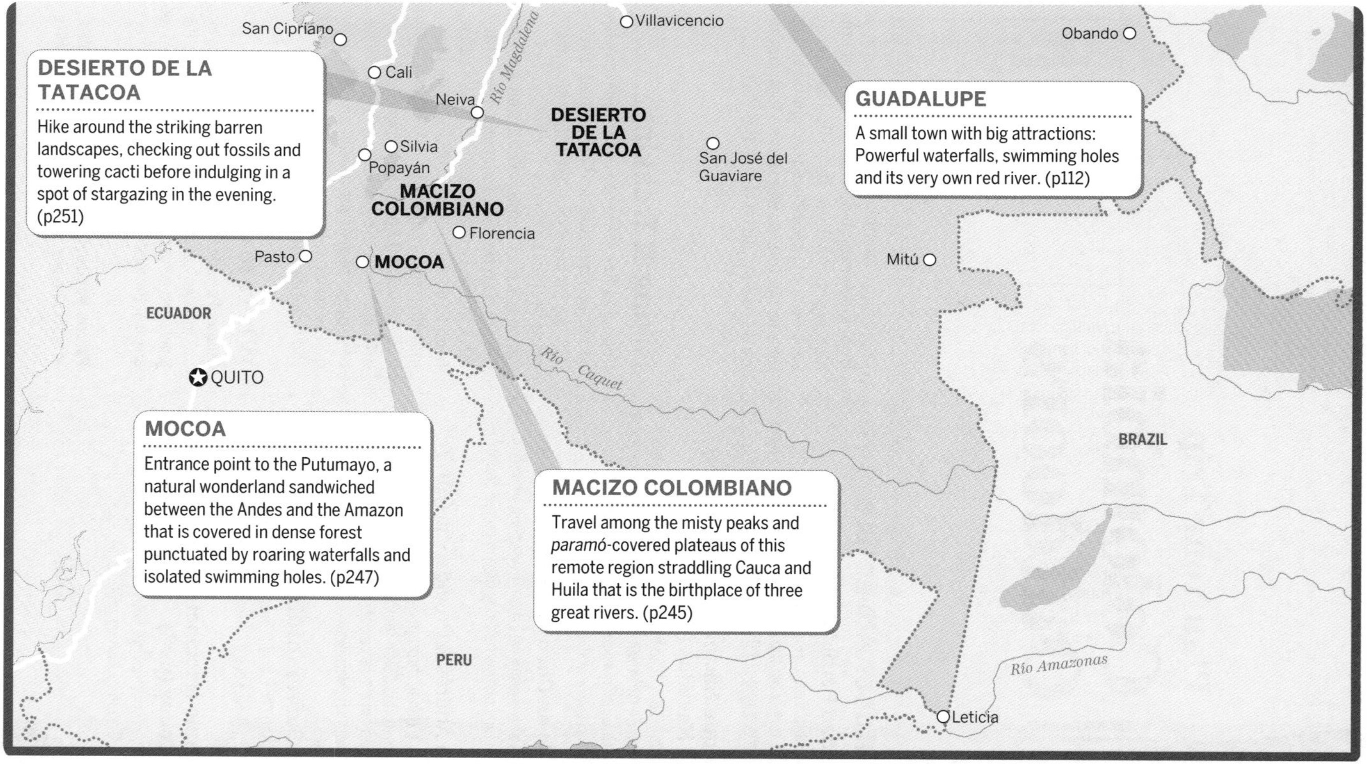
DESIERTO DE LA TATACOA
Hike around the striking barren landscapes, checking out fossils and towering cacti before indulging in a spot of stargazing in the evening. (p251)
GUADALUPE
A small town with big attractions: Powerful waterfalls, swimming holes and its very own red river. (p112)
MOCOA
Entrance point to the Putumayo, a natural wonderland sandwiched between the Andes and the Amazon that is covered in dense forest punctuated by roaring waterfalls and isolated swimming holes. (p247)
MACIZO COLOMBIANO
Travel among the misty peaks and *paramó*-covered plateaus of this remote region straddling Cauca and Huila that is the birthplace of three great rivers. (p245)
San Cipriano
Cali
Neiva
Río Magdalena
Villavicencio
Obando
DESIERTO DE LA TATACOA
San José del Guaviare
Silvia
Popayán
MACIZO COLOMBIANO
Florencia
Pasto
MOCOA
Mitú
ECUADOR
QUITO
Río Caquet
BRAZIL
PERU
Río Amazonas
Leticia

Plan Your Trip

Colombia Outdoors

Outdoor Adventures

Ciudad Perdida (p152)

Colombia's most popular trek: a four- to six-day, 44km-long walk through jungle to the remarkably preserved ruins of the lost city of the Tayronas.

Parque Nacional Natural (PNN) Los Nevados (p212)

The three-day hike from Parque Ucumari up to Laguna de Otún will take your breath away as you pass through gorgeous *páramo* landscapes surrounded by magnificent peaks.

Valle de Cocora (p225)

Gawk at towering wax palm trees through misty green hills on this half-day hike in coffee country.

San Andrés & Providencia (p169)

Superb diving through warm Caribbean waters awaits at this 35km reef, home to spectacular colored corals, large pelagic fish, portly eels and long-lost shipwrecks.

Río Suárez (p102)

Near San Gil, Class IV and V white-water rapids lure thrill seekers to the country's wildest river.

Parque Nacional Natural (PNN) El Cocuy (p98)

Highly restricted, but with 15 peaks above 5000m it's still a cloud-kissing highlight.

Exploring Colombia's dramatic landscapes, from glacier-topped peaks to lowland jungles, is a highlight of any visit. Discover the best ways to experience these natural wonders to the fullest, whether on foot, in the water or soaring on thermal winds.

Hiking & Trekking

Colombia has some of South America's best trekking opportunities. The casual hiker looking for good one-day walks also has many options to choose from – most of which, such as Laguna Verde and Valle de Cocora, can be done independently without a guide. Guided day-hike prices range from COP$40,000 to COP$100,000. For multiday treks expect to pay COP$100,000 to COP$150,000 per day, depending on the difficulty and the guide's experience. The best times of year for a walk are February on the coast and December to February in the mountains.

Where to Go

Ciudad Perdida On the Caribbean coast; this long trek involves a sweaty, multiday hike through the jungle and across waist-high rivers. At the end you arrive at the long-forgotten ruins of the Tayrona civilization.

Parque Nacional Natural (PNN) El Cocuy With at least 12 peaks above 5000m and phenomenal high-altitude landscapes, this national park offers rich rewards for intrepid trekkers. Those with the lungs for it should not miss a trek here.

Parque Nacional Natural (PNN) Tayrona Offers accessible short hikes through tropical dry forest with the opportunity to eat, drink and swim along the way.

Valle de Cocora Near Salento; the country's best half-day hike takes you up into the national park amid wax palms.

Tierradentro A spectacular one-day walk in the south that traverses a triangular ridgeline and visits all of the nearby tombs.

Volcán Puracé Near Popayán; can be summited in one day (weather permitting).

Parque Nacional Natural (PNN) Farallones de Cali Near Cali; offers a day-long hike to the summit of Pico de Loro.

Laguna Verde Between Pasto and Ipiales; this five-hour hike takes you to a stunning green lake hidden in the crater of a rugged volcano.

Diving & Snorkeling

Colombia's Caribbean coast offers clear waters and bright coral formations, while the Pacific region offers close encounters with large marine animals.

On the Caribbean coast you'll find diving at budget prices with two tank dives starting from around COP$175,000. Prices in the Pacific tend to be significantly higher.

Where to Go

San Andrés & Providencia Classic Caribbean diving, with excellent visibility, fine coral reefs and a variety of marine life. There are even two sunken ships you can visit. The snorkeling is also top-notch with a lot of marine life in shallow waters.

Taganga On the Caribbean coast, Taganga offers some of the cheapest diving courses on the planet. Here you can get your PADI or NAUI certification from around COP$800,000 for a four-day course. The diving itself is second rate, but at these prices it's hard to complain.

Cartagena Boasts good diving around Bocachica, Tierrabomba and Punta Arena.

Islas de Rosario Famous for its diving and snorkeling, although warm-water currents have somewhat damaged the reef.

Capurganá and Sapzurro These small Pacific-coast towns are just minutes from the Panamanian border and offer good diving in clear Caribbean waters.

Isla Malpelo A small Pacific island 500km west of the continent that's home to schools of more than a thousand sharks. It can only be reached by joining a minimum eight-day live-aboard dive cruise from Buenaventura, on Colombia's Pacific coast, or Panama.

Playa Huína There are some diving opportunities near Bahía Solano, where a warship that survived Pearl Harbor has been sunk to create an artificial reef.

Hyperbaric Chambers

There are several hyperbaric chambers around the country – including at the Hospital Naval (p136) in Cartagena – should you experience decompression sickness (ie 'the bends'). Additional chambers are located in Providencia, San Andrés, Bahía Málaga and Bahía Solano; as well as Panama, if necessary.

In an emergency, your first response should be to contact local emergency services (telephone 123) who will stabilize the diver and help to locate the nearest treatment facility. For additional advice contact the **Divers Alert Network** (emergency hotline in US 1-919-684-9111; www.diversalertnetwork.org).

ORGANIZED ADVENTURES

If you fancy joining up with local outdoor enthusiasts while exploring Colombia, check out the following nonprofit organizations that arrange group excursions into the countryside.

Sal Si Puedes (p51) Runs weekend walks in rural areas around Bogotá.

Ecoaventura (p229) This Cali organization offers a variety of outdoor activities all over southern Colombia, including night hikes and abseiling trips.

White-water Rafting, Canoeing & Kayaking

Canoeing and kayaking aren't especially popular in Colombia, but opportunities are growing. Experienced paddlers can rent kayaks in both San Gil and San Agustín for white-water runs, the former's Río Suárez offering some of the best rapids (several Class IV and V) in South America. For some high-altitude paddling, rent a kayak in Guatapé to explore its extensive artificial lake.

Rafting trips range from COP$45,000 to COP$130,000 depending on length and adrenaline level.

Where to Go

Top rafting spots include the following:

San Gil This is the white-water rafting capital. The Río Fonce is fairly leisurely while the Río Suárez offers some serious thrills on Class IV and V rapids.

San Agustín A close second to San Gil. Here you can go white-water rafting on the Río Magdalena, one of Colombia's most important rivers. There are easy Class II and III trips, and longer, more difficult trips for experienced rafters.

Río Claro Offers a quiet paddle through the jungle with some minor Class I rapids. It's a fine spot to admire the flora and fauna instead of obsessing about falling out of the raft.

Rock Climbing & Abseiling

The birthplace of Colombian rock climbing is Suesca, a quick day trip from Bogotá. You'll find a 4km-long sandstone wall formation standing up to 120m high that's home to 300 climbing routes, both traditional and bolted. Suesca-based **Colombia Trek** (☎320-339-3839; www.colombiatrek.com) offers courses and/or guided climbing for COP$250,000 (including equipment). In Medellín, Psiconautica (p191) runs a rock-climbing/abseiling/canyoning school as well.

If you want to test your skills before committing to a full-on rock-climbing adventure, Gran Pared (p57), in Bogotá, offers a challenging climbing wall where you can get a feel for the sport.

Canopying

Sometimes called 'ziplines' in North America, canopying involves strapping yourself into a harness and zipping around the forest canopy on cables. You use a heavy leather glove on top of the cable to brake. The popularity of this sport exploded in Colombia in recent years, particularly in the mountain regions.

Where to Go

One of the best places for canopying is in Río Claro, halfway between Medellín and Bogotá, where a series of canopy lines zigzags across the river.

Other spots where you can go canopying include Los Yarumos near Manizales, the shores of Embalse del Peñol, near Medellín, Termales San Vicente near Pereira and Peñon Guane near San Gil. There are also several canopy lines near Villa de Leyva.

Paragliding

Colombia's varied mountain terrain means there are lots of great thermals to ride if you want to try *parapentismo* (paragliding). Tandem flights in Bucaramanga are cheap – starting from a mere COP$80,000. You can also enroll in a 10-day paragliding course for COP$3,400,000 and become an internationally accredited paragliding pilot.

Where to Go

Bucaramanga Arguably the country's paragliding capital, attracting paragliders from around the world.

Parque Nacional del Chicamocha One of the most spectacular spots, with longer rides ranging from 30 to 45 minutes of gliding.

Medellín Urban paragliders can test their wings on Medellín's outskirts, where a number of schools offer tandem flights and instruction.

Horseback Riding

With their deep rural roots, Colombians love riding horses. In almost every town that's frequented by domestic tourists, you'll find rentals and guided tours. While most tours are short half-day trips to local attractions, there are also some epic multiday adventures on offer, especially in the south of the country where the rolling green hills and temperate climate make for fantastic rides.

BIRDWATCHING IN COLOMBIA

Clocking in just shy of 2000 bird species (the number so far recorded; new species are still being discovered), Colombia is the world's number-one country in bird diversity and easily holds its own against Peru and Brazil in endemic species. The Andean mountains are full of hummingbirds (more than 160 species); the Amazonian jungle is full of toucans, parrots and macaws; and Parque Nacional Natural (PNN) Puracé, near Popayán, is home to condors, which the wardens will tempt down with food so you can see them up close. The Pacific coast is flooded with swarms of pelicans, herons and other water birds; as well as rare and skulky antbirds in the jungle.

Some 70% of the country's birds live in the Andean cloud forest, one of the world's most endangered ecosystems. The single-best birdwatching spot in the country is Montezuma Peak, located inside Parque Nacional Natural (PNN) Tatamá in the Cordillera Occidental between the departments of Chocó, Valle del Cauca and Risaralda. Here you'll find the best mix of Chocó and Andean birds in the country; it's packed with endemics, regional specialties and megarare birds. Access to the park itself is often restricted due to conservation; fortunately nearby Planes de San Rafael and Montezuma near Pueblo Rico (Risaralda) are reliable alternatives.

Other great bets include Reserva Ecológica Río Blanco above Manizales, and Km18 near Cali. The Amazon basin near Leticia is also an excellent spot for jungle birds, as is the Chocó. Colombia also features the western third of the Los Llanos area, shared by Venezuela, and it's a fine spot to see the diverse mix of birds this region attracts. The isolated Santa Marta massif in the north, along with the Perijá mountains, is packed with endemics. Several new species have recently been discovered in the Guyanese/Amazonian white-sand forest in Mitú, and in the east slope of the Andes in Putumayo where local guides now roam freely due to improved security in the region.

The country's most recent accolade in the birding world was winning the 2017 Global Big Day (www.ebird.org/ebird/globalbigday) event, with an amazing 1487 species recorded countrywide in a single day by nearly 2000 birdwatchers.

ProAves (☎1-340-3229; www.proaves.org; Carrera 20 No 36-61) is a Colombian nonprofit organization dedicated to preserving vital bird habitat. It runs a number of private reserves in Important Bird Areas (IBAs) around the country.

Finding birdwatching guides in Colombia isn't as difficult as it used to be. In many remote areas, locals can take you where they know birds are, but it'll be up to you to find them. For Andean birdwatching, especially in the Cordillera Occidental, you may be able to find a guide through **Mapalina** (www.facebook.com/mapalina birdingtrails), a nonprofit initiative based in Cali.

One reputable birdwatching tour company is **Colombia Birding** (☎314-896-3151; www.colombiabirding.com), run by a bilingual Colombian whose network of local guides can show you around many of the country's most popular birdwatching areas. It does private and small-group tours, charging around US$100 per person per day plus expenses. Its website has information on birds by region.

Robin Restall's *Birds of Northern South America* (2007), with full-color plates for every bird you're likely to see, and Fernando Ayerbe's *A Field Guide to the Birds of Colombia* (2014), are essential birdwatcher's field guides to Colombian birds.

For online information, check out Colombia's official tourism portal, www.colombia.travel, which does a surprisingly good job with birdwatching.

Where to Go

San Agustín Travel between remote pre-Columbian monuments in stunning natural settings. Most horses here are strong and in excellent condition.

Jardín Ascend steep, narrow mountain paths on the way to the spectacular Cueva del Esplendor.

Providencia Pick up your mount in Southwest Bay and trot along beaches and rural paths all over the island.

Desierto de la Tatacoa Bring your spaghetti western fantasies to life among striking arid landscapes.

Laguna de Magdalena Ride from San Agustín high into the *páramo* (high-mountain plains) of the Macizo Colombiano to the source of the mighty Río Magdalena on this multiday expedition.

Valle de Cocora Make your way beneath wax palms on the circuit to Reserva Natural Acaime.

Filandia Explore local coffee farms on horseback.

Mountain Biking

Cycling is very popular in Colombia, although most of it is road cycling. Prices for bike rental vary across regions, depending on the quality of the bike – expect to pay anywhere from COP$20,000 to COP$50,000 per half-day bike rental.

Where to Go

There's something about mountains that makes cyclists want to conquer them. Mountain biking per se is most popular in San Gil and Villa de Leyva, where several adventure companies and bike-rental shops can facilitate your adrenaline fix.

Some other great routes:

Minca Offers exciting mountain-bike runs in the Sierra Nevada mountains.

Coconuco to Popayán Take a dip in the thermal pools then cruise back down the mountain.

A WHALE OF A VIEW

Every year, whales living near Chile's Antarctic waters make the 8000km-plus journey to Colombia's Pacific coast to give birth and raise their young. These are humpback whales (yubartas, sometimes called jorobadas), and more than 800 have been recorded off the Colombian coast. They grow to 18m long and weigh up to 25 tons; there are few things cuter than spotting a *ballenato* (baby whale) already the size of a small truck, nosing its way through the surface.

The best whale-watching is from July through October, though arrivals begin in June. Whales can be seen all along the Pacific coast, and there are comfortable resorts where you can relax before and after a boat tour. Sometimes whales come so close to shore they can be seen from the beach, or from lookouts in the hills. Most whale-watching tours last 1½ to two hours and cost around COP$80,000 to COP$100,000 per person (although these prices can vary widely depending on the operator).

Where to Go

Humpback whales can be seen all along Colombia's Pacific coast but are not always easy to spot from the beach. We list the best places to observe whales up close.

Bahía Solano & El Valle While it's possible to spot whales right from the beach here, there are also a number of lookouts in the hills that offer better vantage points. Alternatively, organize a boat trip for an even closer look.

Parque Nacional Natural (PNN) Ensenada de Utría This narrow inlet of water, in the Chocó, is one of the best places to see whales up close while staying on dry land. During the calving season the whales enter the *ensenada* (inlet) and play just a few hundred meters from shore.

Isla Gorgona Whales come very close to the shore at this island national park; boat trips are available.

Guachalito There are a variety of accommodations ranging from rustic to high end on this long beach near Nuquí and all can arrange whale-watching trips.

Diving off San Andrés (p170)

Otún Quimbaya to Pereira The run from Santuario de Flora y Fauna Otún Quimbaya back to town passes through spectacular scenery.

Salento Full-day adventures take riders up to the Andean divide from where you'll cruise down the far side to the biggest wax palm forest in the region. You'll then be bought back up to the peak in a truck for the ride down the mountain to Salento.

Kitesurfing & Windsurfing

Colombia's vast water resources and tropical climate make it an ideal place for kitesurfing (kiteboarding) and windsurfing.

The casual traveler will find the learning curve for windsurfing much shorter than for kitesurfing; it's also a fair bit cheaper. Prices vary considerably. Expect to pay roughly COP$100,000 per hour for windsurfing instruction and COP$120,000 to COP$145,000 per hour for individual kitesurfing instruction (prices are lower in groups). Kite rentals go for around COP$100,000 per hour. If you've got your own gear, you'll pay COP$20,000 to COP$30,000 for each water entrance.

The most comprehensive guide to kitesurfing in Colombia can be found at www.colombiakite.com.

Where to Go

On the Caribbean coast, winds are best from January to April. Good spots include the following:

Lago Calima The star kitesurfing spot is not where you might think: Lago Calima is an artificial reservoir (elevation 1800m) lying 86km north of Cali. The appeal is year-round 18- to 25-knot winds, which attract world champions to its competitions held every August and September. There's no beach here; access to the water is via the grassy slopes along the lake.

La Boquilla Just near Cartagena.

Cabo de la Vela Terrific remote beaches; stunning backdrops.

San Andrés Launch from the island's famous white-sand beaches.

Regions at a Glance

Colombia offers a beautifully diverse potpourri of landscapes and a laundry list of varied experiences within them. Big cities like Bogotá, Cali and Medellín are epicenters of gastronomy and nightlife; the Caribbean Coast and the islands of San Andrés and Providencia are tropical paradises; wildlife thrives in the Amazon rainforest, the wetlands of Los Llanos and the Pacific Coast; and colonial villages, ancient ruins and coffee plantations are peppered around the country as well. With excellent transportation infrastructure, it's possible to bounce between the jungles, the mountains and the sea, giving Colombia a trifecta of dazzling settings within its borders. From the snowcapped peaks of the Andes to the translucent waters of the Caribbean, South America's comeback kid beckons jetsetters with cinematic sundry of travel joy.

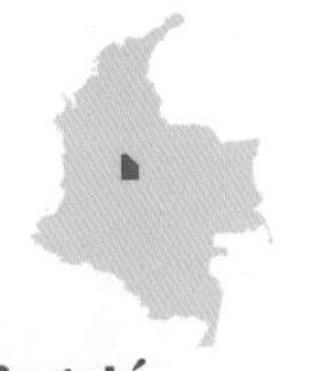

Bogotá

Architecture
Museums
Wining & Dining

Colonial Epicenter

Bogotá's historic colonial center of 300-year-old homes, churches and buildings known as La Candelaria is a preserved mix of Spanish and baroque architecture.

World-class Museums

Anchored by one of South America's most brilliantly curated and designed museums, the fascinating Museo del Oro, Bogotá boasts more than 60 museums.

Local Specialties

From its classic regional specialties such as *ajiaco* (an Andean chicken stew with corn), to modern takes on gourmet fare that have begun to employ Colombia's wealth of native ingredients, the city is enjoying a bona fide foodie resurgence.

p39

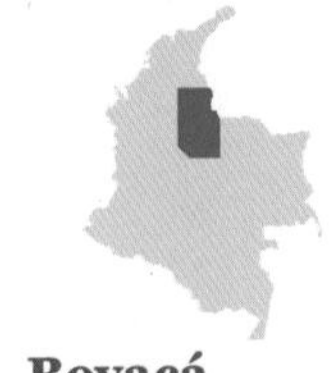

Boyacá, Santander & Norte de Santander

Villages
Adventure
Nature

Colonial Villages

This region has four of Colombia's most striking colonial villages: Barichara and Villa de Leyva, and sleepier Monguí and Playa de Belén.

Thrilling Adventures

Whether seeking a challenging high-altitude trek or white-knuckle adventure, Boyacá and Santander deliver. In Parque Nacional Natural (PNN) El Cocuy, visitors can hike among at least 12 peaks above 5000m.

Great Outdoors

Nature enthusiasts should flock to Villa de Leyva and Barichara for their excellent natural surroundings. Lago de Tota ups the ante with mountain trekking and a sky-high beach.

p81

Caribbean Coast

Beaches
Architecture
Trekking

White Sands

The idyllic beaches of Colombia's Caribbean coast and islands are Colombia's best. Here, white sands are fringed with seething jungle, dramatic deserts or palm trees. Whatever your poison, there's sun and sand for all.

Colonial Architecture

The walled city of Cartagena offers ornate churches and romantic, shaded squares, while hidden Mompós has a restored colonial heart.

Lost City

The multiday trek to Ciudad Perdida (Lost City) is one of the continent's classic hikes; the destination is a mysterious ancient city belonging to a disappeared culture.

p119

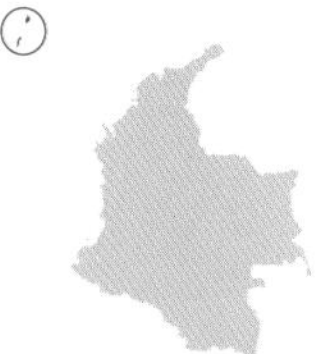

San Andrés & Providencia

Diving
Beaches
Hiking

Coral Reefs

Both islands have extensive coral reefs totaling 50km with a biodiversity that equals any in the region. Sharks are the standout, but there are also turtles, barracudas, stingrays, manta rays and eagle rays just offshore.

Idyllic Coasts

Take your pick of idyllic beaches bordering the archipelago's famed sea of seven colors. San Andrés offers a vibrant atmosphere and water sports, while Providencia is tranquil and remote.

El Pico

San Andrés and Providencia don't just cater for beach bums and divers: the island's interior is mountainous, and El Pico Natural Regional Park on Providencia offers walkers a breathtaking 360-degree Caribbean view.

p169

Medellín & Zona Cafetera

Coffee
Nightlife
Hiking

Coffee Fincas

Throughout Caldas, Risaralda and Quindío departments, some of Colombia's best coffee *fincas* (farms) welcome visitors onto their plantations.

Bright Discos & Bohemian Bars

Going out in Medellín is all about seeing and being seen. *Paisas* (people from Antioquia) love to dress up and go out, from the bright discos of Parque Lleras to the bohemian bars downtown.

Walks & Treks

With high-altitude treks in PNN Los Nevados and more sedate strolls through regional nature reserves, the Zona Cafetera offers hikes to match all energy levels. Don't miss the Valle de Cocora, near Salento, with its towering wax palms.

p183

Cali & Southwest Colombia

Archaeology
Culture
Architecture

Pre-Columbian Ruins

More than 500 mysterious stone statues are scattered around San Agustín, while at Tierradentro, archaeologists have unearthed more than 100 underground tombs.

Salsa

From small barrio bars to the sweaty *salsatecas* (salsa dance clubs), high-energy salsa is the beat that drives Cali. Take classes at one of the city's many academies.

Spanish-Colonial Architecture

Boasting whitewashed mansions and splendid churches, Popayán is a superb example of Spanish-colonial architecture. Continue the colonial theme in Cali's Barrio San Antonio.

p227

Pacific Coast

Marine Life
Beaches
Nature

Whales, Turtles & Sharks

Get close to massive humpback whales at Parque Nacional Natural (PNN) Ensenada de Utría or head out at night to watch sea turtles lay their eggs near El Valle.

Gray-sand Beaches

Framed by jungle-covered mountains, the rugged gray beaches of the region are breathtaking and mostly deserted. Guachalito and Playa Almejal both have fine resorts wedged between the jungle and the sea.

Trekking & Canoeing

The Chocó boasts fantastic off-the-beaten-track treks to waterfalls deep in the jungle. Check out the region's amazing biodiversity while paddling up the Río Joví or Río Juribidá in a dugout canoe.

p259

Los Llanos

Nature
Archaeology
Swimming

Wild Rivers & Waterfalls

There are few regions in Colombia as pristine and well protected as Caño Cristales, where tours take you deep into the national park to see gorgeous waterfalls and rushing rivers.

Pre-Columbian Cave Paintings

Pre-Columbian cave paintings can be seen in great abundance in the countryside around San José del Guaviare, and often involve exciting treks through the jungle.

Pools, Pozos & Swimming Holes

Places for a dip abound in Los Llanos, with various gorgeous pools and swimming holes (often complete with waterfalls) in Caño Cristales and the fabulous *pozos naturales* around San José del Guaviare.

p273

Amazon Basin

Wildlife
Jungle
Ecovillages

Wild Kingdom

While human encroachment have pushed the Amazon's wildlife population in the wrong direction, it remains an incomprehensibly gigantic hotbed of biodiversity, the world's largest collection of living plants and animal species.

Amazon Rainforest

The mother of all jungles, no word conjures up a more alluring mix of enigmatic rainforest, enormous rivers, indigenous folklore and tropical wildlife than the Amazon.

Puerto Nariño

The ecological village of Puerto Nariño is a charming, architecturally interesting, near-perfect place to chill out in the rainforest.

p281

On the Road

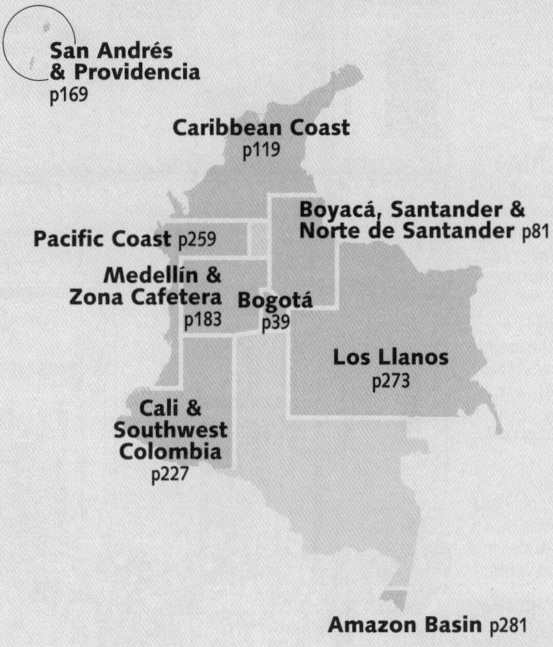

San Andrés & Providencia p169

Caribbean Coast p119

Boyacá, Santander & Norte de Santander p81

Pacific Coast p259

Medellín & Zona Cafetera p183

Bogotá p39

Los Llanos p273

Cali & Southwest Colombia p227

Amazon Basin p281

AT A GLANCE

POPULATION
7.6 million

ELEVATION
2640m

BEST EDGY ART
Espacio KB (p47)

BEST CRAFT BEERS
Cervecería Gigante (p68)

BEST BOUTIQUE HOTEL
Casa Legado (p58)

WHEN TO GO

Jun & Jul
Temperatures aren't as high as in May, but rainfall drops dramatically.

Aug
Typically the month with the least rainfall, the city's residents enjoy the many parks and plazas.

Dec
Bogotanos fall hard for Christmas, when the city sparkles in a festival of lights.

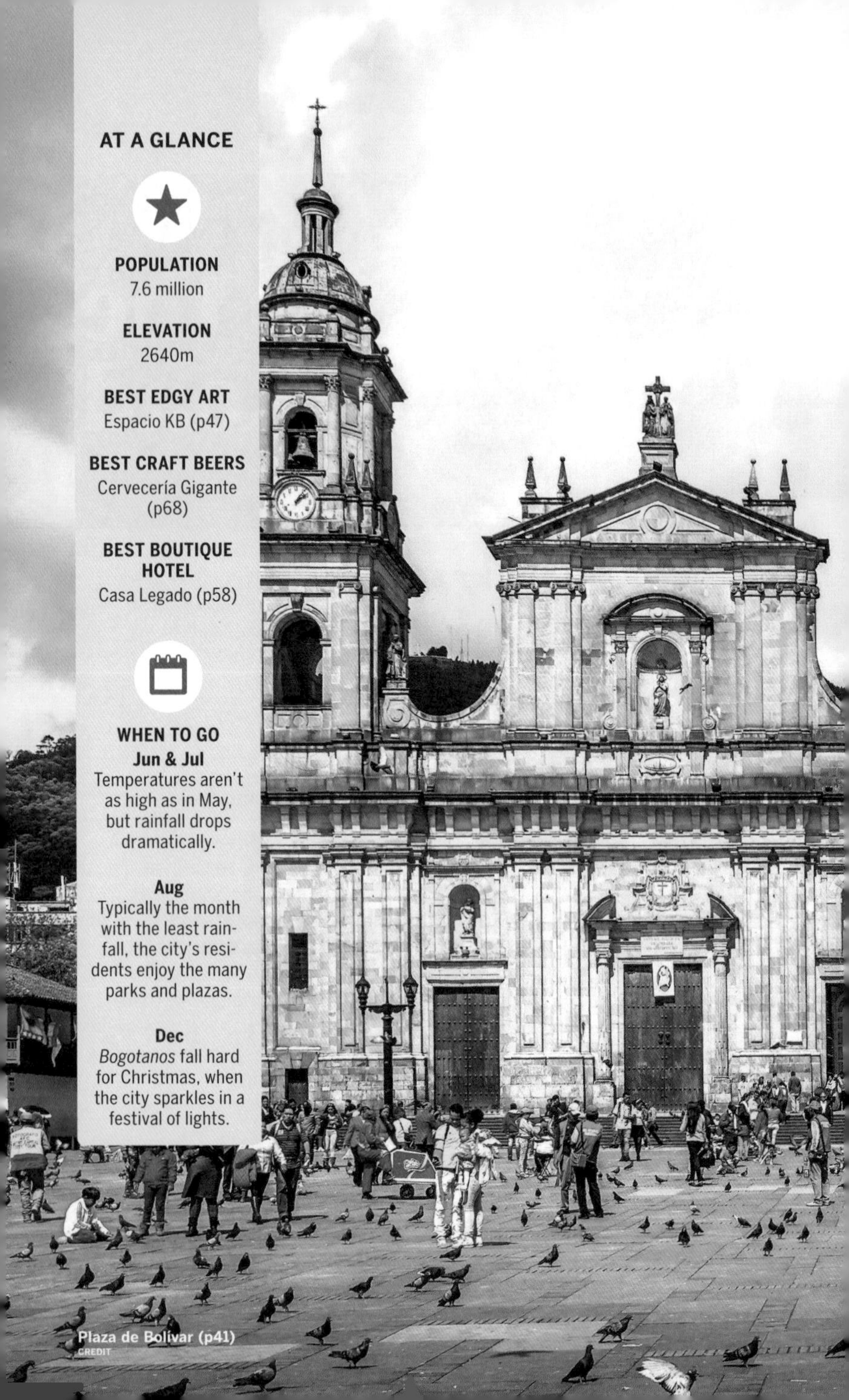

Plaza de Bolívar (p41)
CREDIT

Bogotá

Bogotá is Colombia's beating heart, an engaging and vibrant capital cradled by chilly Andean peaks and steeped in sophisticated urban cool. The city's cultural epicenter is La Candelaria, the cobbled historic downtown to which most travelers gravitate. Here, a potpourri of carefully preserved colonial buildings is home to museums, restaurants, hotels and bars, peppered amid 300-year-old houses, churches and convents. Nearly all of Bogotá's traditional attractions are here, radiating from Plaza de Bolívar, and gorgeous Cerro de Monserrate is just east.

The city's grittier sides sit south and southwest, where working-class barrios continue to battle their (sadly, deserved) reputations for drugs and crime. In the ritzier north you'll find boutique hotels, and well-heeled locals piling into chic entertainment districts such as the Zona Rosa and Zona G.

INCLUDES

History 41
Sights 41
Activities 50
Courses 51
Tours 51
Festivals & Events 53
Sleeping 56
Eating 59
Drinking & Nightlife 66
Entertainment 71
Shopping 72

Bogotá Highlights

1. **Museo del Oro** (p46) Pondering Colombia's El Dorado myths at one of the continent's top museums.
2. **Andrés Carne de Res** (p64) Stepping into the nightlife world at this extraordinary bar.
3. **Cerro de Monserrate** (p52) Trekking up the towering symbol of Bogotá for sweeping capital views.
4. **Museo Botero** (p42) Appreciating the beauty of heft at this fantastic collection donated by the artist himself.
5. **Museo Santa Clara** (p43) Genuflecting at the interiors of this 17th-century ecclesiastical masterpiece.
6. **Iglesia de San Francisco** (p46) Marveling at the gilded altar in the city's oldest surviving church.
7. **Cafe culture** (p69) Experiencing Colombia's coffee reawakening in Bogotá's northern neighborhoods.
8. **Bogotá Bike Tours** (p52) Attacking Bogotá by bike on fascinating tours.

History

Long before the Spanish Conquest, the Sabana de Bogotá, a fertile highland basin that today has been almost entirely taken over by the city, was inhabited by one of the most advanced pre-Columbian indigenous groups, the Muisca. The Spanish era began when Gonzalo Jiménez de Quesada and his expedition arrived at the Sabana, founding the town on August 6, 1538, near the Muisca capital, Bacatá.

The town was named Santa Fe de Bogotá, a combination of the traditional name, Bacatá, and Quesada's hometown in Spain, Santa Fe. Nonetheless, throughout the colonial period the town was simply referred to as Santa Fe.

At the time of its foundation Santa Fe consisted of 12 huts and a chapel, where a Mass was held to celebrate the town's birth. The Muisca religious sites were destroyed and replaced by churches.

During the early years Santa Fe was governed from Santo Domingo (on the island of Hispaniola, the present-day Dominican Republic), but in 1550 it fell under the rule of Lima, the capital of the Viceroyalty of Peru and the seat of Spain's power for the conquered territories of South America. In 1717 Santa Fe was made the capital of the Virreinato de la Nueva Granada, the newly created viceroyalty comprising the territories of present-day Colombia, Panama, Venezuela and Ecuador.

Despite the town's political importance, its development was hindered by the area's earthquakes, and also by the smallpox and typhoid epidemics that plagued the region throughout the 17th and 18th centuries.

After independence, the Congress of Cúcuta shortened the town's name to Bogotá in 1821 and decreed it the capital of Gran Colombia. The town developed steadily and by the middle of the 19th century it had 30,000 inhabitants and 30 churches. In 1884 the first tramway began to operate in the city and, soon after, railway lines were constructed to La Dorada and Girardot, giving Bogotá access to the ports on the Río Magdalena.

Rapid progress came only in the 1940s with industrialization and the consequent peasant migrations from the countryside. On April 9, 1948, the popular leader Jorge Eliécer Gaitán was assassinated, sparking the uprising known as El Bogotazo. The city was partly destroyed; 136 buildings were burnt to the ground and 2500 people died.

Tranquil life in Bogotá was rocked again on November 6, 1985, when guerrillas of the M-19 (Movimiento 19 de Abril) revolutionary movement invaded the Palace of Justice in Bogotá and made hostages of the 300-plus civilians in the building. By the next day, 115 people were dead, including 11 Supreme Court judges.

Colombia's historic 2016 peace deal with Revolutionary Armed Forces of Colombia (FARC), which ended a 52-year civil war, has Bogotá breathing a long-awaited sigh of relief. Dramatically improved safety, along with a host of progressive projects under successive mayors (eg the 350km of CicloRuta bike lanes), have helped the city make major strides toward positioning itself as not only a cultural capital but a destination in its own right.

Sights

Most attractions are in historic La Candelaria, where Bogotá was born, and you'll probably want more than a day to look around the area.

If you're thinking of going to a museum on a Sunday, think again: Bogotá has half-a-hundred options, and most get crammed with locals, particularly on free day (the last Sunday of the month); 45-minute lines outside second-stringer museums aren't unheard of. It's quieter during the week.

When walking around, pop into random churches, too. Most are beauties, frequently dating from the 17th and 18th centuries, and often with more elaborate decoration than the exterior would suggest. Some show off a distinctive Spanish-Moorish style called Mudejar (mainly noticeable in the ceiling ornamentation) as well as paintings by Colombia's best-known colonial-era artist, Gregorio Vásquez de Arce y Ceballos.

La Candelaria

Blissfully alive and chock-full of key things to see, La Candelaria is Bogotá's colonial barrio, with a mix of carefully restored 300-year-old houses, some rather dilapidated ones, and still more marking more modern eras.

The usual place to start discovering Bogotá is **Plaza de Bolívar** (Map p48; btwn Calles 10 & 11), marked by a bronze statue of Simón Bolívar (cast in 1846 by Italian artist Pietro Tenerani). It was the city's first public monument. The square has changed considerably over the centuries and is no longer lined

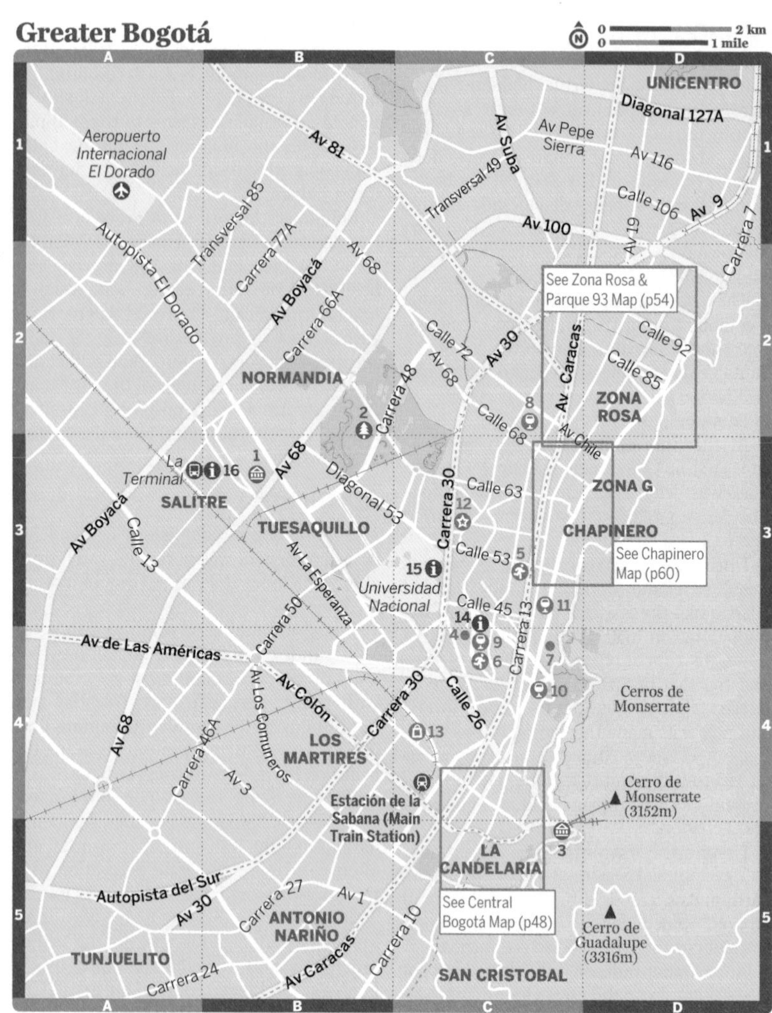

by colonial buildings; only the Capilla del Sagrario dates from the Spanish era. Other buildings are more recent and feature different architectural styles.

Some of La Candelaria's most popular sights, as well as the **Centro Cultural Gabriel García Márquez** (☎1-283-2200; www.fce.com.co/CCGGM; Calle 11 No 5-60; ⏰7am-9pm Mon-Fri, 9am-9pm Sat, 10am-6pm Sun) **FREE**, are within a couple of blocks east of the plaza. The slightly confusing web of museums run by the Banco de la República, including the Museo Botero, Casa de Moneda, the Colección de Arte and the Museo de Arte del Banco de la República, are essentially one massive and labyrinthine interconnected museum complex and form what is easily one of Bogotá's top attractions. Plan ahead: last admission to the complex is 30 minutes before closing.

★ **Museo Botero** MUSEUM

(Map p48; www.banrepcultural.org/museo-botero; Calle 11 No 4-41; ⏰9am-7pm Mon & Wed-Sat, 10am-5pm Sun) **FREE** Even if you've never heard of Fernando Botero, you'll probably recognize some of his highly distinctive paintings of oversized (read: chubby) characters, including dodgy dictators, fleet-footed dancers, dogs and birds. Colombia's most famous

Greater Bogotá

Sights
1 Maloka B3
2 Parque Metropolitano Simón Bolívar B2
3 Quinta de Bolívar C5

Activities, Courses & Tours
4 De Una Colombia Tours C4
5 Gran Pared C3
6 ProAves C4
7 Universidad Javeriana's Centro Latinoamericano C4

Drinking & Nightlife
8 Cerveceria Gigante C2
9 Cervecería Statua Rota C4
10 Cine Tonalá C4
11 La Negra C3

Entertainment
12 Estadio El Campín C3

Shopping
13 Plaza de Mercado de Paloquemao C4

Information
14 Instituto Distrital de Turismo C3
15 Instituto Geográfico Agustín Codazzi C3
16 Punto de Información Turística B3

living artist is also a prolific sculptor and his curvaceous bronze statues display equally generous girth.

The museum, which belongs to the Banco de la República de Colombia, was founded in 2000 when Botero donated more than 100 of his own works, along with 85 from his personal collection of other artists' work – a haul that includes pieces by Picasso, Monet, Matisse and Klimt. The painter curated the museum himself.

Botero paintings to look out for include a parody of Di Vinci's *Mona Lisa* (1978), the wonderfully intimate *Pareja Bailando* (1987) and the haunting studies of Colombia's drug-cartel violence in the 1980s and '90s.

Audio guides (COP$10,000) in English, French and Spanish are available from the museum complex's main entrance on Calle 11. Other than that, there's no cost.

Museo Santa Clara CHURCH

(Map p48; www.museocolonial.gov.co; Carrera 8 No 8-91; adult/child COP$4000/2000; 9am-5pm Tue-Fri, 10am-4pm Sat & Sun) One of Bogotá's most richly decorated churches, the Santa Clara is also its oldest (along with Iglesia de San Francisco). Deconsecrated in 1968, it was acquired by the government and is now run as a museum, with paintings by some of Colombia's most revered baroque artists. The church was once part of an adjoining Franciscan convent that was demolished in the early 20th century.

Built between 1629 and 1674, the single-nave construction features a barrel vault coated in golden floral motifs that looks down over walls entirely covered by 148 paintings and sculptures of saints. Interactive panels are available in Spanish, English, French and Portuguese.

Casa de Nariño HISTORIC BUILDING

(Map p48; http://visitas.presidencia.gov.co; Plaza de Bolívar) On the south side of Plaza de Bolívar, beyond the Capitolio Nacional and reached via Carreras 8 or 7, this is Colombia's neoclassical presidential building, where the country's leader lives and works. To visit, you'll need to email or go to the website and scroll down to 'Visitas Casa de Nariño' under 'Servicios a la Ciudadanía'. No permission is needed to watch the changing of the presidential guard – best seen from the east side – held at 3:30pm Wednesdays, Fridays and Sundays.

The building is named for Antonio Nariño, a colonial figure with ideas of independence and who secretly translated France's human-rights laws into Spanish – and went to jail for it, a couple of times. In 1948 the building was damaged during El Bogotazo riots and only restored in 1979. Register in advance for 45-minutes tours at 9am, 10:30am, 2:30pm and 4pm during the week; 2:30pm and 4pm on Saturday; and 3pm and 4pm on Sunday. Note: guards around the president's palace stand at barriers on Carreras 7 and 8. It's OK to pass them, just show the contents of your bag and stay clear of the fence-side sidewalks.

Colección de Arte MUSEUM

(Map p48; www.banrepcultural.org; Calle 11 No 4-14; 9am-7pm Mon & Wed-Sat, 10am-5pm Sun) FREE Most of Banco de la República's permanent art collection, which features 800 pieces by 250 different artists spread over 16 exhibition halls at two addresses, is reached via elaborate staircases within the same museum complex as Casa de Moneda (p44) and Museo Botero (p42). The collection has been reorganized into five time periods spanning the 15th century to modern day, each separately curated. The collection's contemporary art exhibition is located inside **Biblioteca Luis Ángel Arango** (Map p48; ☎1-343-1224) on Calle 12.

Most of it sticks with modern splashes of oils by Colombian artists, including giant figurative paintings by Luis Caballero (1943–95) on the first floor. A bit at odds with the rest are the two first-floor halls toward the east, which focus on 17th- and 18th-century religious objects, including two extraordinary *custodias* (monstrances). The largest was made of 4902g of pure gold encrusted with 1485 emeralds, one sapphire, 13 rubies, 28 diamonds, 168 amethysts, one topaz and 62 pearls. But who's counting?

Casa de Moneda MUSEUM

(Mint; Map p48; www.banrepcultural.org; Calle 11 No 4-93; ⏰9am-7pm Mon & Wed-Sat, 10am-5pm Sun) FREE This historic museum inside the Banco de la República complex houses the **Colección Numismática** as well as the Colección de Arte (p43). The former exhibit starts with pre-Columbian exchanges of pots and lead chronologically to misshapen coins, the introduction of a centralized bank in 1880, and the making of the cute tree art on the current 500 peso coin in the late 1990s.

Museo Histórico Policial MUSEUM

(Museum of Police History; Map p48; www.policia.gov.co; Calle 9 No 9-27; ⏰8am-5pm Tue-Sun) FREE This surprisingly worthwhile museum not only gets you inside the lovely ex-HQ (built in 1923) of Bogotá's police force, but gives you 45 minutes or so of contact time with English-speaking,18-year-old local guides who are serving a one-year compulsory service with the police (interesting tales to be heard).

The best parts otherwise follow cocaine kingpin Pablo Escobar's demise in 1993 – his Harley Davidson (a gift to a cousin) and his personal Bernardelli pocket pistol, otherwise known as his 'second wife.'

Museo Colonial MUSEUM

(Map p48; www.museocolonial.gov.co; Carrera 6 No 9-77; adult/student COP$3000/2000; ⏰9am-5pm Tue-Fri, 10am-4pm Sat & Sun) This museum occupies a one-time Jesuit college and traces the evolution of how religious and portrait art pieces are made, particularly by Colombia's favorite baroque artist, Gregorio Vásquez de Arce y Ceballos (1638–1711). It reopened in 2017 after an extensive, three-year renovation and now features five permanent galleries.

Capitolio Nacional HISTORIC BUILDING

(Map p48; www.senado.gov.co; Plaza de Bolívar; ⏰tours by appointment) FREE On the southern side of the plaza stands this neoclassical seat of congress. It was begun in 1847 but, due to numerous political uprisings, not completed until 1926. Its square-facing facade was built by English architect Thomas Reed. To take a free three-hour tour, email at least a week ahead; otherwise, you can wander around the stone courtyard.

Plazoleta del Chorro de Quevedo PLAZA

(Map p48; cnr Carrera 2 & Calle 12B) No one agrees exactly where present-day Bogotá was founded – some say by the Catedral Primada on the Plaza de Bolívar; others say here, in this wee plaza lined with cafes, a small white church and many boho street vendors (or hacky-sack players).

It's a cute spot at any time of day, but particularly as dark comes – when students pour onto the scene – in the narrow, funnel-like alley leading past pocket-sized bars just north. On Friday afternoon (at 5pm) there are Spanish storyteller sessions – well worth a visit for the atmosphere.

Observatorio Astronómico OBSERVATORY

(Map p48; obsan_fcbog@unal.edu.co; ⏰9am & noon Mon & Wed) FREE Conceptualized by celebrated Colombian botanist José Celestino Mutis, the 1803 tower is reputedly the first astronomical observatory built on the continent. It's possible to visit at set times, but you must reserve three days ahead. Email the names, telephone numbers, passport numbers and makes, serial numbers and colors of any cameras (phones or otherwise) of all in your party to reserve a spot.

Catedral Primada CATHEDRAL

(Map p48; www.catedral.arquibogota.org.co; Plaza de Bolívar; ⏰Mass noon Tue-Sat, 10am, noon & 1:30pm Sun) This neoclassical cathedral stands on the site where the first Mass *may* have been celebrated after Bogotá was founded in 1538 (some historians argue that it happened at Plazoleta del Chorro de Quevedo, just east). Either way, it's Bogotá's largest cathedral. It's also the main plaza's most dominating building, facing from the northeastern corner.

The original simple thatched chapel was replaced by a more substantial building from 1556 to 1565; this later collapsed due to poor foundations. In 1572 the third church went up, but the earthquake of 1785 reduced it to ruins. Only in 1807 was the massive

BOGOTÁ IN...

Two Days

Start in La Candelaria, with a snack at La Puerta Falsa (p59), a look at Plaza de Bolívar (p41) and a visit to the sculptures of chubby bodies at the Museo Botero (p42). Lunch at Prudencia (p62) or Capital Cocina (p62), then take in Colombia's golden past at Museo del Oro (p46). Feast on cutting-edge Colombian food in **Chapinero Alto** or **Quinta Camacho** (or fine dine in **Zona G**), before drinking to your liver's content in **Zona Rosa** or **Parque 93**.

On your second day, you'll want to leg it up Monserrate (p52) for massive capital views, and then grab a nap. At night, enter the surreal world of Andrés Carne de Res (p64), a 23km taxi ride north in Chía.

Four Days

Follow the two-day itinerary, then take a day trip to the salt cathedral (p58) at Zipaquirá, easily reached by public transportation. On your last day, start with brunch in Usaquén (p66) before heading to the city for a tour on two wheels with Bogotá Bike Tours (p52). Afterward, grab a hot cup of *canelazo* (made with aguardiente, sugarcane, cinnamon and lime) in a cafe in La Candelaria (p67), and have a farewell meal at an innovative Colombian restaurant – the bohemian foodie neighborhoods of Chapinero Alto (p63) and La Macarena (p62) are good bets.

building that stands today initiated, and it was successfully completed by 1823. It was partly damaged during the Bogotazo riots in 1948. Unlike those of many Bogotá churches, its spacious interior has relatively little ornamentation. The tomb of Jiménez de Quesada, the founder of Bogotá, is in the largest chapel off the right-hand aisle.

Museo de la Independencia – Casa del Florero MUSEUM
(Casa del Florero; Map p48; www.museoindependencia.gov.co; Calle 11 No 6-94; adult/student COP$3000/2000, free Sun; ⌚9am-5pm Tue-Fri, 10am-4pm Sat & Sun) Just after Napoleon overcame Spain in 1810, local Creole Antonio Morales supposedly came to this late-16th-century home and demanded an ornate vase from its Spanish owner, which led to a fistfight on the street (plus one shattered vase) – eventually spurring a rebellion. In these hallowed halls you can see the broken vase in question.

The story is known as 'the broken vase was heard around the world.'

Teatro Colón THEATER
(Map p48; ☎1-284-7420; www.teatrocolon.gov.co; Calle 10 No 5-32; ⌚box office 10am-7pm Mon-Sat, to 4pm Sun) The Teatro Colón, with its adorable Italian-style facade, has had various names since its birth in 1792; this latest version opened as Teatro Nacional in 1892 and was designed by Italian architect Pietro Cantini. Its lavish interiors reopened mid-2014 after it underwent a six-year makeover. The theater hosts concerts, opera, ballet, plays – and even electronica DJ sets.

Tours are available in Spanish only at 3pm on Wednesday and Thursday and noon and 3pm Saturday (COP$8000).

Museo Militar MUSEUM
(Military Museum; Map p48; http://museo-militar.webnode.com.co/; Calle 10 No 4-92; ⌚9am-4pm Tue-Fri, 10am-4pm Sat) FREE This two-floor museum is run by military guys in fatigues, and features playful models sporting the history of military uniforms (note the 'anti-terrorist' outfit and the insane diving suit); a Korean War room; and a courtyard of artillery and aircraft including a presidential helicopter.

Newer, postpeace agreement installations have been added, including a timeline of Colombia's armed conflict and Alex Sastoque's *Metamorfosis,* a copper AK-47 turned shovel, an idea – converting a tool of destruction into a tool of creation – which has come to symbolize the end of civil war in Colombia. ID required.

City Center

Bogotá's scrappy business center – busiest along Calle 19 and Carrera 7 – is easiest to deal with on Sunday, when Ciclovía shuts down Carrera 7 for cyclists and pedestrians (a permanent pedestrianization between Plaza de Bolívar and Calle 26 was completed in 2018), and the **Mercado de San Alejo** (www.facebook.com/MercadoSanAlejo; Carrera 7 btwn Calles 24 & 26; ⏲9am-5pm Sun) flea market is in force. Some of the district's most visited parts (notably the Museo del Oro (p46)) cluster near La Candelaria by Av Jiménez.

★Museo del Oro MUSEUM

(Map p48; www.banrepcultural.org/museo-del-oro; Carrera 6 No 15-88; adult/child COP$4000/free, Sun free; ⏲9am-6pm Tue-Sat, 10am-4pm Sun) Bogotá's most famous museum and one of the most fascinating in South America, the Gold Museum contains more than 55,000 pieces of gold and other materials from all of Colombia's major pre-Hispanic cultures. The collection is laid out in logical, thematic rooms over three floors; descriptions are in Spanish and English.

Second-floor exhibits break down findings by region, with descriptions of how pieces were used. There are lots of mixed animals rendered in gold (eg jaguar-frog, human-eagle); note the female figurines indicating how women of the Zenú in the pre-Columbian north played important roles in worship.

The 3rd-floor 'Offering' room exhibits explain how gold was used in ceremonies and rituals. Some of the displayed *tunjos* (gold offerings, usually figurines depicting various aspects of social life) were thrown into the Laguna de Guatavita; the most famous one, found near the town of Pasca in 1969, is the unlabeled gold boat called the Balsa Muisca. It's uncertain how old it is, as generally only gold pieces that include other materials can be carbon dated.

There's more to understanding the stories than the descriptions can convey, so try taking a free one-hour tour (11am and 4pm Tuesday through Saturday; in Spanish and English) – tours vary the part of the museum to be highlighted. Audio guides (COP$8000) are available in Spanish, English, French and Portuguese.

The museum gets exceedingly busy on Sunday, when entry is free.

> **GREEN PEOPLE**
>
> While walking around La Candelaria – while keeping an eye out for fresh dog feces and missing pothole covers at street level – look up for a unique art project that peers down from rooftops, window ledges and balconies. Assembled in the past decade from recycled materials, the artworks – green figures representing the area's *comuneros* (commoners) – come from local artist Jorge Olavé.
>
> Note the guy watching over Plaza de Bolívar from atop the **Casa de Comuneros'** southwestern corner – he's got the best seat in town.

★Iglesia de San Francisco CHURCH

(Map p48; www.templodesanfrancisco.com; cnr Av Jiménez & Carrera 7; ⏲6:30am-10:30pm Mon-Fri, 6:30am-12:30pm & 4-6:30pm Sat, 7:30am-1:30pm & 4:30-7:30pm Sun) Built between 1557 and 1621, the Church of San Francisco is Bogotá's oldest surviving church. In the atmospherically dark interior, with its extravagant pews and steady trickle of praying pilgrims, your eye is immediately drawn to the gilded, U-shaped 17th-century altarpiece, the largest and most elaborate of its kind in the capital.

Casa Museo Quinta de Bolívar MUSEUM

(Map p42; www.quintadebolivar.gov.co; Calle 20 No 2-91 Este; adult/child COP$4000/2000, Sun free; ⏲9am-5pm Tue-Fri, 10am-4pm Sat & Sun) Bringing a bit of the country into the middle of high-rise Bogotá, this lovely historic home-museum is set in a garden at the foot of the Cerro de Monserrate. The mansion was built in 1800 and donated to Simón Bolívar in 1820 in gratitude for his liberating services. Bolívar spent 423 days here over nine years. Rooms are filled with period pieces, including the liberator's sword. Less is said about its later days as a psychiatric institution.

There are English- and Spanish-language audio guides for COP$2000, and guided tours in English on Wednesday at 11am.

Mirador Torre Colpatria VIEWPOINT

(Map p48; Carrera 7 No 24-89; COP$7500; ⏲6-8:30pm Fri, 2-7:30pm Sat, 11am-4:30pm Sun) From the 48th-floor outside deck of the Colpatria Tower you can catch a superb view of the bullring, backed by office buildings and the mountains – there are also fine 360-degree vistas across the city. The 162m-high skyscraper was Colombia's tallest building from 1979 until 2016, when it was usurped by the 246m BD Bacatá tower. Expect queues.

BOGOTÁ FOR CHILDREN

Bogotá isn't any more or less kid-friendly than other South American cities of its size and the usual quirks apply. Generally speaking, the capital is a safe destination for kids, though you shouldn't expect facilities on par with those in European or North American destinations. Diaper-changing rooms aren't guaranteed but are a fairly common sight in non-basic establishments. With its wealth of museums, Bogotá is a wonderful spot for teaching moments, giving young travelers valuable insight into culture and history at every turn. The obvious standout kid destination, Maloka (p50), is a child-oriented science museum with a dome cinema, but Botero's chubby art at Museo Botero (p42) can be fun as well. Parque Metropolitano Simón Bolívar (p47), Bogotá's signature green space, is perfect for picnics, a game of tag or throwing a frisbee around, and popping up to the top of Monserrate (p52) is a surefire winner. Vendors sell birdseed for the (many) pigeons in Plaza de Bolívar (p41). And you can marvel at the hats at the changing of the presidential guard at nearby Casa de Nariño.

Friendly and fun food options include diner chain Crepes & Waffles (p63), fast-food burgers at El Corral (p63) and popsicles at **La Paletteria** (Map p54; www.lapaletteria.co; cnr Carrera 13 & Calle 84; popsicles COP$4500-6000; ⏲11am-9pm Mon-Thu, 10am-10pm Fri & Sat, 11am-7:30pm Sun). And don't miss Andrés Carne de Res (p64). Better yet, if your little one has a birthday, Andrés is set up to throw the party of a lifetime!

Centro Internacional

Offices look over Carrera 7 in this busy pocket of the city, where you'll find a few attractions and lots of business meetings.

Museo Nacional MUSEUM

(National Museum; Map p48; www.museonacional.gov.co; Carrera 7 No 28-66; adult/child COP$4000/2000, Sun free; ⏲10am-6pm Tue-Sat, to 5pm Sun) Housed in the expansive, Greek-cross-shaped building called El Panóptico (designed as a prison by English architect Thomas Reed in 1874), the Museo Nacional explores Colombia's past via archeology, history, ethnology and art. The collection is spread across 17 galleries that will eventually be themed by floor – the museum is undergoing a major modernization that will last through to 2023.

The first two galleries, Memoria y Nación and Tierra como Recurso, are open and present a strikingly modern contrast to the whitewashed walls and dated galleries elsewhere in the museum. On the 3rd floor, room 16 gives the best sense of prison life – with old cells now presenting various exhibits. The first on the right centers on Jorge Gaitán, the populist leader whose 1948 assassination set off the Bogotazo violence – and, coincidentally, delayed the opening of this museum. Afterward, check out the lovely gardens and their pleasant glass Juan Valdez cafe. There are many good eating options on nearby Calle 29bis.

Northern Bogotá

Espacio KB GALLERY

(Map p54; www.facebook.com/kbespacioparalacultura; Calle 74 No 22-20; ⏲9am-midnight Mon-Sat) FREE One of several edgy art galleries that have sprung up in San Felipe, Bogotá's next cusp-of-cool barrio, this house-turned-gallery is a magnet for the city's hipster and cultural brigade, most of whom are using cutting-edge art as an excuse to drink the night away: DJs, pints of Club Colombia and 2-for-1 gin and tonics fuel the sporadically announced late-night parties. No tourists here!

Plaza Central de Usaquén PLAZA

(Los Toldos de San Pelayo, Carrera 6A, btwn Calles 119 & 119A) It's best coming on Sunday for the flea market (Mercado de las Pulgas; from 9am to 5:30pm).

Western Bogotá

Parque Metropolitano Simón Bolívar PARK

(Map p42; www.idrd.gov.co/sitio/idrd/node/233; Calle 63 & 53, btwn Carreras 48 & 68; ⏲6am-6pm) At 360 hectares, the Parque Metropolitano Simón Bolívar is slightly larger than New York's Central Park, something that more than a few of the weekend draw of 200,000 local park-goers like to point out. It's a pleasant spot, with lakes, bike paths and walkways, public libraries, stadiums, and many events,

Central Bogotá

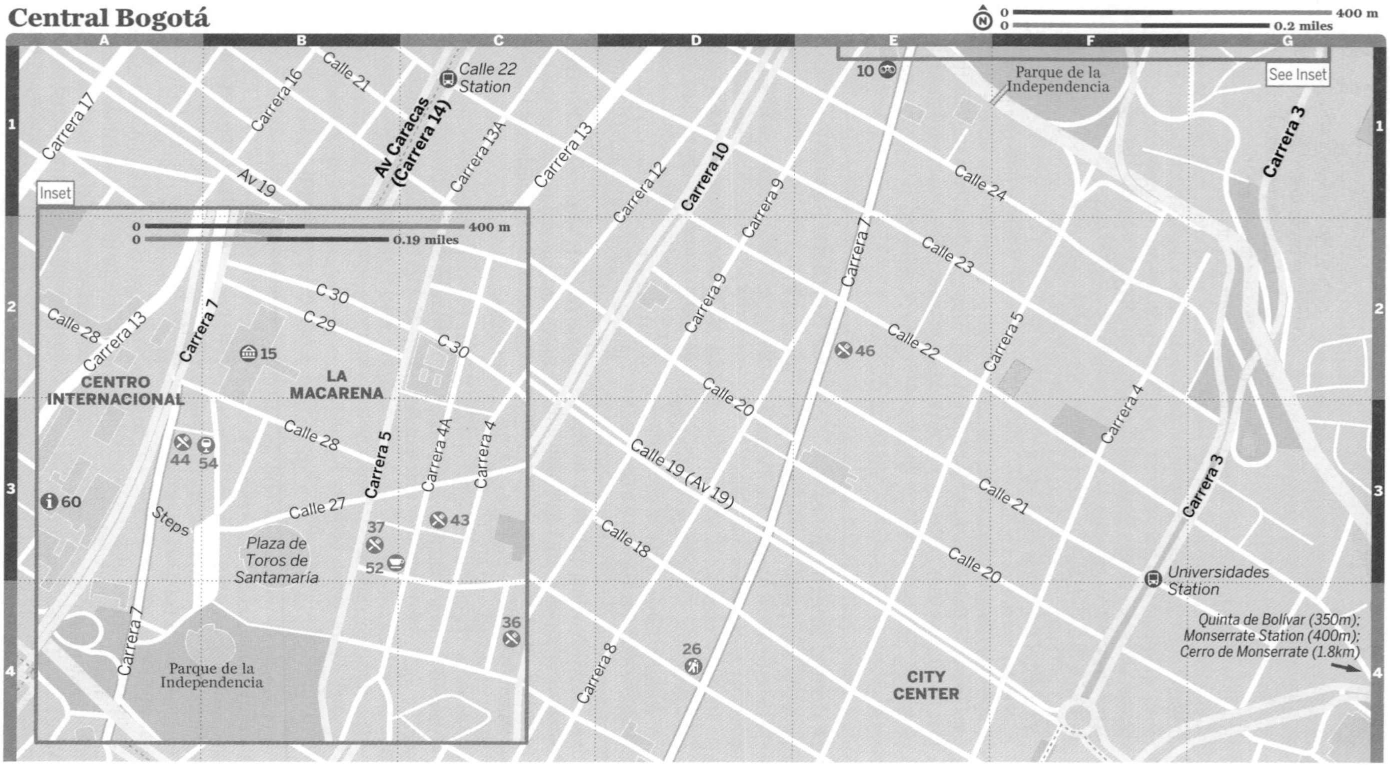

0 — 400 m
0 — 0.2 miles

A B C D E F G
1 2 3 4

Calle 22 Station
Av Caracas (Carrera 14)
Carrera 17
Carrera 16
Calle 21
Av 19
Carrera 13A
Carrera 13
Carrera 12
Carrera 10
Carrera 9
Carrera 7
Carrera 5
Carrera 4
Carrera 3
Carrera 8
Calle 24
Calle 23
Calle 22
Calle 21
Calle 20
Calle 19 (Av 19)
Calle 18
Parque de la Independencia
10
46
26
CITY CENTER
Universidades Station
Quinta de Bolívar (350m); Monserrate Station (400m); Cerro de Monserrate (1.8km)

See Inset

Inset

0 — 400 m
0 — 0.19 miles

CENTRO INTERNACIONAL
LA MACARENA
Calle 28
Carrera 13
Carrera 7
C 30
C 29
C 30
Calle 28
Carrera 5
Carrera 4A
Carrera 4
Calle 27
Steps
Plaza de Toros de Santamaría
Parque de la Independencia
Carrera 7
15
44
54
60
37
52
43
36

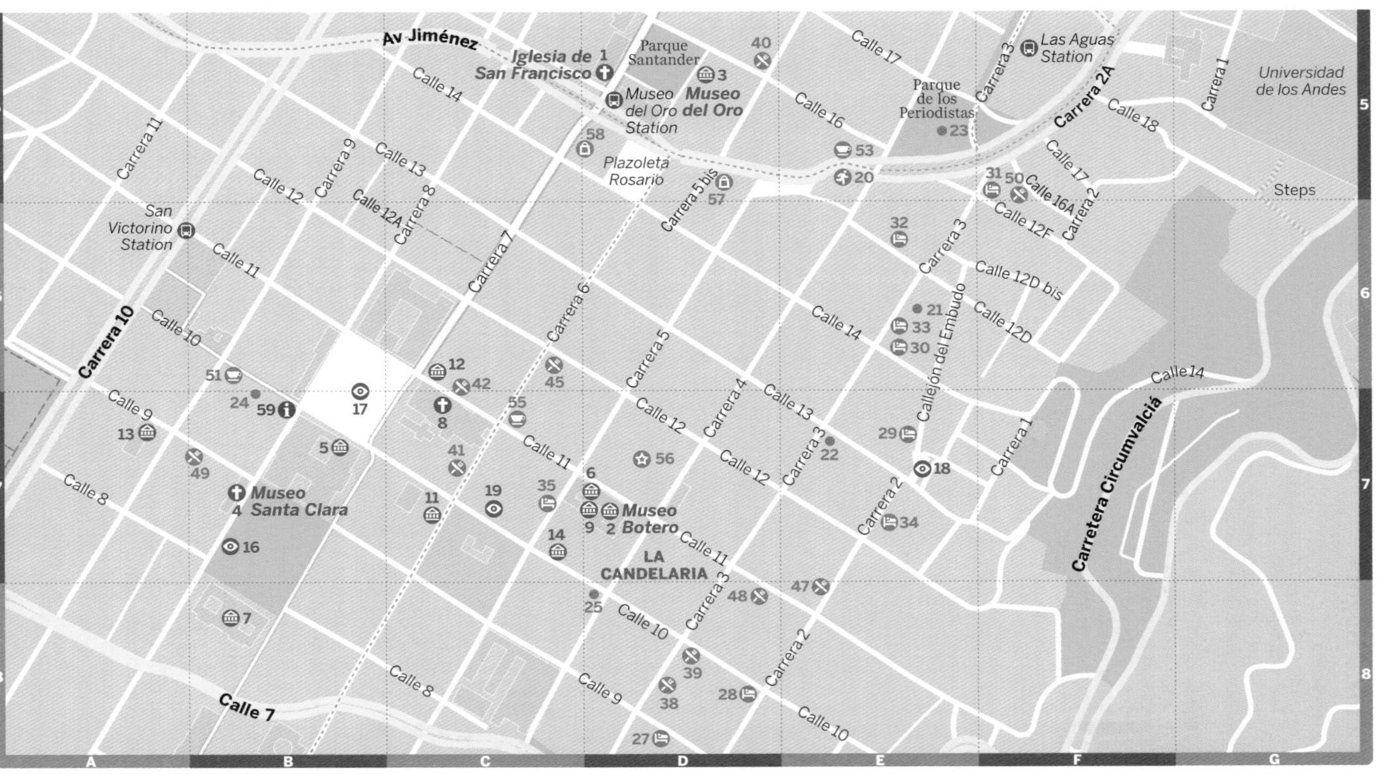

Av Jiménez
Iglesia de San Francisco 1
Parque Santander
Museo del Oro Station
Museo del Oro 3
40
Calle 17
Las Aguas Station
Carrera 3
Parque de los Periodistas
23
Carrera 2A
Calle 18
Carrera 1
Universidad de los Andes
Calle 14
Calle 16
Carrera 11
Carrera 9
Calle 13
58
Plazoleta Rosario
53
20
Calle 17
31
50
Calle 16A
Carrera 2
Steps
Calle 12
Calle 12A
Carrera 8
Carrera 5 bis
57
Calle 12F
San Victorino Station
Calle 11
Carrera 7
32
Carrera 3
Calle 12D bis
Carrera 10
Calle 10
Carrera 6
Calle 14
21
33
30
Callejón del Embudo
Calle 12D
51
24
59
17
12
42
45
Carrera 5
Carrera 4
Calle 13
Calle 14
Calle 9
13
55
8
Calle 12
29
Carretera Circumvalciá
5
41
Calle 11
56
Carrera 3
22
Calle 12
18
Carrera 1
49
Calle 8
Museo Santa Clara 4
11
19
35
6
Museo Botero 2
9
Carrera 2
34
16
14
Calle 11
LA CANDELARIA
47
25
48
7
Calle 10
Carrera 3
39
Carrera 2
Calle 8
Calle 9
38
28
Calle 7
27
Calle 10
A
B
C
D
E
F
G
5
6
7
8

Central Bogotá

Top Sights
1 Iglesia de San Francisco D5
2 Museo Botero D7
3 Museo del Oro D5
4 Museo Santa Clara B7

Sights
5 Capitolio Nacional B7
6 Casa de Moneda D7
7 Casa de Nariño B8
8 Catedral Primada C7
9 Colección de Arte D7
10 Mirador Torre Colpatria E1
11 Museo Colonial C7
12 Museo de la Independencia – Casa del Florero C6
13 Museo Histórico Policía A7
14 Museo Militar C7
15 Museo Nacional B2
16 Observatorio Astronómico B7
17 Plaza de Bolívar B7
18 Plazoleta del Chorro de Quevedo E7
19 Teatro Colón C7

Activities, Courses & Tours
20 Aventure Colombia E5
21 Bogota & Beyond E6
22 Bogotá Bike Tours E7
Bogotá Craft Beer Tour (see 21)
23 Bogotá Graffiti Tour E5
Breaking Borders (see 18)
24 Escuela de Artes y Oficios Santo Domingo B7
25 International House Bogotá D8
26 Sal Si Puedes D4

Sleeping
27 Anandamayi Hostel D8
28 Botanico Hostel D8
29 Casa Bellavista E7
30 Casa Deco E6
31 Casa Platypus F5
32 Cranky Croc E6
33 Hostal Sue Candelaria E6
34 Masaya Bogota Hostel E7
35 Orchids C7

Eating
36 Agave Azul C4
37 Ázimos B3
38 Café de la Peña Pastelería Francesa D8
39 Capital Cocina D8
40 Chantonner Delikatessen D5
41 La Condesa Irina Lazaar C7
42 La Puerta Falsa C6
43 La Tapería C3
44 Leo Cocina y Cava A3
45 Madre C6
Papaya Gourmet (see 21)
46 Pastelería Florida E2
47 Prudencia E8
48 Quinua y Amaranto D8
49 Restaurante de la Escuela Taller B7
50 Sant Just F5

Drinking & Nightlife
51 Arte y Pasión Café B6
52 Café Origami B3
53 Contraste Coffee Lab E5
54 El Bembe B3
55 Juan Valdéz C7

Entertainment
56 Biblioteca Luis Ángel Arango D7

Shopping
57 Emerald Trade Center D5
58 Gems Metal D5

Information
59 Punto de Información Turística B7
60 Punto de Información Turística A3

including the beloved Rock al Parque (p53). Simón Bolívar station on the TransMilenio's E line is at the eastern end of the park (at Av Ciudad de Quito and Calle 64).

Maloka MUSEUM
(Map p42; ☎1-427-2707; www.maloka.org; Carrera 68D No 24A-51; combined tickets COP$29,000-40,000; ⏲8am-5pm Mon-Fri, 10am-7pm Sat & Sun) A short walk from the bus station in the planned neighborhood of Salitre, Maloka is a kid-oriented interactive center of science and technology. Lots of school kids in uniform amble about the eight rooms – using physics to lift a car, or playing in the life-size toy-block park.

There are two high-tech cinemas: Cine Domo, which plays 40-minute films on a huge domed ceiling, and a 3D cinema.

Activities

If you're looking for a place to kick around a football or go for a jog, try Parque Simón Bolívar, or go for a climb up Monserrate (p52). And don't be afraid to get out on two wheels – Bogotá has some extremely bike-friendly options.

Bogotá's incredible 376km CicloRuta network consists of separate bike lanes that cross the city. **Ciclovía** (www.idrd.gov.co) opens about 121km of city roads to cyclists and pedestrians from 7am to 2pm on

Sunday and holidays for a well-run event that gets Bogotá on their bikes. Fruit-juice and street-food vendors, performers, and bike-repair stands line the cross-town event, which has a street-party vibe whether you're with or without a bike. Wednesday night's **Ciclopaseo de los Miercoles** is a free, good-time bike ride that meets at **Plaza CPM** (Map p54; www.facebook.com/ruedodeciudad; cnr Carrera 10 & Calle 96) at 7pm.

Gran Pared CLIMBING

(Map p42; ☎316-578-2653; www.granpared.com; Calle 52 No 15-27; full day with/without equipment COP$25,000/20,000; ⏲2-9:45pm Mon-Fri, 10am-6:45pm Sat, 10am-5:45pm Sun) Bogotá rock climbers head to nearby Suesca, but if you want to hone your skills in town, long-standing climbing haunt Gran Pared has built a state-of-the-art facility that includes 11 leading climbing lines (22 routes), 16 top-rope climbing lines (32 routes) and a boulder zone.

Sal Si Puedes HIKING

(Map p48; ☎300-436-1196, 1-283-3765; www.fundacionsalsipuedes.org; Carrera 7 No 17-01, oficina 640; ⏲8am-5pm Mon-Thu, to 2pm Fri) This association of outdoor-minded people organizes weekend walks in the countryside (COP$55,000 per person, including transportation, health insurance and Spanish-speaking guides). Most walks last nine or 10 hours. Drop by for a yearly schedule.

Courses

Nueva Lengua LANGUAGE

(Map p60; ☎corporate 1-813-8674, mobile 315-855-9551; www.nuevalengua.com; Calle 69 No 11A-09, Quinta Camacho) This language school offers a number of study programs, including at its branches in Medellín and Cartagena. A 20-hour week in group classes ranges from US$120 to US$185 per week depending on the number of weeks and includes cooking lessons as well.

Escuela de Artes y Oficios Santo Domingo CRAFTS

(Map p48; ☎1-282-0534; www.eaosd.org; Calle 10 No 8-65; courses from COP$494,000; ⏲shop 7am-5pm Mon-Sat) This donation-sustained organization offers one- and two-month (and beyond) courses in woodwork, leatherwork, silversmithing, embroidery and weaving in a pretty restored building in La Candelaria. And, though technically not a store, its shop is one of the best spots in town for well-made, gorgeous handicrafts.

International House Bogotá LANGUAGE

(Map p48; ☎1-744-1993; www.ihbogota.com; Carrera 13 No 72-23; ⏲7am-8pm Mon-Fri, to 1pm Sun) Offers group Spanish-language courses (US$230 per week for five four-hour morning classes, plus US$40 for materials) in its new location just north of Chapinero. Courses start every Monday. Private tutors are US$30 per hour.

Universidad Javeriana's Centro Latinoamericano LANGUAGE

(Map p42; ☎1-320-8320 ext. 4612; www.javeriana.edu.co/centro-lenguas; Transversal 4 No 42-00, piso 6) Bogotá's best-known school of Spanish language offers private lessons (per hour COP$122,000) or 80-hour courses (per person COP$2,608,000).

Tours

Free walking tours in English depart at 2pm Tuesday and Thursday from the Punto de Información Turística (p74) branch in La Candelaria. Bookings required at least 24 hours ahead.

★**Breaking Borders** CULTURAL

(Map p48; ☎Diana 321-279-6637, Jaime 304-686-0755; Plaza del Chorro del Quevedo) Bogotá's most fascinating tour is through the Barrio Egipto with members of La 10ma gang, who have given up a life of crime in favor of this cultural-tourism initiative, started by the Universidad Externado de Colombia in cooperation with Impulse Travel (p53).

Former gang members such as Jaime Roncancio (street name 'El Calabazo' or 'The Pumpkin') will take you on an engrossing tour through the 'hood, which is controlled by four gangs and remains a no-go zone – unless you're under the guides' protection. You'll learn the history of organized crime in the neighborhood (*bazuco,* a cheap but highly dangerous drug made from cocaine remnants, brick dust, acetone and even human bones, and dudes with names like Carlos Gasolina, both feature heavily), take in outstanding city views, visit the homes of former gang members and, if you're lucky, try some local *chicha* (homemade hooch made from fermented corn). Spanish speakers can go without a translator – two- to three-hour tours leave Tuesday and Thursday at 11am from Plaza del Chorro del Quevedo (call Jaime or Diana ahead); otherwise, tours can also be arranged (with hotel transfers and a translator) through Impulse Trav-

DON'T MISS

CERRO DE MONSERRATE

Bogotá's proud symbol – and convenient point of reference – is the white-church-topped 3150m **Monserrate peak**. It flanks the city's east, about 1.5km from La Candelaria, and is visible from most parts across the Sabana de Bogotá (Bogotá Savannah; sometimes called 'the valley'). The top has gorgeous views of the capital's 1700-sq-km sprawl. On a clear day you can even spot the symmetrical cone of Nevado del Tolima, part of the Parque Nacional Natural (PNN) Los Nevados volcanic range in the Cordillera Central, 135km west.

The **church** up top is a major mecca for pilgrims, due to its altar statue of the Señor Caído (Fallen Christ), dating from the 1650s, to which many miracles have been attributed. The church was erected after the original chapel was destroyed by an earthquake in 1917. You'll also find two restaurants (Santa Clara and San Isidro) and a cafe – make a day of it.

The steep **1500-step hike** – past snack stands – to the top (60 to 90 minutes' walk) is open from 5am (closed Tuesday). It's a popular weekend jaunt for *bogotanos;* on weekdays it used to be dangerous, as thefts occurred all too regularly, but an increase in police presence in recent years has curbed that considerably. If you're traveling solo or don't feel like walking, the regular *teleférico* (cable car) and funicular alternate schedules up the mountain from **Monserrate Station** (www.cerromonserrate.com; Sendero Peatonal Monserrate; round trip Mon-Sat from COP$20,000, Sun COP$12,000; ⏲5:30am-11:30pm Mon-Fri, to 6:30pm Sun). Generally, the funicular goes before noon (3pm on Saturday), the cable car after.

The funicular base station is a 20-minute walk up from the Iglesia de las Aguas (along the brick walkways with the fountains – up past the Universidad de los Andes), at the northeastern edge of La Candelaria. Safety along this route has also improved, although you're still best advised to make the trip at weekends, particularly in the morning, when many pilgrims are about.

el for COP$120,000. Tips help support the community; COP$20,000 is a good amount.

★**Bogotá Bike Tours** CYCLING
(Map p48; ☎312-502-0554; www.bogotabiketours.com; Carrera 3 No 12-72; tours from COP$40,000, bike rental per hour/day COP$9000/45,000) In what is probably the best cycling city in South America, this is the best bike outfit. You can rent your own and take advantage of 375km of dedicated trails or choose from an array of tours that, on occasion, pedal into neighborhoods that would otherwise be no-go. Tours leave daily at 10:30am and 1:30pm from the La Candelaria office.

Highlights include La Candelaria, a fruit market – watch those spice vendors with their super-hot wares! – graffiti tours, a caffeine-fueled spin around the local coffee roasters, the red-light district, and day and multi-day tours outside Bogotá.

Aventure Colombia TOURS
(Map p48; ☎1-702-7069; www.aventurecolombia.com; Av Jiménez No 4-49, oficina 204; ⏲8am-5pm Mon-Sat) Run by a charming French expat, Aventure Colombia specializes in far-flung, off-the-beaten-path destinations nationwide, such as the fascinating Cerros de Mavecure, Parque Nacional Natural (PNN) El Tuparro and Caño Cristales (July to November) in Los Llanos; Punta Gallinas on the Guajira Peninsula; and indigenous homestays in the Sierra Nevada of Santa Marta.

Bogota & Beyond TOURS
(Map p48; ☎319-686-8601, 304-455-9723; www.bogotaandbeyond.com; Carrera 3 No 12C-90; tours from COP$20,000; ⏲noon-5pm Mon, 12:30-9:30pm Wed-Sat, 12:30-7pm Sun) Join the rollicking Septima Challenge (you and your team gallivant along the Ciclovía route practicing your Spanish on unsuspecting locals in a race to complete as many tasks as possible in two hours) and other good-time tours run by this agency, the brainchild of two friendly Australians.

Other options include exploring Bogotá's emerging craft-beer scene on the Bogota Craft Beer Tour (p53), or heading into the wilds on a weekly hike up the mountains behind Chapinero, to La Chorrera waterfall, or to Guatavita Lake and the Salt Cathedral.

Impulse Travel TOURS
(Map p60; 1-753-4887; www.impulsetravel.co; Calle 65 No 16-09; 9am-5pm Mon-Fri) Long-standing city-tour experts Destino Bogotá have gone national: the rebranded Impulse Travel is an excellent choice for two- to-five-day round-trip excursions from Bogotá to must-see destinations such as Caño Cristales and PNN Tayrona; playful city and area tours, including salsa lessons, *tejo* (type of sport which involves throwing metal discs into holes in a wooden target box) nights and food tours; and social initiatives like the highly recommended Breaking Borders (p51) tour to Barrio Egipto.

Visits to Guatavita/Zipaquirá, La Chorrera hikes and coffee-farm trips are also offered. The office is inside the very hip Tierra Firme co-working space.

Bogotá Craft Beer Tour FOOD & DRINK
(Map p48; www.bogotacraftbeer.com; Carrera 3 No 12C-90; COP$75,000; 4pm Mon-Fri, 2pm Sat) Two beer-loving Australians are behind this fun tour that takes in at least four local nano- and microbreweries, including Cervecería Gigante (Bogotá's best) and Madriguera Brewing Co (not otherwise open to the public). Tours include tasting and a beer in each stop.

5Bogotá CULTURAL
(313-278-5898, 314-411-1099; www.5bogota.com) This upstart agency run by young *bogotanos* takes a hands-on approach to exploring the city and stands out among the standard fare. It creates sensorial experiences from the daily activities of everyday people. Unique tours include exploring truly local markets rather than touristy ones; learning how to make empanadas or *patacones*; salsa lessons in a local's home, and the like.

Bogotá Graffiti Tour TOURS
(Map p48; 321-297-4075; www.bogotagraffiti.com; tours 10am & 2pm) FREE A fascinating 2½-hour walking tour through Bogotá's considerable and impressive urban art, starting from Parque de los Periodistas. The tour itself is free, but a COP$20,000 to COP$30,000 gratuity is recommended for the guide.

Festivals & Events

Festival Iberoamericano de Teatro de Bogotá THEATER
(FITB; www.facebook.com/FITBogota; Mar/Apr) Biannual 17-day festival that counts itself as the largest performing-arts festival in the world – the world's most important theater companies from five continents participate. Events, at various venues around the city, include street theater, international concerts, classical dance, children's and youth theater and storytelling, among others.

The event is on an even-year cycle.

Rock al Parque MUSIC
(www.rockalparque.gov.co; Parque Metropolitano Simón Bolívar; Aug) Three days of (mostly South American) rock/metal/pop/funk/reggae bands at Parque Metropolitano Simón Bolívar. It's free and swarming with fans.

Alimentarte FOOD & DRINK
(1-236-1329; www.alimentarte.site; Parque El Virrey; Aug) Some of Colombia's best chefs and most devout foodies descend on Parque El Virrey for five gluttonous days of food and drink at this good-time northern Bogotá festival. The first few days are focused on an invited country (France in 2017) while the last two days hone in on an invited Colombian region (Altiplano Cundiboyacense in 2017).

Festival de Verano CULTURAL
(www.idrd.gov.co; Parque Metropolitano Simón Bolívar; Aug) Eight days of free music and culture in Parque Metropolitano Simón Bolívar.

Festival de Jazz MUSIC
(www.teatrolibre.com; Calle 62 No 9A-65; Sep) Now held in Chapinero, this festival features local and national Latin jazz artists, plus an occasional US or European star.

Hip Hop al Parque MUSIC
(www.hiphopalparque.gov.co; Parque Metropolitano Simón Bolívar; Oct) Two days of hip-hop taking over Parque Metropolitano Simón Bolívar.

Festival de Cine de Bogotá FILM
(1-545-6987; www.bogocine.com; Oct) With a nearly 35-year history, the city's cinema festival attracts films from all around the world, including a usually strong Latin American selection.

Zona Rosa & Parque 93

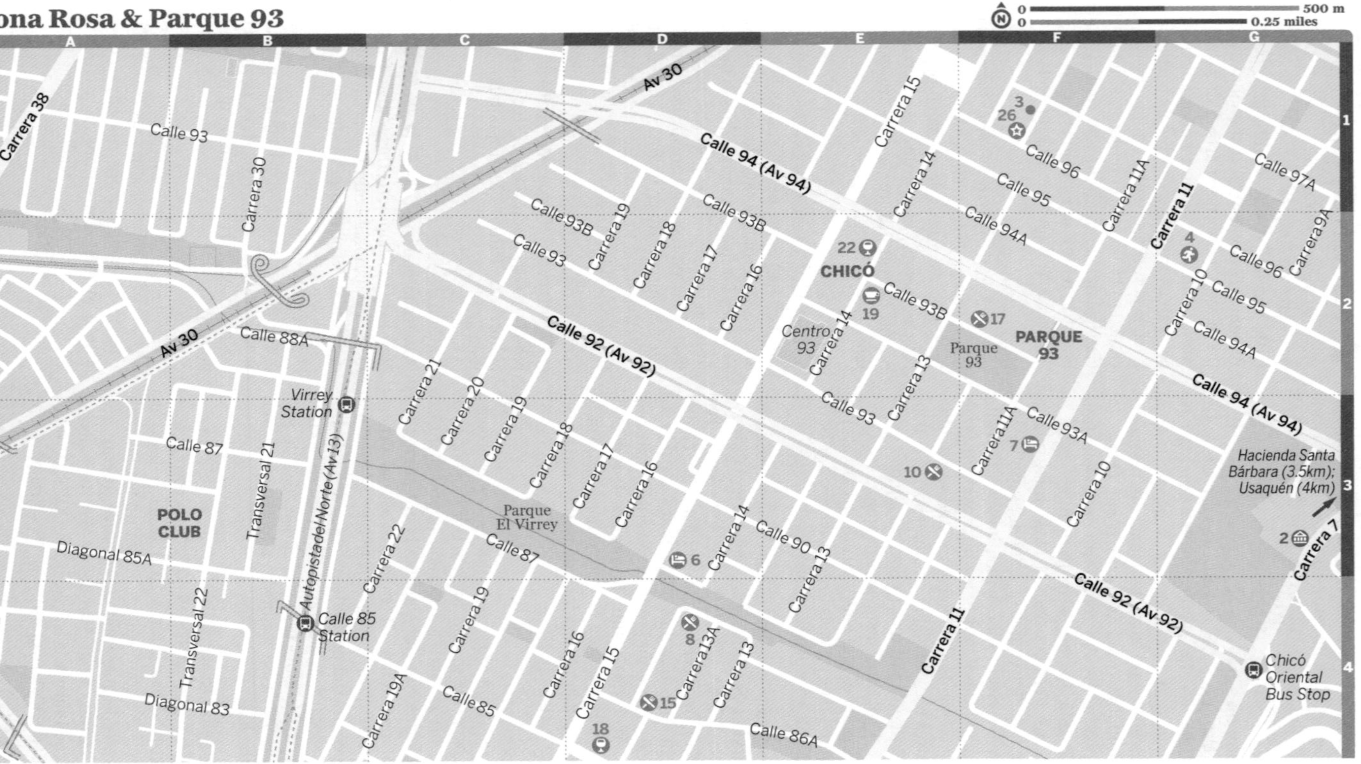

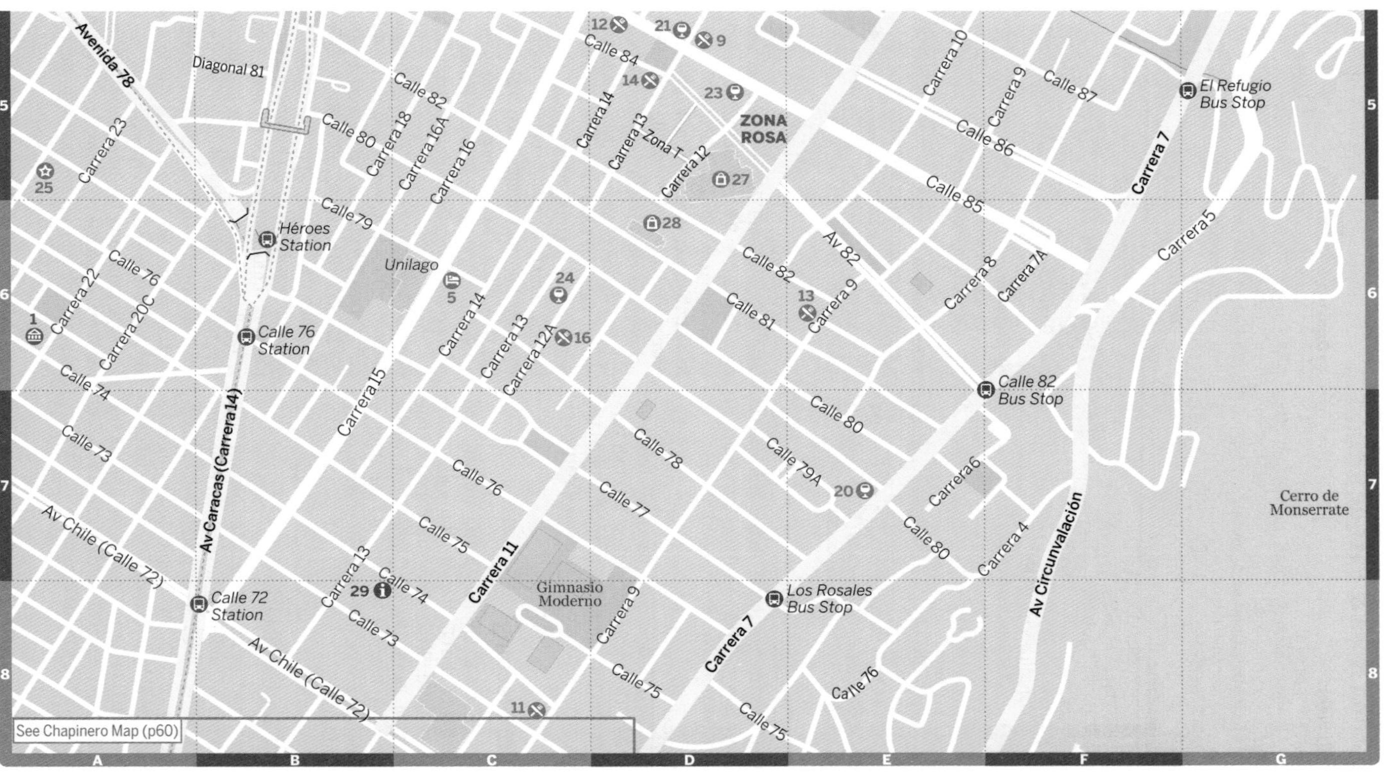

Avenida 78
Diagonal 81
Calle 82
Calle 84
Carrera 10
Carrera 9
Calle 87
El Refugio Bus Stop
Carrera 23
Calle 80
Carrera 18
Carrera 16A
Carrera 16
Carrera 14
Carrera 13
Zona T
Carrera 12
ZONA ROSA
Calle 86
Carrera 7
Calle 85
Calle 79
Héroes Station
Unilago
Av 82
Calle 82
Carrera 8
Carrera 7A
Carrera 5
Calle 76
Carrera 22
Carrera 20C
Calle 76 Station
Carrera 14
Carrera 13
Carrera 12A
Calle 81
Carrera 9
Calle 74
Carrera 15
Calle 82 Bus Stop
Calle 80
Calle 73
Calle 78
Calle 79A
Carrera 6
Calle 76
Calle 77
Cerro de Monserrate
Av Chile (Calle 72)
Av Caracas (Carrera 14)
Calle 75
Calle 80
Carrera 4
Av Circunvalación
Carrera 13
Calle 74
Carrera 11
Gimnasio Moderno
Carrera 9
Los Rosales Bus Stop
Calle 72 Station
Calle 73
Carrera 7
Av Chile (Calle 72)
Calle 75
Calle 76
Calle 75
See Chapinero Map (p60)
1
5
9
11
12
13
14
16
20
21
23
24
25
27
28
29
A
B
C
D
E
F
G
5
6
7
8

Zona Rosa & Parque 93

Sights
1 Espacio KB ... A6
2 Museo El Chicó ... G3

Activities, Courses & Tours
3 Colombian Journeys ... F1
4 Plaza CPM ... G2

Sleeping
5 Chapinorte Bogotá ... C6
6 Cité ... D3
7 Hotel Click-Clack ... F3

Eating
8 Canasto Picnic Bistró ... D4
9 Central Cevicheria ... D5
10 Container City ... E3
11 Crepes & Waffles ... C8
12 El Corral ... D5
13 Home Burger ... E6
14 La Paletteria ... D5
15 Les Amis Bizcochería ... D4
16 Raw ... C6
17 Wok ... F2

Drinking & Nightlife
Andrés D.C ... (see 28)
18 Armando Records ... D4
19 Azahar Café ... E2
20 Bistro El Bandido ... E7
21 Bogotá Beer Company ... D5
22 Chelarte ... E2
23 El Mozo ... D5
24 El Recreo de Adàn ... C6
Tap House ... (see 10)

Entertainment
25 Club de Tejo La 76 ... A5
26 Gaira Café ... F1

Shopping
27 Centro Comercial Andino ... D5
28 Centro Comercial El Retiro ... D6

Information
29 Parques Nacionales Naturales (PNN) de Colombia ... B8

Salsa al Parque SALSA
(www.salsaalparque.gov.co; Parque Metropolitano Simón Bolívar; Nov) A salsa extravaganza in Parque Metropolitano Simón Bolívar.

Expoartesanías ARTS & CRAFTS
(www.expoartesanias.com; Carrera 37 No 24-67; Dec) This crafts fair gathers together artisans and their products from all around the country. Crafts are for sale and it's an excellent place to buy them.

Sleeping

Boutique and business hotels are scattered north of Calle 65, many within walking distance of the lively scenes of Zona G, Zona Rosa or Parque 93. La Candelaria is where most of Bogotá's attractions and budget lodgings are located – including many excellent hostels.

La Candelaria

In the past couple of years, the historic suburb of La Candelaria has seen an explosion in hostels. Generally, private rooms in hostels are better than cheapies in the district's dated, grubby hotels. In the higher-end price bracket there are a couple of fine locales with more colonial spirit than you'll find anywhere else in the capital.

Botanico Hostel HOSTEL $
(Map p48; 313-419-1288; www.botanicohostel.com; Carrera 2 No 9-87; dm COP$27,000, r with/without bathroom COP$130,000/110,000; @) In a rambling, creaky wooden-floored house once called home by notable Colombian painter Gonzalo Ariza, this new-in-2017 Candelaria offering oozes colonial character and charm. Original touches like wood-beamed ceilings and optimal hang spaces (fire-lit lounge, jungly garden, supreme rooftop with city and mountain views) make leaving difficult; a spacious private room with wood-burning stove doesn't help, either.

There's yoga on the rooftop at 10am daily.

Casa Bellavista HOSTEL $
(Map p48; 1-334-1230; www.bellavistahostelbogota.com; Carrera 2 No 12B-31; incl breakfast dm from COP$25,000, s/d from COP$70,000/80,000; @) Shoehorned into hippy-dippy Callejón de Embudo, this small hostel in a historic house has plenty of antiquated character. Creaky hardwood floors lead to six- to nine-bed dorms that have their own bathrooms, and the three spacious private rooms are chock-full of detail such as original tile flooring – the standout is loft-style with a spiral staircase.

Flags, maps and the odd musical instrument embellish the communal areas, where you can sink into a hammock with the wi-fi or ditch the electronics for a game of chess.

It's steps from Plazoleta del Chorro de Quevedo, with a facade covered in ever-changing urban graffiti (a giant frog at last visit).

★Cranky Croc HOSTEL $
(Map p48; 1-342-2438; www.crankycroc.com; Calle 12D No 3-46; dm COP$36,000-54,000, s/d COP$110,000/140,000, without bathroom COP$75,000/110,000; @) Perennial favorite the Cranky Croc, run by a friendly Aussie and styling itself as a backpacker hostel, has kept up with the times and doesn't lack space or natural light, which hits you as soon as you enter the brightly tiled lobby. The four- to 10-bed dorms feature lockers, reading lamps and individual electric outlets for device charging.

★Masaya Bogotá Hostel HOSTEL $
(Map p48; 1-747-1848; www.masaya-experience.com; Carrera 2 No 12-48; dm from COP$40,000, r with/without bathroom from COP$170,000/120,000; @) Taking flashpacker luxury to a new level, this large French-owned hostel has notably comfortable dorms, with privacy curtains, beanbags, and fluffy pillows and duvets, while the hotel-quality private rooms are very spacious and exhibit first-rate wardrobes and flat-screen TVs. You'll also find great common areas, piping-hot high-pressure showers and a wealth of cultural activities, including cooking classes.

Casa Platypus GUESTHOUSE $$
(Map p48; 1-281-1801; www.casaplatypusbogota.com; Carrera 3 No 12F-28; dm/s/d/tr COP$55,000/160,000/182,000/220,000; @) Looking like a colonial home brought over from Villa de Leyva, this upscale guesthouse is an ideal flashpacker choice right in the heart of Bogotá. The interior patio exudes charm, the common areas (a handsome breakfast room and a relaxing terrace) invite guest interaction, and the small but tidy rooms come with comfy beds equipped with deluxe headboards.

Anandamayi Hostel HOSTEL $$
(Map p48; 1-341-7208; www.anandamayihostel.co; Calle 9 No 2-81; dm/s/d without bathroom COP$40,000/108,000/140,000, d COP$150,000, all incl breakfast; @) South of most hostels, this lovely whitewashed and turquoise-trimmed colonial home has very well-furnished rooms with wood-beam ceilings, plenty of wool blankets and colonial furniture. Rooms and the 13-bed dorm surround a few semileafy central stone courtyards with hammocks. A top Candelaria choice for those seeking peace and quiet in their hostel and a less gringo-centric experience.

★Orchids BOUTIQUE HOTEL $$$
(Map p48; 1-745-5438; www.theorchidshotel.com; Carrera 5 No 10-55; r/ste incl breakfast COP$360,000/680,000; @) Behind a mauve facade hides La Candelaria's most discerning and upscale choice, an intimate six-room boutique hotel bursting with historic character. Every generously proportioned room has a different design scheme: period furniture (some original to the historic mansion), four-poster beds, porcelain sinks and thick wooden writing desks are just some of the features.

★Casa Deco BOUTIQUE HOTEL $$$
(Map p48; 1-282-8640; www.hotelcasadeco.com; Calle 12C No 2-36; s/d incl breakfast from COP$210,000/252,000; @) A 22-room gem run by an Italian emerald dealer, this discerning option is a serious step up from the sea of hostels surrounding it. Rooms come in seven bright colors and are laced with bespoke hardwood art deco–style furniture, desks, futon beds and newly installed soundproof doors and windows.

There's a guitarist at breakfast, adorable staff, and a mesmerizing terrace with Monserrate and Cerro de Guadalupe views.

Chapinero

★12:12 Hostel HOSTEL $$
(Map p60; 1-467-2656; www.1212hostels.com; Calle 67 No 4-16; dm incl breakfast COP$35,000-48,000, r/ste COP$98,000/138,000; @) This artsy hostel epitomizes the cutting-edge Chapinero Alto scene: recycled materials such as discarded bikes, which are mounted like fun-house art installations, and tossed-aside books, which pepper the walls instead of wallpaper, are the backbone of this design-forward choice.

The colorful dorm beds are some of Bogotá's most comfortable, with reading lamps, privacy curtains and cozy bedding; the big, modern communal kitchen and slate bathrooms are above and beyond for a hostel.

WORTH A TRIP

ZIPAQUIRÁ

Far and away the most popular day trip from Bogotá is to head 50km north of the city to the **Salt Cathedral** (Salt Cathedral; 315-760-7376; www.catedraldesal.gov.co; Parque de la Sal; foreigners/Colombians COP$55,000/34,000; 9am-5:45pm) of **Zipaquirá**. This underground cathedral carved out of salt is one of only three such structures in the world (the other two are in Poland).

In the mountains about 500m southwest of Zipaquirá there are two salt cathedrals: the first opened in 1954 and was closed in 1992 for safety reasons, but you can visit its stunning replacement. Between 1991 and 1995, around 250,000 tons of salt were cleared away to carve out the moody, ethereal underground sanctuary, hailed as one of Colombia's greatest architectural achievements. You'll descend to 180m below ground through 14 small chapels representing the Stations of the Cross – Jesus' last journey – each an evocatively lit triumph of both symbolism and mining. But nothing prepares you for the trail's culmination in the main nave, where a mammoth cross (the world's largest in an underground church) is illuminated from the base up. The tradition of mixing religion with salt has logical roots: work in the mines was dangerous, so altars were made.

All visitors must join regularly departing groups on hour-long tours – you can leave the tour once you're inside if you want. The 75m-long mine can accommodate 8400 people and holds services on (very busy) Sundays at noon. In addition to the Salt Cathedral, there are a Brine Museum and other minor attractions on the premises. Zipaquirá's main plaza is lined with cafes and has a lovely church worth peeking into.

To reach Zipaquirá, hop on a frequent bus from the Portal del Norte TransMilenio station at Calle 170, which is about a 45-minute ride from the city center. From here, buses to Zipaquirá (COP$5400, 45 minutes) leave every four minutes or so until 11:30pm from Portal's Buses Intermunicipales platform. You can also catch an hourly direct bus from *módulo* 3 (red) at Bogotá's bus station (COP$5400, 1½ hours). Alternatively, take the Turistren (p335), which runs Saturday and Sunday from Bogotá to Zipaquirá. The train departs Bogotá's main train station, **Sabana Station** (Estación de la Sabana; Calle 13 No 18-24), at 8:15am, stops briefly at Usaquén Station at 9:05am and reaches Zipaquirá at 11:05am.

From Zipaquirá it's possible to catch a few daily buses on to Villa de Leyva.

A round-trip taxi from Bogotá should run between COP$140,000 and COP$160,000 including around 2½ hours' waiting time; one way in an off-peak UberX runs COP$75,000 or so.

About 15km northeast of Zipaquirá, the town of **Nemocón** is also home to a smaller (and less touristy) salt mine that can be visited daily. This one has been in use for 400 years and once served as the town hall. Head there by taxi.

Fulano Backpackers HOSTEL **$$**
(Map p60; 1-467-2530; www.facebook.com/fulanobackpackers; Carrera 10A No 69-41; dm from COP$30,000, r with/without bathroom from COP$120,000/95,000; @) An Italian-Colombian affair inside a historic Quinta Camacho mansion, this boutique hostel is easy on the eyes. It calls on juxtapositions of hardwoods, minimalistic design schemes and artistic bathroom tilings to foster an aesthetically impressive environment for a hostel. DJs, live music sets and spontaneous BBQs on the custom-built grill aren't uncommon, and an air of cultural awareness pervades throughout.

Zona G

Casa Legado BOUTIQUE HOTEL **$$$**
(Map p60; 318-715-9519; www.casalegadobogota.com; Carrera 8 No 69-60; r incl breakfast COP$650,000-1,300,000; P @) Find your way to this renovated 1950s art deco home in Quinta Camacho and you'll fall in love with your host, Helena, and her seven-room dream pad. An exotic fruit garden, a communal dining room and a guest-use kitchen, plus an ivy-draped courtyard, are perfect companions to stylish rooms, decked out according to the personalities of Helena's nieces and nephews.

An interior designer by trade, Helena has painstakingly accented the experience with local Colombian products wherever possible (luxurious Loto del Sur amenities, beautiful ceramics from Tybso, aromatic Libertario coffee). There's a lot to love here, not least the treats that are included in the price: gourmet breakfast, food and drinks from the well-stocked kitchen, city bikes, picnic baskets and access to five deluxe common areas.

Four Seasons Casa Medina HISTORIC HOTEL **$$$**

(Map p60; ☎1-325-7900; www.fourseasons.com/bogotacm; Carrera 7 No 69A-22; r from COP$1,323,000; @ 📶) Easily the most interesting of Bogotá's two new Four Seasons hotels (the other is in Zona Rosa, both converted from previous hotels), this Zona G hotel occupies two historic mansions boasting Spanish colonial accents (beamed ceilings, original tiling) and a gorgeous sunlit breakfast room/bar with a lush vertical garden.

Four Seasons couldn't change much when it revamped the former Charleston Casa Medina in 2015, but rich hardwood flooring and leather-accented desks, nightstands and antiques in some rooms keep things historically luxurious. The in-house Spanish restaurant, Castanyoles, does a bang-up Sunday brunch with unlimited mimosas (COP$89,000).

Zona Rosa & Parque 93

Chapinorte Bogotá HOSTEL **$$**

(Map p54; ☎317-640-6716; www.chapinortehostelbogota.com; Calle 79 No 14-59, Apt 402; s/d COP$90,000/170,000, without bathroom COP$75,000/220,000; @ 📶) In a nondescript residential building just beyond the northern edges of Chapinero, this five-room guesthouse, run by a friendly Spaniard, is a great anti-Candelaria choice. Some of the hostel's stylish rooms have enormous bathrooms and cable TVs, and surround a cute island kitchen in the living room. No breakfast.

★ **Hotel Click-Clack** BOUTIQUE HOTEL **$$$**

(Map p54; ☎1-743-0404; www.clickclackhotel.com; Carrera 11 No 93-77; r incl breakfast COP$379,000-688,000; ❄ @ 📶) This high-design haven, the boutique hotel of choice for Colombia's trendsetters, has a sophisticated aesthetic vaguely based around vintage TVs and photographic equipment. The best of the five room sizes (extra small to large) are the 2nd-floor mediums, which open onto spacious patios with small patches of grass and a vertical garden.

There's no spa or fitness center: everything here – from Apache, the high-class miniburger bar on the roof, with stupendous views, to 100 Grams, the trendy basement restaurant where everything is served in 100g portions (like larger-size tapas) – is focused on a good time, not on R & R. There's a Lust kit and a Hangover kit in each room, depending on how things go.

Cité BOUTIQUE HOTEL **$$$**

(Map p54; ☎1-646-7777; www.citehotel.com; Carrera 15 No 88-10; r incl breakfast COP$320,000-380,000; ❄ @ 📶 🏊) Part of a small Bogotá chain, this 56-room business-hip boutique hotel located between Zona Rosa and Parque 93 boasts rarely seen advantages such as a heated rooftop pool, extra-large rooms with lots of natural light and even some with bathtubs, a true rarity.

Perhaps coolest of all is that there are bicycles for guests to use for free – handy as you are on a CicloRuta bike path.

Eating

Fusion is the watchword of many Bogotá restaurateurs, who are running Mediterranean, Italian, Californian or pan-Asian influences through typical Colombian dishes, but reinvented homegrown cuisine is on the rise. The best dining destinations include Zona Rosa, Nogal and Zona G; also recommended is the slightly boho scene in La Macarena, just north of La Candelaria.

La Candelaria

La Puerta Falsa FAST FOOD **$**

(Map p48; www.restaurantelapuertafalsa.inf.travel; Calle 11 No 6-50; snacks COP$6000-8000; ⏲7am-9pm Mon-Sat, 8am-7pm Sun) If it ain't broke, don't fix it. Maybe that's why, after two centuries, the 'False Door' is still successfully knocking out the same one-page menu, dominated by two epoch-spanning snacks: *tamales,* and the practically sacred *chucula y almojábanas*, a simple plate of sweet bread and soft cheese accompanied by a cup of steaming hot chocolate.

The punters obviously like it. On an average morning you'll have to wait patiently for a table outside this diminutive two-story cafe–pastry shop just off the Plaza de Bolívar. Inside, pull up a small stool at an even smaller table and partake in a tasty piece of Bogotá history.

Chapinero

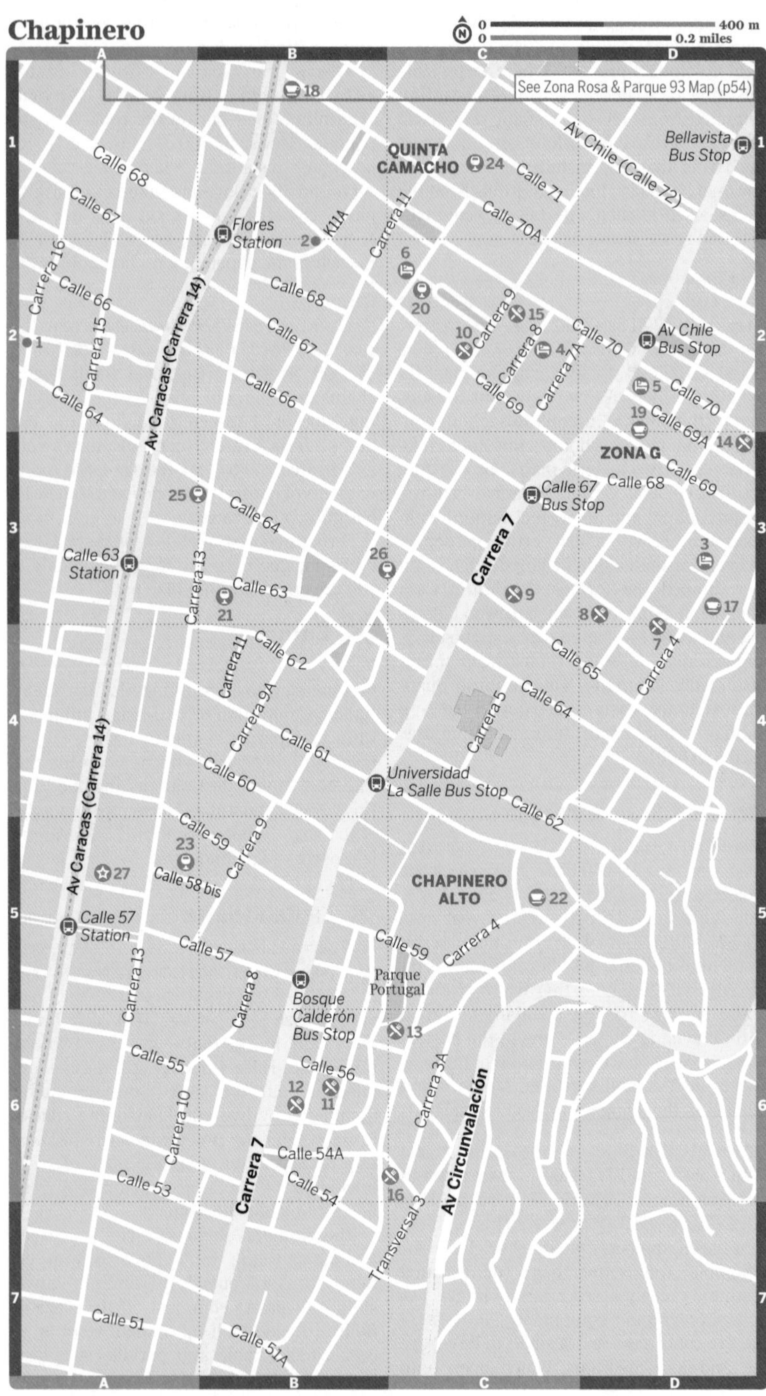

0 400 m
0 0.2 miles
See Zona Rosa & Parque 93 Map (p54)
QUINTA CAMACHO
ZONA G
CHAPINERO ALTO
Flores Station
Calle 63 Station
Calle 57 Station
Bellavista Bus Stop
Av Chile Bus Stop
Calle 67 Bus Stop
Universidad La Salle Bus Stop
Bosque Calderón Bus Stop
Parque Portugal
Av Chile (Calle 72)
Av Caracas (Carrera 14)
Carrera 7
Av Circunvalación
Transversal 3

Chapinero

Activities, Courses & Tours
1 Impulse Travel ... A2
2 Nueva Lengua ... B2

Sleeping
3 12:12 Hostel ... D3
4 Casa Legado ... C2
5 Four Seasons Casa Medina ... D2
6 Fulano Backpackers ... C2

Eating
7 Arbol del Pan ... D4
8 Cantina y Punto ... D3
9 De/Raíz ... C3
10 Guerrero ... C2
11 Insurgentes Taco Bar ... B6
12 Mesa Franca ... B6
13 Mini-Mal ... C6
14 Rafael ... D3
15 Restaurante La Herencia ... C2
16 Salvo Patria ... C6

Drinking & Nightlife
17 Amor Perfecto ... D3
18 Bourbon Coffee Roasters ... B1
19 Café Cultor ... D2
20 El Mono Bandido ... C2
21 Mi Tierra ... B3
22 Taller de Té ... C5
23 Theatron ... A5
24 Tierra Santa Cerveza Artesanal ... C1
25 Video Club ... A3
26 Village Café ... B3

Entertainment
27 Latino Power ... A5

Café de la Peña Pastelería Francesa CAFE **$**
(Map p48; www.cafepasteleria.com; Carrera 3 No 9-66; items COP$2200-6900; 9am-7pm Mon-Sat, 9am-6pm Sun;) Colombians run this fabulous French-style bakery, but you'd never know it. They make some of the nicest *pan de chocolate,* éclairs and almond croissants in the area; and they roast their own excellent coffee. Local art adorns the walls of the garden and there are a couple of seating areas.

Restaurante de la Escuela Taller COLOMBIAN **$**
(Map p48; www.escuelataller.org; Calle 9 No 8-71; mains COP$16,500-26,800; noon-3pm Mon-Sat;) This great lunch hot spot is tucked away inside a culinary (among other skills) workshop for disadvantaged youth and feels like a find. Dining here in the sunlit courtyard supports student efforts, who not only run the kitchen, but have carved the restaurant's wooden furniture as well. Modern, fairly sophisticated takes on traditional Colombian recipes fill the menu.

The excellent, award-winning *ajiaco* (COP$19,000) is hard to beat, but there are daily changing lunch specials (COP$13,500), *panela*-barbequed pork ribs, grilled tilapia with tamarind sauce and a whole lot more, which can be washed down with *panela* lemonade and enjoyed alongside native potato chips and spicy *ají,* which arrive table side for free.

Papaya Gourmet CAFE **$**
(Map p48; www.facebook.com/cpapayagourmet; Carrera 3 No12C-90; pints COP$10,000; noon-5pm Mon, 12:30-9:30pm Wed-Sat, 12:30-7pm Sun; Las Aquas TransMilenio Station | Museo del Oro TransMilenio Station) This bright and extra cozy hole-in-the-wall travel cafe dishes up burritos (COP$10,000 to COP$13,500) and tacos (COP$9500 to COP$12,500) as vehicles for soaking up featured local craft beer from three refrigerator taps. It's one of the only spots in town to get Cerveceria Gigante (p68) outside of its brewery; and top suds from Madriguera Brewing Co. are also usually tapped.

The first-rate Aussie-friendly service and two-for-one Happy Hour (4pm to 6pm) means hopheads can happily sip away in La Candelaria without having to schlep north or to Parkway. It also stocks Golden Lion Colombian cider, produced by the country's only cidery. Bogota & Beyond (p52) and Bogotá Craft Beer Tour (p53) are also run from here.

★**Sant Just** FRENCH **$$**
(Map p48; 314-478-1460; www.santjustbogota.com; Calle 16A No 2-73; mains COP$20,000-37,000; 11am-4pm Mon-Wed, to 8pm Thu & Fri, 11:30am-4:30pm Sat;) This wonderful French-owned cafe serves a daily changing menu of Colombian-leaning French fare. Whatever the kitchen makes that day – fresh juices, sustainably caught seafood, wonderful lamb served alongside previously out-of-favor veggies such as *cubio* (an Andean root) – it nails it, both in presentation and in the comfort-food stakes. Expect a wait.

Madre PIZZA **$$**
(Map p48; Calle 12 No 5-83; pizza COP$26,000-38,000; noon-10pm Tue-Sat, noon-4pm Sun;) You'd never notice this hip pizzeria and bar

from the street – it's tucked away within an unassuming shopping plaza that does little to catch anyone's attention. Madre will grab yours, however, if you venture into its industrial-artsy environs flush with dilapidated exposed brick, jungly exotic plants, hanging birdcages and contemporary street art.

Good brick-oven pizza and cocktails (COP$28,000) are slung to a bohemian crowd in the know, accompanied by cool tunes set just loud enough to get your knees bouncing. On Sundays when the shopping plaza is closed, security will open the gate for you.

Quinua y Amaranto VEGETARIAN **$$**
(Map p48; www.quinuayamaranto.com.co; Calle 11 No 2-95; set lunch COP$17,000; 8:30am-7pm Tue-Fri, to 4pm Mon & Sat;) This sweet spot – run by women in an open-front kitchen – offers tasty set lunches, as well as empanadas, salads and coffee. Fare is all vegetarian during the week, but there's often *ajiaco* (chicken, corn and potato soup) on weekends. A small selection of coca leaves, baked goods and tempting chunks of artisanal cheese (on Saturday) rounds out the cozy offerings.

Capital Cocina COLOMBIAN **$$**
(Map p48; Calle 10 No 2-99; mains COP$23,000-34,000; 12:15-3pm & 6:45-9pm Mon, to 10pm Tue-Fri, 12:15-3pm & 6-10pm Sun;) Prepare to fight for tables at this quaint cafe serving a few takes on simple Colombian comfort food – fish of the day, pork chop, steak, grilled chicken – that are in fact anything but simple. The daily menu (COP$20,500) is a three-course steal considering the quality of chef Juan Pablo's food; and there are artisanal beers, decent wines and single-origin coffee.

★ **Prudencia** INTERNATIONAL **$$$**
(Map p48; 1-394-1678; www.prudencia.net; Carrera 2 No 11-34; prix fixe COP$45,000-56,000; noon-4pm Mon-Sat;) This doozy of dining and design is run by Colombian-American husband-and-wife team Mario and Meghan. The sunlit canopy, an unorthodox marriage of bamboo and steel designed by noted architect Simón Vélez, is a striking setting for the weekly changing four-course menus (vegetarian or non), forged with local ingredients and an often wood-fired international flair.

Menus are never repeated, but vegetarian dishes have included wood-braised fennel and zucchini with saffron and tomato, polenta and fresh-cured buffalo mozzarella; proteins have ranged from Jamaican-spiced pulled pork to pastrami rib-eye steaks. Desserts, such as the one combining white-chocolate mousse, organic honey and peanut butter, leave the sweetest of aftertastes.

City Center

Chantonner Delikatessen DELI **$**
(Map p48; www.chantonner.com.co; Carrera 5 No 16-01; sandwiches COP$11,400-15,600; 7am-7pm Mon-Wed, to 8pm Thu-Fri, to 5pm Sat;) Once a small *tienda* (shop) selling cigarettes and sweets, Chantonner Delikatessen is now a popular lunch hangout for those attracted to the house specialty: 12-hour smoked meat and cheese boards; and a wealth of sandwiches like pulled pork and several smoked options (trout, brisket, pancetta).

A newer location in Quinta Camacho TK has just opened complete with their own eight-tap craft beer bar, **Tierra Santa** (Map p60; www.facebook.com/pg/tierrasanta cervezaartesanal; Calle 71 No 10-47; pints COP$11,000; 10am-9pm Mon-Wed, to 11pm Thu-Sat) (good stouts, IPAs).

Pastelería Florida COLOMBIAN **$**
(Map p48; www.facebook.com/PasteleriaFlorida; Carrera 7 No 21-46; mains COP$6600-24,500, chocolate completo COP$12,500; 6am-midnight) Those needing a bit of pomp or history with their *chocolate santafereño* (hot chocolate served with cheese) should make the hike to this classic snack shop-restaurant (a legendary spot for hot chocolate since 1936). Overwhelmed uniformed waiters serve up Tolimenses- and Santandereanos-style tamales to legions of fans for breakfast and cakes and pastries throughout the day (COP$2200 to COP$7500).

Macarena

Ázimos CAFE **$**
(Map p48; www.azimos.com; Carrera 5 No 26C-54; breakfast COP$6500-13,000; 8am-8pm Mon-Sat, 8am-2pm Sun;) Start your day adorably with a series of regional breakfasts at this organic cafe and supermarket in La Macarena, where hip vegetarians and other sustainably minded warriors dine under cardboard boxes reborn as lampshades and glass-jar chandeliers. For lunch, choose from several *menú del dia* options (COP$18,200) – green pea falafel one day, physalis-glazed pork ribs the next. Quaint and cool.

La Tapería TAPAS $$
(Map p48; www.lataperia.co; Carrera 4A No 26D-12; tapas COP$12,000-31,000; noon-3pm & 6-11pm Mon-Wed, noon-3pm & 6pm-midnight Thu-Sat, 1-5pm Sun;) To the delight of those in the know, delectable tapas such as cherry tomatoes wrapped in blue cheese and bacon with a balsamic reduction are churned out under the guidance of a Dutch music fiend in this cool, loft-aesthetic lounge. There's flamenco on Thursday and Saturday, and Friday's neighborhood-curated Música del Barrio playlist draws a young crowd.

Reserve ahead online.

★ **Agave Azul** MEXICAN $$$
(Map p48; 315-277-0329; www.restauranteagaveazul.blogspot.com.co; Carrera 3A No 26B-52; tasting menu COP$75,000; noon-3pm & 6:30-10pm Tue-Fri, 1-4pm & 7-10pm Sat;) This outstanding restaurant is a trip, both literally and figuratively, through truly authentic Mexican cuisine by way of Chicago, New York and Oaxaca. Chef Tatiana Navarro has no set menu – just a daily open-ended tasting menu – and no sign. Agave Azul is hidden inside a residential La Macarena home, offering a handful of tables and highly personalized service. Advance reservations essential.

Once you're inside, a culinary coup awaits: possibilities include slow-braised Jalisco short ribs with chile ancho, habanero-laced ceviche with passionfruit reduction or mini *carnitas* sandwiches with *chicharones* (pork cracklings). Even the simple things (guacamole) are done well, and there's always a surprise among the seven courses. Chase the meal with outstanding chipotle margaritas – surely Colombia's best – and you've reached nirvana *cocina mexicana*.

★ **Leo** COLOMBIAN $$$
(Map p48; 1-286-7091; http://restauranteleo.com; Calle 27B No 6-75; mains COP$52,000-87,000; noon-3:30pm & 7-11pm Mon-Sat;) Chef Leo Espinosa is the culinary priestess for innovative Colombian fine dining. Her epic 12-course tasting menu (COP$210,000) paired with wine and artisanal beverages (COP$280,000) is a belt-loosening, multihour journey through exotic regional ingredients, many of which are ignored by most Colombian kitchens. A meal here is revelatory, with bold colors and striking flavors unlike those of anything previously plated.

Chapinero & Chapinero Alto

Insurgentes Taco Bar MEXICAN $
(Map p60; Calle 56 No 5-21; tacos COP$5500-8000; noon-midnight;) Occupying a former Chapinero Alto mansion now split between two restaurants, hip newcomer Insurgentes is a high-design, good-time taco bar that draws a cool and artsy crowd chasing excellent and fairly priced *carnitas, al pastor* and fish tacos with *micheladas* and mezcal.

BOGOTÁ CHAINS

Bogotá has some surprisingly worthy chain eateries, many of which once dominated their speciality before the rise of movements like Third Wave coffee, gourmet burgers and craft beer. The best of the lot by a landslide is **Wok** (Map p54; www.wok.com.co; Calle 93B No 12-28, Parque 93; mains COP$15,900-34,900; noon-10:30pm Mon-Sat, to 9pm Sun;); its excellently executed, sustainably sourced Asian-fusion food is some of the best you'll find in South America. Other Bogotá-born staples to keep an eye out for include **El Corral** (Map p54; www.elcorral.com; Calle 85 No 13-77; burgers from COP$19,900; 24hr;), with excellent fast-food hamburgers; **Crepes & Waffles** (Map p54; www.crepesywaffles.com.co; Carrera 9 No 73-33; mains COP$10,900-28,400; 11:45am-9:30pm Mon-Thu, to 10pm Fri & Sat, to 9pm Sun;), a do-it-all, diner-like chain; **Bogotá Beer Company** (Map p54; www.bogotabeercompany.com; Calle 85 No 13-06; pints COP$16,900; 12:30pm-2am Sun-Wed, to 3am Thu-Sat;), with corporate craft-beer pubs; and Juan Valdez (p69), a Starbucks-like coffee chain – and there are more where those came from (La Hamburguesería for burgers, Julia for authentic Italian pizza, Tostao' for coffee and bakery items – you get the idea.)

You'll find branches in most neighborhoods, particularly in the north, and a few have even gone international. They're a solid bet for a quick, dependable and consistent bite, pint or pick-me-up.

DON'T MISS

ANDRÉS CARNE DE RES

You cannot describe the indescribable, but here goes: the legendary **Andrés Carne de Res** (☎1-861-2233; www.andrescarnederes.com; Calle 3 No 11A-56, Chía; steaks COP$49,600-59,000, cover Fri & Sat COP$21,000; ⏰11am-3am Thu-Sat, to midnight Sun; 📶) bar-restaurant is an otherworldly entertainment cocktail that's equal parts Tim Burton, Disneyland and Willy Wonka – with a dash of junkyard kitsch and funhouse extravaganza. No, wait; a Swedish tourist said it better: 'It's like eating dinner in a washing machine.' Whatever! Andrés blows everyone – even repeat visitors – away with its all-out fun atmosphere, awesome steaks (the menu is a 75-page magazine) and surreal decor. For most, it's not so much a meal but an up-all-night, damn-the-torpedoes spectacular.

The catch is that it's out of town – in Chía, 23km north toward Zipaquirá. An Uber from Bogotá costs COP$27,000 to COP$48,000 depending on demand (skip the restaurant's highly overpriced taxi service). A party bus to Andrés on Friday (COP$70,000) and Saturday (COP$80,000) leaves at 10pm from **Hostal Sue Candelaria** (Map p48; ☎1-344-2647; www.hostalsuecandelaria.com; Carrera 3 No 12C-18; incl breakfast dm COP30,000-35,000, r without bathroom COP$80,000; @📶), returning in the wee hours – prices include admission and booze on the bus. Alternatively, save a bit of money getting there by catching a Chía-bound bus from inside the TransMilenio's **Portal del Norte** (cnr Carrera 45 & Calle 174) station from the Buses Intermunicipales platform; buses leave every two minutes until 11pm (COP$2700, 30 minutes). See for yourself if a visit to Andrés isn't the most insane night you've ever had.

For a more sedate location closer to town, **Andrés D.C** (Map p54; ☎1-863-7880; www.andrescarnederes.com; Calle 82 No 12-21, Centro Comercial El Retiro; steaks to share COP$36,700-98,900, cover Fri & Sat COP$21,000; ⏰noon-3am; 📶). is also an option, but it lacks that certain something.

Arbol del Pan BAKERY $

(Map p60; www.facebook.com/panaderiaarboldelpan; Calle 66 No 4A-35; pastries COP$2500-7800; ⏰8am-8pm Mon-Fri, to 6pm Sat; 📶) You'll feel like your sweet nighttime dreams have extended into breakfast at this all-natural bakery and pastry shop that pumps out an array of just-baked breads and a slew of delectable pastries, including superflaky almond croissants. There's also heartier breakfast fare (COP$9000 to COP$15,000), such as prosciutto-wrapped asparagus and that old hipster standby: avocado and poached egg on toast.

Mesa Franca COLOMBIAN $$

(Map p60; ☎1-805-1787; www.facebook.com/mesafrancabogota; Carrera 6 No 55-09; small plates COP$17,000-42,000; ⏰noon-10pm Mon-Wed, to 11pm Thu-Sat) 🌿 Colombian chef Iván Cadena evokes the come-one, come-all banquet-style of his Araucanian farm upbringing at this hot Bogotá newcomer, a beautiful example of both the Bogotá and, more specifically, Chapinero Alto, food evolution.

Churning out delectable farm-to-table small plates inside a hip converted mansion (the kitchen sits in the former garage), ingredients procured direct from local producers seize the spotlight: Cundinamarcan goat cheese with sweet *criolla*-style apple and sourdough crumble, Santa Rosa chorizo agnolotti with *hogao* confit emulsion etc. Dishes are designed to share and the English-Polish mixologist knows his cocktails – making this an easy spot to call it a night.

Salvo Patria CAFE $$

(Map p60; ☎1-702-6367; www.salvopatria.com; Carrera 54A No 4-13; mains COP$16,000-32,000; ⏰noon-11am Mon-Sat; 📶) This Chapinero Alto stalwart of coolness and quality helped pioneer Bogotá's now well-established farm-to-table food scene (local producers are listed on a chalkboard at the entrance).

It's one part very serious coffeehouse (the *bogotano* owner honed his barista skills in Australia, so even Australians don't complain about the coffee!), and one part bar-restaurant dishing up sophisticated Mediterranean-French bistro fare to artsy hipsters in the know. Great cocktails, rarer Colombian craft beer and great-value *menú del día* (from COP$22,000).

★**Mini-Mal** COLOMBIAN $$

(Map p60; ☎1-347-5464; www.mini-mal.org; Carrera 4A No 57-52; mains COP$27,900-38,000; ⏰noon-

3pm & 7-10pm Mon-Thu, noon-11pm Fri & Sat;) You'll be hard-pressed to find a more creative Colombian menu than at this excellent Chapinero Alto hot spot, which has resurrected some of the country's more interesting regional ingredients – sustainably sourced and fiercely artisan – and breathed new life into contemporary Colombian cuisine. The menu is an intriguing triumvirate of Caribbean, Altiplano and jungle-sourced food.

Count on beef braised with *tucupí* (a spicy, *adobo*-like sauce derived from poisonous yuca root, enhanced with chilies and ants); chicken sautéed with *chicha* (fermented corn hooch) and raw sugar glaze; and wild mushrooms with coastal cheese and nasturtium pesto – it's all outstanding and totally without precedent. Save room for the delectably moist cornbread cake with guava sauce.

Zona G

Guerrero SANDWICHES **$**

(Map p60; www.facebook.com/guerrero.cia; Carrera 9 No 69-10; sandwiches COP$13,000-20,000; noon-9:30pm Mon-Sat;) Guerrero is a trendy-ish sandwich joint in Quinta Camacho that does a mouthwatering menu of gourmet sandwiches (a fantastic burger, fried trout, chicken or pork, a pork loin, beef and portobello mushroom) on wonderful buns, accompanied by fries or native potato chips. It's a great spot for a quick bite.

Cantina y Punto MEXICAN **$$**

(Map p60; 1-644-7766; www.cantinaypunto.co; Calle 66 No 4A-33; mains COP$12,300-49,800; noon-11pm Mon-Wed, to 11:30pm Thu-Sat, noon-6pm Sun;) From Michelin-starred Mexican chef Roberto Ruíz (of Punto MX fame), this high-end destination for *comida mexicana* is not to be missed: dig into fiery and tangy fresh salsas and guacamole served in a traditional *molcajete* (a stone mortar) while agonizing over the menu: *cochinita pibil* or brisket tacos? Habanero, ancho and pasilla-chili braised pork shank or a blessed pork confit?

Restaurante La Herencia COLOMBIAN **$$**

(Map p60; 1-249-5195; http://restaurantelaherencia.com; Carrera 9 No 69A-26, Quinta Camacho; mains COP$16,500-43,000; 7am-10pm Mon-Sat, 9am-5pm Sun; Flores TransMilenio Station | AK 7 - CL 70A) La Herencia takes the very best of traditional Colombian cuisine and serves it up within a sophisticated and friendly atmosphere. From the comfort of this pleasantly decorated restaurant, sit back and take a gastronomy tour of Colombia, sampling dishes and drinks ranging from as far afield as the Caribbean and Pacific Coast to the high Andean mountains.

De/Raíz VEGETARIAN **$$**

(Map p60; Calle 65 No 5-70; mains COP$16,000-21,500; 10am-9pm Mon-Tue, to 10pm Wed-Sat, to 4pm Sun;) This stylish plant-based bistro was born out of the upstart owner's MBA thesis project and is seriously steeped in fostering relationships with local producers as much as possible. The menu features a small but delectable handful of staples (think quinoa and kale salad, grilled veggie plate) and one daily changing special. Organic wines from Chile are also available.

Rafael PERUVIAN **$$$**

(Map p60; 1-255-4138; www.rafaelosterling.pe/en/bogota.html; Calle 70 No 4-63/65; mains COP$34,500-69,500; 12:30-3pm & 7:30-11pm Mon-Sat;) *Bogotano* foodies and chefs are nearly unanimous in calling Peruvian Chef Rafael Osterling's creative homegrown cuisine some of city's most consistently innovative. The contemporary space melds cold aesthetics like concrete ceilings with a warm and intimate garden; and the food leaves no one unsatisfied.

Favorites like sticky duck rice braised in black beer or a crunchy cochinillo (suckling pig) are staples on the ever-changing menu, but leave room for dessert. Osterling's creative take on the traditional *suspiro de limeña* (layered meringue and dulce de leche; in this case with soursop, raspberry and port meringue) is a fitting end to a dazzling travel meal, especially if Peru isn't in your travel plans.

Zona Rosa & Parque 93

Les Amis Bizcochería CAFE **$**

(Map p54; www.lesamisbizcocheria.com; Carrera 14 No 86A-12, piso 2; pastries COP$500-6500; 8:30am-7:30pm Mon-Fri, 9am-5pm Sat; TransMilenio Station Calle 85) More an extended living room than a coffee shop, Les Amis has a homey atmosphere that begs for quiet, intimate conversations, interrupted only by a deep and often indecisive inspection of the freshly baked savoury tarts, cakes, croissants and biscuits that spill over a large kitchen table.

All of the baked goods are made in an open-plan kitchen, so you can witness the magic of the creation process unfold while you munch. There's another branch on Calle 70A, Un Cafe de les Amis, offering similar fare, minus the on-site kitchen.

Home Burger BURGERS **$**
(Map p54; www.homeburgers.com.co; Carrera 9 No 81a-19; burgers COP$10,500-15,500; noon-9pm Mon-Thu, to 10pm Fri & Sat, to 8pm Sun) What some say is the pinnacle of Bogotá's off-the-charts burger wars, hipster-ish Home Burger eschews gourmet nonsense for down-home simplicity: folks line up for single or double patties with cheese and/or bacon; skinny, nicely seasoned fries and little else.

The small space means most folks take away (nearby Parque El Nogal makes for a decent meal setting) but you can throw some elbows in for a table as well.

★ **Canasto Picnic Bistró** COLOMBIAN **$$**
(Map p54; www.facebook.com/canastopicnic bistro; Calle 88 No 13A-51; breakfast COP$4100-15,900, mains COP$16,100-34,000; noon-10pm Mon, 7am-10pm Tue-Sat, 7am-6pm Sun;) This artistically driven and sustainably minded bistro near Parque El Virrey is all the rage in the city. Breakfast items like avocado toast with smoked trout and a long and colorful list of organic egg dishes are perfectly accompanied by strong espresso served in gorgeous blue ceramic cups from Chía's Santa Paloma.

As the day wears on, the vegan- and vegetarian-minded menu covers couscous and quinoa-based salads, wonderful sandwiches and heartier mains. The potted-plant-strewn patio is a see-and-be-seen venue for Bogotá's bold, beautiful and breakfast-minded set.

Central Cevicheria SEAFOOD **$$**
(Map p54; 1-644-7766; www.centralcevicheria.com; Carrera 13 No 85-14; ceviche COP$20,000-30,000; noon-11pm Mon-Wed, noon-midnight Thu-Sat, noon-10pm Sun;) This large, high-concept cevicheria is insanely popular with the upscale Bogotá set. Choose your fish (octopus, shrimp, mixed seafood etc), then add one of a dozen sauces split into spicy and nonspicy categories, of which there are more than 10 inventive offerings. Reservations recommended.

A favorite sauce is the kick-laced *picoso,* swimming in two peppers, cilantro and fresh corn. But it doesn't stop there: there are numerous *tiraditos* (long-cut ceviches without onions), tartares, fresh seafood main dishes and good Latin cocktails (COP$22,800). It's Colombian coastal cuisine on overdrive. Save room for the deliciously dense coconut flan.

Container City FOOD HALL **$$**
(Map p54; www.facebook.com/ContainerCity93; Calle 93 No 12-11; 7:30am-11pm;) A gourmet food court fashioned from 10 or so shipping containers, this atmospheric food court includes Mexican, gourmet burgers, Latin-inspired tapas and craft beer, among others.

Usaquén

★ **Abasto** BREAKFAST **$$**
(1-620-5262; Carrera 6 No 119B-52; mains COP$20,000-37,000; 7am-10pm Mon-Thu, to 11pm Fri, 9am-10:30pm Sat, 9am-5pm Sun;) Make a pilgrimage to Usaquén to indulge in the creative breakfasts and delectable mains and desserts at this rustic-trendy restaurant. Inventive *arepas* (corn cakes) and seriously good egg dishes such as *migas* (scrambled eggs with bits of *arepas* and *hogao,* a concoction of onion, tomato, cumin and garlic) are washed down with organic coffee by true morning-sustenance connoisseurs.

Whatever you order, sprinkle a bit of the punch-packing Wai Ya organic Amazonian pepper in it.

80 Sillas CEVICHE **$$**
(1-644-7766; www.80sillas.com; Calle 118 No 6A-05; ceviche COP$19,900-22,900; noon-11pm Mon-Sat, noon-10pm Sun;) Usaquén's busiest spot is all about putting a modern spin on traditional ceviche, set in a redone colonial farmhouse on the southwestern corner of the plaza. You can pick from a host of ceviche styles (such as ginger or a hearty *criollo* with bacon, potato, lime and cheese). Yes, there are 80 seats.

Drinking & Nightlife

Atmospheric 300-year-old homes with corner fireplaces and old tile floors dot La Candelaria. Watering holes turn up the trend as you head north: especially in Chapinero Alto, Zona Rosa and Parque 93. Bohemian barrios west of Av Caracas, such as Parkway in La Soledad, have become stomping grounds for craft brewing and other hipster trends in the last few years.

La Candelaria

Arte y Pasión Café COFFEE

(Map p48; www.arteypasioncafe.com; Calle 10 No 8-87; coffee COP$3500-18,000; 7am-7pm Mon-Fri, 8am-5pm Sat;) What began as a way to educate Colombians about the wonders of specialty coffee became a successful, hands-on barista training school plus a chic, specialized coffee shop where 'art and passion' and Colombian coffee come together for a fun, unique experience. This second, newer location offers 12 Colombian single-origins, eight brewing methods and sharply dressed baristas working their magic.

Try ordering the signature drink, Irish coffee, which comes with a fascinating preparation experience. Their somewhat worn-down original location is near Museo del Oro.

City Center

Contraste Coffee Lab COFFEE

(Map p48; www.facebook.com/contrastelab; Calle 16 No 4-51; coffee COP$3500-15,000; 8am-7pm Mon-Fri, 9am-5pm Sun;) Hidden away in the Hotel Continental shopping center, you'll find this tiny but serious java joint run by the soft-spoken Manual, an expert Colombian barista who prepares the best flat white this side of the Pacific. His daily roasted, single-origin coffee hails from Viotá (Cundinamarca) and can be enjoyed via all the serious methods and preparations (pour over, espresso, cold brew).

Macarena

Café Origami CAFE

(Map p48; www.planetaorigami.com; Carrera 4A No 26C-04; cofee COP$3000-6000; 3:30-9pm Mon-Wed, to 10:30pm Thu-Sat, 1:30-8pm Sun; TransMilenio CL26) Japanese art, Lebanese cuisine and Colombian coffee flawlessly collide to create this charming conceptual cafe where coffee and origami have become best friends. Blending into the so-called international neighborhood of La Macarena, it's a great place to relax and sip a coffee while you transform a scrap of paper into an origami masterpiece.

The cafe also holds art and design expositions and creative workshops.

El Bembe BAR

(Map p48; www.facebook.com/elbembebar; Calle 27B No 6-73; cover Fri & Sat COP$25,000; noon-9pm Mon-Wed, to 1am Thu, to 3am Fri & Sat) Cuba and Colombia share a loose cultural alliance, especially when it comes to music, as this little piece of *tropicalia* ably demonstrates. Head up the multicolored stairs off a cobbled street in La Macarena for rum and salsa, live bands and potent mojitos (COP$25,000 to COP$42,000), all of which seem to flow more freely on Friday. Skip the food.

Chapinero, Chapinero Alto & Quinta Camacho

Taller de Té TEAHOUSE

(Map p60; www.tallerdete.com; Calle 60A No 3A-38; tea COP$4000-10,000; 10am-8pm Mon-Sat;) This adorable cafe is unique in Bogotá for serious tea. Owner Laura sources more than 70 teas and infusions from plantations around the world and blends them with local herbs, flowers, spices, teas and traditional plants. There are organic, vegetarian and vegan light bites from trusted culinary artisans around Colombia to pair with them.

As with many Chapinero businesses, the street profile is more private home than commercial cafe.

La Negra CLUB

(Map p42; www.facebook.com/LaNegraBta; Carrera 7 No 47-63; cover COP$15,000; 9:30pm-2:30am Fri & Sat) With its flashy retro logo and a soundtrack that hopscotches between salsa, vallenato, reggaeton, cumbia and rarer Colombian genres, La Negra is an informal but wildly popular crossover magnet for upper-middle-class university students and young professionals, who take turns swigging from their bottles of aguardiente (Colombia's anise-flavored local firewater) between the frenetic and contagious beats.

CLUBBING IN BOGOTÁ

Strap yourself in: Bogotá boogies. There's all sorts of ambience and musical rhythm on offer – from rock, techno and metal to salsa, vallenato and samba. If you don't know how to dance, be prepared to prove it. Strangers frequently ask each other to dance and everyone seems to know the words to every song played.

GAY & LESBIAN BOGOTÁ

Bogotá has a large and frequently changing gay-nightlife scene. It's mostly centered in Chapinero, nicknamed 'Chapi Gay', between Carrera 7 and 13 from Calles 58 to 63. If you want to make an event of it, **Queer Scout** (www.thequeerscout.co) claims to offer Colombia's only gay-nightlife tour.

Browse **Guia Gay Colombia** (www.guiagaycolombia.com/bogota) for details on dozens of varied clubs and bars, or check online listings from **Colombia Diversa** (☎1-483-1237; www.colombiadiversa.org; Calle 30A No 6-22, oficina 1102), a not-for-profit organization promoting gay and lesbian rights in Colombia. Lesbian-only places haven't really caught on here yet, so most gay bars and clubs attract a mixed crowd, including Video Club (p68), which throws Sunday parties on bank-holiday weekends.

Get there before 10pm or prepare to wait. COP$6000 of the cover is can be recuperated in *cerveza*.

Cervecería Statua Rota CRAFT BEER
(Map p42; Calle 40 No 21-34; pints COP$15,500-17,000; ⏲noon-11pm Mon-Wed, to midnight Thu-Fri, to 1am Sat; 📶) It once would have been odd to travel west of Av Caracas, but this Parkway microbrewery and bar attracts a fiercely dedicated army of beer-loving alt-hipsters content to swill house-brewed double red IPAs and summer Witbiers – often brewed with Colombian fruits and other local ingredients – to indie, alternative rock and metal until the wee hours.

Amor Perfecto CAFE
(Map p60; www.amorperfectocafe.net; Carrera 4 No 66-46; ⏲8am-9pm Mon-Sat, 10am-7pm Sun; 📶) Pick your single-origin regional Colombian specialty bean, select your method of preparation (Chemex, Siphon, AeroPress or French press), and let the highly knowledgeable and national-champion baristas at this hip Chapinero Alto coffeehouse do the rest. You can also pop in for tastings and courses.

Mi Tierra BAR
(Map p60; Calle 63 No 11-47; ⏲4pm-3am) Find a space among the busted typewriters, sombreros, moose heads, musical instruments and televisions at this friendly Chapinero bar that resembles a licensed flea market. It's popular with a chilled crowd, so you don't need to be too concerned about the collection of old machetes, and the music is particularly well curated.

It's shoehorned beneath a small shopping mall.

🍷 Northern Bogotá

★**El Mono Bandido** PUB
(Map p60; www.elmonobandido.com; Carrera 10A No 69-38; pints COP$9500-10,500; ⏲4pm-midnight Mon-Wed, to 1am Thu-Sat, noon-8pm Sun; 📶) Having commandeered a Quinta Camacho mansion and flipped it into one of Bogotá's most cinematic pubs, El Mono Bandido has atmosphere in spades. Enjoy house-brewed craft suds inside the two-floor space teeming with exposed, loose-end pipes illuminated with Edison lighting, or at one of a handful of oil-candle-lit tables in the surrounding garden.

Its original location at Carrera 4 No 54-85 in Chapinero also offers a very good time indeed.

Cervecería Gigante CRAFT BEER
(Map p42; www.cerveceriagigante.com; Carrera 22 No 70A-60; pints from COP$8000; ⏲5-11pm Thu-Sat; 📶) American nanobrewer Will Catlett has created what feels like an underground brewer's lair at Bogotá's top craft-beer destination, a simple, unsigned place west of Carrera 14 with 12 taps (three dedicated to its own craft sodas). But it's more than a drinking den: house-made chicken and pork chorizo (with leeks, mango and jalapeño), burgers and wings make for unmissable pub grub.

The Citra Pale Ale and Sequioa Roja IPA come especially recommended, as do the gluten-free Oatmeal Pale Ale and the smoked Saison from invitees Madriguera Brewing Co and Viteri Cervecería, respectively. Make it a pilgrimage (in a taxi!).

Video Club CLUB
(Map p60; ☎1-474-7000; www.facebook.com/pg/videoclubbogota; Calle 64 No 13-09; cover COP$25,000-45,000; ⏲10pm-5am Fri & Sat) Fortunately for club kids, the unfortunately

named Video Club is much cooler than its name (and facade) suggest. The two-floor former warehouse space in Chapinero draws a vehemently mixed crowd, who mingle on the wood-accented ground floor to salsa and other Latin-infused experimental dance tunes before gravitating to the electronica-heavy 2nd floor, replete with brick archways and exposed rebar.

It's here, on a moonlit, open-air terrace, that some of Bogotá's trendiest clubbers – gay, straight, uncertain – shake it off until breakfast. Check ahead for info on gay Sunday parties on bank-holiday weekends.

★ **Azahar Café** CAFE

(Map p54; www.azaharcoffee.com; Calle 93B No 13-91; coffee COP$4000-16,000; ⏲7am-8pm Mon-Fri, 9am-8pm Sat & Sun; 📶) 🍃 Possibly the finest shrine to coffee in Colombia, the recently amplified Azahar exudes taste, expertise and an undying passion for the country's second-most-famous homegrown product (after cocaine). Busy baristas work behind a huge counter like alchemists in a chemistry lab, experimenting with French press, Chemex, pour-over and espresso. The attention to detail jumps out of the cup.

Sit at one of the lovely wooden tables and watch as staff custom-brew your request and bring it to you in a fancy pot, cup or flask. The breakfasts – Spanish-style *migas* (bread salad), açai bowls and the requisite avocado on toast – are available all day and hard to pass up. Lunches mainly involve sandwiches and chicken.

BOGOTÁ'S COFFEE EVOLUTION

Colombia may be *muy famosa* for coffee, but in reality it's just been remarkably astute at coffee marketing. Despite international renown and a loveable figurehead in the fictional Juan Valdez (created by the National Federation of Coffee Growers of Colombia in 1958), Colombian coffee in Colombia was terrible for decades. The ubiquitous preparation, known as *tinto*, is a barely drinkable swill resulting from the fact that Colombians are accustomed to drinking what the rest of the world ain't got no time for – the best beans were always exported, and the dregs were roasted, ground, sweetened into oblivion and sold countrywide in colorful thermoses that definitely do not proclaim, 'Singular coffee experience!'.

Despite coffee's Third Wave (in which it's treated as a high-quality commodity and served in artisanal espresso bars by career baristas who make coffee art with your latte) dating back to the early Noughties in most countries, Colombia lagged woefully behind. And it faced a tourism dichotomy due to its reputation: once the world started visiting Colombia, it naturally expected amazing coffee. But while destination Colombia was a major hit, *tinto* failed to deliver.

Things started looking up in 2002, when the first **Juan Valdez** (Map p48; www.juanvaldezcafe.com; Centro Cultural Gabriel García Márquez, Carrera 6 No 11-20; coffee COP$3600-7900; ⏲8am-8pm Mon, 7am-8pm Tue-Sat, 9am-6pm Sun; 📶) café opened in Bogotá. Although little more than a Colombian Starbucks, the Second Wave had arrived and Colombians began to get a taste for something other than *tinto*. Still, the evolution was slow – it would still take more than a decade before the Third Wave arrived.

As recently as 2012, the United States Department of Agriculture (USDA) estimated that Colombia was importing 90% of the coffee it consumed (Colombia's statistics bureau pegged the number closer to 80%, but still, the numbers were considerable). Why? Essentially because it was cheaper, as even commodity-quality Colombian arabica beans traded for a premium on the international market. But the tide has begun to turn.

With Juan Valdez having laid the foundation (as few as 10% of Colombians drank coffee at cafes in 2007; today that figure is 50%), and growing disposable income among the country's middle class along with newfound national pride in consuming their world-renowned product, Colombian coffee is now amazing on both sides of the border.

By 2017 there were more than 50 specialty coffee cafes in Bogotá. With options such as Amor Perfecto (p68) and Azahar Café (p69) offering coffee every bit as good as anything in Seattle or Turin, caffeine fiends will never have to suffer at the hands of *tinto* again.

After all, as Azahar put it from the beginning: *Porque Colombia Merece su Mejor Café* (Because Colombia Deserves the Best Coffee).

Bourbon Coffee Roasters CAFE

(Map p60; www.bourboncoffeeco.tumblr.com; Calle 70A No 13-83, Quinta Camacho; coffee COP$3200-12,000; ⏲8am-8pm Mon-Fri, 10am-6:30pm Sat; 📶; 🚇Calle 72 TransMilenio Station | Flores TransMilenio Station) Even before you enter the softly lit, Victorian-style red-brick house, the quaint surrounding neighborhood lays down high expectations. A haven for hipsters and conversationalists, the cafe has done well to create the perfect match of professionalism and style without attitude. Single-origin Colombian coffee is roasted and ground on-site and served according to preference by trained baristas.

Chelarte CRAFT BEER

(Map p54; www.chelarte.com; Carrera 14 No 93B-45; pints from COP$12,600; ⏲10am-11pm Mon-Wed, to 1am Fri & Sat; 📶) Chelarte – a portmanteau word combining Mexican slang for beer ('chela') and 'artesanal' – helped pioneer craft beer in Bogotá when brewer Camilo Rojas decided six years ago that Club Colombia and Aguila just weren't up to snuff. Today, their candlelit craft beer lounge is one of Bogotá's most atmospheric.

Nine taps include staples like their summer ale, pale ale and brown ale (all named after fictional females like Pamela, Rachel and Carmela) with rotating one-offs (look for the India pale ale and organic ale) and invited local nanobreweries. Good burgers and bar snacks as well.

Café Cultor COFFEE

(Map p60; www.cafecultor.co; Calle 69 No 6-20; ⏲8am-7:30pm Mon-Thu, 9:30am-3:30pm Sat, to 3pm Sun; 📶; 🚇TransMilenio AK 7 - CL68) Fuelled by the motto that life is too short to drink bad coffee, this recycled coffee-container-turned-cafe, complete with a pretty rooftop deck, continually delivers its nationally recognised top-notch brews. Located in Bogotá's trendy Zona G, Café Cultor rotates among 10 different single-origin Colombian beans, all of which come from sustainable, fair-trade agreements with local farmers.

Tap House CRAFT BEER

(Map p54; www.facebook.com/TapHouseBog; Carrera 14 No. 83-57; pints COP$13,000; ⏲4-10pm Mon-Wed, to 2am Thu-Sat; 📶) A partnership between two local craft breweries (the American-Colombian-run Tomahawk and more traditional Tierra Alta), this craft beer haunt is a good spot to acquaint yourself with the new wave of Colombian *cerveza artesanal.*

The 13 taps are more or less spread evenly among the house brews and invited guests, all easily enjoyed on the long bar illuminated by hipster Edison lighting. There's nothing daring or risky going on here yet (no barrel-aged brews or anything particularly funky), but the fuse is lit and the music isn't afraid to rock.

★Cine Tonalá CLUB

(Map p42; www.cinetonala.co; Carrera 6A No 35-37; films COP$7000; ⏲noon-2:30am Tue & Thu-Sat, to 8pm Wed; 📶) Bogotá's only independent cinema champions Latin and Colombian films and international cult classics, but this Mexico City import refuses to be categorized. The multifaceted cultural center, set in a renovated 1930s La Merced mansion, is a shelter for artistic refugees, who retreat here for a very hip bar scene, excellent Mexican food and rousing club nights from Thursday to Saturday.

The red-brick, bay-windowed facade looks more like an old English manor house than a Latin American cinema. Inside, it's more pub-like, with parquet floors and lashings of Stanley Kubrick memorabilia.

Armando Records CLUB

(Map p54; www.armandorecords.org; Calle 85 No 14-46; cover Thu-Sat COP$17,000-30,000; ⏲8:30pm-2:45am Tue-Thu, from 8pm Fri & Sat) Still a Bogotá hot spot after several years, this multilevel den of nocturnal delight features the 2nd-floor Armando's All Stars, which skews younger for crossover tunes and includes a back garden packed with patrons; and the 4th-floor retro rooftop, where the likes of LCD Soundsystem and Empire of the Sun guide your evening.

Bistro El Bandido BAR

(Map p54; ☎1-212-5709; www.elbandidobistro.com; Calle 79B No 7-12; mains COP$34,000-65,100; ⏲noon-1am Mon-Sat; 📶) Step back in time at this popular high-end bar and brasserie hidden behind residential shrubbery in Nogal. DJ's spin oldies (think Big Band, Elvis) between live jazz/swing sets while a well-heeled crowd laps up classic cocktails (from COP$23,000). An excellent menu of brasserie standbys, including a chorizo appetizer, *coq au vin* and fish *meunière,* come highly recommended.

It all surrounds a big and beautiful social bar – somewhat of a novelty in Bogotá – but don't forget to peek in the back, where the tiny and gorgeous Bar Enano (the bar within the bar!) is one of the city's hot spots. Reservations essential after 7pm.

Entertainment

Bogotá is home to a well-established arts, theater and music scene. The city's best theaters are found in La Candelaria, while live-music venues dot the north, from grittier/trendier Chapinero to more mainstream venues in the Zona Rosa.

Check out the online '*entretenimiento*' sections of local papers **El Tiempo** (www.eltiempo.com/cultura/entretenimiento) and **El Espectador** (www.elespectador.com/entretenimiento/eventos), as well as Civico (www.civico.com/bogota), for event listings. For cultural events and commentary in English, pick up the free monthly **City Paper** (www.thecitypaperbogota.com). For schedules and tickets to many events (theater, rock concerts, football games), check **Tu Boleta** (www.tuboleta.com).

Live Music

Clubs across town stage live music nightly, and outdoor festivals such as Rock al Parque (p53) are huge events that attract fans from all over the continent. Posters around town tout big-name acts, who play at Estadio El Campín, Parque Simón Bolívar, and Parque Jaime Duque (on the way to Zipaquirá, north of the city).

Latino Power LIVE MUSIC
(Map p60; Calle 58 No 13-88; cover COP$10,000-35,000; ⏰9pm-3am Fri & Sat) Despite this graffiti-covered disco space undergoing an

HOW TO BUY EMERALDS

Some of the world's highest-quality emeralds are mined chiefly in the Muzo and Chivor areas of Boyacá. Colombia is the world's largest exporter of emeralds, making these precious stones a coveted item on tourists' 'to buy' lists when visiting Bogotá and surrounding regions.

In years past the beauty of Colombia's emeralds was overshadowed by the dangerous conditions in which they were mined. Some locals compared Colombia's emerald market with the diamond industry in Africa. In 2005 the government abolished tariffs and taxes associated with mining, effectively ending the power of the black market and associated elements.

Travelers can now buy emeralds in good conscience. In the capital, emeralds are sold in the flourishing **Emerald Trade Center** (Map p48; Av Jiménez No 5-43; ⏰7:30am-7pm Mon-Fri, 8am-5pm Sat), where dozens of *comisionistas* (traders) buy and sell stones – sometimes on the sidewalk. You will also be offered emeralds on the street. Don't do it: glass imitations these days look a lot like the real thing (and even if they're genuine emeralds, you'll surely overpay). Serious buyers should consider a two-hour city tour with **Colombian Emerald Tours** (☎313-317-6534; www.colombianemeraldtours.com; downtown tour per person COP$80,000) that will introduce you to the *comisionistas* and educate you on cut, quality and the like inside the Emerald Trade Center. There's no pressure to buy, but if you do, the COP$80,000 tour price will be credited back. The outfit also offers a long day trip into the emerald mine in Chivor, Boyacá (COP$1,700,000 for two people all inclusive; the price lowers with bigger groups), an ecotourism initiative run by the community there.

Tips to keep in mind while shopping for emeralds:

- Inspect the person selling you the emerald as closely as the emerald itself. Find a seller that you feel comfortable with. You'll be surprised at how obvious it is to either run away or relax when you devote some attention to the seller.
- Gems and jewelry are very subjective; often when looking at emeralds in the shops or with dealers your first impression is the best and most reliable one. Don't be in a hurry when buying. The quality of the gem in any Colombian shop is regulated by the tourist industry, so just concentrate on the price. Don't be afraid to walk away if you feel that the price is too high.
- Assess the harmony between a stone's color, clarity, brightness and size.
- If you find a jeweler or dealer you like, invite him or her for tea or a *tinto* (black coffee). You'll hear good stories and will have an ally in the emerald business.

unfortunate name change (from the far-superior Boogaloop), its mantra perseveres: a shelter for indie-rock kids to take in eclectic alternative DJ sets and energetic live performances (ska, punk, vallenato) by talented local musicians.

Gaira Café LIVE MUSIC

(Map p54; ☎1-746-2696; www.gairacafe.co; Carrera 13 No 96-11; cover COP$10,000-30,000; ⊙noon-2am Mon-Sat, to 5pm Sun;) Vallenato legend Carlos Vives' ultra-fun dancehall-restaurant hosts live vallenato, cumbia and porro – or modern takes on them. Locals pack in for food and rum drinks, and dance in the tight spaces around tables to an 11-piece band. Music begins nightly at 9pm.

Sports

Many outsiders equate Colombia's national sport – football (soccer) – with the shooting of Andrés Escobar after his own goal eliminated Colombia from the 1994 World Cup, but seeing games here is generally a calm affair (wearing neutral colors isn't a bad idea, though). The two big rivals are **Los Millonarios** (in blue and white; www.millonarios.com.co) and **Santa Fe** (in red and white; www.independientesantafe.co).

The principal venue is the 36,343-seat **Estadio El Campín** (Map p42; ☎1-315-8728; Carrera 30 No 57-60). Games are played on Wednesday night and Sunday afternoon. Reserve your seats online in advance for big matches (decent seats go for between COP$200,000 and COP$350,000); otherwise, turn up at the ticket window before match time. For international matches, check with the **Federación Colombiana de Fútbol** (www.fcf.com.co) for locations that sell tickets or head online to **StubHub** (www.stubhub.co).

Bullfighting was banned in Bogotá in 2012 by Mayor Gustavo Petro, making the city's 1931 red-brick ring, Plaza de Toros de Santamaría, little more than an impressive historical circle. The decision was overturned by a Colombian constitutional court in 2014, however, and the battle continued through 2017 until bullfights recommenced, amid widespread protests.

Club de Tejo La 76 TEJO

(Map p54; Carrera 24 No 76-56; per hr COP$70,000; ⊙10am-10:30pm) Drawing a healthy mix of locals and foreigners, this tejo club is friendly enough to welcome novices who aren't as skilled as *bogotanos* when it comes to being drunk in a room full of live explosives and throwing heavy metal objects around. You must drink to play – one *petaca* (a case of 30 350ml bottled beers) every hour.

Priorities for a lane are given to larger groups for obvious reasons.

Shopping

Locals love malls – **Centro Comercial El Retiro** (Map p54; www.elretirobogota.com; Calle 81 No 11-84; ⊙10am-8pm Mon-Thu, 10am-9pm Fri & Sat, noon-7pm Sun) and **Centro Comercial Andino** (Map p54; www.centroandino.com.co; Carrera 11 No 82-71; ⊙8am-10pm Mon-Thu, 7am-3am Fri-Sun) are the best – but Sunday flea markets are more inviting attractions. Also look along Carrera 9, south of Calle 60, for Chapinero's antique shops.

For cutting-edge Colombian fashion, there are boutiques in Chapinero on Carrera 7 between Calles 54 and 55.

Orientation

Sprawling Bogotá stretches mostly north–south (and west in recent years), with the towering peaks of Monserrate and Guadalupe providing an easterly wall.

Locating an address in the city is generally a breeze…after you get your head around the mathematical precision of it all. Calles run east-west, rising in number as you go north, while Carreras go north–south, increasing in number as they go west (away from the mountains). Handily, any street address (almost) always indicates the nearest cross streets; Calle 15 No 4-56, for example, is on 15th St, 56m from the corner of Carrera 4 towards Carrera 5.

Central Bogotá has four main parts: the partially preserved colonial sector La Candelaria (south of Av Jiménez and between Carreras 1 and 10), with lots of students, bars and hostels; aged business district the 'city center' (focused on Carrera 7 and Calle 19, between Av Jiménez and Calle 26); the high-rise Centro Internacional (between Carreras 7, 10 and 13 from Calles 26 to 30); and just east, toward the hills, the bohemian restaurant district of La Macarena.

Beginning 2km north of Centro Internacional, northern Bogotá is known as the wealthiest part of the city. With theaters, antique shops and many gay bars, the sprawling Chapinero (roughly between Carrera 7 and Av Caracas, from Calle 40 to Calle 67 or so) is scruffier than areas further north, which begin with Zona G, a pint-sized strip of high-end eateries (east of Carrera 7 and Calle 80). Chapinero Alto is an artsy mini-enclave in Chapinero between Carrera 7A and Av Circunvalar from Calles 53 to 65.

Ten blocks north, lively Zona Rosa (or 'Zona T'; the name stems from the T-shaped pedestrian mall between Carreras 12 and 13, at Calle 82A) is a zone of clubs, malls and hotels. A more sedate version – with many restaurants – rims the ritzier Parque 93 (Calle 93 between Carreras 11A and 13), part of the Chicó neighborhood, and the one-time pueblo plaza at Usaquén (corner Carrera 6 and Calle 119). The rather unappealing modern buildings of the so-called 'financial district' line Calle 100 between Av 7 and Carrera 11.

The most popular links between the center and the north are Carrera Séptima (Carrera 7; 'La Séptima') and Carrera Décima (Carrera 10), which are crowded with city buses. Av Caracas (which follows Carrera 14, then Av 13 north of Calle 63) is the major north–south route for the TransMilenio bus system. Calle 26 ('Av El Dorado') leads west to the airport and bus terminal.

ℹ Information

SAFE TRAVEL

Since the mid-'90s Bogotá has made many significant advances, among them reducing its homicide rate from 80 murders per 100,000 residents in 1993 to 15.8 in 2016 (mobile-phone theft fell by 20% from the previous year as well). These statistics mirror the downward trend of the overall Colombian murder rate for the same year (it was the lowest in four decades). Today Bogotá is one of the safest urban areas in Latin America – so safe, in fact, that Pope Francis visited in 2017.

In 2016 the Colombian government and the Fuerzas Armadas Revolucionarias de Colombia (FARC; Revolutionary Armed Forces of Colombia) signed a historic cease-fire deal, so Bogotá potentially sees fewer bombings than it did at the height of Colombia's armed conflict, but that doesn't mean the bombings have stopped entirely: an explosion at Centro Comerical Andino killed three people in 2017. (The bomb was attributed to members of a smaller urban guerrilla group known as the Movimiento Revolucionario del Pueblo, or MRP; this was its first attack to cause fatalities). Also in 2017, a bomb injured 29 (26 were police officers) in La Macarena. Though no arrests have been made, known members of the National Liberation Army (ELN) are wanted for the attack. While tourists are not specifically targeted, it's easy to be in areas where these things happen. Thankfully, the Colombian government announced a cease-fire with ELN in late 2017, and wavering peace talks in Havana, Cuba, continued through 2018; Bogotà – and Colombia – breathed a sigh of relief.

Hostel owners report a considerable drop in robberies in La Candelaria, which is generally safe during the day but can still be dicey at night. Always be aware of your surroundings. Be wary of handling your phone near the edge of streets, as thieves on motorcycles and bikes have been known to ride by and snatch them. If you opt to stay in La Candelaria, choose accommodations based not only on your general criteria but also on security. Avoid walking alone or with anything valuable after dark – these days the area has more of a police presence at night, though it's still a far cry from the show of force during the day.

Muggings are common around Calle 9 up the hill nearer the poorer neighborhood of Barrio Egipto, which remains a notable hot spot. Although tours of the barrio are now offered, under no circumstances should you wander there on your own. Do not stray beyond Carrera 1. At the Barrio Egipto's northern end there's private security in Parque de los Periodistas (you'll see personnel walking around with dogs) hired by the universities, so this once-sketchy area is now a lot safer. Solo travelers should always exercise caution on the road between the Universidad de Los Andes and Monserrate, though a police presence on the mountainside trails from 6am has curbed incidents here dramatically.

Police presence has been stepped up in La Macarena as well, though it's still a good idea to take a taxi and stick to the main restaurant streets – La Perseverancia barrio, just north of La Macarena, has a very dodgy reputation and it's not difficult to stray into it if you're unfamiliar with the area.

Generally speaking, Bogotá's south is a bit more dangerous, while the north is, on the whole, a different story. Many locals walk well after dark between, say, Zona Rosa and Parque 93's club and restaurant scene, whereas in La Candelaria you'd want to be way more cautious.

- Always be on guard – pickpocketing is rampant on buses and the TransMilenio.
- Avoid deserted streets and take taxis after hours – the extra security of a taxi app is always best.
- Police posts known as Comando de Acción Inmediata (CAI) are strategically placed around the city – use them in an emergency.

EMERGENCY

Ambulance	☎125
Police	☎112
Fire	☎119

INTERNET ACCESS

Wi-fi is ubiquitous among bars, restaurants and, of course, hotels and hostels. Bogotá also runs a hot-spot scheme with various access points around town; look for the network called *Wi-Fi Gratis para la Gente* or check the website for the zone nearest you (http://micrositios.mintic.gov.co/zonas-wifi).

MEDICAL SERVICES

It's preferable to use private clinics rather than government-owned institutions, which, though cheaper, may not be as well equipped.

Clinica Santa Fe (☎1-603-0303; www.fsfb.org.co; Calle 119 No 7-75) Highly recommended private hospital.

Clínica de Marly (☎1-343-6600; www.marly.com.co; Calle 50 No 9-67) A recommended clinic with doctors covering most specialties; sometimes handles vaccinations.

Aerosanidades (☎1-220-5674; www.aerosanidadsas.com; Aeropuerto Internacional El Dorado) Emergency health services at Bogotá's airport.

MONEY

There are two exchange houses in the Emerald Trade Center (p71), but it's best to use one of the plentiful ATMs.

Banco de Bogotá (Calle 11 No 5-60)

Bancolombia (Carrera 8 No 12B-17; ⏰9am-4pm Mon-Fri)

Western Union (www.westernunion.com; Calle 28 No 13-22, local 28; ⏰9am-5:30pm Mon-Fri, to 1pm Sat)

TOURIST INFORMATION

Colombia's energetic **Instituto Distrital de Turismo** (Map p42; ☎1-800-012-7400; www.bogotaturismo.gov.co; Carrera 24 No 40-66; ⏰7am-4:30pm Mon-Fri) is making visitors feel very welcome, with a series of Puntos de Información Turística (PIT) branches opening at key locations around Bogotá, operated by very friendly English-speaking staff. A couple of PIT locations offer free walking tours (scheduled separately in English or Spanish). There are PITs at each of the airport terminals as well as other locations around the city including:

Casa de Las Comuneros (PIT; Map p48; ☎1-555-7627; www.bogotaturismo.gov.co; Carrera 8 No 9-83, Casa de Las Comuneros; ⏰8am-6pm Mon-Sat, to 4pm Sun)

Centro Internacional (PIT; Map p48; ☎1-800-012-7400; www.bogotaturismo.gov.co; Carrera 7 No 26-07; ⏰9am-5pm Mon-Thu & Sat, 1-8pm Fri)

Terminal de Transportes (PIT; Map p42; ☎1-800-012-7400; www.bogotaturismo.gov.co; Diagonal 23 No 69-60, La Terminal, módulo 5; ⏰7am-7:30pm Mon-Sat, 8am-4pm Sun)

Getting There & Away

AIR

Bogotá's shiny airport, Aeropuerto Internacional El Dorado (p329), which handles nearly all domestic and international flights, is located 13km northwest of the city center. It received a massive US$900-million face-lift in 2014, and an expansion in 2017 to accommodate an additional 12 million passengers annually.

Terminal T1, which replaced the old El Dorado terminal, serves all international flights, Avianca's main domestic routes (Barranquilla, Cali, Cartagena, Medellín and Pereira) and domestic routes from other airlines.

Terminal T2 (commonly referred to as Puente Aéreo), 1km west of T1 and reached by airport shuttle, serves the remainder of Avianca's domestic routes (Armenia, Barrancabermeja, Bucaramanga, Cúcuta, Florencia, Ibagué, Leticia, Manizales, Montería, Neiva, Pasto, Popayán, Riohacha, San Andrés, Santa Marta, Valledupar, Villavicencio and Yopal).

BUS

Bogotá's main bus terminal, **La Terminal** (Map p42; ☎1-423-3630; www.terminaldetransporte.gov.co; Diagonal 23 No 69-11), about 5km west of the city center in the squeaky-clean planned neighborhood of Salitre, is one of South America's best and most efficient, and it's shockingly unsketchy. It's housed in a huge, arched red-brick building divided into five *módulos* (units). Southbound buses leave at the western end from *módulo* 1 (color-coded yellow); east and westbound buses from *módulo* 2 (blue); and northbound buses from *módulo* 3 (red). *Colectivo* vans leave for some nearby towns such as Villavicencio from *módulo* 4, while all arrivals come into *módulo* 5 (at the station's eastern end).

There are plenty of fast-food options, ATMs, left-luggage rooms, (clean) bathrooms and even showers (COP$7000), and a PIT information center in *módulo* 5, which will help you track down bus times or call for accommodations.

Each *módulo* has a number of side-by-side ticket vendors from various companies, and these folks sometimes try to hassle you for their buses. For some long-distance destinations – particularly to the Caribbean coast – you can sometimes haggle in low season. The usual type of bus is the *climatizado*, which is air-conditioned. Various companies are not the best at displaying destinations, fares and departure schedules – the best resource for that is La Terminal's official website.

Domestic Buses

For most domestic destinations there are frequent departures during the day by several companies; departures are usually half-hourly for destinations such as Medellín, Cali and Bucaramanga). Shop around for prices and departure times, as they will vary wildly depending on season, company and quality of service.

Expreso Bolivariano (☎1-424-9090; www.bolivariano.com.co; La Terminal, Diagonal 23 No 69-11) is Colombia's best national bus company, with comfortable buses. For online booking, **PinBus** (https://pinbus.com) sell

SAMPLE DOMESTIC BUS FARES & ROUTES

DESTINATION	PRICE (COP$)	DURATION	MÓDULO (NO)	COMPANIES
Armenia	43,000-68,000	7hr	yellow (1)	Bolivariano, Magdalena, Velotax
Barranquilla	80,000-100,000	17-20hr	red (3) & blue (2)	Brasilia, Continental Bus, Ochoa
Bucaramanga	60,000-70,000	8-9hr	red (3)	Autoboy, Berlinas, Copetran & others
Cali	60,000-70,000	8-10hr	yellow (1)	Bolivariano, Magdalena, Palmira, Velotax
Cartagena	100,000-110,000	12-24hr	red (3)	Autoboy, Berlinas, Brasilia, Copetran
Cúcuta	90,000-115,000	15-16hr	red (3) & blue (2)	Berlinas, Bolivariano, Copetran, Cotrans, Ormeño
Ipiales	148,000	22hr	yellow (1) & red (3)	Bolivariano, Brasilia, Continental Bus, Ormeño
Manizales	50,000-64,000	8-9hr	yellow (1), blue (2) & green (4)	Bolivariano, Palmira, Tax La Feria, Tolima
Medellín	60,000-80,000	9hr	blue (2)	Arauca, Bolivariano, Brasilia, Magdalena
Neiva	30,000-50,000	5-6hr	yellow (1)	Bolivariano, Coomotor, Cootranshuila, Magdalena, Taxis Verdes, Tolima
Pasto	120,000-140,000	18-20hr	yellow (1) & blue (2)	Continental Bus, Cruz del Sur
Pereira	50,000-75,000	7-9hr	yellow (1)	Bolivariano, Magdalena, Velotax
Popayán	95,000-110,000	12hr	yellow (1)	Continental Bus, Cruz del Sur, Velotax
Ráquira	22,000	3-4hr	red (3)	El Carmen, Coflonorte, La Verde
Riohacha	100,000-107,000	18-19hr	red (3)	Copetran
San Agustín	65,000	9-10hr	yellow (1)	Coomotor, Taxis Verdes
San Gil	50,000	6-7hr	red (3)	Omega
Santa Marta	80,000-90,000	16-17hr	red (3)	Berlinas, Brasilia, Copetran
Tunja	22,000	3hr	red (3) & green (4)	Autoboy, Los Muiscas, Nueva Flota Boyaca
Villa de Leyva	25,000	4hr	blue (2) & red (3)	Aguila, Alianza, El Carmen, Cundinamarca & others
Villavicencio	26,000	3hr	blue (2)	Arimena, Autollanos, Bolivariano, Macarena, Velotax

tickets for many of the country's most popular routes.

International Buses

Expreso Ormeño (☎1-410-7522; La Terminal, Diagonal 23 No 69-11) and **Cruz del Sur** (☎1-428-5781; www.cruzdelsur.com.pe; La Terminal, Diagonal 23 No 69-11) sell tickets for most destinations around South America.

ℹ Getting Around

Rush hour in the morning and afternoon can really clog roads – and space on the buses.

TO/FROM THE AIRPORT

The most economical and efficient route from the airport is the TransMilenio (p77). You'll need to buy a *tarjeta tullave* from the attendants in

SAMPLE INTERNATIONAL BUS FARES & ROUTES

DESTINATION	PRICE (COP$)	DURATION	DEPARTURE
Buenos Aires	1,120,000	6 days	11am Mon & Wed, 9am Fri
Guayaquil	335,000	36hr	11am Mon & Wed, 9am Fri
Lima	472,000	3 days	11am Mon & Wed, 9am Fri
Mendoza	1,030,000	5 days	11am Mon & Wed, 9am Fri
Quito	450,000	28hr	11am Mon & Wed, 9am Fri
Rio de Janeiro	1,275,000	8½ days	11am Mon & Wed, 9am Fri
Santiago	900,000	5½ days	11am Mon & Wed, 9am Fri
São Paulo	1,300,000	8 days	11am Mon & Wed, 9am Fri

blue-and-yellow jackets outside Puerta 8 of the arrivals area next to where the buses depart.

If you're staying in Chapinero or points to the north, bus M86/K86 departs from outside Puerta 8 in the arrivals hall every seven minutes between around 4:30am and 10:45pm Monday to Friday, 6am to 10:45pm Saturday and 6am to 9:45pm Sunday, and heads towards Centro Internacional before turning north and carrying on up Carrera 7 to Calle 116.

If you're staying in La Candelaria, you'll need to change buses. From the airport, catch bus K86 to Portal El Dorado, and switch to TransMilenio 1 to Universidades, which is attached to **Las Aguas Station** (Map p48; cnr Carrera 3 & Calle 18) via an underground tunnel. To the airport, catch 1 from Universidades to Plaza de la Democracia and switch to bus K86 to the airport.

Either way, plan on a solid hour's travel at the best of times, allowing longer during rush hour.

Taxi Imperial (☎ 317-300-3000; www.taxiimperial.com.co) manages a fleet of white airport taxis – look for the folks in orange jackets – which are pricier (more comfortable! working seat belts!), but regular yellow taxis are fine as well. Estimated fares from the airport are La Candelaria COP$30,000 to COP$32,000, Chapinero COP$35,000 to COP$37,000 and Zona Rosa COP$35,000 to COP$38,000. The (usually lengthy) taxi line is right outside the main terminal. You pay a *sobrecargo* (surcharge) of COP$4900 for taxi trips to or from the airport and there's also sometimes a nominal add-on fee for luggage. Uber is also an (often cheaper) option.

TO/FROM THE BUS TERMINAL

The fastest and most convenient option to La Terminal is a TransMilenio–short walk combo. El Tiempo station, on the TransMilenio M86/K86 line to the airport, is 950m from the terminal. To reach La Terminal, exit El Tiempo station on the footbridge to the right and then head right again down to the sidewalk. Walk straight along for 1½ blocks to Carrera 69 and turn left (between the Cámara de Comercio Bogotá and World Business Port buildings). Walk five blocks, passing Maloka on the left and traversing two pedestrian footbridges (over Calle 24A and Av La Esperanza, respectively), then continue on the sidewalk for 300m towards the 't' tower. Do not follow Google maps, which does not account for the footbridges and will take you the long way round. Follow the directions in reverse to leave La Terminal.

Módulo 5 of La Terminal has an organized taxi service; it has outrageous lines, but you pay by the meter. Rates are around COP$14,000 to COP$16,000 to La Candelaria or Chapinero Alto and COP$15,000 to COP$16,000 to Zona Rosa. Uber is usually cheaper. There's a COP$2000 surcharge between 8am and 5am.

BICYCLE

Bogotá has one of the world's most extensive bike-route networks, with more than 375km of separated, clearly marked bike paths called CicloRuta. Free Bogotá maps from PIT information centers show the CicloRuta paths.

In addition, about 121km of city roads are closed to traffic from 7am to 2pm on Sunday and holidays for the citywide Ciclovía (p50), a well-run event to get Bogotá out on two wheels. You can rent a bike at Bogotá Bike Tours (p52). Ciclovía runs along Carrera 7 all the way from La Candelaria to Usaquén – it's worth witnessing even on foot.

BUS

In addition to its TransMilenio (p77), Bogotá's public transportation is operated by **SiTP** (www.sitp.gov.co) and consists mainly of *servicio urbano* (blue buses, nicknamed *'azules,'* covering routes not served by TransMilenio), *servicio complementario* (orange buses; serving routes to and from nearby TransMilenio stations), *servicio alimentador* (green buses; serving routes to and from TransMilenio portals) and *servicio troncal* (red buses; basically extensions of TransMilenio lines).

Payment is by smart card, known as **tarjeta tullave** (www.tullaveplus.com); these can be purchased and recharged at stations and some markets/newsstands. Flat fares, regardless of distance traveled, are COP$2100 to COP$2300. Stops are marked.

There are also *servicio especial* buses (burgundy in color, or 'red wine' as SiTP refers to them), which serve outlying areas. Occasional older buses known as *colectivos* or *busetas*, which do not follow fixed schedules or stop at designated stops, are also seen along major thoroughfares like Carreras 7, 11 and 15 and in La Candelaria. Many of these have been granted *'provisional'* status and are being integrated into the SiTP network, while others are being phased out. Fares run between COP$1450 and COP$1600 and can be paid in cash on board.

To help make sense of it all, **TransmiSitp** (www.movilixa.com/english) is a popular app that coordinates routes between TransMilenio and SiTP. Buses run the length and breadth of the city, usually at full speed if traffic allows.

TAXI

Bogotá's impressive fleet of Korean-made yellow taxis are a safe, reliable and relatively inexpensive way of getting around. In 2018 the city changed from traditional taxi meters to a digital-pricing scheme similar to those implemented by taxi apps like Uber. Not 100% popular with Bogotá's large army of *taxistas*, the new GPS-based app calculates routing and fares. For those hailing taxis off the street (something you really shouldn't ever do), taxis are required to install tablets on the passenger-side back seat to display the route and fare in advance.

Traditionally, the minimum unit fare is '50,' which equates to COP$4450. Taxi trips on Sunday and holidays, or after dark, include a COP$2000 surcharge; trips to the airport have a COP$4900 surcharge. There is a COP$700 surcharge for booking taxis.

If you're going to make a couple of trips to distant places, it may be cheaper to hire a taxi for about COP$18,500 per hour.

Don't even think about waving down a taxi in the street unless you are with a local. When you do so, you're not registered and therefore forfeit all the security measures put in place to protect you, increasing your chances of robbery exponentially. You can call numerous companies that provide radio service, such as **Taxis Libres** (☎1-311-1111; www.taxislibres.com.co) or **Tax Express** (☎1-411-1111; www.taxexpress.com.co), but popular taxi apps **Uber** (www.uber.com), **Tappsi** (www.tappsi.co) and **Cabify** (www.cabify.com) are even better and eliminate the language barrier.

Some drivers, particularly in late hours, will round fares up a bit. Drivers don't often get tips.

TRANSMILENIO

The ambitiously named **TransMilenio** (www.transmilenio.gov.co), modeled after a similar groundbreaking system in Curitiba, Brazil, revolutionized Bogotá's public transportation when it opened in 2000. Numerous plans and studies were made to build a metro, but after 30 years the project was buried and a decision was taken to introduce a fast urban bus service instead. Today the TransMilenio is the world's largest BRT (Bus Rapid Transit) system.

The system is, in essence, a bus network masquerading as a subway. Covering 112km with a fleet of over 2000 buses, the TransMilenio has 12 lines and approximately 147 self-contained stations, which keeps things orderly and safe (and some stations have wi-fi). Buses use dedicated lanes, which keeps them free from car traffic. The service is frequent and cheap (fares run COP$2300). Generally speaking, lines run from 4:30am to midnight Monday to Saturday, 6am to 11pm Sunday, though some lines begin earlier and run later.

TransMilenio serves up to 2.2 million people daily – well over capacity – so buses get *very* crowded at rush hour (locals jokingly refer to it as the *TransmiLLENO*, which would translate to *TransFULL*); transfers at Av Jiménez resemble punk-rock mosh pits. TransMilenio's current plans project completion by 2031, with lines canvassing 388km. Meanwhile, Bogotá mayor Enrique Peñalosa is planning a raised railway to complement (and relieve) the system by 2022.

AROUND BOGOTÁ

Most *bogotanos* looking for a break from the city also look for warmth, fleeing for lower elevations further afield. Outside the capital district, there are also significant changes in landscape, where you can find lakes, waterfalls, cloud forests, mountains and a maze of small towns and villages, many of which hold on to their colonial fabric.

North of Bogotá

Many day-trippers out of the Bogotá head this way. It's possible to combine a trip to Zipaquirá and Guatavita in a day – agencies such as Impulse Travel (p53) offer combo day trips.

Suesca

One of Colombia's most popular rock-climbing destinations lies just south of Suesca, 65km north of Bogotá. Although the *pueblo* itself is unremarkable, the stunning 4km-long sandstone wall formation standing up to 120m high along the Río Bogotá is home to 300 (and counting) routes and worthy of a postcard home in its own right.

Many visitors come on day trips from Bogotá, particularly at weekends, when the half-a-dozen or so outfitters open their doors to greet a hundred climbers daily. There are also mountain-biking options.

Veteran climber and mountaineer Rodrigo Arias (p99), who lives in Suesca when he's not climbing in Parque Nacional Natural El Cocuy, is a great guide and can arrange multiday rock-climbing (from COP$170,000 per day), mountain-biking and hiking excursions.

Sleeping

Niddo CAMPGROUND **$$$**
(☎1-357-5943; www.niddo.co; tents Sat & Sun/Mon-Fri from COP$340,000/210,000;) This six-tent glamping option high above Suesca's massive rock wall is easily the area's most cinematic sleep. Luxurious teepee-like accommodations feature double beds, sofas and heaters, and there are more than 40 activities, including climbing, horseback riding, yoga and spelunking. Meals (plans run COP$90,000 extra) are in an atmospheric tent, and there's a small reception, a bar and firepits throughout.

Information

Tourist Information (☎350-653-6203; Carrera 4 No 2-20; ⌚9am-5pm) Small but helpful municipality tourist-information office. Some English spoken.

LAGUNA DE GUATAVITA: LAKE OF (FOOLS') GOLD

Traditionally, the Muisca believed that **Laguna de Guatavita** – once set in a perfectly round crater rimmed by green mountains – was created by a crashing meteor that transported a golden god who resided in the lake's floor. It's now believed volcanoes are more likely to be the lake's creator. Many hopes of finding El Dorado once converged on this small, circular lake about 50km northeast of Bogotá. Lovely Guatavita was the sacred lake and ritual center of the Muisca people. Here, half a millennium ago, the gold-dust-coated Zipa – the Muisca *cacique* (indigenous tribal head) – would throw precious offerings such as elaborate *tunjos* (ornate gold pendants and figurines) inscribed with wishes into the lake from his ceremonial raft. He'd then plunge into the waters to obtain godlike power. You can see many such *tunjos* at Bogotá's Museo del Oro.

This led to a gold frenzy for the Spaniards, and many other outsiders, who felt they'd reached a watery El Dorado. Over the years many painstaking, fruitless efforts were made to uncover the treasures lurking below. In the 1560s a wealthy merchant, Antonio de Sepúlveda, cut a gap on one side – still visible today – to drain the lake, yielding a mere 232 pesos of gold. Sepúlveda died bankrupt. By the late 19th century an English company managed to drain the lagoon, finding only 20-odd objects – not nearly enough to pay off the £40,000 and eight years invested in the project.

In the 1940s US divers with metal detectors searched out treasures, and the Colombian authorities – finally – banned such activities in 1965. Not to say that all treasure seekers obeyed. In the 1990s access to the lake required a permit in order to keep track of visitors (especially those illegally coming with scuba gear to search out fortunes).

Despite its fame, Guatavita never yielded much gold. Colombia's best-known piece – the Balsa Muisca (housed at the Museo del Oro) – was actually found in a cave near the village of Pasca.

Today you can't follow the Zipa's lead (no swimming allowed), but there are several lookouts on a trail above the water. The area is higher up than Bogotá – and you'll feel the difference in altitude on the mandatory 90-minute guided tours from the **site entrance** (www.colparques.net/lguatavita; Colombian/foreigner COP$12,000/17,000; ⌚8:30am-4pm Tue-Sun).

Getting There & Away

To get to Suesca from Bogotá, take the TransMilenio to its northern terminus at Portal del Norte, then catch one of the frequent buses (COP$7000, one hour), which depart inside the Portal's Buses Intermunicipales platform every 12 minutes from 5:25am to 11pm.

West of Bogotá

Those who go west from Bogotá are heading to the beach, Medellín or coffee country. Many don't stop, but there are a few places that qualify as destinations. If you're traveling by your own means, note that two highways head out of Bogotá – take the northerly route via La Vega (west on Calle 80), a nicer drive than the southern route via Facatativa, which hooks up with the La Vega route (after many suburbs and truck jams) at Villeta, about 65km west.

The best reason to come out this way is the gorgeous privately owned **Parque Natural Chicaque** (1-368-3114; www.chicaque.com; admission COP$15,000; 8am-3pm), where *bosque de niebla* (cloud forest) hikes await only 20km west of Bogotá.

The 3-sq-km area features half a dozen walks (about 20km altogether), which are among the nation's best marked. The park is home to one waterfall (best during rainy season, of course), over 300 species of birds, nocturnal monkeys and sloths, a 340m-long zipline, and several lodging **options** (1-368-3114; www.chicaque.com; Parque Nacional Chicaque; campsite COP$77,700, cabin s/d COP$283,000/360,000, tree house COP$202,000-515,000, all incl meals), including a mountain hostel, cabins and two fantastic treehouses (advance reservations require a bank deposit, which is a pain for foreigners). Meals are served at one of two restaurants, Arboloco (mains COP$19,500 to COP$38,000) and Refugio (daily special COP$13,000). You can also camp near the entrance at the Portería Camp Site for COP$31,700 (no meals).

On weekends (or by previous arrangement during the week) you can hire a horse to ride back up the steep hill paths.

The reserve is a few kilometers off the Soacha–La Mesa road. To get there from Bogotá's center, take the TransMilenio to Terreros, where weekend buses leave at 7am, 8am, 9am, 11am, 2:15pm, 3:15pm and 4:15pm, returning at 9am, 2pm, 3pm and 4pm (COP$6000, minimum six passengers). You can find the bus by heading to the Servientrega office across the pedestrian bridge and looking for a person wearing an orange vest with the Chicaque written in green. Outside of weekends, you can almost get there by a complicated combination of *colectivos*, but it's easier to simply hire Chicaque's shuttle privately for COP$25,000 for up to four people (COP$6000 each for more than four).

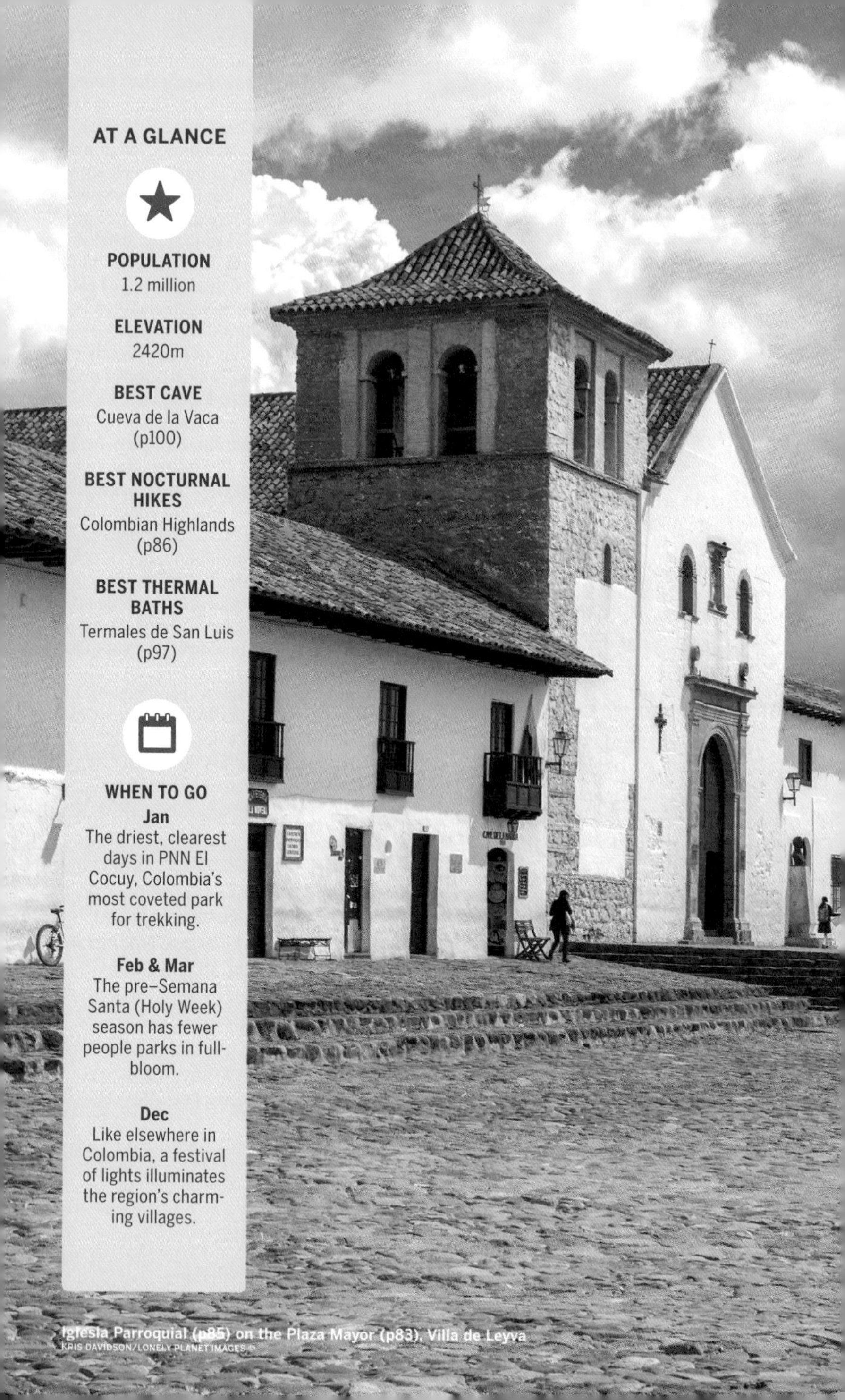

AT A GLANCE

POPULATION
1.2 million

ELEVATION
2420m

BEST CAVE
Cueva de la Vaca (p100)

BEST NOCTURNAL HIKES
Colombian Highlands (p86)

BEST THERMAL BATHS
Termales de San Luis (p97)

WHEN TO GO

Jan
The driest, clearest days in PNN El Cocuy, Colombia's most coveted park for trekking.

Feb & Mar
The pre–Semana Santa (Holy Week) season has fewer people parks in full-bloom.

Dec
Like elsewhere in Colombia, a festival of lights illuminates the region's charming villages.

Iglesia Parroquial (p85) on the Plaza Mayor (p83), Villa de Leyva
KRIS DAVIDSON/LONELY PLANET IMAGES ©

Boyacá, Santander & Norte de Santander

Boyacá, Santander and Norte de Santander together form one of the first areas settled by Spanish conquistadores and its calling as Colombia's heartland cannot be understated. It's here that the seeds of revolution were sowed, culminating in the victory at Puente de Boyacá that ultimately led to Colombia's independence.

Amid its deep gorges, fast-flowing rivers and soaring, snowcapped mountains, extreme is the game in Colombia's outdoor adventure capital, San Gil, and the glacial peaks of Parque Nacional Natural El Cocuy. But it's the region's bucolic colonial villages evoking life inside a living museum that forge the most lasting impressions – immensely beautiful Villa de Leyva; fiercely authentic Monguí; unadulterated Playa de Belén; and cinematic, perfectly preserved Barichara.

INCLUDES

Boyacá 83
Villa de Leyva 83
Santuario de Iguaque 91
Monguí 92
Sierra Nevada del Cocuy 94
Santander 100
San Gil 100
Barichara 104
Bucaramanga 108
Guadalupe.................. 112
Pamplona.................... 114
Playa de Belén 116

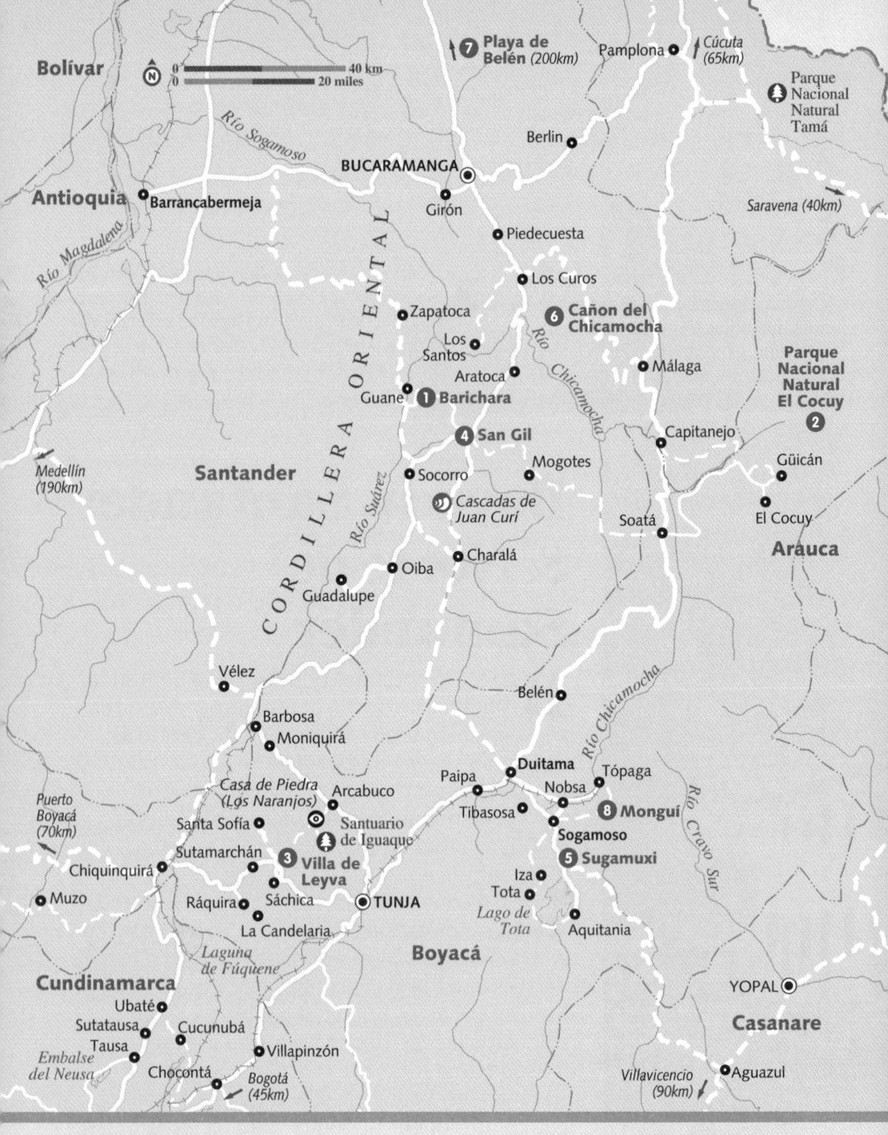

Boyacá, Santander & Norte de Santander Highlights

1. **Barichara** (p104) Wandering the cinematic streets lined with colonial splendor.
2. **Parque Nacional Natural El Cocuy** (p98) Hiking beneath glaciers in this rarely visited national park.
3. **Villa de Leyva** (p83) Exploring cobblestone streets, hidden waterfalls and prehistoric fossils.
4. **San Gil** (p100) Tackling the epic Cañón del Río Suárez via white-water rafting or extreme mountain biking.
5. **Sugamuxi** (p93) Trekking the extraordinary *páramo and* visiting sky-high Lago de Tota.
6. **Cañon del Chicamocha** (p108) Soaring on a paragliding flight over this spectacular dry canyon.
7. **Playa de Belén** (p116) Exploring funky rock formations around this postcard-perfect village.
8. **Monguí** (p92) Losing yourself in this color-coordinated village.

History

The Muiscas (Boyacá) and the Guane people (Santander) once occupied the regions north of what is now Bogotá. Highly developed in agriculture and mining, the Muisca traded with their neighbors and came into frequent contact with Spanish conquistadores. It was their stories of gold and emeralds that helped fuel the myth of El Dorado. The conquistadores' search for the famed city also sparked settlements and the Spanish founded several cities, including Tunja in 1539.

Several generations later, Colombian nationalists first stood up to Spanish rule in Socorro (Santander), stoking the flames of independence for other towns and regions. It was also here that Simón Bolívar and his upstart army took on Spanish infantry, winning decisive battles at Pantano de Vargas and Puente de Boyacá. Colombia's first constitution was drawn up soon after in Villa del Rosario, between the Venezuelan border and Cúcuta.

Getting There & Away

Boyacá is extremely well linked by frequent buses to Bogotá to the south and Santander to the north. The region's capital and transportation hub Tunja is just two hours from the northern edge of Bogotá. Frequent buses also run directly from Bogotá to Sogamoso for visiting in the Sugamuxi region.

While there are airports in Tunja and Paipa, they don't get much traffic. Aeroboyaca (www.aeroboyaca.com) offers service twice a week between Paipa and Bogotá. The closest place with regular flights to other destinations is El Dorado in Bogotá.

BOYACÁ

The department of Boyacá evokes a sense of patriotism among Colombians; it was here that Colombian troops won their independence from Spain at the Battle of Boyacá. The department is dotted with quaint colonial towns; you could easily spend a few days bouncing between them. Boyacá's crown jewel is the spectacular Parque Nacional Natural (PNN) El Cocuy, located 249km northeast of the department capital, Tunja, though access has been cut back by park officials.

Villa de Leyva

☎8 / POP 17,500 / ELEV 2140M

One of the most beautiful colonial villages in Colombia, Villa de Leyva is a city frozen in time. Declared a national monument in 1954, the photogenic village has been preserved in its entirety, with cobblestone roads and whitewashed buildings.

Villa's physical beauty and mild, dry climate have long attracted outsiders. The town was founded in 1572 by Hernán Suárez de Villalobos, and early on it was mainly a retreat for military officers, clergy and the nobility.

In recent years an influx of wealthy visitors and expats has slowly transformed this once-hidden gem. Boutique hotels, gourmet restaurants and tacky tourist shops are replacing many of the old family *hosterías* (inns) and cafes, and the authenticity. On weekends the narrow alleys can get downright crammed with day-trippers from Bogotá. But, thankfully, on weekdays it reverts to a peaceful, bucolic village.

Sights

Villa de Leyva is a leisurely place made for wandering – roam the charming cobblestone streets, listen to the church bells and enjoy the lazy rhythm of days gone by. It's also famous for its abundance of **fossils** from the Cretaceous and Mesozoic periods, when this area was underwater. Look closely and you'll notice that fossils have been used as construction materials in floors, walls and pavements.

As you stroll around, pop into the **Casa de Juan de Castellanos** (Carrera 9 No 13-15), Casona La Guaca (p85) and Casa Quintero (p88), three meticulously restored colonial mansions just off the plaza that now house quaint cafes, restaurants and shops.

★**Plaza Mayor** PLAZA

At 120m by 120m, Plaza Mayor is one of the largest town squares in the Americas. It's paved with massive cobblestones and surrounded by magnificent colonial structures and a charmingly simple parish church. Only a small, central Mudejar fountain, which provided water to the villagers for almost four centuries, interrupts the vast expanse. In most Colombian cities the main square is named after a historic hero, but this one is traditionally and firmly called Plaza Mayor.

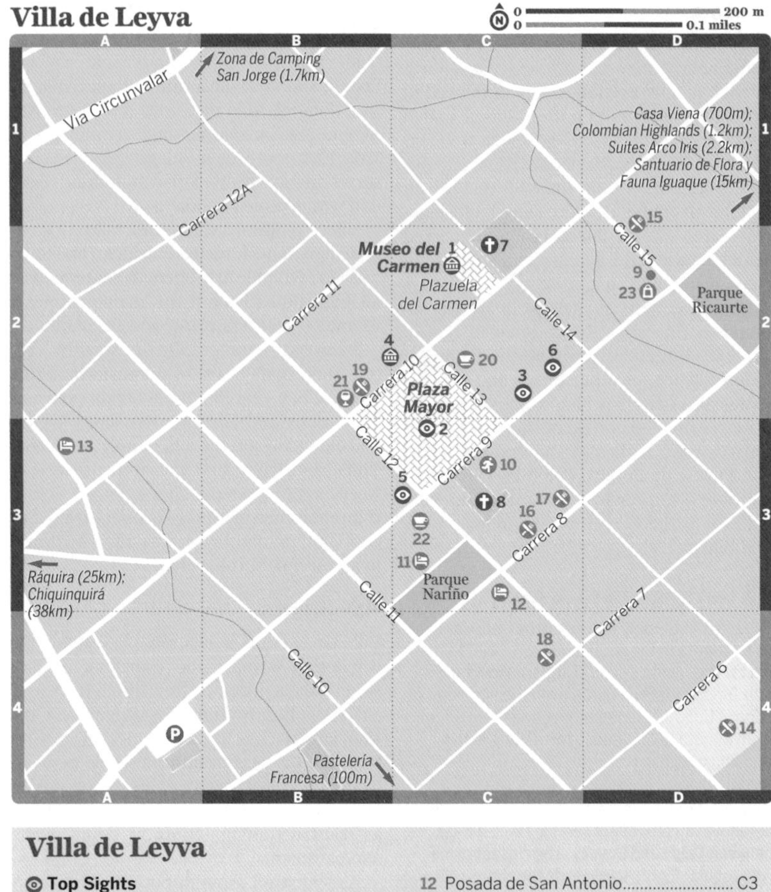

Villa de Leyva

Top Sights

1 Museo del Carmen....C2
2 Plaza Mayor....C3

Sights

3 Casa de Juan de Castellanos....C2
4 Casa Museo de Luis Alberto Acuña....B2
5 Casa Quintero....C3
6 Casona La Guaca....C2
7 Iglesia del Carmen....C2
8 Iglesia Parroquial....C3

Activities, Courses & Tours

9 Ciclotrip....D2
10 Colombia Natural Sport....C3

Sleeping

11 Alfondoque....C3
12 Posada de San Antonio....C3
13 Villa del Angel....A3

Eating

14 Don Salvador....D4
15 Entre Panes....D1
16 Mercado Municipal....C3
17 miCocina....C3
18 Restaurante Coreano....C4
19 Tartas y Tortas de la Villa....B2

Drinking & Nightlife

20 Cafe del Gato....C2
21 La Cava de Don Fernando....B2
22 Sybarrita Cafe....C3

Shopping

23 La Tienda Feroz....D2

Museo del Carmen MUSEUM
(☎8-732-0214; Plazuela del Carmen; COP$4000; ⏲10am-1pm & 2-5pm Wed-Mon) Apparently one of best museums of religious art in the country, the Museo del Carmen is housed in the **convent** (Calle 14 No 10-04; ⏲Mass 7am Mon-Fri, 6pm Tue, 7am, 11am & 6pm Sat, 6am, 7am, 11am & 6pm Sun) of the same name. The fairly average

collection of paintings, carvings, altarpieces and other religious objects dates from the 16th century onward. Some of the pieces are a little soiled and many of them are anonymous, but there are several notable works by colonial-era Colombian artists Gaspar Figueroa and Gregorio Vázquez.

Casona La Guaca NOTABLE BUILDING
(Carrera 9 No 13-57) This colonial mansion has an intimate courtyard with an abundance of plants and trees surrounding a fountain. The front section houses shops, and there's a large patio with restaurants out the back.

Casa Museo de Luis Alberto Acuña MUSEUM
(☎8-732-0422; Plaza Mayor; adult/child COP$6000/4000; ⏲9am-6pm) Villa de Leyva's best museum features works by one of Colombia's most influential painters, sculptors, writers and historians, Luis Alberto Acuña (1904–93), who was inspired by sources ranging from Muisca mythology to contemporary art. Set up in the mansion where Acuña lived for the last 15 years of his life, this museum is the most comprehensive collection of his work in Colombia.

There's a fine patio containing some of Acuña's indigenous-themed murals and a little shop out front. If the door's closed, ring the bell.

Iglesia Parroquial CHURCH
(Plaza Mayor; ⏲Mass 6pm Mon, Wed, Thu & Fri, noon & 7pm Sat, 7am, 10am, noon & 7pm Sun) This parish church facing the main square was built in 1608 and has hardly changed since that time. The interior is plain, except for the marvelous baroque main retable.

Activities

Activity options around Villa de Leyva include hiking, cycling, horseback riding and swimming, along with more extreme sports such as rappelling, canyoning and caving.

There are many hiking possibilities around Villa de Leyva, as well as some longer treks in the Santuario de Iguaque. A great hike begins directly behind the Renacer Guesthouse (p87), just outside town. It's open to nonguests – ask at reception for permission to cross the property and the staff will lend you a map and point you to the path. The trail passes two small waterfalls to reach a spectacular bird's-eye view of the village; the round-trip hike takes less than two hours.

Elsewhere, it's perfectly feasible to hike to many of the surrounding sights on quiet country lanes. A little Spanish will come in handy when asking for directions.

Swimming holes can be found beneath some of the nearby waterfalls or just outside town at Pozos Azules (p91). The most spectacular falls in the area are **El Hayal**, Guatoque (p91) and La Periquera, but the last of these was officially closed at research time after too many accidents and deaths over the years.

Cycling and horseback riding can be arranged at numerous outlets. Bikes cost about COP$90,000 per day for a decent setup. Horse riding is COP$25,000 to COP$30,000 per hour, plus you'll be expected to pay for a horse for the guide for each group. If you plan to see various nearby attractions, it's often cheaper (once you take waiting time into account) to book a horseback tour from an outfitter.

Cycling is a good way to access the town's surrounding sights, most of which are linked by relatively quiet country tracks and lanes.

Colombia Natural Sport ADVENTURE SPORTS
(☎311-850-8324; www.colombianaturalsport.com; Carrera 9 No 12-68; ⏲8:30am-noon & 2-6pm Wed-Mon) This high-adrenaline agency run by an enthusiastic Colombian named Oscar will get you rappelling down waterfalls and canyoning in the surrounding region. There's no English-speaking infrastructure in the office, but English and German guides are available.

Tours

Taxis at the bus terminal offer round trips to the surrounding sights – expect to pay around COP$25,000 to COP$30,000 per attraction including waiting time, although if you visit various sights you can negotiate a better deal. The price is per vehicle so it makes sense to get a small group together.

If you want to learn more about the attractions consider taking a tour. The standard routes offered by local operators include El Fósil (p90), **Estación Astronómica Muisca** (El Infiernito; adult/child COP$8000/6000; ⏲8am-5pm Tue-Sun) and Convento del Santo Ecce Homo (p90) (COP$142,000), and Ráquira and **Monasterio de La Candelaria** (☎1-223-7276; adult/child COP$6000/4000; ⏲9am-noon & 1-5pm) (COP$152,000). Prices, which include transportation, guide and insurance (but not entrance fees), are per person based on two people and drop with larger groups.

WORTH A TRIP

TUNJA

Often ballyhooed by Colombians and overlooked by travelers rushing on to Villa de Leyva, Tunja, the capital of Boyacá and a bustling student center, can't compete with Boyacá's big guns, but it does offer an imposing central square, Plaza de Bolívar, elegant mansions adorned with some of South America's most unique artwork and a plethora of standout colonial-era churches.

Tunja was founded by Gonzalo Suárez Rendón in 1539 on the site of Hunza, the pre-Hispanic Muisca settlement. Almost nothing is left of the indigenous legacy, but much colonial architecture remains.

Several colonial mansions in Tunja, including the **Casa del Fundador Suárez Rendón** (Carrera 9 No 19-68; 8am-noon & 2-5pm Tue-Sun) FREE and the **Casa de Don Juan de Vargas** (313-208-6176; Calle 20 No 8-52; COP$3000; 9-11:30am & 2-4:30pm Tue-Fri, 9am-3:30pm Sat & Sun), have ceilings adorned with paintings featuring a strange mish-mash of motifs taken from very different traditions. They include mythological scenes, human figures, animals and plants, coats of arms and architectural details. You can spot Zeus and Jesus amid tropical plants, and an elephant under a Renaissance arcade.

The source of these bizarre decorations seems to have been the scribe Juan de Vargas. He had a large library with books on European art and architecture, ancient Greece and Rome, religion and natural history, and it appears that the books' illustrations inspired the anonymous painters who worked on the ceilings. Since the original illustrations were in black and white, the ceilings' color schemes are entirely the design of these unknown artisans.

Tunja is also a trove of colonial-era churches, noted for their Mudejar art, an Islamic-influenced style, developed in Christian Spain between the 12th and 16th centuries. One stunning example is the richly decorated **Iglesia de Santo Domingo** (Carrera 11 No 19-55; 9am-noon & 2-7pm Mon-Fri, 7am-noon Sat & Sun). Most churches are open to visitors in the afternoon.

If you come through, dress for the weather: Tunja is the highest and coldest departmental capital in Colombia. Its mountain climate can be windy or wet any time of year.

The bus terminal is on Av Oriental, a short, hilly walk southeast of Plaza de Bolívar. Buses to Bogotá (COP$19,000, 2½ to three hours) depart every 10 to 15 minutes. Northbound buses to San Gil (COP$20,000, 4½ hours), Bucaramanga (COP$35,000, seven hours) and beyond run at least every hour.

Minibuses to Villa de Leyva (COP$7000, 45 minutes) depart regularly between 6am and 7pm, and to Sogamoso (COP$8000, 1½ hours) from 5am to 8pm.

Ciclotrip CYCLING

(320-899-4442; www.ciclotrip.com; Carrera 9 No 14-101; 9am-6pm Mon-Fri, 8am-8pm Sat & Sun) This highly recommended bike outfitter and tour agency gets you out on two wheels to all the popular attractions but also to more obscure waterfalls and mountain trails. Owner Francisco is trained in first aid and mountain rescue. Guided day trips run COP$120,000 to COP$300,000. The half-day trip to the Periquera waterfall (COP$130,000) is also popular.

If you want to go it alone, Ciclotrip also rents bikes (COP$90,000 per day) that are a step up from those found elsewhere around town. Staff will help you plan a route and give you a marked-up map to follow and even a cell phone so you can call for mechanical support if you run into difficulties.

Colombian Highlands ECOTOUR

(310-552-9079, 8-732-1201; www.colombianhighlands.com; Av Carrera 10 No 21-Finca Renacer) Run by biologist and Renacer Guesthouse (p87) owner Oscar Gilède, this agency runs a variety of offbeat tours, including ecotours, mountain trips, nocturnal hikes, birdwatching, rappelling/abseiling, canyoning, caving and hiking. It also rents bikes and horses. English spoken.

Festivals & Events

Festival de las Cometas CULTURAL

(Aug) Locals and foreign kite fans compete in this colorful kite festival.

Festival de Luces FIREWORKS
(⏲Dec) This fireworks festival is usually held on the first or second weekend of December.

Sleeping

Villa de Leyva has a large selection of hotels in all price ranges. Note that prices increase on weekends, when it may be hard to find a room. During the high seasons, including Semana Santa and December 20 to January 15, prices can more than double. Plan ahead. Camping around the area runs about COP$20,000 per person.

★**Renacer Guesthouse** HOSTEL $
(☎8-732-1201, 311-308-3739; www.renacerhostel.com; Av Carrera 10 No 21-Finca Renacer; campsites per person from COP$18,000, dm from COP$32,000, s/d from COP$70,000/90,000; @🛜🏊) Located 1.2km northeast of Plaza Mayor, this delightful 'boutique hostel' is the creation of biologist and tour guide extraordinaire Oscar Gilède of Colombian Highlands (p86). Everything about this place feels like home – hammocks surrounding an immaculate garden, a communal, open-air kitchen with brick pizza oven, and spotless dorms and rooms. Staff will even donate herbs from the garden toward your cooking needs.

There's a natural swimming pool in the back, and a little cafe if you don't fancy going into town to eat.

Casa Viena HOSTEL $
(☎8-732-0711, 314-370-4776; www.hostel-villadeleyva.com; Carrera 10 No 19-114; s/d without bathroom COP$30,000/45,000; @🛜) This little guesthouse a 10-minute walk from the main village has just two simple private rooms with a shared bathroom and rustic views. It's quiet and cheap, if not as plush as some of the town's other hostels, although the management is helpful in imparting local info. There are a good guest kitchen and a lounge-like social area downstairs.

Zona de Camping San Jorge CAMPGROUND $
(☎8-732-0328; campingsanjorge@gmail.com; Vereda Roble; campsites per person high/low season COP$22,000/20,000; 🛜) Located approximately 2km northeast of town, this huge grassy field has lovely views of the surrounding mountains and space for 120 tents. Amenities include a small restaurant (meals COP$14,000 to COP$18,000) and shop, and spotless bathrooms with hot water.

It's a 25-minute walk from Plaza Mayor: walk north on Carrera 9, passing the Museo Paleontológico. At the T-intersection, turn right, then make an immediate left down the well-signed gravel road to the campground.

Villa del Angel HOTEL $$
(☎8-732-1506; www.hotelvilladelangel.co; Calle 9 No 11-52; s/d COP$110,000/127,000) Convenient to both the center of town and the bus station, this cozy little 2nd-floor hotel offers a fine base from which to explore Villa. The five spotless, well-appointed, modern rooms are full of natural light and are big on comfort. The included breakfast is served in a dining area with mountain views.

★**Suites Arco Iris** BOUTIQUE HOTEL $$$
(☎311-254-7919; www.suitesarcoiris.com; Km2 Vila la Colorada; r mountain/village view incl breakfast from COP$260,000/280,000; 🛜) Perched on a hilltop above town and surrounded by a fine garden, this romantic 26-room hotel tops the charts in Villa de Leyva for personality. The massive rooms, each unique but all equally drenched in color, art and character, are snazzy affairs, with Jacuzzis, terraces,

BOLÍVAR'S BRIDGE

The **Puente de Boyacá** is one of the most important battlefields of Colombia's modern history. On August 7, 1819, and against all odds, the armies of Simón Bolívar defeated Spanish troops led by General José María Barreiro, sealing Colombia's independence.

Several monuments have been erected on the battlefield. The centerpiece is the **Monumento a Bolívar**, an 18m-high sculpture topped by the statue of Colombia's hero and accompanied by five angels symbolizing the *países bolivarianos* (countries liberated by Bolívar): Venezuela, Colombia, Ecuador, Peru and Bolivia. An eternal flame for Bolívar burns nearby.

The Puente de Boyacá, the bridge that gives its name to the battlefield and over which Bolívar's troops crossed to fight the Spaniards, is just a small, simple span reconstructed in 1939.

The battlefield is on the main Tunja–Bogotá road, 15km south of Tunja. To get here, take a local bus from Tunja headed to Tierra Negra; most intercity express buses won't stop here.

fireplaces and kaleidoscopically tiled bathrooms. Views, be they mountain or town, are stupendous.

The bummer here is that if you don't have your own wheels, you'll spend an additional COP$24,000 to COP$30,000 round trip going to and from town. Thankfully, the hotel is relatively self-contained, with its own restaurant and spa. Rates drop on weekdays.

Posada de San Antonio BOUTIQUE HOTEL **$$$**
(☎8-732-0538; www.hotellaposadadesanantonio.com; Carrera 8 11-80; s/d incl breakfast from COP$301,000/342,000; @) Natural light permeates all the nooks and crannies of this antique-packed, charismatic 1860 colonial home, one of Villa's most discerning choices. Rooms feature exposed glimpses of original brick and there's a lovely open kitchen, a character-filled restaurant/living room, a small portable altar and, of course, a lovely courtyard.

Eating

Villa is the most sophisticated foodie destination in Boyacá. There are a few gourmet food courts in the village, with **Casa Quintero** (cnr Carrera 9 & Calle 12) and Casona La Guaca (p85) offering the best and most diverse options.

During low season a lot of higher-end restaurants offer discount lunch menus, but these all but disappear once the crowds arrive.

Pastelería Francesa BAKERY, FRENCH **$**
(Calle 10 No 6-05; items COP$1500-3600; 8am-7pm Thu-Sun, closed Feb & Sep) You can smell the sweet scent of baked goodness a block away from this authentic French bakery with croissants (oh, those almond ones!), baguettes, tarts, quiches, mini-pizzas, coffees and hot chocolate. It's great if you can catch it open – the owner likes his vacation time – and a classy redo of the place approaches legitimately chic.

Don Salvador COLOMBIAN **$**
(meals COP$5000-10,000; 6am-3pm Sat) Don Salvador does the best *mute* (puffed-corn soup, served with a side of cow foot or chicken thigh) and *carne asada* (grilled steak) at Villa's bustling Saturday market (p89).

Entre Panes SANDWICHES **$$**
(entrepanesbistro@gmail.com; Calle 15 No 9-58; sandwiches COP$19,000-26,000; 1-9pm Mon & Tue, 1-10pm Fri, 10am-10pm Sat, 10am-5pm Sun) A couple of blocks from the plaza you'll find this appealing outdoor cafe serving up some of the best sandwiches in Colombia. Take your pick from French classics or more gourmet options all served on homemade bread with the outrageously good house mayo. Try the lamb and tzatziki version.

Restaurante Savia VEGETARIAN **$$**
(☎322-474-9859; www.restaurantesavia.com; Calle 10 No 6-67; mains COP$14,000-34,000; noon-9pm Sun-Thu, to 11pm Fri & Sat;) The delightful Savia specializes in inventive vegetarian, vegan and organic fare and local eco-artisanal products of the same ilk. Carnivores aren't left behind, though – there's fresh seafood and poultry dishes (but no red meat). It's located in a gorgeous old colonial house with a large courtyard and massive back garden.

There's also a small grocer on site selling organic foodstuffs and some handicrafts.

Restaurante Coreano KOREAN **$$**
(☎320-285-5755; Carrera 7 No 11-83; mains COP$19,000-20,000; noon-9pm Thu-Mon;) It's not the most imaginatively named place in town, but this Korean-run restaurant is worth a visit for authentic Asian cuisine. There are only eight dishes on the menu but they're all good, especially the homemade spicy tofu. Vegetarians are well catered for.

★**Mercado Municipal** COLOMBIAN **$$$**
(☎318-363-7049; Carrera 8 No 12-25; mains COP$24,000-65,000; 1-10pm Mon-Sat, to 9pm Sun) On its way to becoming Boyacá's most interesting dining experience, this chef-driven restaurant in the gardens of a colonial house (1740) has resurrected ancient techniques of cooking meat in a 1m-deep underground wood-burning *barbacoa* (barbecue). Among the specialties are rich pork ribs in apricot barbecue sauce – the tender meat slides effortlessly off the bone.

miCocina COLOMBIAN **$$$**
(www.academiaverdeoliva.com; Calle 13 No 8-45; mains COP$22,000-73,000; 11am-4pm Sun-Thu, to 9pm Fri & Sat;) This colorful restaurant/culinary school prides itself on being 100% Colombian and is indeed the best place to sample Colombian gastronomy at levels beyond *sancocho* (soup) and *patacones* (fried plantains). Being dedicated to local cuisine, there's little joy on the menu for vegetarians, but carnivores have a wide selection to choose from. Its salad dressing is easily the best in town.

Drinking & Nightlife

The drinking scene in Villa centers on the charming plaza – locals and visitors alike plop down on the steps along Carrera 9, an area that turns into a full-on street party in the early evening.

Sybarrita Cafe CAFE

(Carrera 9 No 11-88; coffee COP$1600-5000; 8:30am-9pm) Villa de Leyva's most popular java joint, serving daily changing single-origin coffees from around Colombia's best regions in an old-school environment that feels a lot more classic than this upstart cafe's age. The few tables are usually crammed with village old-timers mingling with nomadic caffeine connoisseurs.

La Cava de Don Fernando BAR

(Carrera 10 No 12-03; 4pm-1am Sun-Thu, to 2am Fri & Sat;) On the corner of Plaza Mayor, this cozy bar has excellent tunes, atmospheric candles and one of the better beer selections in town.

Shopping

A market is held every Saturday on the square three blocks southeast of Plaza Mayor (p83). It's best and busiest early in the morning. There's also an organic market in that location on Thursday.

Villa de Leyva has quite a number of handicraft shops noted for fine basketry and good-quality woven items. Many craft shops open only on weekends.

La Tienda Feroz ARTS & CRAFTS

(www.latiendaferoz.com; Carrera 9 No 14-101; 9am-6pm Mon-Fri, 8am-8pm Sat & Sun) This great little shop features the unique art of 27 Colombian artists and is the spot to pick up items that aren't typical tourist wares. The owners have backgrounds in illustration, animation and industrial design, so they know their creativity.

Getting There & Away

You can walk from Villa de Leyva to some of the nearest sights, or go by bicycle (highly recommended) or on horseback. You can also go by taxi or arrange a tour with Villa de Leyva's tour operators. If you choose to go by taxi, make sure you confirm with the driver all the sights you want to see and agree on a price before setting off. A round-trip taxi (for up to four people) from Villa de Leyva to El Fósil (p90), Estación Astronómica Muisca (p85) and Ecce Homo (p90) should cost about COP$75,000, including waiting time.

DON'T MISS

SUTAMARCHÁN

While traveling about around Villa de Leyva, it's worth stopping in Sutamarchán, the longaniza capital of Colombia, 14km west of Villa on the road to Ráquira. Longaniza is a regional sausage similar to Portuguese *linguiça*. In town, it's grilled up everywhere – follow your nose.

The best spots to try longaniza are **Fabrica de Longaniza & Piqueteadero Robertico** (Carrera 2 No 5-135; longaniza portion from COP$7000; 8am-8pm) – for the more rustic, spicier version – and **La Fogata** (312-355-8677; www.lafogatasutamarchan.com; Av Principal, salida a Tunja; longaniza portion COP$6000; 9am-7:30pm), a more clean-cut operation.

Local buses pass close to some of the attractions but are not particularly regular, so it's important to check timetables before heading out.

Around Villa de Leyva

Archaeological relics, colonial monuments, petroglyphs, caves, lakes and waterfalls are among the attractions surrounding the picturesque colonial village of Villa de Leyva. Endowed with gentle pastoral fields and crisscrossed by quiet country lanes, the area is ideal for walking and cycling.

Sights & Activities

Centro de Investigaciones Paleontológicas MUSEUM

(CIP; 321-978-9546, 314-219-2904; info@centropaleo.com; adult/child COP$9000/5000; 8am-noon & 2-5pm Tue-Thu, 8am-5pm Fri-Sun) Just across the main road from the famed El Fósil (p90) site, this sleek center combines an open-window research facility with a collection of impressive fossils, including an amazing full-body plesiosaurus (a Jurassic sea dragon), the oldest known turtle fossil and the only tooth of a saber-tooth tiger ever discovered in Colombia. Everything is signed in English.

It's gloriously geeky fun and there are a number of awesome hands-on activities for young travelers, including excavation classes where kids can unearth fossil replicas and workshops creating imitation fossils from molds, which the budding paleontologists can then take home.

★**Paso de Angel** MOUNTAIN

(COP$3000) This vertigo-inducing mountain path running along a ridge on the way to the Guatoque (p91) waterfall is a popular attraction in its own right. At its narrowest point, the **Angel's Step**, it's only around 33cm wide for about a meter and a half, with vertical drops of over 100m on one side and 30m on the other. Views on both sides are amazing.

Visitors with a fear of heights will do best to admire it from a distance – there have been many cases of panic-stricken travelers getting stuck on the other side after having plucked up the courage to make the initial crossing. At the entrance you'll usually find the elderly landowner collecting an admission fee; it's not unheard of for his wife to collect another fee further down the path. (Bear in mind that it's a small amount and their main source of income.)

The path is accessible from the small village of Santa Sofía. From where the bus arrives, cross the plaza and take the road past the cemetery for 1.5km until you reach a signed turnoff by an orange house. Continue 3.5km past the sugar mill and school to the trailhead.

The Paso de Angel hike is offered as a one-day guided hike by Colombian Highlands (p86) in Villa de Leyva.

Convento del Santo Ecce Homo CHURCH

(COP$5000; ⊙8am-5pm Tue-Sun) Founded by the Dominican fathers in 1620, this convent is a large stone-and-adobe construction with a huge, faintly regal courtyard. The floors are paved with stones quarried in the region, so they contain ammonites and fossils, including petrified corn and flowers. There are also fossils in the base of a statue in the chapel.

The chapel is endowed with a magnificent gilded main retable with a small image of Ecce Homo. The original wooden ceiling is full of fascinating details: note the images of pineapples, eagles, suns and moons (used to help convert indigenous peoples); the skull and crossbones with a Bolivian-style winter cap in the sacristy; and the crucifix in the **Capitulary Hall** showing Christ alive (his eyes are open), a rarity in South America. Look out for the drawing of Christ in the west cloister – from different angles it appears that the eyes open and close.

The convent is 13km from Villa de Leyva. Any bus to Santa Sofía will drop you off at the access road, from where it's a 15-minute walk to the convent. Alternatively, it makes for a beautiful bike ride along quiet country lanes.

The convent has a small cafe and shop.

El Fósil ARCHAEOLOGICAL SITE

(☎310-629-1845; adult/child COP$8000/5000; ⊙8am-6pm) This impressive 120-million-year-old baby-kronosaurus fossil is the world's most complete specimen of this prehistoric marine reptile. The fossil is 7m long – the creature was about 12m in size, but the tail did not survive – and it remains in place exactly where it was found in 1977. Museum staff can explain how the fossil was found and direct you around several other paleontological specimens in the same museum.

JUST ANOTHER CERAMIC SUNDAY...

Twenty-five kilometers southwest of Villa de Leyva, Ráquira is the pottery capital of Colombia, where you'll find everything from ceramic bowls, jars and plates to toys and Christmas decorations. Brightly painted facades, a jumble of craft shops and stacks of freshly fired mud and clay pots make a welcoming sight along the main street of this one-horse town. There are many workshops in and around the village where you can watch pottery being made. The best time to visit is Sunday, when the local produce market is in full swing, but the souvenir shops are open every day.

Ráquira is 5km off the Tunja–Chiquinquirá road, down a side road branching off at Tres Esquinas. Four minibuses run Monday to Friday between Villa de Leyva and Ráquira (COP$6000, 45 minutes, 7:30am, 12:45pm, 3pm and 4:50pm), with a fifth added on weekends.

Returning from Ráquira to Villa de Leyva, the majority of buses do not enter the town – you'll need to jump off at the Muisca Sol monument at the Sáchica intersection and grab a passing bus on the Tunja-Villa run.

A handful of buses from Bogotá also call here daily.

A round-trip taxi from Villa de Leyva with an hour or so to explore will set you back about COP$80,000, or COP$100,000 if you want to also swing by La Candelaria (p85).

WORTH A TRIP

IT'S A MIRACLE!

Chiquinquirá is the religious capital of Colombia, attracting flocks of devoted Catholic pilgrims due to a 16th-century miracle involving a painting of the Virgin Mary. It is the oldest documented Colombian painting.

The Virgin of the Rosary was painted around 1555 by Spanish artist Alonso de Narváez in Tunja. It depicts Mary cradling baby Jesus and flanked by St Anthony of Padua and St Andrew the Apostle. Soon after it was completed, the image began to fade, the result of shoddy materials and a leaky chapel roof. In 1577 the painting was moved to Chiquinquirá, put into storage and forgotten. A few years later, Maria Ramos, a pious woman from Seville, rediscovered the painting. Though it was in terrible shape, Ramos loved to sit and pray to the image. On December 26, 1586, before her eyes and prayers, the once faded and torn painting was miraculously restored to its original splendor. From then on its fame swiftly grew and the miracles attributed to the Virgin multiplied.

Dominating the Plaza de Bolívar, the **Basílica de la Virgen de Chiquinquirá** houses the sacred image. Construction of the huge neoclassical church began in 1796 and was completed in 1812. The spacious three-naved interior boasts 17 chapels and an elaborate high altar where the painting – measuring 113cm by 126cm – is displayed.

There are eight buses a day between 7am and 4pm from Villa de Leyva to Chiquinquirá (COP$8000, one hour). Buses to Bogotá depart every 15 minutes (COP$18,000, three hours).

The fossil is off the road to Santa Sofía, 6km west of Villa de Leyva. You can walk here in a bit more than an hour, or take the Santa Sofía bus, which will drop you off 80m from the fossil.

Cascada Guatoque WATERFALL

Accessible by the nerve-racking Paso de Angel (p90) path outside the small town of Santa Sofía, this pretty 80m waterfall empties into a fine pool. The final parts of the trail are very steep and are bordered by sheer drops. Go with a guide from Villa de Leyva. The path finishes at the top of the waterfall; under no circumstances should visitors attempt to make their way down to the base of the falls without a professional guide – the descent is highly dangerous.

The only safe path to get down to the pool winds through the mountains a fair distance from the top of the falls. It's a tricky two-hour hike, but the reward is a refreshing dip in a wonderfully isolated swimming hole.

Pozos Azules SWIMMING

(Via Santa Sofía; with/without swimming COP$10,000/5000; ⌚8am-6pm) Not to be confused with the other collection of blue ponds of the same name nearby, this site has a number of brightly colored pools, including a large one that visitors are able to swim in. It gets quite deep in the middle. Note: these are not thermal springs.

ℹ Getting There & Away

You can walk from Villa de Leyva to some of the nearest sights, or go by bicycle (highly recommended) or on horseback. You can also go by taxi or arrange a tour with Villa de Leyva's tour operators. If you choose to go by taxi, make sure you confirm with the driver all the sights you want to see and agree on a price before setting off. A round-trip taxi (for up to four people) from Villa de Leyva to El Fósil (p90), Estación Astronómica Muisca (p85) and Ecce Homo (p90) should cost about COP$75,000, including waiting time.

Local buses pass close to some of the attractions but are not particularly regular, so it's important to check timetables before heading out.

Santuario de Iguaque

High above the surrounding valley and shrouded in mist is a pristine wilderness that Muiscas consider to be the birthplace of humankind. According to Muisca legend, the beautiful goddess Bachué emerged from Laguna de Iguaque with a baby boy in her arms. When the boy became an adult they married, bore children and populated the earth. In old age, the pair transformed into serpents and dove back into the sacred lake.

Today this Muisca Garden of Eden is a 67.5-sq-km national park called **Santuario de Flora y Fauna de Iguaque** (foreigners/Colombians COP$46,500/17,500; ⌚8am-5pm).

There are eight small mountain lakes in the reserve sitting at an altitude of between 3550m and 3700m, although the only one accessible to visitors is **Laguna de Iguaque**. This unique *páramo* (high-mountain plains) neotropical ecosystem contains hundreds of species of flora and fauna but is most noted for the frailejón, a shrub typical of the highlands.

It can get pretty cold here, with temperatures ranging between 4°C and 13°C. It's also very wet, receiving an average of 1648mm of rain per year. The best months to visit are January, February, July and August. Come prepared.

The only place to sleep in the reserve is at the **visitors center** (dm COP$50,000, campsites per person COP$10,000; 8am-5pm). Lodging reservations via **Naturar** (318-493-5704, 312-585-9892; naturariguaque@yahoo.es) are required in December, January, June and the second week of October, and during any holidays; otherwise, you can just stroll up. It's a supreme place to chill out in the mountains, with nightly visits from wild turkeys.

To get to the park from Villa de Leyva, take the Arcabuco-bound bus (departs 6am, 7am and 8am) and tell the driver to drop you at Casa de Piedra (also known as Los Naranjos; COP$4000) at Km12, from where it's a 3km hike up the rough road to the visitors center (p92). The 6am service is the best choice, as it passes closer to the access road.

Returning to Villa, make sure you're at Casa de Piedra no later than 4pm in order to catch the last bus. Colombian Highlands (p86) runs full-day tours from Villa de Leyva for COP$170,000 per person for two people (less for larger groups). Alternatively, you can negotiate a rate with a taxi driver in Villa de Leyva.

Sogamoso

8 / POP 112,287 / ELEV 2569M

Sogamoso was a religious center of the Muiscas and is the jumping-off point for explorations further afield around Lago de Tota. The city also boasts the only archaeological museum (p92) of the Muisca people in Colombia. Despite its past importance, Sogamoso is now a distinctly uninspiring working-class Colombian city.

Sights & Activities

Museo Arqueológico Eliécer Silva Célis MUSEUM

(1-770-3122; Calle 9A No 6-45; adult/child COP$8000/6000; 9am-noon & 2-5pm Mon-Sat, 9am-3pm Sun) This very well-done archaeological museum was built on the remains of Sogamoso's Muisca cemetery and highlights this very important Chibcha-speaking culture – among others – through art, ceramics, sculpture, music and paleontology. The most interesting exhibits include the mummified remains of a *cacique* (tribal leader) and the spine-shivering shrunken-head techniques of the Jivaros and Shiworas peoples.

Sleeping

La Cazihita HOSTEL $

(314-411-6104; Carrera 8 No 9-66, Barrio Santa Ana; dm COP$35,000, s/d COP$50,000/100,000, without bathroom COP$35,000/68,000;) In one of the few old streets left in Sogamoso is this welcoming, homey hostel run by a local couple. Rooms tend to be on the small side, but the place is neat and tidy and has a pleasant, fire-warmed social area to hang out in. The owners are a good source of regional information.

Make contact ahead, as there's no 24-hour reception.

Getting There & Away

Regular buses serve Sogamoso from Bogotá (COP$27,000, three to four hours, hourly) and Tunja (COP$8000, one hour, every 15 minutes). From Sogamoso, **Cootracero** (8-770-3255) serves Iza (COP$2800, 40 minutes) and Monguí (COP$4000, one hour) every 20 minutes, and Lago de Tota (COP$9000, 1½ hours) hourly. There are six buses a day to San Gil (COP$50,000, six hours).

Monguí

8 / POP 4984 / ELEV 2900M

Once voted the most beautiful village in Boyacá, Monguí is just 14km east of Sogamoso but feels far removed from the latter's industrial landscapes. The first missionaries appeared in the region around 1555, but the town wasn't founded until 1601. It later became a catechetic center of the Franciscan monks – as evidenced by one of Monguí's most striking buildings, the Convento de los Franciscanos (p93), which dominates the gorgeous plaza.

WORTH A TRIP

THE VALLEY OF THE SUN

Some 130km east of Villa de Leyva is the largely unexplored region known in the indigenous Muisca language of Chibcha as 'Sugamuxi' – the Valley of the Sun. Ecotourism is blossoming in this area, which remains locked in traditions and offers a side of Colombia relatively unaffected by mass tourism.

There are several wonderfully preserved colonial villages here. While Monguí is the belle of the ball, **Iza** is her worthy deputy. This tiny village 15km southwest of Sogamoso is particularly notable for its desserts. It all started when *merengón* (meringue with local fruits) began to be sold from the back of cars and grew into a tradition, especially on weekends, when it's a sweet-tooth free-for-all in the plaza. The rest of the week, Iza is supremely tranquil, and is worth bedding down in for a night if you're looking to bliss out in a colonial hamlet untouched by big tourism.

Set in a scenic valley 3km from town, the professionally run **El Batan** (☎312-592-3325, 321-242-7511; www.elbatan.travel; Vereda La Vega, Cuítiva; d/q incl breakfast COP$190,000/330,000; P 📶 ≋) spa complex has the best rooms in the area. Accommodations are housed in colonial-style buildings and feature king beds, flat-screen TVs and elegant wooden furniture. Guests have access to an exclusive set of thermal pools – the water here is dark green and scent-free.

There are also a number of other settlements in the area worth a visit: **Tópaga**, famous for its devil sculpture inside the local church and handicrafts made from coal; **Nobsa**, well known for Boyacá handicrafts; and **Tibasosa**, the feijoa – pineapple guava – capital of Colombia.

Nature is another major drawcard in Sugamuxi, with great sightseeing around **Lago de Tota**, Colombia's largest lake, and an out-of-the-blue white-sand Andean beach, the 3015m-high **Playa Blanca** (admission free, parking COP$4000), sweetening the deal.

Regular buses run between Iza and Sogamoso (COP$3000, 35 minutes) from 6:30am to 7pm. Buses to Playa Blanca (p93) (COP$6500, one hour) pass along the main road one block from the park.

Today this idyllic Christmas-colored village boasts uniform green-and-white colonial architecture only interrupted by the occasional newer brick construction that evokes the English countryside. Either way, the beautiful facades drip with colorful red-rose-scented geraniums and ivy. It's a truly lovely pueblo adhering to a fiercely authentic ethos.

Sights

Convento de los Franciscanos MONASTERY
(Plaza Principal; foreigner/Colombian COP$12,000/7000; ⏲10am-noon & 2-4pm Tue-Fri, 9am-4pm Sat & Sun) Construction on this Franciscan monastery, the most dominating building in Monguí, began in 1694 and took 100 years to complete. The stunning redstone marvel was recently refurbished and, aside from its pretty cloister, houses a religious-art museum with important works by Gregorio Vázquez. The convent is attached to the **Basílica Menor de Nuestra Señora de Monguí**, a massive church for such a small village; its three-nave interior displays a richly gilded main retable.

The image of the Virgen de Monguí, crowned in 1929 as the patron saint of Monguí, sits above the altar. Access to the church and convent is via the Despacho Parroquial on Calle 5, just east of the main square. Guided tours are given in Spanish.

Activities

Monguí is the base for some satisfying but little-trodden high-altitude hikes. It's the main starting point for the 18km journey on foot through the unique alpine tundra of **Páramo de Ocetá**. Due to disputes with local landowners, for this hike it is important to hire a local guide who knows which lands are open.

A slightly easier option is the half-day trek to the **Laguna Colorada**, which passes through some gorgeous *páramo* landscapes with six species of frailejón.

Bear in mind that both hikes ascend to altitudes of close to 4000m. Acclimatize with a night in Monguí first.

Monguí Travels (p94) offers great itineraries for both hikes.

Monguí Travels HIKING
(☎313-424-8207; www.monguitravels.com; Plaza Principal, cnr Carrera 4 & Calle 5; ⏰7am-8pm) Monguí's go-to tour operator is run by a group of enthusiastic young guides who offer a variety of activities, the highlight of which is an 18km trek through the incredible alpine tundra of the Páramo de Ocetá. They also offer cycling trips and rock climbing. Swing by the ultra-friendly office to discuss your options.

Full-day hikes in the *páramo* run at around COP$40,000 per person, with meals available for COP$10,000. This is a intermediate hike that ascends to a height of 3915m. There's also a day trip to Laguna Colorado for COP$60,000 per hiker, all-inclusive. Cycling trips in the surrounding countryside start at COP$40,000 for a 20km circuit.

Sleeping & Eating

Mongui Plaza Hotel HOTEL $$
(☎313-209-0067; monguiplaza@gmail.com; Carrera 4 No 4-13; s/d incl breakfast from COP$60,000/120,000; P 📶) In a prime position on the main square, the Mongui Plaza is housed a colonial mansion decked out in the town's characteristic green, red and gold trim. Despite the building's age, the refurbished rooms have parquet floors, fresh linens and modern bathrooms equipped with big showerheads that pump out piping-hot solar-powered water. All rooms have heaters (and you'll need them here).

Breakfast is served in the handsome central patio.

Calicanto Real Hostal GUESTHOUSE $$
(☎311-811-1519; calicantoreal.hostal@gmail.com; Carrera 3; r per person incl breakfast COP$50,000; P 📶) Overlooking one of Monguí's most magical scenes – the stone Puente Real de Calicanto bridge and the grumbling Río Morro – this six-room guesthouse is in a stuck-in-time *casona* (large, rambling old house) that doesn't lack character. The rooms, chock-full with period-style furnishings, are starting to look a bit scuffed and ready for a refurb, however.

There's a riverside garden, free parking and a cluttered common lounge. The atmospheric cafe-bar next door is a great place for a drink.

Pizza Cabubara PIZZA $
(Carrera 3 No 2-85; pizza slice COP$3500; ⏰6-10:30pm) An extremely friendly family-run shop that serves surprisingly good pizza by the slice, alongside lasagna and burgers. One of the few places you can get a bite to eat late at night in Monguí.

Information

The nearest ATM is in Sogamoso.

Cafe Net (Calle 3A No 2-12; per hour COP$1200; ⏰9am-7pm)

Monguí Tourist Office (☎350-653-6191; Calle 5 No 3-24; ⏰8am-12:30pm & 2-6pm Mon-Fri, 10am-noon & 2-4pm Sat & Sun) Has basic information in Spanish and some maps.

Getting There & Away

Minibuses to Sogamoso (COP$4000, every 20 minutes) depart from the northwestern corner of Monguí's plaza. There are two daily buses to Bogotá, but a *super directo* from Sogamoso is a much quicker bet.

Sierra Nevada del Cocuy

Relatively unknown outside of Colombia, the Sierra Nevada del Cocuy is one of the most spectacular mountain ranges in South America. This gorgeous slice of heaven on earth has some of Colombia's most dramatic landscapes, from snowcapped mountains and raging waterfalls to icy glaciers and crystal-clear blue lakes.

It's the highest part of the Cordillera Oriental, the eastern part of the Colombian Andes. The Sierra Nevada del Cocuy contains 21 peaks, of which 15 are higher than 5000m. The tallest peak, Ritacuba Blanco, reaches 5330m.

The mountains are quite compact, relatively easy to reach and ideal for trekking, though they're best suited to experienced hikers. The starting points for these hikes are the pretty villages of Güicán and El Cocuy, both of which have scenic beauty that hikes and nonhikers alike will appreciate.

El Cocuy

☎8 / POP 5157 / ELEV 2750M

Dramatically surrounded by soaring mountains, the pretty colonial village of El Cocuy is the most traveler-friendly entry point to Parque Nacional Natural (PNN) El Cocuy, with several hotels, some good restaurants and decent logistical support. El Cocuy has preserved its colonial character: nearly every building in town is painted white with sea-green trim and topped by red Spanish tiled roofs.

Sierra Nevada del Cocuy

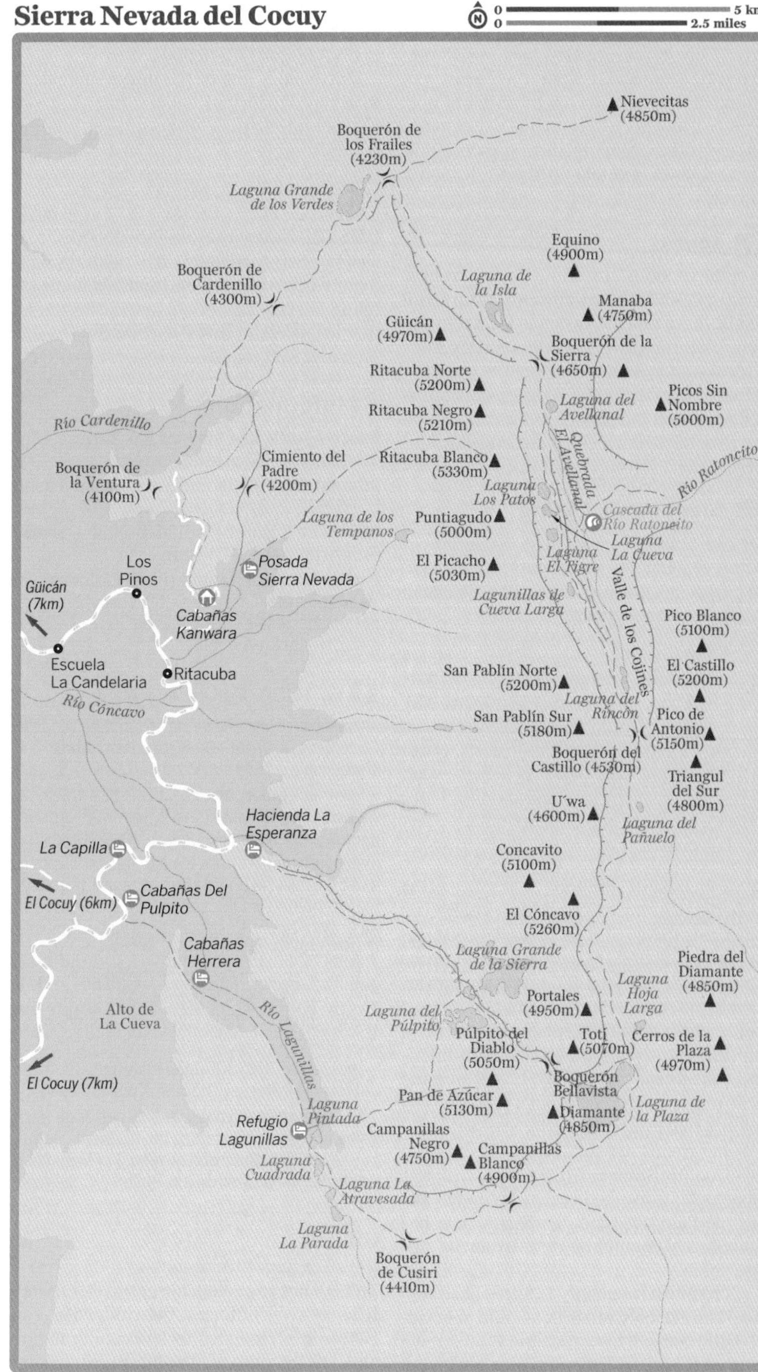

The closure of PNN El Cocuy (p98) in 2016 dealt a hammer blow to the local economy. Many visitor-oriented businesses were forced to close and, despite the recent reopening of the park, the town has yet to fully recover. However, it remains a gloriously peaceful place from which to organize outdoor activities and take in the fresh mountain air.

 Tours

Convite Travel CULTURAL
(☎310-294-9808; www.convitetravel.com.co; Calle 4 No 3-52, Guacamayas) A dynamic local tour operator that runs a variety of interesting tours in towns throughout the region. You can learn to make your own ruana (woollen poncho) in El Cocuy, meet indigenous weavers in Guacamayas or check out some of the endemic bird species in the surrounding forests.

Sleeping & Eating

Most restaurants are located inside hotels. In the evening, street vendors sell *comida corriente* (set menus of the day) in small shops around the square.

Hotel San Gabriel HOTEL **$**
(☎320-984-3629; sangabrielcocuy@gmail.com; Calle 8 No 2-55; r per person COP$35,000-50,000; 📶) A charming little guesthouse on a narrow street, San Gabriel has just six warm and inviting rooms with polished wood floors, perfect paint jobs and modern bathrooms. Two of the top-floor rooms have private balconies.

★**La Posada del Molino** HISTORIC HOTEL **$$**
(☎8-789-0377; http://elcocuycasamuseo.blogspot.com; Carrera 3 No 7-51; r per person high/low season COP$60,000/35,000, cabañas high season COP$300,000; 📶) This 230-year-old renovated colonial mansion gives plenty of comfort and a whole lotta atmosphere for the peso. The building's bright blue-and-yellow interiors evoke its colorful history. It was once the local police post (check out the preserved holding cell) and is reputedly haunted.

Some rooms are decorated with tasteful wooden furnishings, while simpler, newer cabañas offer five beds each. Try to get the Paso de Balcones room upstairs, which has phenomenal mountain views from its private porch.

All rooms have quality features like satellite TV, wi-fi, hardwood floors and renovated bathrooms. The gorgeous fossil-strewn courtyard with a babbling brook will lull you to sleep. Service is top notch and it's also one of the best places in town to eat (meals COP$7000 to COP$18,000).

The hotel is one of the town's few places to accept credit and debit cards; staff can also organize a cash advance if you run out of funds.

Las Empanadas de Mamá FAST FOOD **$**
(☎313-252-3370; Carrera 3; empanadas COP$1000-2500, burgers COP$3000-7500; ⏲2-9pm Mon-Sat) A friendly little cafeteria serving a variety of good empanadas alongside filling burgers and other snacks. It's one of the few places in town you can find freshly prepared fruit juices.

Information

Banco Agrario de Colombia (cnr Carrera 4 & Calle 8) Only ATM in town.

Internet Central (Carrera 5 No 7-72; per hour COP$1500; ⏲8am-noon & 2-8pm)

Oficina de Seguros (☎312-531-9031; Carrera 5; ⏲7-11:45am & 1-4:45pm)

Parque Nacional Natural (PNN) El Cocuy Headquarters (☎8-789-0359; cocuy@parquesnacionales.gov.co; Calle 5A No 4-22; ⏲7-11:45am & 1-4:45pm)

Getting There & Away

All buses arrive at and depart from their respective offices (many of which are convenience stores) on the town square along Carrera 5.

Luxurious **Libertadores** (☎313-829-1073; www.coflonorte.com; Carrera 5 No 7-28; ⏲8am-noon & 2-8pm) buses to Bogotá (COP$60,000, nine hours) depart from the square at 6:30pm and 8pm daily; in Bogotá buses depart from the main terminal for El Cocuy at 6pm and 8:50pm. All Bogotá-bound buses will drop you in Tunja (COP$32,000, seven hours).

Another company servicing the Bogotá–Cocuy–Guicán route is **Expreso Paz del Río** (www.expresopazderio.com), with around five daily buses,

To Güicán (COP$3000, 30 minutes), Cootradatil buses depart at 11:30am, 4pm and 8pm.

To Bucaramanga you're usually better off going to Tunja and catching the frequent northbound buses to Buca and beyond. For Medellín you'll also need to change in Tunja.

Güicán

☎8 / POP 6701 / ELEV 2880M

Though not as photogenic or traveler friendly as its rival El Cocuy, the chilly village of Güicán is surrounded by spectacular nature and has become a popular starting point for trekkers heading up to the mountains, mainly because it provides a closer and easier hike to Parque Nacional Natural El Cocuy (p98). Nonhikers should note that Güicán offers a number of attractions that don't necessarily involve strenuous mountain paths.

The town is a gateway to the traditional lands of the indigenous U'wa community. Religious tourism associated with the miracle of the Virgen Morenita de Güicán (p97) is also a major source of revenue.

Sights & Activities

Güicán's most famous attraction is the Virgen Morenita de Güicán (p97). The shrine to the Morenita is located inside the **Nuestra Señora de la Candelaria** church on the town square, Parque Principal. The brown-brick and faux-marble church isn't much to look at outside, but inside it's richly decorated and painted in pastel pinks, greens and blues.

East of town is a 300m-high cliff known as **El Peñón de los Muertos**, where U'wa people chose to jump to their deaths upon the arrival of the conquistadores rather than live under Spanish rule. The trail to the cliff begins at the end of Carrera 4. A hike to the top of the cliff takes about two hours. The **Monumento a la Dignidad de la Raza U'wa**, depicting the mass suicide, is located at the town's entrance.

In the canyon heading out of town there are **petroglyphs** left behind by pre-Columbian indigenous communities.

A good acclimatization hike runs to the **Cerro Monseratte** – the site of a religious sanctuary on a mountaintop overlooking the town. Alternatively, the loop to **Alto de San Ignacio** provides views of the glaciers.

Just outside town are four rock-climbing sites, complete with pegs, set among spectacular scenery. Aseguicoc (p98) can organize guides and equipment; you'll pay around COP$80,000 per climb.

Termales de San Luis THERMAL BATHS
(320-222-3705; COP$12,000; 9am-8pm) Located in a dramatic valley on the road into Güicán, these tasteful developed thermal baths are the perfect place to relax after a strenuous hike. There's one big pool and two smaller baths set in an appealing garden next to a rushing stream that attracts butterflies and birds.

Just outside the gates you'll find El Chorro – a shower of thermal waters surrounded by rocks that's free to bathe in.

Sleeping

Casa del Colibri GUESTHOUSE $
(319-297-4148; www.hotelcasadelcolibri.com; Calle 2 No 5-19; r per person COP$25,000-35,000) Set in a lovely colonial house, this welcoming little hotel has large rooms surrounding a pleasant courtyard complete with tables and umbrellas for chilling out. All rooms have wooden floors and flat-screen TVs and some have mountain views. Meals are available (COP$5500 to COP$10,000).

Hotel Ecológico El Nevado INN $$
(310-297-7166, 310-806-2149; www.econevado.com; Km3 Carretera Güicán–Panqueba, San Luis;

VIRGEN MORENITA DE GÜICÁN

Güicán is known throughout Colombia for the miracle of the Virgen Morenita de Güicán, which was an apparition of a dark-skinned Virgin Mary that appeared to the indigenous U'wa people. The story begins in the late 17th century, when Spanish conquistadores arrived in the area and set about converting the U'wa to Christianity. Rather than bow to Spanish rule, U'wa chief Güicány, for whom the town is named, led his tribe to their deaths by leaping off the cliff now called El Peñol de Los Muertos. Güicány's wife Cuchumba was spared because she was pregnant. Cuchumba and a handful of survivors fled to the mountains and hid in a cave. On February 26, 1756, an apparition of the Virgin Mary mysteriously appeared on a cloth. The image of Mary had a dark complexion, and features just like those of the U'wa, who quickly converted to Christianity.

A small chapel was built in Güicán to house the Virgen Morenita. During one of the many civil wars between the rival towns of Güicán and El Cocuy, the Virgen was stolen and hidden in El Cocuy, supposedly behind a wall in what is now the hotel La Posada del Molino. The family residing there was haunted until they returned the Virgen to Güicán, where it resides today under lock and key.

The grand **Festival of the Virgen Morenita** is celebrated from February 2 to 4, attracting pilgrims from far and wide.

r COP$140,000-180,000) Just off the highway to Güicán set among spectacular mountains, this spacious rural hotel is a great place to relax before or after a trip to the park. The building is a new construction that replicates classic farmhouses of the region and features comfortable modern rooms with small private balconies. There's also a large thermal pool on the property.

It's about a 15-minute drive from Güicán. If you don't have a vehicle, you'll be dependent on the infrequent buses that run along the highway.

Information

Banco Agrario de Colombia (Carrera 5) Güicán's only ATM.

Cafeteria La Principal (Carrera 5 No 3-09; per hour COP$2000; 8am-8pm;) Internet access.

Parque Nacional Natural El Cocuy (8-789-7280; cocuy@parquenacionales.gov.co; Transversal 4A No 6-60; 7am-11:45am & 1-4:45pm)

Getting There & Away

Two main companies run to/from Bogotá: **Libertadores** (320-448-9181; www.coflonorte.com; Casa Cural, cnr Carrera 5 & Calle 4) and Expreso Paz del Río (www.expresopazderio.com).

Luxurious Libertadores buses to Bogotá (COP$60,000, 11 hours) depart from Güicán's plaza at 6pm and 7pm; buses to Güicán depart Bogotá's main bus terminal at 6pm and 8:50pm. Less comfortable Expreso Paz del Río buses run around five times a day. All call at El Cocuy and Tunja.

To El Cocuy (COP$3000, 40 minutes), local **Cootradatil** (320-330-9536; Carrera 3 No 4-05) buses depart at 3am, 7am, 11am and 2pm. Alternatively, take one of the Bogotá-bound buses, which all pass through El Cocuy on their way to the capital.

To Bucaramanga you're usually better off going to Tunja and catching the frequent northbound buses to Buca and beyond. For Medellín you'll also need to change in Tunja.

Parque Nacional Natural El Cocuy

Covering an enormous 306,000 hectares, **Parque Nacional Natural (PNN) El Cocuy** (foreigners/Colombians COP$61,000/30,500) is home to some of Colombia's most impressive landscapes and is the main attraction of the Sierra Nevada del Cocuy region. It has 15 peaks that are at least 5000m, the highest of which is Ritacuba Blanco at 5330m.

Once off-limits because of the security situation, the park is now safe to visit, but access can still be complicated. In 2013 the main attraction, the Güicán–El Cocuy Circuit Trek, was closed to visitors indefinitely, and in 2016 the park was closed completely while the government negotiated with local indigenous communities. The park reopened in early 2017 but with even more restrictions. It's no longer possible to touch any of the glaciers, making climbing the peaks impossible, and overnight stays are no longer permitted. Check ahead to see if the situation has changed by the time you visit.

Tours

You can hire guides from any of the cabañas near the mountains or through the excellent community guide association **Aseguicoc** (Asosciacion de Servicios Turisticos de Guican y El Cocuy; 311-255-1034, 314-252-8977; aseguicoc@gmail.com) in El Cocuy and Güicán. For up to six people, expect to pay about COP$100,000 a day for a *campesino* or interpreter (who can merely show you the way), or COP$120,000 to COP$150,000 for an accredited trekking guide. Porters cost about COP$100,000 per day (horses were banned above 4000m in 2013). Solo hikers and small groups can be paired with others to keep costs down.

While the main circuit is closed, there are now three day treks open to visitors; these are located in the north, central and southern reaches of the park.

In order to hike the trails you'll need to be at the corresponding control point by 9am, after which no visitors will be admitted. First entry is at 5am. All hikers must commence their return leg by 1pm, in order to be back outside the park by closing time.

Access to each of the trails is limited to a set number of hikers per day, so in high season it's a good idea to register at the park offices with as much notice as possible. Your guide may be able to reserve your spot, but you'll still need to register in person upon arrival in El Cocuy or Güicán.

The northernmost hike is a 15.2km round trip from the ranger office to the edge of the glacier of **Ritacuba Blanco**, the highest peak in the Cocuy range, beginning at around 4000m and reaching a peak of 4800m. It's about an eight-hour round trip at a relaxed pace.

More spectacular is the 21km hike through the center of the range to **Laguna Grande** and the edge of the glacier of

Nevado Concavo at 4700m, which offers spectacular views of many of the peaks in the southern section of the park. It's a long 10-hour round trip that requires plenty of stamina. The first 2km of the trail passes through high Andean forest before arriving at La Cuchumba; this waterfall and cave just outside the park boundaries is a site of religious pilgrimage. From La Cuchumba the trail remains fairly flat through the Valle de los Frailejones before climbing up Laguna Grande at 4400m. From the lake to the edge of the glacier is another hour-long hike.

The final trail open to visitors is the trail from Laguna Pintada up to the Púlpito del Diablo and the Pan de Azúcar glacier at 4800m in the southern reaches of the park. At 8.6km and six hours, it's not a long hike, but it does contain the most difficult climb of the three trails: a 600m section from Hotelito up to Alto del Conejo. The highlight of the trek is the imposing rectangular formation of the Púlpito backed by dramatic snowcapped peaks.

There are also a couple of acclimatization hikes you can do just outside the park boundaries. The southern version is a mostly flat hike that runs for 3km to 4km from the Refugio Lagunillas (p99) alongside a river in the Valle de Lagunillas past several small lakes nestled amid wonderful *páramo* landscapes. Although the vast majority of the trek is outside the park boundaries, there's one stretch toward the end that crosses into the park; while technically park admission is required, this is not usually enforced. Check the latest in Cocuy before heading out.

The northern acclimatization trek is a four-hour round-trip hike from the northern cabañas along the road to Parada de Romero. It's a fairly easy, flat hike with fine mountain panoramas and views down to Güicán.

Veteran climber and mountaineer Rodrigo Arias of Colombia Trek (☎320-339-3839; www.colombiatrek.com; 2/3/4-day trek from COP$650,000/800,000/1,100,000) is an experienced, highly recommended guide and one of the few English speakers in the mountains. He can arrange personalized tours and all-inclusive packages for individuals or groups. Trekking packages begin from Güicán and include transportation, meals, park entrance, accommodations and guides. If restrictions are lifted, he can organize the Paso del Conejo multiday trek, which passes through some of the park's most impressive scenery. He also rents camping gear and equipment.

Sleeping & Eating

After a visit to El Cocuy or Güicán, most hikers choose to adjust to the altitude by staying overnight at one of several cabañas located just outside the park boundaries. The most comfortable are located in the northern end of the park near Güicán, but you'll also find good options in the mountains halfway between El Cocuy and Güicán and at the southern end of the park.

There are no restaurants inside the park boundaries. Carry some snacks in your bag – and make sure to take the trash out with you.

Hacienda La Esperanza FARMSTAY **$**
(☎320-328-1674; haciendalaesperanza@gmail.com; r per person incl breakfast COP$45,000) Halfway between El Cocuy and Güicán, at 3600m, you'll find the rustic working farmhouse of Hacienda La Esperanza. It is a large, classic colonial-style building made of rammed earth, with rooms set around an internal patio. It's convenient for the hike to Laguna Grande and El Cóncavo. Other meals are available for COP$15,000.

Refugio Lagunillas GUESTHOUSE **$$**
(Cabañas Sisuma; ☎311-255-1034; aseguicoc@gmail.com; r per person with/without bathroom COP$50,000/40,000) Run by the local guide association, this five-room lodge in the southern region at 3980m is the closest accommodations to the park boundaries. It's a good base from which to explore Lagunillas on an acclimatization hike or launch the trek to Púlpito del Diablo and Pan de Azúcar. Meals are available for COP$15,000.

Note that the *refugio* has the only cabañas without road access; you'll need to hike the last 3km with your gear, but it's a fairly gentle trip along mostly flat terrain.

Cabañas Kanwara GUESTHOUSE **$$**
(☎311-237-2660, 311-231-6004; kabanaskanwara@gmail.com; r per person COP$45,000) Comfortable cabañas located in the northern end of the park near Güicán. The four A-frame cabins each have eight to 14 beds, a fireplace, a kitchen and a bathroom. Breakfast is COP$15,000; other meals run between COP$20,000 and COP$25,000.

Getting There & Away

If you're on a budget, the best way to get into the park is to hike from El Cocuy or Güicán; this will also help you acclimatize before you attempt one of the park trails.

From Güicán it's a three-hour hike through lovely countryside to Hacienda La Esperanza (p99) or a five-hour hike straight up to Cabañas Kanwara (p99), where the northern trail begins.

It's pretty much a full-day hike from El Cocuy to the starting point for the Laguna del Púlpito/Pan de Azúcar trail, while the Laguna Grande trailhead is around a six-hour trek from the town. If you hike in you'll need to spend a night in one of the cabañas before entering the park.

If you're short on time, **Corpotuc** (315-860-6083; Carrera 3 No 7-51) in El Cocuy has a fleet of private charter vehicles with white number plates that are available to take visitors anywhere there's a road. A trip to one of the cabañas or trailheads will set you back COP$80,000 to COP$100,000 per vehicle for up to five hikers. You can make a booking through the helpful reception desk at La Posada del Molino (p96) in El Cocuy. Some cabañas can also organize transportation; prices vary depending on destination and group size.

A cheaper, last-resort alternative is to hop a ride on a *lechero* (milk truck; around COP$10,000); these make morning rounds to the mountain farms, though this option shouldn't be considered comfortable or safe. Also, local police are cracking down on the trucks, as they don't have the necessary papers to carry passengers, so you might find it hard to get a ride.

The *lecheros* leave Güicán plaza at 5am, reach El Cocuy plaza at 6am and make a counterclockwise circuit back to Güicán. There are several *lecheros*, so you'll have to ask around to find the one going to your destination. Most *lecheros* do not stop directly at the cabañas; you'll be let off at the nearest intersection, from where you must hike the rest of the way.

SANTANDER

The north-central department of Santander is a patchwork of steep craggy mountains, deep canyons, plummeting waterfalls, raging rivers, unexplored caves and a temperate, dry climate. Mix them together and it's easy to see why Santander has become a favorite destination for outdoor lovers. Extreme-sports nuts can choose from white-water rafting, paragliding, caving, rappelling, hiking and mountain biking. Visitors with more sanity can enjoy exploring the rustic charms of colonial Barichara, strolling the whitewashed streets of Girón or getting their dance on in the nightclubs in the department capital city of Bucaramanga.

San Gil

7 / POP 44,600 / ELEV 1110M

For a small city, San Gil packs a lot of punch. This is the outdoors capital of Colombia and a mecca for extreme-sports enthusiasts. The area is best known for white-water rafting, but other popular pastimes include paragliding, caving, rappelling and trekking. San Gil has a handsome 300-year-old town square and Parque El Gallineral (p101), a beautiful nature reserve on the banks of the Río Fonce.

San Gil may not be the prettiest town in Colombia, but dig beneath the exterior and you'll discover a wonderful city of natural beauty and friendly, welcoming residents. San Gil definitely lives up to its motto, 'La Tierra de Aventura' (The Land of Adventure).

Sights

Cueva de la Vaca CAVE

(Curití; tour COP$35,000; 7am-4:30pm) Located just outside the town of Curití, La Vaca is the most attractive and adventurous cave in the are,a with numerous caverns filled with stalagmites and stalactites. To explore the cave you'll need to go on a guided tour (90 minutes), which can be organized in town. At one point you'll have to swim through a submerged tunnel, although there's a rope to guide you along. Wear old clothes – you'll get muddy. Not for the claustrophobic.

Cascadas de Juan Curi WATERFALL

(COP$9000; 6am-5pm) Take a day trip to this spectacular 180m-high waterfall where you can swim in the natural pool at its base or relax on the rocks. Adventure junkies can rappel the sheer face of the falls; book this activity with one of the tour companies. Juan Curi is 22km from San Gil on the road to Charalá. Charalá buses (COP$6300, one hour) depart twice hourly from the local bus terminal.

Ask to be let off at 'Las Cascadas,' where two 20-minute trails lead up to the falls. Most travelers choose the cheaper (though slightly less beautiful) trail at Juan Curi Parque Ecologico, which is the first entry coming from San Gil. It's the only trail that allows access to higher sections of the falls; both paths give access to the swimming hole below.

If you like food, combine a trip here with a stop in Valle de San José for the famous chorizo cooked in *guarapo* (fermented sugarcane juice) at Piqueteadero Doña Eustaquia (p103).

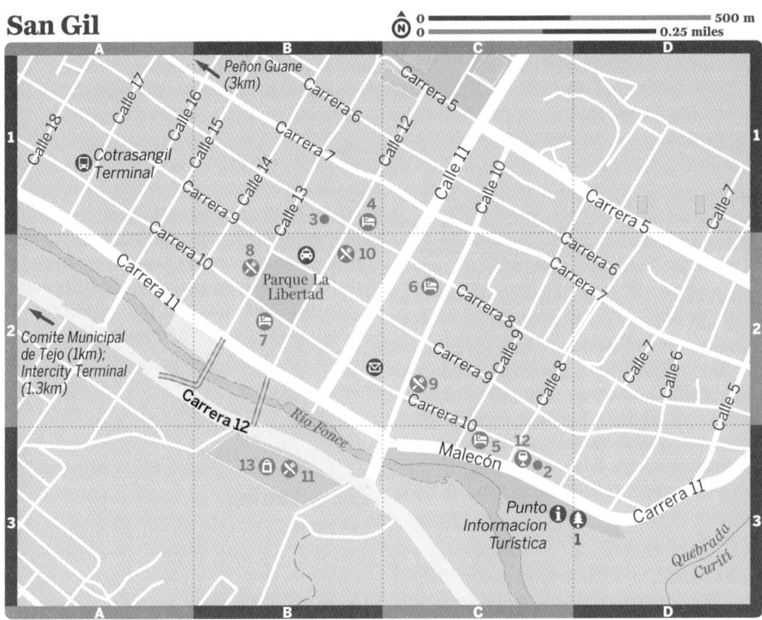

San Gil

Sights

1 Parque El Gallineral ... D3

Activities, Courses & Tours

2 Colombia Rafting Expeditions ... C3
3 Connect4 ... B1
Macondo Adventures ... (see 6)

Sleeping

4 Hostel Casa Rome ... B1
5 La Posada Familiar ... C3
6 Macondo Guesthouse ... C2
7 Sam's VIP ... B2

Eating

8 Autoservice Veracruz ... B2
9 El Maná ... C2
10 Gringo Mike's ... B2
11 Metro ... B3

Drinking & Nightlife

12 La Habana ... C3

Shopping

13 Centro Comercial El Puente ... B3

Parque El Gallineral PARK
(7-724-4372; cnr Malecón & Calle 6; with/without swimming COP$10,000/6000; 8am-6pm) San Gil's showpiece is the salubrious Parque El Gallineral, a 4-hectare park set on a triangular island between two arms of the Quebrada Curití and Río Fonce. Many of the 1900 trees are covered with long, silvery tendrils of moss called barbas de viejo (old man's beard), hanging from branches to form translucent curtains of foliage and filtered sunlight. It's like a scene set in JRR Tolkien's Middle Earth.

Several paths and covered bridges snake through the urban forest and over the rushing streams. Two large chlorinated pools have been constructed to replace the natural pool that was closed due to health issues. While the new pools are a bit at odds with the glorious natural surroundings, they're nevertheless good places to cool off. Otherwise, just come to sip a *cerveza* (beer) at one of the restaurants or cafes. Upon paying admission you'll be given a wristband permitting access throughout the day until last entry at 5pm.

Activities

Several tour agencies in San Gil run white-water rafting on local rivers. A 10km run on Río Fonce (Class I to III) costs

COP$45,000 per person and takes 1½ hours; experienced rafters can tackle the rapids of the Río Suárez (COP$130,000, up to Class V). Most operators also offer paragliding, caving, horseback riding, rappelling/abseiling, mountain biking, bungee jumping and ecowalks.

★Colombian Bike Junkies MOUNTAIN BIKING
(☎316-327-6101; www.colombianbikejunkies.com; day trips from COP$270,000) Modeled after Gravity in Bolivia, this Colombian-Ecuadorean-owned extreme-mountain-bike company offers a 50km downhill adrenaline overdose on two wheels through the Cañón del Río Suárez (with a stop in Barichara) or the equally spectacular Cañon de Chicamocha. It's an all-day affair that takes in absolutely epic countryside. Lunch is included; a celebratory beer is de rigueur.

There's no physical office in San Gil. Book via the website.

Macondo Adventures ADVENTURE SPORTS
(☎7-724-8001; www.macondohostel.com; Carrera 8 No 10-35) A one-stop adventure shop, this professional tour desk inside the Macondo hostel (p102) organizes the full gamut of adventure activities. The helpful staff have tried all the activities themselves and can recommend a variety of options depending on your interests and sanity. Choose from rafting, paragliding, mountain biking, kayaking and caving.

Colombia Rafting Expeditions RAFTING
(☎7-724-5800; www.colombiarafting.com; Carrera 10 No 7-83; rafting from COP$130,000; ⌚8am-5pm) The rafting specialist for the Río Suárez; also offers hydrospeeding and kayaking.

Pescaderito SWIMMING
FREE This group of five swimming holes is a great little place to relax the day away. Skip the first one – they get better the further up you go (the fifth is the best; no diving from the third!). It's also a nice camping spot.

To reach here, catch a bus from the local terminal to Curití's main square (COP$2700, every 15 minutes), walk four blocks past the church and take the road leading out of town for about 40 minutes upriver.

Peñon Guane ADVENTURE SPORTS
(Km2 Via San Gil–Barichara; zipline COP$50,000) For high-adrenaline views, check out these two 300m-long ziplines on the mountainside high above the town on the road to Barichara. There's also a massive extreme swing that launches participants out over the abyss. The on-site bar has fine views and is popular with couples in the evening who come to romance while gazing at the city lights.

Courses

Connect4 LANGUAGE
(☎7-724-2544; www.connect4.edu.co; Carrera 8 No 12-19) A professionally run language center offering intensive and well-structured 12-hour Spanish courses (COP$320,000) designed to teach travelers the basics they'll need during their journey. You can take each three-hour module whenever you want, which leaves plenty of time for adventure activities between classes. You can also take a one-day course (COP$80,000) or private lessons (COP$42,000 per hour).

Sleeping

San Gil has plenty of downtown budget and moderately priced lodgings. Private rooms in most hostels are so comfortable that it's not usually necessary to splurge on midrange accommodations. There are many basic cheapie hotels on Calle 10, but if you're looking for luxury, check out the resorts on the outskirts of town along Vía Charalá or Vía Mogotes; alternatively, head to Bogotá.

★Macondo Guesthouse HOSTEL $
(☎7-724-8001; www.macondohostel.com; Carrera 8 No 10-35; dm COP$22,000-28,000, d COP$100,000, without bathroom COP$65,000; @📶) The original San Gil hostel is still easily the best in town. It's a laid-back but secure place (with CCTV) that feels a bit like crashing at a friend's. There's a wonderful leafy courtyard with a 10-person Jacuzzi and a variety of dorm and room options, including three upgraded private rooms that punch above their hostel weight class.

While it's not the flashiest choice around, it absolutely nails the San Gil vibe. The helpful management and staff know the area inside out and have tried all the adventure activities themselves so are able to offer quality advice. Don't miss Tejo Tuesdays and don't even think about showing up without a booking.

Hostel Casa Rome HOSTEL $
(☎7-723-8819; www.hostelcasarome.com; Carrera 8 No 11-90; r per person COP$40,000; 📶) In a small colonial-style building, Casa Rome has inviting rooms with wood-beamed ceilings, bright tiled floors and exposed stone walls.

Private rooms have flat-screen TVs and modern bathrooms (some external to the rooms); some rooms have small balconies. The quadruple room functions as a dorm.

Common areas with hammocks and rocking chairs encourage lazy contemplation. That said, the hostel offers all manner of San Gil–style activities, paragliding and bungee jumping among them.

La Posada Familiar GUESTHOUSE **$$**
(☎301-370-1323, 7-724-8136; laposadafamiliar@hotmail.com; Carrera 10 No 8-55; r per person COP$40,000; @ 📶) Señora Esperanza dotes on her guests at this most Colombian of choices, a lovely six-room guesthouse wrapped around a plant-jammed courtyard with a gurgling fountain. Well-maintained rooms are unembellished but offer modern bathrooms and hot water, and there's a small but pleasant guest kitchen with a hardwood sink.

Sam's VIP HOSTEL **$$**
(☎7-724-2746; www.samshostel.com; Carrera 10 No 12-33; dm COP$30,000, s/d COP$85,0000/110,000, without bathroom COP$65,000/90,000; @ 📶 🏊) There aren't many hostels that claim VIP status, but Sam's does, at least, make you feel like a VIB (very important backpacker). The dark garage entry off the main square doesn't promise much, but things get infinitely brighter when you climb the two flights of stairs to enter a sunny, plaza-facing lounge-lobby-terrace.

Eating

San Gil isn't a gourmet destination, but it does have a collection of restaurants serving home-cooked local cuisine alongside some good international fare. For self-catering there's **Autoservice Veracruz** (Calle 13 No 9-24; ⏰8am-9pm Mon-Sat, to 2pm Sun) on the plaza (better for fresh fruit and veggies) and **Metro** (⏰8am-9pm Sun-Fri, to 10pm Sat) – San Gil's biggest; better for dry goods – inside Centro Comercial El Puente (p103), San Gil's modern shopping center.

★**El Maná** COLOMBIAN **$**
(Calle 10 No 9-42; set meals COP$15,000; ⏰11am-3pm & 6-8:30pm Mon-Sat, to 3pm Sun) This popular, word-of-mouth favorite is the best Colombian restaurant in town. You can taste the extra love in the fantastic set meals – seven or so to choose from daily – featuring traditional dishes like chicken in plum sauce, *estofado de pollo* (chicken stew) and grilled mountain trout. The bummer is that it closes early – no good if you're out all day.

Piqueteadero Doña Eustaquia COLOMBIAN **$**
(Calle 3 No 5-39, Valle de San José; chorizo COP$1300; ⏰7am-8pm) Located in the village of Valle de San José on the way to the Juan Curi (p100) falls, this place is famous for its chorizo sausage cooked in *guarapo* (fermented sugarcane juice). It has a branch in the food court at the mall in San Gil, but it's not the same.

★**Gringo Mike's** AMERICAN **$$**
(☎7-724-1695; www.gringomikes.net; Calle 12 No 8-35; burgers COP$18,500-24,500; ⏰8am-11pm; 📶 🌿) What *isn't* good here? In a moody, candlelit courtyard you'll find this US-UK operation thrilling homesick travelers with a surplus of American-portioned gourmet burgers, bacon-heavy sandwiches, breakfast burritos and French-press coffee. You may need a knife and fork to dismember the spicy jalapeño burger and the Mexican beef-fillet burrito.

Honorable mentions should go to the great cocktails, ample vegetarian choices (all burgers have veggie alternatives), and the spectacular mango, peanut and blue-cheese salad with prawns. Far more than a footnote are the desserts, led by the giant, freshly baked chocolate-chip cookie served hot in the pan with ice cream: all are fully justifiable if you just returned from some white-knuckle San Gil–style activity.

Drinking & Entertainment

Several cafes on the plaza have proper espresso machines, but the best coffee, including a branch of Juan Valdez, is in **Centro Comercial El Puente** (www.elpuente.com.co; Calle 10 No 12-184; ⏰9am-9pm). Drinking beer in the plaza used to be one of the town's favorite pastimes, but new laws mean it's no longer permitted. However, numerous bars surrounding the park serve cold beers with a view.

La Habana BAR
(☎300-407-5138; Calle 8 No 10-32; ⏰3pm-midnight Mon-Thu, to 1am Fri & Sun, 9am-1am Sun) With a wall display that pays homage to Che Guevara and The Beatles and an agreeably unkempt location overlooking the *malecón* (jetty/promenade), this unpretentious 2nd-floor bar is where San Gil's extreme adventurers go to wind down (or up). If you've been sitting on too many Colombian buses listening to local radio, you'll appreciate the edgy reggae, rock and blues soundtrack.

Comite Municipal de Tejo SPORTS
(☎7-724-4053; Carrera 18 No 26-70; ⏲4-10:30pm) Throw rocks at explosives at San Gil's local tejo courts. If you don't know what you're doing, it's best to come on a tour to avoid offending serious players.

Information

There are several ATMs in and around the plaza (avoid the problematic Banco Agrario one). For listings of hotels and adventure companies, check out www.sangil.com.co.

4-72 (Carrera 10 No 10-50; ⏲8am-noon & 2-6pm Mon-Fri, 9am-noon Sat) Post office.

Bancolombia (Calle 12 No 10-44)

BBVA (Carrera 10 No 12-23)

Davivienda (cnr Carrera 10 & Calle 11)

Punto Información Turística (Malecón contiguo a Parque Gallineral; ⏲10am-5pm)

Tourist Police (☎7-724-3433, 320-302-8489; cnr Carrera 11 & Calle 7; ⏲24hr)

Getting There & Around

San Gil has two bus stations with numerous names, but you'll most likely arrive at the **intercity bus terminal** (Vía San Gil-Bogotá) (known locally as *terminal principal*), located 3km west of downtown on the road to Bogotá. Local buses shuttle regularly between the terminal and the city center, or you can take a taxi (COP$4000).

Minibuses leave for Bucaramanga (COP$16,000, 2½ hours) via Parque Nacional del Chicamocha (p108) every half-hour from 4am to 8pm, after which time you can also jump on passing long-distance services.

Frequent buses depart to Bogotá (COP$35,000, seven hours) via Tunja (COP$25,000, four hours). Less frequent direct services call at Barranquilla (COP$70,000, 13 hours), Cartagena (COP$80,000, 15 hours), Santa Marta (COP$70,000, 12 hours), Medellín (COP$80,000, 12 hours) and Cúcuta (COP$50,000, nine hours), with most departures in the evening. Direct buses to other destinations leave from Bucaramanga, but you can make reservations at the company offices in the San Gil terminal. **Copetran** (☎313-333-5740; www.copetran.com.co) has the most regular services.

The **Cotrasangil Terminal** (Terminalito; ☎7-724-2155; www.cotrasangil.com; cnr Calle 17 & Carrera 10) – known locally as *'terminalito'* – has frequent buses to Barichara (COP$5000, 45 minutes) from 6am to 6:45pm. This terminal also serves Guane (COP$7300, one hour, eight per day), Curití (COP$2700, 20 minutes, every 15 minutes from 6am to 7:30pm) and Charalá (COP$6300, one hour, every 30 minutes from 6:30am to 4pm), among other places.

Local **taxis** (Carrera 9) congregate on the north side of the park.

Barichara

☎7 / POP 7100 / ELEV 1336M

Barichara is the kind of town that Hollywood filmmakers dream about. A Spanish colonial town saturated with atmosphere, it boasts cobblestone streets and whitewashed buildings with red-tiled roofs that look almost as new as the day they were constructed some 300 years ago. It's no wonder that many Spanish-language films and *telenovelas* are shot here. Granted, the movie-set appearance owes a debt to considerable reconstruction efforts made since the town was declared a national monument in 1978.

The town is located 20km northwest of San Gil, high above the Río Suárez. Founded in 1705, its natural beauty, temperate climate and bohemian lifestyle have long attracted visitors. In recent years Barichara has become a magnet for affluent Colombians. Compared to Villa de Leyva, Barichara is more upscale but less touristy. It is, without a doubt, one of the most beautiful small colonial towns in Colombia.

Sights & Activities

The main attractions of Barichara are its architecture and its haunting cobbled streets.

Parque Para Las Artes PARK
A lovely little park decorated with impressive water features (although they were out of service when we visited), statues carved by local sculptors and an outdoor amphitheater that occasionally hosts live music concerts. From the park you can enjoy breathtaking views of the neighboring valley.

Catedral de la Inmaculada Concepción CHURCH
(Parque Principal; ⏲5:45am-7pm) This 18th-century sandstone church is the most elaborate structure in Barichara, looking somewhat too big for the town's needs. Its golden stonework (which turns deep orange at sunset) contrasts with the whitewashed houses surrounding it. The building has a clerestory (a second row of windows high up in the nave), which is unusual for a Spanish colonial church.

Taller Centro Dia WORKSHOP
(Museo Parra; cnr Carrera 2 & Calle 6; ⏲8am-3pm) Inside the courtyard of the **Museo Aquileo Parra**, this collective of 24 senior citizens weaves bags and other artisanal products from fique fibers using traditional looms. Come and watch them work and buy a bag

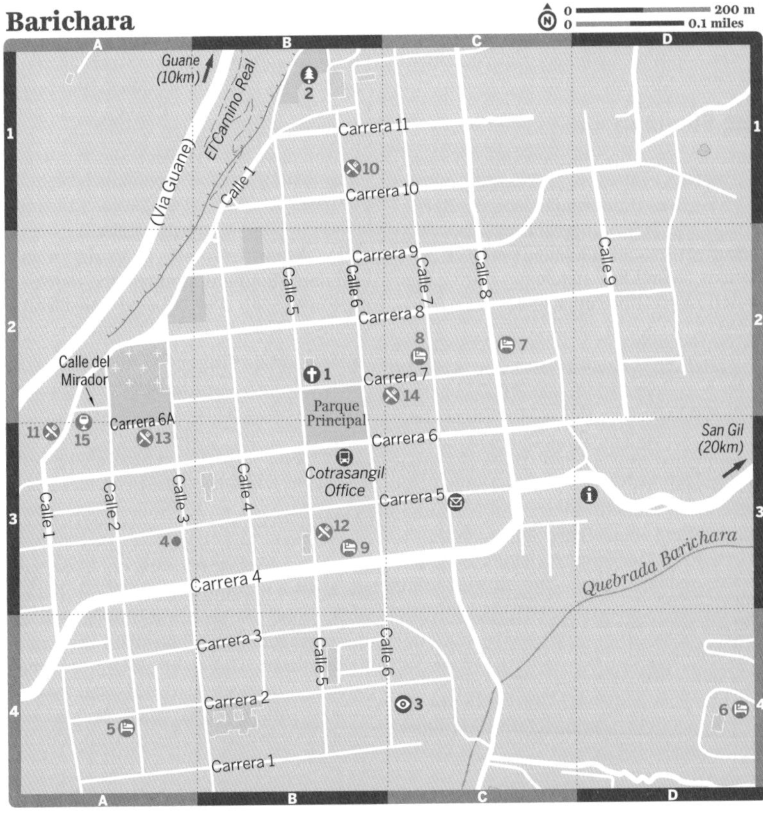

Barichara

Sights

1 Catedral de la Inmaculada Concepción....B2
2 Parque Para Las Artes....B1
3 Taller Centro Dia....C4

Activities, Courses & Tours

4 Fundación San Lorenzo....A3

Sleeping

5 Artepolis....A4
6 Color de Hormiga Posada Campestre....D4
7 La Mansión de Virginia....C2
8 La Nube Posada....C2
9 Tinto Hostel....B3

Eating

10 7 Tigres....B1
11 Carambolo....A3
12 El Compa....B3
13 Ristorante Al Cuoco....A3
14 Shambalá....C2

Drinking & Nightlife

15 Iguá Náuno....A3

on your way out – they're cheap and the group makes ends meet with the proceeds.

★ **Fundación San Lorenzo** TOURS
(Taller de Papel; ☎7-726-7234; www.fundacionsanlorenzo.wordpress.com; Carrera 5 No 2-88; tour with/without paper making COP$5000/3500; ⏱7:30am-1pm & 3-5:30pm Mon-Fri, 8am-1pm & 3-6pm Sat, 10am-1pm Sun) This small paper factory run by a single-mothers' cooperative offers visitors a fascinating glimpse of the four-month-long process of making artisanal paper from fique, a natural fiber that grows in the leaves of the Andean fique plant, and pineapple leaves. Visitors are able

to take part in a basic workshop to make their own sheet of paper.

The resulting stationery and paper products make great souvenirs.

Sleeping

Barichara isn't the cheapest (budget travelers are better off staying in San Gil), but the town rewards those who hang around. Prices can spike 30% or more during *temporada alta* (high season), roughly December 20 to January 15 and Semana Santa. During high season reservations are a must.

★Tinto Hostel HOSTEL $
(7-726-7725; www.tintohostel.com; Carrera 4 No 5-39; dm COP$23,000-27,000, s/d from COP$80,000-120,000;) Barichara's best hostel occupies a great multilevel home with a productive fruit garden. There are three dorms and five private rooms with good bathrooms, vaulted ceilings and hot water. The common areas – guest kitchen with artsy ceramic pottery, lounge, hammock space, terrace and small pool – are all wonderful, and the latter has views over the red roofs of Barichara.

The house is old but well-kept with plenty of deft artistic touches (copper sinks and tree branches as balustrades), while the reception acts like a mini information office for the area.

Artepolis HOTEL $
(300-203-4531; www.artepolis.info; Calle 2 No 1-50; d/tr/q from COP$68,000/85,000/100,000;) Set on a hillside on the town's periphery with outstanding views of the countryside, this unusually designed hotel looks like four joined-up colonial-style houses fronted by a porch studded with hammocks, tables and sofas. Rooms are on the 2nd floor and accessed by a wide spiral staircase. All rooms are large, with private open-air bathrooms and a shared balcony.

The hotel, which has a strong artistic bent (check out the wooden horse out front), also organizes locally run art and craft workshops (two to four hours).

Color de Hormiga Posada Campestre GUESTHOUSE $$
(315-297-1621; Vereda San José; s/d incl breakfast COP$100,000/180,000, dm/s/d without bathroom COP$22,000/40,000/60,000;) Set on a gorgeous 29-hectare nature reserve a short walk from town, this wonderful guesthouse features four rustic, character-filled rooms in the main house, with boutique beds and memorable outdoor bathrooms sporting rain-style showers. The surrounding countryside is great to take a stroll in and is dotted with many nests of the region's famous hormigas culonas (p107).

Meals here are excellent and the whole setup is designed for maximum relaxation. Cheaper rooms are available in a separate building with shared bathrooms.

It's a 1½km uphill walk along the Camino Real past astounding views; the path begins on the southern edge of Calle 7. Alternatively, take a moto-taxi for COP$6000.

La Mansión de Virginia GUESTHOUSE $$
(315-625-4017; www.lamansiondevirginia.com; Calle 8 No 7-26; r per person COP$50,000;) A tranquil, friendly establishment with clean, comfy rooms with TV and renovated private bathrooms and the requisite courtyard.

La Nube Posada BOUTIQUE HOTEL $$$
(7-726-7161; www.lanubeposada.com; Calle 7 No 7-39; s/d COP$240,000/275,000;) Hidden behind the simple exterior, this old colonial home has been transformed into an unassuming boutique hotel with sleek, minimalist decor. The eight simply furnished rooms, with queen-sized beds and vaulted ceilings with exposed wood beams, surround an abstract courtyard with rotating art exhibitions.

The on-site gourmet Colombian restaurant-bar is one of the best in town and it boasts a 14-country rum collection under lock and key. A new annex houses suites and a spa. The one outright flaw is the bathrooms – they are fine for a Holiday Inn, but you deserve better in Barichara.

Eating & Drinking

Barichara has a good selection of international flavors and traditional regional dishes like *cabrito* (grilled baby goat) and the famous hormigas culonas (p107). A lot of places close early in the week, especially on Tuesday, when there are very limited dining options.

El Compa COLOMBIAN $$
(Calle 5 No 4-48; meals COP$16,000-30,000; 8am-6pm) The best local restaurant – unpretentious and not pandering to tourists; indeed, not pandering to anyone much. No matter. The key here is the food: 15 or so workhorse Colombian meals led by *cabrito* (baby goat) and backed up by *sobrebarriga*

(flank steak), trout, chicken and *carne oreada* (sun-dried beef), all served with a host of sides such as salad, yuca and potatoes.

Carambolo SPANISH **$$**
(313-210-1257; www.elcarambolo.com; Calle 1 No 6-39; mains COP$25,000-32,000; 7-10pm Thu & Fri, noon-2:30pm & 7-10pm Sat & Sun;) Barichara's finest dining option is an elegant open-air affair with phenomenal views over the canyon of Río Suárez. The gregarious Spanish owner prepares a variety of Mediterranean-influenced dishes, and prices are very reasonable considering the quality and ambience.

There's also a good bar serving a decent range of drinks with which to toast the spectacular scenery.

Shambalá VEGETARIAN **$$**
(Carrera 7 No 6-20; mains COP$20,000-30,000; 12:30-4pm & 6-9:30pm Thu-Tue;) An extremely popular and consciously retro cafe doing made-to-order, mostly vegetarian dishes. Choose from wraps, rice and pasta in Mediterranean, Indian or Thai styles (you can add chicken or shrimp), and accompany your meal with an excellent juice or tea.

7 Tigres PIZZA **$$**
(312-521-9962; Calle 6 No 10-24; pizzas COP$19,000-21,000; noon-3pm & 6-10pm) Colombians love their crispy thin-crust 'pita' pizzas, and the pies at this semi-alfresco place with its open kitchen and exclamation marks of artsy decor are piled with fresh ingredients sautéed immediately before they're slung in the oven. Great lasagna, too.

Ristorante Al Cuoco ITALIAN **$$$**
(320-232-5422; Carrera 6A No 2-54; mains COP$28,000-35,000; noon-9:30pm Mon-Sat, to 6pm Sun) This fairly elegant one-man Italian show is run out of the home of an amicable Roman chef. Though the menu is limited (some raviolis, cannelloni, gnocchi, risotto, a couple of mains and some desserts), the house-made pasta excels, both as a deviation from the status quo and as a culinary journey to the Mother Boot. Reservations recommended weekends and holidays.

Don't leave without trying the house creation – Parmesan ice cream (COP$13,000); the cheese contrasts perfectly with blackberries and almonds to create a taste sensation.

Iguá Náuno BAR
(cnr Calle del Mirador & Carrera 7; 5-11pm) This is the one spot where the town's trendy gather for drinks. It's not even a dedicated bar, but imported beers (good *micheladas*), a few cocktails and an atmospheric garden make for a fine watering hole. Folks eat here, too, and there's a fair selection of vegetarian dishes.

BARICHARA'S BOOTYLICIOUS BUGS

Of Colombia's culinary traditions, perhaps none is as peculiar as Santander's delicacy, *hormigas culonas* (literally, 'fat-bottom ants'). The tradition dates back more than 500 years to when the indigenous Guane people cultivated and devoured the ants for their supposed aphrodisiac and healing properties.
The giant dark-brown ants are fried or roasted and eaten whole, or ground into a powder. Containers of fried-ant snacks are sold in just about any corner shop in Santander, but especially in Barichara, San Gil and Bucaramanga. The ants are normally in season during spring but can now be found year-round. Their flavor is like crunchy dirt mixed with old coffee grounds. It's definitely an acquired taste – but one you must attempt to cultivate.

Information

There are two ATMs on the plaza:

Banco Agrario (Parque Principal)

Banco de Bogotá (Parque Principal)

4-72 (cnr Carrera 5 & Calle 7; 8am-noon & 2-6pm) Postal agent inside a grocery shop.

Police (8-726-7173; cnr Calle 7 & Carrera 4) The tourist police also sometimes operate from a kiosk on Parque Principal.

Punto Información Turística (315-630-4696; Carrera 5, Salida San Gil; 9am-5pm Wed-Mon)

Getting There & Away

Buses shuttle between Barichara and San Gil (COP$5000, 45 minutes) every 30 minutes from 5am to 6:45pm. They depart from the **Cotrasangil office** (8-726-7132; www.cotrasangil.com; Carrera 6 No 5-70) on the main plaza. There are 10 buses to Guane (COP$2300, 15 minutes) between 5:30am and 5:45pm.

Guane

A sleepy town that feels stuck in another era, Guane is a decidedly pretty place for a stroll. It has a handsome main square featuring a fine rural church, the **Santa Lucía Iglesia**, built in 1720. Check out the fossils in the rocks lining the plaza in front of the church.

There's a great lookout point with lovely views of the Río Suárez valley on the western edge of town. To find it, cross the plaza from the church and take Calle 9 to the left.

The unique **Museum of Paleontology & Archaeology** (Carrera 6 No 7-24; COP$3000; 8am-noon & 2-6pm) has a collection of more than 10,000 fossils, a 700-year-old mummy, a few conehead skulls, Guane artifacts and religious art. The curator locks the front door and gives a personal tour (in Spanish) whenever someone shows up, so just hang tight.

Set in a renovated colonial home that was once a stopover for mule drivers traveling around the country, Guane's best hotel, **Casa Misiá Custodia** (316-566-3187; misiacustodiahotelboutique@gmail.com; Carrera 5 No 7-21; s/d from COP$150,000/180,000;), offers plenty of rest at a good price. In addition to the elegant and spacious rooms, there's an open-air restaurant area and a small pool and Jacuzzi in the rear courtyard.

During daylight hours, most travelers opt to hike to Guane from Barichara and catch a bus back. Don't forget water, sunscreen and proper footwear.

Buses to Barichara (COP$2200, 20 minutes) and on to San Gil (COP$7000, one hour) depart from Guane's plaza 10 times daily between 6am and 6:15pm.

Cañon del Chicamocha

Halfway between San Gil and Bucaramanga is the spectacular canyon of Río Chicamocha, an arid landscape of majestic mountains standing guard over the cappuccino-colored river way down below. The cliff-hugging road between the two cities is one of the most wonderful (and windy) drives in Santander.

Sights

The biggest attraction is the canyon itself, which is best viewed from the cable car (p108) that runs from Panachi to Mesa de Los Santos.

Parque Nacional del Chicamocha AMUSEMENT PARK
(7-639-4444; www.parquenacionaldelchicamocha.com; Km54, Vía Bucaramanga-San Gil; adult/child COP$25,000/18,000; 10am-6pm Wed-Fri, 9am-7pm Sat & Sun;) Don't be fooled by the name: Parque Nacional del Chicamocha, or 'Panachi' as it's known by locals, isn't a national park in the conventional sense. It's really a slightly tacky amusement park built atop some spectacular mountains. There are no hiking trails here, but there is a *mirador* (lookout) offering magnificent 360-degree views. The highlight of the park is the 6.3km-long, 30-minute **teleférico** (return ticket incl park entrance adult/child COP$50,000/32,000; 10:30-11am, 12:30-1pm, 2:30-3pm & 4:30-5pm Wed-Fri, 9am-6pm Sat & Sun;), which descends to the base of the canyon, then ascends to the top of the opposite rim.

Other activities include an extreme swing and a zipline. The park also houses the mildly diverting **Museum of Guane Culture** (full of pre-Colombian Guane ceramics), several restaurants, a 4D cinema, a children's playground, a forgettable ostrich farm and the strange but striking *Monumento a la Santandereanidad,* a huge multistatue sculpture (with running commentaries in Spanish and English) commemorating the revolutionary spirit of santanderians (inhabitants of Santander province).

The most recent addition is an incongruous US$6-million water park (admission including national park adult/child COP$38,000/32,000) – an interesting thing to build on the top of an arid mountain range that regularly suffers from severe drought. The park is accessed via an underground road tunnel.

Getting There & Away

Any bus between San Gil (COP$10,000, one hour) and Bucaramanga (1¾ hours, COP$12,000) will drop you off at the entrance to the park. To get back to either city, just flag a passing bus from the bus stop on the highway.

In other areas of the canyon along the main highway there are few safe places to disembark: there's no footpath and there are sheer drops on the side of the road.

The paragliding site is just off the main highway south of the park, but the companies include private transportation with flight purchases.

Bucaramanga

7 / POP 528,500 / ELEV 960M

Dubbed 'The City of Parks,' Santander's capital has some fine green spaces and is a suitable spot to recharge your batteries. It comes to life at night, when dozens of clubs, hundreds of bars and the students of 10 universities don their party hats.

Buca, as it's known to locals, is one of Colombia's major cities, with a greater-metropolitan population of about a million; it's packed with skyscrapers and surrounded by mountains. While it may not be the most interesting city in the country, it's not overrun with visitors and is a pleasant place to get a taste of the region's culture.

The city was founded in 1622 and developed around what is today the Parque García Rovira, but most of its colonial architecture is long gone. Over the centuries the city center moved east, and today Parque Santander is Bucaramanga's heart. Further east are newer, posh neighborhoods with hotels and nightspots.

Sights & Activities

Jardin Botánico Eloy Valenzuela GARDENS
(☎7-648-0729; Av Bucarica, Floridablanca; COP$5000; ⏰8am-4:30pm) Located a short walk from the park in Floridablanca, this lush botanic garden beside a pretty stream is a good place to take a break from the city, although you can still hear the frenzied traffic in the distance. In addition to wonderful trees covered with drooping moss, it has two small lakes and a population of turtles.

Admission includes the services of a guide, but you're also free to explore on your own.

Museo Casa de Bolívar MUSEUM
(☎7-630-4258; www.academiadehistoriadesantander.org; Calle 37 No 12-15; COP$2000; ⏰8am-noon & 2-6pm Mon-Fri, 8am-noon Sat) Another piece in the historical jigsaw of Simón Bolívar's life (Colombia is full of them), this slightly musty museum is housed in a colonial mansion where the *libertador* stayed for two months in 1828. One room is dedicated to Bolívar and his exploits, while the rest of the suites tell the story of Santander province and the Guane people who once inhabited it. Take your time to peruse archaeological exhibits, weapons, yellowed documents, faded paintings, and frighteningly real mummies.

The house – if you're able to see past the unsightly temporary tin roof – has a mossy, dusty elegance and is anchored by a proud bust of Bolívar guarded by several flags in the central patio.

Colombia Paragliding PARAGLIDING
(☎312-432-6266; www.colombiaparagliding.com; Km2 Via Mesa Ruitoque; 15/30min tandem rides COP$80,000/150,000) Try Bucaramanga's most popular sport on a tandem ride, or go all out and become an internationally licensed paragliding pilot: 12-day courses including lodging begin at COP$3,400,000. Rides and courses are held atop the Ruitoque mesa, Buca's paragliding hub.

Sleeping & Eating

Kasa Guane Bucaramanga HOSTEL $
(☎7-657-6960; www.kasaguane.com; Calle 11 No 26-50, Barrio Universidad; dm COP$35,000, s/d from COP$65,000/75,000; @ 📶) Bucaramanga's best hostel has bright rooms with Guane-themed murals, cable TV and hot-water bathrooms alongside cheery dorms. Management is great for information and organizing all kinds of guest activities, including paragliding, but the real star here is the ample rooftop bar, which is a good place to hang out with locals.

All the dorms have only four beds and each has its own bathroom; there are colorfully painted doubles, too. Ask about the hostel's Goals for Peace project, which works with disadvantaged children through football. The location isn't super-duper for bars and restaurants, but it's right next to a Metrolínea (p112) terminal, so getting around is a breeze.

Nest HOSTEL $$
(☎7-678-2722; www.thenesthostel.com; Km2 Vía Mesa Ruitoque; dm COP$40,000, s/d from COP$60,000/90,000; @ 📶 🏊) This fly-site hostel is perched on a hilltop with amazing views of the city; it's next to one of Bucaramanga's best paragliding launch pads, 20 minutes' drive from downtown. The majority of guests are paragliding students (p109), but it's also a good choice for anyone seeking peace and quiet.

Rates include a good breakfast, and there's a wonderful kitchen for guests, plus a small pool. It's located next to the Aguilas Parapenting complex – look for the bird's-nest sculpture above the brown gate. You can get here by suburban bus from the Papi Quiero Piña bus stop. A taxi from Bucaramanga will run around COP$20,000.

Hotel Tamarindo HOTEL $$
(☎7-643-6502; www.hoteltamarindobucaramanga.com; Carrera 34 No 46-104; s/d/tr COP$130,000/160,000/190,000; ❄ 📶) A small welcoming hotel in a quiet street next to the nightlife district, the Tamarindo has comfortable rooms set around a leafy courtyard and far more character than many of the business-orientated accommodations nearby.

Bucaramanga

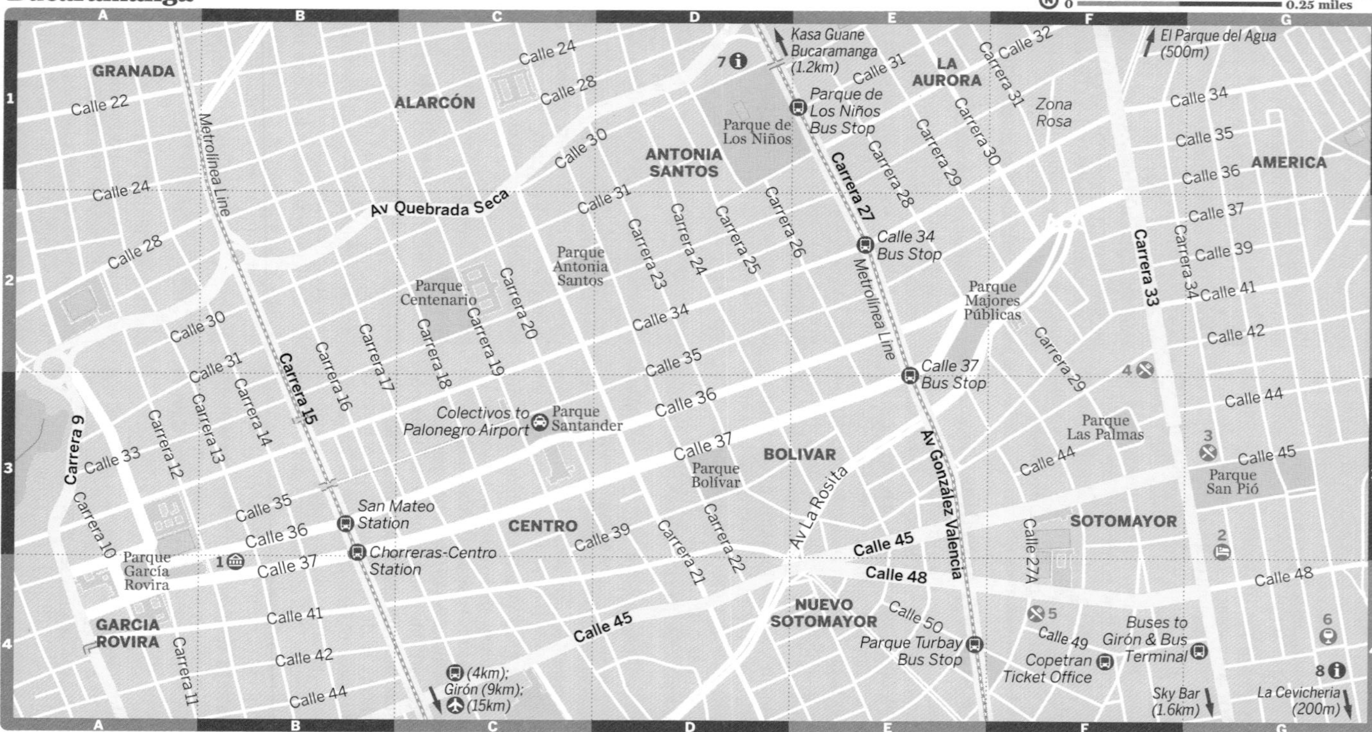

Bucaramanga

Sights
1 Museo Casa de Bolívar B4

Sleeping
2 Hotel Tamarindo G3

Eating
4 Mercagán F2
3 Mercagán G3
5 Penelope Casa Gastronómica............ F4
SazonArt .... (see 5)

Drinking & Nightlife
6 Vintrash G4

Information
7 Oficina de Turismo............................... D1
8 Punto Información Turística............... G4

SazonArt COLOMBIAN $
(cnr Calle 48 & Carrera 27A; set meals COP$8500-12,000; 7am-2pm Tue-Sat, 8am-3pm Sun & Mon) One of the better set-meal spots you'll come across in Santander, this very popular, very clean corner restaurant dishes out a few choices daily, conveniently written in Spanish on the board to help those along who can read better than they can *hablar.*

★**Penelope Casa Gastronómica** INTERNATIONAL $$
(7-643-1235; Carrera 27A No 48-15; mains COP$20,000-35,000; 11:30am-10:30pm) A diverse selection of gourmet plates from faraway lands awaits at this small but seriously hip restaurant run by talented young chefs. Among the options are naan bread topped with lamb and baked vegetables, *causa limena* (savory Peruvian potato cakes), and chicken tikka served with almond rice and chickpeas. All plates are spectacularly presented and combine many subtle flavors.

Many of the dishes use organic produce trucked in from Villa de Leyva. Be sure to try the homemade fruit sodas. Reservations highly recommended.

★**Mercagán** STEAK $$
(7-632-4949; www.mercaganparrilla.com; Carrera 33 No 42-12; steak COP$21,500-47,500; 11:30am-11pm Mon & Thu-Sat, to 3pm Tue & Wed, to 4pm Sun) Often touted as serving the best steak in the whole of Colombia, this traditional *parrilla* (grilled-meat restaurant) run by a team of brothers is all it's cracked up to be. Perfect slabs of meat from the brothers' own farm come in 200g, 300g or 400g (good luck!) sizes, served on sizzling iron plates.

It's all about the *lomo finito* (tenderloin). Don't let them butterfly it – you want it *en bloque!* Another location at nearby **Parque San Pío** (7-643-5630; www.mercaganparrilla.com; Carrera 34 No 44-84; steak COP$21,500-47,500; 11:30am-11pm Tue, Wed & Fri, to 3pm Mon & Thu, to 10pm Sun) should be open on the nights this one is closed.

La Cevicheria SEAFOOD $$
(7-647-4739; www.lacevicheria.co; Carrera 37 No 52-17; ceviche COP$19,500; noon-10pm Mon-Thu, to 11pm Fri & Sat, 6-10pm Sun;) Colorful, cute and happening, this build-your-own ceviche and salad spot is a great escape from meat, rice and yuca. There are six predetermined choices, which is the way to go to avoid a head explosion laboring over the perfect combination. It's not gourmet but it's tasty and fast. There's also sushi and great house-concocted juices, teas and smoothies.

Drinking & Nightlife

La vida nocturna (the nightlife scene) attracts clubbers from around the region. The area between Calles 48 and 49 running from Carreras 34 to 39 is a sure bet for happening options. For more traditional choices (salsa, vallenato and merengue), head to between Calle 34 and 36 around Carrera 32.

★**Vintrash** BAR
(Calle 49 No 35A-36; cover Fri & Sat COP$10,000; 4-11pm Mon-Wed, to midnight Thu, to 3am Fri & Sat;) Among vintage oil barrels, hanging bicycles and a wisp of street cred, this bar sucks in the indie cool kids and those drawn to them for great music and alternative attitude. Electronica is the main sound, decent food plates are served and dancing is de rigueur. Entry is for those 21 and over.

Sky Bar BAR
(cnr Transversal Oriental & Calle 93, 18th fl; cocktails COP$18,000-20,000; 9:30am-10:30pm Sun-Thu, to 11:30pm Fri & Sat) Bucaramanga's trendiest bar is on the 18th floor of the new Holiday Inn (never thought we'd write *that!*). It's an open-air affair decked in white with stupendous city views. Definitely a nice spot for a drink.

Information

There's no shortage of ATMs; many are clustered near Parque Santander along Calle 35, and in Sotomayor on Carrera 29.

Bancolombia (Carrera 18 No 34-28; 24hr)
BBVA (cnr Carrera 19 & Calle 36; 24hr)

DON'T MISS

GIRÓN

The cobbled streets, horse carts and lazy atmosphere of whitewashed San Juan de Girón are a world away in time, but just 9km from bustling Bucaramanga. The pleasant town was founded in 1631 on the banks of the Río de Oro. In 1963 it was declared a national monument. Today it's a magnet for artists and day-trippers, anxious to escape the city but in exchange for an increase in temperature – Girón sits in a breezeless hole in the valley and bakes most of the year.

Stroll Girón's narrow cobblestone streets, looking at whitewashed houses, shaded patios, small stone bridges and the waterfront *malecón* (promenade). The **Catedral del Señor de los Milagros** on Parque Principal (the main plaza) was begun in 1646 but not completed until 1876. Don't miss the pleasant plazas, **Plazuela Peralta** and **Plazuela de las Nieves**, which features a charming village church, the 18th-century **Capilla de las Nieves**.

There are frequent city buses from Bucaramanga (COP$2000) to Girón. A taxi from Bucaramanga runs around COP$14,000.

Davivienda (cnr Calle 49 & Carrera 29)

Oficina de Turismo (☎7-634-1132, ext 112; www.imct.gov.co; Calle 30 No 26-117, Biblioteca Pública Gabriel Turbay, Piso 4; ⏰8am-noon & 1-5pm Mon-Fri) Main tourism office.

Getting There & Away

AIR

The **Palonegro airport** (BGA; Lebrija) is on a *meseta* (plateau) high above the city, 20km west in Lebrija. The landing here is quite breathtaking. The airport has direct flights to Bogotá, Barranquilla, Medellín, Cali and Cartagena, and international services from Panama City.

Colectivo taxis (Parque Santander; ⏰6am-6pm Mon-Sat) to the airport (COP$11,000) park off Parque Santander on Carrera 20 and leave every 15 minutes between 5am and 6pm. A taxi from the city center is a fixed COP$32,000.

Coming from San Gil, get off the bus at the Papi Quiero Piña bus stop to pick up a taxi to the airport.

BUS

Bucaramanga's **Terminal TB** (☎7-637-1000; www.terminalbucaramanga.com; Transversal Central Metropolitana) is situated southwest of the city center, midway to Girón; frequent city buses marked 'Terminal' go there from Carrera 15 (COP$2100), or take a taxi (COP$10,000).

Copetran (☎7-644-8167; www.copetran.com.co; Terminal de Transporte) is the big bus company here, serving most major destinations, such as Bogotá (COP$60,000 to COP$80,000, 10 hours), Cartagena (COP$80,000, 13 hours), Medellín (COP$95,000, eight hours), Santa Marta (COP$70,000, 12 hours), Pamplona (COP$30,000, four hours) and Cúcuta (COP$35,000, six hours). There's a convenient **ticket office** (☎7-685-1389; Calle 49 No 28-64; ⏰8am-noon & 2-6pm Mon-Sat) in the center of town.

Cootrasangil (www.cotrasangil.com; Terminal de Transporte) heads to San Gil (COP$16,000, three hours) via Parque Nacional del Chicamocha (COP$10,000, 1½ hours). It's usually quicker to pick up San Gil buses at the Papi Quiero Piña bus stop at the edge of town near Floridablanca rather than going all the way to the terminal.

Cootransunidos (☎7-637-3811; Terminal de Transporte) has hourly buses to Ocaña (COP$40,000, five hours) for onward transportation to Playa de Belén.

Buses to Girón (cnr Carrera 33 & Calle 49) leave from the corner of Carrera 33 and Calle 49.

Getting Around

Metrolínea (www.metrolinea.gov.co; per trip COP$2100; ⏰4:30am-10pm Mon-Fri, to 9pm Sat & Sun), modeled on Bogotá's TransMilenio, runs from Bucaramanga to Piedecuesta. The main lines run north–south along Carrera 15, with smaller buses running along Carrera 27 and Carrera 30 (along which they remain traditional bus stops rather than stations). Of little use yet to tourists, the system is mainly used en route to Mesa de los Santos or to get to the Papi Quiero Piña bus stop to pick up services to San Gil.

Passengers must purchase a rechargeable *tarjeta inteligente* (COP$3000) before boarding. A single ride costs COP$2100 and you can transfer between buses without charge.

Guadalupe

☎7

Just one hour off the main Bogotá–Bucaramanga highway, the sleepy agricultural town of Guadalupe has recently become something of a tourism hot spot, with busloads of Colombian visitors and a steady trickle of backpackers descending on its pretty palm-filled plaza.

The influx is due to Quebrada Las Gachas (p113), also known as the Caño Cristales of Santander, a shallow river running over reddish rocks with dozens of tiny swimming holes. But Guadalupe offers plenty of other attractions for nature lovers, including other less-visited rivers, natural pools and majestic waterfalls.

The town itself is attractive and friendly but very quiet and is unlikely to hold your attention for long once you've seen the surrounding sights.

Sights & Activities

Las Gachas RIVER

Santander's answer to Caño Cristales, Las Gachas is a clear, shallow stream that emerges from a spring in lush countryside and runs along a red stone riverbed falling into dozens of individual-sized swimming holes – or jacuzzis as locals call them – along the way. Unlike its spectacular rival in the Macarena, the red color here comes from mineral deposits on the rocks rather than algae, but it is still an impressive sight and a delightful place to relax.

Las Gachas is best early in the morning when there are few other visitors around. It's about a 45-minute walk from town along a trail that begins just past the gas station on the road to Oiba. The path is paved in stones in parts and in other areas is a bit muddy. You'll come to a couple of other streams before reaching Las Gachas – don't deviate from the path; when you reach the real deal you'll see two of the swimming holes just to your right.

Don't jump into the first two holes: they are somewhat dangerous and difficult to get out of. When walking up the river, socks work better than sandals or shoes for maximum traction – bring an extra pair.

Cascada Los Caballeros WATERFALL

The most impressive waterfall in the area, Los Caballeros is a thunderous high-volume wall of water tumbling off a spectacular 90m-high cliff in three stages. It's a one-hour drive on an unpaved road from town; the road passes very close to the falls so there's no need to hike far.

Cascada La Llanera WATERFALL

While not the tallest or highest-volume waterfall in the area, La Llanera is worth a visit for its mystical remote setting surrounded by magnificent nature. The rock face juts out into the air, making it possible to walk through the grotto behind the waterfall to the other side.

Half the fun of visiting La Llanera is getting there – it's an 8km hike through lush countryside from the trailhead, which is a 20-minute drive from town.

★ **José Navarro** HIKING

(☎311-833-0526, 311-835-1573; j.navarro151@hotmail.com) Experienced guide José Navarro

HIGH ADVENTURE IN MESA DE LOS SANTOS

On the far side of the Chicamocha canyon, the Mesa de Los Santos is a large plateau with a coolish climate and many activities that attract crowds from Bucaramanga on weekends. It offers far more to do than Chicamocha (rock climbing, hiking, waterfalls, coffee *fincas*) in a far less Disneyfied way and is a popular place to spend a relaxing day or two.

Clinging to the mountainside, views from the little **Refugio La Roca** (☎313-283-1637; www.refugiolarocacolombia.com; Km22.7 Mesa de Los Santos; r COP$150,000-200,000, without bathroom COP$60,000-80,000; @ 🛜) 🌿 hostel are predictably jaw-dropping, especially from the private rooms with open-air bathrooms that make using the restroom a postcard-worthy experience. The fiercely sustainable hostel is located next to La Mojarra, the best rock-climbing spot in the area, and climbing courses are on offer. Alexandra and Ricardo, the young couple who run the place, also offer rappelling, highline, yoga, a properly trained chef in the kitchen (mains COP$25,000 to COP$32,000) and a whole lot of homespun hospitality.

To get there from Bucaramanga, catch Metrolínea (p112) P8 or one of the private buses on Carrera 33 to Piedecuesta, from where direct **La Culona** (☎7-655-1182; Carrera 6 No 12-60, Piedecuesta) buses to Los Santos leave hourly from 6am to 7:45pm (COP$8000, 1½ hours). Ask the driver to let you off at La Mojarra/Refugio La Roca.

From San Gil, take the teleférico (p108) in Panachi. Someone from the hostel will pick you up at the *teleférico* for COP$30,000, but you must reserve in advance.

is a Guadalupe native who helped put the town on the map for backpackers thanks to his energy and enthusiasm. A trip with José combines nature and adventure; he'll show you the best swimming holes and the most slippery rocks to slide down as well as the best places just to enjoy the view.

He also rents rooms (per person COP$20,000 to COP$25,000) in a couple of unsigned houses around town and works with other homeowners when things fill up.

Sleeping & Eating

During the day there are a few restaurants serving *comida corriente* but come nightfall eating options are drastically reduced. You may be able to get a full meal if you're prepared to eat early, otherwise you'll be tucking into fast food.

Hotel Colonial HOTEL $
(313-394-4335; r per person COP$25,000;) The best hotel in town is far from a luxurious affair but is clean and comfortable. It has small, neat rooms with high wooden ceilings, flat-screen TVs and private bathrooms. Meals can be prepared with advance notice.

Information

Banco Agrario (Parque Principal) Only ATM in town.

Getting There & Away

Guadalupe is just 24km off the main Bogotá–Bucaramanga highway from the turnoff at the town of Oiba. Pickups (COP$7000, one hour) run every hour or two between the two towns from 6am to 7pm.

Coming from Bucaramanga there are a couple of direct bus services. Omega (COP$30,000, 4½ hours) leaves the terminal at 12:15pm and passes San Gil around 3pm, while Cotrasaravita (COP$28,000, 4½ hours) departs at 1:30pm passing San Gil around 4pm. Direct services from Guadalupe to San Gil and Bucaramanga leave from the main plaza at 4am and 6am.

From Bogotá, Omega runs a direct bus at 10:30pm (COP$50,000, eight hours); alternatively take any Bucaramanga-bound bus and change at Oiba.

NORTE DE SANTANDER

Norte de Santander is where the Cordillera Oriental meets the hot, lowland plains that stretch into neighboring Venezuela. The scenic road from Bucaramanga climbs to 3300m at the provincial border town of Berlin before it begins its rapid descent toward Venezuela; it calls at pleasant Pamplona along the way before arriving at the departmental capital and largest city of Cúcuta, nestled right up against the Venezuelan border. Nearly 300km northeast, tiny Playa de Belén stands out as the department's most picturesque moment.

Pamplona

7 / POP 58,200 / ELEV 2290M

Spectacularly set in the deep Valle del Espíritu Santo in the Cordillera Oriental, colonial-era Pamplona, founded by Pedro de Orsúa and Ortún Velasco in 1549, is a delightful town of old churches, narrow streets and bustling commerce. With an average temperature of just 16°C, this university town is not a major destination in its own right, but is a welcome respite from the heat of nearby Bucaramanga and Cúcuta, and a nice stopover en route to or from Venezuela. Unfortunately, an 1875 earthquake wiped out a good part of the town. Today, the inviting plaza is a mix of reconstructed colonial and modern architecture and there's a surprising number of trendy cafes, bars and restaurants catering to the young population.

Sights

Pamplona has quite a collection of museums and almost all are set in restored colonial houses. There are some 10 old churches and chapels in town, reflecting Pamplona's religious status in colonial days, though not many have retained their splendor.

Museo de Arte Moderno Ramírez Villamizar MUSEUM
(Calle 5 No 5-75; COP$1000; 9am-noon & 2-5pm Tue-Sat, 9am-4pm Sun) In a 450-year-old mansion, this museum has about 40 works by Eduardo Ramírez Villamizar, one of Colombia's most outstanding artists, born in Pamplona in 1923. The collection gives an insight into his artistic development from expressionist painting of the 1940s to geometric abstract sculpture in recent decades.

Casa Colonial MUSEUM
(Calle 6 No 2-56; 8am-noon & 2-6pm Mon-Fri) FREE One of the oldest buildings in town, Casa Colonial dates from the early Spanish days. The collection includes some pre-Columbian pottery, colonial sacred art,

artifacts of several local indigenous communities including the Motilones and U'wa, plus antiques.

Casa de las Cajas Reales NOTABLE BUILDING
(cnr Carrera 5 & Calle 4; ⏲8am-6pm Mon-Sat) One of Pamplona's finest colonial mansions, La Casa de las Cajas Reales is currently occupied by a college, but visitors can ask the guard for permission to look around.

Sleeping & Eating

El Solar HOTEL $$
(☎7-568-2010; Calle 5 No 8-10; r per person from COP$50,000-65,000; 📶) A well-run hotel in a big colonial house offering fantastic value. The cheaper bottom-floor rooms here are simpler; up the creaky staircase, the more expensive 2nd floor has extremely spacious modern rooms with big kitchens and small balconies overlooking the street.

El Solar has an excellent bar-restaurant that is warmed by a cozy, hanging fire pit at night. It has the town's most popular *menú del dia* for COP$10,000 – get there before 1pm or forget it!

1549 Hostal GUESTHOUSE $$
(☎7-568-0451; www.1549hostal.com; Calle 8B No 5-84; s/d incl breakfast COP$80,000/130,000; @📶) One of Pamplona's most discerning options, this friendly 10-room boutique guesthouse is set in a colonial home on a pleasant side street with a good, spacious bar-restaurant in the rear courtyard. Some rooms are a tad small, but character-driven touches like local art, creative bric-a-brac, candles and bathrobes give it a leg up in both design and intimacy.

The downside is the electric showers. Staff lay it on extra thick for foreigners.

London Coffee CAFE $
(cnr Carrera 6 & Calle 8B; coffee COP$2000-7000, cocktails COP$15,000; ⏲1:30-11:30pm Sun-Thu, to 1am Sat; 📶) The town's best cafe, a small and trendy little number with good espresso, cocktails and imported beers, alongside sweet and savory waffles, tapas and a gourmet *michelada* (beer served with salt and lemon juice) menu. The drinks are good but the food and service are hit-and-miss.

Piero's ITALIAN $$
(Carrera 5 No 8B-67; pizza COP$15,000-46,000, pasta COP$11,000-20,000; ⏲5-11:30pm Mon-Sat, noon-3pm & 5-11:30pm Sun) Who knows how an actual Italian ended up here, but he did, and now there is good Italian food to show for it. Oddly, though, the classics are missing (where is the pizza margarita?), but what's here, somewhat curbed for Colombian tastes, is solid. The pick of the menu are the tasty pastas.

There is also pizza by the slice and sweets and fresh baked goods at the attached Caffè Romaní and, if you're still peckish, a gelato counter around the corner.

VENEZUELA BORDER

We do not recommend traveling to Venezuela at present. Most government-sanctioned travel advice is to avoid visiting the country due to civil unrest and violence. The border region with Colombia is particularly dangerous, and should be avoided.

Information

ATMs cluster in and around Parque Agueda Gallardo.

Bancolombia (Calle 7 No 5-70)

Davivienda (Calle 6 No 6-70)

Servibanca (Calle 5 No 5-23)

4-72 (Calle 8 No 5-33; ⏲8am-noon & 1-6pm Mon-Fri, 9am-noon Sat) Post office.

Navegar (Carrera 7 No 7-42; per hour COP$1000; ⏲1-7pm) Internet cafe in the center.

Punto Informacíon Turística (cnr Calle 5 & Carrera 6; ⏲8am-noon & 2-5pm Mon-Fri)

Getting There & Away

Pamplona's **bus terminal** (Terminal de Transporte) is just 750m east of the main square.

Pamplona is on the Bucaramanga–Cúcuta route. **Cotranal** (☎7-568-2421; Terminal de Transporte) goes to Cúcuta (COP$17,000, two hours) every 30 minutes. There are regular Bucaramanga buses (COP$25,000, four hours). There are several direct buses per day to Bogotá (COP$65,000, 14 hours) as well as the Caribbean coast. For Ocaña, for onward travel to Playa de Belén, switch in Cúcuta, where Cootraunidos buses depart every 30 minutes for Ocaña (COP$35,000, five hours).

Right-hand-side bus windows afford dramatic views along the spectacular road from Bucaramanga to Pamplona. Passengers prone to motion or altitude sickness should consider taking motion-sickness medication. And bring a sweater.

Playa de Belén

☎7 / POP 8559 / ELEV 1450M

The tiny color-coordinated patrimonial pueblo of Playa de Belén evokes a perfectly chiseled chin, dramatically carved out of an otherworldly landscape created by eroded rock formations in the far north of Norte de Santander. The gorgeous and sleepy village saddles right up against Área Natural Única Los Estoraques (p116), one of Colombia's smallest protected areas, and everything in the village – the architecture, the streets, the sidewalks – is precision-planned, right down to the carefully placed potted wall plants that pepper the outside of the buildings around town.

Playa de Belén is not a Colombian secret, but very few foreigners make it this far north in Norte de Santander. If you go, you'll find a friendly village unaffected by international tourism.

Sights

Área Natural Única Los Estoraques NATIONAL PARK
(COP$2000; ⏲7am-6:30pm) This 6-sq-km protected area, one of Colombia's smallest, is an otherworldly delight of eroded and weathered brownstone rock formations sprouting skyward – columns, pedestals and caves – that have formed over time due to rainfall and tectonic shifts. If you use your imagination, it's vaguely reminiscent of Cappadocia (without all the folks living in fairy chimneys). The park is 350m north of where the pavement ends on Carrera 3.

At present the park is the subject of a dispute between the government and the local landowners and, if you ask the authorities, it is technically closed. However, you can still go in – one of the landowners runs a small kiosk by the access point and charges a small admission fee.

Guides are not obligatory but a few locals hang around working for tips only and can guide you on a walk through the area. Budget on paying around COP$20,000 per group for a short circuit and COP$30,000 for a longer tour. Beware of the snakes!

Mirador Santa Cruz VIEWPOINT
For a bird's-eye view of the pueblo and surrounding rock formations, head up to this lookout point above town, a straight 15-minute ascent east on Calle 4.

Activities

Yaragua ADVENTURE SPORTS
(☎314-315-4991; Carrera 3 No 3-58; zipline COP$20,000; ⏲7am-6pm) Right on the edge of the town center, this little adventure park has a 400m zipline and a mirador with views of Los Estoraques (p116). Also rents some well-equipped cabañas (s/d COP$60,000/100,000).

Sleeping & Eating

Casa Real GUESTHOUSE $
(☎318-278-4486; karo27_03@yahoo.es; Vereda Rosa Blanca; r per person with meals COP$50,000) This small *finca* (farm) offers neat and comfortable accommodations with plenty of space and fresh air for relaxing. It's a trade-off – you're outside the idyllic pueblo, but there's something to be said for the terrace strung with hammocks and guest kitchen, both of which have views across to Los Estoraques (p116) that are especially evocative in the late afternoon light.

Rations for meals are often plucked from the farm's organic garden. It's a 700m walk from town north along Carrera 1.

Posada Marmacrisli GUESTHOUSE $
(☎322-310-3435, 313-369-5123; www.posadaenlaplaya.com; Calle Central No 5-65; r COP$70,000; 📶) The coziest spot in the village, with six super-comfortable rooms decked out in dark hardwood furniture surrounding a tiny brick courtyard. The stylish bathrooms feature real gas hot water. Breakfast is an additional COP$8000.

El Portal COLOMBIAN $
(Carrera 1; mains COP$12,000; ⏲10am-9pm) The best restaurant in town prepares both fast food and more-filling typical Colombian plates in an open-air dining room under a big thatched roof. It's a five-minute walk from the plaza heading north out of town.

Information

The nearest ATM is in Ocaña.

Punto Información Turística (☎310-572-2012; www.laplayadebelen-nortedesantander.gov.co; cnr Carrera 1 & Calle 3; ⏲9am-noon & 3-5pm Thu-Mon) Helpful and well-stocked tourism office.

Telecom (cnr Carrera 2 & Calle 4; per hour COP$1500; ⏲8am-9pm) Internet right on the park.

Getting There & Away

Cootrans Hacaritama (☎314-215-5316; Carrera 1 No 5-01) has four set van departures daily to Ocaña (COP$6000, 45 minutes) from Playa de Belén at 5:30am, 6am, 8am and 2:30pm, which return from Ocaña when full. Otherwise, *colectivo* taxis leave when full for the same price until around 6pm.

Coming from Cúcuta or Bucaramanga, you don't have to go all the way to Ocaña – ask the driver to drop you off at the crossroads for Playa de Belén, where moto-taxis hang about the store across the road and can take you the remaining 11km (COP$5000, 15 minutes), even with luggage.

AT A GLANCE

POPULATION
9 million

AREA
132,000 km²

BEST WATERSPORTS
Kitesurf Colombia (p128)

BEST BOOKSHOP
Ábaco (p134)

BEST SEAFOOD
Donde Chucho (p143)

WHEN TO GO

Dec & Jan
The beaches are at their best at Christmas when the humidity drops.

Feb–Apr
The dry season means that you'll rarely have your day interrupted by a downpour.

Sep & Oct
Prices are at their lowest and you'll have many places to yourself.

Parque Nacional Natural Tayrona (p148)

Caribbean Coast

Sun soaked and rich in culture, Colombia's dramatic Caribbean coastline is its dazzling crown, capping the country with myriad ecosystems, from the dense jungles of the Darién Gap on the border with Panama to the hauntingly atmospheric desert of La Guajira near Venezuela.

The jewel along the coast is the colonial city of Cartagena, its beauty and romance unrivaled anywhere in Colombia despite the enormous number of visitors it attracts. A yet-undiscovered version can be enjoyed by journeying inland to find gorgeously isolated Mompós, a sleepy colonial hamlet lost in the jungle whose star is truly in the ascendant. Other attractions are more natural: the PNN Tayrona, a stretch of perfect beach and virgin rainforest, and the thrilling and arduous Ciudad Perdida (Lost City) trek, which will satisfy adventurers keen to discover the remnants of an ancient civilization.

INCLUDES

Cartagena 122
Santa Marta 139
Minca 144
Taganga 147
Parque Nacional Natural Tayrona 148
Palomino 150
Ciudad Perdida 152
Cabo de la Vela 157
Mompós 160
Tolú 163
Capurganá & Sapzurro 165

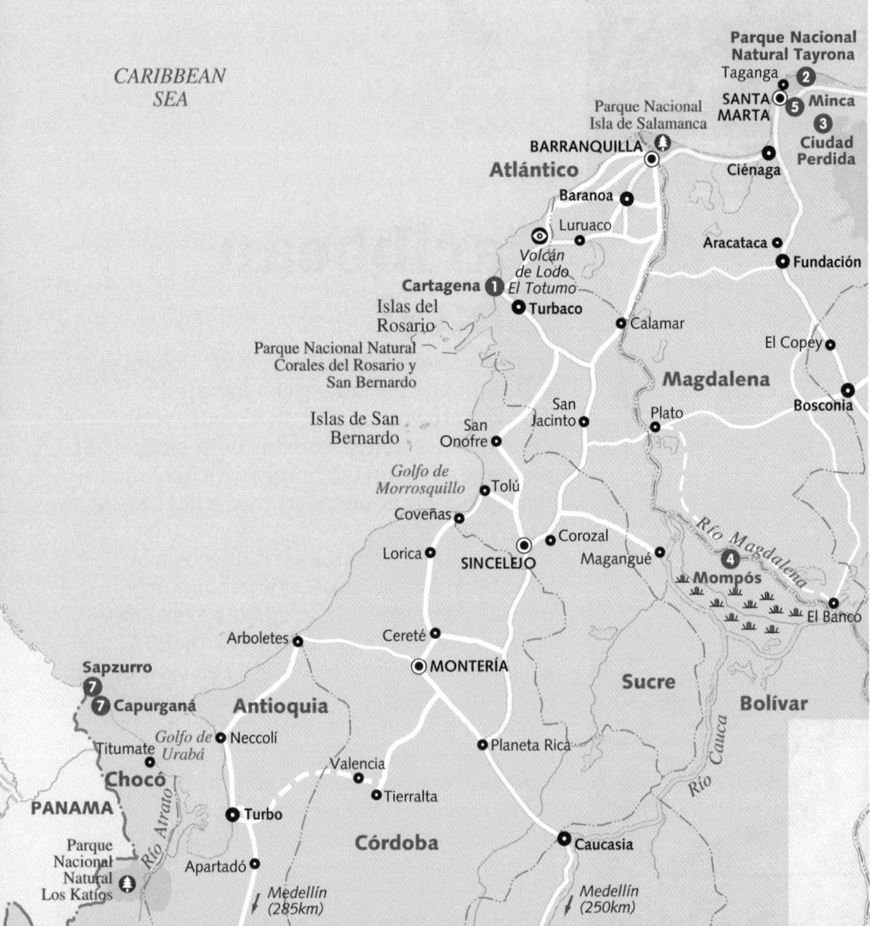

Caribbean Coast Highlights

1 Cartagena (p122) Soaking up the history as you stroll the colorful colonial streets of this unforgettable Spanish-fortress city.

2 Parque Nacional Natural (PNN) Tayrona (p148) Beach-hopping through the magical coves of this coastal national park.

3 Ciudad Perdida (p152) Trekking through thick Colombian jungle to the mysterious pre-Columbian capital of the Tayrona people.

4 Mompós (p160) Discovering the region's most charming colonial town and – as word gets out – site of a tourism boom.

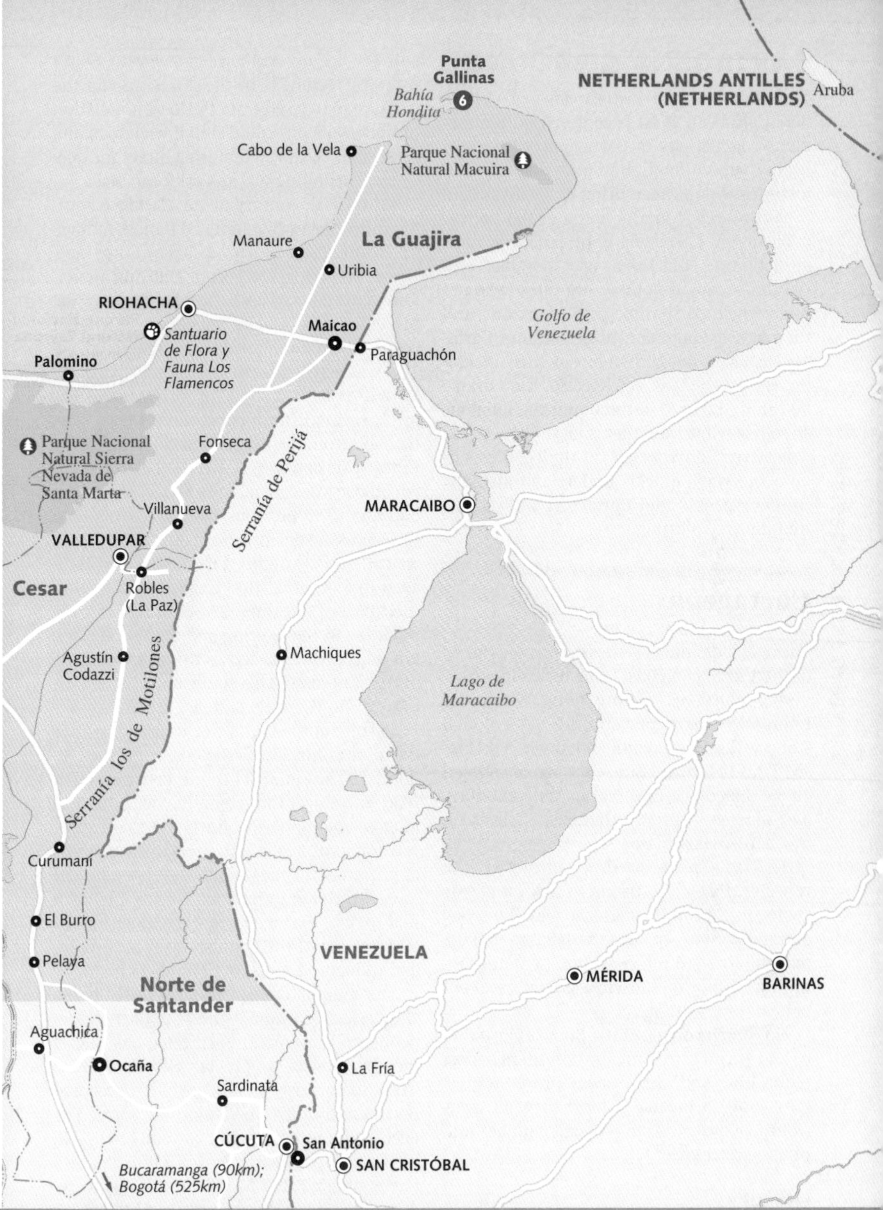

5 **Minca** (p144) Escaping the heat of the coast in this wonderful mountain refuge and chilled-out backpacker haunt.

6 **Punta Gallinas** (p159) Traversing the feral seaside desertscape of La Guajira Peninsula to the stunning sand-dune beaches of its northern tip.

7 **Capurganá and Sapzurro** (p165) Straddling the Colombia–Panama border in the tranquil villages and excellent beaches around the Darién Gap.

CARTAGENA & AROUND

This dramatic and historic slice of Colombia's Caribbean coast is centered on the fabulous colonial city of Cartagena, whose raw beauty, superb food, thumping nightlife and historical significance bring a steady stream of visitors year-round. Capital of the Bolívar department, Cartagena is by far the biggest attraction in this area of Colombia, and rightly so: few in number are those who are underwhelmed by this gritty, romantic and thoroughly Colombian place. Around Cartagena is a slew of worthwhile day trips, including the lovely Islas del Rosario, the curious Volcán de Lodo El Totumo and the fabulous stretch of white sand that is Playa Blanca. You won't ever find yourself off the beaten path here, but you'll quickly understand just why so many people find Cartagena and its surroundings so alluring.

Cartagena

☎5 / POP 971,500 / ELEV 2M

Cartagena de Indias is the undisputed queen of the Caribbean coast, a historic city of superbly preserved beauty lying within an impressive 13km of centuries-old colonial stone walls. Cartagena's Old Town is a Unesco World Heritage Site – a maze of cobbled alleys, balconies covered in bougainvillea, and massive churches that cast their shadows across leafy plazas.

This is a place to drop all sightseeing routines. Instead of trying to tick off all the sights, just stroll through the Old Town day and night. Soak up the sensual atmosphere, pausing to ward off the brutal heat and humidity in one of the city's many excellent bars and restaurants.

Holding its own against Brazil's Ouro Preto and Peru's Cuzco for the continent's most enthralling and impressively preserved historic city, Cartagena is hard to walk away from – it seizes you in its aged clutches and refuses to let go.

History

Cartagena was founded in 1533 by Pedro de Heredia on the site of the Carib settlement of Calamari. It quickly grew into a rich town, but in 1552 an extensive fire destroyed a large number of its wooden buildings. Since that time, only stone, brick and tile have been permitted as building materials.

Within a short time the town grew into the main Spanish port on the Caribbean coast and the major northern gateway to South America. It came to be the storehouse for the treasure plundered from the local population until the galleons could ship it back to Spain. As such, it became a tempting target for buccaneers operating on the Caribbean Sea.

In the 16th century alone, Cartagena suffered five sieges by pirates, the most famous (or infamous) of which was led by Sir Francis Drake. He sacked the port in 1586 and 'mercifully' agreed not to level the town once he was presented with a huge ransom of 10 million pesos, which he shipped back to England.

It was in response to pirate attacks that the Spaniards built a series of forts around the town, saving it from subsequent sieges, particularly from the biggest attack of all, led by Edward Vernon in 1741. Blas de Lezo, a Spanish officer who had already lost an arm, a leg and an eye in previous battles, commanded the successful defense. With only 2500 poorly trained and ill-equipped men, don Blas managed to fend off 25,000 English soldiers and their fleet of 186 ships. The Spaniard lost his other leg in the fighting and died soon after, but he is now regarded as the savior of Cartagena. You can see his statue outside the Castillo de San Felipe de Barajas.

In spite of the high price it had to pay for the pirate attacks, Cartagena continued to flourish. The Canal del Dique, constructed in 1650 to connect Cartagena Bay with the Río Magdalena, made the town the main gateway for ships heading to ports upriver, and a large part of the merchandise shipped inland passed through Cartagena. During the colonial period, Cartagena was the most important bastion of the Spanish overseas empire and influenced much of Colombia's history.

The indomitable spirit of the inhabitants was rekindled again at the time of the independence movement. Cartagena was one of the first towns to proclaim independence from Spain, early in 1810, which prompted Bogotá and other cities to do the same. The declaration was signed on November 11, 1811, but the city paid dearly for it. In 1815, Spanish forces under Pablo Morillo were sent to reconquer and 'pacify' the town, and they took it after a four-month siege. More than 6000 inhabitants died of starvation and disease.

In August 1819, Simón Bolívar's troops defeated the Spaniards at Boyacá, bringing freedom to Bogotá. However, Cartagena had to wait until October 1821 for liberation, when the patriot forces eventually took the city by sea. It was Bolívar who gave Cartagena its name La Heroica (the Heroic City).

Cartagena began to recover and was once again an important trading and shipping center. The city's prosperity attracted foreign immigrants, and many Jews, Italians, French, Turks, Lebanese and Syrians settled here. Today their descendants own many businesses, including hotels and restaurants.

Sights

Old Town

Without a doubt, Cartagena's old city is its principal attraction, particularly the inner walled town consisting of the historical districts of El Centro and San Diego. El Centro in the west was traditionally home to the upper classes, and San Diego in the northeast was previously occupied by the middle classes. Both sections of the Old Town are packed with perfectly preserved colonial churches, monasteries, plazas, palaces and mansions, with balconies and shady patios that overflow with bright flowers.

With its modest architecture, the outer walled town of Getsemaní is less obviously impressive, but as it's far more residential and less sanitized, it offers plenty of atmosphere and is well worth exploring. In recent years it has become a backpacker hub, and gentrification has come astonishingly quickly – the area is full of trendy restaurants, packed cocktail bars and salsa clubs, and almost as many boutique hotels as the inner walled town. A beautiful walkway alongside the **Muelle Turístico de los Pegasos** links Getsemaní with the Old Town.

The Old Town is surrounded by **Las Murallas**, the thick walls built as protection against enemies. Construction began towards the end of the 16th century, after a siege by Francis Drake; until that time Cartagena was almost completely unprotected. The project took two centuries to complete due to repeated damage from storms and pirate attacks. It was finally finished in 1796, just 25 years before the Spaniards were eventually expelled.

Palacio de la Inquisición MUSEUM
(Plaza de Bolívar; adult/child COP$20,000/17,000; 9am-6pm Mon-Sat, 10am-4pm Sun) The Palace of the Inquisition may today be one of the finest buildings in the city, but in the past it housed the notoriously grisly Inquisition, whose bloody task it was to stamp out heresy in colonial Cartagena. The palace is now a museum, displaying the inquisitors' instruments of torture, some of which are quite horrific. The museum also houses pre-Columbian pottery and plots a historical trajectory of the city using armaments, paintings, furniture and even church bells.

Although the site was the seat of the Punishment Tribunal of the Holy Office from 1610, the palace wasn't completed until 1776. It's a good example of late-colonial architecture, noted particularly for its baroque stone gateway topped by the Spanish coat of arms, and the long balconies on the facade.

On the side wall, just around the corner from the entrance, you'll find a small window with a cross on top. Heretics were denounced here, and the Holy Office would then instigate proceedings. The principal 'crimes' were magic, witchcraft and blasphemy. When culprits were found guilty, they were sentenced to death in a public auto-da-fé (execution of heretics, often by burning them at the stake). Five autos-da-fé took place during the Inquisition until independence in 1821. About 800 folk were condemned to death and executed. The Inquisition did not judge the indigenous people.

A good model of Cartagena from the beginning of the 19th century and an interesting collection of old maps of the Nuevo Reino de Granada from various periods are also on display. There are some English translations, but guides (COP$40,000 in English) are available for a fuller experience. Go in a group if you can: these prices cover up to five people.

Convento & Iglesia de San Pedro Claver MUSEUM
(5-664-4991; Plaza de San Pedro Claver; adult/child COP$13,000/8000; 8am-5:30pm) Founded by Jesuits in the first half of the 17th century as Convento San Ignacio de Loyola, this convent later changed its name to honor Spanish-born monk Pedro Claver (1580–1654), who lived and died here. Called the 'Apostle of the Blacks' or the 'Slave of the Slaves,' the monk spent his life ministering to enslaved people brought from Africa. A series of lucid paintings inside the building relates his life story.

The convent is a monumental three-story building surrounding a tree-filled courtyard, and much of it is open as a **museum**. Exhibits include religious art and pre-Columbian ceramics; a section devoted to contemporary Afro-Caribbean pieces includes wonderful Haitian paintings and African masks.

You can visit the cell in the convent where San Pedro Claver lived and died, and also climb a narrow staircase to the choir loft of

Cartagena Old Town

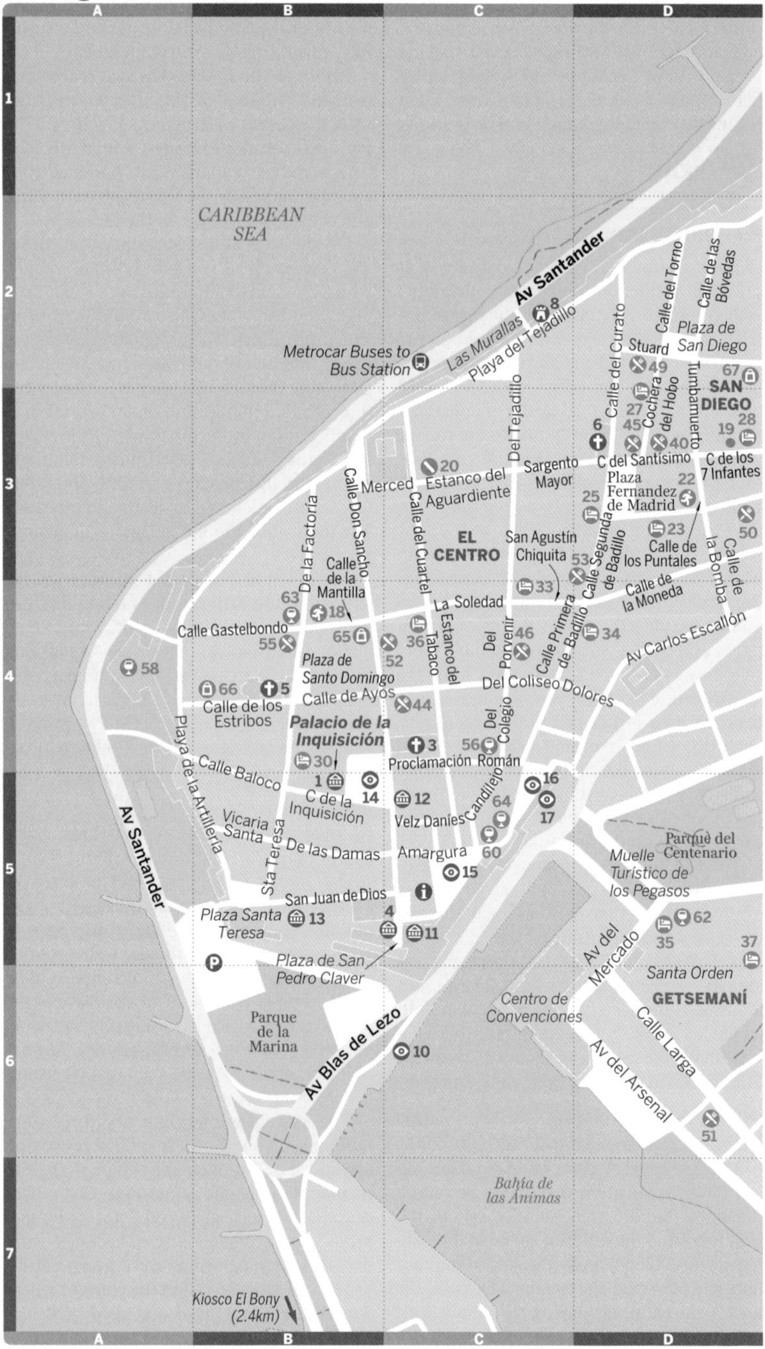

A B C D
1 2 3 4 5 6 7

CARIBBEAN SEA
Av Santander
Las Murallas
Playa del Tejadillo
8
Metrocar Buses to Bus Station
Calle del Curato
Calle del Torno
Calle de las Bóvedas
Plaza de San Diego
Stuard
49
67
SAN DIEGO
Cochera del Hobo
Tumbamuerto
27
45
40
19
28
6
Del Tejadillo
20
Merced
Estanco del Aguardiente
Sargento Mayor
C del Santísimo
C de los 7 Infantes
Plaza Fernandez de Madrid
22
25
23
50
Calle de la Factoría
Calle Don Sancho
Calle del Cuartel
EL CENTRO
San Agustín Chiquita
53
Calle Segunda de Badillo
Calle de los Puntales
Calle de la Bomba
Calle de la Mantilla
63
18
La Soledad
33
Calle de la Moneda
Calle Gastelbondo
55
65
52
36
Estanco del Tabaco
Del Porvenir
46
Calle Primera de Badillo
34
Av Carlos Escallón
58
Plaza de Santo Domingo
66
5
Calle de los Estribos
Calle de Ayos
44
Del Coliseo
Dolores
Playa de la Artillería
Palacio de la Inquisición
3
Del Colegio
56
30
Proclamación
Román
Calle Baloco
1
14
12
16
17
C de la Inquisición
Candilejo
64
Av Santander
Vicaria Santa
Velz Daníes
Sta Teresa
De las Damas
Amargura
60
15
Parque del Centenario
Muelle Turístico de los Pegasos
San Juan de Dios
4
Plaza Santa Teresa
13
11
62
35
37
Av del Mercado
Plaza de San Pedro Claver
Santa Orden
GETSEMANÍ
Centro de Convenciones
Calle Larga
Parque de la Marina
Av Blas de Lezo
10
Av del Arsenal
51
Bahía de las Animas
Kiosco El Bony (2.4km)

the adjacent church. Should you need one, guides (COP$32,000 in English for a group of up to seven) are available at the ticket office. Completed in the first half of the 18th century, the Iglesia de San Pedro Claver has an imposing stone facade, and inside there are fine stained-glass windows and a high altar made of Italian marble. The remains of San Pedro Claver are kept in a glass coffin in the altar – his skull is visible.

Plaza de Bolívar — PLAZA

Formerly the Plaza de Inquisición, this leafy and shaded plaza is surrounded by some of the city's most elegant balconied colonial buildings. It's one of Cartagena's most alluring plazas and offers wonderful respite from the Caribbean heat. A statue of the eponymous Simón Bolívar stands in the middle of the square.

Museo del Oro Zenú — MUSEUM

(Plaza de Bolívar; 9am-5pm Tue-Sat, 10am-3pm Sun) FREE This museum is like a miniature version of Bogotá's world-class gold museum, the Museo del Oro (p46). Though small, it offers a fascinating collection of the gold and pottery of the Zenú (also known as Sinú) people, who inhabited the region of the present-day departments of Bolívar, Córdoba, Sucre and northern Antioquia before the Spanish Conquest. Some pieces are exquisitely detailed.

Should you be heading to Bogotá, this gold museum offers a taste of the bigger and grander one there. It's also a superb spot to take a break from Cartagena's oppressive humidity: the air-con is refreshingly arctic.

Iglesia de Santo Domingo — CHURCH

(Plaza de Santo Domingo; 9am-7pm Tue-Sat, noon-8pm Sun) Reputedly the oldest church in the city, Santo Domingo was built in 1539 in Plaza de los Coches, but the original building succumbed to fire and the church was rebuilt in its present location in 1552. Builders gave it a particularly wide central nave and covered it with a heavy roof, but it seems they weren't too good at their calculations, as the vault began to crack afterwards.

Massive buttresses had to be added to the walls to support the structure and prevent it from collapsing. The builders also had problems with the bell tower, which is distinctly crooked.

The interior is bright if unremarkable, save for a metallic spiral staircase providing access to a mezzanine. A wood carving of Christ is set in the baroque altar at the head

Cartagena Old Town

Top Sights
1 Palacio de la Inquisición ... B5

Sights
2 Casa de Rafael Núñez ... F1
3 Catedral ... C4
4 Convento & Iglesia de San Pedro Claver ... C5
5 Iglesia de Santo Domingo ... B4
6 Iglesia de Santo Toribio de Mogrovejo ... D3
7 Las Bóvedas ... E1
8 Las Murallas ... C2
9 Monumento a la India Catalina ... F3
10 Muelle Turístico de la Bodeguita ... C6
11 Museo de Arte Moderno ... C5
12 Museo del Oro Zenú ... C5
13 Museo Naval del Caribe ... B5
14 Plaza de Bolívar ... B5
15 Plaza de la Aduana ... C5
16 Plaza de los Coches ... C5
17 Puerta del Reloj ... C5

Activities, Courses & Tours
18 Aventure Colombia ... B4
19 Centro Catalina Spanish School ... D3
20 Diving Planet ... C3
21 Nueva Lengua ... E6
22 Sico ... D3

Sleeping
23 Bantú ... D3
24 Casa Canabal ... E4
25 Casa La Fe ... D3
26 Casa Villa Colonial ... E5
27 El Genovés Hostal ... D3
28 El Viajero Cartagena ... D3
29 Friends To Be ... E5
30 Hostal Santo Domingo ... B4
31 Hostel Mamallena ... E5
32 Hotel Casa de las Palmas ... E7
33 Hotel Casa San Agustin ... C4
34 Hotel Don Pedro de Heredia ... D4
35 Hotel Monterrey ... D5
36 La Passion ... C4
37 Mama Waldy Hostel ... D5
38 Media Luna Hostel ... E5
39 San Pedro Hotel Spa ... E3

Eating
40 Agua de Mar ... D3
41 Beiyu ... E6
42 Caffé Lunático ... F5
Cevichería Chipi Chipi ... (see 40)
43 Demente ... E6
44 El Bistro ... C4
45 El Boliche ... D3
46 Espíritu Santo ... C4
47 Gastrolab Sur ... F5
48 Interno ... E2
49 La Cevichería ... D2
50 La Mulata ... D3
51 Oh Là Là ... D6
52 Pastelería Mila ... C4
53 Pezetarian ... D3
54 Restaurante Coroncoro ... E5
55 Señor Toro ... B4

Drinking & Nightlife
56 Alquímico ... C4
57 Bazurto Social Club ... E5
58 Café del Mar ... A4
59 Café Havana ... E5
60 Donde Fidel ... C5
61 León de Baviera ... E7
62 Quiebra-Canto ... D5
63 The Beer Lovers ... B4
64 Tu Candela ... C5

Shopping
65 Ábaco ... B4
66 Colombia Artesanal ... B4
67 El Arcón ... D2

of the right-hand aisle. The floor in front of the high altar and in the two aisles is paved with old tombstones dating mostly from the 19th century.

Puerta del Reloj GATE

Originally called the Boca del Puente, this was the main gateway to the inner walled town and was linked to Getsemaní by a drawbridge over the moat. The side arches of the gate, which are now open as walkways, were previously used as a chapel and armory. The republican-style tower, complete with a four-sided clock, was added in 1888.

Plaza de los Coches PLAZA

Previously known as Plaza de la Yerba, the triangular plaza just behind Puerta del Reloj was once used as a market for enslaved people. It is lined with old balconied houses with colonial arches at ground level. The arcaded walkway, known as El Portal de los Dulces, is today lined with confectionery stands selling local sweets. The statue of the city's founder, Pedro de Heredia, is in the middle of the plaza.

Plaza de la Aduana PLAZA

This is the largest and oldest square in the Old Town and was used as a parade ground. In colonial times all the important governmental and administrative buildings were here. The old Royal Customs House has been restored and is now the City Hall. A statue of Christopher Columbus stands in the center of the square.

Museo de Arte Moderno MUSEUM
(Museum of Modern Art; Plaza de San Pedro Claver; adult/child COP$8000/4000; ⌚9am-noon & 3-7pm Mon-Fri, 10am-1pm Sat, 4-9pm Sun) The Museum of Modern Art is a perfectly sized museum, housed in a beautifully converted part of the 17th-century former Royal Customs House. It presents rotating exhibitions from its own collection, including works by Alejandro Obregón, one of Colombia's most remarkable painters, who was born in Cartagena, and Enrique Grau, another local painter who left a legacy to the museum on his death. There's also a range of sculpture, abstract art and temporary exhibitions.

Museo Naval del Caribe MUSEUM
(Calle San Juan de Dios No 3-62; COP$16,000; ⌚9am-5pm) Opened in 1992 on the 500th anniversary of Columbus' arrival in the New World, the Naval Museum occupies a great colonial building, which was once a Jesuit college. It features, for the most part, a grand collection of reconstructed cityscapes and boat models from throughout the centuries, but woefully lacks much in the way of actual artifacts (although there are some nice torpedoes).

Catedral CHURCH
(Calle de los Santos de Piedra) Work on Cartagena's cathedral began in 1575, but in 1586, while still under construction, it was partly destroyed by the cannons of Francis Drake. The structure known officially as the Basilica Santa Catalina de Alejandría wasn't completed until 1612, although the distinctive terracotta dome visible all over town was added later. Further alterations were carried out in the early 20th century by Cartagena's first archbishop, who covered the church with stucco and painted it to look like marble.

Notable inside are the huge stations of the cross skillfully carved in stone on either side of the nave, and four saintly statues (of San Pedro, Pablo, Gregorio and Sebastián) that used to decorate the facade but were restored and placed inside near the main door in 2000.

Iglesia de Santo Toribio de Mogrovejo CHURCH
(Calle del Curato, San Diego; ⌚10am-10pm) Erected between 1666 and 1732, this gorgeous church received a full renovation in 2015. Its ceiling is covered with Mudejar paneling, while its pink-and-gold baroque altar is the only one of its kind in Cartagena. During Vernon's attack on the city in 1741, a cannonball was fired through a window into the church during mass, but miraculously nobody was killed. The offending cannonball is now displayed in a glass box on the left wall.

Casa de Rafael Núñez MUSEUM
(⌚9am-5pm Tue-Fri, 10am-4pm Sat & Sun) FREE This charming mansion, just outside the walls of Las Bóvedas, was the home of the former president, lawyer and poet Rafael Núñez. He wrote the words of Colombia's national anthem and was one of the authors of the constitution of 1886, which was in use (with some later changes) until 1991. The beautiful white-and-green wooden mansion is now a museum featuring some of Núñez's documents and personal possessions.

It's hard not to envy his lovely outdoor covered dining room or the huge walk-out balcony. The chapel opposite the house, known as the Ermita del Cabrero, holds his ashes.

Monumento a la India Catalina STATUE
The monument at the main entrance to the Old Town from the mainland is a tribute to the Carib people, the group that inhabited this land before the Spanish Conquest. The lovely bronze statue depicts Catalina, a beautiful Carib woman who acted as interpreter to Pedro de Heredia upon the arrival of the Spaniards. The statue was forged in 1974 by Eladio Gil, a Spanish sculptor living in Cartagena.

Spanish Forts

Cartagena's old city is a fortress in itself, yet there are several more fortifications built at strategic points outside the city, many of which are worth visiting. The most famous of these is, of course, the massive Castillo de San Felipe de Barajas, which looms over the city and is perhaps the most impressive colonial fortress in South America. Other less-known fortresses are worth visiting for history buffs, but always check the latest safety information with your hotel or a travel agency, as some remote fortresses may not be safe for you to visit alone.

★ **Castillo de San Felipe de Barajas** FORTRESS
(Av Arévalo; adult/child COP$25,000/10,500; ⌚8am-6pm) The greatest fortress ever built by the Spaniards in any of their colonies, the Castillo de San Felipe de Barajas still dominates an entire section of Cartagena's cityscape. It should definitely be the first fortress you visit. The original edifice was quite small. It was

commissioned in 1630, and construction began in 1657 on top of the 40m-high San Lázaro hill. In 1762 an extensive enlargement was undertaken, which resulted in the entire hill being covered with this powerful bastion.

It was truly impregnable and was never taken despite numerous attempts to storm it. A complex system of tunnels connected strategic points to allow provisions to be distributed and to facilitate evacuation. The tunnels were constructed so that any noise reverberated all the way along them, making it possible to hear the slightest sound of an approaching enemy's feet, and also making internal communication easy.

Some of the tunnels are lit and are open to visitors – an eerie walk not to be missed. Take an audio tour (COP$10,000 in English) or hire a guide (Spanish/English COP$15,000/20,000) if you want to learn more about the curious inventions of Antonio de Arévalo, the military engineer who directed the construction of the fortress.

The fortress is a short walk over the bridge from Getsemaní.

Convento de la Popa

Convento de la Popa CHURCH

(adult/child COP$11,000/8000; 8am-6pm) On a 150m-high hill, the highest point in Cartagena, stands this convent. The views from here are outstanding and stretch all over the city. The convent's name literally means the 'Convent of the Stern,' after the hill's similarity to a ship's back end. Founded by Augustine fathers in 1607, it was initially just a small wooden chapel, but when the hill was fortified two centuries later it was replaced by a stouter construction.

A beautiful image of La Virgen de la Candelaria, the patroness of the city, is in the convent's chapel, and there's a charming flower-filled patio. There is also a chilling statue of a speared Padre Alonso García de Paredes, a priest who was killed along with five Spanish soldiers while trying to convert indigenous peoples to Christianity.

There's a zigzagging access road leading up to the convent (no public transportation), which is located 3km outside the old city walls. It takes 30 minutes to walk to the top, but for safety reasons it's not recommended – the road skirts one of Cartagena's dicier neighborhoods. Take a cab and expect to pay up to COP$60,000. Haggle politely but insistently and you might get it for half that.

Mercado Bazurto

Mercado Bazurto MARKET

(Av Pedro de Heredia; 24hr) For adventurous souls only, Cartagena's labyrinthine central market, 4km outside the old city walls, is both dirty and enthralling – an all-out assault on the senses. If it's marketable, it's for sale here: there are endless stalls of fruit and vegetables, meat and fish, and plenty of options for grabbing a quick bite or chilled beverage. Pay close attention to your belongings and don't wear flashy jewelry. Grab a taxi (COP$7000 from the Old Town) and explore away.

Activities

Cartagena has grown into an important scuba-diving center, taking advantage of the extensive coral reefs along its coast. La Boquilla, just outside town, is also popular for kitesurfing.

Diving Planet DIVING

(310-657-4926, 320-230-1515; www.divingplanet.org; Calle Estanco del Aguardiente No 5-09; 8am-6pm Mon-Sat) This five-star PADI diving school offers two-tank dives in the Islas del Rosario, including transportation, equipment, lunch and instructors, for COP$408,000. Discounts of 10% are available if you pay in cash.

It also offers one-day mini-courses (COP$428,000) and three-day open-water courses (COP$1,578,000). Dive boats leave daily at 8am and return around 4:30pm. Book one day in advance.

Kitesurf Colombia KITESURFING

(311-410-8883; www.kitesurfcolombia.com; Carrera 9, behind Edificio Los Morros 922, Cielo Mar) This kitesurfing school is located beyond the airport, off the main road to Barranquilla. It also offers windsurfing, surfing, kayaking and other activities from its beachside premises.

Sico CYCLING

(300-339-1728; www.sicobikerental.com; Calle Puntales 37-09; 9am-10pm) This friendly outfit in the middle of the Old Town offers two-hour guided bicycle tours of the city and its surroundings. It also rents out good-quality hybrids and mountain bikes (COP$24,000 per half-day). Multilingual two-hour city tours depart at 8am and 4:30pm daily.

Tandem bikes and kids' bikes available. Locks, helmets, maps and a bottle of water also provided.

Courses

Centro Catalina Spanish School LANGUAGE
(☎310-761-2157; www.centrocatalina.com; Calle de los 7 Infantes No 9-21) This recommended Spanish school has an enviable location right in the heart of the walled city. It offers a range of courses; a one-week course with 20 hours' tuition starts at US$239 plus a US$60 enrollment fee. Accommodations can also be arranged and a whole slew of activities is available.

Nueva Lengua LANGUAGE
(☎315-8559-551, 1-813-8674; www.nuevalengua.com; Callejón Ancho No 10b-52, Getsemaní) Language courses at this casual but friendly school start for as little as US$185 per week for 20 hours of instruction. This tariff includes one hour's cooking class per week, to help you improve more than just your Spanish skills.

Festivals & Events

Hay Festival Cartagena ART
(www.hayfestival.com; ⏲Jan) The Colombian version of the acclaimed literature-and-arts festival takes place in January over a four-day period, and includes invited international luminaries giving talks and readings.

Fiesta de Nuestra Señora de la Candelaria PROCESSION
(⏲Feb 2) On the day of Cartagena's patron saint, a solemn procession is held at the Convento de la Popa during which the faithful carry lit candles. Celebrations, the so-called Novenas, begin nine days earlier, when pilgrims flock to the convent.

Sleeping

Cartagena has a huge choice of places to sleep, though you'll pay a pretty penny for anything above a hostel or a very simple midrange hotel. Catering to wealthy Colombian and US weekenders, the town's top-end accommodations have truly stratospheric rates, and there's an enormous number of beautifully restored boutique colonial options to choose from. Getsemaní, especially Calle de la Media Luna, is the main place to find budget accommodations.

El Genovés Hostal HOSTEL $
(☎5-646-0972; www.elgenoveshostal.com; Calle Cochera del Hobo No 38-27, San Diego; dm COP40,000-49,000, r from COP$160,000, all incl breakfast; ❄📶🏊) This charming, colorful place has several dorms as well as a number of private double and triple rooms with their own bathroom. The hostel surrounds a plunge pool and is topped off with a small roof terrace. There's also a full communal kitchen.

Mama Waldy Hostel HOSTEL $
(☎5-645-6805, 300-696-9970; mamawaldyhostel@gmail.com; Calle La Sierpe No 29-03, Getsemaní; incl breakfast dm with/without air-con COP$30,000/40,000, d COP$120,000; ❄📶) This popular and pleasant hostel in a converted colonial house is a great place to enjoy Cartagena from a chilled and friendly Getsemaní perch. All dorms have their own bathrooms, while private rooms are rather small and a big step up price-wise. Breakfast is included for all guests except on Sundays, when you'll need to forage up your own.

Hostel Mamallena HOSTEL $
(☎5-670-0499, 5-660-9969; www.mamallena.travel; Calle de la Media Luna No 10-47, Getsemaní; dm/d/tr/q incl breakfast COP$40,000/120,000/160,000/200,000; 📶) This clean and simple Getsemaní establishment has well looked-after rooms surrounding at prettily painted courtyard. The staff speaks English, can arrange tours and buses in Colombia and boats to San Blas and Panama. Laundry is available, lockers are backpack sized and there's cheap and decent food and drink available on site.

Friends to Be BOUTIQUE HOTEL $$
(☎5-660-6486; www.friends-to-be.hotels-cartagenacolombia.com; Calle del Espíritu Santo No 29-101; dm COP$40,000, s/d incl breakfast COP$160,000/180,000; ❄📶🏊) One of Getsemaní's best midrange deals, this charming place is like an urban hacienda, with a large, rustic wooden courtyard hidden behind the walls of a colonial mansion. The most impressive rooms are the two at the front of the house, both of which are spread over two floors, and one of which has a private roof terrace and sleeps four.

Bedrooms, including a spacious dorm, have starched sheets and exposed brick walls. There's a tiny pool.

★ **Casa Villa Colonial** HOTEL $$
(☎5-664-5421; www.casavillacolonial.co; Calle de la Media Luna No 10-89; s/d/tr incl breakfast COP$130,000/220,000/250,000; ❄📶🏊) Despite steadily rising prices in Getsemaní, rates here remain reasonable and you'll get personal, four-star service, beautiful communal areas with comfortable sofas and air-con for your money. The best rooms have small balconies onto the courtyard. There's a small kitchen for guests' use and endless great coffee.

The icing? A small, inviting rooftop pool and adjacent terrace – and boy, do you need them in this hot, humid city!

Hotel Don Pedro de Heredia HOTEL **$$**
(☎5-664-7270; www.hoteldonpedrodeheredia.com; Calle Primera de Badillo No 35-74; r incl breakfast from COP$235,000; ❄📶🏊) An excellent choice if you want somewhere in the Old Town with more than a whiff of history about it, but can't afford the truly sumptuous boutique-luxury experience that most places in this area offer. The Don Pedro represents great value for money, and included is a good breakfast on the breezy rooftop restaurant. Rooms are spacious, spotless and tastefully decorated.

El Viajero Cartagena HOSTEL **$$**
(☎5-660-2598; www.elviajerohostels.com; Calle de los 7 Infantes No 9-45; incl breakfast dm COP$50,000-56,000, d COP$220,000, without bathroom COP$175,000; ❄📶) This backpacker blockbuster is the most centrally located hostel and one of the most social pads in the city. All rooms have air-con – an absolute dream in this heat and at this price. The beds are firm, the kitchen is well organized and spotless, and there's a very friendly, social vibe in the lovely open courtyard.

Media Luna Hostel HOSTEL **$$**
(☎5-664-3423; www.medialunahostel.com; Calle de la Media Luna No 10-46; dm/r incl breakfast COP$45,000/160,000; ❄@📶🏊) Cartagena's ultimate party hostel is paradise for some and rather too much noise for others. Etched with a grand colonial feel, it's undoubtedly the hub of the backpacking scene in Getsemaní and a good place to meet the international bus set. Standout features include a big courtyard, a pool table and a roof terrace where fiestas kick off on Wednesday nights.

Rooms are generally clean and well kept, with crisp linens and good mattresses, and there's an ever-busy dipping pool surrounded by loungers, palms and pop-art murals.

Hostal Santo Domingo HOSTEL **$$**
(☎5-664-2268; hsantodomingopiret@yahoo.es; Calle Santo Domingo No 33-46, El Centro; s/d/tr incl breakfast COP$110,000/150,000/180,000; ❄📶) Walk through a handicrafts shop to get to this friendly little place. If it were located in Getsemaní, it could only charge half this much for what is relatively simple accommodations, but it's on a beautiful street in the old town and is steps away from some of the most beautiful buildings in Latin America.

★ **Hotel Casa San Agustin** LUXURY HOTEL **$$$**
(☎5-681-0621; www.hotelcasasanagustin.com; Calle de la Universidad; r incl breakfast from COP$1,350,000; ❄📶🏊) Firmly established as Cartagena's finest hotel, the Casa San Agustin enjoys a central location that would be wonderful for any establishment. However, it's the unique building (through which the city's former aqueduct cuts over an angular swimming pool) that creates such an unusual and atmospheric space, not to mention its superengaged and polite staff and club-like atmosphere.

Overflowing with formal, old-world fittings, such as its dazzling library, the hotel has unsurprisingly palatial rooms, including tiled marble bathrooms that heave with designer goodies and boast rain showers. In-room iPads, huge balconies and heavy wooden canopy beds complete the scene.

★ **Bantú** HOTEL **$$$**
(☎5-664-3362; www.bantuhotel.com; Calle de la Tablada No 7-62; s/d incl breakfast COP$550,000-630,000; ❄@📶🏊) Two wonderfully restored 15th-century homes make up this lovely 28-room, open-air boutique hotel, replete with exposed-brick archways, original stone walls and lush vegetation. Smartly appointed rooms are full of local artistic touches that blend sympathetically with the building. There's also a rooftop pool, as well as a musical fountain and a swing hanging from the towering courtyard mango tree.

Hotel Monterrey HISTORIC HOTEL **$$$**
(☎5-650-3030, 318-695-1837; www.hotelmonterrey.com.co; Av del Mercardo No 25-100; s/d incl breakfast COP$320,000/330,000; ❄📶🏊) With magnificent views of the walled city, Hotel Monterrey is perfectly located with Getsemaní on one side and El Centro on the other. Rooms are spacious, with high ceilings, comfortable beds and impressive furnishings. Breakfast is particularly good, though it's also hard to beat an evening cocktail on the rooftop.

★ **San Pedro Hotel Spa** BOUTIQUE HOTEL **$$$**
(☎5-664-5800; www.sanpedrohotelspa.com.co; Calle San Pedro Mártir No 10-85; r incl breakfast from COP$460,000; ❄📶🏊) An arresting seven-room boutique hotel wrapped in a handsome colonial mansion, the San Pedro manages to balance authentic historical touches with genuine modern luxury. Excitement mounts with the mosaic-tiled atrium pool and extends through large bedrooms beautified with Chinese screens, antique bed chests and elegant chairs. The rooftop

terrace with plunge pool and quiet bookish lounge is spectacular, as is the service.

Expansive breakfasts appear like magic from a modern open kitchen (or they'll serve you in your room), high-pressure showers wipe away the grime of Cartagena's hot streets, and there's a free half-hour foot massage for all guests.

Casa Canabal BOUTIQUE HOTEL **$$$**
(☎5-660-0666; www.casacanabalhotel.com; Calle Tripita y Media No 31-39, Getsemaní; r incl breakfast from COP$330,000; ❄📶🏊) Luxury without absurd cost can be found at this Getsemaní bolthole where sleek design combines with old-world care from attentive staff. Beautiful, minimalist rooms come with high ceilings, lots of wood and stylish bathrooms. The highlight is definitely the wonderful roof terrace, complete with bar, pool and spa (with a free welcome massage for each guest, naturally).

La Passion HOTEL **$$$**
(☎5-664-8605; www.lapassionhotel.com; Calle Estanco del Tabaco No 35-81, El Centro; r incl breakfast from COP$327,000; ❄📶🏊) Run by a French movie producer and his Colombian partner, this republican-style home features eight uniquely decorated rooms, some with Roman baths and outdoor showers. It's the canoe-swing in the courtyard, though, that really sets the eccentric, albeit stylish, tone. The pool and rooftop terrace with front-row views of the cathedral clinch it.

Casa La Fe B&B **$$$**
(☎5-660-0164, 5-660-1344; www.kalihotels.com/casa-la-fe/; Calle Segunda de Badillo No 36-125, San Diego; r incl breakfast from COP$359,000; ❄📶🏊) A British-Colombian pair run this boutique B&B decorated with tasteful religious art right in the heart of the Old Town. Eat in the jungly interior courtyard, sun yourself on a lounger or soak in the rooftop plunge pool. Higher-priced rooms have balconies overlooking Plaza Fernández de Madrid.

Hotel Casa de las Palmas HOTEL **$$$**
(☎5-664-3630; www.hotelcasadelaspalmas.com; Calle de las Palmas No 25-51, Getsemaní; s/d/tr incl breakfast COP$168,000/193,000/235,000; ❄📶🏊) This converted colonial mansion on the edge of Getsemaní oozes charm with its multiple small courtyards, walls heaving with Colombian folk art and a small pool to cool off in during the heat of day. The rooms are a little on the small side, but they're clean and comfortable. It's a good place for children, with lots of enclosed space.

Eating

Food in Cartagena is fabulous, with enormous choice and high quality at all levels. Backpackers should look out for *comida corriente* (daily set menu) places at midday, where you can eat for around COP$15,000 per person.

Cartagena is strong on street food: plenty of snack bars all across the Old Town serve local snacks such as *arepas de huevo* (fried maize dough with an egg inside), *dedos de queso* (deep-fried cheese sticks), empanadas and *buñuelos* (deep-fried maize-and-cheese balls). Try the region's sweets at confectionery stands lining El Portal de los Dulces on the Plaza de los Coches (p126).

Espíritu Santo COLOMBIAN **$**
(Calle del Porvenir No 35-60; mains COP$16,000; ⏲11:30am-3:30pm) In a city full of tourists, Espíritu Santo is where you come to meet the locals – hundreds of 'em in one sitting. (The restaurant is small from the outside but deceptively large within.) Choose your protein plus three sides and, in the true spirit of *comida corriente* (set menu of the day), it'll arrive in the blink of an eye.

Service is sharp, the atmosphere is nicely noisy, and it's always crowded for the lunchtime rush. The fish fillet in coconut milk is a perennial menu favorite, and it comes in large portions.

Restaurante Coroncoro COLOMBIAN **$**
(☎5-664-2648; Calle Tripita y Media No 31-28; mains COP$9000-17,000; ⏲7:30am-10pm) Unashamedly basic, Coroncoro has plastic chairs, crummy tables and an eccentric collection of wall-mounted paraphernalia that looks as though it was stolen from a garage sale. The menu is a little more straightforward: lots of filling starch, plenty of fried fish and an array of cheap prices (flavor comes a little further down the list).

The clientele is mainly local, with the odd bemused backpacker thrown in.

Beiyu CAFE **$$**
(Calle del Guerrero No 29-75; breakfast COP$10,000-13,000; ⏲7am-9pm Mon-Sat, 9am-6pm Sun; 📶🖋) 🍃 A simple little cafe plying excellent Colombian coffee, fresh juices, full breakfasts and an innovative selection of lunch and dinner dishes, Beiyu is a slice of organic, sustainable heaven in the heart of Getsemaní. It's top pick as the place to slowly eat off the effects of a late night. Portions are supergenerous. Don't miss the açai bowl.

Oh Là Là FRENCH $$
(☎5-664-4321; Calle Larga No 4-48, Getsemaní; mains COP$18,000-38,000; ⏲8am-10pm Mon-Sat; 📶✍) This fabulous addition to Getsemaní's increasingly varied and interesting dining options brings a slice of Gallic culture. In a gorgeous converted space with high ceilings and comfortable seating, the restaurant also offers popular cookery classes and focuses on healthy, sugar-free dishes. Its breakfasts are superb, while its seasonally changing lunch and dinner menus offer sublime, innovative dishes.

Pezetarian SUSHI $$
(☎5-668-6155; www.pezetarian.com; Calle Segunda de Badillo No 36-19; mains COP$17,000-23,000; ⏲8am-10pm; 📶✍) 🍃 Feast on affordable and delicious sushi, ceviche, wok dishes and salads at this ultracentral location. You'll find little else in this area at this price at all, let alone something totally organic, healthy and fresh. The place looks a little like a fast-food restaurant at first glance, but don't let this put you off. Service is swift and friendly.

Caffé Lunático TAPAS $$
(☎320-383-0419; Calle Espíritu Santo No 29-184; tapas COP$12,000-20,000, mains COP$26,000-53,000; ⏲11am-3pm & 7-11pm; 📶✍) There's nothing remotely looney about this artsy little spot in the hosteling hub of Gestemaní that pays homage to Amy Winehouse in a head-and-shoulders mural that takes up a whole wall. The perfect solution to minor lunchtime hunger pangs, midafternoon cake yearnings or early-evening cocktail urges, the Lunático does a full range of small plates and desserts exceedingly well.

The traditional Spanish tapas – aubergine sticks and croquettes never fail to impress – make a solid afternoon spread. The generous cocktails pave the way for dinner.

Demente PIZZA, TAPAS $$
(☎5-660-4226; Plaza de la Trinidad, Getsemaní; tapas COP$15,000-30,000, pizzas from COP$20,000; ⏲6pm-midnight Sun-Thu, 6pm-2am Fri & Sat; 📶✍) Right in the heart of the Getsemaní action, Demente is an open-air (well, has a retractable roof), rather trendy spot where craft beer and great cocktails are served up alongside excellent tapas and some of Cartagena's best pizza. Service is friendly and swift, and you're just moments from the party atmosphere outside in the square.

Pastelería Mila BAKERY $$
(Calle de la Iglesia No 35-76; breakfasts COP$16,500-28,000, mains COP$17,500-35,000; ⏲8am-10pm; 📶) Cartagena's fanciest patisserie serves up breakfasts and lunches at this fashionable spot in the heart of the Old Town. The distressed walls and wooden beams create a contemporary vibe, while the leather banquettes are grander in style. The combo breakfast (pancakes with *dulce de leche,* sour cream, scrambled eggs and crispy bacon) might be considered a crime in less permissive jurisdictions.

Kiosco El Bony SEAFOOD $$
(Av 1 Bocagrande; mains COP$15,000-30,000; ⏲10am-10pm Mon-Sun) Owned by ex-Olympic boxer Bonifacio Ávila, this beachside Cartagena institution is famous for its vast fish lunches. It's thronged with Colombians on weekends.

La Mulata COLOMBIAN $$
(☎5-664-6222; Calle Quero No 9-58, El Centro; set meal COP$20,000-25,000; ⏲11am-4pm & 6:30-10pm; 📶) This stylish and rather eccentric *comida corriente* option is still outstanding, even if its prices have risen in recent years. A daily set menu offers a handful of excellent choices and fresh juices in an atmosphere entirely too hip for Cartagena's Old Town. The staff are absolute charmers, the ceiling fans whir and mains are served on pieces of whittled wood.

La Cevichería SEAFOOD $$$
(☎5-664-5255; Calle Stuart No 7-14; mains COP$39,000-120,000; ⏲noon-11pm Wed-Mon; 📶) A once little-known spot prized by locals, La Cevichería was given ample publicity in an episode of Anthony Bourdain's *No Reservations* in 2008. Cue the crowds but, thankfully, no real slide in the excellent quality of the food. Each dish is prepared with panache; the octopus in peanut sauce is incredible, as is the black-squid-ink rice and Peruvian ceviche.

Señor Toro STEAK $$
(☎5-656-4077; Calle Santo Domingo No 35-55; mains COP$25,000-70,000; ⏲noon-midnight; 📶) This centrally located steakhouse is the most rigorous in the city in terms of sourcing and preparing meat. Nowhere else will you find such perfectly cooked medium-rare porterhouse or entrecôte in the city. There are also ceviche and burgers on the menu if steak isn't your thing.

★**El Boliche** CEVICHE $$$
(☎5-660-0074, 310-368-7908; Cochera del Hobo No 38-17; mains COP$48,000-60,000; ⏲12:30-3pm & 7-11pm Mon-Sat; 📶) Small, delightful

and not so well known that it's inundated, El Boliche basks in its relative obscurity. If you're reticent about raw fish, Boliche offers hot and cold ceviche daubed with bold and adventurous ingredients such as tamarind, coconut milk and mango. The handsome six-table interior features a glass waterfall and a bar that dispatches spot-on mojitos.

★Interno COLOMBIAN $$$
(☎310-260-0134, 310-327-3682; www.restauranteinterno.com; Cárcel San Diego, Calle Camposanto; 3-course set meal COP$90,000; ⏲7-11pm Tue-Sun) Interno is a restaurant inside Cartagena's women's prison that raises money for the rehabilitation of its inmates, who cook for and wait on you. Trained by a top Bogotá chef, the cooks prepare set meals that are delectable takes on modern Colombian cuisine. Meals are served on a gorgeously repurposed open-air patio.

You'll need to make reservations 24 hours ahead with your passport number, and you'll need to bring your passport with you when you come.

Cevichería Chipi Chipi CEVICHE $$$
(☎5-660-1156; Cochera del Hobo No 38-86; mains COP$30,000-52,000; ⏲11:30am-3pm & 6:30-11pm Mon-Sat, 3-11pm Sun; 📶) As if to underscore this place's ceviche credentials, its dining room enjoys a somewhat writ-large nautical theme, but it remains a stylish and cool place for a meal. The ceviche is superfresh and delicious, with a big choice of flavors and ingredients. There's also outdoor dining on the plaza nearby come the evening.

Lobo de Mar TAPAS $$$
(☎5-664-5798; Calle del Santísimo No 8-15; tapas COP$18,000-35,000, mains COP38,000-46,000; ⏲6-11pm Tue-Sun; 📶🖉) This gorgeous and inventive place is one of Cartagena's most interesting restaurants, sporting titular water features and a very cool gin bar (the friendly owner will create a mind- and wallet-blowing gin-and-tonic combination just for you). The gourmet tapas menu is full of interesting flavors, and is particularly strong on seafood, as well as having plentiful vegetarian choices.

Drinking & Nightlife

There's a long-standing bar scene centered on the Plaza de los Coches (p126) in El Centro for salsa and vallenato, while most of the hotter and hipper action can be found in thumping Getsemaní, where the venues are bigger and the crowd younger. Weekends are best, though the action doesn't really heat up until after midnight.

★Alquímico COCKTAIL BAR
(☎318-845-0433; www.alquimico.com; Calle del Colegio No 34-24; ⏲5pm-2am Sun-Thu, to 3:30am Fri & Sat) Anyone remotely hip ultimately gravitates to this Old Town bar with a pharmaceutical theme. Occupying a gorgeous colonial building, the bar is spread over three floors: the ground floor is a sleek, low-lit lounge perfect for an aperitif, while upstairs there's a kitchen and pool table. One more floor up is the always-packed roof-terrace bar, serving imaginative aguardiente cocktails.

The entire space is easily one of Cartagena's most sophisticated options and the roof terrace is perfect for tropical nights.

★Café Havana CLUB
(cnr Calle del Guerrero & Calle de la Media Luna; cover COP$30,000; ⏲8:30pm-4am Thu-Sat, 5pm-2am Sun) Havana has it all: live salsa from horn-blowing Cubans, strong drinks, a gorgeous horseshoe-shaped bar surrounded by brilliant eccentrics, wood-paneled walls and a ceiling full of whirring fans. While it's no secret these days, it's still worth a pilgrimage. Expect sweaty crowds and the odd elbow in the ribs when you're trying out your salsa moves at 1am. No shorts.

Bazurto Social Club CLUB
(www.bazurtosocialclub.com; Av del Centenario No 30-42; cover COP$5000; ⏲8pm-4am Wed-Sat) Join the crowds at this lively spot where locals dance in unison under an enormous glowing red fish to live *champeta* music, sip knockout cocktails and catch up on the Getsemaní gossip. The music's great, and after a few drinks you'll find yourself being dragged in, though your ears will likely ring for days.

Donde Fidel BAR
(☎5-664-3127; El Portal de los Dulces No 32-09; ⏲11am-2am) Old salts meet salsa-seeking tourists at this usually packed and always loud Old Town bar characterized by glaring florescent lighting and busy walls covered with photos of owner Fidel posing with a Wikipedia's worth of Latin celebrities from A-list to D-list. Order a bottle of rum along with an ice bucket and some mixers and hunker down.

Tu Candela CLUB
(☎5-664-8787; El Portal de los Dulces No 32-25; ⏲8pm-4am) With wall-to-wall reggaeton, vallenato, merengue and some decent salsa, Tu Candela's always cramped, but the atmosphere's cool and anything goes. The

interior is dark and cave-like, punctuated by a long, backlit bar. The place has recently become known for its sweet and spicy ceviche, made out front before your eyes. Cocktails are expensive.

The Beer Lovers CRAFT BEER
(☎5-664-2202; esq Calles Gastelbondo & Factoría; ⏰9am-11pm, until 1am Thu-Sat; 📶) This raucous and rather dark place has a huge selection of craft beers from around the world, including dozens of local brews, and is the best bar in town to explore the craft beers of Colombia and beyond.

Quiebra-Canto CLUB
(☎5-664-1372; Camellón de los Mártires, Edificio Puente del Sol, Getsemaní; ⏰7pm-4am Tue-Sat) It gets tight with an eclectic crowd of all shapes and sizes at this excellent Getsemaní spot for salsa, son and reggae. It's on the 2nd floor overlooking Pegasos and the clock tower. Purists insist the salsa here is hotter than at rival bar Café Havana (p133), but its crowd tends to be less exciting.

León de Baviera BAR
(☎5-664-4450; Av del Arsenal No 10B-65; ⏰4pm-4am Tue-Sun; 📶) Run by an expat German named Stefan, this is one of the city's few true watering holes. The intimate space fills quickly with locals swilling back 3L tubes of European and local brews. The waitresses are dressed in their St Pauli Girl's best.

Café del Mar BAR
(☎5-664-6513; Baluarte de Santo Domingo, El Centro; cocktails COP$20,000-35,000; ⏰5pm-1am; 📶) Ocean breezes swoop in off the coast and bring a relaxing freshness to this touristy outdoor lounge perching on the western ramparts of the Old Town. Dress up a notch or two and be prepared to pay COP$10,000 for a beer if you want to blend in. The view is unbeatable.

☆ Entertainment

Cartagena's local football team, Real Cartagena, plays games at **Estadio Olímpico Jaime Morón León** (Villa Olímpico), located 5km south of the city. Games run throughout the year. Buy tickets at the stadium. A taxi there will cost around COP$12,000.

Shopping

Cartagena has a wide range of shops selling crafts and souvenirs, and the quality of the goods is usually high. The biggest tourist shopping center in the walled city is **Las Bóvedas** (Playa del Tejadillo), which offers handicrafts, clothes and kitschy souvenirs. You'll find more interesting things for sale by wandering in Getsemaní, San Diego and El Centro, however.

Ábaco BOOKS
(☎5-664-8338; cnr Calle de la Iglesia & Calle de la Mantilla; ⏰8am-10pm Mon-Sat, 10am-8pm Sun; 📶) An erudite-looking bookshop-cafe that's short on space but big on atmosphere, with the obligatory ladder to reach the higher shelves. Search carefully and you'll encounter Cervantes tomes, English-language titles and pretty much everything Gabriel García Márquez ever wrote. There's also Italian beer, Spanish wine and strong espresso.

El Arcón ANTIQUES
(☎5-664-1197; www.arconanticuario.com; Calle del Camposanto No 9-46, San Diego; ⏰9am-noon & 1-7pm Mon-Sat) This impressive place housed in a handsome colonial mansion is the best antiques shop in the walled city, a veritable treasure trove of art, furniture and various curios that's well worth searching out if you'd like a truly memorable souvenir of your time in Colombia.

Colombia Artesanal ARTS & CRAFTS
(www.artesaniasdecolombia.com.co; Callejón de los Estribos No 2-78; ⏰10am-8pm Mon-Sat, 11am-7pm Sun) A set of several stores in the Old Town offers an excellent selection of brightly hued Colombian handicrafts from all over the country. The salespeople are extremely knowledgeable and can offer fascinating insights into the making and background of each piece.

Orientation

Travelers tend to focus on the walled city, made up of El Centro, San Diego and Getsemaní. To the south, the peninsula of Bocagrande – Cartagena's Miami Beach – is where fashionable *cartageneros* sip coffee in trendy cafes, dine in glossy restaurants and live in the upscale luxury condos that line the area like sentries. Few visitors stay here, but it's a viable, safe and glamorous alternative to the walled city.

Cartagena's streets have both names and numbers. Listings use street names, as these are the identifiers most commonly posted on the streets themselves.

Information

SAFE TRAVEL

Cartagena is the safest metropolis in Colombia – around 2000 police officers patrol the old city alone. That said, don't flaunt your wealth, and stay alert at night in less-populated areas such La Matuna, the modern strip between Getsemaní and the old city. You're more likely to be irritated by peddlers than to become a victim of any crime. Aggressive hassling in the streets by unofficial vendors selling tourist tat, cocaine or the services of prostitutes is definitely the main nuisance here. A simple '*No quiero nada*' ('I don't want anything') should shoo them away.

MEDICAL SERVICES

Hospital Naval de Cartagena (☎8-655-4306; Carrera 2 No 14-210; ⏰24hr) Has a hyperbaric chamber.

MONEY

Casas de cambio (currency exchanges) and banks are ubiquitous in the historic center, especially around Plaza de los Coches and Plaza de la Aduana. Compare rates before buying. There are many street 'money changers' around Cartagena offering fantastic rates; they are all, without exception, expert swindlers, so don't even think of changing money on the street. There's a real lack of ATMs in El Centro and San Diego; however, there's a proliferation on Av Venezuela.

TOURIST INFORMATION

The city's main **tourist office** (Turismo Cartagena de Indias; ☎5-660-1583; Plaza de la Aduana; ⏰9am-noon & 1-6pm Mon-Sat, 9am-5pm Sun) can be found on Plaza de la Aduana. There are also small booths in Plaza de San Pedro Claver and Plaza de los Coches.

VISA INFORMATION

Migracíon Colombia (☎5-670-0555, 5-666-0172; www.migracioncolombia.gov.co; Carrera 29D No 20-18; ⏰8am-noon & 2-5pm) can be found some way from the Old Town, but this is where you should head for immigration issues and visa extensions.

ℹ Getting There & Away

AIR

All major Colombian carriers operate flights to and from Cartagena's **Aeropuerto Internacional Rafael Núñez** (☎5-693-1351; www.sacsa.com.co; Calle 71 No 8-9), 3km from the city, in Crespo. There are flights to Bogotá, Cali, Medellín, San Andrés and many other major cities with **Avianca** (☎5-655-0287; www.avianca.com; Av Venezuela No 8B-05; ⏰8am-12:30pm & 2-6pm Mon-Fri, 8am-1pm Sat). **Copa** (☎5-655-0428; www.copaair.com; Calle 71 No 8-9; ⏰8am-6pm Mon-Fri, to 5pm Sat & Sun) connects to Panama City, American Airlines to Miami and JetBlue Airways to New York. Air Canada Rouge has seasonal flights to Toronto.

The terminal has four ATMs, a *casa de cambio* (currency exchange; in domestic arrivals) and multiple car-hire agencies in the terminal building or immediately nearby.

BOAT

Sailboat is a great way to get to Panama and also a unique way to experience the San Blas Islands. Various boats leave Cartagena for Panama via the San Blas Archipelago and vice versa; the schedule is set a few months ahead and has boats departing almost every day in both directions. The trip normally takes five days and includes three days in San Blas for snorkeling and island-hopping. Trips cost around US$550 per person but can range from US$450 to US$650, as there are many factors involved.

Most boats arrive at the Panamanian ports of Porvenir, Puerto Lindo or Portobello. It's easy to connect to Panama City from all three.

The industry has been transformed in recent years by **Blue Sailing** (☎310-704-0425, 300-829-2030; www.bluesailing.net; Calle San Andrés No 30-47; 5-day trips US$450-650; ⏰9am-5pm Mon-Sat), a Colombian-American-run agency that has sought to legalize what had been an unregulated business. Blue Sailing currently represents more than 22 boats and ensures that all have proper safety equipment for open-sea navigation. It monitors boats' locations and uses licensed captains. It's therefore highly recommended that you find your boat through Blue Sailing to ensure a safe and legal crossing.

Other agencies and hostels in Cartagena offer boat crossings, but do ask about safety equipment and the captain's license. Ideally, check online for reviews of the boat and crew before you commit to anything.

Different boats depart each week, even in low season; email an operator with your preferred departure dates and the staff will hook you up with a boat that best fits your needs. It's important to book ahead, especially December through March, as boats tend to book out weeks before departure.

The sailboat trip is a popular way to visit San Blas even for those who didn't originally plan to travel to Panama. A few airlines offer cheap flights back to Colombia from Panama City; try Wingo, Air Panama and Avianca.

For those passengers traveling with vehicles, various shipping companies offer container sharing or 'roll on, roll off' services between Cartagena and Colón (US$700 to US$1200, six to eight days including loading/unloading). Passengers can take the sailboat across to meet their vehicle. It's easy and inexpensive to reach Colón from Puerto Lindo or Portobello.

Visas are not generally required for stays of up to 90 days in Panama.

BUS

If you're heading to Barranquilla or Santa Marta, the easiest option is to leave from the **Berlinastur Terminal** (☎318-724-2424, 318-354-5454; www.berlinastur.com), a short taxi ride from the Old Town. Air-conditioned minibuses depart from here every 20 minutes from 5am to 8pm, stopping first in Barranquilla (COP$20,000, two hours) and then in Santa Marta (COP$40,000, four hours).

An even better, but pricier, option for this route is the **MarSol** (☎5-656-0302; Carrera 2 No 43-111) bus to Santa Marta (COP$50,000, three hours), Taganga (COP$52,000, three hours), PNN Tayrona (COP$67,000, four hours) and Palomino (COP$77,000, five hours). It picks you up from any hotel or hostel in Cartagena, skips Barranquilla entirely and then drops you at any hotel or hostel in Santa Marta or beyond. There are two buses a day; call a day ahead to reserve your seats.

For other destinations, including for cheaper tickets to Barranquilla and Santa Marta, you'll need to head to Cartagena's **Terminal de Transportes de Cartagena** (☎304-577-5743; www.terminaldecartagena.com; Calle 1A No 3-89). It's on the eastern outskirts of the city, far away from the center – give yourself 45 minutes to get there in all but the darkest hours.

Several bus companies serve Bogotá and Medellín throughout the day. Among them, **Copetran** (www.copetran.com) heads to Bogotá (from COP$110,000, 21 hours, six buses daily). **Unitransco** (☎5-663-2067, 5-663-2665; Terminal de Transportes de Cartagena, Calle 1A No 3-89) serves Barranquilla (COP$14,000, 2½ hours, hourly), with continuing services to Santa Marta (COP$35,000, four hours, hourly). There's also a 7:30am service to Mompós (COP$46,000, six hours, daily) and an hourly service to Montería (COP$40,000, five hours, daily). For Riohacha on La Guajira Peninsula, Expreso Brasilia and **Rápido Ochoa** (☎312-843-1249, 5-693-2133; Terminal de Transportes de Cartagena, Calle 1A No 3-89) both have hourly departures (COP$42,000, eight hours). The latter also has four daily departures to Medellín (COP$125,000, 13 hours).

On overland trips to Panama, take one of the hourly buses to Montería (COP$40,000, five hours), where you can switch to one of the hourly buses to Necocli (COP$25,000, 2½ hours) and Turbo (COP$35,000, 3½ hours). It's worth noting that if you don't leave Cartagena before 11am, you risk missing the last bus for Necocli/Turbo and will have to sleep in Montería. From both ports, you can take the boat to Capurganá the following morning, from where there are regular launches to Obaldia in Panama.

Buses to Playa Blanca (Calle de la Magdalena Concolón) (COP$1500, 70 minutes), for those who aren't keen to take the boat excursion (p135) there, leave throughout the day. Look for vehicles marked 'Pasocaballos' and tell the driver where you're headed so you can be let off.

Getting Around

TO/FROM THE AIRPORT

The route to and from the airport is serviced by frequent local buses. There are also *colectivos* (COP$2000), as well as nicer air-conditioned shuttles called **Metrocar** (Av Luis Carlos López; COP$2000), both of which depart from Monumento a la India Catalina in the Old Town. (For Metrocar, look for the green-signed buses.)

By taxi, there's a surcharge of COP$5000 on airport trips. It costs COP$10,000 to COP$15,000 from the center to the airport; coming from the airport, official taxis charge set amounts according to distance and time of day. Expect to pay between COP$10,000 and COP$15,000 to Getsemaní, San Diego and El Centro, but be sure to get a receipt from the dispatch office at the airport first, to ensure you know how much the journey should cost.

TO/FROM THE BUS STATION

Large green-and-red-signed **Metrocar buses** (Av Santander; COP$2000) shuttle between the city and the bus terminal every 15 to 30 minutes (COP$3000, 40 minutes). In the center you can catch them on Av Santander. A taxi from the bus station to El Centro costs COP$15,000, plus COP$5000 after 8pm.

In 2016 Cartagena inaugurated BRT Transcaribe, a rapid-transit system similar to Bogotá's Transmilenio, with buses operating in special busways. Further development is expected, but for the time being the network's single line is tailored more to locals than visitors.

Islas del Rosario

An archipelago about 35km southwest of Cartagena, the Islas del Rosario consist of 27 small coral islands, including some tiny islets. The islands are surrounded by coral reefs, where the color of the sea is an incredible combination of cerulean and turquoise. The whole area has been declared a national park, the PNN Corales del Rosario y San Bernardo. Sadly, warm-water currents have eroded the reefs, and the diving isn't as good as it once was. But water sports are still popular, and the two largest islands, Isla Grande and Isla del Rosario, have inland lagoons and some tourist facilities, such as hotels and a resort. The islands can be visited in a day trip from Cartagena, although to really appreciate them and to avoid the crowds, consider spending a night or two here.

Tours

The usual way to visit the park is on a one-day boat tour of the islands. Tours depart year-round from the Muelle Turístico de la Bodeguita in Cartagena; contact the cruise office at the *muelle* (pier; tours from COP$60,000 per person). Boats leave between 8am and 9am daily and return roughly between 4pm and 6pm.

Around Cartagena

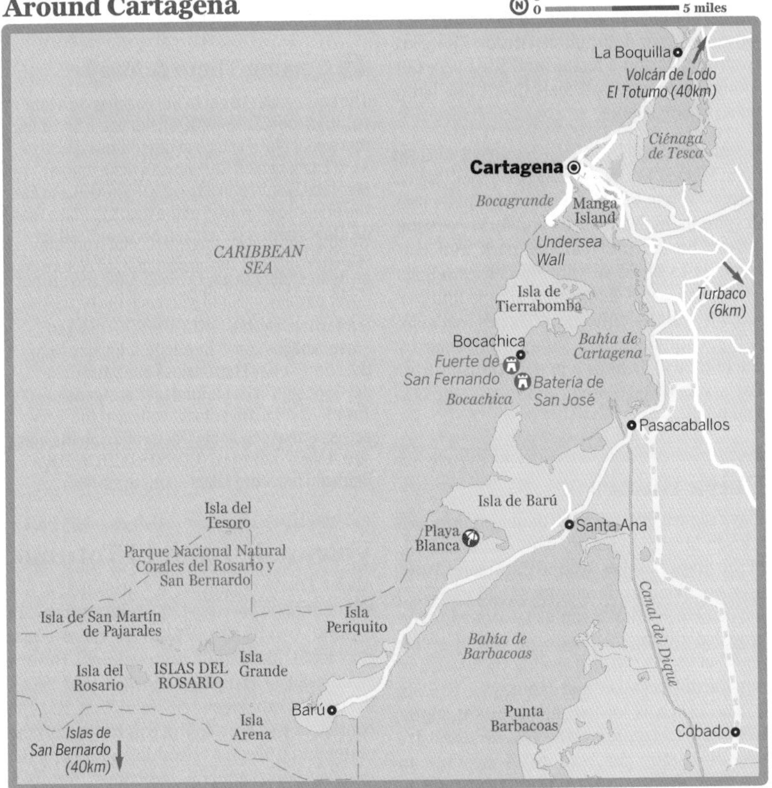

A number of smaller operators at the pier offer cheaper tours. Popular budget hotels in Cartagena sell tours, too, and may offer lower prices – COP$50,000 per person is common.

Tours all take a similar route to the islands, though the trip may differ a little between small and large boats. All vessels go through the Bahía de Cartagena and into the open sea through the Bocachica strait, passing between Batería de San José and, directly opposite, the Fuerte de San Fernando. Boats then cruise among the islands (there's generally Spanish commentary along the way) and stop at the tiny **Isla de San Martín de Pajarales**. Here there's an aquarium (COP$30,000) and a shady wooded area to chill out in or a beach to swim at while you wait for the trip to continue. Boats then go to Playa Blanca, on the Isla de Barú, for lunch and two hours or so of free time.

Tours usually include lunch but not port taxes, the national-park entrance fee and aquarium entry; check with your operator to confirm. Some higher-end hotels offer their own boat transfers from Cartagena.

Sleeping

Most hotels are on Isla Grande, and tend to be very rustic no matter how much you pay – and at the top end this is not an insignificant amount.

Eco Hotel Las Palmeras GUESTHOUSE **$$**
(☎314-584-7358; Isla Grande; hammock/r per person incl full board COP$80,000/120,000) This Isla Grande ecotourism option is run by the charming Ana Rosa. It's all very basic and rustic, but it's a wonderful place to disconnect from the world. Canoe tours are offered on the nearby lagoons; there's good snorkeling nearby; and you're just a five-minute walk away from Playa Bonita, the best on the island.

Hotel San Pedro de Majagua HOTEL **$$$**
(☎5-693-0987; www.hotelmajagua.com; Isla Grande; r & bungalows from COP$520,000;)

This high-end option offers stays on Isla Grande in chic stone bungalows with fiber-woven roofs and minimalist decor. There are two beaches and a restaurant. It's a very fabulous experience and feels much like being on a private island.

Coralina Island BOUTIQUE HOTEL $$$

(☎313-245-9244; www.coralinaisland.com; Isla del Rosario; r from COP$680,000;) This place, despite its high price, is actually very rustic, located inside the national park and constructed to blend in with the surroundings. The cabañas are charmingly simple and perfect for real disconnection. There's free snorkeling equipment and some lovely beaches: the hotel will arrange a private transfer from Cartagena if you'd prefer not to take the normal boat.

Playa Blanca

Playa Blanca lives up to its name – it is indeed a lovely stretch of sugary white sand and one of the finest beaches around Cartagena. However, encroaching development and incessant hawkers mean that it can feel extremely overcrowded during high season and at weekends, so it's best to visit during the week and outside of December and January.

The beach is located about 20km southwest of Cartagena, on the Isla de Barú. It's usually a stop for boat tours heading to the Islas del Rosario (p136). Beware: when the boats arrive, peddlers descend in their droves, offering everything from beach chairs to massages (most of them ridiculously overpriced). Keeping these folks at bay can be an irksome challenge. The only thing worth buying is *cocada,* a sweet coconut treat available in a variety of flavors.

Playa Blanca is also good for snorkeling – if you can see past the Jet-skis.

Sleeping & Eating

The beach has some rustic places to stay, and before 10am and after 4pm the place is wonderfully deserted.

A few simple beach restaurants serve up fresh fish and rice for around COP$20,000. Lunch is usually included if you're on a tour; check with your operator.

La Estrella CABIN $

(☎312-602-9987; hammocks COP$10,000, d from COP$50,000) If you want to stay close to the water, friendly local José offers appealing tents under thatched roofs that sleep three to four, hammocks (with mosquito nets), and a sand-floored hut or two.

Getting There & Away

The easiest way to get to the beach is on a tour (p136) (from COP$40,000), but you'll find it far more peaceful if you go at other times. Head to Av El Lago, behind Cartagena's main market, Mercado Bazurto, in a taxi (COP$8000) and ask the driver to let you off at the boats to Playa Blanca. Boats depart (when full) between 7:30am and 9:30am daily except Sunday. The trip takes an hour. Expect to pay COP$25,000 and up, but never pay anyone until you reach the beach.

Alternatively, buses (COP$1800) marked 'Pasocaballos' leave throughout the day from the corner of Av Luis Carlos López and Calle del Concolon in La Matuna (in Cartagena's Old Town). Ask the driver to let you off at the ferry across Canal del Dique. Once you're on the other side, take a moto-taxi (COP$15,000) to Playa Blanca. This route takes about three hours.

Volcán de Lodo El Totumo

About 50km northeast of Cartagena, a few kilometers off the coast, is an intriguing 15m **mound** (mud bath COP$10,000; ⏲dawn-dusk) that looks like a miniature volcano. However, instead of erupting with lava and ashes, it spews forth lukewarm mud that has the consistency of cream. You can climb into the crater and frolic in a refreshing mud bath; the mud contains minerals acclaimed for their therapeutic properties. Once you've finished you can wash off in the lagoon, just 50m away.

Bring plenty of small bills to tip (COP$5000) the various locals who will wait on you during your time here – massaging you rather inexpertly, rinsing you off, holding your camera and taking photos. All in all, it's a lot of fun and a rightly popular day trip from Cartagena.

Getting There & Away

A tour is by far the most convenient and fastest way of visiting El Totumo, and it's no more expensive than getting there on your own. Several operators in Cartagena organize minibus trips to the volcano (COP$30,000 to COP$40,000, depending on whether lunch is included). Tours can easily be purchased through hotels.

NORTHEAST OF CARTAGENA

The departments of Atlántico and Magdalena sit northeast of Cartagena, where the highest coastal mountain range in the world, the Sierra Nevada de Santa Marta, begins to rise from the sea. The increasingly charming Santa Marta, a colonial city, and the beautiful coastal and mountainous attractions around it – namely Parque Nacional Natural (PNN) Tayrona, Ciudad Perdida, Minca and Palomino – are some of Colombia's most visited attractions.

Santa Marta

5 / POP 450,000 / ELEV 2M

Santa Marta is South America's oldest European-founded town and the second-most-important colonial city on Colombia's Caribbean coast. Despite its long history and charming center, it gets a bad rap from many travelers, who cite its unlovely urban sprawl and terrible traffic as reasons not to hang about here. The secret to Santa Marta is to use it for what it does well: hotels, restaurants and bars, and then get out to the slew of superb nearby destinations during the daytime.

That said, following an impressive sprucing up of its colonial heart, Santa Marta has gained a bit more of its own charm, and you might well find yourself spending more time here than you imagined. The climate is hot, but the heat here is drier than in Cartagena, and the evening sea breeze keeps the city cool after dark.

History

Rodrigo de Bastidas planted a Spanish flag here in 1525, deliberately choosing a site at the foot of the Sierra Nevada de Santa Marta to serve as a convenient base for the reputedly incalculable gold treasures of the indigenous Tayrona.

As soon as the plundering of the Sierra began, so did the inhabitants' resistance. By the end of the 16th century the Tayrona had been wiped out, and many of their extraordinary gold objects (melted down for rough material by the Spaniards) were in the Crown's coffers.

Santa Marta was also one of the early gateways to the interior of the colony. It was from here that Jiménez de Quesada set off in 1536 for his strenuous march up the Magdalena Valley to found Bogotá two years later.

Engaged in the war with the Tayrona and repeatedly ransacked by pirates, Santa Marta didn't have many glorious moments in its colonial history and was soon overshadowed by its younger, more progressive neighbor, Cartagena. Despite this, on December 17, 1830, Simón Bolívar died here, having brought independence to six Latin American countries. His body was later returned to Venezuela in 1842, where it continues to lie in a mausoleum in his native Caracas.

Sights

There's little to see in Santa Marta itself, though it's worth having a stroll along the seaside boulevard Av Rodrigo de Bastidas (Carrera 1C) and Av Campo Serrano (Carrera 5), the main commercial street. The beach resort of **El Rodadero**, 5km south of the center, is popular with vacationing Colombians.

★Quinta de San Pedro Alejandrino MUSEUM

(5-433-1021; www.museobolivariano.org.co; Av Libertador; foreigners/Colombians COP$21,000/15,000; 9am-4:30pm) This hacienda is where Simón Bolívar spent his last days in 1830 before succumbing to either tuberculosis or arsenic poisoning, depending on whom you believe. The hacienda was owned by a Spanish supporter of Colombia's independence who invited Bolívar to stay and take a rest before his journey to exile in Europe, but Bolívar died before he could complete the journey.

Several monuments have been built on the grounds in remembrance of Bolívar, the most imposing of which is a massive central structure called the **Altar de la Patria**, inside which a haughty Bolívar looks down.

Just to the right of this is the **Museo Bolivariano**, which features works of art donated by Latin American artists, including those from Colombia, Venezuela, Panama, Ecuador, Peru and Bolivia, the countries liberated by Bolívar.

Highlights among the wares in the house include an absolutely decadent marble bathtub. The hacienda was established at the beginning of the 17th century and was engaged in cultivating and processing sugarcane. It had its own *trapiche* (sugarcane mill) and a *destilería* (distillery).

The outstanding grounds, home to Santa Marta's 22-hectare, iguana-filled **Jardín Botánico**, are also worth a stroll. Some of the property's trees alone warrant a trip out here. The *quinta* is in the far-eastern suburb of Mamatoco, about 4km from the city center. To get here, take the Mamatoco bus from the waterfront (Carrera 1C); it's a 20-minute trip (COP$1600) to the hacienda.

Santa Marta

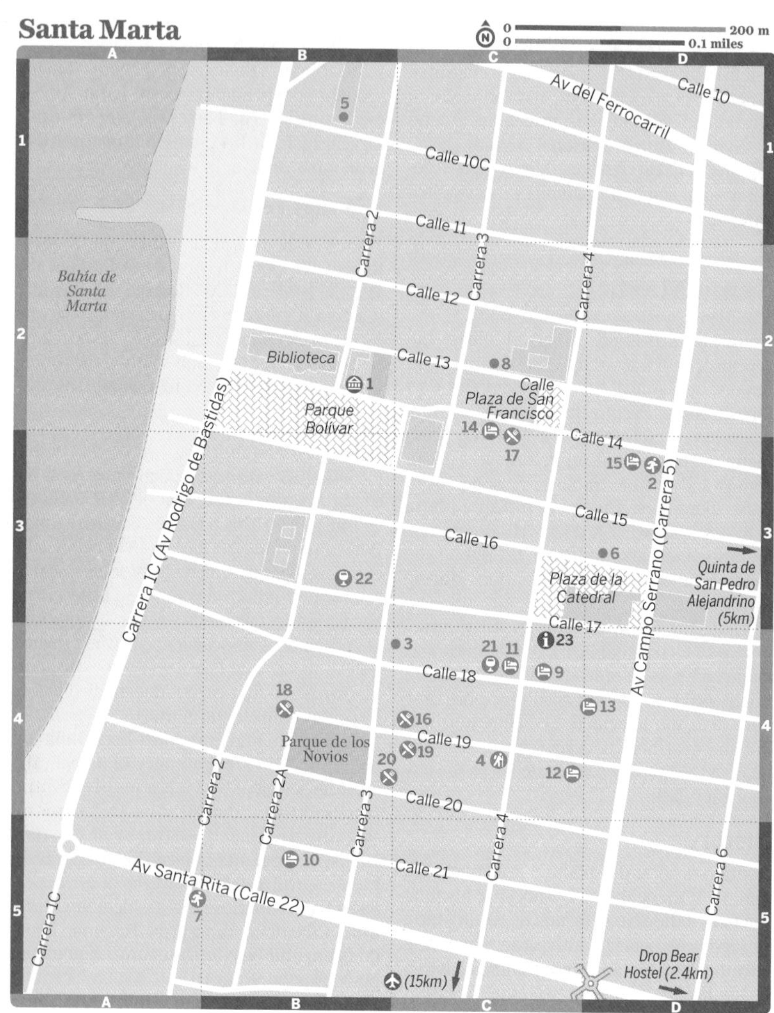

Museo del Oro MUSEUM

(Calle 14 No 1-37; 9am-5pm Tue-Sat, 10am-3pm Sun) FREE *Oro* (gold) is only half of what this fabulous museum is about. Housed in the impressively renovated Casa de la Aduana (Customs House), which features in the Gabriel García Márquez novel *No One Writes to the Colonel*, the displays lure you in with ceramics and jewelry from the Nahuange and Tayrona periods, backed by a comprehensive history of metalwork in the pre-Columbian Sierra Nevada.

Upstairs the history lesson continues in Spanish and English with the full story of Santa Marta's past, including a tribute to Simon Bolívar, who died here in 1830.

Tours

Santa Marta's tour market revolves around Ciudad Perdida treks, but the same agencies that offer these can also arrange various other hiking trips, plus birdwatching, mountain biking and visits to Minca and PNN Tayrona. Highly recommended agencies for local tours include Magic Tours (p154) and Expotur (p154).

Santa Marta

Sights

1 Museo del Oro B2

Activities, Courses & Tours

2 Aventure Colombia D3
3 Expotur C4
4 Guías Indígenas Tours C4
5 Guías y Baquianos Tours B1
6 Magic Tours D3
7 Osprey Expeditions A5
8 Turcol C2

Sleeping

9 Casa del Agua C4
10 Casa del Árbol B5
11 Casa del Farol C4
12 Casa del Piano C4
13 Casa Verde D4
14 La Brisa Loca C2
15 Masaya Santa Marta D3

Eating

16 À Deriva C4
17 Amargo C3
18 Donde Chucho B4
19 Ikaro C4
20 Ouzo B4

Drinking & Nightlife

21 Crabs C4
22 La Puerta B3

Information

23 Parques Nacionales Naturales de Colombia C4

Sleeping

Santa Marta's tourism industry is booming, so there's a wide range of hotels and hostels, many of which are some of the best on the coast. There's lots of choice in the town center but also plentiful options outside the center that are worth considering.

★ Masaya Santa Marta HOSTEL $

(5-423-1770; www.masaya-experience.com; Carrera 14 No 4-80; dm COP$40,000-50,000, r incl breakfast COP$120,000-200,000;) This fabulous hostel in the town center takes some beating. A clever and stylish multilevel conversion of an old mansion, it has superb-value dorms and gorgeous private rooms. Dorm beds have individual curtains for increased privacy; private rooms are adorned with interesting art. There are three plunge pools, a busy rooftop bar, a large outdoor kitchen, billiards and a cinema room.

Rooms are named after famous Colombians of yore. The staff is kind and knowledgeable and the vibe superb.

Drop Bear Hostel HOSTEL $

(5-435-8034; www.dropbearhostel.com; Carrera 21 No 20-36, Barrio Jardín; dm with air-con/fan COP$35,000/30,000, r with air-con/fan from COP$120,000/80,000;) Although it's housed in the former mansion of a drug cartel family, there couldn't be anything less shady about this bright and breezy hostel. Ask for a tour if you're interested – Australian owner Gabe believes there's still money hidden somewhere in the walls. Despite being located in a suburb, the big rooms, great pool and superfriendly atmosphere keep travelers returning.

Some of the private rooms, barely changed since their '80s heyday, are quite fabulous, and you might find you have a bathroom larger than most hotel rooms in Colombia. Definitely a quirky place, it's a good mix of a chill-out and party hostel, and will appeal to anyone who enjoys character. A taxi here from the center is COP$6000.

Dreamer HOSTEL $

(300-251-6534, 5-433-3264; www.thedreamerhostel.com; Diagonal 32, Los Trupillos; dm/d from COP$38,000/126,000;) A very high-end, self-contained and intelligently designed hostel, the Dreamer has rooms clustered around one of Santa Marta's best swimming pools. Even the dorms get air-con, a clean shared bathroom and good beds. It's hugely popular with discerning travelers. The Italian owners oversee the kitchen, so the food's great, too.

It's a little way out of town, but in fact it's well located for trips to Ciudad Perdida, PNN Tayrona, Minca and some of the area's better beaches, which means you don't have to face the crush of the city's traffic every time you head somewhere.

Casa Verde HOTEL $$$

(313-420-7502, 5-431-4122; www.casaverdesantamarta.com; Calle 18 No 4-70; d/ste incl breakfast COP$254,000/315,000;) If you're what the relaxed and attentive live-in owner calls 'a retired backpacker,' then this cute nine-room spot – with pebble-lined walls and floors, smart bathrooms, crisp bed linen, and intelligently designed, pristine whitewashed rooms – is for you. Lounge in the refreshing pool near the lobby or enjoy city views on the new roof terrace.

A RITUAL HIGH: COCA LEAVES

As you travel up and down the Caribbean coast, you might see Kogi people hopping on local buses with bags full of seashells – but they're not collecting them as ornaments. The indigenous groups of the Sierra Nevada de Santa Marta collect them for a sacred, ritualized method of consuming coca known as the *poporo*.

The active alkaloids in coca leaves are a powerful stimulant when chemically refined into cocaine. When the leaves alone are chewed, they have little effect. However, when chewed together with an alkaline substance, their active ingredients are multiplied, enabling users to walk many miles without rest or food, even at altitude – handy if you live in the world's highest coastal mountain range.

For the *poporo*, thousands of seashells called *caracucha* are collected, roasted over a fire and pounded into a fine powder. This powder is then placed into a hollowed-out gourd known as a *totuma*, which represents femininity. Men receive this as they come of age.

Women of these tribes collect coca leaves and dry them by placing them into *mochilas* (woven, bucket-shaped shoulder bags) packed with hot stones. Men take a large wad of leaves, put them into their mouths, and dip a small stick into the *totuma* to gather some of the powdered shell, which they suck off the stick. Any excess spittle-and-powder mix is wiped on the outside of the gourd, causing it to grow – symbolizing wisdom. The men then chew the mixture for up to 30 minutes; as their basified saliva causes the coca leaves to release their active components, users experience a slightly cocaine-like high. It is believed that the *poporo* instills knowledge, just as reading a book or going to college increases students' intelligence.

La Brisa Loca HOSTEL **$$**
(317-585-9598, 5-431-6121; www.labrisaloca.com; Calle 14 No 3-58; dm with/without air-con from COP$45,000/30,000, r with/without bathroom COP$150,000/120,000;) The 'Crazy Breeze' is the choice of a young, festive crowd, who pack out the 100 or so beds. Dorms sleep four to 10, and there's an array of private rooms, too, all with firm mattresses, high ceilings, ancient tile work, and in-room lockers that allow you to charge your phone securely while you're out.

The hostel is centered on the lively bar, which has a friendly vibe, a pool table and lewd cartoons on the wall. The large rooftop hosts big parties on weekends.

★ **Casa del Farol** BOUTIQUE HOTEL **$$$**
(5-423-1572; www.lacasadelfarol.com; Calle 18 No 3-115; r/ste incl breakfast from COP$275,000/330,000;) A superb hotel that could almost be recommended as a city highlight, the Farol hides a wealth of little luxuries behind its plain red facade. The large, funky-modern rooms are named and decorated after various cities (the Beijing and NYC rooms stand out), and the polite, courteous staff members are as helpful as tour guides.

Raising the bar further are the glorious common areas, which include an intimate patio (with pond), an inviting lobby (with books), and a lovely roof terrace with curvaceous loungers, creative marine murals and a cute little dip pool.

The owner, from Barcelona, also runs **Casa del Árbol** (5-422-4817; www.lacasadelarbol.com.co; Calle 21 No 2A-38; r incl breakfast COP220,000-395,000;) and **Casa del Piano** (5-420-7341; www.xarmhotels.com; Calle 19 No 4-76; r incl breakfast COP$215,000-395,000;), two similarly priced and stylish converted mansions in the city center.

Eating

Santa Marta has some of the best food on the coast. An influx of Latin and North American restaurateurs has simplified menus and moved the focus to ambience, classic cooking and stylish presentation. Parque de los Novios is the heart of Santa Marta's eating scene.

★ **Ikaro** VEGETARIAN **$$**
(5-430-5585; www.ikarocafe.com; Calle 19 No 3-60; mains COP$12,000-28,000; 8am-9pm Mon-Sat, 9am-9pm Sun;) Ikaro draws you in with its freshly baked bread and micro-roasted coffee and then entreats you to stay with its giant lounging 'beds' (ideal for sprawling with your headphones) and interior green wall dripping with foliage. The cafe menu is vegetarian, but carnivores will also find it appealing, and there are vegan options and craft beer, too.

Fill up on pad Thai noodles, mango ceviche or vegetable gyozas, and quench your thirst with inventive smoothies, South American wines and at least a dozen ways of imbibing your coffee.

Ouzo MEDITERRANEAN $$

(☎5-423-0658; www.ouzosantamarta.com; Carrera 3 No 19-29; mains COP$26,000-44,000; ⏲noon-10:30pm Mon-Thu, to 11pm Fri & Sat; 📶) Ouzo offers a stripped-back, classic Greek and Italian menu that includes superb pizza from a wood-fired oven and a good wine list. The octopus is slow-cooked for two hours in a garlicky broth, then slammed on the coals to sear and seal in the flavor. There's great service, and the superbly designed interior means the heat stays in the kitchen.

The place's immense popularity has spawned an upstairs section called Il Balcon, with outdoor seating overlooking the Parque de los Novios. Reservations aren't a bad idea for the evenings.

Donde Chucho SEAFOOD $$

(☎5-421-4663; Calle 19 No 2-17; mains COP$35,000-55,000; ⏲11am-11pm Mon-Sat) Serving the best seafood on the coast, Donde Chucho is a local legend. Start with the signature *ensalada Chucho* (shrimp, octopus, calamari and manta ray smoked in olive oil) and move on to *róbalo au gratin* (mozzarella and Parmesan). It's divine, though budget plenty of time for your meal: service is relaxed and dishes are prepared to order.

Drinking & Nightlife

With a young population, Santa Marta has lots going on after dark. Lively bars and clubs are scattered throughout the center. **Parque de los Novios** serves as an informal gathering place where young and old can meet before dancing until dawn.

La Puerta CLUB

(Calle 17 No 2-29; ⏲6pm-1am Tue & Wed, to 3am Thu-Sat) Here students and gringos eye each other up and get happily trashed in beautifully benign Colombian style. Soca, salsa, house, hip-hop and reggae warm up the packed dance floor. The gusting fans surrounding it will make you and other dancers look dramatically windswept.

Crabs BAR

(Calle 18 No 3-69; ⏲8pm-3am Wed-Sat) Less to do with crustaceans and more to do with rock and roll, the whimsically decorated Crabs is considered one of Colombia's best rock and blues bars, with cold beer, friendly staff and live sounds most nights. There are plenty of icons on the wall, a pool table, and even a bath to sit in (a reference to Jim Morrison, perhaps?).

BARRANQUILLA: COLOMBIA'S BIGGEST PARTY

Barranquilla, Colombia's fourth-largest city, is a hardworking port town located on the delta of the massive River Magdalena and laid out in a tangled ribbon along mangroves and the Caribbean Sea, sweltering and hustling in the blinding sun. The birthplace of Colombian pop goddess Shakira, Barranquilla is actually most famous for its annual **carnaval** (www.carnavaldebarranquilla.org; ⏲Feb), when the town clocks off, puts on its glad rags and goes wild as it throws the country's biggest street party.

The Mardi Gras celebration is held in February on the four days before Ash Wednesday, so the date changes each year. Much like the carnival in Rio de Janeiro, there are street bands, masquerade and fancy dress, live performances, and a riotous, slightly unhinged atmosphere as the town drinks and dances itself into the ground. It can be rough and ready, and you need to keep an eye on your possessions and your companions, but let your hair down and it could be a highlight of your trip.

The center of budget accommodations is on and around Paseo Bolívar (Calle 34), but this area is seedy. If you're coming for Carnaval, be sure to secure your hotel reservations months in advance, or you'll have no chance at all. The charming Italian-run **Meeting Point Hostel** (☎320-502-4459, 5-318-2599; www.themeetingpoint.hostel.com; Carrera 61 No 68-100; dm/r from COP$30,000/90,000; ❄📶) is probably the best value and certainly the most sociable place to stay on Baranquilla's otherwise lackluster accommodations scene. There's an excellent breakfast, clean rooms, friendly multilingual service and a very pleasant backyard to relax in.

While Barranquilla attracts big crowds for Mardi Gras, at any other time of the year there are very few visitors, and most travelers skip the town altogether (there's very little to see compared with elsewhere on the coast). If you do come, you'll find a city proud to be the home of *costeño* culture, and one full of excellent restaurants, lively bars and a smattering of decent museums.

WORTH A TRIP

ARACATACA: MAGIC & REALITY

Welcome to Macondo. Locals, maps, bus drivers and government officials will tell you it's really named Aracataca, and residents themselves rejected a name change in a 2006 referendum, but anyone who has read Gabriel García Márquez's masterpiece, *One Hundred Years of Solitude*, might be interested to know that the great author's place of birth was also the inspiration for the fictional town of Macondo, so beautifully described in the novel.

While Cartagena and Mompós are the main Gabriel García Márquez destinations in Colombia, with gorgeous Mompós looking today pretty much as Macondo is described, Aracataca is a place for diehard fans to head to. This workaday and fairly unlovely town may not have much in terms of atmosphere or architecture, but it boasts the interesting and well-curated **Casa Museo Gabriel García Márquez** (☎(5) 425-6588; http://casamuseogabo.unimagdalena.edu.co; Carrera 6 No 5-46; ⏱8am-1pm & 2-5pm Tue-Sat, 9am-2pm Sun) FREE, a faithful reconstruction of the Nobel Prizewinner's childhood home.

The museum is housed in a reconstruction of the house where García Márquez was born in 1927. The original house was sold by the family and knocked down decades ago, and even though the current structure is a fake, each building has been faithfully recreated. Panels (in Spanish only) describe various scenes from books that were set there and link the various buildings to episodes in Gabo's work.

There are several simple places to eat around the museum, including a number of *panaderías* (bakeries) on the main square, Plaza Bolívar. There's also a highly recommended restaurant, **El Patio Mágico de Gabo & Leo Matiz** (☎301-571-7450, 301-739-7516; Calle 7 No 4-57; set meals: COP$25,000; ✎), for those who'd prefer a longer lunch.

It's possible to visit Aracataca independently by bus from Santa Marta's market (COP$9000 1½ hours, hourly) or from Baranquilla's bus station (COP$17,000, 2½ hours, hourly). There are also two buses a day to/from Cartagena (COP$29,000, five hours). Leaving from Aracataca, head for the **Berlinave Terminal** (Carrera 1 & Carrera 2E).

Information

4-72 (☎5-421-0180; Calle 22 No 2-21; ⏱8am-noon & 2-6pm Mon-Fri, to noon Sat) Post office.

Aviatur (☎5-423-5745; www.aviatur.com; Calle 15 No 3-20; ⏱8am-noon & 2-4pm Mon-Fri) A place to reserve accommodations run by the agency inside PNN Tayrona.

Parques Nacionales Naturales de Colombia (☎5-423-0758; www.parquesnacionales.gov.co; Calle 17 No 4-06) This office of the national-park service gives some basic information about PNN Tayrona.

Policía Nacional (☎5-421-4264; Calle 22 No 1C-74)

Getting There & Away

AIR

The **Aeropuerto Internacional Simón Bolívar** (☎5-438-1360; http://smr.aerooriente.com.co; Vía Ciénaga Santa Marta, Km18) is 16km south of the city on the Barranquilla–Bogotá road and must be one of the few airports in the world right on the beach. City buses marked 'El Rodadero Aeropuerto' will take you there in 45 minutes from Carrera 1C. Flight destinations include Bogotá and Medellín.

BUS

The **bus terminal** (Calle 41 No 31-17) is on the southeastern outskirts of the city. Frequent minibuses go there from Carrera 1C in the center, or you can take a cab (COP$6000).

The main bus companies all offer several daily connections to the following destinations.

Destination	Fare (COP$)	Duration (hours)	Frequency
Barranquilla	14,000	2	hourly
Bogotá	80,000-90,000	16-17	hourly
Bucaramanga	70,000	9-12	2 daily
Cartagena	35,000	4	hourly until 5:30pm
Medellín	126,000	15	5 daily
Riohacha	20,000	2½	every 30min
Tolú	51,000	7	3 daily

To get to Palomino, take the Mamatoco bus from the market in Santa Marta (COP$9000, two hours).

Minca

☎5 / POP 1200

Perched 600m high up in the Sierra Nevada above Santa Marta, Minca is a small mountain village famous for its organic coffee, incredibly varied birdlife and – perhaps more importantly – much cooler temperatures than on the scorching coast below. The town, which until a few years ago could only be reached via a dirt road, is delightful, surrounded by thick cloud forest and soaring mountain peaks. Despite being recognized by Unesco as a biosphere reserve since 1980, it's only in the last few years that Minca has grown as a traveler destination, with a slew of new hostels and hotels.

It's now well and truly on the map, however, and specializes in ultraremote traveler retreats scattered amid the surrounding steep mountainsides. A great base for mountain biking, birdwatching and hiking, Minca also offers delightfully warm locals who seem genuinely happy to see visitors.

Sights

Cascada de Marinka WATERFALL
(COP$4000; 8am-6pm) This lovely spot is a 1½ hour walk from Minca – or a 10-minute moto-taxi ride (COP$9000) – and is a surprisingly impressive set of two waterfalls, with rather cold bathing pools beneath each. It can get crowded, so go early in the day or after 4pm. There's also a small **cafe**.

Finca La Victoria FARM
(tour COP$15,000; 9am-5pm) Founded in the late 19th century, this family-run coffee plantation offers interesting 40-minute tours (usually available in English) in which the coffee-production process is carefully explained. Upstairs there's a charming cafe perfect for a cup of the plantation's coffee accompanied by a moist piece of cake. It's a steep 1½-hour walk from Minca, or take a motorbike (COP$10,000).

Pozo Azul NATURAL POOL
FREE This fun natural pool and small waterfall is a popular sight for locals and tourists alike, though it can get very full on weekends and during high season. It's a 30-minute walk from town: simply continue straight on and follow the road once you've crossed the yellow bridge in the middle of Minca. A moto-taxi costs COP$7000.

Activities

Birdwatching, hiking and mountain biking are the most popular activities in Minca, and can be organized by almost any hostel or hotel. Minca is also well located for the Ciudad Perdida (p152) trek, and makes for a good place to relax and unwind afterwards.

Marcos Torres López BIRDWATCHING
(314-637-1029; marcostorres92@yahoo.com.co) Marcos doesn't speak English, but he has the sharpest eye in Minca, so much so that he gets international clientele traveling here just to birdwatch with him. He charges just COP$160,000 for a full-day birdwatching trip to El Dorado, including lunch and transport.

Fidel Travels TOURS
(321-589-3678; www.fideltravels.com) Fidel Travels has an office just by the church and offers birdwatching tours, visits to the La Victoria coffee farm (p145) and trips to Pozo Azul (p145), a gorgeous spot for swimming. There's also a highly recommended full-day combo tour, which takes in all the main sights of Minca in one day.

Lucky Tours MOUNTAIN BIKING
(310-397-5714) Based in the Tienda Café de Minca, this mountain-bike specialist outfit is run by Andrés, who can take you on some superb trips, including a route called the Kraken, a ride that takes you through 11 different ecosystems, and the Clockwork Orange, another world-class bike route.

Jungle Joe Minca Adventures TOURS
(317-308-5270; www.junglejoeminca.com) If you're short on time or are just keen to immerse yourself in Minca's diversity, English-speaking Joe Ortiz can fix you up with an excellent tour incorporating a coffee farm, cacao production, hiking, a local lunch and a swim near a waterfall, all for a very reasonable COP$130,000. There are also more specialised tubing and birdwatching trips.

Sleeping

Minca has blossomed in recent years and now has some of the best hostels along the coast – and certainly many of those with the best views. There are many hostels in the town itself, but the very best options are in the mountains, and often involve a motorbike ride to get there.

Mundo Nuevo HOSTEL $$
(300-360-4212; www.mundonuevo.com.co; hammocks COP$30,000, dm COP$40,000-55,000, d COP$150,000-200,000) This fantastic place is all about creating an environmentally friendly project that gives back to its community. Housed on a former cattle farm, Mundo Nuevo seeks to be self-sustainable in relation to food, water and energy. Its mountain setting is gorgeous, and visitors immediately feel that they're part of a team. The hostel is a COP$20,000 moto-taxi ride from Minca.

Activities include bread making, permaculture tours and visits to an indigenous Wiwa village.

★ Casa Elemento HOSTEL $
(☎ 313-587-7677, 311-655-9207; www.casaelemento.co; hammocks/dm COP$25,000/40,000, cabañas from COP$150,000;) When they say the location here is 'above Minca' they're not kidding – just getting to this fantastic place is an adventure and ensures that only the intrepid arrive. Created and run by an international crew, Casa Elemento has an incredible position with extraordinary views and is the perfect place to escape the world. It's a 30-minute, COP$25,000 motorbike ride from Minca.

Accommodations are simple and hostel-like, with a small pool, toilets that have views direct into the jungle, and a busy restaurant-bar-hangout. The centerpiece is an enormous hammock where a dozen people can comfortably fit and drink in the views. Ziplines connect tree platforms that are perfect for birdwatching. There's no wireless, which makes for an extremely social atmosphere. Walk back down to Minca by all means, but only masochists walk up – take a motorbike.

Casas Viejas HOSTEL $
(☎ 321-523-7613, 310-828-0761; www.casasviejasminca.com; dm COP$35,000, tents for 2 COP$40,000, d with/without bathroom COP$130,000/90,000) This extraordinary place is perfect for isolating yourself in the mountains above Minca. It has a self-contained hippyish feeling, with a spectacular location, a communal fire pit and good food. Choose from rooms in a dorm, double tents to share and private rooms. Activities include yoga, massage and admiring sunsets. Meals are served communally. The locally grown coffee is free.

Appropriately, the hostel is just uphill from the Finca La Victoria coffee farm (p145), but fear not: you're properly isolated here. A moto-taxi from Minca costs COP$20,000 (35 minutes) and is quite a thrilling ride (try to keep your luggage to a minimum). The arduous walk takes at least two hours.

Minca Ecohabs CABAÑAS $$
(☎ 317-586-4067; www.mincaecohabs.com; r incl breakfast from COP$196,000;) On a steep hillside with views toward the Caribbean and Santa Marta, this long-standing hotel was recently taken over by a Santa Marta hotelier who has attempted to reinvigorate the place. The two-story rooms are made of entirely natural fibers, have screened windows, balconies, fans, electricity and fridges. It's a wonderful place to really drink in Minca's unique location.

Hotel Minca HOTEL $$
(☎ 317-437-3078; www.hotelminca.com; s/d incl breakfast COP$85,000/150,000;) This 13-room place is the closest thing Minca has to a formal hotel. It has large, simple rooms in a colonial-style building that was once a convent, surrounded by thick vegetation. Breakfast on the balcony is an incredible spectacle as dozens of hummingbirds come to feed from sugar water put out for them by staff.

Eating

There are a few restaurants and plenty of small cafes and bakeries in Minca, but as yet there's none of the culinary sophistication that can be found in Santa Marta or Cartagena. Most hotels and hostels serve meals, so there's never any problem finding somewhere to eat.

Lazy Cat INTERNATIONAL $
(Calle Principal Diagonal; mains COP$13,000-20,000; 9am-9pm;) You can slink into the Lazy Cat at any time of day for all kinds of hunger relief, from breakfasts (COP$8000 to COP$10,000) to superb local coffee, smoothies, sandwiches, burgers, quesadillas and wok dishes. There's a lovely balcony overlooking the green valley below, and the eponymous cat can usually be found lounging around the place somewhere.

★ Casa d'Antonio SPANISH $$$
(☎ 312-342-1221; www.hotelrestaurantecasadantonio.com; mains COP$22,000-60,000; noon-3pm & 6-11pm;) Handily situated in the middle of town overlooking the river, this hotel-restaurant serves authentic Málagan food – something of an apparition in these parts. Get (re)acquainted with delicious Spanish-style seafood such as *paella de mariscos* or *pulpo a la gallega* (Galician-style octopus) if you have time for a leisurely meal. The meat *a la parrilla* is equally robust.

Getting There & Away

Colectivos and shared taxis to/from Santa Marta arrive at and depart from the center of Minca throughout the day (COP$8000, 30 minutes), and you'll rarely have to wait longer than 20 minutes for them to fill up and depart. A taxi to Santa Marta is around COP$40,000.

In Santa Marta, Minca-bound *colectivos* and shared taxis leave from outside the market at the corner of Calle 11 and Carrera 12. A faster option for the same price is the moto-taxi to Minca. However, these depart from Yucal, a barrio on the outskirts of town, so you'll need to take a COP$6000 taxi from anywhere in Santa Marta to get there.

Taganga

5 / POP 5000

Once a tiny fishing village, Taganga seemed to have hit the jackpot when it became a big backpacker destination in the early 2000s. It drew a diverse crowd of locals and travelers, and quietly boomed. Hostels and restaurants prospered with the endless stream of visitors.

Taganga today is something of a cautionary tale about the overdevelopment of small towns, though, and in the past few years the village has gone from a near-obligatory backpacker stop to a rather depressing place where poverty is rife and much of what originally attracted visitors has disappeared. That said, some travelers still come here for cheap accommodation, partying and diving; there are also those who love being so close to PNN Tayrona (p148), just a short boat ride away. The town's hostel owners are a determined bunch and are doggedly fighting to restore Taganga to its former glory.

Activities

Taganga is a popular scuba-diving center due to its low low prices. Several schools offer diving and courses (four-day open-water PADI around COP$1,150,000).

Poseidon Dive Center DIVING

(5-421-9224, 314-889-2687; www.poseidondivecenter.com; Calle 18 No 1-69) One of the best reasons to visit Taganga is this friendly but professional diving operator. It offers mini-courses allowing beginners to dive up to 12m (COP$300,000), PADI open-water courses (COP$1,150,000) and two-tank dives (COP$240,000). Boats leave most mornings for the pristine waters in and around Tayrona National Park (p148).

Expotur TOURS

(5-421-9577; www.expotur-eco.com; Calle 18 No 2A-07; 8am-6pm) The Taganga office of this excellent Santa Marta–based agency sells Ciudad Perdida (p152) treks, tours of La Guajira (p155) and PNN Tayrona (p148), and mountain-biking and birdwatching trips.

Tours

Taganga remains a popular and competitive place to buy Ciudad Perdida (p152) tours; a couple of Santa Marta–based tour companies have offices here selling trips.

Sleeping & Eating

Casa de Felipe HOSTEL $

(5-421-9120, 316-318-9158; www.lacasadefelipe.com; Carrera 5A No 19-13; dm COP$20,000-25,000, s/d from COP$50,000/70,000;) Feeling like a bit of the old, mellower Taganga, this French-run hostel is the best budget option hereabouts. It's also very secure, though be sure to take a taxi after dark. It's in a beautiful house on lush grounds above the bay, and has great staff, pleasant rooms, a good bar, a kitchen, numerous hammocks, and friendly folk from around the world.

Hearty breakfasts are COP$8000 extra.

Divanga B&B GUESTHOUSE $$

(5-421-9092; www.divanga.com; Calle 12 No 4-07; incl breakfast with/without air-con dm COP$47,000/42,000, r COP$120,000/90,000;) Run by French resident Lucie, who has spent 20 years in Taganga and is a passionate campaigner for the town, this charming and colorful place has 13 rooms, most of which surround a swimming pool, as well as two 'kiosks' (raised, thatched-roof cabins). There's a rooftop deck and bar that catches the sea breeze and serves up a large breakfast.

★ **Pachamama** FRENCH $$

(5-421-9486; Calle 16 No 1C-18; mains COP$20,000-37,000; 5pm-midnight Mon-Sat;) With tiki stylings and a laid-back vibe, Pachamama may look like an indoor beach bar, but casual as it may be, this is easily the culinary highlight of Taganga. The French chef has produced one of the most creative menus on the coast; the tenderloin in red-wine-and-mushroom sauce is sensational, and the tuna carpaccio is perfect.

Babaganoush INTERNATIONAL $$

(Carrera 1C No 18-22; mains COP$20,000-30,000; 1-11pm Thu-Sun, 6:30-10:30pm Wed;) This cosy rooftop restaurant has great bay views and an eclectic menu that keeps the crowds returning. Try the excellent falafel, the perfectly cooked filet mignon or the sublime Thai green curry. It's up the hillside on the road towards Santa Marta.

Information

In recent years Taganga's security situation has deteriorated seriously. Be mindful at any time of day, and don't leave the main streets if you're on your own. Do not try to walk to Playa Grande, even though it's only a 1km stroll from the town; there have been numerous reports of robberies in broad daylight here. Always take taxis after dark.

There's only one ATM in Taganga, and it's usually broken or empty. The nearest reliable ATMs are in Santa Marta.

The **tourist information point** (Carrera 1; ⏲9am-6pm Mon-Sat) usually staffed by tourist police is directly on the beachfront as you arrive from Santa Marta.

Getting There & Away

Taganga is easily accessible; there are frequent minibuses (COP$1600, 15 minutes) from Carreras 1C and 5 in Santa Marta. A taxi costs COP$10,000.

From Taganga there's a daily boat to Cabo San Juan del Guía in PNN Tayrona. This leaves at 11am each day, and returns at 4pm from Cabo San Juan, though in the high season the boat makes three trips in both directions per day. The one-way cost is COP$50,000; the trip takes an hour and boats leave from the tourist information point.

Parque Nacional Natural Tayrona

Parque Nacional Natural Tayrona is a magical slice of Colombia's Caribbean coast, with stunning stretches of golden sandy beach backed by coconut palms and thick rainforest. Behind it all rise the steep hillsides of the Sierra Nevada de Santa Marta, the world's highest coastal mountain range. The park stretches along the coast from the Bahía de Taganga near Santa Marta to the mouth of the Río Piedras, 35km east, and covers some 12,000 hectares of land and 3000 hectares of coral-rich sea.

The park gets extremely crowded in high season (December and January), and vicious currents mean that most of the gorgeous beaches aren't suitable for swimming, though you can take a dip and snorkel (with great care) at a select, safer few. Despite these issues, Tayrona is an immensely attractive place and one that's rewarding and exciting to explore.

Sights

The **Parque Nacional Natural Tayrona** (www.parquetayrona.com.co; foreigners/Colombians COP$54,500/23,000; ⏲8am-5pm) can be entered at several points, but wherever you enter, you'll need to pay the entrance fee (foreigners/Colombians COP$54,500/23,000). This fee is valid for as long as you care to stay inside the park, and you can also leave the park and re-enter at another entrance until 5pm on the day of purchase. Upon entering you may be searched for alcohol and glass bottles, neither of which are permitted.

★Cabo San Juan del Guía BEACH

Cabo San Juan del Guía is a beautiful cape with a knockout beach. It's also by far the most crowded area of the park, although lack of road access deters casual day-trippers. The area has a **restaurant** and a campsite (p149), with hammocks and cabins, in a spectacular lookout on a rock in the middle of the beach. It's possible to spend a very atmospheric night here. Swimming is also possible most of the time, but don't go in too deep.

Playa Cristal BEACH

(Bahía Neguange) This gorgeous boat-in beach on Bahía Neguange used to be known as Playa

Parque Nacional Natural Tayrona

del Muerto (Beach of the Dead) – little wonder they decided on a name change. It's a wonderful place to spend the day on the sand, and there are several **shacks** serving up fresh fish and cold beers. You'll need to take a boat from Cabo San Juan del Guía (p148) (COP$60,000 for up to 10 people, so it's worth hanging around for other potential punters).

La Arenilla BEACH

La Arenilla is an attractive beach in a tiny cove framed by massive boulders, with chunky sand and glints of fool's gold dancing in the water. It has a sweet little **restaurant** with great sea views from its tables. It's a good alternative to the throngs at nearby San Juan del Guía (p148).

Cañaveral BEACH

Cañaveral is as far as you can go in the park by road. From the car park a trail leads west to **Arrecifes** and Cabo San Juan del Guía (p148). The beaches in Cañaveral are very beautiful – golden sand and blue water – but there's no shade, and swimming can be dangerous because of treacherous offshore currents. There are several places to stay here.

Pueblito VILLAGE

From Cabo San Juan del Guía (p148) a scenic path goes inland and uphill to the small indigenous village of Pueblito, providing some splendid tropical-forest scenery and getting you to Pueblito in 1½ hours. In the tranquil village you can see traditional houses and various sites sacred to residents, making for an interesting change of pace from the beach.

The path from Cabo San Juan del Guía is definitely more challenging than others in the park – the majority of the uphill climb is over stones, some of them massive. It's not an easy trail, and you can forget about it when it rains or if you have a large pack. You can hire a guide for the walk in Cabo San Juan del Guía from COP$50,000. It's also possible to reach Pueblito from the main road at the Calabazo entrance, from where it's a two-hour hike.

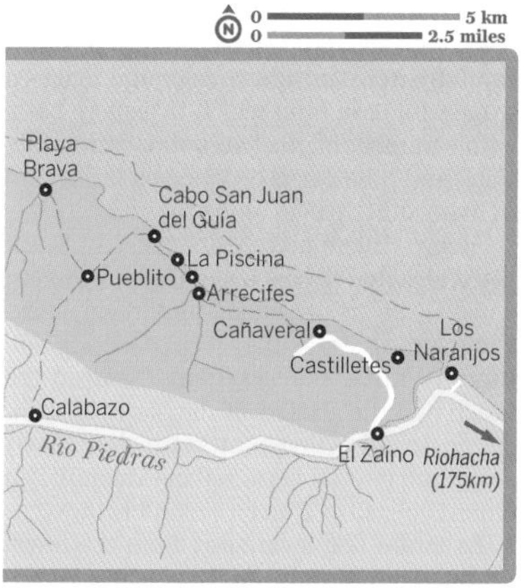

Sleeping

There are multiple options for spending a night or two in the park, though they are either exceptionally expensive or very basic. **Castilletes** (☎300-405-5547, 313-653-1830; www.campingcastilletespnntayrona.blogspot.com; campsites/tents per person COP$20,000/30,000, hammocks COP$25,000, cabins COP$110,000; P), the first point reached after entering from El Zaíno, offers peaceful camping with sea views; Cañaveral (p149) is where the fancier options are, while Arrecifes (p149) and Cabo San Juan del Guía (p149) are the most popular spots for backpackers.

Camping Don Pedro CAMPGROUND $

(☎317-253-3021, 315-320-8001; campingdonpedro@hotmail.com; Arrecifes; hammocks COP$15,000, campsites per person with/without tent hire COP$20,000/18,000, cabañas per person incl breakfast COP$60,000) Of the three places to stay and eat in Arrecifes, this is the best. It's reached via a 600m split off the main trail just before Arrecifes. The spacious grounds are well maintained and have an abundance of fruit trees. Cooking facilities are available to guests, while excellent meals, including superb fresh fish, cost an average COP$15,000. The welcome is warm.

Camping Cabo San Juan del Guía CAMPGROUND $

(☎333-356-9912; www.cabosanjuantayrona.com; Cabo San Juan del Guía; campsites COP$20,000, hammocks COP$40,000-50,000, rent-a-tents COP$60,000, cabins COP$200,000) Most backpackers end up at this campground, which has the air of a music festival in high season. There are two gorgeous swimming beaches as well as a busy but mediocre restaurant. For COP$50,000 you can sleep in the hammocks high atop the *mirador* (lookout) on the rocks above the beach, giving fantastic views of the sea, beaches and mountains.

There are also two private double rooms on the top floor of the *mirador*.

★**Finca Barlovento** HOTEL $$$

(☎314-626-9789; http://barloventotayrona.com; Via Riohacha, Km33; s/d/tr incl half board from

COP$330,000/450,000/695,000) Finca Barlovento may be the single most beautiful spot in the area, and it's located just outside PNN Tayrona right on the beach at Playa Los Naranjos. Here, where the Río Piedras bursts out of the Sierra Nevada and empties into the Caribbean, you'll find this architecturally unique home, clinging to a cliff face.

The property consists of the original house and the *maloka*, an indigenous-style thatched structure divided into private rooms. Both feature open-air beds that jut out on a deck over the sea, and the food is simply sensational.

★ **Ecohostal Yuluka** HOSTAL **$$**
(☎310-361-9436; www.aviatur.com; Via Santa Marta, Km28; incl breakfast dm COP$40,000, r from COP$160,000;) This gorgeous place very stylishly caters for discerning backpackers who want to explore the park without giving up all comforts. It's very rustic but supremely comfortable, with large private bathrooms, spacious dorms and even a slide into the pool. All beds come with mosquito nets, and the food is great.

It's located on the main road just before the main El Zaíno park entrance if you're coming from Santa Marta.

Cayena Beach Villa BOUTIQUE HOTEL **$$$**
(☎314-800-5471; www.cayenabeachvilla.com; Villa Troncal Caribe, Km39; r incl half-board from COP$750,000;) Located a few kilometers east of PNN Tayrona, this recently constructed beach villa with its gabled thatched roof and exquisite tropical garden is a self-contained luxury option. Right on the seafront, with one of Colombia's most gorgeous pools (which you can actually swim laps in), it has huge rustic-chic rooms, high-quality furniture and gourmet dinners (included in the price).

Among the many highlights are the open-air bathrooms, the rejuvenating yoga classes and the romantic beach a short walk away. With only six rooms and a team of warm, friendly staff, this place will spoil you rotten.

Ecohabs CABIN **$$$**
(☎5-344-2748; www.aviaturecoturismo.com; Cañaveral; 4-person cabañas incl breakfast from COP$695,000;) This group of 14 rustic-chic cabañas is a five-minute walk from the car park that marks the end of the road into Tayrona national park. Each two-story cabaña is in the style of a Tayrona hut, with conical thatched roof, minibar, large shaded terrace, flatscreen TV and spectacular views. It's by far the nicest place to stay inside the park.

There's also a gourmet restaurant (mains COP$29,000 to COP$39,000).

Eating

There are several beachside restaurants within the park, serving fresh fish and less-fresh chicken dishes. Campers can try to self-cater, but facilities are very basic, so most people eat at the simple campsite restaurants. It's forbidden to bring your own alcohol into the park, but it's for sale at most places.

Estadero Doña Juana SEAFOOD **$$**
(Playa Cristal; mains COP$20,000-40,000; ⊙11am-4pm low season, 7am-4pm high season) Take a boat from Bahía Neguange to gorgeous Playa Cristal and head straight for Doña Juana's makeshift beach restaurant. You'll be taken to the kitchen, shown various fish and asked to choose one; it will arrive 20 minutes later, mouthwateringly prepared.

Getting There & Away

You can get to El Zaíno (COP$7000, one hour) on Palomino-bound buses that depart regularly from Santa Marta's market; just let the driver know where you want to get out. From El Zaíno, catch the jeep that shuttles between the park entrance and Cañaveral (COP$3000, 10 minutes) or walk the 2.5km.

Palomino

☎5 / POP 6000

Palomino doesn't look like much as you pass through it on the main Santa Marta–Riohacha highway, but lurking on one side of its urban sprawl is one of Colombia's most perfect beaches, while on the other are the dramatic Sierra Nevada mountains, a place the local indigenous people still guard carefully from outsiders. Palomino makes a wonderful base from which to explore both, with a number of great accommodations options and a backpacker vibe you'll not find in many other places along the coast.

Along Palomino's palm-backed beach you'll also find fishers using traditional nets, while in its mountainous hinterland indigenous tribes live as they have done for centuries. With seven ecosystems between the beach and the glaciers of the Sierra Nevada, it's no surprise that ecotourism has slowly come into its own here, making Palomino an almost obligatory stop for Colombia travelers.

Be aware that swimming from the beach in Palomino is only rarely possible, as the

currents are treacherous: look out for the red flags, and don't go into the water beyond the shallows if they're flying. Take care even at other times, too. Other than beach-lounging, the main activity here is tubing down the river from the mountains to the coast.

Sleeping

Palomino has some of the best traveler hostels and most laid-back beach hotels in the country. Most listings are on the beach, but all can arrange trips into the mountains for activities, including hiking, tubing or white-water rafting.

★Tiki Hut Hostel Palomino HOSTEL **$**
(☎314-794-2970; www.tikihutpalomino.co; dm/d incl breakfast COP$40,000/160,000;) Like a backpacker hostel relocated to a tropical beach setting, Tiki Hut is paradise on a budget, a beautifully designed place set around a large pool, with charming staff and comfortable, rustic rooms that feature mosquito nets and artsy splashes of color. Less brilliant are the not-fully-enclosed toilets in the big dorms.

The bar is a blast during happy hour, and there's an essential billiard table where you can competitively introduce yourself to other guests. The beach is a mere two-minute stroll away.

Dreamer Hostel HOSTEL **$$**
(☎300-609-7229, 320-556-7794; www.thedreamerhostel.com; dm/d incl breakfast from COP$45,000/180,000;) Like a resort for backpackers, the Dreamer has a kidney-shaped pool, a large, florid garden and a restaurant that knocks out good pizzas. The supersocial ambience is reminiscent of a refined beach party, and there are plenty of activities on offer. The tile-floored, fan-cooled dorms have thatched roofs and are spacious, if lacking in luxury touches.

All in all, it's a great place to hang and make friends. The beach is a short walk away.

It's the sister property to Santa Marta's Dreamer hostel (p141).

Finca Escondida HOSTEL **$**
(☎310-456-3159, 315-610-9561; www.fincaescondida.com; hammocks COP$30,000, dm COP$40,000, d COP$170,000-210,000;) The football pitch, outdoor gym, yoga classes and surf school suggest that this large beachfront complex is run by a bunch of fitness fanatics, but it also rewards guests in search of tranquility, with inviting hammocks, relaxing gardens and largish rooms complete with beautiful heavy beds and psychedelic murals. The feel is rustic, with wooden buildings set in grounds full of fruit trees.

The attached restaurant, which has tables on the beach, is one of the best in town, and does excellent fresh fish and seafood served with ice-cold beers.

La Sirena LODGE **$$**
(☎310-718-4644; www.ecosirena.com; r/cabañas incl breakfast from COP$160,000/240,000;) Aiming for the romantic crowd, La Sirena is a collection of beachfront eco-cabins with a healthy, holistic vibe. Employing the local building materials (palm thatch, bamboo) in a more stylish way than its competitors, the lodge has comfy-rustic rooms with super-soft bedding, mosquito nets and outdoor bathrooms. Set amid a peaceful palm-studded garden, the complex takes its environmental impact seriously.

The small, mainly vegetarian cafe does exceptional French toast for breakfast.

There's a minimum two-night stay (three in high season).

Reserva Natural El Matuy CABIN **$$$**
(☎315-322-0653, 317-504-9340; www.elmatuy.com; cabañas per person incl full board COP$230,000;) Matuy is the quintessential 'anti-resort' resort, where the 'disconnect' is taken literally: there's no electricity in its 10 inconspicuous cabins shaded by lean palms and built right on the beach. The rest of the complex operates on candlelight and cold outdoor showers. (Plug-ins and wi-fi are available at reception.)

Perhaps surprisingly, Matuy is an all-inclusive of sorts. All meals and non-alcoholic drinks are included in the rates, and you can enjoy them sprawled on beanbags, or swinging from hammocks under gnarly old trees and shapely palms illuminated by candles. If you like your accommodation simple, tranquil and close to nature (and an unruffled beach), this will seem like heaven.

Aité Eco Hotel HOTEL **$$$**
(☎321-782-1300; www.aite.com.co; d/cabañas/bungalows incl breakfast from COP$511,000/430,000/610,000;) Compared to Palomino's other backpacker-oriented places, Aité is a bit more grown up and manicured. Set on a secluded hillside with closely cropped grass and well-tended plants, this 15-room pleasure garden has common areas perched atop a small ridge, though the loveliest rooms are

arguably the beachside cabañas, which open onto the sea.

Design-wise the place is something of a tropical Ikea, with local thatch and bamboo mixed with starched sheets and stylish sofas. There's a curvy pool, a fancy spa and piles of activities in which to indulge.

Eating

Nearly all hostels and hotels serve three meals a day, so many travelers simply eat where they're staying. Nearly all hostels allow nonguests to dine with them as well, and as such there are relatively few independent restaurants in Palomino, with a couple of notable exceptions.

★Suá COLOMBIAN **$$**
(☎310-251-5738; mains COP$18,000-35,000; ⊙noon-11pm Wed-Sun;) Set in a lovely garden, Suá is a collectively run project with impeccable environmental and sustainability credentials, including a great vegetarian selection. Ironically, it also does one of the best steaks on the Caribbean coast. Altogether the fare is rather inventive, with a fully translated English menu that includes specialties such as prawns marinated in garlic, sea salt and butter.

Pizzería La Frontera PIZZA **$$**
(Carrera 6 Calle 1A-90; pizzas COP$10,000-30,000; ⊙noon-11pm;) If you can prise yourself away from your dreamy Palomino beach shack, this semi-alfresco place between the main road and the beach serves the best pizza in town. It might not look much by day, but come evening it's usually packed and buzzing with a friendly, sociable vibe.

Getting There & Away

There's no bus station in Palomino, but regular buses in both directions run along the main road. Destinations include Santa Marta (COP$9000, two hours), PNN Tayrona (COP$6000, one hour) and Riohacha (COP$8000, 1½ hours). The best place to pick them up is at the top of Carrera 6.

If you're arriving in Palomino, you can walk down to the beach or grab a moto-taxi to drive you the 500m there (COP$2000). Buses and motorbikes run all day and until late at night – not a bad option if you have luggage.

Ciudad Perdida

What could be more intriguing than an ancient abandoned city? Ciudad Perdida (literally 'Lost City') disappeared into the jungle around the time of the Spanish Conquest and was only 'discovered' again in the 1970s. Deep in the Sierra Nevada de Santa Marta mountains, it remains accessible only on foot in what is easily one of Colombia's most exciting and breathtaking hikes. Known locally by its indigenous name of Teyuna, the city was built by the Tayrona people on the northern slopes of the Sierra Nevada de Santa Marta. Today it's one of the largest known pre-Columbian towns in the Americas, and the focus of Colombia's most popular multiday hike. Doing the hike is a fantastic experience, and you don't need to be particularly strong or experienced to do it, either. The landscapes and the sense of remoteness will stay with you long after you return.

Ciudad Perdida lies on the steep slopes of the upper Río Buritaca valley at an altitude of between 950m and 1300m. The central part of the city is set on a ridge from which various stone paths lead down to other sectors on the slopes. Although the wooden houses of the Tayrona are long gone, the stone structures, including terraces and stairways, remain in remarkably good shape.

There are around 170 terraces, most of which once served as foundations for the houses. The largest terraces are set on the central ridge and these were used for ritual ceremonies. The vast majority of the site is totally unexcavated, as the indigenous people will not allow further investigation.

Recent surveys have pinpointed the location of about 300 other Tayrona settlements scattered over the slopes, once linked by stone-paved roads. Of all these, Ciudad Perdida is the largest and is thought to have been the Tayrona 'capital.'

Archaeological digs have uncovered Tayrona objects (fortunately, the *guaqueros* didn't manage to take everything). These are mainly various kinds of pottery (both ceremonial and utilitarian), goldwork and unique necklaces made of semiprecious stones. Some of these objects are on display in the Museo del Oro (p140) in Santa Marta and in Bogotá. It's a good idea to visit the museum in Santa Marta before going to Ciudad Perdida.

Tours

Previously, just the one agency, Turcol, had access to Ciudad Perdida. However, in 2008 the Colombian military cleared out the paramilitaries in the area, which has effectively opened up the route to Ciudad Perdida to healthy competition. There are now six

THE LOST CIVILIZATION

In pre-Columbian times the Sierra Nevada de Santa Marta on the Caribbean coast was home to various indigenous communities, of which the Tayrona, belonging to the Chibcha linguistic family, was the dominant and most developed one. The Tayrona (also spelled Tairona) are believed to have evolved into a distinctive culture since about the 5th century AD. A millennium later, shortly before the Spaniards came, the Tayrona had developed a civilization based on complex social and political organization and advanced engineering.

Ciudad Perdida was built between the 11th and 14th centuries, though its origins are much older, going back to perhaps the 7th century. Spread over an area of about 2 sq km, it's the largest known Tayrona city; it was most probably the civilization's biggest urban center and its major political and economic center. Some 2000 to 4000 people are believed to have lived here at its peak.

The Tayrona civilization was the first advanced indigenous culture that the Spaniards encountered in the Americas, in 1499. It was here in the Sierra Nevada that the conquerors were for the first time astonished by the local gold, and the myth of El Dorado was born. The Spaniards crisscrossed the Sierra Nevada, meeting with brave resistance from the indigenous people. The Tayrona defended themselves fiercely but were almost totally wiped out in the course of 75 years of uninterrupted war. A handful of survivors abandoned their homes and fled into the upper reaches of the Sierra. Tayrona settlements were soon engulfed by the jungle.

For four centuries Ciudad Perdida lay untouched and forgotten, until local man Florentino Sepúlveda and his two sons, Julio César and Jacobo, stumbled upon the city in the early 1970s, on one of their grave-robbing expeditions. Word spread like wildfire and soon other *guaqueros* (grave robbers) came to Ciudad Perdida. Fighting broke out between rival gangs, and Julio César was one of the casualties.

In 1976 the Colombian government sent in troops and archaeologists to protect the site and learn its secrets, but sporadic fighting and looting continued for several years. During this time the *guaqueros* dubbed the site the Infierno Verde (Green Hell).

licensed agencies, all based in Santa Marta, guiding groups of travelers on the four- to six-day hike to the ancient ruins. You cannot do the trip on your own or hire an independent guide. If you're not sure about the legitimacy of your guide or agency, be sure to ask for the Operación de Programas Turísticos (OPT) certificate, the essential document needed by any guide.

Once the market opened in 2008, the race to the bottom began, and prices and quality fell. The government intervened by regulating prices and service, and the official price of the tour is now set at COP$950,000.

The price includes transportation, food, accommodations (usually mattresses with mosquito nets, though some agencies still use hammocks on one night), porters for your food, non-English-speaking guides and all necessary permits. The price does not go down if you complete the walk in fewer days. Most groups tend to do the trek in four days, but less fit walkers and those who want to take their time often do it in five. Six-day trips are the maximum and are only really necessary for the very slow and easily exhausted; the four-day version is recommended.

Take the strongest mosquito repellent you can find and reapply it every few hours. Local brand Nopikex is excellent and will protect you better than many stronger foreign brands. Take some long pants and a long-sleeved T-shirt, both of which are advisable at Ciudad Perdida itself, where the mosquitoes are particularly hungry.

Tours are in groups of four to 15, and depart year-round as soon as a group is assembled. In high season expect a tour to set off every day. In low season the agencies tend to pool resources and form a joint group, even if each agency still has its own guides. Other companies are agents for these outfits and there's really no reason to use them.

Note that all access to Ciudad Perdida is closed (and thus no hikes depart) for much of September, when indigenous peoples meet to perform cleansing ceremonies at the site.

The Hike

After meeting your tour group (obligatory) in Santa Marta in the morning, you'll be driven to the village of El Mamey (also known as Machete), the end of the road from Santa Marta, where you'll have a leisurely lunch before setting off. The walk normally takes 1½ days uphill to Ciudad Perdida, with a half-day at the site on the morning of the third day, then one full day's walking back downhill that is split over two days. The round trip is just shy of 45km, but it feels like a lot more as you scramble uphill, slide through mud downhill and generally exhaust every leg muscle you have. In the dry season the schedule can vary. Ask your tour company for a detailed itinerary. You walk in and out along the same route; travel agencies are continuing to negotiate with the indigenous Wiwa people to grant access to a different route out, but the Wiwa understandably remain extremely protective of their lands.

The normal hike is challenging but not mercilessly so; although each day covers only 5km to 8km, it's nearly all very steep ascent or descent. If you've never hiked before in your life, you'll find it tough, but even unfit first-timers complete the journey. At times you'll be scrambling alongside vertiginous river banks, clutching onto vines, and most people find that carrying a stick helps with balance. The rainy season brings its own challenges, such as surging rivers; heavy, boot-caking mud; and collapsed walkways.

There are significant uphill slogs that can be brutal in the scorching jungle heat. When the sun isn't blazing, it's likely to be muddy, so you'll trade sweat for loose traction. The driest period is from late December to February or early March. Depending on the season, on day three you might have to cross the Río Buritaca multiple times, at times going in up to your waist, and finally you'll have to slog up Ciudad Perdida's mystical but slippery, moss-strewn rock steps – all 1260 of them – that lead to the site.

Along the way, the food is surprisingly good and the accommodations are comfortable, often located by rivers, where you can cool off in natural swimming pools. The scenery is (obviously) nothing short of astonishing: this is a walk that is done at least as much for the journey as for the destination.

The site itself, a high plateau surrounded by blindingly brilliant jungle, is fascinating, and you'll likely only be sharing it with your group and the few Colombian soldiers stationed there when you arrive.

It's important to be aware that the mountains are sacred to all the indigenous people who live there, so it's essential to leave absolutely no litter (and by all means pick up any you find on the route), and behave with respect within the Ciudad Perdida site.

Tour Operators

★ Expotur HIKING

(☎5-420-7739; www.expotur-eco.com; Carrera 3 No 17-27) Expotur treats its staff in exemplary fashion, and it has worked hard to ensure that all its guides become qualified. Its certified indigenous guides, with whom radio contact is maintained during the hike, are delightful, even if they don't speak English, though translators are usually provided. With its years of Ciudad Perdida experience, you're in good hands here.

There are also offices in Taganga (p147) and Riohacha (p156).

Magic Tours HIKING

(☎5-421-5820, 317-679-2441; www.magictourcolombia.com; Calle 16 No 4-41) A very highly recommended operator, Magic Tours has led the way in terms of treating its guides well, providing them with social-security coverage, health care and pensions, while also doing much to ensure that tourism benefits the indigenous communities it affects. Guides are from the mountains, and are knowledgeable and certified.

It does all the classic local trips, including forays into Tayrona national park, Ciudad Perdida and Minca.

Guías Indígenas Tours HIKING

(☎321-742-7902, 5-422-2630; www.guiasindigenas.com; Calle 19 No 4-12, Santa Marta) This new agency has only been operating since 2017, but as its name suggests, it's entirely run and staffed by indigenous people and has superb access to sites in the Sierra Nevada. The company offers Ciudad Perdida tours, including an option to take the circular route through the jungle.

Guías y Baquianos Tours HIKING

(☎316-745-8947, 5-431-9667; www.guiasybaquianos.com; Hotel Miramar, Calle 10C No 20-42, Santa Marta) Located inside Hotel Miramar, this was the original agency to offer treks to Ciudad Perdida. Using guides that have at least a decade of experience (and often twice that), the company has strong relationships to the indigenous communities with which it works. Many of the guides themselves have farms in the Sierra Nevada.

Turcol HIKING

(☎5-421-2256; www.turcoltravel.com; Calle 13 No 3-13 CC San Francisco Plaza, Santa Marta) Turcol has the most experience on the Ciudad Perdida route, starting in the 1990s, and has professional guides who work hard with

HIKING TO CIUDAD PERDIDA: WHAT TO BRING

The following items are broken down into the essential and less essential. Most camps have some kind of generator-powered recharging facilities, so it's not ridiculous to bring your phone and charger (for taking photos, at least – there's no mobile reception along the way!). However, do carry as little as possible, as you'll find the trip miserable if you take too much.

Must Have

- Flashlight
- 1.5L water bottle
- Insect repellent
- Sunscreen
- Sunglasses
- Long pants
- A different T-shirt for each day's walking
- Multiple pairs of socks and underwear
- Two pairs of shoes (ideally, walking shoes for the hiking and strap sandals for river crossings)
- Multiple plastic bags (very useful for carrying wet clothing)
- Towel
- Ciprofloxacin and Loperamide (antibiotic and antidiarrhea medicines)

Nice to Have

- Playing cards
- Band-Aids or bandages for blistered feet
- Peaked cap
- Swimming costume
- Waterproof bag cover
- Sweatpants or pyjamas for the evenings
- Ziplock bags to keep things dry
- Antihistamine pills to soothe mosquito bites, and cream to treat blisters
- Five extra pairs of socks
- A book or journal for the evenings
- Earplugs (for the communal sleeping experience)

its groups. Most of its guides don't speak English, but they ensure there's a translator available if you don't speak Spanish (do check before you book your tour).

Osprey Expeditions TOURS
(☎300-478-7320; www.ospreyexpeditions.com; Calle 22 & Carrera 2) After years of experience in Venezuela, Osprey Expeditions have opened an office in Colombia and offer tours throughout the country, including Ciudad Perdida and PNN Tayrona trips. They also offer transport services to Venezuela, one of the few agencies to do so in the current climate. Owner Ben Rodriguez speaks fluent English and is a superb source of travel information.

Getting There & Away

Ciudad Perdida lies about 40km southeast of Santa Marta as the crow flies. It's hidden deep in the thick forest amid rugged mountains, far away from any human settlement, and without access roads. The only way to get there is on foot. The trail begins in El Mamey (Machete), a 90-minute drive from Santa Marta.

LA GUAJIRA PENINSULA

English pirates, Dutch smugglers and Spanish pearl hunters have all tried to conquer the Guajira Peninsula – a vast swath of barren sea and sand that is Colombia's northernmost point – but none were able to overcome the indigenous Wayuu people, who wisely traded with, or waged war upon, the invaders. The Wayuu's complex and autonomous political and economic structures meant they were ready to mount a staunch defense of their lands – on horseback and with firearms.

Even today, this is a diesel-and-dust landscape with more than a whiff of *Mad Max*–like lawlessness. Sadly, the roadsides around the small towns in the west are littered with rubbish – indeed, the symbol of modern-day Guajira might well be a plastic bag caught in a leafless bush. Fortunately, as you head east the litter fades away until you fall upon the end-of-the-world paradise of Punta Gallinas, an immaculate collision of desert dunes and crashing waves.

Access to La Guajira is normally via Riohacha, and to Middle and Upper Guajira via the small town of Uribia, the transport hub for the peninsula proper. There are no scheduled buses, and transportation is always in 4WD jeeps that leave when full. In general, it's never a good idea to rely on public services in this part of Colombia; travel on a tour that includes transportation.

Riohacha

5 / POP 278,000

Riohacha, traditionally the end of the line, is the gateway to the northern, semiarid desert region of La Guajira and retains more than a little frontier-town feeling. As tourism in the peninsula has developed in recent years, Riohacha has become an unlikely traveler hub of sorts and you may find yourself spending the night here on the way to or from more isolated and beautiful parts of Colombia. The town isn't teeming with things to do, but it's pleasant enough; there's a 5km-long beach strewn with palm trees, and the long pier, constructed in 1937, makes for a lovely evening stroll. Despite Riohacha's oppressive daytime heat, there's generally a cool breeze coming in off the Caribbean, and the town is friendly and welcoming.

Sights

Beachfront Calle 1 is the town's principal thoroughfare, with Riohacha's main plaza, **Parque José Prudencio Padilla**, two blocks inland between Carreras 7 and 9. On weekend evenings the **malecón** and its parallel street, Carrera 1, fill with revelers taking in the waterfront restaurants and bars.

Santuario de Fauna y Flora Los Flamencos NATURE RESERVE
(www.parquesnacionales.gov.co; Camarones) FREE Pink flamingos inhabit this tranquil, 700-hectare nature preserve in great numbers: up to 10,000 in the wet season (usually September through December). Groups of up to 2000 birds can usually be seen in one of the park's four lagoons. If you want to see the flamingos you'll need to take a canoe trip (COP$30,000 for one to three people; COP$15,000 per extra person). The reserve is in the town of Camarones, 25km from Riohacha.

Skippers usually know where the flocks are hanging out, but they won't take you if they're beyond a reasonable distance.

Camellón de Riohacha PIER
(Camino de Playa) Built in 1937, this impressive wooden pier is lovely for a stroll late in the day.

Tours

Expotur ADVENTURE
(5-728-8232; www.expotur-eco.com; Carrera 5 No 3A-02) This outpost of the excellent Santa Marta–based agency specializes in tours to Punta Gallinas and all over La Guajira Peninsula. It has excellent relationships with the Wayuu people and offers English-speaking guides.

Kaí Ecotravel ADVENTURE
(311-436-2830,5-729-2936; www.kaiecotravel.com; Calle 5 No 7-24) Kai Ecotravel has spent years fostering relationships with the Wayuu to get access to Punta Gallinas. It's a great resource for peninsula tours as well as homestays with indigenous families. Transportation-only deals to Cabo de la Vela are available if it has spare seats in its 4WD vehicles.

Alta Guajira Tours ADVENTURE
(5-729-2562, 311-678-4778; www.altaguajiratours.com; Calle 1 No 9-63) Another experienced and reliable operator offering all-inclusive trips to Upper Guajira, starting at a two-night trip to Cabo de la Vela for CO$250,000 per person. They also offer indigenous home stays, tours of Cabo de la Vela's mine and – naturally – trips to Punta Gallinas.

Sleeping & Eating

★ **Bona Vida Hostel Tercera** HOSTEL $
(314-637-0786; www.bonavidahostel.com; Calle 3 No 10-10; dm incl breakfast COP$30,000-38,000, d with/without bathroom COP$110,000/95,000;) La Bona Vida is so good that it had to add a second branch in 2017, only a year

after opening the first. Behind the turquoise colonial facade lies a diminutive, well-laid-out interior sporting dorms (with curtained bunks and personal fans) and private doubles (with air-con and – drumroll – Netflix!).

But this place is about the little details: freebies at half-a-dozen local restaurants, straight-off-the-hot-plate breakfasts, dinner on demand, and super-quick laundry service. Nothing is too much trouble for these guys. Best hostel on Colombia's Caribbean coast? Possibly.

The new branch of the hostel, Bona Vida Quinta, offers the same fabulous deal a couple of blocks away.

Taroa Hotel HOTEL **$$$**
(☎5-729-1122; www.taroahotel.com; Calle 1 No 4-77; s/d/ste incl breakfast COP$255,000/280,000/464,000; ❄📶) Branded a 'Wayuu lifestyle hotel,' this modern tower on the seafront is by far the smartest place to bed down in Riohacha. An all-Wayuu staff welcomes you to enormous and spotless rooms, each with minibar, flat-screen TV, coffee machine and balcony, and there's a rooftop bar and restaurant. It's the perfect place to recharge before a La Guajira trip.

★ **Lima Cocina Fusión** FUSION **$$**
(☎5-728-1313; Calle 13 No 11-33; mains COP$15,000-35,000; 📶🌱) The cool interior of this polished place exerts a magnetic force on hungry walk-by traffic. While the name's a little misleading (there's not much gourmet Peruvian cuisine to be had), the food quality and service are certainly worthy of comparisons to Lima. The menu revolves around a selection of 'pitas' (thin-crust mini-pizzas), backed by some of the best salads in Colombia.

It's styled as a boutique cafe, with casual tables and a few alfresco perches.

La Casa del Marisco SEAFOOD **$$**
(☎5-728-3445; Calle 1 No 4-43; mains COP$20,000-50,000; ⏲11am-10pm Mon-Sat, 11am-9pm Sun; 📶) This place, right on the seafront, attracts local families all day long with its deliciously prepared, freshly landed fish and seafood. Specialties include several types of fish casserole, *calamari al gusto* and *fritura de mariscos* (fried seafood).

Information

Hospital Nuestra Señora de los Remedios (☎5-727-3312; www.hospitalnsr.gov.co; cnr Calle 12 & Carrera 15)

Policía de la Guajira (☎5-727-3879; Carrera 5 No 15-79)

Tourist Office (☎5-727-1015; Carrera 1 No 4-42; ⏲8am-noon & 2-6pm Mon-Fri)

Getting There & Away

AIR

The airport is 3km southwest of town. A taxi there from town costs COP$6000. **Avianca** (☎5-727-3627; www.avianca.com; Calle 7 No 7-04; ⏲8am-noon & 2-6pm Mon-Fri, 9am-2pm Sat) operates two flights daily to/from Bogotá.

BUS

The **bus terminal** (cnr Calle 15 & Carrera 11a) is about 1km from the center. A taxi from the center is COP$5000.

Expreso Brasilia (☎5-727-2240; Terminal de Transporte Riohacha) has buses to Santa Marta (COP$20,000, 2½ hours) and Barranquilla (COP$31,000, five hours) every 30 minutes; hourly services to Cartagena (COP$42,000, seven hours); and services every 45 minutes to Maicao (COP$10,000, one hour), on the border with Venezuela. There's a daily bus to Bogotá (COP$100,000 to COP$107,000, 18 hours) at 3pm, which also passes through Valledupar (COP$30,000, four hours).

Coopetran (☎313-333-5707; Terminal de Transporte Riohacha) offers similar services to Santa Marta, Cartagena and Bogotá. It also has a connection to Bucaramanga (COP$90,000, 12 hours, three daily).

Cootrauri (☎5-728-0000; Terminal de Transporte Riohacha) runs *colectivos*, leaving as they fill up, every day from 5am to 6pm to Uribia (COP$14,000, one hour), where you switch for the final leg to Cabo de la Vela (COP$12,000 to COP$18,000, 2½ hours). Just let the driver know you're heading to Cabo and they will drop you off at the switch point. The last car for Cabo de la Vela leaves Uribia at 1pm. Private rides to Cabo are available (COP$400,000; haggle and you might get it for less) and will take you and three friends there and back in a day, rushing through the highlights at breakneck speed, which kind of misses the point. You can also hitch a lift with Kaí Ecotravel (p156) for COP$50,000 if it has a spare seat; rides depart daily.

To visit the Santuario de Fauna y Flora Los Flamencos (p156), you must catch a *colectivo* (COP$5000) bound for the town of Camarones from the Francisco El Hombre traffic circle, at the corner of Calle 14 and Carrera 8. Tell the driver where you're going and they'll drop you at the entrance to the park.

Cabo de la Vela

☎5 / POP 1500

The fishing village of Cabo de la Vela, 180km northwest of Riohacha, was until recently little more than a remote rural community, its Wayuu inhabitants living in traditional huts made from cactus right up against the sea. But in the last couple of years Cabo has become a hotbed of ecotourism and kitesurfing and now boasts a wealth of indigenous-style accommodations. Nevertheless, the village still has electricity by generator only, and there are few fixed phone lines. Internet access is sporadic at best.

The surrounding area is a highlight of the Upper Guajira and one of the most starkly beautiful spots in Colombia. The cape for which it's named is full of rocky cliffs above and sandy beaches below, all set against a backdrop of stunning desert ochres and aquamarines.

If you're looking for peace, Cabo is best avoided around Easter, December and January.

Sights & Activities

Cabo de la Vela is a notable center for kitesurfing, with half a dozen Wayuu-run outfits offering tuition.

Cabo de la Vela has a large concentration of La Guajira's sights within easy reach, giving you plenty to keep you occupied for a day if kitesurfing isn't your thing. Most sights are reachable from the village via a 30- to 90-minute walk.

Playa del Pilón BEACH

Playa del Pilón, far and away the most beautiful beach in Cabo, is a vivid orange-sand beach lapped by surprisingly cool waters and framed by low, rocky cliffs. Spectacular at any time of day, the colors are especially impressive at sunrise and sunset. In the wet season add lush desert flora to the mix and the whole scene is rather cinematic.

Wayuu people sell drinks and hire hammocks from open-sided huts at the edge of the car park overlooking the beach.

Pilón de Azúcar VIEWPOINT

Pilón de Azúcar looms over the eponymous beach and provides the area's most telescopic viewpoint, with the whole of Alta Guajira displayed before you and the Serranía del Carpintero mountain range in the distance. A statue of La Virgen de Fátima, erected here in 1938 by Spanish pearl hunters, stands at the top of the viewpoint as the patron saint of Cabo.

It's a short 10-minute scramble to the 95m-high summit from the car park. Hold onto your hat – it can be windy.

El Faro LIGHTHOUSE

Wayuu and tourists alike head to El Faro, a small lighthouse at the edge of a rocky promontory, for stiff winds and tangerine sunsets. The view is stunning. It's a 3.5km walk from town, or you can wrangle a ride with a local for COP$30,000 or so round trip. Take plenty of water, insect repellent and a hat.

Sleeping & Eating

A government-sponsored ecotourism project has resulted in more than 60 rustic posadas (hotels) in Cabo. Lodging is generally in Wayuu huts fashioned from *yotojoro*, the core of the cardon cactus that grows in the desert here. Choose between smaller hammocks, larger and warmer traditional *chinchorros* (locally crafted hammocks) or beds with private bathrooms (note: running water is scarce). Bring your own towel.

Nearly all posadas double as restaurants, and more or less serve the same thing: fish or goat. Breakfasts are around COP$8000, lunch and dinner COP$20,000 each. Lobster is often available – for a price.

Ranchería Utta GUESTHOUSE $

(☎312-678-8237, 313-817-8076; www.rancheriautta.com; hammocks/chinchorros/cabañas per person COP$20,000/30,000/45,000) On the far side of the village, within walking distance of El Faro lighthouse (p158), is the best *ranchería* in town. The adjoining rooms, fashioned from the traditional Wayuu cactus, have a few splashes of color, with hung blankets and the like. Bonuses are a large, clean restaurant and an owner who's happy to greet his guests.

Budget travelers can choose from *enramadas* (opened-sided shelters) where you can sling hammocks or *chinochorros* (deluxe hammocks), and 'shower' with a bucket of water and a ladle that staff will politely bring to you.

Utta is right on the beach and hosts the odd spontaneous Wayuu cultural event.

Hostería Jarrinapi GUESTHOUSE $

(☎311-683-4281; hammocks COP$20,000, r per person COP$35,000) One of the more central options in Cabo, this little complex has rustic private rooms with their own bathrooms housed in traditional Wayuu cabins. There's a handy shop out front, a restaurant serving three meals a day (mains COP$18,000 to COP$40,000) and generator that provides electricity between 6pm until 6am meaning your fan whirs and you can sleep. Hammocks also available.

Water (cold only) is provided at certain times. Wi-fi? Forget it!

Getting There & Away

Getting to Cabo de la Vela isn't the easiest trip you'll make in Colombia, so most folks come on a tour. That said, it's possible to come on your own: from Riohacha, you must catch a colectivo (p157) to Uribia; it will depart as it fills up every day from 5am to 6pm (COP$15,000 to COP$20,000, one hour). The driver will let you out in front of Panadería Peter-Pan at the entrance to Uribia, from where trucks and 4WDs leave for Cabo (COP$25,000, 2½ hours). Non-4WD vehicles are a definite no-go on these dusty, rocky tracks.

Punta Gallinas

Punta Gallinas is South America's most northerly point and offers one of the continent's most dazzling landscapes. Its access point, Bahía Hondita, is where burnt-orange cliffs surround an emerald bay with a wide and wild beach, beyond which is a large colony of pink flamingos. Otherwise the bay is home to just eight Wayuu families, who dwell in an exceptionally harsh environment peppered with vibrant green vegetation and shared only with herds of goats and locusts.

As the continent gives way to the Caribbean, sand dunes topping 60m high push right up against the turquoise sea, like a five-story sand tsunami in reverse. This is Playa Taroa, perhaps Colombia's most beautiful and certainly its least trampled-upon beach, accessed by sliding down a towering sand dune right into the water.

Sleeping

Hospedaje Alexandra GUESTHOUSE $
(315-538-2718, 318-500-6942; hospedajealexandra@hotmail.com; hammocks/chinchorros/cabañas per person COP$20,000/20,000/35,000) In a wonderful position right on the bay, Hospedaje Alexandra offers views of wild flamingos and thick mangrove forests below. It has basic but charming wooden huts and superb food.

Getting There & Away

There's virtually no way to reach Punta Gallinas without the help of a tour, though it is technically possible: for much of the year 4WD vehicles from Cabo de la Vela can make the three- to four-hour drive to La Boquita, the top of the bay across the water from the posadas. With notice, someone from the posadas can come and pick you up from there by boat (it's free for guests). When roads are impassable due to rains, access is by three-hour boat ride from Puerto Bolívar, a short drive from Cabo de la Vela near the El Cerrejón coal mine. Contact Kaí Ecotravel (p156) or Expotur (p156) in Riohacha to make the trip. Both Kaí Ecotravel and Expotur offer transport-only deals to Punta Gallinas; contact them for prices and availability around the time you want to travel.

VALLEDUPAR

Valledupar lies in the long, fertile valley formed by the Sierra Nevada de Santa Marta to the east and Venezuela's Serranía del Perijá to the west. It has remained off the traveler radar as it's not a hugely touristic town, and was landlocked during the darker days of the Colombian civil conflict, when Valledupar was held virtual hostage by the guerrillas that controlled the mountains.

These days Valledupar sees some travelers every now and again with its small, well-preserved colonial center, some great outdoors activities nearby and a bustling nightlife.

This is cattle-and-cowboy country, and Valledupar is mythologized and venerated by Colombians as the birthplace of vallenato, the coast's ubiquitous, manic, accordion-driven folk music that sings of love, politics, and the pain of losing your woman (or horse) to another man.

Activities

Valledupar is a place to chill out, relax and recharge. It makes a great overnight stop if you're completing a circuit around Santa Marta, La Guajira Peninsula and Mompós.

Balneario La Mina SWIMMING
(COP$10,000; dawn-5pm) The Río Badillo carves a bizarre, brain-like path through the riverbed down from the Sierra Nevada to make this a great swimming hole. Take plenty of strong insect repellent and beware the surging currents in wetter months. Take a *colectivo* from Carrera 6 in the center of town to Atanquez and jump out at La Mina; service runs from 11am to 2pm. To return take a moto-taxi for COP$15,000, no later than 4pm.

There's a really worthwhile women's cooperative here, run by María Martínez, whom everyone calls La Maye. All proceeds benefit local women who lost their husbands and sons in the years of conflict, and the woven bags are of very high quality. She also serves a cheap (COP$12,000) fantastic *sancocho de gallina,* or cockerel stew, cooked over a wooden fire and served in the yard of her simple home.

Balneario Hurtado SWIMMING

FREE On Sundays and holidays, the vallenatos come here to bathe in the Río Guatapurí, cook and socialize. There are a few simple restaurants and wandering snack vendors, and all in all it's a superchilled family day out. It lies alongside the Parque Lineal; buses head there from Cinco Esquinas in the center of town.

Festivals & Events

Festival de la Leyenda Vallenata MUSIC

(www.festivalvallenato.com; Apr) The city's Festival de la Leyenda Vallenata is a four-day orgy of vallenato and Old Parr whisky – the favored tipple here. The latter is so beloved that locals call the town Valle de Old Parr.

Sleeping & Eating

Valledupar has one excellent hostel, which also has a number of private rooms. Room prices everywhere quadruple – and book out a year in advance – during the city's Festival de la Leyenda Vallenata in April.

★ **Provincia Hostel** HOSTEL $$

(5- 580-0558, 300-241-9210; www.provinciavalledupar.com; Calle 16A No 5-25; dm/s/d/tr COP$ 30,000/75,000/94,000/125,000;) Friendly, safe, clean and charming, this is the best place in town whatever your budget. The private rooms lack natural light, and can get some noise from the kitchen and social area right outside, but are superbly comfortable, while the dorms are great value. Bicycle rental is also available and the owner can give great day-trip advice.

Joe Restaurante GRILL $$

(5-574- 9787; Calle 16A No 11-67; mains COP$20,000-40,000; 5:30-11pm) A Valledupar institution, El Joe is a heaven for meat lovers. The mixed grill is big enough for two and features a mountain of locally sourced beef, pork and goat for the price, while the restaurant itself is extremely clean and staff outgoing and friendly.

El Varadero CUBAN $$$

(5-570-6175; Calle 12 No 6-56; mains COP$30,000-50,000; noon-3pm & 6-10pm;) Cuban seafood is the fare in this restaurant, where photographs of local celebrities deck the walls, and it's very good seafood indeed: the lobster salad to start is great, as are the garlic mussels. To complete the continent-hopping menu, try the seafood Al Macho, served Peruvian-style with yellow peppers.

Getting There & Away

The **bus station** (Carrera 7 & Calle 44) is a 30-minute taxi ride (COP$5000) from the center, or take any bus with 'Terminal' as its destination from Carrera 7 and Calle 17. Buses go to the following:

Destination	Fare	Duration (hrs)	Frequency (daily)
Bucaramanga	COP$89,000	8	2
Cartagena	COP$45,000	5½	4
Medellín	COP$100,000	12	1
Mompós	COP$55,000	5	1
Riohacha	COP$25,000	3	1
Santa Marta	COP$28,000	2	hourly

MOMPÓS

5 / POP 44,000 / ELEV 33M

Mompós is one of Colombia's most perfectly preserved colonial towns. Remotely located deep inland on the banks of the Río Magdalena, the town (also known by its original Spanish name of Mompox) has essentially been in decline since river transport patterns changed in the mid-19th century, leaving it – quite literally – a backwater. Its similarities to García Márquez' fictional town of Macondo are striking, and Mompós, ironically, is a far better place to soak up the atmosphere of *One Hundred Years of Solitude* than García Márquez' nearby hometown of Aracataca. The 21st century finds this forgotten gem rising again, with a steady proliferation of boutique hotels and restaurants in recent years. It's easily the most charming town in northern Colombia, its decaying facades and multicolored churches reminiscent more of Havana's old town than of polished-and-buffed Cartagena.

History

Founded in 1540 by Alonso de Heredia (brother of Cartagena's founder, Pedro de Heredia) on the eastern branch of the Río Magdalena, Santa Cruz de Mompox was an important trading center and active port through which all merchandise from Cartagena passed via the Canal del Dique and the Río Magdalena to the interior of the colony.

The town initially flourished, minting coins for the colony, and becoming famous for its goldsmiths; traces of this goldsmithing legacy can still be seen today in the town's

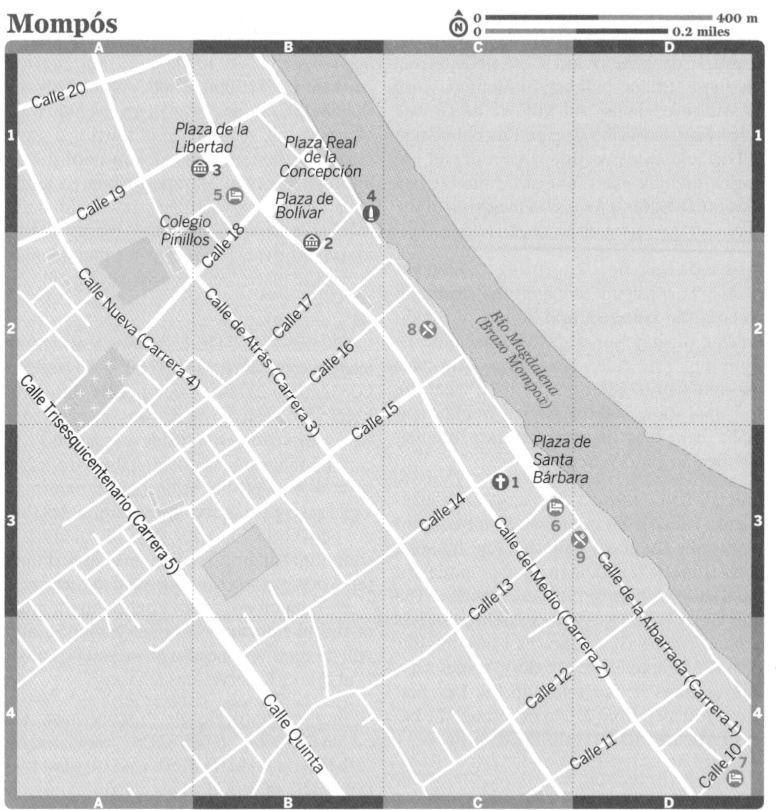

Mompós

Sights

1 Iglesia de Santa Bárbara C3
2 Museo del Arte Religioso B2
3 Palacio San Carlos B1
4 Piedra de Bolívar B1

Sleeping

5 Bioma Boutique Hotel B1
6 Casa Amarilla C3
7 Hostal La Casa del Viajero D4

Eating

8 Casa Sol del Agua C2
9 El Fuerte San Anselmo D3
Restaurante Mompoj .... (see 5)

superb filigree jewelry. Mompox declared its independence from the Spanish Empire in 1810, the first town in Colombia to do so, and at this time began to use the name Mompós. During the War of Independence, Mompós became an important military town and saw Simón Bolívar himself come and go eight times between 1812 and 1830, the dates and details of which are immortalized on the riverside Piedra de Bolívar.

Towards the end of the 19th century, disaster struck Mompós as shipping was diverted to the other branch of the Río Magdalena, the Brazo de Loba. This fateful decision immediately turned Mompós into an isolated backwater in Colombia's interior, a biographical detail that repeats itself in Gabriel García Márquez' *One Hundred Years of Solitude*, in which many readers see echoes of Mompós' fate despite the novel's actually being based on the author's hometown of Aracataca. At this point Mompós entered a century-long sleep, broken only by the jingling of the tourist dollar in the early 21st century.

Sights

There's little to see in terms of attractions here, so your time is best spent wandering the gorgeous streets, strolling along the Río Magdalena's fine embankment and taking in the vibrant colors, sounds and smells.

Iglesia de Santa Bárbara CHURCH
(cnr Carrera 1 & Calle 14) Dating from 1613, this unusual riverside church is undoubtedly the most striking building in Mompós, with its wide-eyed lions and griffins, its strange balcony-ringed bell tower, and its population of bats and swallows that stream in and out during evening mass. You can climb the bell tower (COP$2000) for a sweeping view of the river and the surrounding countryside.

Piedra de Bolívar MONUMENT
(Calle 1) This solemn stone on the riverbank records the comings and goings of Simón Bolívar during the wars of independence from Spanish rule. Most important was his first trip to Mompós in 1812, when he recruited some 400 troops that would eventually help him liberate Caracas, bringing independence to Venezuela.

Palacio San Carlos HISTORIC BUILDING
(Carrera 2 & Calle 18) A former Jesuit convent that's now the town hall, this fine building dates from 1600 and has a notable statue of a freed slave with broken chains outside it. The line *'Si a Caracas debo la vida, a Mompox debo la gloria'* (If to Caracas I owe my life, then to Mompox I owe my glory) comes from Bolívar himself and refers to the fact that some 400 men from Mompós formed the basis of his victorious revolutionary army.

Museo del Arte Religioso MUSEUM
(Carrera 2 No 17-07; COP$5000; ⏲8-11:45am & 2-4pm Tue-Sat) Mompós' main museum is a decent collection of religious paintings, gold and silver crosses and other religious objects, all displayed in several rooms of an impressive colonial mansion.

Festivals & Events

Two annual events are well worth traveling for: the town's **Semana Santa** (⏲Mar/Apr) celebrations are some of the most elaborate in the country, while the relatively recently established **Mompox Jazz Festival** (www.facebook.com/mompoxjazzfestival; ⏲late Sep) is one of Colombia's best music events and attracts big crowds. For both events it's important to arrange your accommodations months in advance.

Sleeping & Eating

There are a number of boutique hotels in town catering to wealthy weekenders, while budget travelers are also covered with dozens of smaller hostels.

Hostal La Casa del Viajero HOSTEL $
(☎320-406-4530; http://lacasadelviajeromompox.business.site; Calle 10 No 1-65; incl breakfast dm from COP$20,000, d with/without bathroom COP$85,000/55,000; ❄📶) This friendly traveler hangout at the edge of town is a great budget option and has all you need for an affordable stay in Mompós: a shared kitchen, a rather messy garden strewn with hammocks, a karaoke machine, roomy dorms and cozy private rooms. Owner Juan Manuel keeps the place sociable and gay friendly.

★ **Casa Amarilla** BOUTIQUE HOTEL $$
(☎310-606-4632, 5-685-6326; www.lacasaamarillamompos.com; Carrera 1 No 13-59; r incl breakfast COP$135,000-250,000; ❄📶) This beautiful hotel was created by a British journalist and his *momposina* wife inside a restored 17th-century mansion overlooking the river. It has several wonderfully atmospheric rooms, as well as a couple of roomy upstairs suites that are perfect for romantic stays. Breakfast is a communal affair served up on a large dining table overlooking the courtyard garden.

Staff members speak English, are a mine of useful information about Mompós, and will do their very best to make you feel totally at home. Reservations advised.

Bioma Boutique Hotel BOUTIQUE HOTEL $$$
(☎316-625-0669, 5-685-6733; www.bioma.co; Calle Real del Medio No 18-59; r incl breakfast from COP$230,000; ❄📶🏊) This delightful property is a fully restored and transformed colonial house in the heart of Mompós with 11 simple but gorgeous rooms surrounding a charming courtyard and a much-needed pool to cool down in. There's also an excellent dining option, Restaurante Mompoj (p163), on site.

Casa Sol del Agua CAFE $
(Carrera 1 No 15-101; breakfasts COP$3500-6000, sandwiches COP$6000-11,000; ⏲7am-7pm; 📶🌱) Do as the menus of this sweet little riverside cafe suggest: read a book, drink a coffee and enjoy the river – from one of its outdoor rocking chairs, no less. You'll find great breakfasts, fresh fruit juices, toasted sandwiches and delicious cakes at this simple place, where the kind owner fusses over her guests. Bicycles are available for COP$6000 per hour.

The *casa* also rents rooms.

★ **El Fuerte San Anselmo** EUROPEAN $$$
(☎5-685-6762, 314-564-0566; www.fuertemompox.com; Carrera 1 No 12-163; mains from COP$40,000; ⏲6:30-11pm) With its beautifully crafted interior and spacious, airy garden

overlooked by a towering banana tree, El Fuerte really is a highlight of Mompós. Try the excellent pizza cooked in a wood-fired oven, one of its lovingly prepared pasta dishes or the excellent gazpacho. Come in good time to ensure you get an outdoor table.

Restaurante Mompoj INTERNATIONAL **$$$**
(☎5-685-6733; www.bioma.co; Bioma Boutique Hotel, Calle Real del Medio No 18-59; mains COP$35,000; ⏱noon-3pm & 6-10pm; 📶) Named after the original name of the area before the Spanish conquest, the Mompoj is an excellent restaurant with an interesting and eclectic menu. Try pork curry, chicken stew or baby beef medallions in tamarind sauce. It's important to reserve ahead, as the restaurant often isn't open unless there are some confirmed guests.

Getting There & Away

Mompós is remote, there's no denying that, but it can be reached by direct bus from Cartagena and several other major towns. Most travelers arrive from Cartagena with **Ulnitransco** (www.unitransco.co), which runs a daily bus at 7:30am (COP$46,000, six hours).

It's also possible to travel to Mompós from Bucaramanga (COP$65,000, seven hours, 10am and 9:45pm) and from Bogotá (COP$90,000, 15 hours, three times daily). All these services are operated by Copetran.

There are direct door-to-door services from Mompós to Barranquilla, Cartagena and Santa Marta, all taking between five and six hours, with a cost ranging from COP$75,000 to COP$85,000. If you want to use these services, ask your hotel to book you a pickup.

SOUTHWEST OF CARTAGENA

Unspoiled beaches and the road less traveled characterize the Caribbean coast southwest of Cartagena, an area that, due to security concerns, has seen little international tourism in the last two decades. Secure and at the ready these days, areas like Tolú and the Islas de San Bernardo, which previously catered to Colombians only, are now wide open for foreign exploration.

There is quite a notable change in the landscape here from the northern coast through the departments of Sucre, Córdoba, Antioquia and Chocó. Swampy pasturelands dotted with billowing tropical ceiba trees, ground-strangling mangroves and crystalline lagoons flank the seaside around the Golfo de Morrosquillo; while the jungle near the Darién Gap rides right up against cerulean waters and beaches where the Golfo de Urabá gives way to Panama, near the serene villages of Capurganá and Sapzurro.

Transport here can be a rather tricky thing, with long distances, isolated locations and a lack of roads making things rather arduous. Everywhere is accessible by bus or boat (and often a combination of both), but you'll need to give yourself plenty of travel time, and you'll not always enjoy the most comfortable travel conditions.

Tolú

☎5 / POP 48,000 / ELEV 2M

You'd never know it, but the tranquil pueblo of Tolú, the capital of the Golfo de Morrosquillo, is one of Colombia's most visited tourist destinations. Colombians flock here throughout the high season for its small-town feel and surrounding beaches, but there's rarely a foreigner in sight. The rest of the year, it's a quiet backwater. The beaches aren't particularly impressive, but they're pleasant enough if you're passing through.

Tolú's lengthy *malecón* (boardwalk), full of seaside bars, restaurants and small artisan stalls, is worth a stroll, but the main draw for foreign tourists is the town's proximity to the idyllic Islas de San Bernardo (p164), part of Parque Nacional Natural (PNN) Corales del Rosario y San Bernardo.

Sights & Activities

Tolú is the main jumping-off point for day tours to Islas de San Bernardo (p164). In nearby Coveñas there is less infrastructure but better beaches, many of which are dotted with thatched-roof tables fit for drinking an afternoon away.

Ciénega la Caimanera NATURE RESERVE
(km 5, Via Tolú-Coveñas) **FREE** This 1800-hectare nature reserve is a part-freshwater, part-saltwater bog with five varieties of mangroves. The red mangrove's roots twist and tangle in and out of the water like hyperactive strands of spaghetti. The canoe trip here is a pleasant and beautiful way to spend an hour and a half, meandering through artificial mangrove tunnels and sampling oysters right off the roots.

To reach the Ciénega, grab any bus (COP$2500) heading toward Coveñas and ask to be let off at La Boca de la Ciénega. Canoe guides wait for tourists on the bridge, and charge COP$30,000 for one to two people and as little as COP$10,000 per person for larger groups.

Playa Blanca BEACH

If you're looking for a good slice of local beach, then Playa Blanca is your best bet. It is accessed via moto-taxi from Coveñas (COP$6000).

Punta Bolívar BEACH

This stretch of sand is a good choice if you want to spend the day on the beach. It's rather remotely located, so you'll need to hire a moto-taxi from Coveñas to get here (COP$5000).

Mundo Mar TOURS

(312-608-0273, 321-809-7009; www.clubnauticomundomartolu.com; Carrera 1 No 14-40) This well-run agency does daily tours departing at 8:30am to Islas de San Bernardo for COP$45,000. You'll be back by 4pm.

Sleeping & Eating

Villa Babilla HOSTEL $$

(312-677-1325; www.villababillahostel.com; Calle 20 No 3-40; s/d from COP$40,000/80,000;) Three blocks from the waterfront, this German-run hostel/hotel offers a friendly space highlighted by its thatched-roof outdoor TV lounge. There's a kitchen, laundry service and free coffee all day. There's no sign outside but it's the tallest building on the block.

Doña Mercedes COLOMBIAN $

(Plaza Pedro de Heredia; arepas from COP$5000; 8am-6pm Mon-Sat) Do not leave Tolú without eating the country's most sublimely perfect arepa, filled with egg and spiced meat, from Doña Mercedes' food stand. It's on the southeast corner of the square next to the Expreso Brasilia office. Crunchy, savory perfection.

Information

There are plenty of ATMs in town, including **Bancolombia** (Calle 14 No 2-88) on Calle 14.

You can find helpful staff at the **Tourist Office** (5-286-0192; Carrera 2 No 15-43; 8am-noon & 2-6pm) on Carrera 2.

Getting There & Around

Expreso Brasilia/Unitransco (5-288-5180; Calle 15 No 2-36), **Rápido Ochoa** (5-288-5226; Calle 15 No 2-36) and **Caribe Express** (5-288-5223; Calle 15 No 2-36) share a small bus station on the southwest side of Plaza Pedro de Heredia. Buses depart hourly for Cartagena (COP$35,000, three hours) and Montería (COP$25,000, two hours). If you are continuing on to Turbo and the Panamanian border beyond, you must take a bus to Montería and switch there for Turbo.

Tolú is a small town where residents choose bicycles over vehicles, and bicycle taxis, known as *bicitaxis*, are an art form: each one is decked out with individual personality and flair – and feature massive, cranked-up speakers playing salsa and reggaeton.

Colectivos to Coveñas depart every 10 minutes daily (COP$2500) from near Supermercado Popular at the corner of Carrera 2 and Calle 17 in Tolú.

Islas de San Bernardo

The 10 archipelagoes that make up the Islas de San Bernardo, set off the coast of Tolú, are a far more spectacular and interesting addition to the PNN Corales del Rosario y San Bernardo than their neighbors to the north, the Islas del Rosario.

Carib *indígenas* (indigenous Caribbeans) once called the islands home, but they are more trampled on today by vacationing Colombians, who have done well to keep the islands a secret from foreign tourists. Known for their crystalline waters, mangrove lagoons and white-sand beaches, these picturesque islands stand out on the Caribbean coast as a little oasis of rest and relaxation.

Tours

The full-day tour of the islands leave Tolú each morning. It includes a fly-by of one of the world's most densely populated islands, **Santa Cruz del Islote**, where up to 1000 people, mostly fisherfolk, live in a tropical aquatic shantytown measuring just 1200 sq meters; and Isla Tintipan, the largest of the archipelago's islands.

Most of the tourism infrastructure is on **Isla Múcura**, where tours stop for three hours of free time. Here you can rent snorkeling equipment for COP$5000, kick back and have lunch and a beer (not included in the tour), or simply wander around the mangroves.

Sleeping

Hostal Isla Múcura HOSTAL $

(316-620-8660; www.hostalislamucura.com; Isla Múcura; tent/hammock COP$15,000 per person, dm/r/cabaña COP$20,000/50,000/60,000 per person) This excellent option offers you the chance to stay on the islands at an affordable price. Right on the beach, this place has a laid-back vibe and superfriendly staff. The sleeping options range from pitching your own tent and hammocks to the super popular 'private kiosks,' which are thatched huts on stilts with lovely views and a great breeze.

Meals cost COP$20,000 and are delicious. Volunteers are welcome year-round and help serve breakfast, arrange events, tend the bar and collect guests.

★ **Casa en el Agua** HOTEL $$
(www.casaenelagua.com; off Isla Tintipán; hammock/dm COP$70,000/80,000 d from COP$180,000) This incredible place lives up to its name – it's literally a house in the middle of the water – a wooden holiday home built on an artificial island that has been colonized by corals and subsequently transformed into an ecologically conscious hostel. Accommodations are rustic but comfortable, food is good, there are activities and the cocktails are great value.

Capurganá & Sapzurro

☎4 / POP 2200

Colombia ends its desert-to-jungle Caribbean coastline with a flourish: the idyllic, laid-back villages of Capurganá and Sapzurro, and their surrounding beaches, are hidden in a half-forgotten corner of Colombia's northwest, just a stroll from the Panamanian border. Hemmed in by jungle-covered mountains and washed by fabulously azure waters, the villages are littered with the colorful quirks that characterize wild, isolated settlements. Cars are banned, electricity gets turned off almost daily and ATMs remain a distant urban rumor.

Part of the adventure is just getting here: both villages are only accessible by a choppy 1½- to 2½-hour boat ride from Turbo or Necoclí, or by a tiny plane from Medellín. Consequently, the beaches remain pleasantly unkempt and the jungle deliciously impenetrable. While in-the-know Colombians and a trickle of foreign backpackers might have discovered the area, the vibe is still decidedly casual, unhurried and locally led.

Activities

Several diving schools are exploring the coast's magnificent reef and logging new sites. Capurganá arguably has the best diving on mainland Colombia's Caribbean coast, with a better-preserved reef and visibility up to 25m common from August to October. The sea is rough from January to March. At **Dive & Green** (☎316-781-6255, 311-578-4021; www.diveandgreen.com; Capurganá; 1/2 dives COP$140,000/210,000) and **Centro de Buceo Capurganá** (☎314-861-1923; centrodebuceocapurgana@gmail.com; Luz de Oriente, Capurganá; 1/2 dives COP$100,000/170,000), two-tank dives cost between COP$170,000 and COP$210,000.

The town beaches in both Capurganá and Sapzurro are lovely and relatively clean. Sapzurro's is much quieter and complemented by the wilder Cabo Tiburón about 15 minutes' walk around a rocky peninsula.

A short hike over the hillside from Sapzurro into Panama takes you to the most famous beach in the area, **La Miel** (bring your ID – there's a military checkpoint). It's a quick walk up a series of steep steps across the border and back down the other side (turn right at the bottom of the hill and follow the sidewalk). The small beach has white sand, cerulean waters and several small shacks where you can eat fresh fish and drink a cold beer. Sadly, it's a little marred by litter and noise pollution at times.

Walk for 30 minutes along the coast beyond Capurganá's town beach and you'll reach the beautiful rocky lookout of **Coquitos**, where an enterprising local man has built a rustic set of swimming holes (two freshwater and one saltwater). He charges COP$3000 entry and serves fabulous snacks with homemade lemonade. It's a fabulously tranquil spot.

The recently upgraded 4km **jungle trail** between Capurganá and Sapzurro has wonderful views from a lookout tower at the halfway point. This is the region's best hike by far.

El Cielo, a 3km jungle hike into the mountains from Capurganá, passes several natural swimming pools and waterfalls along a trail where you might see howler and squirrel monkeys, toucans and parrots. Pick up the path at the end of the airstrip.

The pleasant but sometimes strenuous coastal hike to **Aguacate**, 3.5km south of

WORTH A TRIP

THE GOLFO DE URABÁ

The Golfo de Urabá has a few tiny towns nestled on the fringes of the Darién Gap. Acandí, Triganá and San Francisco have decent, affordable accommodations, quiet beaches and amazing hiking. All are accessible by boat from Turbo. In Acandí between March and May hundreds of leatherback turtles, measuring as much as 2m in length and weighing up to 750kg, come ashore to lay their eggs.

Capurganá, stops at quiet beaches along the way, while the delightful **Playa Soledad** can be accessed by a 8km walk east of Capurganá, or on a short boat trip negotiated with one of the fishers on Capurganá's main beach.

Sleeping & Eating

There's a good range of hotels, hostels and campsites in the twin villages, with new establishments opening as the tourism boom continues. Hotel owners often hang around the dock; in general these folk aren't touts, and they may even offer discounted rooms outside high season.

★Posada del Gecko GUESTHOUSE **$$**
(☎314-525-6037, 314-629-1829; www.posadadelgecko.com; Capurganá; s/d/tr/q COP$30,000/80,000/110,000/140,000; ❄📶) Megapopular Gecko has simple wooden rooms that are great value; smarter options include rooms with air-con and private bathroom. The place is known for its garden bar-restaurant serving authentic Italian pizzas and pastas. It's a fine place for a drink, too, with a soundtrack that's a little more subtle than Capurganá's default skull-splitting reggaeton.

The owner can organize three-day trips to the San Blas Islands.

La Gata Negra GUESTHOUSE **$**
(☎321-572-7398; www.lagatanegra.net; Sapzurro; r per person COP$50,000-55,000, without bathroom COP$35,000-45,000) This Spanish-owned guesthouse, recently under new management, occupies a gorgeous timber chalet set back a short distance from the beach. Two of the fan-cooled rooms share a bathroom, while a larger cabin has its own. The cabaña sleeps four in a double bed and two bunks. The home cooking (dinners COP$25,000), courtesy of owners Jordi and Imma, is a definite plus.

★La Posada HOSTEL **$$**
(☎310-410-2245; www.sapzurrolaposada.com; Sapzurro; r per person incl breakfast COP$75,000-95,000,

GETTING TO PANAMA

It's not possible to drive from Colombia to Panama – the Pan-American Hwy does not extend through the swamps of the Darién Gap. Various foolhardy maniacs have ignored the dangers and attempted to cross the 87km distance in all-terrain vehicles and even on foot, risking encounters with guerrillas, paramilitaries or drug traffickers – don't attempt this.

It is possible and fairly safe, however, to reach Panama (mostly) overland, with just a few sea trips and a short flight. At research time the following route was secure and calm, but always check ahead for security updates before setting out, and stick to the coast.

First, make your way to Turbo or (far better) Necocli. The Medellín–Turbo bus route (COP$70,000, eight hours) is now safe, but daytime travel is still advised. From Cartagena, you'll have to go to Montería (COP$50,000, five hours) and change there for Necocli (COP$35,000, 2½ hours). Buses run regularly from 7am to 5pm. Ensure you leave Cartagena before 11am to avoid getting stuck overnight in Montería. You'll have to spend the night in either Turbo or Necocli, as boats only depart for Capurganá in the mornings. Necocli is the more pleasant town by far.

Next, catch a boat from Turbo or Necocli to Capurganá. The cost for each is COP$70,000, although the Necocli crossing is an hour shorter (taking 1½ hours total). Arrive at the dock at least an hour early to secure a ticket. Hang onto your hat: this can be a bumpy ride. There's a 10kg baggage limit – a COP$1000-per-kilogram excess charge applies – and a COP$2600 port tax.

Then, take a boat from Capurganá to Puerto Olbaldía in Panama (COP$35,000, 30 minutes). The day before you depart, get your Colombian exit stamp at **Migración Colombia** (☎311-746-6234; www.migracioncolombia.gov.co; Capurganá; ⏲8am-5pm Mon-Fri, 9am-noon Sat & Sun), near Carpuganá's harbor (the office will not be open in time on the day you leave). Boats depart Capurganá daily at 7:30am; be at the docks for 7am. This is another bumpy journey, depending on sea conditions. Note: the boat journey costs a minimum of COP$100,000, so you'll have to pay the full amount if you're the only passenger.

Obtain your Panama entry stamp at Panamanian immigration in Puerto Olbaldía, though you might be asked for two copies of your passport. (There's a copy place here if you need it.) Then fly to Panama City's domestic Albrook terminal. There are flights on Tuesday, Thursday and Sunday (US$115, one hour). Puerto Olbaldía has very little to offer tourists: avoid spending any more time here than necessary, and head straight to Panama City.

campsite or hammocks per person COP$15,000-20,000;) The most comfortable, well-run spot in Sapzurro has beautiful gardens with flourishing guava, coconut and mango trees; open-air showers for campers; and beautiful, airy rooms with wooden floors, exposed beams and hammocks on the balconies. Owner Mario speaks great English, and his wife, Lena, prepares meals (mains COP$20,000 to COP$35,000 – call ahead if you plan to eat).

They have recently opened a new guesthouse called **Dule**, 200m along the beach, with three modern air-con rooms (COP$40,000 to COP$55,000 per person).

Eco Hotel Punta Arrecife GUESTHOUSE **$$**
(314-666-5210, 320-687-3431; luzdelaselva52@yahoo.es; Sapzurro; r per person incl breakfast COP$75,000-100,000) Built beside a reef at the edge of the village, this wonderful place is set in an alluringly unkempt garden and presided over by Rubén and Myriam, two charming recluses from the modern world. They host guests in color-themed, cabin-like rooms that are crafted from wood and full of tasteful arts and crafts.

The owners grow much of their own food here, and they encourage guests to disconnect as much as possible.

It's not the easiest place to find: follow the concrete walkway at the eastern end of Sapzurro beach and enter via a small, hard-to-spot gate. A little beyond the hotel toward Panama is another, quieter beach at Cabo Tiburón where there's a small beach-shack bar and good snorkeling.

The owners can help arrange transport from Capurganá or Acandí.

★ **Josefina's** SEAFOOD **$$**
(Capurganá; mains COP$22,000-40,000; noon-9:30pm) Scour the coast and you won't find better seafood – or a warmer welcome – than at Josefina's. Her medium-sized *pargo* (red snapper) practically fills the plate and is a succulent joy, supported by coconut rice, tangy salad and crispy *patacones* (plantain chips); the *crema de camerón* (cream-of-shrimp soup) isn't far behind.

You'll find Josefina in a simple beach shack, complete with multicolored chairs dug into the sand, on Capurganá's Playa Caleta.

Capurgarepa COLOMBIAN **$$**
(Capurganá; mains COP$15,000-25,000; 8am–9pm;) This simple window-in-the-wall place with the silly name does do great *arepas* (corn cakes), but owner-chef Amparo will prepare more elaborate dishes, including veritable feasts of veggies, if you order a few hours ahead. Breakfast is also available.

Information

Be aware that there are no ATMs in either Capurganá or Sazurro, so it's important to bring as much cash as you'll need for your stay. In a pinch, you can get cash advances on a credit card from **Hostal Capurganá** (318-206-4280, 316-482-3665; www.hostalcapurgana.net; Calle de Comercio, Capurganá; s/d/f incl breakfast COP$75,000/125,000/225,000;). The same place (and a few others) also change US dollars, but both transactions will cost you.

AT A GLANCE

POPULATION
61,000

AREA
52km²

BEST DIVING
Banda Dive Shop (p172)

BEST LATE NIGHT COCKTAILS
Banzai (p175)

BEST BEACH
Bahía Suroeste (p177)

WHEN TO GO

Jan–Jun
Dry season and the best time to visit to avoid the Caribbean's increasingly common hurricanes.

Apr–Jul
Crabs migrate and Providencia roads can be closed to protect them.

Dec
Christmas is peak time on both islands book ahead.

Aug
Also peak travel season. Prices spike.

Johnny Cay Natural Regional Park (p170)

San Andrés & Providencia

The archipelago of San Andrés and Providencia is geographically located near Nicaragua, historically tied to Great Britain and politically part of Colombia. Here you'll find isolated beaches, unspoiled coral reefs and an alluring island flavor, and with just a little digging the 300-year-old English-Creole-speaking Raizal culture.

San Andrés, the largest island in the archipelago and its commercial and administrative hub, attracts many Colombian tourists seeking duty-free shopping sprees. The crowds, however, are not difficult to escape.

Providencia offers the same turquoise sea and extensive coral reefs but is much less commercialized. Its colonial heritage is thriving in hamlets of colorful wooden homes peppered about the island.

Both islands offer a total change of pace to the mainland and are well worth the effort of getting there.

INCLUDES

San Andrés 170
Providencia 176

San Andrés

☎8 / POP 70,000

Just 150km east of Nicaragua and some 800km northwest of mainland Colombia, the seahorse-shaped island of San Andrés is best known as Colombia's favorite weekend getaway, where mainlanders love to come to drink, tax-free shop, sunbathe and party. San Andrés Town, the focus of the action, won't be splashed across postcards any time soon, though it does boast an attractive beach promenade and has in recent years begun to address what might be charitably termed its beauty gap.

Indeed, San Andrés is best appreciated outside the downtown hubbub. Whether you take a boat trip to one of the idyllic offshore cays, check out the excellent scuba-diving and snorkeling opportunities or head down the scenic 30km road encircling the rest of the island, this quirky place – where Anglo-Caribbean Raizal culture grinds up against the far more recently imported Colombian one – often manages to charm visitors in the end.

Sights

Johnny Cay Natural Regional Park BEACH
(COP$2000) This protected 4-hectare coral islet sits about 1.5km north of San Andrés Town. It's covered with coconut groves and surrounded by a lovely white-sand beach that's easily the best in San Andrés. The sunbathing is good, but be careful swimming here as there are dangerous currents. Boats leave from the main San Andrés Town beach (round trip on a *colectivo*/private boat COP$10,000/30,000 per person). The last boat back is at 5pm in high season, 3:30pm in low season.

As well as the taxi fare and entry to the cay, you'll be charged for food and drink you consume during your stay. Most of the time you'll be met by an unofficial waiter/fixer who will arrange refreshments for you during your stay and will keep a tab for you that you can pay at the end. Bear in mind that the cay can fill up far beyond capacity, and tourists fight for space with the estimated 500 iguanas that call the place home.

San Luis VILLAGE
Located on the island's east coast, San Luis boasts white-sand beaches and some fine traditional wooden houses. The sea here is good for snorkeling, though conditions can be a little rough. San Luis has no center as such and is really just a 3km string of mostly ramshackle houses along the coast, but it's a tranquil alternative to San Andrés Town.

Cayo El Acuario BEACH
Off the east coast of San Andrés and right next to Haynes Cay, Acuario is a sandbank frequently visited by boat (round trip COP$15,000). The surrounding sea is shallow and calm, and good for snorkeling. If you forget to bring your snorkeling gear, you can rent some here on the beach.

Haynes Cay ISLAND
This small, rocky island doesn't offer beaches, but it's an idyllic and wild spot full of iguanas and great for snorkeling. There're a couple of restaurants and it's a fun day trip for much of the year, though it can get crowded on weekends and during the August holidays. Boat trips cost COP$15,000 from San Andrés Town.

Hoyo Soplador GEYSER
At the southern tip of the island, the Hoyo Soplador is a small geyser where sea water spouts into the air (up to 20m at times) through a natural hole in the coral. This phenomenon occurs only at certain times, when the winds and tide are right, but it's worth hanging around to see.

La Piscinita BEACH
(West View; COP$5000) Located just south of El Cove, La Piscinita is a good site for snorkeling. It has usually calm water, plenty of fish (which will eat out of your hand) and some facilities, including a restaurant serving seafood and renting snorkel gear.

La Loma VILLAGE
This small town in the inner part of San Andrés, also known as the Hill, is one of the most traditional places on the island. It's noted for its 1847 Baptist church, the first to be established here. Be sure to take a stroll and absorb the unique atmosphere – it's the least Colombian-influenced part of the island.

Activities

Due to the beautiful coral reefs all around it, San Andrés is an important diving center, with more than 35 dive spots. Otherwise, most visitors are focused on beach-hopping, day trips to various islands, water sports and partying in San Andrés Town.

Crucero Riviel BOATING
(☎8-512-8840; Av Newball, San Andrés Town) Offers daily tours that combine Acuario and Johnny Cay and leave at 8:30am

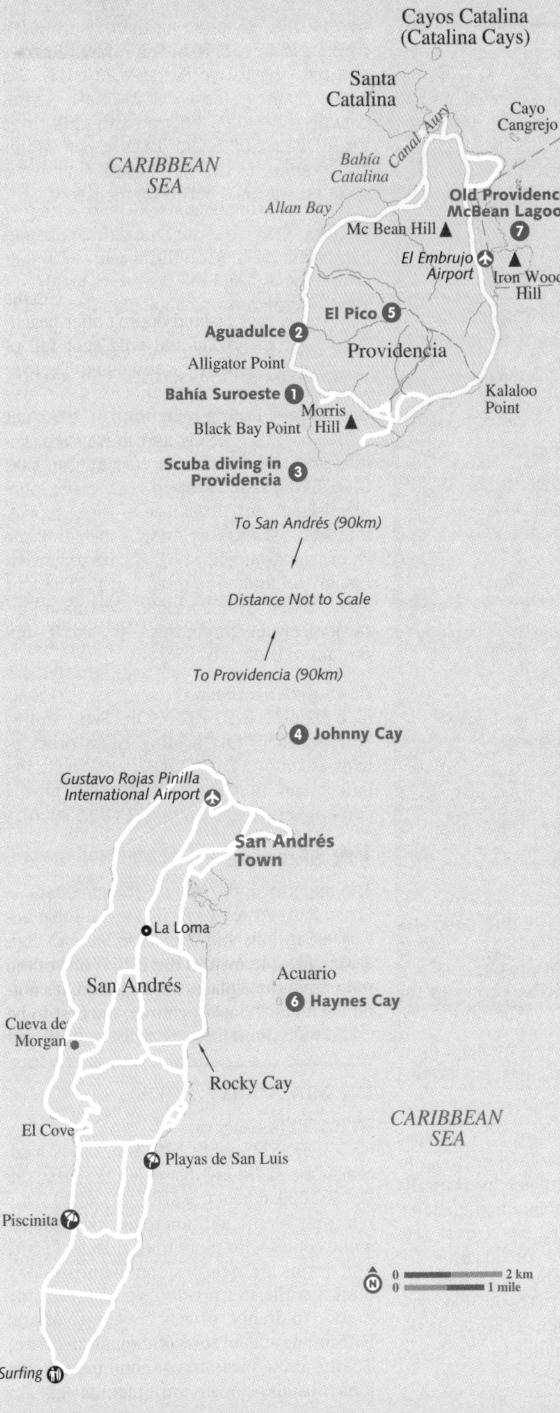

San Andrés & Providencia Highlights

1 Bahía Suroeste (p177) Drinking *coco locos* on this gorgeous stretch of sand while watching the sunset.

2 Bahía Aguadulce (p177) Lying on Providencia's busiest beach still means you'll see only a few dozen other people.

3 Scuba diving (p175) Gawking at Colombia's prettiest coral reefs and marine life in Providencia's blue waters.

4 Johnny Cay (p170) Digging your toes into the pristine sands of the stunning 4-hectare Johnny Cay Natural Regional Park.

5 El Pico (p179) Trekking through iguana and crab country for stunning views from Providencia's highest point.

6 Haynes Cay (p170) Swimming with the stingrays at sunset off San Andrés.

7 Old Providence McBean Lagoon (p177) Exploring the thick mangrove swamps off the coast of Providencia by boat.

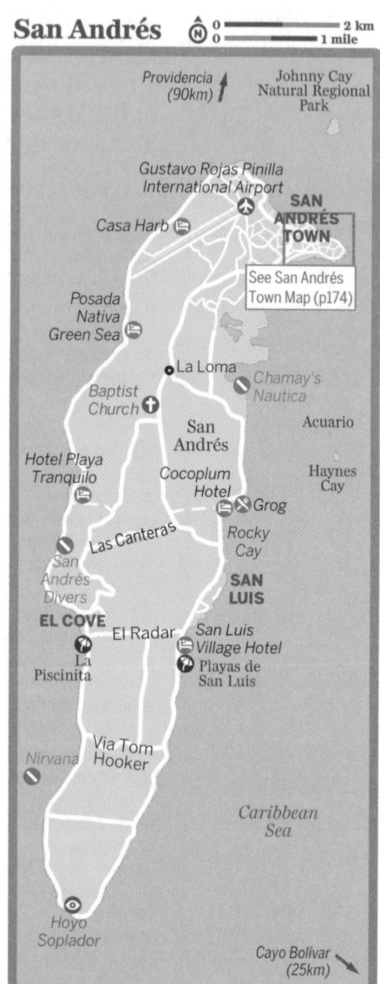

(COP$30,000). Also runs less frequent tours to other hard-to-access islets, snorkeling sites and remote beaches.

San Andrés Divers DIVING
(☎312-448-7230; www.sanandresdivers.com; Av Circunvalar, Km 10) Though not as centrally located as other dive shops on the island, this large shop and school has a great reputation and offers PADI certification for COP$850,000. A two-tank dive with all equipment included is COP$165,000. The office is located at Hotel Blue Cove, while the training pool and dive center can be found further down the main road.

Banda Dive Shop DIVING
(☎8-513-1080, 315-303-5428; www.bandadiveshop.com; Hotel Lord Pierre, Av Colombia, San Andrés Town; ⏰8am-6pm Mon-Sat) Extra-friendly dive shop offering two-tank dives for COP$235,000 and PADI Open Water certification for COP$1,300,000. One of the most professional outfits on the island.

Karibik Diver DIVING
(☎318-863-9552, 8-512-0101; www.karibik-diver.com; Av Newball No 1-248, San Andrés Town) This small German-run school provides quality equipment and personalized service. A two-tank dive is COP$170,000 without equipment. PADI certification costs COP$900,000.

San Andrés Diving & Fishing SNORKELING
(☎316-240-2182; sites.google.com/site/sanandresfishinganddiving; Portofino's Marina; 3hr tours COP$75,000) Jaime Restrepo runs a very popular island tour that takes in three snorkeling sites around San Andrés, including the chance to swim with stingrays. It's somewhat casual and limited to groups of 10. The tour leaves at 2pm from Portofino's Marina at Barracuda Park in San Andrés Town and it's important to book ahead.

Coonative Brothers BOATING
(☎8-512-1923, 8-512-2522) On San Andrés Town's beach, this boating co-op provides trips to Johnny Cay (COP$20,000 including entry) and Acuario (COP$15,000), plus a combined tour to both cays (COP$25,000).

Sleeping

The majority of the island's accommodations are in San Andrés Town. There are some hotels in San Luis, but elsewhere there are relatively few places to stay. For the most part, options on the island are more expensive than on the mainland, although there are now several hostels. Rates rise steeply in high season.

San Andrés Town

★**Karibbik Haus Hostel** HOSTEL $
(☎300-810-3233, 8-512-2519; www.karibbikhaus.com; Calle 11 No 1a-1, Barrio los Almedros; dm COP$60,000, d from COP$175,000; ❄📶) This relatively recent addition to the local budget scene comes with more than a dash of style. The dorms are spacious and feature quality bunks, while the private rooms are firmly in the midrange category, with sparkling bathrooms and all sorts of thoughtful extras. There's also a pleasant common room and a large upstairs balcony with hammocks.

Next door you'll find the hostel's own restaurant, which serves all meals. The staff are very keen to help arrange tours around the island.

Cli's Place GUESTHOUSE **$$**
(8-512-0591; luciamhj@hotmail.com; Av 20 de Julio No 3-47, San Andrés Town; d/tr COP$165,000/205,000;) This Raizal-run place is part of the island's *posada nativa* program, where you stay with locals. English-speaking Cli has eight simple rooms, some with kitchenettes. The guesthouse is reached via a gated alleyway off the park. Breakfast costs COP$10,000 per person.

Apartahotel Tres Casitas HOTEL **$$**
(8-512-5880; Av Colombia No 1-60, San Andrés Town; r per person incl half board COP$145,000;) A cute yellow-and-blue clapboard hotel with extra-large rooms, all with kitchenettes and separate living areas. Rates include breakfast and dinner, and some rooms have balconies over the sea. One of the more charming options in San Andrés Town.

Posada Henry 2 GUESTHOUSE **$$**
(8-512-6150; libiadehenry@hotmail.com; Av 20 de Julio No 1-36, San Andrés Town; s/d COP$60,000/120,000) This centrally located guesthouse is part of the *posada nativa* program, which allows travellers to stay with locals on the island. The fan-cooled, tile-floored rooms all have bathrooms and fridges, and are decorated in bright island colors. Breakfast is not available.

Decameron Los Delfines BOUTIQUE HOTEL **$$$**
(8-512-4083; www.decameron.com; Av Colombia No 16-86; per person all-inclusive from COP$528,000;) The first boutique hotel on the island, as well as within the Decameron chain, this stylish 36-room hotel is quiet, discreet and very popular with couples. It features an over-water restaurant, a small pool and smart furniture, all housed in a design-forward structure that wouldn't be out of place in Los Angeles.

San Andrés Island

★ **Hotel Playa Tranquilo** BOUTIQUE HOTEL **$$$**
(8-513-0719; www.playatranquilo.com; Km 8 Via El Cove; r incl breakfast from COP$360,000;) Buddha overlooks a small pool and sets the tone for this boutique place, which has gorgeous rooms combining modern and traditional touches. Kitchens and communal sitting areas are on offer in some rooms, making it a great place to come with kids. However, the beach of the hotel's name is nowhere in evidence: despite the seafront location, there's no sand. There's also a dive school on-site.

★ **Cocoplum Hotel** HOTEL **$$$**
(8-513-2121; www.cocoplumhotel.com; Via San Luis No 43-39; s/d incl breakfast COP$362,000/500,000;) On a gorgeous private white-sand beach shaded with palms, this multicolored, low-key beach resort sports Caribbean architecture. The restaurant, serving fresh meals all day, is also open to nonguests. Rocky Cay, a good spot for snorkeling, is nearby.

Eating

The Creole-Caribbean influence means staples include breadfruit, which takes the place of *patacones* (fried plantains) as the starch of choice, and the ubiquitous conch, which can be found on almost every menu. Be sure to try the most traditional dish, rundown (*rondon* in the local Creole), a soupy dish of lightly battered fish, plantains, yucca and other gooey starches, all slow-cooked in a healthy dose of coconut milk.

Perú Wok PERUVIAN **$$**
(www.peruwok.com; Av Colombia, Big Point; mains COP$20,000-50,000; noon-11pm;) This restaurant offers dishes of Peruvian-Asian fusion including ceviches, seafood, rice dishes, wok dishes and grills, with a sleek, modern design sets it apart from much of the competition. Choose between the cool dining room or the breezy sea-view terrace.

Mr Panino ITALIAN **$$**
(Edifico Breadfruit, local 106-107, Av Colón; mains COP$20,000-50,000; 10am-10pm Mon-Sat, 4pm-10pm Sun) Despite the touristy-sounding name, this place in San Andrés Town is the real deal. You can expect to find Parma ham and amazing cheeses in its Italian specialty deli, as well as sandwiches (not to mention olive-oil-drenched panini), pasta, pizza, risotto and even octopus carpaccio on the menu.

Miss Celia O'Neill Taste SEAFOOD **$$**
(8-513-1062; Av Newball, San Andrés Town; mains COP$20,000-40,000; noon-3pm & 6-10pm) This rather cute place in a colorful and traditional Caribbean house with a big garden and a breezy patio is a good choice for local food such as *rondon*, stewed crab and stewed fish.

Fisherman Place SEAFOOD **$$**
(8-512-2774; Av Colombia; mains COP$15,000-50,000; noon-4pm) Visiting this open-air, beachside San Andrés Town restaurant is a great way to support local fisherfolk and

San Andrés Town

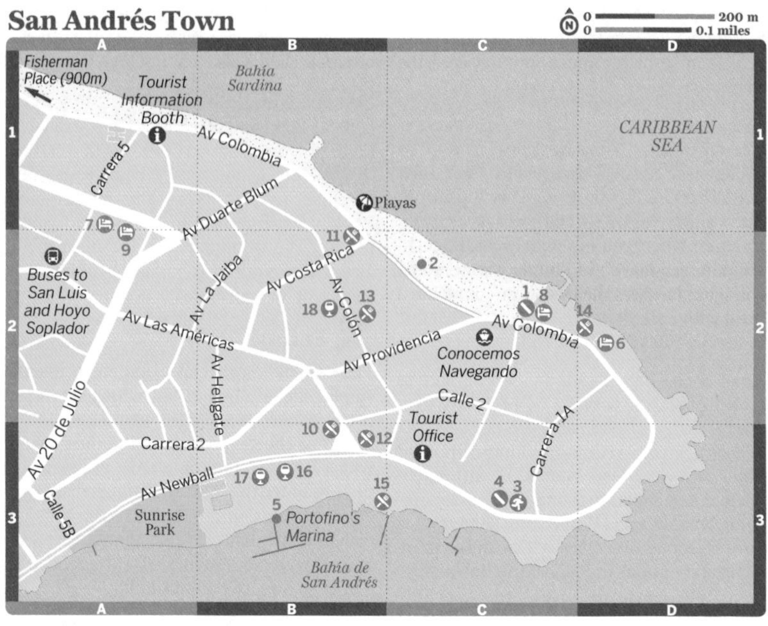

San Andrés Town

Activities, Courses & Tours

1 Banda Dive Shop C2
2 Coonative Brothers C2
3 Crucero Riviel C3
4 Karibik Diver C3
5 San Andrés Diving & Fishing B3

Sleeping

6 Apartahotel Tres Casitas D2
7 Cli's Place A1
8 Decameron Los Delfines C2
9 Posada Henry A2

Eating

10 Gourmet Shop Assho B3
11 Mahi Mahi B2
12 Miss Celia O'Neill Taste B3
13 Mr Panino B2
14 Perú Wok D2
15 Restaurante La Regatta B3

Drinking & Nightlife

16 Banzai B3
17 Blue Deep B3
18 Éxtasis B2

eat well. *Rondon* and fried fish are the most popular dishes, but the lobster is the clear winner for the price.

Grog SEAFOOD $$
(Rocky Cay; mains COP$20,000-40,000; ⏲10am-6pm Wed-Mon) With shade-dappled tables scattered all over the beach, this friendly little locale does a range of mean seafood dishes, including ceviche, rice and wok options, and tasty starters. Unsurprisingly, the titular drink (represented here by Aguila and Club Colombia) is also very popular.

★ **Gourmet Shop Assho** EUROPEAN $$$
(Av Newball; mains COP$30,000-85,000; ⏲noon-3pm & 6-11pm Mon-Sat, noon-11pm Sun; 📶) Streets ahead of the competition, this strangely named place stands out with its delightful decor and impressive menu: here you'll find rare steak, beautifully seasoned seafood dishes, and a range of salads, tapas and vegetarian options. There's an excellent wine list, great coffee and killer desserts, too – do not miss.

★ **Restaurante La Regatta** SEAFOOD $$$
(☎317-744-3516; www.restaurantelaregatta.com; Club Náutico, Av Newball, San Andrés Town; mains COP$30,000-100,000; ⏲noon-3pm & 6.30-11pm; ✍) The island's best restaurant, La Regatta is housed on a wooden pontoon over the sea at Club Náutico. Despite a healthy dose of pirate kitsch, it has a formal, white-linen-tablecloth atmosphere and the food is heavenly. The *langosta regatta* (lobster tails with

three sauces) is nothing short of perfection. Book a table for the evenings.

★Donde Francesca SEAFOOD $$$

(San Luis; mains COP$30,000-60,000; ⏲10am-6pm; 📶) Right on the beach, this breezy place may be little more than a shack, but it serves up absolutely delicious traditional Caribbean food, such as *langostinos al coco* (breaded crayfish deep-fried with coconut), *pulpo al ajillo* (octopus cooked in garlic) and tempura calamari. Even better, showers and changing facilities mean you can combine a meal with a swim.

Mahi Mahi THAI $$$

(Hotel Casablanca, Av Colombia; mains COP$30,000-95,000; ⏲noon-11pm; 📶) This chic Thai spot on the waterfront, part of Hotel Casablanca, provides a welcome break from Colombian staples with its seasoned curries and island-tinged dishes. As well as the cheaper Thai menu, there's a pricey Colombian seafood menu, too.

El Paraíso SEAFOOD $$$

(San Luis; mains COP$30,000-60,000; ⏲9am-5pm; 📶) On a great strip of white-sand beach, El Paraíso is a slightly more upmarket restaurant than some of the simpler beach shacks, but its fresh seafood is of the same excellent quality. There are shower and changing facilities here, so it's a great spot to hang out for the day.

Drinking & Nightlife

There are many nightspots in San Andrés Town along the eastern end of Av Colombia, but expect drunk holidaying Colombians and ear-bleeding music that may not appeal to foreigners much.

Banzai COCKTAIL BAR

(Av Newball, local 119, San Andrés Town; ⏲7pm-2am) If you want a late-night drink without going to a club, Banzai is a great cocktail bar that's popular with locals. The well-mixed drinks are served expertly to a reggae backbeat, and it's chic and rather alternative without being try-hard.

Éxtasis CLUB

(Hotel Sol Caribe San Andrés, Av Colón, San Andrés Town; ⏲9:30pm-3am Mon-Thu, to 4am Fri & Sat) The busiest and best-established club in San Andrés, Éxtasis, on the top floor of the Hotel Sol Caribe, has a huge dance floor that is always packed at weekends and a capacity of 500 people. You can recoup COP$15,000 of the varying cover charge in cocktails.

DIVING ON SAN ANDRÉS & PROVIDENCIA

While courses or individual dives may be cheaper on the mainland, the richness of the corals and the variety of marine life here rivals almost any place in the Caribbean.

Both San Andrés and Providencia have extensive coral reefs – 15km and 35km respectively – and they're notable for their sponges, which appear in an amazing range of forms, sizes and colors. Other aquatic inhabitants include barracudas, sharks, turtles, lobsters, rays and red snappers. Wreck divers will want to check out the two sunken ships, *Blue Diamond* and *Nicaraguense*, both off the coast of San Andrés.

The top five dive spots:

Palacio de la Cherna A wall dive southeast of San Andrés that begins at 12m and drops off some 300m more. Midnight parrot fish, tiger fish, king crabs, lobsters and even nurse and reef sharks are common sightings.

Cantil de Villa Erika Southwest of San Andrés. Depths range from 12m to 45m along this colorful reef full of sponges, soft and hard corals, sea turtles, manta and eagle rays, and sea horses.

La Piramide A shallow dive inside the reef on San Andrés' north side, this is a haven for stingrays. The quantity of fishes, octopuses and moray eels make it one of the most active spots on the island.

Tete's Place Large schools of mid-sized goatfish, grunt fish, schoolmasters and squirrel fish frequent this aquarium-like site 1km offshore at Bahía Suroeste in Providencia.

Manta's Place Despite its name, there are no manta rays at this Providencia site, but rather southern stingrays with wingspans up to 1.5m. As you survey the sands between coral mounds, you'll pass fields of ghost feather dusters, where brown garden eels withdraw into the sand for protection.

Information

There's plentiful information for visitors to San Andrés in both the main **tourist office** (Secretaría de Turismo; 8-513-0801; Av Newball; 8am-noon & 2-6pm Mon-Fri) and the smaller **tourist-information booth** (cnr Avs Colombia & 20 de Julio; 8am-6pm) on the seafront.

Getting There & Away

AIR

Gustavo Rojas Pinilla International Airport (Aeropuerto Internacional Sesquicentenario; 8-512-6112) is right in the town center and the runway ends at the beach. You must buy a tourist card (COP$105,000) on the mainland before boarding your San Andrés–bound flight, but the cards are sold at the gate and there's no chance you'll be allowed to board without one. Airlines that connect to San Andrés include **Avianca** (8-512-3216; www.avianca.com; Gustavo Rojas Pinilla International Airport), **LATAM** (1-800-094-9490; www.latam.com) and **Copa** (8-512-7619; www.copaair.com; Gustavo Rojas Pinilla International Airport), and cities with direct flights here include Bogotá, Barranquilla, Cali, Cartagena, Medellín and Panama City.

Satena (8-512-1403; www.satena.com) operates two flights per day between San Andrés and Providencia in low season (round trip from COP$600,000) and up to six per day in high season.

BOAT

Conocemos Navegando (toll free 01-8000-111-500; www.conocemosnavegando.com; Centro Comercial New Point L.111, Av Providencia; 1 way/return COP$213,000/378,000; 8am-12:30pm & 2-6pm Mon-Fri, 8am-1pm Sat) provides pricey catamaran services between San Andrés and Providencia daily, except Tuesday, in both directions. Services depart from **Muelle Toninos** (Tonino Marina) at 8am and return at 2:30pm the same day. You're supposed to arrive a full hour and a half before departure for registration. The journey takes three hours, and can be extremely rough. It's possible to visit Providencia on a day trip with this service, but it would be very rushed. Seats often sell out, even in low season, so it's important to book ahead.

Getting Around

TO/FROM THE AIRPORT

The airport is a 10-minute walk from the town center, or a flat-fare COP$15,000/7000 ride by taxi/moto-taxi. If you don't have much luggage, it's an easy walk. There's a left-luggage room at the airport (COP$5000 per item per 24 hours).

BICYCLE

Cycling around San Andrés is a great way to get a feel for the island. Roads are paved, there are very few hills and there's little traffic to contend with. Rentals start at around COP$10,000/20,000 per half/full day.

BUS

Local buses circle the island and run along the inland road to El Cove; they're the cheapest way to get around (COP$2000 per ride). They can drop you off close to all the major attractions.

A bus marked 'San Luis' travels along the east-coast road to the southern tip of the island; take this bus to **San Luis and Hoyo Soplador**. The bus marked 'El Cove' runs along the inner road to El Cove, passing through La Loma. It'll drop you in front of the Baptist church, within easy walking distance of La Piscinita. You can catch both buses at the end of Carrera 5 in San Andrés Town.

SCOOTER

The best way to travel independently around the island is by scooter (from COP$70,000 per day, but as much as COP$120,000 in high season) or golf buggy (known locally as a *mula;* from COP$100,000 per day). Many of the dozens of rental businesses are on Av Newball in San Andrés Town and are concentrated around the tip of the island. Most will also deliver to your hotel. Shop around, as prices and conditions vary.

TAXI

A taxi for a sightseeing trip around the island will cost about COP$70,000.

Providencia

8 / POP 5000

Providencia, 90km north of San Andrés, is a wonderfully remote and traditional Caribbean island with breathtaking scenery, gorgeous golden-sand beaches, friendly locals and superb diving. Best of all, it's a pain to get to, ensuring that you'll only have to share this slice of paradise with the other intrepid travellers happy to fly here in a rickety 20-seater plane or brave the often-rough three-hour catamaran ride.

Without a direct connection to the Colombian mainland, Providencia hasn't seen nearly the same levels of cultural invasion as San Andrés, leaving its traditions and customs more or less intact. You'll still hear the local English Creole spoken all over the island, and road signs direct you using the old English town names rather than their Spanish counterparts. All this, combined with beautiful topography standing sentinel over swaths of turquoise-blue sea, gives Providencia no small claim to being a quirky paradise.

Sights

Parque Nacional Natural (PNN) Old Providence McBean Lagoon PARK

(COP$17,000) To protect the unique marine life here, a 10-sq-km nature reserve in the island's northeast was established in 1995. About 10% of the park's area covers a coastal mangrove system east of the airport; the remaining 905 hectares cover an offshore belt including the islets of Cayo Cangrejo and Cayo Tres Hermanos. An 800m-long eco-path helps you identify different species of mangroves and the fauna that inhabit them.

Cayo Cangrejo ISLAND

(Crab Quay) Cayo Cangrejo, a small island that's part of Parque Nacional Natural Old Providence McBean Lagoon, rises sharply and dramatically off the coast. There's no beach here, but there is terrific snorkeling and diving, and a couple of bars serving drinks and seafood. Boat captains will take you across from Maracaibo, where they hang around outside the Hotel Deep Blue (p180). Pick-up is whenever you tell them. A trip costs COP$44,000 per person, plus a COP$17,000 fee to enter the national park.

Bahía Manzanillo BEACH

(Manicheel Bay) This very lovely stretch of white-sand beach is also Providencia's wildest, with no development at all, save the much-loved Roland Roots Bar (p181). The water here can be rough, and the beach is often strewn with seaweed, but the entire place is magical. It's generally safe to swim, but avoid going too far out as there are strong currents.

Bahía Aguadulce BEACH

(Freshwater Bay) This sleepy hamlet offers peace, quiet and a charming sandy beach. There are more than a dozen places to stay here, many right on the beach, and also a couple of diving schools.

Bahía Suroeste BEACH

(Southwest Bay) This gorgeous bay boasts a magnificent palm-lined beach backed by steep hills. There are just a couple of hotels here, so it's a great spot for true escape. If you're on the island on a Saturday afternoon, be sure to come here for the weekly bareback horse race along the beach, which starts around 2pm.

Almond Bay BEACH

A relatively little-known beach a five-minute walk downhill from the main island road, tiny Almond Bay has lovely white sand, calm clear water and very few visitors. There are a few stands serving drinks and simple snacks, and you can also hire snorkeling equipment. However, the beach has almost no shade, so consider bringing an umbrella.

Santa Catalina ISLAND

Some tiny, deserted beaches exist on the island of Santa Catalina. It's worth a look if only to see Morgan's Head, a rocky cliff in the shape of a human face, best seen from the water. An underwater cave is at the base of the cliff. The shoreline changes considerably with the tides; during high-tide, beaches get very narrow and some totally disappear. To explore the island's attractive coastline, take the path to the left after the pontoon bridge.

Lighthouse GALLERY

(☎313-380-5866; www.lighthouseprovidencia.com; High Hill; ⏲5-9pm Tue-Sat) With a great lookout to the sea, this community-run arts space serves as a small educational center, gallery, cafe and hangout. It shows documentaries on a projector after dark (ask to see the fascinating – if bizarre – doc about the local crab migration, COP$10,000 per person); serves up good coffee and a range of island snacks; and promotes environmental awareness.

Santa Isabel VILLAGE

Strangely, Santa Isabel doesn't see much tourism, despite its gorgeous location in a picturesque bay attached by a pontoon bridge to the little island of Santa Catalina. Its lack of a beach might be the explanation, but it's well worth coming up here to wander around the quaint town and see the locals going about their business.

Activities

The main activity in Providencia is kicking back and enjoying the beaches. The very best are Bahía Suroeste, Bahía Aguadulce, and Bahía Manzanillo at the southern end of the island, but there are several other lovely places to swim.

Diving & Snorkeling

Snorkeling and diving are the island's two biggest attractions, and you shouldn't miss the opportunity to do either here. The clear water and stunning reef life make this one of the Caribbean's best places for these activities. Diving trips and courses can be arranged with local operators, dive sites tend to be fairly standardized, and there's an ever-increasing number of outfits on the island, which keeps competition healthy.

Providencia

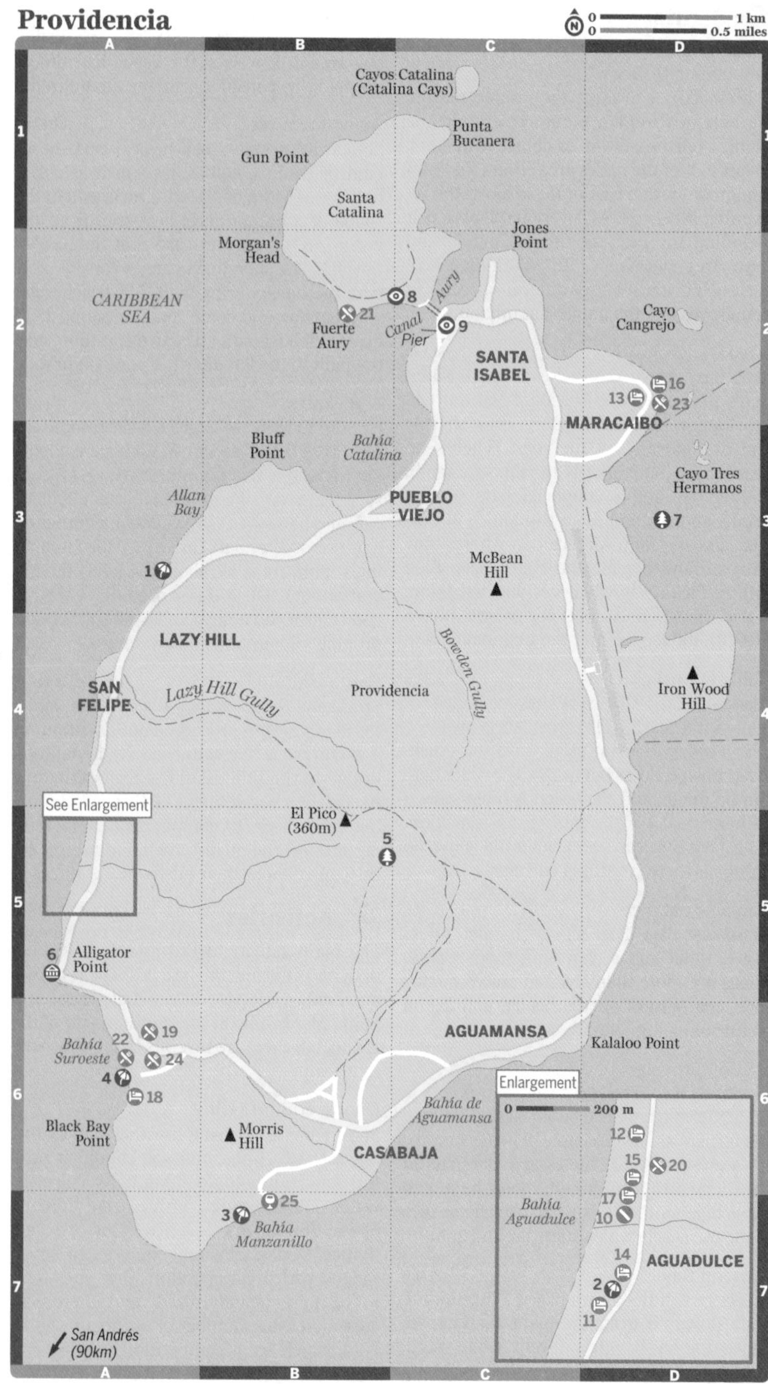

Providencia

Sights
1 Almond Bay........A3
2 Bahía Aguadulce........D7
3 Bahía Manzanillo........B7
4 Bahía Suroeste........A6
5 El Pico Natural Regional Park........B5
6 Lighthouse........A5
7 Parque Nacional Natural (PNN) Old Providence McBean Lagoon........D3
8 Santa Catalina........C2
9 Santa Isabel........C2

Activities, Courses & Tours
Felipe Diving Shop........(see 11)
Sirius Dive Shop........(see 18)
10 Sonny Dive Shop........D7

Sleeping
11 Cabañas El Recreo........D7
Cabañas Miss Elma........(see 11)
12 Frenchy's Place........D6
13 Hotel Deep Blue........D2
14 Hotel El Pirata Morgan........D7
Hotel Miss Mary........(see 4)
15 Mr Mac........D6
16 Posada Coco Bay........D2
17 Posada del Mar........D7
18 Sirius Hotel........A6
Sol Caribe Providencia........(see 2)

Eating
19 Café Studio........A6
20 Caribbean Place........D6
21 Don Olivo........B2
22 El Divino Niño........A6
23 Restaurante Deep Blue........D2
24 Salt Wata........A6

Drinking & Nightlife
25 Roland Roots Bar........B7

Felipe Diving Shop DIVING
(☎8-514-8775; www.felipediving.com; Aguadulce) Diving trips and courses can be arranged with this recommended operator run by a native Raizal. An open-water or advanced course can be arranged for COP$880,000. As well as leading dives to one of dozens of sites daily, Felipe also offers night dives (COP$200,000).

Sirius Dive Shop DIVING
(☎8-514-8213; www.siriushotel.net; Bahía Suroeste) This dive shop, located in the grounds of the Sirius Hotel (p180), offers an open-water or advanced course for COP$800,000. A two-tank dive with quality equipment is COP$200,000. Night dives are also offered (COP$220,000).

Sonny Dive Shop DIVING
(☎313-430-2911, 318-274-4524; www.sonnydiveshop.com; Aguadulce) Sonny's Dive Shop in Aguadulce offers an open-water or advanced course for COP$850,000. Two-tank dives cost COP$190,000, while a night dive is COP$150,000.

Hiking

The mountainous interior of the island is impressive in terms of its vegetation and small animal life, making it great for walking. There's perhaps nowhere else in Colombia that you will see so many colorful lizards, iguanas and black crabs scampering through bushes. Beware of a common shrub with spectacular hornlike thorns; ants living inside have a painful bite. Mosquitoes also abound in the interior.

One superb hike takes you through the thick mountain forests of **El Pico Natural Regional Park** FREE for outstanding 360-degree views of the Caribbean from El Pico mountain (360m). The most popular trail begins in Casabaja. Ask for directions as several paths crisscross on the lower part (further up there are no problems), or ask in Casabaja for an informal guide. It's a steady 90-minute walk to the top, best done early. Carry drinking water (there is none along the way), sun cream and a hat.

Festivals & Events

Crab Migration NATURE
This event takes place twice a year for a week or two between April and July. First, the adult black crabs descend to the beaches and lay their eggs, before returning to the mountainside. Then, several weeks later, the juvenile crabs leave the sea and follow in their path. Roads usually close to allow safe crossing for the crabs.

Cultural Festival CULTURAL
Providencia's major cultural event takes place in the last week of June. It includes music and dance, a parade of motorcycles and, just for kicks, an iguana beauty pageant.

Sleeping

Accommodations in Providencia tend to be disappointing, with poorly run hotels coasting by on the island's charms. Most options can be found in Aguadulce or Bahía Suroeste, where there's a growing number of small cottages, hotels and cabañas. There are places to stay all over the island, however, and the north – which is virtually traveller-free – can make for a pleasant contrast to the tourist enclaves down south.

Posada Coco Bay GUESTHOUSE **$$**
(☎311-804-0373; posadacocobay@gmail.com; Maracaibo; s/d from COP$100,000/150,000; ❄📶) A rustic spot with a view of Cayo Cangrejo and hammocks on the timber balconies, this is a good choice for a chilled island vibe. The shipshape rooms come with mosquito nets and some even have kitchens. While there's no beach here, it's still possible to swim directly from the property.

Mr Mac CABAÑAS **$$**
(☎316-567-6526, 318-695-9540; posadamistermack@hotmail.com; Aguadulce; bungalows/apt per person COP$100,000/110,000; ❄) The island's cheapest option is also one of its friendliest, where host Laudina warmly welcomes guests. The green-painted timber house is over the water, with hammocks strewn along the veranda. Rooms are large and the enormous apartments have kitchenettes. It's possible to swim in the sea from the garden here, though the beach is a five-minute walk away. No wi-fi.

Cabañas Miss Elma CABAÑAS **$$**
(☎310-566-3773, 8-514-8229; Aguadulce; r per person incl breakfast COP$150,000; ❄) Right on Aguadulce's lovely palm-backed beach, this friendly family-run place has colorful common areas and a wonderfully casual seaside restaurant. The six wood-panelled cabañas are simple but spotless and spacious. Some have sea views and all have fridges and TV.

Cabañas El Recreo CABAÑAS **$$$**
(☎317-425-5389; capbryan@hotmail.com; Aguadulce; s/d/tr incl breakfast COP$120,000/206,000/292,000; ❄📶) These orange-painted timber cabins spread out along the edge of the beach in Aguadulce may not exactly exude charm in themselves, but they have a dreamy location with the waves just meters away. Each one includes a fridge and a TV, and the rooms right on the beach are no extra cost, so book early!

Posada del Mar HOTEL **$$$**
(☎8-514-8454; www.decameron.com; Aguadulce; s/d incl breakfast from COP$140,000/250,000; ❄📶) This place, run by hotel chain Decameron, still feels small-scale, though it's rather larger than it appears from the street. It's brightly painted and well maintained, rooms have smallish balconies overlooking the sea and there's a garden from where you can swim.

Hotel Deep Blue HOTEL **$$$**
(☎315-324-8443, 321-458-2099; www.hoteldeepblue.com; Maracaibo; d/ste incl breakfast from COP$610,000/770,000; ❄📶🏊) Providencia's smartest hotel by some distance, the Deep Blue offers 12 spacious rooms complete with marble floors, rain showers, flat-screen TVs and smart bathroom products. The higher categories even have mini-infinity pools on their balconies and there's a communal rooftop pool with amazing views towards Cayo Cangrejo, as well as a highly recommended restaurant on the waterfront.

Frenchy's Place APARTMENT **$$$**
(☎315-709-6910, 318-306-1901; posadafrenchysprovidencia@gmail.com; Aguadulce; s/d/tr COP$190,000/250,000/310,000) Run by Parisienne Marie (known as 'Frenchy'), this charmingly rustic, wood-crafted apartment is perhaps the most characterful place to stay on the island. There's a gorgeous balcony overlooking the sea, two bedrooms (one double, one single), a full kitchen, a bathroom and a living area crammed full of eccentric knickknacks. Book in advance.

Sirius Hotel HOTEL **$$$**
(☎8-514-8213; www.siriushotel.net; Bahía Suroeste; s/d/tr incl breakfast from COP$190,000/310,000/400,000; ❄📶) Sirius has a dreamy location on Bahía Suroeste. Its rooms are extremely clean, and some have lovely sea views and even balconies. It's a perfect choice if you want to spend quiet days on the beach or diving with the in-house school.

Hotel El Pirata Morgan HOTEL **$$$**
(☎8-514-8232; www.elpiratamorganhotel.org; Aguadulce; s/d/tr incl breakfast COP$180,000/220,000/310,000; ❄📶🏊) A solid option in the heart of Aguadulce, the Pirata Morgan may lack the Caribbean flair of some of its neighbors and has rather dated interiors, but the welcome is friendly and the rooms are clean. There's a pleasant pool and a garden that's perfectly located to watch sunsets, and the beach is just a short wander away.

Eating

Generally speaking, food is more expensive on Providencia than on the mainland, but the island has a couple of excellent options that won't break the bank. For self-caterers there are rather pricey supermarkets with an extremely limited range of foodstuffs in Aguadulce and Santa Isabel; you may do better to bring some supplies from San Andrés.

El Divino Niño SEAFOOD **$$**
(Bahía Suroeste; mains COP$20,000-44,000; ⏲ noon-6pm) It's easy to see why this restaurant on Providencia's best beach is so popular – palm-shaded tables dot the sand with waves lapping at your feet, while the teams serve up fresh fish, lobster, crab and conch dishes. If in doubt, order the superb seafood *plato mixto*. The loud music is a shame at such a peaceful spot, but hey, you're in Colombia.

Salt Wata SEAFOOD **$$**
(☎ 311-253-5087; Bahía Suroeste; mains COP$20,000-60,000; ⏲ 8am-10pm, noon–3pm & 6-10pm Wed-Mon) With just two tables outside on the terrace and two more inside the brightly lit dining room-kitchen, this tiny place serves up traditional Creole seafood dishes from a large menu that includes ceviche, sandwiches and tacos. Breakfasts, desserts and a children's menu can also be ordered.

★**Café Studio** SEAFOOD **$$$**
(☎ 8-514-9076; Bahía Suroeste; mains COP$30,000-60,000; ⏲ 11am-10pm Mon-Sat) Providencia's most popular restaurant is run by a Canadian–Raizal couple and the food is generally delightful, both memorable and reasonably priced given where you are. It gets fearsomely crowded come evening – not least with mosquitoes, making repellent a must – so get here in good time to secure a table, or try visiting at lunch to avoid the rush.

★**Caribbean Place** SEAFOOD **$$$**
(Donde Martin; ☎ 311-287-7238; Aguadulce; mains COP$40,000-78,000; ⏲ 12:30-4pm & 7-10pm Mon-Sat) Follow the pathway that leads to this charming place, and discover one of the island's culinary highlights. Though you'll pay handsomely for the seafood here, Bogotá-trained chef Martin Quintero has succeeded in producing serious gastronomy in a casual atmosphere. Highlights include black crab cooked many ways, crawfish, shrimp and various seafood casseroles.

Restaurante Deep Blue CARIBBEAN **$$$**
(☎ 321-215-4818, 321-458-2099; Maracaibo; mains COP$28,000-60,000; ⏲ 7am-10pm) Its waterfront tables have gorgeous views towards Cayo Cangrejo, and this upmarket place boasts a very impressive and inventive menu, taking in crunchy coconut prawns, garlic crab claws and a superb mixed seafood platter for two. Service can be on the slow side, so come with plenty of time for a relaxed meal. Reserve ahead for the evening, as they will often close early if they're not expecting guests.

Don Olivo SEAFOOD **$$$**
(☎ 310-230-5260; Santa Catalina; mains COP$35,000-65,000; ⏲ noon-5pm Wed-Mon, dinner by reservation) Don Olivo hails from Mauritania and delights in preparing his morning's catch for lunch, which he serves up on the terrace of his seafront home on the island of Santa Catalina. The menu changes daily and dishes include conch ceviche and lobster in Olivo's own secret sauce, though it's the warm welcome and conversation that make this place particularly special.

Drinking & Nightlife

Providencia may be the sleepiest corner of Colombia, but it's still Colombia, so you'll often be able to find the odd impromptu beach party or some loud music after dark. Ask around, and if in doubt head to Roland Roots Bar or wander around Santa Isabel and see what the locals are up to.

Roland Roots Bar BAR
(Bahía Manzanillo; ⏲ 10am-midnight, to 2am Fri & Sat) This travelers' icon encapsulates island life in one ridiculously atmospheric beach bar. Booths fashioned from bamboo sit beneath ramshackle thatched roofs spread amid the sands, and it's all set to a booming reggae soundtrack. Roland is an island legend for his late-night parties and his *coco locos* – jazzed-up piña coladas served in coconuts. There's also excellent seafood (mains COP$20,000 to COP$35,000).

Information

The island's **hospital** and only two ATMs are in Santa Isabel (**Banco Agrario** and **Banco de Bogotá**: ⏲ 8-11:30am & 2-4pm Mon-Fri).

Getting There & Away

Satena (p176) flies between San Andrés and Providencia (round trip from COP$600,000) twice daily in low season, with several more flights in high season. Be sure to buy your ticket in advance in high season. Note that, due to the small planes used on this route, the luggage allowance is 10kg; you'll need to pay for any extra, though it's not expensive and generally no issue to do so.

The Conocemos Navegando (p176) catamaran connects Providencia to San Andrés daily, except Tuesday, in both directions (COP$378,000 return, three hours).

Getting Around

Providencia has just one circular road around it, with a few offshoots.

AT A GLANCE

POPULATION
2.5 million

ELEVATION
1495m

BEST COFFEE FARMS
Ecosistemas (p208)

BEST ESCOBAR TOUR
Paisa Road (p191)

BEST FUSION FOOD
Osea (p193)

WHEN TO GO

Jan–Mar
Clear conditions expose the peaks of Parque Nacional Natural (PNN) Los Nevados.

Aug
The streets of Medellín explode with the vibrant colors of the Feria de las Flores.

Oct–Dec
Coffee pickers converge on farms throughout the Zona Cafetera for the main harvest.

Medellín (p186)
ALEXANDER CANAS ARANGO/SHUTTERSTOCK ©

Medellín & Zona Cafetera

Welcome to *país paisa* – *paisa* country – a vibrant region made up of coffee plantations and flower farms, lush cloud forest, dynamic student towns and the busy city of Medellín. It is one of Colombia's most dynamic regions, and is not to be missed.

In Medellín, the country's second-largest metropolis, towers soar skyward in the center of a deep valley, concrete examples of the ambition that has placed the city at the vanguard of Colombia's revival. It is an attractive city that seduces most travelers instantly, with its just-perfect climate, great restaurants, museums, public artwork and thumping discos.

Further south is the Zona Cafetera, a rich tapestry of historic villages, charming coffee farms, fantastic nature reserves and grand mountain peaks. Coffee is more than a cash crop here – it is a way of life. You'll never look at your morning cup the same way again.

INCLUDES

Medellín ... 186
Guatapé ... 199
Santa Fe de Antioquia ... 201
Jardín ... 203
Zona Cafetera ... 205
Manizales ... 205
Parque Nacional Natural Los Nevados ... 212
Pereira ... 215
Armenia ... 219
Salento ... 222
Valle de Cocora ... 225

Medellín & Zona Cafetera Highlights

❶ **Valle de Cocora** (p225) Craning your neck to see the tops of the majestic wax palms.

❷ **Medellín** (p186) Riding the Metrocable high above the rooftops before sampling the city's many fine restaurants and bars.

❸ **Zona Cafetera** (p205) Heading out into the plantation to pick your own coffee.

❹ **Termales San Vicente** (p217) Bathing in piping-hot thermal springs high in the mountains.

❺ **Río Claro** (p205) Spending the night in your hotel room open to the jungle, the river roaring below.

❻ **Parque Nacional Natural Los Nevados** (p212) Hiking to a mystic lagoon beneath majestic mountains.

❼ **Piedra del Peñol** (p200) Scaling the rock for amazing views over the Embalse Guatapé.

❽ **Jardín** (p203) Sipping a mug of local arabica in the vibrant central plaza.

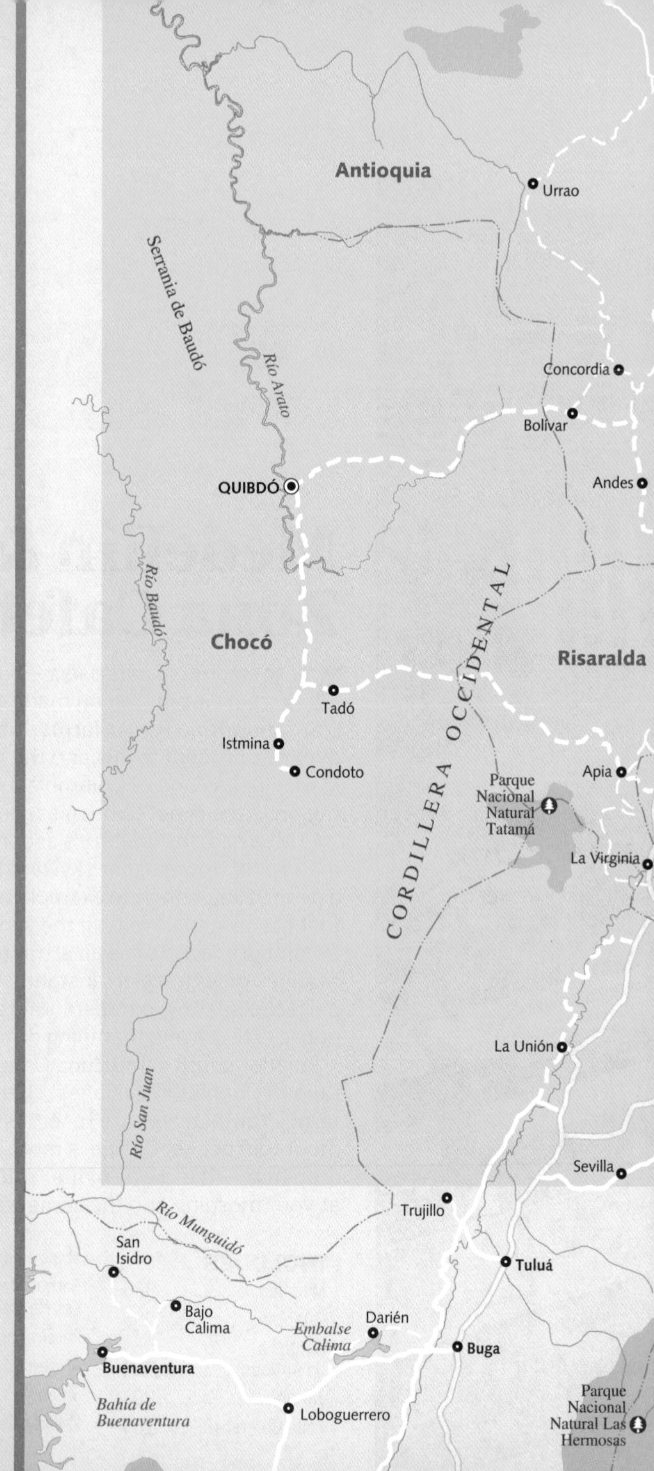

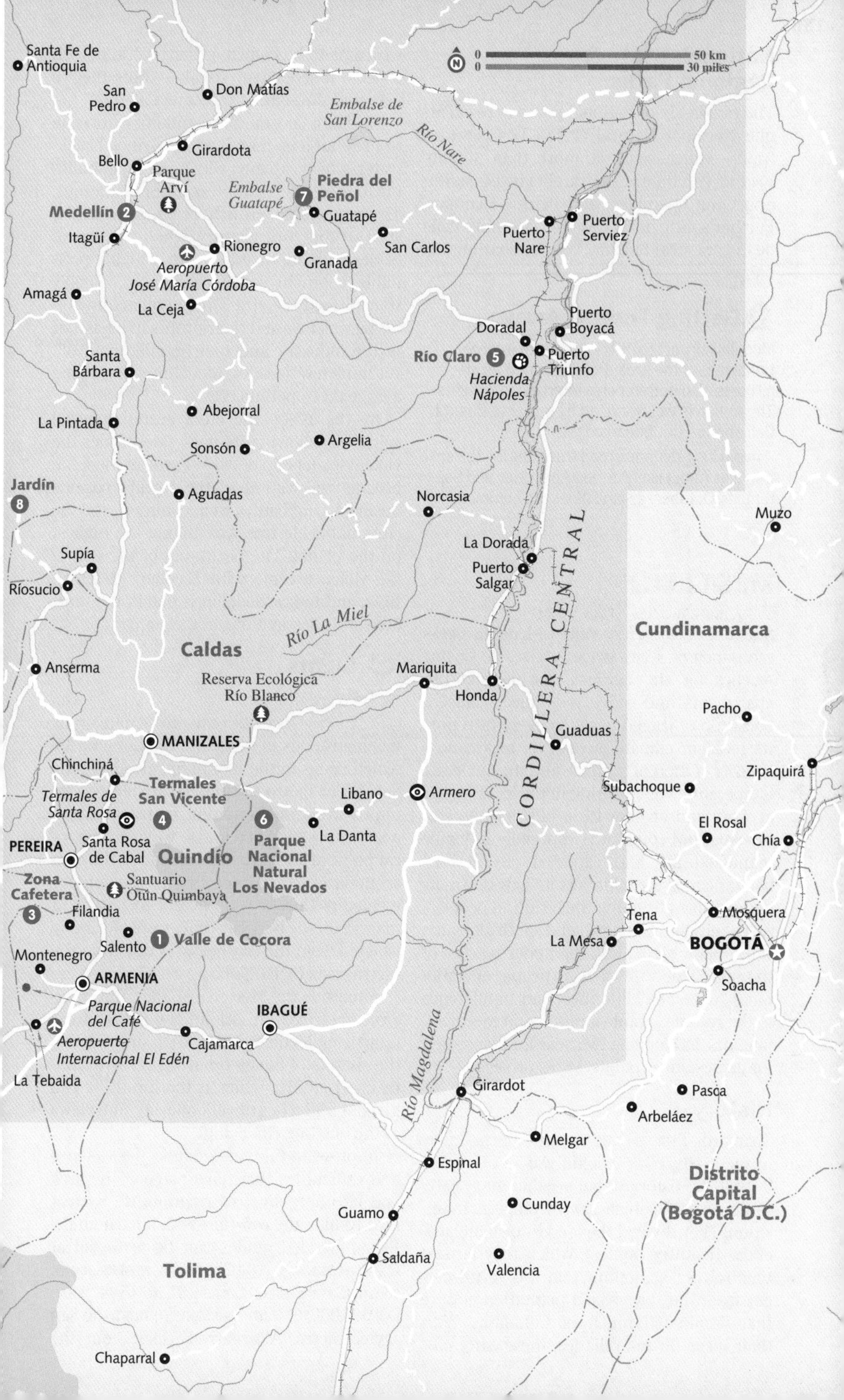
0 50 km
0 30 miles
Santa Fe de Antioquia
San Pedro
Don Matías
Embalse de San Lorenzo
Río Nare
Girardota
Bello
Parque Arví
Embalse Guatapé
7 Piedra del Peñol
Medellín 2
Guatapé
Itagüí
Rionegro
San Carlos
Granada
Aeropuerto José María Córdoba
Puerto Nare
Puerto Serviez
Amagá
La Ceja
Doradal
Puerto Boyacá
Río Claro 5
Puerto Triunfo
Hacienda Nápoles
Santa Bárbara
La Pintada
Abejorral
Sonsón
Argelia
Jardín 8
Aguadas
Norcasia
Muzo
La Dorada
Supía
Puerto Salgar
Ríosucio
CORDILLERA CENTRAL
Río La Miel
Cundinamarca
Caldas
Anserma
Mariquita
Reserva Ecológica Río Blanco
Honda
Pacho
MANIZALES
Guaduas
Chinchiná
Termales San Vicente
Zipaquirá
Termales de Santa Rosa
4
Libano
Armero
Subachoque
6
La Danta
El Rosal
PEREIRA
Santa Rosa de Cabal
Quindío
Parque Nacional Natural Los Nevados
Chía
Zona Cafetera 3
Santuario Otún Quimbaya
Filandia
Mosquera
Tena
Salento
1 Valle de Cocora
La Mesa
BOGOTÁ
Montenegro
ARMENIA
Soacha
Parque Nacional del Café
IBAGUÉ
Aeropuerto Internacional El Edén
Cajamarca
La Tebaida
Río Magdalena
Girardot
Pasca
Arbeláez
Melgar
Espinal
Distrito Capital (Bogotá D.C.)
Cunday
Guamo
Saldaña
Valencia
Tolima
Chaparral

National, State & Regional Parks

The big daddy of national parks here is Parque Nacional Natural (PNN) Los Nevados (p212), which soars at more than 5000m. East of Pereira are the rarely visited Santuario Otún Quimbaya and Parque Ucumarí. Further south, don't miss the stunning Valle de Cocora, near Salento, with its soaring wax palms.

Getting There & Away

Medellín airport (p198) is the main international hub of the area. Pereira and Armenia airports also both receive international flights. The region is well serviced by buses to Bogotá, Cali and the Caribbean coast.

Avoid long-distance road travel during torrential rains (most likely during April/May and September/October) as landslides are common.

MEDELLÍN

4 / POP 2 MILLION / ELEV 1495M

Situated in a narrow valley, Medellín packs the punch of a city twice its size. Its skyline reaches for the heavens, setting high-rise apartments and office buildings against a backdrop of jagged peaks in every direction. Its pleasant climate gives it its nickname – the City of Eternal Spring – and the moderate temperatures put a spring in the locals' steps, at work and at play. It's a bustling place of industry and commerce, especially in textile manufacturing and exported cut flowers. On weekends Medellín lets its hair down, its many discos attracting the beautiful people.

The city sprawls north and south along the valley floor; slums hug the upper reaches of the hills. True to its *paisa* (people of Antioquia) roots, Medellín affects an indifference to the rest of Colombia, putting on metropolitan airs and looking overseas for inspiration for its next great public-works projects.

History

Spaniards first arrived in the Aburrá Valley in the 1540s, but Medellín was not founded until 1616. Historians believe that many early settlers were Spanish Jews fleeing the Inquisition. They divided the land into small haciendas (country estates), which they farmed themselves – something that was very different from the slave-based plantation culture that dominated much of Colombia. With their focus on self-reliance, these early *paisas* came to be known as hard workers with a fierce independent streak – traits they've exported throughout the Zona Cafetera.

Medellín became the capital of Antioquia in 1826 but long remained a provincial backwater, which explains why its colonial buildings are neither sumptuous nor numerous. The city's rapid growth began only at the start of the 20th century, when the arrival of the railroad, together with a highly profitable boom in coffee production, quickly transformed the city. Mine owners and coffee barons invested their profits in a nascent textile industry, and their gamble paid off. Within a few decades, Medellín had become a large metropolitan city.

By the 1980s the city's entrepreneurial spirit was showing its dark side. Under the violent leadership of Pablo Escobar, Medellín became the capital of the world's cocaine business. Gun battles were common, and the city's homicide rate was among the highest on the planet. The beginning of the end of the violence came with Escobar's death in 1993, and today Medellín is one of the most accessible destinations in the country.

Sights

★**La Comuna 13** AREA

(221i, 225i) Once one of the most dangerous neighborhoods in Medellín, the Comuna 13, which clings to the mountainside above the San Javier metro station, has undergone an impressive transformation in recent times and is now considered safe to visit. The focal point of a trip to the *comuna* is the area around the *escaleras electricas,* the outdoor escalators that provide access to homes in marginalized barrios that were formerly isolated from the city below. A taxi from the metro costs COP$5500.

Alongside the Metrocable lines, the *escaleras electricas* are one of the icons of the rebirth of Medellín. The area surrounding the six sets of escalators is awash with murals and graffiti, while at the top there is a lookout and a boardwalk offering fine views of the bustling city below.

In order to fully understand the violence and difficulties that have plagued the area and its impressive reformation, it's a great idea to hike the *comuna* with a local guide. Recommended guides can be arranged at **Casa Kolacho** (4-252-0035; www.facebook.com/LaCasaKolacho; Carrera 97 No 43-41; tours COP$35,000; 11am-7pm Mon-Fri) near the San Javier metro. Alternatively, check out the barrio's artwork with the **Comuna 13 Graffiti Tour** (www.comuna13tours.com; Calle 10; COP$70,000; ⏲10am & 4pm), departing twice daily from the Poblado metro.

To reach the *escaleras* take either bus 221i or 225i from the stop by the traffic lights on the right as you leave the San Javier metro. Buy an integrated ticket at the station where you board the metro.

★Museo Casa de la Memoria MUSEUM

(☎4-385-5555; www.museocasadelamemoria.gov.co; Calle 51 No 36-66; ⏲9am-6pm Tue-Fri, 10am-4pm Sat & Sun) FREE This harrowing museum dedicated to the urban conflict in Medellín is a must-visit for travelers wanting to fully understand the city (and Colombia). There are interesting displays on the geopolitical origins of the conflict, but the most moving parts are the life-size video screens, where survivors recount their experiences as if they were standing in front of you, and the Wall of Memory outside, which pays homage to local residents killed in the violence, their names etched onto the bricks.

Cerro Nutibara VIEWPOINT

(Map p188; ☎4-260-2416, 4-385-8017; ⏲6am-11pm; 🚍1, 2) On top of this 80m-tall hill, 2km southwest of the city center, sits the kitschy **Pueblito Paisa**, a miniature version of a typical Antioquian township, complete with tacky gift stalls. Views across the city from the adjacent platform are stunning on a good day. Take a taxi to the top (or a Metroplus bus to the Nutibara stop) and check out the Parque de las Esculturas – a handful of modern abstract sculptures by South American artists – on the way down.

Next to the lookout you'll find the **Museo de la Ciudad** (Map p188; Cerro Nutibara; COP$2000; ⏲10am-6pm; 🚍1, 2), a small museum dedicated to the history of Medellín, which often showcases old photographs of the city.

Casa Museo Pedro Nel Gómez MUSEUM

(Map p188; ☎4-444-2633; Carrera 51B No 85-24; ⏲9am-5pm Mon-Sat, 10am-4pm Sun) FREE Located in the house where the artist lived and worked, this fine museum has an extensive collection of pieces by prolific local painter Pedro Nel Gómez (1899–1984), as well as occasional major exhibitions. It also organizes painting workshops for visitors (COP$80,000 per group) where you can take classes in the studio of the artist, which is adorned with a wonderful mural. Book in advance.

Many of the houses lining the road up to the museum from the neighborhood of Moravia have had reproductions of works by Nel Gómez painted on their facades – it's worth walking up rather than taking a taxi or bus.

Museo de Arte Moderno de Medellín GALLERY

(☎4-444-2622; www.elmamm.org; Carrera 44 No 19A-100; adult/student COP$10,000/7000; ⏲9am-6pm Tue-Fri, 10am-6pm Sat, 10am-5pm Sun) Set around a refurbished industrial building in Ciudad del Río, 'El MAMM' showcases changing exhibitions of contemporary art. The large new wing houses pieces from the permanent collection, which includes many works by local painter Débora Arango. It also has a cinema showing independent films.

Monumento a la Raza MONUMENT

(Map p188; Calle 44, Centro Administrativo La Alpujarra) Rodrigo Arenas Betancur, Colombia's favorite designer of monuments, has a number of pieces around Medellín, but the most impressive work is this one in front of the municipal building that tells the story of Antioquia in dramatically twisting metal.

Plazoleta de las Esculturas PLAZA

(Plaza Botero; Map p192; Plazoleta de las Esculturas) This public space in front of the Museo de Antioquia (p189) is home to 23 large, curvaceous bronze sculptures by renowned local artist Fernando Botero, including some of his most iconic works.

El Cerro de Moravia HILL

(Map p188; Barrio Moravia) The densely populated neighborhood of Moravia was once Medellín's municipal rubbish dump with an open-air mountain of trash surrounded by a large shanty town whose residents once rummaged through the detritus. However, it has since been transformed into a model urban center, with the mound of trash turned into a foliage-covered hillside. You can take a guided tour of the neighborhood and find out about the fascinating transformation by contacting the **Centro de Desarollo Cultural de Moravia** (Map p188; ☎ext 108 4-213-2809; www.centroculturalmoravia.org; Calle 82A No 50-25; ⏲by appointment) FREE.

While the hill now has a green hue and looks natural, underneath the pile of rubbish still smolders and locals say it's a couple of degrees hotter here than elsewhere in the city.

Medellín

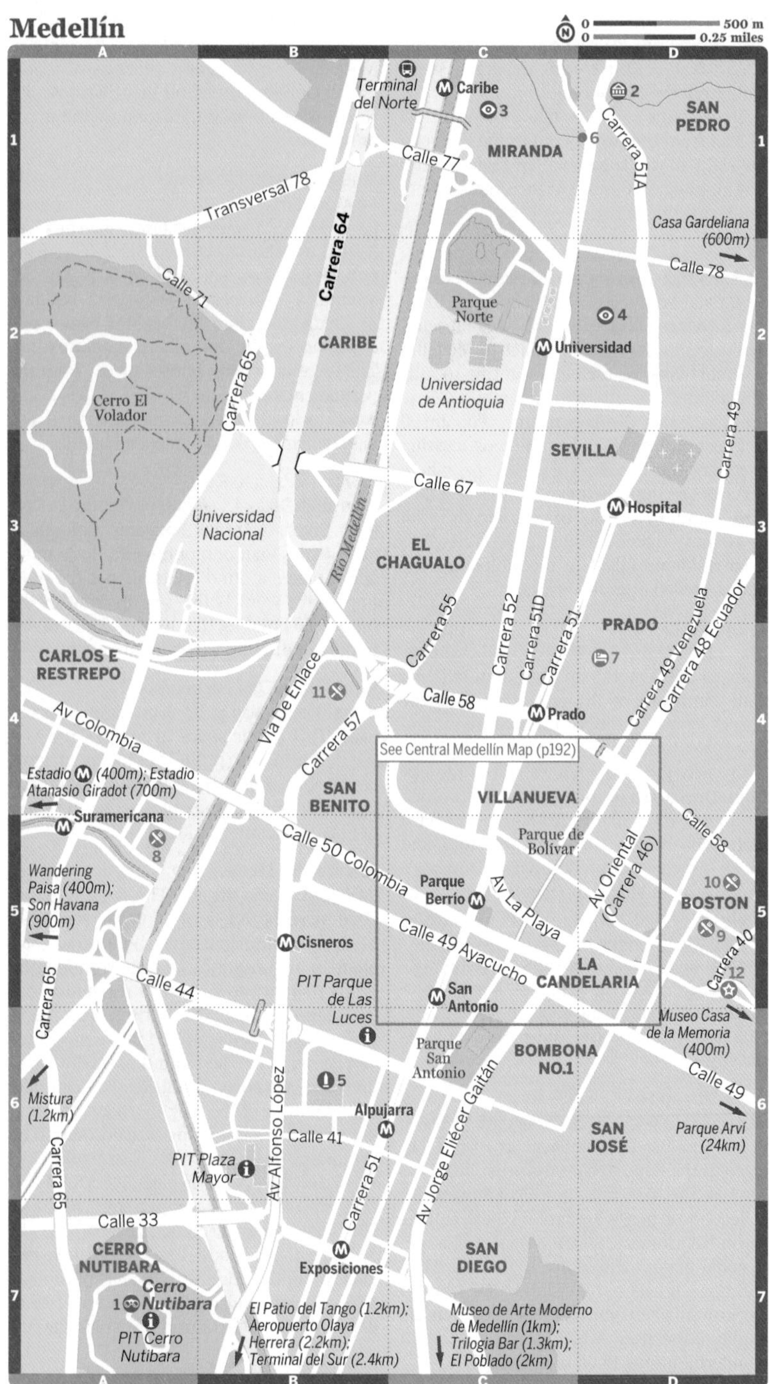

MEDELLÍN & ZONA CAFETERA MEDELLÍN

Medellín

Top Sights
1 Cerro Nutibara....................................A7

Sights
2 Casa Museo Pedro Nel Gómez............D1
3 El Cerro de Moravia.............................C1
4 Jardín Botánico....................................D2
5 Monumento a la Raza..........................B6
Museo de la Ciudad.......................(see 1)

Activities, Courses & Tours
6 Centro de Desarollo Cultural de Moravia...D1

Sleeping
7 61 Prado...D4

Eating
8 Ciao Pizza Gourmet.............................A5
9 Itaca...D5
10 Pizzeria Centro...................................D5
11 Plaza Minorista José María Villa.........B4

Entertainment
12 Teatro Pablo Tobón Uribe...................D5

Palacio de la Cultura Rafael Uribe Uribe NOTABLE BUILDING
(Map p192; ☎4-320-9780; www.culturantioquia.gov.co; Carrera 51 No 52-03; ⊙8am-5pm Mon-Fri, to 4pm Sat) FREE Adjacent to the Berrío metro station, this striking black-and-white Gothic Revival building designed by Belgian architect Agustín Goovaerts is one of Medellín's most interesting landmarks. Construction on the project began in 1925 although only a quarter of the original design was completed. Visitors are free to stroll along its majestic corridors and through the ornate rooms, some of which hold rotating art exhibitions.

If you want to take a peak inside the majestic dome, come on Tuesday or Thursday afternoon when there are free international films shown in the interior at 4pm. Downstairs you can get access to the lovely central courtyard, which features a fountain surrounded by azaleas.

Jardín Botánico GARDENS
(Map p188; www.facebook.com/JardinBotanicoMedellin; Calle 73 No 51D-14; ⊙9am-4:30pm; M Universidad) FREE One of Medellín's nicest green spaces, the botanic gardens cover 14 hectares, showcase 600 species of trees and plants, and include a lake, a herbarium and a butterfly enclosure. Events often take place beneath the **Orquideorama** – an organically expanding meshwork of wooden flowers.

Behind the park, the **Esquina de las Mujeres** pays tribute to notable women from the area from the colonial era onwards.

★ **Museo de Antioquia** MUSEUM
(Map p192; ☎4-251-3636; www.museodeantioquia.co; Carrera 52 No 52-43; adult/student COP$18,000/9000; ⊙10am-5:30pm Mon-Sat, to 4:30pm Sun) In the grand art deco Palacio Municipal, Colombia's second-oldest museum (Museo Nacional in Bogotá is the oldest) houses one of the country's most important art collections. The permanent collection spans 19th-century and contemporary Colombian art, as well as pre-Columbian pieces. The highlight is the 3rd floor, where there are many sculptures and paintings by native son Fernando Botero as well as other artists' work from his personal collection. Look out for the wonderful Pedro Nel Gómez murals around the building.

Activities

Zona de Vuelo PARAGLIDING
(☎4-388-1556, 301-535-8330; www.zonadevuelo.com; Km5.6 Via San Pedro de los Milagros) This experienced operator offers 15- and 20-minute tandem flights (COP$130,000/160,000) and photos/videos of your flight for an extra COP$40,000. Also on offer are 15-day courses (COP$3,500,000). It also provides round-trip transportation to the launch point in San Felix from Medellín (COP$90,000 for up to four passengers).

Dance Free DANCING
(Map p196; ☎4-204-0336, WhatsApp 316-288-7063; www.dancefree.com.co; Calle 10A No 40-27; individual classes per hour COP$65,000, group classes per month COP$100,000) A hugely popular dance school offering salsa and bachata classes in a large space in El Poblado. Teachers are enthusiastic and professional and both private and group classes are available. At night it turns into a disco so you can practice your moves.

Psiconautica ADVENTURE SPORTS
(☎312-795-6321, 300-212-0748; www.aventurapsiconautica.com; Km 5.6 Via San Pedro de los Milagros; rock climbing COP$150,000-350,000) In the same complex as Zona de Vuelo (p189), this one-stop adventure shop specializes in rock climbing, canyoning and abseiling and offers 'zip-trekking' – multi-discipline tours around the mountain. Its experienced bilingual guides arrange mountaineering and trekking trips around the country.

Courses

Toucan Spanish School LANGUAGE
(Map p196; ☎4-311-7176; www.toucanspanish.com; Carrera 41A No 10-28; 20hr courses COP$625,000) A well-organized Spanish school right in the heart of El Poblado with bright air-conditioned classrooms and extracurricular social activities. There's also a fine cafe downstairs with a good tour desk.

Tours

★**Bicitour** CYCLING
(Map p196; ☎312-749-2581, 312-512-0690; www.bicitour.co; Carrera 36 No 7-10, Casa Kiwi; tours COP$70,000) Bicitour offers in-depth cycle tours of Medellín, visiting a variety of interesting sights pertinent to local history, politics and culture, on a 19km route through diverse neighborhoods. They're a healthy and ecological way to see a side of the city you might otherwise miss. Tours begin and end in El Poblado.

Tours start at 9am, take around five hours in total and prices include a refreshment.

★**Real City Tours** WALKING
(☎319-262-2008; www.realcitytours.com) Run by enthusiastic young locals, this company offers a free walking tour through the city center, with detailed explanations in English of the stories behind the main points of interest. Tips for the guides are expected. You need to reserve online to secure your spot.

It also runs a paid fruit-themed tour (COP$70,000) to Medellín's largest market and a 'Barrio Transformation Tour' (COP$70,000), which visits Moravia, one of the city's most densely populated neighborhoods.

BOTERO SCULPTURES

Around the city center you'll frequently bump into the distinctive voluptuous sculptures of *paisa* artist Fernando Botero, whose larger-than-life figures have become emblems of the city. Among those worth checking out is the iconic **La Gorda**, in front of the Banco de la República in Parque Berrío. There are three more Botero sculptures in Parque San Antonio, including the **Pájaro de Paz** (Bird of Peace), which sits alongside its earlier incarnation that was destroyed in a terrorist bomb attack.

Festivals & Events

Festival Internacional de Tango DANCE
(Festitango; ☎4-385-6563; cultura.ciudadana@medellin.gov.co; ⊙Jun) The city celebrates its love for tango with competitions, concerts and workshops.

Feria de las Flores CULTURAL
(www.feriadelasfloresmedellin.gov.co; ⊙Aug) This weeklong festival is Medellín's most spectacular event, with numerous parades and concerts. The highlight is the Desfile de Silleteros, when up to 400 *campesinos* (peasants) come from the mountains to parade along the streets with flowers on their backs.

Festival Internacional de Jazz MUSIC
(Medejazz; www.festivalmedejazz.com; ⊙Sep) Many North American bands come for this festival. There are usually a couple of free concerts.

Sleeping

Wandering Paisa HOSTEL **$**
(☎4-436-6759; www.wanderingpaisahostel.com; Calle 44A No 68A-76; dm COP$25,000-29,000, r COP$75,000; @) Right by the bars and restaurants of La 70, this dynamic hostel is a great choice for those wanting to find a middle ground between the bright lights of El Poblado and downtown. There is a small bar and roof terrace and the enthusiastic management is constantly arranging social events and group outings. Bikes are available to explore the neighborhood.

★**Los Patios** HOSTEL **$$$**
(Map p196; ☎305-323-9897; www.lospatioshb.com; Carrera 43E No 11-40; dm COP$62,400-71,400, r/tr COP$195,000/234,000;) Setting the standard for flashpacker comfort, this large hostel in Manila features slick industrial-chic design and some of the best common areas you'll find on your travels. The open kitchen offers great views over town, but the panoramas are even better from the upstairs lounge and phenomenal rooftop. Modern dorms are equipped with privacy curtains and male/female bathrooms.

There's also an on-site Spanish school and tour desk, while on the ground floor the hip food market means you won't have to go far to get something to eat.

Rango HOSTEL **$$**
(Map p196; ☎4-480-3180; www.hostelrango.com; Calle 8 No 42-25; dm COP$59,000-64,000, tw/d COP$236,000/247,000;) An industrial-chic

PROFITING FROM PABLO

Even after his death, infamous cocaine warlord Pablo Escobar Gaviria keeps on making money. When backpackers started flowing back into Medellín – something only made possible by the fall of the Medellín Cartel boss – a couple of young local entrepreneurs sensed an opportunity. They began running Escobar-themed tours, visiting the pivotal places from his bloody reign over the city: his luxurious homes and offices, the suburban house where he was shot, and his grave. More mainstream tour operators soon latched on, and even members of Escobar's family have begun running tours where you can discuss the *capo's* (boss's) favorite things with his brother.

Needless to say, plenty of Colombians are unimpressed with what they see as the glorification of a bloodthirsty terrorist who blew up planes and once paid his henchmen for every police officer they killed. Others accept that Escobar is an important historical figure and compare the tours to those dedicated to mobsters in Chicago.

Most tours last around half a day, but note that prices and quality vary widely. If you do decide to take an Escobar-themed tour, **Paisa Road** (☎317-489-2629; www.paisaroad.com) gets positive reviews for its informative and impartial tours. Even better, pay a visit to the Museo Casa de la Memoria (p187) in downtown Medellín to learn about just how disastrous Escobar's reign was for the city.

If you're not done with Escobar after that, you can get an idea of the sheer scale of his wealth and ambition at Hacienda Nápoles, a huge farm four hours from Medellín that he turned into a private kingdom complete with several mansions, a bullring, and exotic pets including giraffes, zebras and several hippopotamuses. When the government turned up the heat on Escobar, Hacienda Nápoles was abandoned. These days it is home to the safari-themed **Hacienda Nápoles Adventure Park** (☎1800-510-344; www.haciendanapoles.com; Km165 Autopista Medellín–Bogotá; COP$39,000-75,000; 👪), and vestiges of Escobar's ownership are being removed, but you can still check out the hippos.

hostel-hotel hybrid overlooking Parque La Presidenta, with polished concrete floors and wood features throughout. It offers comfortable dorms with top facilities including big solid lockers and hotel-class private rooms complete with minibars. There's no guest kitchen but the fusion restaurant downstairs earns accolades from locals and visitors alike.

Happy Buddha HOSTEL **$$**

(Map p196; ☎300-831-7565, 4-311-7744; www.facebook.com/HappyBuddhaHostel; Carrera 35 No 7-108; dm/r/tw incl breakfast COP$35,000/120,000/130,000; 📶) Boasting a sleek, modern design and large terrace bar, this hostel on the edge of the *zona rosa* (nightlife zone) in El Poblado has less of a party vibe than it used to, though it's still a sociable place. Some dorms have poor ventilation. In the mornings there are inevitable lines for the bathroom facilities, but staff are welcoming and helpful.

Black Sheep HOSTEL **$$**

(Map p196; ☎317-518-1369, 4-311-1589; www.blacksheepmedellin.com; Transversal 5A No 45-133, Patio Bonito; dm COP$34,000-40,000, s/d COP$90,000/110,000, without bathroom COP$75,000/95,000; @📶; Ⓜ Poblado) One of Medellín's original hostels and still one of its best, this well-run and welcoming place is conveniently located and has a pleasant social vibe without being rowdy, but there are frequent lines for the too-few bathrooms. There is a variety of common areas, including a lovely terrace, and a good selection of comfortable, modern, private rooms.

61 Prado GUESTHOUSE **$$**

(Map p188; ☎4-254-9743; www.61prado.com; Calle 61 No 50A-60; s/d/ste COP$73,000/99,000/113,000 r/tr without bathroom COP$71,000/94,000; 📶) This elegant place in the historic Prado neighborhood is a great base from which to explore the sights around the center. The spacious renovated rooms have high-beamed ceilings and touches of art throughout and there is a fine rooftop terrace. The decent on-site restaurant is open around the clock. Light sleepers might want a room at the rear.

Casa Kiwi HOSTEL **$$**

(Map p196; ☎4-268-2668; Carrera 36 No 7-10; dm COP$37,000-40,000, s/d COP$125,000/145,000, without bathroom COP$85,000/110,000; @📶🏊) With an enviable location overlooking a stream on the edge of the *zona rosa* in El Poblado, Casa Kiwi is close to the action. There's

Central Medellín

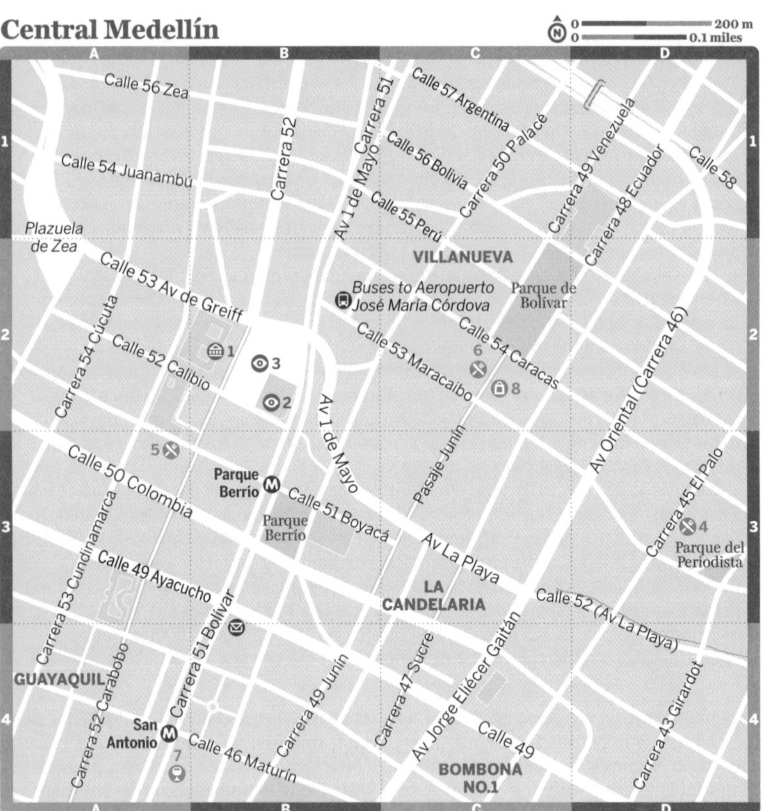

Central Medellín

Sights
1 Museo de Antioquia B2
2 Palacio de la Cultura Rafael Uribe Uribe B2
3 Plazoleta de las Esculturas B2

Eating
4 Café Colombo Credenza D3
5 Govinda's A3
6 Salón Versalles C2

Drinking & Nightlife
7 Salon Malaga A4

Shopping
8 Centro Artesanal Mi Viejo Pueblo C2

a range of elegant private rooms alongside more standard dorms (some don't have much natural light). The appealing common areas include a spacious hammock terrace, a cinema-like TV room and a rooftop dipping pool.

La Playa HOSTEL $$
(Map p196; ☎4-352-0748; www.laplayahostel.com.co; Carrera 35 No 7-69; dm COP$40,000-50,000, r COP$150,000;) A cute little hostel right in the middle of Poblado's action, La Playa is bright and spotlessly clean. Rooms are comfortable and boast excellent bathrooms but the best feature is the great rooftop bar overlooking the road – the perfect place from which to launch your night.

El Alternativo HOSTEL $$
(Map p196; ☎4-266-3049; www.el-alternativo.com; Carrera 43E No 11A-13; dm COP$30,000-37,000, r with/without bathroom from COP$110,000/85,000;) With a good location in the heart of Manila and a laid-back arty vibe, this French-run place is a fine spot for those looking for a quiet hostel with a bit of character. Rooms feature neat paint jobs and touches of art, while the rooftop terrace has fine views, plenty of space to hang out and a guest kitchen.

In House Hotel HOTEL $$

(Map p196; ☎4-444-1786; www.inhousethehotel.com; Carrera 34 No 7-109; s/d/tr incl breakfast COP$156,500/174,000/258,000;) This excellent-value small hotel stands out from the crowd in busy El Poblado. Its stylish, bright rooms feature pine furniture, work desks and big windows. Service is friendly and professional, and a continental breakfast is included. Rooms at the front have private balconies while those at the rear are quieter.

Hotel Dann Carlton HOTEL $$$

(Map p196; ☎4-444-5151; www.danncarlton.com; Carrera 43A No 7-50; s/d COP$280,000/395,000, ste from COP$575,000;) This slick, professionally run hotel is a cut above the rest with quality accommodations and plenty of extra touches including elegant flower displays in the lobby. The suites in particular are huge, with attached sitting room, walk-in closet and massive bathroom.

Eating

Plaza Minorista José María Villa MARKET $

(Map p188; cnr Carrera 57 & Calle 55; 7am-4pm) This huge, bustling undercover market has more than 2500 stalls, selling mostly food. It was established in 1984 to remove hawkers from the streets. It's a good place for self-caterers to stock up on fresh fruit and veg.

★ **Arte Dolce** GELATO $

(Map p196; ☎4-352-0881; www.facebook.com/artedolcemde; Carrera 33 No 7-167; gelati COP$4500-8000; noon-8pm Mon, 8:30am-9:30pm Tue-Sat, 8:30am-7pm Sun) Swing by this little corner cafe to try some of the fabulous gelato made right on the premises. Lorenzo the confectioner manages to evoke the tastes and texture of Italian gelato; our favorite flavor is the Mediterranean, which blends pistachios, caramelized almonds, lemon, orange and olive oil.

★ **Restaurante Itaca** COLOMBIAN $

(Map p188; ☎4-581-8538; www.facebook.com/RestauranteItaca; Carrera 42 No 54-60, Boston; set lunch COP$14,000, mains COP$16,000-33,000; noon-3pm & 6-10pm Mon-Sat, noon-5pm Sun;) This tiny hole-in-the-wall restaurant on the outskirts of downtown prepares fantastic, fairly priced gourmet plates bursting with flavor. At lunch there are a couple of set options while in the evening there is no menu – the friendly chef Juan Carlos will tell you what he has; go for a *picada* (mixed grill) if you can.

Vegetarians are well catered for while meat lovers should not leave without trying a portion of the homemade sausages, which have been proclaimed the best in Antioquia. On Sunday there's a big barbecue on the street outside. There's no sign – look for the blue door.

Salón Versalles COLOMBIAN $$

(Map p192; ☎4-511-9148; www.versallesmedellin.com; Pasaje Junín 53-39; breakfast COP$6000-16,000, mains COP$20,000-35,000; 7am-9pm Mon-Sat, 8am-6pm Sun) Famous for its scrumptious Argentine-style empanadas, this Medellín institution also serves monster portions of steak *milanesa* and nicely seasoned *churrasco*. It is frequented by everyone from hard-up pensioners to young entrepreneurs and is worth checking out just to observe the crowd. At breakfast time you can fill your boots for a pittance.

Govinda's VEGETARIAN $

(Map p192; ☎4-293-2000; Calle 51 No 52-17; meals COP$9000-10,000; 11:30am-7pm;) Part restaurant, part Hare Krishna cultural center, Govinda's has a great-value vegetarian buffet. Choose from a wide range of soups, soy-based mains, salads and vegetable sides. If you arrive late you will probably be limited to the fast-food menu. Upstairs there are regular yoga classes.

Osea FUSION $$

(Map p196; ☎4-268-3964; www.oseamed.co; Calle 9 No 43B-28, El Poblado; mains COP$28,000-40,000; noon-2:30pm & 7-10pm Tue-Sat, 7-10pm Mon) Offering a small, changing menu of inventive modern cuisine at reasonable prices, this neat little restaurant just off Parque Poblado is a real winner. A team of young chefs work away in the open kitchen preparing interesting dishes, such as grilled octopus with salsa verde. It only has six tables so it's best to make a reservation.

Pizzeria Centro PIZZA $$

(Map p188; ☎4-254-4510; www.facebook.com/pizzeriaartesanalmedellin4157; Calle 57 No 41-57; pizzas from COP$30,000; 4:30-11pm Tue-Sat;) Located all alone in a converted house on an average street between the center and Boston, this place serves some of the best thin-crust pizza in Medellín, with a smoky tomato sauce and quality toppings, fired to perfection in the wood-burning oven.

Cafe Zorba PIZZA $$
(Map p196; 2-604-4529; www.facebook.com/cafezorba; Calle 8 No 42-33, Parque La Presidenta; pizza from COP$24,000; 5:30-11:30pm;) Nestled on the edge of Parque La Presidenta, this fashionable open-air cafe is a local favorite for pizza (veggie toppings only) but the quality of both the pizzas and the service is inconsistent. Sometimes the pizza is great, and sometimes promised ingredients never materialise – it's the Russian roulette of dinners.

Verdeo VEGETARIAN $$
(Map p196; 4-476-6941; www.facebook.com/restauranteverdeo; Carrera 36 No10B-33, Manila; mains COP$19,000-25,000; noon-9pm Mon & Tue, to 10pm Wed-Sat;) This vegetarian restaurant does its best to woo diners with its shawarma, burgers, falafel, soups, quinoa dishes and salads. Some of the flavors hit the spot better than others, but the soothing music and plant-filled surrounds make for a peaceful meal, and staff also prepare a nicely presented set lunch (COP$14,000).

Café Colombo Credenza COLOMBIAN $$
(Map p192; 4-251-6251; www.credenzafoods.com; Carrera 45 No 53-24, 10th fl; mains COP$20,000-35,000; noon-10pm Mon-Sat;) This top floor bistro is all neon lights and frosted glass, with a soundtrack that's about a decade behind its *now* image and an ambitious menu that often hits the mark. The good? *Minifritos tradicionales* with a superb *picante* sauce, beautifully cooked fish, homemade maracuya sodas and the panoramic city views. Pasta dishes are somewhat less exciting.

It's a great spot for cocktails early in the evening.

Malevo ARGENTINE $$
(Map p196; 4-580-2150; Calle 11A No 43E-32, Manila; mains COP$23,000-72,000; noon-3pm & 6-10pm Tue-Sat, noon-5pm Sun) Walk off the street and into Argentina at this bustling little steakhouse in a converted house in Manila that serves up choice cuts at reasonable prices. Make sure to order a couple of its famous empanadas to begin with. Service is top-notch and there is sometimes live music.

Bao Bei ASIAN $$
(Map p196; 304-396-2418; www.facebook.com/baobeicolombia; Carrera 36 No 8A-123; mains COP$23,000-27,000; noon-3pm & 6-10pm Tue-Sun) You might have to wait for a table at this tiny place run by a Filipino chef and his Colombian wife, but it's worth it. Dishes are an eclectic Chinese-Korean-Japanese mélange, but their specialty, *bao* – filled steamed buns – are light and fluffy and moreish, and their Korean chicken wings set your mouth on fire in a most welcome way.

Ciao Pizza Gourmet ITALIAN $$
(Map p188; cnr Calle 49 & Carrera 64A, Suramericana; mains COP$12,000-27,000; noon-2pm & 5-9:15pm Mon-Fri, noon-9:15pm Sat, noon-4:30pm Sun) Sit outside on the small plaza at this neighborhood restaurant to enjoy wonderful pizzas and homemade pastas cooked to perfection. It also serves one of our favorite set lunches (COP$13,000 to COP$16,000) full of fresh Italian flavors. It's hidden in a residential area behind the Suramericana building.

Il Castello ITALIAN $$
(Map p196; 4-312-8287; Carrera 40 No 10A-14, Poblado; mains COP$20,000-40,000; noon-2:30pm & 6-10:30pm Mon-Sat) For authentic, quality Italian food, look no further than this unpretentious bistro. The pizzas are tasty but it is the pastas that really excel, especially the ravioli. Accompany your meal with a bottle from the extensive wine list.

★ **Carmen** INTERNATIONAL $$$
(Map p196; 4-311-9625; www.carmenmedellin.com; Carrera 36 No 10A-27, Provenza; mains COP$45,000-60,000; noon-2:30pm & 7-10:30pm Tue-Fri, 7-10:30pm Mon & Sat) Run by an American-Colombian couple, both of whom are Cordon Bleu chefs, Carmen prepares sophisticated international cuisine with a heavy Californian influence. The restaurant itself is made up of distinct dining zones – an intimate dining room overlooking the open kitchen, a conservatory and a rear patio. The knowledgeable English-speaking waiters can offer good wine recommendations to match your meal.

While it is one of Medellín's finest restaurants, prices are very reasonable considering the quality of the dishes. Reservations are essential in the evening.

★ **Tal Cual** FUSION $$$
(Map p196; 316-478-4555; www.talcualrestaurante.com; Calle 12 No 43D-12, Manila; mains COP$27,000-56,000; noon-3pm & 6-10pm;) An unpretentious place in Manila with a casual arty vibe, Tal Cual serves creative fusion cuisine at reasonable prices. The varied menu features a lot of seafood, including some great Peruvian dishes, alongside pastas, risottos, steak and ribs. It's all delicious and well presented, but the ceviches and

tuna *tataki* are outstanding. The service is also excellent.

Rocoto PERUVIAN $$$

(Map p196; ☎4-311-8979; www.facebook.com/rocotorestaurante; Carrera 33 No 8A-14, Provenza; mains COP$34,500-46,000; ⏰noon-10pm Mon-Wed, to 11pm Thu-Sat, to 5pm Sun) This open-air restaurant overlooking a gushing stream in Provenza delivers some solid flavors and good service. The *causas* are moreish and the tuna is beautifully seared, but there are consistency issues: sometimes the ceviche is brutally acidic and the pisco sours are insipid. Dishes are on the dainty side, but the presentation is top-notch, as are the creative cocktails.

Mistura PERUVIAN $$$

(☎4-322-5142; www.misturarestaurante.com; Carrera 39D No 74-62, Laureles; mains COP$34,000-46,000; ⏰noon-3pm & 7-10pm Mon-Wed, noon-3pm & 7-11pm Thu & Fri, noon-4pm & 7-11pm Sat, noon-5pm Sun) Worth a visit for its great grilled octopus and wonderful seafood rice dishes. While the food is good, the ambience is a bit corporate. There's another outlet in Provenza near Parque Lleras.

Drinking & Nightlife

★**Salon Malaga** BAR

(Map p192; ☎4-231-2658; www.salonmalaga.com; Carrera 51 No 45-80; ⏰8am-1am) A Medellín institution, Salon Malaga is more than just a bar, it's a cultural experience. With walls decked out in black-and-white images of long-dead singers and an amazing collection of gramophones, it is a visual feast. But Malaga is all about the tunes, with the senior DJ spinning classic tango and boleros from a collection of old vinyl.

★**Pergamino** COFFEE

(Map p196; ☎4-268-6444; https://us.pergamino.co; Carrera 37 No 8A-37; ⏰8am-9pm Mon-Fri, 9am-9pm Sat, 10am-7pm Sun) It's worth the effort to wait in line for a drink at this popular cafe, which serves the best coffee in Medellín. There is a full range of hot and cold beverages, all made with top-quality beans sourced from small farms around the country. You can also buy coffee in bags to take home.

La Octava BAR

(Map p196; ☎4-583-1783; Calle 8 No 37-49; ⏰5pm-4am) A fairly laid-back bar by Lleras standards, Octava plays good international music, has a 'ball pool' for playing around in and attracts an unpretentious young crowd. Seating is crammed, but if you come early you might snag one of the tables on the porch that are great for people-watching. It's a fine place to begin the evening before hitting the clubs.

Son Havana CLUB

(☎311-339-7175; www.facebook.com/sonhavana; Carrera 73 No 44-56; cover charge COP$8000; ⏰8pm-3am Wed-Sat) The bar of choice for serious *son, la timba* and *la charanga* fans, this popular Cuban-themed place just off La 70 has a great tropical vibe. The small dance floor fills up fast, so most patrons end up dancing around the tables. It's pretty dark so you don't need to worry too much if you lack the moves.

It gets packed from Thursday to Saturday for its live band performances.

Trilogia Bar CLUB

(☎4-204-0562; www.trilogiabar.com; Carrera 43G No 24-08; ⏰8:30pm-3:30am Thu-Sat) For a dynamic night out, head to this friendly club in Barrio Colombia, where bands perform Colombian crossover music from a revolving stage while tipsy locals sing along. Come with a group, and make reservations on the website to avoid missing out. The cover charge varies.

Calle 9 + 1 BAR

(Map p196; www.facebook.com/calle9mas1; Carrera 40 No 10-25; ⏰8pm-4am Thu-Sat) Set around a covered courtyard, this hip alternative hangout has DJs spinning anything from independent electronic music to salsa and house to an arty crowd. It has a different vibe to most of the mainstream bars in the Parque Lleras area.

Entertainment

Casa Gardeliana DANCE

(☎4-444-2633; Carrera 45 No 76-50; ⏰9am-5pm Mon-Fri) FREE Located in Barrio Manrique, Casa Gardeliana was Medellín's main tango venue for years, hosting tango bands and dance shows. It still holds events occasionally but is now basically a small tango museum.

WHAT'S ON IN MEDELLÍN

Opción Hoy (www.opcionhoy.com) Comprehensive activity and entertainment listings with a cultural focus. Look out for the printed version.

Medellín en Escena (www.medellinenescena.com) For theater event listings.

El Poblado

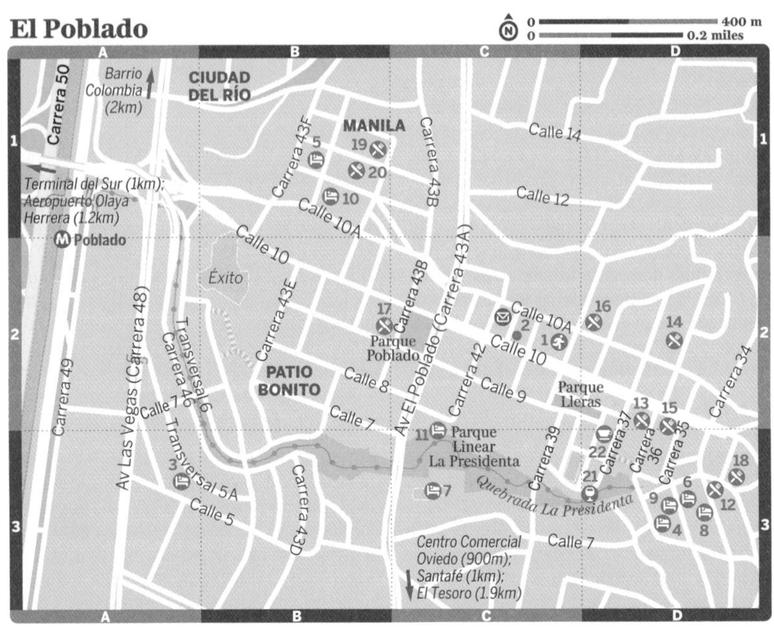

El Poblado

Activities, Courses & Tours

- Bicitour (see 4)
- 1 Dance Free C2
- 2 Toucan Spanish School C2

Sleeping

- 3 Black Sheep A3
- 4 Casa Kiwi D3
- 5 El Alternativo B1
- 6 Happy Buddha D3
- 7 Hotel Dann Carlton C3
- 8 In House Hotel D3
- 9 La Playa D3
- 10 Los Patios B1
- 11 Rango C3

Eating

- 12 Arte Dolce D3
- 13 Bao Bei D2
- Cafe Zorba (see 11)
- 14 Carmen D2
- 15 Casa Clandestino Comedor D2
- 16 Il Castello D2
- Malevo (see 5)
- 17 Osea B2
- 18 Rocoto D3
- 19 Tal Cual B1
- 20 Verdeo B1

Drinking & Nightlife

- Calle 9 + 1 (see 1)
- 21 La Octava D3
- 22 Pergamino D3

On the last Friday of the month, the *casa* hosts the 'Gran Fiesta Tangera' (6pm to 9:30pm) with Argentine empanadas, wine and plenty of dancing. Reserve a table.

It's possible to organize private dance classes here (COP$80,000, 90 minutes) – the price is the same for one dancer or many, so get a group together.

Teatro Pablo Tobón Uribe THEATER
(Map p188; 4-239-7500; www.teatropablotobon.com; Carrera 40 No 51-24) This is Medellín's major mainstream theater. There are free dance classes here on Saturdays and yoga on Tuesday and Thursday mornings – bring your own mat. On Tuesday evenings there's usually theater or dance performances.

El Patio del Tango DANCE
(4-235-4595; www.patiodeltango.com; Calle 23 No 58-38; mains COP$25,000-35,000; noon-8pm Mon-Wed, to 1:30am Thu-Sat) Now tango's major stage in Medellín, this steak restaurant is decorated like a typical Buenos Aires tango dive. Make reservations in advance

for the live shows on Fridays and Saturdays. Check the website for performance details.

Sports

Medellín has two football (soccer) teams: **Independiente Medellín** (www.deportivoindependientemedellin.com), who wear red and are known as 'El Poderoso,' and **Atlético Nacional** (www.atlnacional.com.co), Medellín's biggest football team and one of the most successful in Colombia, who have a green kit. Both play at **Estadio Atanasio Girardot** (www.stadiumguide.com/atanasiogirardot; M Estadio) near the aptly named Estadio metro station.

The greater metropolitan area is also home to **Envigado Fútbol Club**, which plays in the southern municipality of Envigado.

Shopping

For high-end shopping, head to the malls of El Poblado, including **Santafé** (Carrera 43A No 7 Sur-170; 10am-9pm Mon-Sat, 11am-8pm Sun), **Centro Comercial Oviedo** (Carrera 43A No 6 Sur-15; 10am-9pm Mon-Sat, 11am-8pm Sun) and **El Tesoro** (4-321-1010; Carrera 25A No 1A Sur-45; 10am-9pm Mon-Sat, 11am-8pm Sun). Handicrafts and souvenirs can be found at the **Centro Artesanal Mi Viejo Pueblo** (Map p192; www.facebook.com/CentroArtesanalMiViejoPueblo; Carrera 49 No 53-20; 9am-7:30pm Mon-Sat, 10am-5pm Sun) in the center.

Information

SAFE TRAVEL

- While Medellín is for the most part a safe city for visitors, robberies are not unheard of. Take care especially after dark in the center when office workers and retailers head home and the streets empty fast.
- Pickpockets have been reported on buses and the metro – keep a close eye on your belongings.

EMERGENCY & IMPORTANT NUMBERS

Ambulance	125
Fire	119
Police	112

GAY & LESBIAN TRAVELERS

While not as developed as that in Bogotá, Medellín has a small but vibrant gay nightlife scene. Many bars are located in the center and in the area of Calle 33 out near Laureles. For listings of bars and events, visit **Guia Gay Colombia** (www.guiagaycolombia.com/medellin).

INTERNET ACCESS

Most shopping centers and many public places, including some parks, have free wi-fi access points, although speeds are not always the best. Almost all cafes and most restaurants offer wi-fi for clients. Generally all hotels and hostels have good wi-fi available, although it does not always reach into the rooms.

MEDICAL SERVICES

Clínica Las Vegas (4-315-9000; www.clinicalasvegas.com; Calle 2 Sur No 46-55; 24hr) This professional private medical facility is your best option if you need a doctor in a hurry. Staff speak some English.

Clínica Medellín (4-311-2800; www.clinicamedellin.com; Calle 7 No 39-290; 24hr) Private clinic in El Poblado where the staff speak some English. There is another branch in central Medellín.

Congregación Mariana (4-322-8300; www.vid.org.co; Carrera 42 No 52-82; 8am-5pm) Nonprofit clinic with many specialists and low prices.

MONEY

There are numerous ATMs throughout the city including near Parque Berrío in the center, along Av El Poblado and around Parque Lleras.

There are money changers, ATMs and bank branches in Centro Comercial Oviedo (p197).

Banco de Bogotá (Carrera 49 No 49-16) ATM in the center of the city.

Banco de Bogotá (Carrera 43A No 8-84) ATM in El Poblado.

Banco Popular (Carrera 50 No 50-14) Downtown ATMs.

Bancolombia (Calle 43A 65-15, Centro Comercial Oviedo) ATM in El Poblado.

Bancolombia (Carrera 49 No 52-08) Downtown ATM.

Bancolombia (Carrera 39 No 8-100) ATM near Parque Lleras.

Citibank (Carrera 43A No 1A Sur-49) ATM in El Poblado.

Giros & Finanzas (Calle 57 No 49-44, Centro Comercial Villanueva, local 241; 8am-5pm) Currency exchange and Western Union agent.

POST

4-72 (Map p196; www.4-72.com.co; Calle 10A No 41-11; 8am-noon & 1-6pm Mon-Fri, 9am-noon Sat) Post office in El Poblado.

4-72 (Map p192; www.4-72.com.co; cnr Calle 49 & Carrera 51, Centro Commercial Cafetero; 8am-6pm Mon-Fri, 9am-noon Sat) Post office in the center of town.

TOURIST INFORMATION

Medellín makes it easy to get tourist information through a network of Punto Información Turísticas

(PIT) offices, operated by courteous and knowledgeable bilingual staff.

PIT Cerro Nutibara (Map p188; Calle 30A No 55-64; ⌚8:30am-6pm Mon-Fri)

PIT Parque Arví (⌚9:30am-5:30pm Tue-Sun)

PIT Parque de Las Luces (Map p188; cnr Calle 44 & Carrera 54; ⌚9am-5:30pm Mon-Sat)

PIT Plaza Mayor (Map p188; ☎4-261-7277; www.medellin.travel; Calle 41 No 55-80; ⌚8am-6pm Mon-Fri)

There are also branches in each of the airports and bus terminals.

TRAVELERS WITH DISABILITIES

Despite winning plaudits for urban innovation, Medellín still has many areas for improvement when it comes to accessibility for those with reduced mobility.

While all metro stations are now wheelchair accessible, other mass-transit options, including the small buses that link many other destinations, are not. Medellín's topography makes it a challenge for travelers with limited mobility. There are stairs on many public roads, especially in neighborhoods higher up on the hillsides.

Most shopping centers, airports and major museums are accessible for travelers with disabilities and usually have dedicated wheelchair-friendly bathrooms. Private businesses are less likely to have ramps and other facilities, although most top-end hotels and some midrange places have at least some accessible rooms.

VISA INFORMATION

Migración Colombia (☎4-238-9252; www.migracioncolombia.gov.co; Calle 19 No 80A-40, Barrio Belén; ⌚8-11am & 2-4pm Mon-Fri) For visa extensions. From El Poblado take the Circular Sur 302/303 bus heading south along Av Las Vegas.

Getting There & Away

AIR

Medellín has two airports. All international flights (to Miami, Fort Lauderdale, Lima, Madrid, Panama City, Caracas) and most domestic flights to major destinations (Bogotá, Cartagena, Santa Marta, San Andrés) depart from **Aeropuerto Internacional José María Córdova** (☎4-402-5110; www.aeropuertorionegro.co; Rionegro), 35km southeast of the city near the town of Rionegro.

Buses shuttle between the city center and the airport every 15 minutes (COP$9500, one hour, 5am to 9pm). The **bus stop** (Map p192; Carrera 50A No 53-13) in town is behind the Hotel Nutibara, but you can also get onboard near the Centro Commercial San Diego. **Acoa Taxi** (☎2-261-1616; www.acoataxiaeropuerto.com.co) – with blue-and-white-striped vehicles – serves the airport; it's COP$70,000 there and COP$60,000 coming from the airport.

The smaller **Aeropuerto Olaya Herrera** (EOH; ☎4-403-6780; http://aeropuertoolayaherrera.gov.co; Carrera 65A No 13-157) is in town, next door to the Terminal del Sur bus station. Regional domestic flights leave from here, including services to Bogotá, Armenia, Manizales and Pereira.

BUS

Medellín has two bus terminals. **Terminal del Norte** (Map p188; www.terminalesmedellin.com; Autopista Norte; Ⓜ Caribe), 3km north of the city center, handles buses to the north, east and southeast. It is easily reached from El Poblado by metro (alight at Caribe) or by taxi (COP$15,000). Destinations include:

Destination	Price (COP$)	Duration (hr)
Bogotá	66,000-70,000	9-10
Cartagena	139,000-149,000	13½-14
Neiva	80,000-100,000	11-12¼
Santa Fe de Antioquia	11,000-15,000	1½-2
Santa Marta	96,000-119,000	16

Terminal del Sur (www.terminalesmedellin.com; Carrera 65 No 8B-91), 4km southwest of the center, handles all traffic to the west and south. From El Poblado it's a quick taxi ride (COP$6500). Destinations include:

Destination	Price (COP$)	Duration (hr)
Armenia	45,000-49,000	6
Cali	63,000	8
Ipiales	123,000-132,000	22
Manizales	37,000-40,000	5
Pasto	100,000	22-24
Pereira	40,000	5
Popayán	70,000	10

Getting Around

BICYCLE

Medellín has a functional and widespread free public bicycle system called **Encicla** (www.encicla.gov.co). You'll need to register first and pick up a 'Civica' card in any one of the these metro stations: Niquía, San Antonio, Itagüí or San Javier. A network of bicycle paths links many of the stations.

BUS

Medellín is well serviced by buses, although most travelers will find the metro and taxis sufficient for their needs. The majority of routes originate on Av Oriental and from Parque Berrío. Buses stop running around 10pm or 11pm.

METRO

Medellín's **metro** (www.metrodemedellin.gov.co; single ticket COP$2400; ⌚4:30am-11pm Mon-Sat, 5am-10pm Sun) is Colombia's only commuter rail line. It opened in 1995 and consists of a 23km north–south Linea A, that connects El Centro to El Poblado, and a 6km east–west Linea B. Trains run at ground level except for 5km through the central area where they use elevated tracks.

The metro company also operates four cable-car lines, called Metrocable, built to service the impoverished barrios in the surrounding hills and Parque Arví in Santa Elena, with two more under construction at the time of research. The rides themselves afford magnificent views and make for a lovely way to check out the town. The three main Metrocable lines are included in the price of a metro ticket, while the Arví line is separate.

If you're going to spend a while in Medellín it may be worth getting a 'Civica' card, purchased at metro ticket booths, for discounted tickets and faster access.

TAXI

Taxis (☎4-444-4444) are plentiful in Medellín and all are equipped with meters. The minimum charge is COP$5500. A taxi from the center to El Poblado will cost around COP$10,000 to COP$12,000. Alternatively, use ride-share apps such as Uber, Tappsi or Easy Taxi.

AROUND MEDELLÍN

Long off-limits to Colombian tourists who remained trapped in their cities by the civil war, the countryside around Medellín is now secure and bustling with crowds.

Guatapé

☎4 / POP 5500 / ELEV 1925M

The pleasant holiday town of Guatapé is located on the shores of the Embalse Guatapé, a sprawling artificial lake. It is known for the fresco-like adornment of its traditional houses. Brightly painted bas-relief depictions of people, animals and shapes cover the lower half of many dwellings.

Guatapé makes a great day trip from Medellín, a two-hour bus ride away, but there is enough outdoor adventure here to keep you entertained a bit longer if you fancy a peaceful break from the city. Visit on the weekend if you want to experience the festival atmosphere when the town is packed with Colombian tourists, or come during the week to explore the surrounding nature at a more relaxed pace.

Activities

A hydraulic **canopy ride** (Calle 32; per ride COP$15,000; ⌚1-6pm Mon-Fri, 9am-6pm Sat & Sun) runs along the lakeshore from a large hill near the entrance to town. Rock climbing on the southern side of the Piedra del Peñol (p200) is another popular activity; paragliding and kayaking are other fun things to do. Most hostels and hotels can hook you up with local guides.

Tours

A number of boating companies on the *malecón* (promenade) take turns running trips out onto the water.

Most large boats have big sound systems, a bar and a dance floor but do not make any stops where you are able to disembark. In mid-2017 the largest boat on the lake sank in front of town, resulting in several deaths. If you want to take one of the bigger boats, it's recommended to sit on the upper deck so that you can escape in an emergency.

It's more interesting to take a tour on a smaller boat. The standard tours swing past **La Cruz** (a monument to the flooded town of old Peñol, mistakenly believed by many to be part of the old church) and **Isla de las Fantasias**. Both options cost around COP$15,000 per person.

It is also possible to charter smaller boats to see the sights on a private tour. Stops include a visit to a museum dedicated to the creation of the lake and, upon request, Pablo Escobar's abandoned farm, **Finca La Manuela**. Prices vary depending on how far you go but start at around COP$90,000.

Guatape Motos TOURS
(☎313-788-9332; www.guatapemotos.com; Carrera 31 No 22-09; per hour/day COP$20,000/100,000) A professionally run outfit offering motorcycle rentals and guided tours throughout the region. Staff will help you plan a route that takes in sights according to your interests.

Sleeping

★**Hostal Mi Casa Gautape** HOSTEL $
(☎4-861-0632; www.micasaguatape.com; Estadero La Mona; dm COP$30,000, r COP$70,000-80,000;

) Run by an affable Anglo-Colombian couple, this popular small hostel close to the base of Piedra del Peñol is welcoming and comfortable. Some of the spotless, colorful rooms offer lake views and there is a path down to the water's edge where kayaks are available. There's a good kitchen and your hosts can organize rock climbing, kayaking and countryside treks.

Lake View Hostel HOSTEL $$
(4-861-0023; www.lakeviewhostel.com; Carrera 22 No 29B-29; dm COP$19,000-25,000, r/tr from COP$100,000/105,000;) An established local hostel featuring neat, modern rooms. The dorms downstairs open onto the common area and can be noisy, but the private rooms on the 2nd floor with lake views are quality. The sociable owners organize paragliding and mountain-biking excursions and rent out bikes and scooters. On the top floor there's a fine Thai restaurant.

Galeria Hostel HOSTEL $
(4-861-0077; www.galeriahostels.com; Vereda La Piedra, Residencial No 2; dm COP$35,000-40,000;) Perched on a peninsula right below Piedra del Peñol, this hip little hostel is a popular choice among backpackers looking for majestic views on a budget (though overpriced for what it is). It's small and homely and feels somewhat like a private retreat with friends. There's a steep path down to a particularly scenic part of the lake.

The modest breakfast costs COP$5000 and for COP$10,000 they'll store your luggage for you.

Mansion de Oriente HOTEL $$
(4-861-0218; Vereda La Piedra; r/tr/f COP$170,000/255,000/510,000;) A great midrange option near Piedra del Peñol, this rural-style house has neat and spacious rooms opening onto a large wraparound balcony overlooking the lake. But the best part is the large swimming pool and social area down by the water's edge. Packages with meals are also available. Service can be hit and miss.

Eating

Hecho con Amor CAFE $
(321-834-7979; Carrera 27A No 30-71; light meals COP$5000-12,000; noon-7pm Sat-Wed;) Expats swear by this cute little cafe that serves mostly vegetarian plates alongside a bacon wrap for carnivorous visitors. The veggie burgers, tasty dips, soups and quiches are all executed with aplomb. The fantastic desserts – try the cheesecake – warrant a loosening of the corsets.

★ **Pizzeria de Luigi** PIZZA $$
(320-845-4552; Calle 31 No 27-10; pizzas COP$22,000-30,000; 6:30-10:30pm Wed-Sat, 12:30-2:30pm & 6:30-10:30pm Sun;) A friendly Italian-run place near the sports field serving up the best pizzas in Guatapé, nay – the region! Freshly baked, fluffy crusts, high-quality ingredients as toppings, good wine, wonderful service…an immensely satisfying experience overall.

Donde Sam INTERNATIONAL $$
(310-403-1073, 4-861-0171; Calle 32 No 31-57; set lunch COP$11,000-15,000, mains COP$24,000-35,000; 9am-9pm;) This spacious 2nd-floor restaurant has great views of the lake and does its best to recreate a mix of global flavors. Choose from freshly prepared Indian dishes as well as some Italian, Thai, Chinese and Mexican plates. Vegetarians are well catered for, but the quality is inconsistent.

Information

There are two ATMs in town: near the plaza and next to the bus station.

Robin Cell Internet access.

Tourism Office (4-861-0555; Calle 31; 8am-1pm & 2-6pm) Inside the *Alcaldía* (town hall) on the main square.

Getting There & Away

If you're coming on a day trip from Medellín, it makes sense to climb Piedra del Peñol before venturing onward to Guatapé, as it can get cloudy and rainy in the afternoon. Buses to and from Medellín (COP$13,500, two hours) run about once an hour. *Colectivos* shuttle frequently between the turnoff to Piedra del Peñol and Guatapé (COP$2000, 10 minutes) or you can take a moto-taxi all the way to the entrance (COP$10,000).

The last bus back to Medellín is at 6:30pm on weekdays and at 7:45pm on weekends and other peak periods. If returning to Medellín from Guatapé on the weekend, be sure to buy your return ticket immediately upon arrival as buses fill up fast. The ticket office is at the **Terminal de Transporte** (cnr Carrera 30 & Calle 32) on the waterfront.

Piedra del Peñol

Also known as El Peñon de Guatapé, thanks to the fierce rivalry between the towns it straddles, this 200m-high **granite monolith** (off Via El Peñol; per climb COP$18,000; 8am-6pm) rises from near the edge of the Embalse Guatapé. A brick staircase of 659 steps rises up through a broad fissure in the side of the rock. From the top there are magnificent views of the region, the fingers of the lake sprawling amid a vast expanse of green mountains.

Coming from Medellín, don't get off the bus in the town of Peñol – ask the driver to let you off at 'La Piedra,' which is another 10 minutes down the road. Take the road that curves up past the gas station (1km) to reach the parking lot at the base of the rock. Taxi drivers and horse owners will try to convince you that it's a long, exhausting climb but while it's steep, it's not far. At the base there are tourist shacks selling knickknacks and numerous restaurants serving lunch (from COP$8000 to COP$12,000). At the top of the rock, shops sell fruit juice, ice cream and *salpicón* (fruit salad in watermelon juice).

Santa Fe de Antioquia

4 / POP 25,300 / ELEV 550M

This sleepy colonial town, founded in 1541 by Jorge Robledo, is the region's oldest settlement and was once the capital of Antioquia. The clock stands still at 1826, the year the government moved to Medellín. Because it was eclipsed for so long by its neighbor 80km southeast, its colonial center never fell to the wrecking ball and today it looks very much like it did in the 19th century. The narrow streets are lined with single-story, whitewashed houses, many arranged around beautiful courtyards. You'll also see elaborately carved, typically Antioquian woodwork around windows and doorways.

It makes a great day trip from Medellín. Don't miss sampling *pulpa de tamarindo,* the beloved sour-sweet candy made with tamarind from the surrounding valley.

Sights

Puente de Occidente BRIDGE
(Km5, Via Santa Fe de Antioquia-Liborina) This unusual 291m bridge over the Río Cauca is 5km east of town. When completed in 1895, it was one of the first suspension bridges in the Americas. José María Villa, its designer, was also involved in the creation of the Brooklyn Bridge in New York. It's a boring and hot 45-minute walk downhill here. You're best to cycle or take a moto-taxi (round trip COP$15,000). The driver will wait while you walk across.

Be sure to climb the dirt path behind the entrance for aerial photos of the bridge.

Museo Juan del Corral MUSEUM
(4-853-4605; Calle 11 No 9-77; 9am-noon & 2-5:30pm Mon, Tue, Thu & Fri, 10am-5pm Sat & Sun) FREE This perfectly preserved colonial mansion hosts exhibits dedicated to the history of the region, from prehistory to independence from the Spanish. Temporary displays of contemporary Colombian art are also showcased here, and it hosts regular cultural events.

Museo de Arte Religioso MUSEUM
(4-853-2345; Calle 11 No 8-12; COP$3500; 10am-1pm & 2-5pm Fri-Sun) This museum occupies the former Jesuit college constructed in the 1730s, next door to Iglesia de Santa Bárbara (p201). It has a fine collection of colonial religious art, including paintings by Gregorio Vásquez de Arce y Ceballos and silver and gold items from Spanish colonies in the New World.

Iglesia de Santa Bárbara CHURCH
(cnr Calle 11 & Carrera 8; 7-8:30am & 6-7:30pm Mon-Sat, 6-7:30am & 6-7:30pm Sun) Built by Jesuits in the mid-18th century, Santa Fe's most interesting church has a fine baroque facade. The interior has an impressive, if time-worn, retable over the high altar.

Festivals & Events

Semana Santa RELIGIOUS
(Holy Week; Easter) Like most traditional towns dating from the early days of the Spanish Conquest, Santa Fe celebrates Semana Santa with pomp and solemnity. Book accommodations in advance.

Fiesta de los Diablitos CULTURAL
(Dec 22-31) The town's most popular festival runs annually over the last week of the year and has been held continuously since 1653. It includes musical performances, bullfights, dance, parades and – like almost every party in the country – a beauty contest.

Sleeping

Green Nomads HOSTEL $$
(302-434-2163; https://greennomandshostel.com; Calle 9 No 7-63; dm/r/f COP$40,000/120,000/240,000;) The only real hostel in the historic center offers clean and affordable fan-cooled accommodations close to Santa Fe's plaza; the dorms are rather spartan, with bunks packed close together. There's a great pool area with a view

Santa Fe de Antioquia

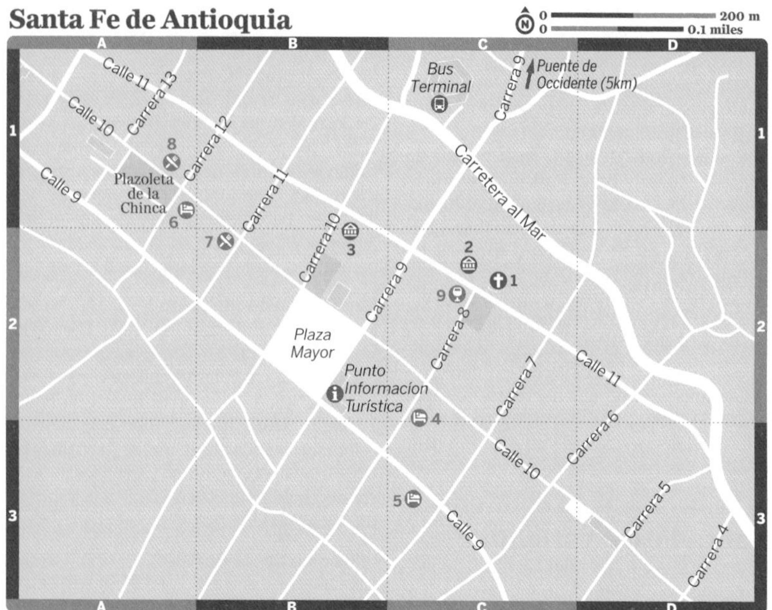

Santa Fe de Antioquia

Sights

1 Iglesia de Santa Bárbara C2
2 Museo de Arte Religioso C2
3 Museo Juan del Corral B2

Sleeping

4 Casa Tenerife C2
5 Green Nomads C3
6 Hotel Mariscal Robledo A1

Eating

7 Restaurante Portón del Parque B2
8 Sabor Español A1

Drinking & Nightlife

9 La Comedia C2

out the back and staff organise paragliding, horseback riding and rafting outings.

★**Hotel Mariscal Robledo** HOTEL $$$
(☎4-853-1563; www.hotelmariscalrobledo.com; cnr Carrera 12 & Calle 10; r incl breakfast COP$335,000-390,000; P❄@🛜🏊) Occupying a privileged place on Parque de la Chinca, Santa Fe's finest hotel oozes character. The spacious rooms are packed with antiques, most of which are for sale, and reflect a simple colonial elegance. There is a rooftop viewpoint, a fantastic large swimming pool and a pretty interior courtyard. The biggest negative is the electric showers.

Casa Tenerife BOUTIQUE HOTEL $$$
(☎4-853-2261; Carrera 8 No 9-50; s/d incl breakfast COP$152,000/244,000; 🛜🏊) Set in a renovated colonial home one block back from the plaza, this fine hotel has elegant and spacious rooms with all the mod cons surrounding a large internal courtyard. There's a good pool area out the back and bicycles for guest use.

Eating & Drinking

Restaurante Portón del Parque COLOMBIAN $$
(☎4-853-3207; Calle 10 No 11-03; mains COP$27,000-33,000; ⏲noon-8pm) This restaurant is in an elegant colonial house with high ceilings and a flowery courtyard, with walls that are covered with the owner's interesting artwork. The kitchen prepares quality traditional food, such as grilled fish with *tostones* (fried green plantains). Vegetarians won't find much here.

Sabor Español SPANISH $$
(☎4-853-2471; www.restaurantesaborespanol.com; Calle 10 No 12-26; mains COP$18,800-74,000, tapas from COP$7400; ⏲noon-3pm & 6-10pm Tue-Fri, noon-10pm Sat, noon-5pm Sun; 🌶) Right on Parque de la Chinca, this top place serves

authentic Spanish food – including excellent paella and *fideuà* – in a large courtyard and patio. The walls are hung with greenery and signed Spanish football shirts and there's flamenco music playing in the background to round out the atmosphere. The service is good and Spanish wines are available.

La Comedia BAR
(Calle 11 No 8-03; noon-late) With a chilled vibe and a low-volume jazz soundtrack, this arty place in front of the Iglesia de Santa Bárbara (p201) serves a full range of hot and cold beverages as well as light meals. In the evening, it is the best place in town for a low-key drink.

Information

Banco Agrario (Calle 9 No 10-51; 9am-5pm Mon-Fri) Has an ATM accepting all cards (Visa, MasterCard etc) but charges a fee.

Bancolombia (Carrera 9 No 10-72) An ATM half a block from the main plaza.

The vast majority of accommodations offer free wi-fi access.

Punto Información Turística (PIT; 4-853-1022; turismo@santafedeantioquia-antioquia.gov.co; Carrera 9 No 9-22; 8am-noon & 2-5:30pm) Friendly tourist office that can organize guides.

Getting There & Away

There are hourly buses (COP$11,000, two hours) and minivans (COP$15,000, 1½ hours) to/from Medellín's Terminal del Norte. The last van back to Medellín from the **bus terminal** (Carretera Medellín-Urabá) leaves around 7:30pm, but after this time you can always flag down a passing intercity service from Turbo (in Urabá) on the highway.

Jardín

4 / POP 14,200 / ELEV 1750M

The self-proclaimed most beautiful town in Antioquia, Jardín lives up to its name. Festooned with greenery, its brightly painted two-story houses are surrounded by small coffee farms that cling impossibly to the slopes of majestic green mountains.

At the center of town life is the breezy cobblestone plaza dominated by the immense neo-Gothic Basilica Menor de la Inmaculada Concepción. It is chock-full of colorful wooden tables and chairs where fruit sellers hawk delicious cocktails and old-timers converse between measured sips of coffee. In the evenings it seems like the entire community comes out to socialize over a drink. While on weekends the town is flooded with visitors from Medellín, the rest of the week it's still full of ye olde colonial charm.

Beyond the small-town Colombia of Jardín lies spectacular countryside with hidden caves, waterfalls and top-notch birdwatching, as well as a wide array of adventure-sport opportunities.

Sights

Basilica Menor de la Inmaculada Concepción CHURCH
(5am-8:30pm) Towering over the central plaza, this imposing 20th-century neo-Gothic church seems more than a little out of place in such a small town. Its gray granite walls topped with aluminum spires contrast markedly with the colorful surrounds. The striking blue interior features gold-plated arches and capitals.

★ **Cerro Cristo Rey** VIEWPOINT
(Via Jardín-Tamesis) You'll spot this lookout point with its white Christ statue from the center of Jardín. Take the modern cable car (round trip COP$5000) up for fantastic views of town and the mountains beyond. There is a shop at the top selling cold beers and snacks.

If the cable car is out of service, which is not uncommon, you can also reach the lookout on foot in 25 to 45 minutes, depending on which path you take. It's also possible to make the trip by bicycle or on horseback.

Reserva Natural Gallito de la Roca NATURE RESERVE
(312-756-2650; Calle 9; COP$10,000; 6-7:30am & 4-5:30pm) This small nature reserve right on the edge of town is the scene of one of Jardín's most impressive natural sights. Early each morning and again in the evening numerous *gallitos de las rocas* (cocks-of-the-rock) fly in to screech, dance and show off their brilliant red plumage in an attempt to impress the ladies of the species. Call Luís to book your visit.

★ **Cueva del Esplendor** CAVE
(316-515-2000; entry COP$7000) Located at 2200m amid beautiful landscapes, this spectacular cave has a 10m waterfall gushing through a large hole in the roof and is Jardín's most famous attraction. The cave is only accessible by foot along muddy, sometimes-narrow mountain paths. The entrance is around a three-hour hike from Jardín, and since 2017 there's been a daily limit of 40 visitors to prevent further damage to the

cave. Only one operator is now allowed to lead hiking tours; book ahead.

The cascade begins about 70m above the entrance, falling in various stages before pouring into a small pool at the bottom of the cave, throwing up clouds of mist. It's possible to take a dip but the water is ice-cold. Note that from the access point it's a 20-minute walk down a steep path to the cave, so visitors need some dexterity.

Expect to pay around COP$70,000 per person for the guided trek, including a traditional lunch.

Activities

Condor de los Andes ADVENTURE
(310-379-6069; condordelosandes@colombia.com; Calle 10 No 1A-62) This dynamic adventure company inside the hostel (p204) of the same name offers a range of high-adrenaline activities around town, including canyoning in **Cascada La Escalera** (Via Jardín-Tamesis) (for COP$80,000).

Tienda de Parapente PARAGLIDING
(311-362-0410; armandovuelo@gmail.com; Calle 15, Av la Primavera; tandem flights COP$130,000; 10am-6pm) Soar over lush green mountains and the neat tiled roofs of town in tandem paragliding flights. The office is behind the stadium; to find it, walk for five blocks up the hill behind the church. Otherwise ask in the Arte Latino jewellery shop half a block from the park on Carrera 4.

Bernardo Lopez HORSEBACK RIDING
(314-714-2021; COP$75,000) Friendly local guide offering horseback-riding trips to Cueva del Esplendor (p203). Bernardo will pick you up in town, from where it's a two-hour ride to the cave entrance. The tour includes a typical lunch.

Sleeping

★**Condor de los Andes** HOSTEL $
(310-379-6069; www.facebook.com/CondordelosandesHostalViajesyAventuras; Calle 10 No 1A-62; dm with/without breakfast COP$32,000/27,000, s/d incl breakfast COP$65,000/99,000;) Offering amazing views and total tranquility in a colonial-style house just a block from Jardín's plaza, this superb hostel is the best choice in town for budget travelers. There's a variety of comfortable rooms with hot water surrounding a stone terrace that overlooks the majestic mountains. Guests have access to the kitchen and a fine open-air common area.

Hotel Jardín HOTEL $$
(310-380-6724; www.hoteljardin.com.co; Carrera 3 No 9-14; s/d COP$70,000/140,000, apt COP$210,000-480,000;) Right on the central plaza, this colorfully painted hotel has rooms and apartments with kitchens, all set around a lovely courtyard. There is a wonderful wide balcony overlooking the park and a rear porch with mountain views. Some of the lower rooms lack natural light; get one upstairs with a window onto the street. Apartments are a bargain for groups/families.

Eating & Drinking

Cafe Europa ITALIAN $$
(302-235-3100; www.facebook.com/cafeeuropacolombia; Calle 8 No 4-02; pasta from COP$15,000, pizzas COP$16,000-20,000; 5-10pm;) You might have to wait for a table at this great-value corner cafe serving a small menu of delicious pizzas and pasta dishes at bargain prices. It's a cozy place, owned by a German travel writer and photographer, with walls lined with European newspaper clippings and Colombian photographic exhibits. It serves wine by the glass or bottle.

★**Cafe Macanas** COFFEE
(313-657-5979; www.facebook.com/Macanasjardin; Parque Principal; 8am-8:30pm) Grab a cup of fantastic locally grown coffee and a pastry, and head out the back to the flower-filled patio right next to the church at this exceptional cafe on the main plaza. There are also cozy spaces inside the colonial building to sit and chill when the rains come down. Also sells bags of Don Darío's coffee to go.

Shopping

Dulces del Jardín FOOD
(4-845-6584; dulcesdeljardin@hotmail.com; Calle 13 No 5-47; arequipe COP$7000; 8am-6pm) This cavity-inducing sweets factory is famous throughout Antioquia for its wide variety of *arequipe* (a sweet dessert of milk and sugar), conserves and fruit candies. Our favorite: Arequipe de Arracacha (an Andean vegetable).

Information

Bancolombia (Calle 9 No 3-33) Reliable ATM.

Punto Informacíon Turística (350-653-6185; piteljardin@gmail.com; cnr Carrera 3 & Calle 10; 8am-noon & 2-5pm) Helpful tourist office around the corner from the church.

Getting There & Away

Around a dozen buses (COP$22,000 to COP$26,000, three hours) head daily to Jardín from Medellín's southern bus terminal. In Jardín the buses depart from the offices on Calle 8, where both **Rapido Ochoa** (☎4-845-5051, 312-286-9768; www.rapidoochoa.com; Calle 8 No 5-24) and **Transportes Suroeste Antioqueño** (☎4-845-5505; Calle 8 No 5-21) operate. Seats sell out during peak periods, so make sure to purchase your round-trip ticket in advance.

If you are continuing south to the Eje Cafetero (Coffee Axis) in the Zona Cafetera, **Cotransrio** (☎311-762-6775; Calle 8 No 5-24) has a direct service from Jardín to Manizales (COP$42,000, six hours) at 6:30am. Alternatively, take the bus to Ríosucio (COP$20,000, three hours) at 8am or 3pm (noon on Saturdays) and pick up a connection to Manizales there.

Río Claro

ELEV 350M

Set 2km south of the Medellín–Bogotá highway, three hours east of Medellín and five hours west of Bogotá, is the **Reserva Natural Cañon de Río Claro** (☎4-268-8855, 313-671-4459; www.rioclaroelrefugio.com; Km152, Autopista Medellín-Bogotá; COP$15,000; 8am-6pm), a small reserve/hotel. Here the crystalline Río Claro rushes through a stunning marble canyon surrounded by lush forest. Be sure to visit the **Caverna de los Guácharos** (guided tour COP$20,000), a spectacular cave next to the river.

You can go rafting in the reserve (COP$25,000), but it's more a gentle cruise through some gorgeous scenery; hard-core rafters may be disappointed. Canopy cables crisscross the river, and make for a diverting afternoon zipping through the jungle (COP$20,000).

Bring a swimsuit, towel and flashlight. On weekends the reserve is often full of Colombian high-school students – you may prefer to come during the week. The reserve offers a variety of accommodation options under the one umbrella, the most impressive of which lie a 15-minute walk upriver from the restaurant. There is also a motel-style property at the edge of the highway, but it is not surrounded by nature and suffers from constant highway noise. If staying overnight, don't even think of showing up without an accommodation reservation – you won't get in.

The reserve is 24km west of Doradal, where you will find a couple of budget hotels and internet cafes near the main plaza, as well as ATMs.

Getting There & Away

Most Medellín–Bogotá buses, with the exception of some of the bigger express services, will drop you at the reserve's entrance as they pass it. Confirm that you will be dropped at the *entrada de la Reserva Río Claro* before purchasing your ticket.

From any other direction, look for transportation to Doradal, from where you can pick up a bus to the main gate (COP$5500, 20 minutes).

ZONA CAFETERA

Colombia is famous for its coffee, but nowhere is the prized bean more important than in the departments of Caldas, Risaralda and Quindío, which together make up the heart of the Zona Cafetera, also called the Eje Cafetero (Coffee Axis). Here you'll find jeeps packed with mustachioed coffee pickers, poncho-wearing senior citizens gossiping in cafes, and, of course, endless cups of piping-hot arabica. Many working *fincas* (coffee farms) have embraced tourism and welcome visitors onto their plantations to learn all about the coffee-growing process. It is particularly interesting to visit during the harvests (April to June, October to December) when the farms are a hive of activity.

The region was colonized by *paisas* in the 19th century during the *colonización antioqueña*, and remains culturally tied to Medellín in everything from its traditional architecture to its cuisine. It's an area of spectacular natural beauty and there are stunning vistas everywhere.

The Zona Cafetera is reachable by frequent direct bus services from Medellín, Cali and Bogotá. Manizales, Armenia and Pereira all have airports; the most accessible facility with the best connections is that of Pereira.

Manizales

☎6 / POP 357,800 / ELEV 2107M

The northern point of the Eje Cafetero (Coffee Axis), Manizales is a pleasantly cool, midsized university town with steep, hilly streets, surrounded on all sides by green mountain scenery. The capital of the Caldas department, Manizales was founded in 1849 by a group of Antioquian colonists looking to escape the civil wars of that time. The town's early development was hindered by

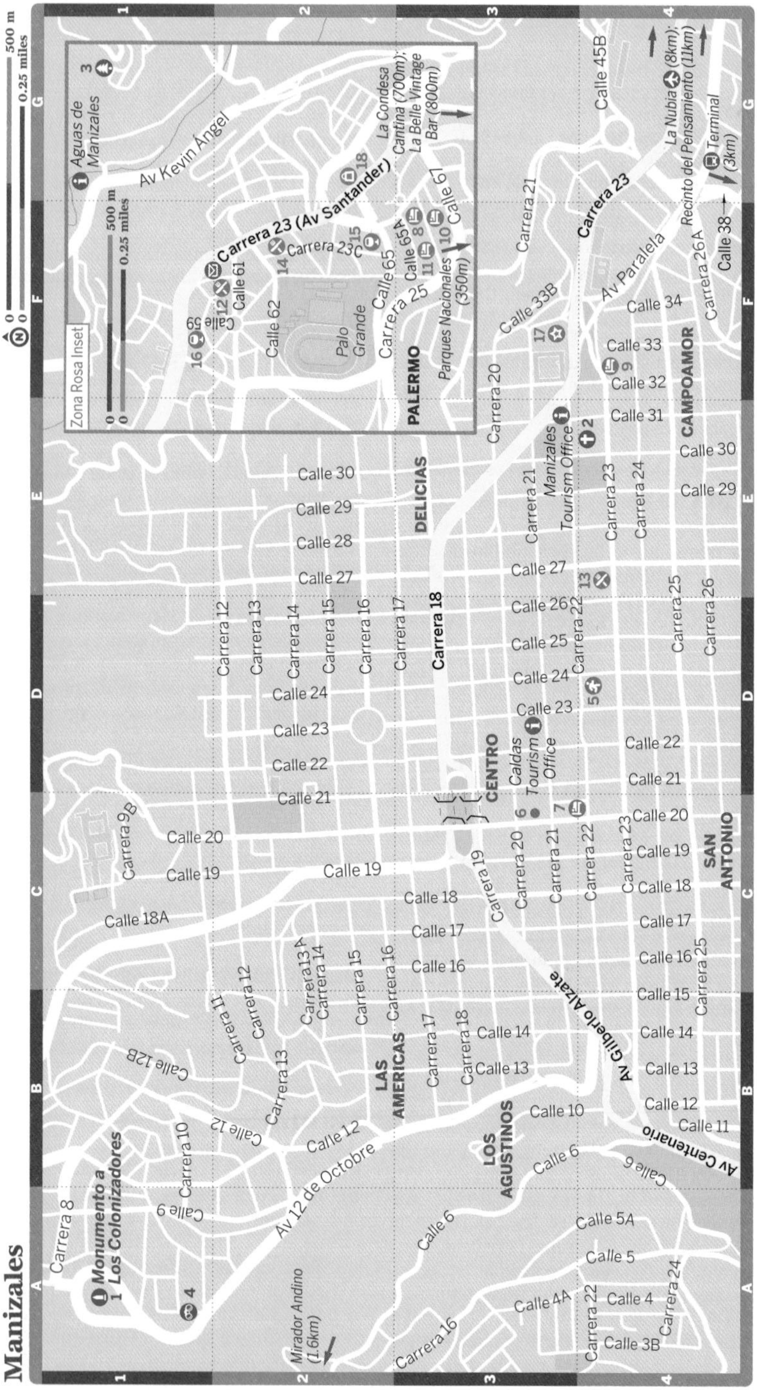

Manizales

0 500 m
0 0.25 miles

Zona Rosa Inset

0 500 m
0 0.25 miles

1 Monumento a Los Colonizadores
4
Mirador Andino (1.6km)
LAS AMERICAS
LOS AGUSTINOS
CENTRO
SAN ANTONIO
DELICIAS
PALERMO
CAMPOAMOR
6
Caldas Tourism Office
7
5
13
Manizales Tourism Office
2
17
9
Aguas de Manizales
3
16
12
14
15
18
8
10
11
Palo Grande
La Condesa Cantina (700m); La Belle Vintage Bar (800m)
Parques Nacionales (350m)
La Nubia (8km); Recinto del Pensamiento (11km)
Terminal (3km)

Carrera 8
Carrera 9B
Carrera 10
Carrera 11
Carrera 12
Carrera 13
Carrera 13A
Carrera 14
Carrera 15
Carrera 16
Carrera 17
Carrera 18
Carrera 19
Carrera 20
Carrera 21
Carrera 22
Carrera 23
Carrera 23 (Av Santander)
Carrera 23C
Carrera 24
Carrera 25
Carrera 26
Carrera 26A
Av 12 de Octobre
Av Gilberlo Alzate
Av Centenario
Av Paralela
Av Kevin Ángel
Calle 3B
Calle 4
Calle 4A
Calle 5
Calle 5A
Calle 6
Calle 9
Calle 10
Calle 11
Calle 12
Calle 12B
Calle 13
Calle 14
Calle 15
Calle 16
Calle 17
Calle 18
Calle 18A
Calle 19
Calle 20
Calle 21
Calle 22
Calle 23
Calle 24
Calle 25
Calle 26
Calle 27
Calle 28
Calle 29
Calle 30
Calle 31
Calle 32
Calle 33
Calle 33B
Calle 34
Calle 38
Calle 45B
Calle 59
Calle 61
Calle 62
Calle 65
Calle 65A
Calle 67

Manizales

Top Sights
1 Monumento a Los Colonizadores..........A1

Sights
2 Iglesia de Inmaculada Concepción.......E4
3 Los Yarumos.........G1
4 Torre de Chipre.........A1

Activities, Courses & Tours
5 Bailongo.........D4
6 Ecosistemas.........C3
Kumanday Adventures.........(see 8)

Sleeping
7 Estelar Las Colinas.........C3
8 Kumanday Hostal.........F3
9 Mirador Andino.........F4
10 Mountain Hostels.........F3
11 Regine's Hotel.........F3

Eating
12 El Bistro.........F2
13 La Suiza.........E4
14 Rushi.........F2

Drinking & Nightlife
15 Bar La Plaza.........F2
16 Prenderia.........F1

Entertainment
17 Teatro Los Fundadores.........F3

Shopping
18 Cable Plaza.........G2

two earthquakes in 1875 and 1878 and a fire in 1925, and for this reason there's not a lot of historical interest left – the real attractions are the surrounding nature activities and the town's vibrant nightlife.

Sights & Activities

★Monumento a Los Colonizadores MONUMENT
(Av 12 de Octobre, Chipre; 10am-6pm) FREE Located atop a hill in the neighborhood of Chipre, this massive monument to the city's founders was crafted from 50 tonnes of bronze (including keys and other implements donated by local residents). It's a very impressive work, but an even bigger attraction is the spectacular view over town and to PNN Los Nevados. Catch a bus marked 'Chipre' along Carrera 23 to get here.

Iglesia de Inmaculada Concepción CHURCH
(cnr Calle 30 & Carrera 22) Built at the beginning of the 20th century, this elegant church has a beautiful carved-wood interior reminiscent of a ship's hull.

Torre de Chipre VIEWPOINT
(Av 12 de Octobre, Chipre; COP$5000; 11am-9pm) The 30m-high spaceship-like lookout point has 360-degree views of the dramatic mountainous terrain surrounding the city. If you're brave you can walk around the perimeter on an external walkway while attached to a harness (COP$15,000). Admission allows you to come and go all day if you want to check the views during the day and after dark. To get here, take any bus running along Av Santander from Cable Plaza (p210) to Chipre; they leave constantly.

Los Yarumos PARK
(Calle 61B No 15A-01; activities COP$12,000-35,000; 8:30am-5:30pm Tue-Sun) This 53-hectare municipal park offers panoramic views of the city and adventure activities. Popular with locals, free activities include a short guided hike along a nature trail and a catapult that launches participants into the air while attached to a rubber sling. Paid options include treks to a waterfall, abseiling, a canopy line and a vertigo-inducing 80m-high Tibetan bridge. It's also a great place to just chill on a clear afternoon, when you can see the peaks of PNN Los Nevados.

A cable car (COP$1900) links the park directly with Cable Plaza (p210), and while it has been plagued by technical problems in the past, it's been revamped and makes for a terrific ride. Otherwise it's a 40-minute walk or COP$4500 in a taxi.

Bailongo DANCING
(314-847-4203; Calle 24 No 22-38, Piso 3; private classes per hour COP$15,000) A dance school in the heart of the 'Calle del Tango' offering private and group tango classes. Also offers lessons in other Latin rhythms.

Tours

Manizales is a good place to organize treks into the PNN Los Nevados and also tours of nearby coffee *fincas* (farms).

Kumanday Adventures ADVENTURE
(315-590-7294, 6-887-2682; www.kumanday.com; Calle 66 No 23B-40) This adventure company runs multiday treks in PNN Los Nevados and mountaineering trips nationwide. It also offers scenic mountain-bike tours through nearby coffee farms (COP$150,000), a high-adrenaline

downhill run from the edge of Nevado del Ruiz back to Manizales, and three-day cycling trips through the Andes. Mountaineering gear and tent rental are available.

Ecosistemas ADVENTURE
(☎312-705-7007, 6-880-8300; www.ecosistemastravel.com.co; Carrera 20 No 20-19; ⊙8am-noon & 2-6pm Mon-Fri, 8am-noon Sat) An experienced and professional outfitter offering excursions and multiday tours to PNN Los Nevados, including hikes to the summits of Nevado de Santa Isabel and Nevado del Tolima. It is one of the only operators with regular day trips into the park (COP$160,000). It also specializes in visits to local coffee farms.

Festivals & Events

Feria de Manizales CULTURAL
(⊙Jan) At Manizales' annual festival you'll find the usual assortment of parades, crafts fairs and, of course, a beauty pageant.

Festival Internacional de Teatro THEATER
(☎6-885-0165; www.festivaldemanizales.com; ⊙Sep) Held annually since 1968, this is one of two important theater festivals in Colombia (the other is in Bogotá). The festival lasts about a week and includes free street performances. Check the website for the schedule.

Sleeping

There's a good mix of hostels that cater to fresh-air fiends, as well as business hotels. Most accommodations are located in the Cable Plaza area, where you will find a large shopping mall and most of the city's best restaurants.

Mountain Hostels HOSTEL $
(☎6-887-4736, 300-439-7387; www.mountainhostels.com.co; Calle 66 No 23B-91; dm from COP$30,000, s/d COP$70,000/80,000, s/d without bathroom COP$60,000/70,000; ᯤ) A short walk from the *zona rosa,* this fine choice spread over two buildings is one of the few hostels where backpackers and Colombian travelers mix. Social areas include a rear patio with hammocks and a replica coffee cottage, but general cleanliness and security could improve. The reception-building rooms are the most comfortable. Staff are helpful with organizing activities.

★**Mirador Andino** HOSTEL $$
(☎310-609-8141, 6-882-1699; www.miradorandino-hostel.com; Carrera 23 No 32-20; dm/r COP$52,000/170,000; ᯤ) Perched on the side of the ridge on the edge of downtown, right next to the cable-car station, this hostel is a superb budget-traveler choice. Rooms are spotless, views from the fine rooftop bar are amazing, and the staff are wonderfully accommodating and superhelpful. Even the dorms come with private bathrooms.

★**Finca Mirador Morrogacho** B&B $$
(☎317-661-6117; www.miradorfincamorrogacho.com; Morrogacho Villa Jordan, enseguida Padres Salvatorianos, Calle 2; incl breakfast dm/s/d from COP$42,000/110,000/140,000, apt from COP$198,000; ᯤ) Located on a mountainside on the outskirts of town, this fantastic small hotel with phenomenal views has a variety of spacious, classy accommodations with polished-wood highlights and loads of natural light; some have guest kitchens. To get here take bus 601 or 619 marked 'Morrogacho' from central Manizales (COP$2000, 20 minutes). A taxi from Cable Plaza costs around COP$10,000.

The breakfast is hearty, and vegetarian meals (COP$20,000) are available.

The enchanting grounds are full of flowers and hummingbirds.There's a path beside the property that winds down through coffee farms to a waterfall and a panoramic yoga space.

Regine's Hotel HOTEL $$
(☎6-887-5360; www.regineshotel.com; Calle 65A No 23B-113; r incl breakfast COP$110,000; ᯤ) A good-value family-run B&B-style hotel offering spacious and comfortable accommodations close to Cable Plaza (p210). The outdoor garden patio is a great place to watch the sun rise. Some rooms are better than others – ask to see a few.

Estelar Las Colinas HOTEL $$$
(☎6-884-2009; www.hotelesestelar.com; Carrera 22 No 20-20; s/d incl breakfast COP$218,000/289,000; P ᯤ) The poshest place in the center, this modern glass-and-concrete hotel isn't pretty to look at, but it has large, comfortable rooms, plus a fine restaurant. Rooms on the upper levels have better views and more natural light. On weekends discounts are available.

Eating

Rushi VEGETARIAN $
(☎6-881-0326; Carrera 23C No 62-73; meals COP$10,000-14,000; ⊙9am-5pm Mon-Sat; 🖉) Rushi is a hip vegetarian restaurant serving great juices and interesting dishes such as

vegetarian lasagna, quinoa couscous and chickpea casserole, prepared with skill and grace before your eyes in the open kitchen. The changing lunch menu is top value. Sometimes there's live music in the evenings.

La Condesa Cantina MEXICAN **$**
(☎300-613-2218; www.facebook.com/LaCondesaCantinaManizales; Carrera 23 No 73-09; items COP$12,000-15,000; ⏲noon-3pm & 5-10pm Mon-Thu, to 11pm Fri, noon-11pm Sat; ✎) A bright little Mexican spot on the edge of the Milan dining strip serving tacos, quesadillas and *elotes* (Mexican grilled corn) with brilliance, flourish and seriously punchy salsa. Wash your meal down with a cold *cerveza michelada* or a margarita the size of a small bathtub.

La Suiza BAKERY **$$**
(☎6-885-0545; www.facebook.com/LaSuizaManizales; Carrera 23 No 26-57; mains COP$18,000-25,000; ⏲9am-8:30pm Mon-Sat, 9:30am-7:30pm Sun; ✎) This scrumptious bakery does great pastries and serves tasty breakfasts plus excellent light lunches, including pastas, gourmet sandwiches and wraps. But it's the sweet stuff they do best. The coffee's not great. There's another branch with great views near Cable Plaza.

El Bistro Francés FRENCH **$$**
(☎313-656-2417, 6-885-0520; Carrera 24A No 60-49; mains COP$20,000-30,000; ⏲noon-2:30pm Mon, noon-2:30pm & 6:30-9:30pm Tue-Sat; ✎) An unpretentious little place with just a handful of tables serving up traditional French fare at good prices. Take your pick from a variety of crepes (including veggie ones) or more filling beef, chicken and salmon dishes. During the day there is a good-value set meal (COP$14,000).

Drinking & Entertainment

La Belle Vintage Bar LOUNGE
(☎310-575-6347; www.facebook.com/labellevintagebar; Carrera 23 No 75-36; ⏲7pm-midnight Wed & Thu, to 2am Fri & Sat) This swanky 2nd-floor bar in the heart of the dining district single-handedly elevated Manizales' status to that of a cosmopolitan metropolis with its globe-spanning selection of gins, tequilas and imported beers. The music volume allows for conversation or seduction, and there's good bar food for when the munchies strike.

Prenderia BAR
(Carrera 23 No 58-42; ⏲8pm-2am Thu-Sat) Wonderfully relaxed bar where talented local musicians play to an older, laid-back crowd.

COLOMBIAN COFFEE

Colombia is the third-largest coffee exporter in the world and the only big producer that grows arabica beans exclusively. The coffee bean was brought to Colombia from Venezuela in the early 18th century by Jesuit priests. It was first cultivated in the area that is now Norte de Santander before spreading throughout the country.

Local conditions proved ideal for growing arabica coffee. Colombia's location near the equator means that coffee can be grown high in the mountains, where the beans mature more slowly. This results in a harder, more dense bean that provides consistent flavor when roasted. Frequent rainfall in the region sees bushes that are almost always flowering, which enables two harvests a year. And the plants thrive in the region's volcanic soils, which contain a high amount of organic material.

The main varieties of arabica coffee grown in Colombia are Tipica, Bourbon, Maragogipe, Tabi, Caturra and Colombia. As the beans on a single plant mature at different times, all Colombian coffee needs to be handpicked. This job is performed by small armies of *recolectores* (coffee pickers) that travel from region to region according to the harvests.

The heavy rainfall means that beans cannot be dried in the open like in other coffee-producing regions. Colombian beans are wet-processed or 'washed,' with the fruit surrounding the bean being removed prior to drying. This process takes much of the acidity out of the bean and gives the end product a richer aroma.

While the country is a major coffee producer, outside the Zona Cafetera Colombians have not traditionally been huge coffee drinkers and traditionally almost all the best beans were picked for export. This is changing as international coffee culture makes a splash in the country's bigger cities, where you'll now find hip coffee houses preparing fine caffeinated beverages using gourmet beans from farms around the country. If you want to purchase coffee to take home, it's best to visit some farms yourself and buy single-origin beans direct from the growers.

Try the lethal *carajillo* – strong espresso spiked with rum – and try not to slide off the bar stools.

Bar La Plaza BAR
(Carrera 23B No 64-80; ⏲11am-11pm Mon-Wed, to 2am Thu-Sat) Delicatessen by day, bar by night, La Plaza fills up fast and by 9pm you'll have to wait for a table. There's a young, student vibe, and it offers gourmet sandwiches (COP$7000 to COP$16,000) and snack platters of quality salami and cheese. The music isn't too loud, so you can have an intimate tête-à-tête over your enormous jug of sangria.

Teatro Los Fundadores THEATER
(☎6-878-2530; cnr Carrera 22 & Calle 33) Manizales' leading mainstream theater; it also has a cinema and hosts concerts.

Information

The area around the central market just north of the city is a favored hangout for thieves and is best avoided.

There are several ATMs inside **Cable Plaza** (Carrera 23 No 65-11).

4-72 (www.4-72.com.co; Carrera 23 No 60-36; ⏲8am-noon & 1-6pm Mon-Fri, 9am-noon Sat) Post office.

Banco de Bogotá (cnr Carrera 22 & Calle 22; ⏲8am-5pm Mon-Fri) ATM in the center.

BBVA (Carrera 23 No 64B-33) ATM in the *zona rosa*.

Caldas Tourism Office (Centro de Información Turística de Caldas; ☎6-884-2400; cnr Carrera 21 & Calle 23, Plaza de Bolívar; ⏲8am-noon & 2-6pm Mon-Fri, 9am-noon Sat) Offers tips on travel throughout the department.

Ciber Rosales Reliable internet access.

Giros y Finanzas Western Union agent; foreign exchange.

Manizales Tourism Office (☎6-873-3901; cnr Carrera 22 & Calle 31; ⏲8am-noon & 2-7pm) City information office.

Getting There & Away

AIR

Aeropuerto La Nubia (☎6-874-5451; Carrera 37) is 8km southeast of the city center, with several daily flights to Bogotá and a couple to Medellín. Take the urban bus to La Enea, then walk for five minutes to the terminal, or grab a taxi (COP$14,000). Delays and cancellations are common because of fog, so don't count on making a tight connection.

BUS

Manizales' sparkling modern **bus terminal** (☎6-878-7858; www.terminaldemanizales.com.co; Carrera 43 No 65-100) is located south of the center and is linked to the downtown area by an efficient **cable car** (www.cableaereomanizales.gov.co; Carrera 23; per trip COP$1800; ⏲6am-10pm) that offers great views of the city. A second cable-car line runs from the terminal across to Villa María on the far side of the valley. If you are staying by Cable Plaza, it is easier to take a taxi direct from the terminal (COP$7000).

Buses depart regularly to Cali (COP$40,000, 4½ hours), Bogotá (COP$56,000 to COP$70,000, eight hours) and Medellín (COP$40,000 to COP$50,000, four to five hours).

Minibuses to Pereira (COP$11,000, 1¼ hours) and Armenia (COP$17,500, 1½ hours) run every 15 minutes or so.

Getting Around

Buses run the length of Manizales along Av Santander from Cable Plaza to Chipre every 30 seconds (yes, that frequently!).

The expanding Cable Aéreo cable-car network (ride COP$1800) runs from 6am to 10pm daily and from the bus terminal to various destinations in the center.

Around Manizales

The lush mountainous countryside surrounding Manizales is home to some of Colombia's most beautiful landscapes and does not lack opportunities for adventure and relaxation. Here you'll find hot thermal baths, volcanic craters, working coffee farms and nature reserves full of birdlife all within a one-hour drive of the city.

Sights

Hacienda Guayabal PLANTATION
(☎314-772-4856, 317-280-4899; www.haciendaguayabal.com; Km3 Via Peaje Tarapacá, Chinchiná; tours Spanish/English COP$35,000/40,000; ⏲tours 8am-5pm) This slow-paced working coffee farm near Chinchiná is a great place to come and unwind while surrounded by *cafetero* culture. It runs an excellent tour that follows the coffee process from the plant to the cup and includes a tasting workshop at the end.

To get here, take an Autolujo bus from Manizales to Chinchiná (COP$3500, 30 minutes). A taxi from Chinchiná direct to the door costs COP$10,000.

The experience here is a bit more personal than those offered by some of the larger outfits and the guides are keen to share their knowledge. Bags of the coffee are available to purchase as souvenirs.

Make sure you stay for lunch – the traditional farm-style food here is absolutely delicious and vegetarians are well catered for. You can hang around afterwards to use the pool.

There's also fine birdwatching on the property with more than 160 species identified, including three endemics. If you want to stay longer, it offers simple, functional accommodations (rooms per person including breakfast COP$70,000) in a modern house set up on a hill, with magnificent views over the surrounding plantations. For more privacy, book one of the fine cabañas (per person including breakfast COP$100,000 to COP$140,000) that cling to the hillside and boast private balconies with breathtaking panoramas. The spacious, light-filled suite is particularly appealing, with its massive windows and attractive indoor/outdoor bathroom.

★**Hacienda Venecia** PLANTATION
(☎6-870-3034, 320-636-5719; www.haciendavenecia.com; Vereda el Rosario, San Peregrino; tours adult/child 12-15yr COP$50,000/40,000; ⊙tours 9:30am) This hacienda has won numerous awards for its coffee. It offers a tour in English that includes an informative presentation about Colombian coffee, an introduction to coffee cupping, a class in coffee preparation and a walking tour through the plantation. You can use the pool afterwards, and a typical lunch is available for COP$15,000. The tour price includes transportation to/from your hotel in Manizales. Barista workshops are available.

The plantation is centered on a well-preserved *paisa* farmhouse with majestic views that has been converted into a lovely boutique hotel (rooms with/without bathroom from COP$374,000/200,000). The gardens are well kept, and there's a pond with lily pads and a round blue pool. The rooms are full of books, antiques and old photographs, while the wraparound verandah has hammocks and rocking chairs to rock away the evening.

There are also cheaper, although slightly less atmospheric, accommodations in a newer building – the Coffee Lodge (rooms COP$180,000 to COP$200,000) – which are across the river from the main house and have a swimming pool. And there's a hostel building a short walk away with breezy dorms (COP$30,000 to COP$35,000), snug rooms (COP$90,000) and a guest kitchen. All accommodations include unlimited farm-fresh coffee and those staying in the hotel or Coffee Lodge are treated to a wonderful breakfast spread.

Recinto del Pensamiento NATURE RESERVE
(☎6-889-7073; www.recintodelpensamiento.com; Km11 Via al Magdalena; COP$17,000; ⊙9am-4pm Tue-Sun) Set in the cloud forest 11km from Manizales, this nature park has a fine mariposario (butterfly enclosure), several short walks through an impressive orchid-populated forest, and a medicinal herb garden. You'll also see plantations of *guadua* and *chusqué* (two kinds of Colombian bamboo). There's even a *telesilla* – a kind of chairlift that takes you up the mountain slope on which the park sits. To get here, take the bus marked Sera Maltería from Cable Plaza in Manizales or take a taxi (COP$12,000).

Admission includes 2½ hours of mandatory guide service; a couple of the guides speak some English. There's impressive birdlife here – book in advance for birdwatching tours run on demand from 6am to 9am and 2pm to 5pm (COP$70,000). Wear brown or green clothes and bring binoculars.

Activities

Termales El Otoño THERMAL BATHS
(☎6-847-0280; www.termaleselotono.com; Km5 Antigua Via al Nevado; adult/child 2-12yr COP$30,000/20,000; ⊙7am-midnight) This high-end resort 5km from Manizales consists of three large thermal pools surrounded by impressive mountain peaks. The pools are set among breezy wooden shelters and there's a cafe serving Colombian standards and booze. Admission from Tuesday to Thursday is half-price. The downside – during peak periods you'll share them with hordes of visitors. From Manizales take the bus marked 'Gallinazo' (COP$2000).

The on-site hotel has rooms ranging from generic hotel-type offerings to luxurious cottages with wooden ceilings, open fireplaces and private thermal spas (single/double rooms including breakfast cost from COP$231,000/302,000).

It is a little too built-up to be a full-on nature experience, but it's still a fine relaxing day away from the city.

Termales Tierra Viva THERMAL BATHS
(☎6-874-3089; www.termalestierraviva.com; Km2 Via Enea-Gallinazo; adult/child 2-10yr COP$20,000/13,000; ⊙9am-11:30pm) Located next to the Río Chinchiná just outside Manizales, this thermal-bath complex has three pools made of rocks set among a pretty garden that attracts hummingbirds and butterflies. The baths are quiet during the week, but on the weekends it can feel a little overcrowded. From Manizales,

WORTH A TRIP

RESERVA ECOLÓGICA RÍO BLANCO

Three kilometers northeast of Manizales lies this 3600-hectare cloud-forest reserve (2150-3700m). It is an area of high biodiversity and protects numerous endangered species, including the *oso andino* (spectacled bear). There are 362 species of bird present in the park, including 13 of Colombia's endemics. It attracts birdwatchers from around the world, but even amateurs will be delighted by the quantities of hummingbirds, butterflies and orchids. It makes a great half-day excursion – best in the morning, as it often rains in the afternoon.

The reserve is one of the most pristine and attractive tracts of forest in the region, but unfortunately visiting is anything but straightforward. Before you can visit you must request permission (free) at least two days in advance from Aguas de Manizales. Staff here are notoriously bad at answering correspondence; you might have to show up to the office and be persistent in order to organize permission.

A taxi to the main gate from Manizales will cost around COP$30,000. Get the number of your driver for the round trip – there is next to no traffic up here.

take a bus marked 'Gallinazo' along Carrera 19 (COP$2000).

There's an elevated, open-air restaurant and a small spa offering a wide range of massages.On weekdays there's often cut-price admission to the thermal baths. There's also a good-value on-site hotel with four spacious, modern rooms (from COP$210,000) sporting full-length windows overlooking a stream.

Sleeping

There are numerous coffee farms in the lush countryside around Manizales that are open to overnight visitors, with lodgings ranging from simple hostel-like digs to plush rooms in historic surrounds. All of the thermal baths in the area also offer accommodations.

★**Termales del Ruiz** SPA HOTEL **$$$**
(☎310-455-3588; www.hoteltermalesdelruiz.com; Paraje de Termales, Villa Maria, Caldas; s/d incl breakfast from COP$315,000/335,000;) Amid stunning landscapes just outside the boundaries of PNN Los Nevados at 3500m, this thermal-baths complex is the place to go for total relaxation. Rooms have the feel of a classic alpine lodge and while not huge they're comfortable. Outside there's a large thermal pool set among otherworldly *páramo* (high-mountain plain) plants. You'll need your own wheels to get here.

Up on a hillside above the complex there's a birding shelter beside a gushing stream where 17 species of hummingbird come to feed. There are also short trails to explore.

Meals are served in an elegant fire-heated dining room, with large windows offering fine views of the mountains and – on a clear day – down to Manizales. The baths are the only ones near Manizales built right at the source – you can see the sulfur-laced waters bubbling out of the mountainside right behind the hotel.

Day-trippers can use one of the pools for COP$30,000. Transportation from Manizales can be arranged for hotel guests for COP$40,000 per visitor one way.

Getting There & Away

Most of the main attractions around Manizales are close enough to reach by taxi or urban bus.

To get to Termales El Otoño (p211) or Termales Tierra Viva (p211), take the white Metropolitano bus marked 'Gallinazo' (COP$2000, 30 minutes) from Av Kevin Ángel below Cable Plaza or Carrera 20 in central Manizales. The last bus back into town leaves around 8:30pm from El Otoño. A taxi from Cable Plaza will set you back around COP$15,000.

Parque Nacional Natural Los Nevados

ELEV 2600-5325M

Following a spine of snow-covered volcanic peaks, this **national park** (☎6-887-1611; www.parquesnacionales.gov.co; foreigners/Colombians COP$43,500/15,500, south of park COP$29,500/10,500; ⏲8am-3:30pm) sits between Manizales, Pereira and Ibagué and provides access to some of the most stunning stretches of the Colombian Andes. Its varied altitude range encompasses everything from humid cloud forests and *páramo* (high-mountain plains) to glaciers on the tallest peaks.

Thirty-seven rivers are born here, providing water to 3.5 million people in four departments. The glaciers in the park have been receding, however, and research is underway to measure the impact on the environment.

Highlights include visits to the beautiful Laguna del Otún, and the ascents of the three snowcapped volcanoes: Nevado del Ruiz, Nevado de Santa Isabel and Nevado del Tolima.

The best months to see snow in Los Nevados are October and November and from March to May. Outside of those times you're more likely to get the dry, windy conditions favorable to trekking and clear views.

Tours

In order to trek into the park, it's obligatory to take a guide registered with Parques Nacionales. For a list of registered guides, contact the **office** (☎6-887-1611; www.parquesnacionales.gov.co; Calle 69A No 24-69; ⏰8am-5pm Mon-Fri) in Manizales.

Public transportation to most entry points of the park is nonexistent. While it's possible to hike into the park from either Parque Ucumarí or Valle de Cocora, it's often more convenient to organize a package including guides and transportation in Manizales or Salento.

If you want to explore Los Nevados by bicycle you'll need to get advance permission from the office of Parques Nacionales (p213) in Manizales. Only limited areas of the park are open to cyclists and designated zones are under constant review.

Nevado del Ruiz

This is the highest volcano in PNN Los Nevados' chain. Its eruption on November 13, 1985, killed more than 20,000 people and swept away the town of Armero on the Río Lagunillas. El Ruiz had previously erupted in 1845, but the results were far less catastrophic; today, the volcano continues to grumble, resulting in restrictions on activities in this part of the park.

The principal access road into the park is from the north. It branches off from the Manizales–Bogotá road in La Esperanza, 31km east of Manizales. The entrance to the park is at Las Brisas (4050m), where you'll need to register at the rangers' office.

Access is only permitted between 8am and 2pm, with all visitors having to leave the park by 3:30pm. At the time of research, visitors were still only permitted to travel a short 5km stretch of road through the *páramo* to **Valle de las Tumbas** (4350m), due to the unrelenting volcanic activity. While tour operators such as Ecosistemas (p208) in Manizales are still running trips (COP$160,000) to this part of the park, tours are more targeted at the photo-op, package-tour crowd than those looking for a nature experience. Visitors spend almost the entire trip in vehicles; it's not permitted to get out and hike even short distances.

If restrictions are lifted, it should be possible to explore more of the area. The volcano actually has three craters: **Arenas**, **La Olleta** and **Piraña**. It is possible to summit the main one, Arenas (5321m). The extinct Olleta crater (4850m), on the opposite side of the road, is covered with multicolored layers of sandy soil and normally has no snow.

Nevado de Santa Isabel

Straddling the departments Caldas, Risaralda and Tolima, this dormant volcano is covered in dome-like formations and topped with a 2-sq-km glacier that is the source of the Río Otún. It's the lowest glacier left in Colombia and the most rapidly retreating.

The volcano is accessed through the village of Potosí near Santa Rosa de Cabal. It's possible to reach the edge of the glacier on a day trip from Manizales although it's pretty intense: you'll travel in a vehicle for about three hours along an unsealed road to a height of 4050m, before hiking uphill through the canyon of Río Campo Alegre for another three hours to the snow line at 4750m. Trips run by the likes of Ecosistemas (p208) usually leave Manizales at around 4am or 5am and don't return until 7pm. Expect to pay around COP$200,000 per hiker, including breakfast and lunch.

If you plan to visit on a day trip, it's important to be aware of the effect the change in altitude will have on your stamina. Pay close attention to the recommendations of your guide.

The climb to the summit (4965m) requires both experience and specialized gear, and it's advisable to hire an experienced guide. It's also recommended to spend a day or two at altitude before attempting the ascent.

Laguna del Otún

This spectacular lake at an altitude of 3950m is surrounded by the gorgeous *páramo* below the magnificent Nevado de Santa Isabel. On the east side of the lake there is a ranger station where you can pitch a tent (COP$10,000 per visitor). You can hike to Laguna del Otún from the north via the park

Parque Nacional Natural Los Nevados

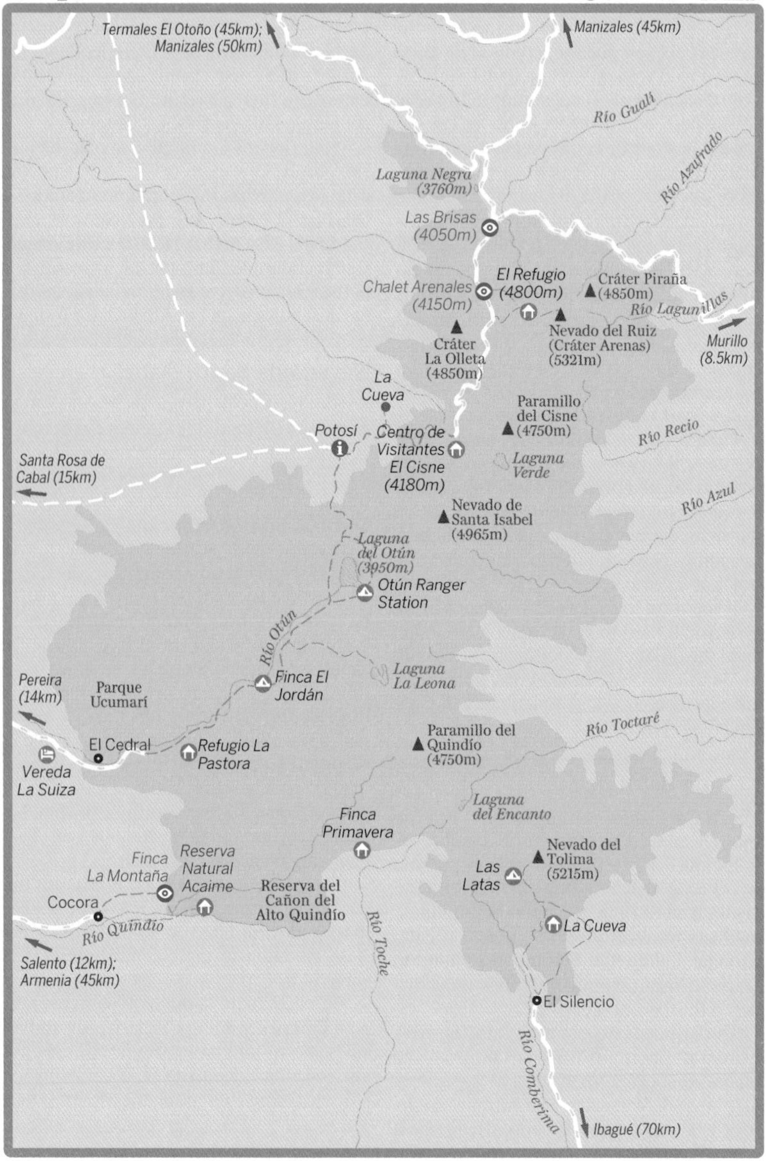

gate at Potosí (three hours one way) or from the south via Refugio La Pastora (seven to nine hours one way). The latter is a popular three-day trek from Pereira, beginning at the settlement of El Cedral and following the valley of the pristine Río Otún for some 19km. While the hike from Potosí is considered easier as it's shorter and begins at a higher altitude, the stiff uphill hike from La Pastora affords better views. If you hike up from La Pastora you'll be required to pay the park entry fee on arrival at Laguna del Otún as there is no gate in this sector.

Some 6km up from El Cedral toward the lake is the Centro de Visitantes La Pastora, with cozy dorms (COP$23,000; bring own sleeping bag; no phone) and hot meals available (from COP$7000).

Halfway along the route from La Pastora you'll find **Finca El Jordán**, home of the Machete family, who offer basic accommodations. It is wise to bring a tent, cooking equipment and food.

It's possible to enter from one access point, spend the night at the lake and then leave along the other route. Note there's no public transportation to Potosí, which is reachable via the road that runs past the Termales San Vicente from Santa Rosa de Cabal; however, Kolibrí Hostel (p216) in Pereira runs day tours to the lagoon via Potosí. El Cedral is reachable via three daily *chivas* with Transportes Florida (p218) from Pereira (COP$5100); at the time of research they made the journey back to Pereira at 11am, 2pm and 5pm.

Nevado del Tolima

Nevado del Tolima (5215m), the second-highest volcano in the chain, is the most handsome of all, with its classic symmetrical cone. On a clear day it can be seen from as far away as Bogotá. Its last eruption took place in 1943.

There are two ways of reaching it. For novices, it's best to do a four-day round trip through the Valle de Cocora. On the first day, you trek for 13.5km from the Valle de Cocora trailhead and up the Río Quindío canyon, overnighting at the Finca la Primavera (COP$10,000) at 3680m. The second day takes you up to a basic campsite at 4400m after a trek of 12km (six to seven hours). The following morning, you start climbing up to the crater at 2am, reaching it at around 7am or 8am, admiring the stupendous views, returning to the Finca La Primavera for the night and to the Valle de Cocora the following day. It's best to go with an experienced guide as the trail is not clearly marked and it's easy to get lost.

Experienced mountaineers might prefer to tackle the southern face accessible through Ibagué, the capital of the Tolima department. The trail begins at Juntas, some 17km from Ibagué and on the first night you can either camp at the Finca Las Nieves (a six-hour hike) or El Vergel (an eight-hour hike). On the second day, it takes around four or six hours to reach the Termales de Cañon campsite from El Vergel or Finca La Nieves, respectively. From there, the volcano can either be summited in one day via the Ingeominas weather station, leaving at 2am, or via an additional overnighter at 4600m, which is best for high-altitude climbers with less technical experience.

Either way it's a challenging multiday trek. Because of the state of the glaciers, it's a more technical climb than the other peaks in PNN Los Nevados, and an experienced guide and mountaineering equipment is essential. A recommended guide is German 'Mancho' of **Excursiones Nevado del Tolima** (☎313-675-1059, 312-211-7677; www.facebook.com/ExcursionesNevadoDelTolima), who is based in Salento and grew up in the area. In Ibagué, try **David 'Truman' Bejarano** (☎315-292-7395; www.truman.com.co), an experienced mountain guide who also offers trips to other peaks around the country.

Pereira

☎6 / POP 440,100 / ELEV 1410M

Hardworking Pereira is not your typical tourist destination. In fact it's not really a tourist destination at all. Almost all visitors to Pereira come for one thing – to do business. Founded in 1863, Pereira is the capital of Risaralda and the economic powerhouse of the Zona Cafetera – a hot commercial center most noted for its throbbing nightlife. Pereira doesn't offer much in the way of attractions, but if you want to experience a fast-paced yet friendly Colombian city away from the gringo trail and with a good dining scene, it certainly fits the bill. Pereira is also the gateway to Parque Ucumarí and Santuario Otún Quimbaya, a pair of top nature reserves, and the relaxing thermal springs of Santa Rosa and San Vicente.

Activities

Finca Don Manolo TOURS
(☎313-655-0196; Vereda El Estanquillo; tours COP$30,000; by appointment) Visit this family-run coffee farm on a mountainside just outside Pereira for an interesting tour covering the entire production process from planting to harvesting and processing. Afterwards you'll enjoy a farm-fresh cup and a brownie while taking in the great views. You'll be shown around by friendly owner Don Manolo, so call ahead to make sure he is home.

A taxi from town costs around COP$15,000 or look for the bus (COP$1800) marked 'Guadales' or 'Vereda El Estanquillo' at the terminal. Ask the driver to let you off at the Centro Logistica Eje Cafetero, from where it's a 1km walk to the farm.

Sleeping

★Kolibrí Hostel HOSTEL $
(☎321-646-9275, 6-331-3955; www.kolibrihostel.com; Calle 4 No 16-35; dm from COP$23,000, r with/without bathroom COP$90,000/60,000; 📶) With a great location just off the main *zona rosa,* this top hostel is sociable without being a party place. Besides comfortable rooms, there's a great terrace with mountain views, a chilled streetside bar area, and coffee from the family *finca* (farm) of one of the owners; the Dutch-Colombian couple is happy to arrange coffee tours, paragliding and cycling excursions.

There's even a self-contained apartment for rent. Our only tiny quibble? Synthetic bedding.

Hotel Condina HOTEL $$
(☎6-333-4225; Calle 18 No 6-26; s/d with air-con COP$166,000/186,000, with fan COP$112,000/149,000; P❄📶) On a bustling traffic-free street in the heart of downtown, this mid-sized hotel offers excellent value. Bright, modern rooms have work desks and even a pillow menu. The facilities are way above what you would normally expect at this price.

Prices include breakfast. Lack of vehicle access might be an issue if you have a lot of luggage.

Hotel Abadia Plaza HOTEL $$$
(☎6-335-8398; www.hotelabadiaplaza.com; Carrera 8 No 21-67; s/d incl breakfast COP$227,000/258,000; ❄📶) This stylish place right in the center of town is a top choice for comfort and professional service. You'll find bilingual staff, original art on the walls, a well-equipped gym, and plush rooms with marble bathrooms and noise-proof windows. Prices drop by around a third on weekends.

Eating

Grajales Autoservicios CAFETERIA $
(☎6-335-6606; Carrera 8 No 21-60; meals COP$15,000; ⏲24hr) At this large 24-hour self-service restaurant/bakery you can put together your own lunch or dinner at the buffet. Alternatively, in the middle of the day choose from a more limited selection of dishes in the good-value lunch special (COP$11,000). It's also a decent option for breakfast.

Vineria San Martino ITALIAN $$
(☎6-346-2481; Carrera 12 No 3-32, La Rebeca; mains COP$15,000-25,000; ⏲noon-3pm & 6-10pm Mon-Thu, to 11pm Fri & Sat; 🖉) A cozy little spot serving fantastic traditional Italian cuisine accompanied by imported Italian wines. Portions aren't huge and the service can be a little slow, but the homemade pasta is absolutely delicious. Other dishes are less consistent.

★Leños y Parrilla GRILL $$
(☎6-331-4676; www.facebook.com/LenosYParrilla; Carrera 12 No 2-78; mains COP$24,000-34,000; ⏲noon-10pm) Just off the Circunvalar, this hugely popular altar to things that go moo delights the carnivorously inclined with its wide selection of both thin- and thick-cut steaks. They're smoky and seared to perfection over hot coals, and the T-bones have crisped ribbons of fat… It's a big place but still gets full so come early or make a reservation.

Drinking & Nightlife

The Circunvalar area is full of bars and small discos and is now Pereira's principal party spot, while downtown has a number of bars popular with a bohemian crowd. The late-night action is a little way outside of the city in La Badea. There's a good coffee scene, too.

★Rincón Clásico BAR
(cnr Carrera 2 & Calle 22; ⏲4-11pm Mon-Sat) Music lovers of all ages descend on this diminutive corner bar to drink and sing along to tango, bolero and other classics from the elderly owner's collection of 7000 records. Don Olmedo has been spinning tunes here for more than half a century. He'll play anything as long as it's classic – don't go asking for reggaeton!

★El Barista COFFEE
(☎6-341-3316; www.facebook.com/elbaristacaf; Carrera 15 No 4-17; ⏲8am-midnight Mon-Thu, to 1am Fri & Sat) This bright and inviting cafe decked out with pine furniture prepares the best coffee in town (COP$3000 to COP$6500) using a variety of different methods. There's a good menu of snacks and light meals and also bags of gourmet beans to go.

El Parnaso BAR
(☎6-334-6420; www.facebook.com/parnaso.bar; Carrera 6 No 23-35; ⏲3:30pm-2am Mon-Sat) Walk down the long corridor to arrive at this arty garden bar with an open fireplace. Skip the pizzas and burgers, and go for a beer instead. The hip indie-rock soundtrack is restrained enough to enjoy a conversation.

Information

There are numerous ATMs in the bus terminal (p217), around Plaza de Bolívar and on the Av Circunvalar.

4-72 (www.4-72.com.co; Carrera 9 No 21-33; ⏲8am-noon & 2-5pm Mon-Fri, 9am-noon Sat) Post office.

Bancolombia (Av Circunvalar No 4-48) ATM in the *zona rosa*.

Tourism Office (☎6-311-6544; cnr Carrera 10 & Calle 17; ⏲8am-noon & 2-6pm Mon-Fri, 9am-3pm Sat) In the Centro Cultural Lucy Tejada.

Getting There & Around

Pereira's international **Aeropuerto Matecaña** (☎6-314-8151; www.aeromate.gov.co; Carrera 12) is 5km west of the city center. It's accessible by MegaBús or urban bus from the bus terminal. A taxi from town costs around COP$15,000. There are numerous daily flights to Bogotá, as well as daily flights to Cartagena and Medellín. Copa (www.copaair.com) has direct flights to Panama twice daily.

The **bus terminal** (☎6-321-5834; www.terminalpereira.com; Calle 17 No 23-157) is 1.5km south of the city center. Many urban buses will take you there in less than 10 minutes. It's a minimum fare by taxi (COP$4500) from the center or the Av Circunvalar.

There are regular departures to Bogotá (COP$48,000 to COP$69,000, nine hours). A number of buses go to Medellín (COP$34,000 to COP$46,000, six hours) and Cali (COP$25,000 to COP$32,000, four hours). Minibuses run every 15 minutes to Armenia (COP$6000 to COP$8000, one hour) and Manizales (COP$11,000, 1¼ hours).

Pereira's **MegaBús** (www.megabus.gov.co; s ticket COP$2000) runs crosstown and out to Dosquebradas. It's similar to Bogotá's TransMilenio and Cali's MIO, but on a smaller scale. It's not hugely useful for travelers staying around the Av Circunvalar, however.

Termales de Santa Rosa

☎6 / ELEV 1950M

High above the town of Santa Rosa de Cabal surrounded by gorgeous mountain scenery is a popular thermal-bath complex: **Termales de Santa Rosa** (☎320-680-3615, 6-365-5237; www.termales.com.co; Km10 Vereda San Ramón, Santa Rosa de Cabal; adult/child COP$36,500/30,000 Mon-Fri, COP$51,000/33,000 Sat & Sun; ⏲9am-11:30pm; 👪). It's divided into two parts, around 1km apart along the same road: the Termales de Hotel at Hotel Termales for the hotel guests, with thermal pools of varying sizes and temperatures along with spa treatments, situated below impressive waterfalls, and **Termales Balneario** (☎6-365-5237; www.termales.com.co; Km10 Vereda San Ramón, Santa Rosa de Cabal; adult/child COP$40,000/20,000; ⏲9am-11:30pm, last entry 10pm; 👪), consisting of three adult thermal pools and one kiddie pool. Both parts of the thermal complex get busy on weekends but during the week the vibe is generally pretty relaxed.

Sleeping & Eating

Hotel Termales HOTEL **$$$**
(☎320-680-3604, 6-365-5500; www.termales.com.co; Termales de Santa Rosa; r incl breakfast from COP$280,000; P📶) On the site of Termales de Santa Rosa (p217), Hotel Termales offers accommodations in a sprawling mansion with one old, renovated wing and two newer wings. Prices include access to both parts of the thermal complex: Termales de Hotel and Termales Balneario, and you can hit the pools at 6am, before day-trippers arrive.

Getting There & Away

The thermal pools are 9km east of Santa Rosa de Cabal, off the Pereira–Manizales road. Urban buses (COP$1700, 25 minutes) leave from the main plaza in Santa Rosa de Cabal every two hours from 6am to 6pm, returning an hour later from the Hotel Termales. A taxi or jeep from Santa Rosa to the thermal complexes costs around COP$25,000.

There's a frequent daytime Santa Rosa–Pereira bus service (COP$2500, 45 minutes). Buses to Manizales (COP$7500, one hour) stop at the gas station on the Pereria–Chinchiná road, four blocks from the plaza.

Termales San Vicente

☎6 / ELEV 2250M

Set at the head of a steep, forested valley and straddling a cold creek, these **thermal pools** (☎320-693-3707; www.sanvicente.com.co; Km17 Via Laguna del Otún y Parque Natural Los Nevados; adult/child 3-10yr COP$50,000/22,000; ⏲8am-midnight) are only 18km east of Santa Rosa de Cabal but feel a world away.

The complex has seven pools, one of which is reserved for hotel guests, and a spa offering a full range of treatments, including mud therapy, facials, peels and massage. Most visitors hang around in the main pools near the restaurant building, but the natural **Piscina de las Burbujas** surrounded by greenery near the main gate is well worth checking out. A short walk further down the valley lies the invigorating **Rio Termal**, where the thermal waters mix with the rushing stream to create amazing natural spas surrounded by thick forest. The complex also has natural saunas built over 80°C to 90°C hot springs. There are also adventure activities, including a canopy line high above the valley (COP$25,000) and abseiling in a waterfall (COP$25,000).

There is a wide range of accommodations (single/double including breakfast from COP$200,000/288,000) on offer inside the complex. Cabins range from split-log rustic to modern minimalist with working fireplaces and private thermal pools. Most have electric shower heads. There are also less appealing hotel-style accommodations and some budget rooms above the reception. Rates include admission and breakfast.

The baths are operated from the **booking office** (6-333-6157; Av Circunvalar No 15-62; 8am-6pm Mon-Sat, to noon Sun) in Pereira, where you can make inquiries. A day package for visitors (adult/child COP$75,000/55,000) runs on Fridays and weekends and includes round-trip transportation from Pereira, admission, lunch and a refreshment. The bus leaves from the office at 9am and returns at 6:30pm.

If you don't have private transportation and don't want to go on the package trip, you can hire a jeep from the market – *la galería* – in Santa Rosa de Cabal (one way for up to six passengers costs around COP$60,000).

Santuario Otún Quimbaya

This nature reserve 18km southeast of Pereira protects a 489-hectare area of high biodiversity between 1800m and 2400m. Set on the Río Otún, it boasts more than 200 species of birds and butterflies and two rare species of monkey, among other wildlife. The reserve has several hiking trails along the river and through the forest, although visitors are not permitted to explore on their own. Guided hikes (COP$7500) leave at 9am, 11:30am and 3pm. Unfortunately the Cascada Los Frailes – a towering waterfall tumbling down a plant-covered mountain – remains closed.

You'll pay the admission fee (COP$6000) at the **visitor center** (Vereda La Suiza; dm/s/d COP$40,000/60,000/90,000). If you're just visiting for the day, a package is available for COP$29,000 that includes admission, lunch and a guided hike along one of the trails.

Reservations can be made through the excellent community tourism organization **Yarumo Blanco** (310-363-5001, 310-379-7719, 314-674-9248; www.yarumoblanco.co).

The visitor center (p218) at La Suiza has two floors of accommodations. There are electric showers (24-hour electricity) but no central heating, and fires are not allowed. Alcohol is also prohibited. Ask for a room on the 2nd floor – rooms have small balconies facing the forest filled with birdsong.

The restaurant at the visitor center (p218) prepares budget meals (COP$10,000 to COP$16,000).

Getting There & Away

Transporte Florida (6-334-2721; Calle 12 No 9-40, La Galería) offers daily *chiva* services (COP$4000, 1½ hours) at 9am and 3pm from Pereira to the Otún Quimbaya visitor center (p218) in the small village of Vereda La Suiza. The *chivas* continue past the visitor center another half hour to El Cedral (COP$5100), where they immediately turn around and head back. On weekends there are additional services at 7am and noon, although the early service does not continue to El Cedral.

The *chiva* terminal in Pereira is in a dangerous part of town; ask your taxi driver to take you all the way into the parking area, or pick the *chiva* up at the Plaza Victoria.

Parque Ucumarí

Established in 1984 just outside the western boundaries of the Parque Nacional Natural (PNN) Los Nevados, this 42-sq-km reserve protects a rugged, forested land around the middle course of the Río Otún, about 30km southeast of Pereira. More than 185 species of bird have been recorded here.

There are ecological paths traced through verdant hills, where you can see lush vegetation and spot some of the park's rich wildlife, or check out the large waterfall about 30 minutes' walk from the base at La Pastora.

There is no phone reception in the park itself but you can call community tourism outfit Yarumo Blanco (p218) in advance to make your reservations for the *refugio* and organize guides for the trek in. It is also able to organize guides (COP$180,000 per day) and rent tents for treks to Laguna del Otún and beyond.

From La Pastora (p219) you can hike up Río Otún, leading through a gorge to PNN Los Nevados. You can even get to Laguna del Otún (3950m), where there's a small rangers' office and a place to pitch a tent (COP$10,000 per visitor). It's a 12km, six- to eight-hour walk uphill but mules are available to carry equipment.

It's best to split the trek and stay in a tent or at El Jordán in the simple house of 'Los

Machetes,' a famously hospitable local family. From El Jordán it's also possible to hire horses (COP$120,000) for the remainder of the trip up to the lake.

If you stay longer around El Jordán, you can also make some side excursions in the *páramo*. Conditions are harsh up here – you'll need to take a guide to show you the way.

The cabins at **Refugio La Pastora** (☎312-200-7711; dm/campsite per person COP$28,000/8000), at an elevation of 2500m, are at the heart of the park and offer simple dormitory accommodations. The ambience here is particularly laid-back; ask the guy who runs the place to build a bonfire – BYO wine and marshmallows.

Getting There & Away

To get here from Pereira, take the Transporte Florida (p218) *chiva* to El Cedral (COP$5100, two hours). From El Cedral it's a 5km, 2½-hour walk up to La Pastora (p219), or rent a horse (COP$35,000 one way).

Armenia

☎6 / POP 315,300 / ELEV 1483M

Armenia feels more like a big town than a departmental capital, far more slow-paced than its coffee-country rivals Manizales and Pereira. There is not much in the way of attractions here for visitors. Devastated by an earthquake in 1999 that flattened much of the city center, Armenia has never fully recovered. The center of the city is makeshift – check out the hastily reconstructed cathedral, made of prefab concrete slabs – and the de facto center has moved north of downtown, along Av Bolívar.

Most travelers will pass through Armenia only long enough to change buses; however, the city has a fine museum and excellent botanical gardens, which make it interesting enough for a day or so.

Sights

Jardín Botánico del Quindío GARDENS
(☎6-742-7254; www.jardinbotanicoquindio.org; Km3 Via al Valle, Calarcá; adult/child COP$30,000/15,000; ⏲9am-4pm) Armenia's excellent 15-hectare botanical garden has the best mariposario in the Zona Cafetera. The 680-sq-meter butterfly house is shaped like a giant butterfly and houses up to 2000 of the insects. There's also a 22m-tall lookout tower, plus ferns, orchids, a *guadua* (bamboo) forest and an extensive collection of palms.

To get here, take the bus marked 'Mariposario' (COP$2000, 40 minutes) from Plaza de la Constitución in central Armenia or along Av Bolívar. A taxi will cost around COP$22,000.

Admission includes the services of a guide – reserve in advance for a tour in English. The best time to visit is in the morning when the butterflies are most active.

★**Museo del Oro Quimbaya** MUSEUM
(☎6-749-8169; www.banrepcultural.org/armenia/museo-del-oro-quimbaya; Av Bolívar 40N-80; ⏲9am-5pm Tue-Sun) FREE This excellent museum showcases the fine work of indigenous pre-Columbian Quimbaya goldsmiths, as well as fine ceramics and ceremonial items. There are thorough explanations in English about the culture of the Quimbaya. It's in the Centro Cultural, 5km northeast of Armenia's center. Grab bus 8 or 12 northbound on Av Bolívar.

Sleeping

Hotel Jardin Cafetero HOTEL $$
(☎6-735-8575; www.hoteljardincafetero.com; Calle 19 No 19-44; s/d/tr incl breakfast from COP$39,000/80,000/104,500;) Close to the heart of downtown, this hotel is good value. While the rooms don't have much character and are not particularly spacious, they are comfortable, contemporary, spotless and well equipped. Staff are happy to provide day-trip info.

Wanderlust Hostel HOSTEL $$
(☎314-588-0182, 6-735-8686; www.wanderlustarmenia.com; Carrera 14 No 1-24; dm COP$25,000-30,000, r COP$90,000;) A friendly hostel with top facilities and excellent service from English-speaking staff. Dorms are bright and comfortable with high-quality bedding, but the best features of the place are the attractive common areas, including a large courtyard out the back with hammocks and a modern lounge/work area. The private rooms at the front of the building are susceptible to street noise.

Armenia Hotel HOTEL $$$
(☎6-746-0099; www.armeniahotelsa.com; Av Bolívar No 8N-67; s/d/tr COP$188,000/231,000/293,000;) The best hotel in town, the Armenia has nine floors built around a vaulted interior atrium with a glass ceiling. The rooms are spacious, decked out with stylish *guadua* (bamboo) furniture, and many offer great views of the Cordillera Central or the city. There is a heated outdoor pool and a full-service restaurant downstairs.

DON'T MISS

DESFILE DE YIPAO

Charge your camera batteries – this is one photo op you don't want to miss. An important part of Armenia's annual birthday celebration, the **Yipao** (Oct) is a fantastic parade in which local working jeeps are loaded down with tonnes of plantain, coffee and household goods, and paraded through town – sometimes on two wheels.

Eating

El Solar COLOMBIAN $$

(6-749-3990; Km2 Via Circasia; mains COP$24,000-40,000; 7:30am-9pm Mon-Thu, to 11pm Fri & Sat, to 7pm Sun) Just a few hundred meters from the *zona rosa* is this restaurant with eclectic decor: kids' bikes, umbrellas and empty wine bottles dangle from the ceiling, and bamboo shoots creep in from the outside. The menu is equally ambitious, but you're better off sticking to the likes of *trucha al ajillo* (trout in garlic sauce) and other Colombian standards.

★**La Fogata** STEAK $$$

(6-749-5501; www.lafogata.com.co; Carrera 13 No 14N-47; mains COP$32,000-64,000; noon-midnight Mon-Sat, to 5pm Sun) This is one of Armenia's finest restaurants and with good reason. Its strengths lie in the carnivore-pleasing, American-style steaks, the melt-in-your-mouth *cordero patagonico* (Patagonia-style slow-cooked lamb), and the crispy beef intestines with guacamole. It also has a good selection of wines and a fantastic choice of locally grown coffee.

Drinking & Nightlife

★**Fonda La Floresta** BAR

(311-631-7731; www.fondalafloresta.com; Av Centenario No 29N-1762; 7pm-3am Fri & Sat) Set up like a traditional Antioquian village and with antiques hanging from the ceiling and party lights everywhere, this popular bar draws a mixed crowd of people, who come to sit around small tables and drink. Once suitably hammered, they then turn the entire place into one big dance floor. It's a 10-minute taxi ride from the center.

★**Cafe Quindio** COFFEE

(6-745-4478; www.cafequindio.com.co; Parque de la Vida, Av Bolívar 7; 11am-9:30pm Mon-Sat, noon-4:30pm Sun) No connoisseur of caffeine should miss a visit to this temple to the coffee bean, dotted with baby coffee plants and serving highland coffee from the surrounding region any way you can think of: Chemex, drip coffee, cold press, French press... The restaurant serves tasty regional dishes and you can buy bags of beans as souvenirs.

Information

4-72 (www.4-72.com.co; Carrera 15 No 22-38; 8am-6pm Mon-Fri, 9am-noon Sat) Post office in the center.

Banco AV Villas (cnr Carrera 14 & Calle 15N) ATM in the north of the city.

Banco de Bogotá (cnr Calle 21 & Carrera 14) ATM on Plaza de Bolívar in the center.

Punto de Información Turística (6-741-7700; Plaza de Bolívar; 9am-noon & 2-6pm Mon-Sat) Moderately helpful tourist office.

Getting There & Around

Aeropuerto Internacional El Edén (6-747-9400) is 15km southwest of Armenia and serves Bogotá, Medellín and Panama City. A taxi here costs around COP$30,000. Spirit (www.spirit.com) has direct flights on Tuesday and Friday to Fort Lauderdale, Florida.

The **bus terminal** (www.terminalarmenia.com; Calle 35 No 20-68) is 1.5km southwest of the center and can be reached by frequent city buses that run along Carrera 19 (COP$2000).

There are plenty of buses to Bogotá (COP$65,000, eight hours), Medellín (COP$47,000, six hours) and Cali (COP$30,000, 3½ hours). Regular minibuses run to Pereira (COP$5000 to COP$8000, one hour) and Manizales (COP$16,000 to COP$19,000, three hours).

During the day the downtown area is full of merchants and shoppers but after dark security is an issue. Taxis are a cheap and secure way to get to your destination. The minimum fare is COP$4500.

Around Armenia

Tiny Quindío department packs plenty into its modest boundaries with enchanting coffee farms, phenomenal vistas and fun theme parks that appeal to visitors of all ages.

Coffee-farm tourism began here, and there are hundreds of *fincas* (farms) catering to a variety of tastes, mostly Colombian. Numerous publications catalog and rate them. The Armenia tourist office (p220) has a lengthy list of options. Also check out **Haciendas del Café** (www.clubhaciendasdelcafe.com), which books accommodations on farms around Quindío.

Sights & Activities

Recuca PLANTATION

(☎310-830-3779; www.recuca.com; Vereda Callelarga, Calarcá; tours COP$21,000; ⏱9am-3pm) This tourism-oriented coffee farm offers tours that provide insight into life on a *finca*. Visitors can throw on traditional clothes and hit the plantation to pick their own beans before returning to the hacienda to learn about the coffee-making process. You can also learn some traditional dances. It's more than a little cheesy but is also good fun. It's best to reserve in advance if you want lunch (COP$17,000).

From Armenia, take any bus (COP$2100) from the terminal to Río Verde and ask to be let off at the entrance to the farm. From here it is a 2km walk through some plantain farms or ask the watchman to call for a jeep (COP$8000 per vehicle). A taxi from Armenia should cost around COP$30,000.

Caficultur TOURS

(Hane Coffee; ☎314-761-0199; www.hanecoffee.com; Finca La Alsacia, Buenavista; tours COP$30,000; ⏱8am-8pm) In the small town of Buenavista, Don Leo runs one of the most informative coffee tours in Quindío on his family farm just outside the urban area. He is an affable and enthusiastic host whose love for coffee is legendary. The tour runs for about three hours and includes a traditional breakfast or lunch depending on what time you arrive.

Call in advance to reserve your tour and Don Leo will meet you in the town plaza.

Sleeping

Finca Villa Nora FARMSTAY $$$

(☎311-389-1806, 310-422-6335; www.quindiofincavillanora.com; Vereda la Granja, Quimbaya; s/d incl breakfast & dinner COP$300,000/400,000;) Located between Armenia and Pereira, this coffee, avocado and guava farm offers comfortable accommodations in a beautiful old white-and-red-trimmed farmhouse that has a wide wraparound verandah. The owners run both the lodging and the farm, providing personalized attention to guests. It's a tranquil option that is full of character. Staff can arrange a private transfer from Armenia or Pereira airports.

A taxi from Quimbaya costs COP$6000.

Hacienda Combia FARMSTAY $$$

(☎310-250-9719, 314-682-5396; www.combia.com.co; s/d incl breakfast from COP$196,000/244,000; @) This hotel on a coffee farm near Jardín Botánico del Quindío (p219) has fantastic mountain views and top-notch facilities, including an infinity pool and spa. It doesn't have the intimacy of some smaller farms, but you won't find better comfort for the price and the coffee here is the real deal – it's been produced by the same family for four generations.

The rooms in the old farmhouse have more character than those in the new wing. There is a spacious open-air restaurant serving typical meals. Even if you don't plan on staying, Combia is worth a visit for the very informative, high-end coffee tour (guests/nonguests COP$93,000/115,000). A taxi here from Armenia costs around COP$35,000.

Getting There & Around

Quindío's bus network is comprehensive and you can get to most local attractions using public transportation from Armenia.

AN ICONIC RIDE: WILLYS JEEP

If you spend any time at all in the Zona Cafetera, it is highly probable that you will take at least a couple of rides in a classic WWII Willys jeep.

These veterans don't just look great parked in formation around the town plaza – they are still the main form of transportation in rural parts of the Zona Cafetera. Willys are used to transport everything from passengers to pigs, *platano* (plantain), furniture and, of course, coffee. And, unlike buses, a Willys jeep is never really full – don't be surprised if your driver packs in 16 passengers or more.

The first jeeps to arrive were army surplus models sent from the US in 1950. In order to sell the vehicles to farmers in the Zona Cafetera, a kind of traveling jeep show was created: expert drivers maneuvered the vehicles up and down the stairs in front of the town churches and moved loads through obstacle courses in the plazas. The locals were sold instantly – and so began a love affair that lasts to this day.

Willys jeeps are such an integral part of rural Colombian culture that a *yipao* – which means a jeep-full – is a legitimate measure of agricultural products in Colombia (it's about 20 to 25 sacks of oranges).

Salento

☎6 / POP 7250 / ELEV 1895M

Set amid gorgeous green mountains 24km northeast of Armenia, this small town survives on coffee production, trout farming and tourists, the last drawn by its quaint streets, typical *paisa* architecture and its proximity to the spectacular Valle de Cocora. It was founded in 1850, and is one of the oldest towns in Quindío.

The main drag is Calle Real (Carrera 6), which is full of *artesanías* (local craft stalls) and restaurants. At the end of the street are stairs leading up to Alto de la Cruz, a hill topped with a cross. From here you'll see the verdant Valle de Cocora and the mountains that surround it. If the skies are clear (usually only early in the morning), you can spot the snowcapped tops of the volcanoes on the horizon.

Activities

★Mountain Bike Salento Colombia MOUNTAIN BIKING

(☎311-333-5936, 316-535-1792; www.salentocycling.com; Calle 7 No 1-04, Plantation House; rides COP$130,000-250,000) Offers excellent full-day mountain-biking adventures that take you up to the Andean divide, from where you'll cruise down the far side to the biggest wax palm forest in the region, before being brought back up to the peak in a truck for the ride all the way back down the mountain to Salento. Includes a picnic lunch with amazing views.

For experienced riders there's also a high-adrenaline single-track route back to town via the Valle de Cocora. The affable manager is straight out of a late-'90s stoner comedy, but is serious when it comes to organization and safety.

Kasaguadua Natural Reserve HIKING

(☎320-425-8075; www.kasaguaduanaturalreserve.org; Via Vereda Palestina; tours COP$25,000) About a 30-minute walk from Salento, this private nature reserve protects 14 hectares of tropical Andean cloud forest. The enthusiastic owners lead informative guided hikes along several trails – participants are asked to book a day in advance. Accommodations in innovative, elevated bamboo-and-recycled-plastic eco-pods (COP$70,000) surrounded by forest are available if you want to spend the night out among nature.

A private jeep out here costs around COP$15,000.

Los Amigos SPORTS

(Carrera 4 No 3-32; ⏲3-11pm) If you are in the mood to drink beer and throw discs at gunpowder, do as the locals do and head to this atmospheric club for *tejo* (a type of sport that involves throwing metal discs into holes in a wooden target box). Wear your best mustache!

Tours

★Finca El Ocaso TOURS

(☎310-451-7329, 310-451-7194; www.fincaelocasosalento.com; Km3.8 Vereda Palestina; tours COP$15,000-65,000) The most polished coffee tour around Salento is set on an expansive farm with fine coffee bushes and a pretty farmhouse. You'll visit the plantation and then follow the process of preparing the beans for market. Tours run for 90 minutes and are offered hourly from 9am to 4pm. To get here, catch an hourly jeep from the plaza (COP$3000).

All tours are in English except those in Spanish (10am and 3pm). If you're really into coffee, you might want to check out the extended three-hour tour (COP$65,000).

Sleeping

Hostal Tralala HOSTEL $

(☎314-850-5543; www.hosteltralalasalento.com; Carrera 7 No 6-45; dm COP$25,000-30,000, r COP$65,000-80,000, without bathroom COP$60,000, apt COP$110,000; 📶) In a brightly renovated colonial house, this small, well-run hostel was clearly created by someone who knows exactly what travelers want. Facilities include comfortable mattresses, piping-hot showers, two kitchens, an extensive DVD library, fast wi-fi and even rubber-boot rental for muddy treks. It's welcoming, spotlessly clean and well organized.

★Coffee Tree Hostel HOSTEL $$

(☎318-390-4415; www.coffeetreebh.com; Carrera 9 No 9-06; dm/r from COP$38,000/230,000; 📶) Coffee Tree well and truly earns its 'boutique hostel' label, with three floors of spacious, well-decorated rooms offering great mountain views alongside a bright social area with high ceilings. Staff are friendly and speak great English and the extensive breakfast spread provides fuel for outdoor adventures.

Hotel Salento Plaza HOTEL $$$

(☎6-759-3066; Carrera 7 No 6-27; r/f from COP$189,000/420,000; 📶) Just half a block from Salento's plaza, this traditional-style small hotel overlooking a manicured garden is an absolute treat. Hardwood floors, king

Salento

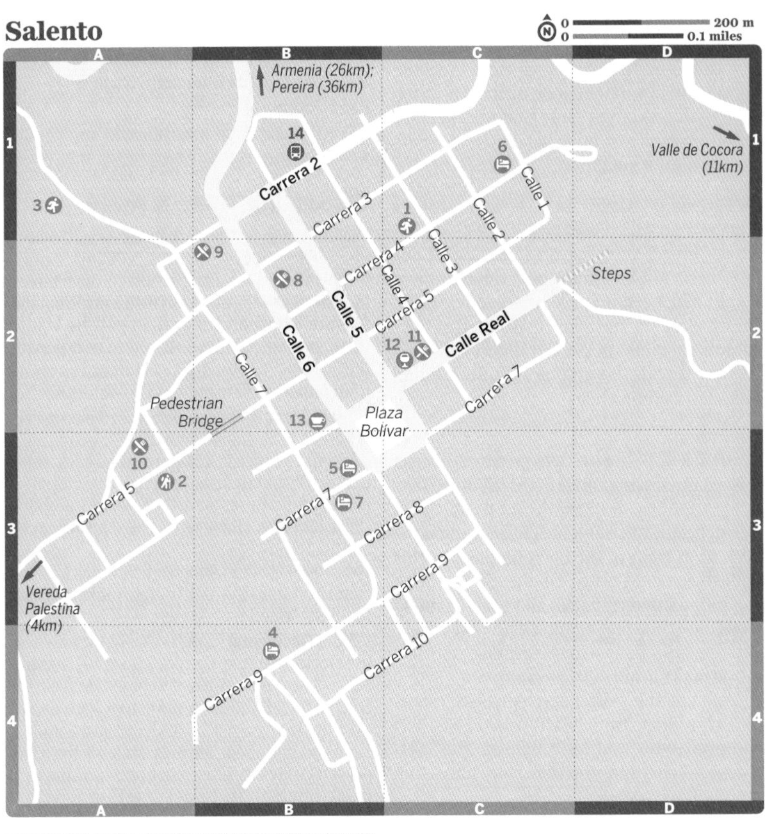

Salento

Activities, Courses & Tours

1 Los Amigos C1
2 Paramo Trek A3
3 Salento Cycling A1

Sleeping

4 Coffee Tree Hostel B4
5 Hotel Salento Plaza B3
6 Las Terrazas de Salento C1
7 Tralala B3

Eating

8 Brunch B2
9 La Eliana B2
10 Luciernaga A3
11 Rincón del Lucy C2

Drinking & Nightlife

12 Billar Danubio Hall C2
13 Café Jesús Martín B2

Transport

Flota Occidental .... (see 14)
14 Salento Transport Office B1

beds and inviting bathrooms make it an excellent deal, but it's the warmth and helpfulness of the owners that raises the hospitality that extra notch.

Las Terrazas de Salento BOUTIQUE HOTEL $$$
(☎317-430-4637; www.facebook.com/HotelTerrazasdeSalento; Carrera 4 No 1-30; s/d from COP$98,000/187,000) Perched high on a hilltop overlooking Salento, this fantastic hotel has elegant rooms with polished wood floors and private balconies. It feels far removed from the bustle of town but is just a short walk down the hill into the heart of the action. The owner is super-helpful, the breakfast is varied and there's a garden chill-out terrace for guests.

Eating & Drinking

Brunch AMERICAN $
(☎311-757-8082; www.facebook.com/brunchdesalento; Calle 6 No 3-25; mains COP$10,500-22,500; ⏲6:30am-9pm) Get your gringo on

at this hugely popular little diner serving big portions of American classics to homesick travelers. Take your pick from excellent burgers, wings, burritos or nachos, and top it off with one of the diner's famous peanut-butter brownies or milkshakes. Great for refueling after a long hike.

★Rincón del Lucy COLOMBIAN **$**
(Carrera 6 No 4-02; breakfast COP$7000, lunch & dinner COP$9000; ⏲7am-8pm) We love Lucy for her gut-busting, best-value-in-town meals: fish, beef or chicken served with rice, beans, plantain and soup, consumed at busy communal tables next to strangers who may become friends. It's a great spot for a filling breakfast before a hike.

Luciernaga BISTRO **$$**
(☎311-438-4281; www.luciernaga.com.co; Carrera 3 No 9-19; mains COP$18,000-32,000; ⏲7am-11:30pm Sun-Thu, to 1:30am Fri & Sat; ☎) Tuck into delicious international cuisine out on the deck or in front of the open fireplace at this fantastic modern bistro. On the diverse menu you'll find burgers, wings and other comfort foods alongside filet mignon with blue cheese and vegan options. Great cocktails and live music make it worth sticking around.

Upstairs the hostel has smallish rooms (dorms/rooms from COP$28,000/80,000) equipped with first-class pillows and mattresses. Those on the far side have fine mountain views.

Casa La Eliana INTERNATIONAL **$$**
(☎321-796-1782; www.facebook.com/CasaLaEliana; Carrera 2 No 6-65; mains COP$15,000-22,000; ⏲noon-9pm; ☎) Prepares gourmet pizzas, pasta and, if you're in the mood for culinary Russian roulette, hit-and-miss Indian curries, all served on a deck overlooking the garden. The portions are generous and prices are very reasonable. There are also a couple of good-value rooms for rent out the back.

Billar Danubio Hall BAR
(Carrera 6 No 4-30; ⏲8am-midnight Mon-Fri, to 2am Sat & Sun) This is every Latin small-town fantasy rolled into one. Old men in ponchos and cowboy hats sip aguardiente (anise-flavored liquor) as they play dominoes, with vallenato tunes playing in the background and younger locals shooting pool. The clientele breaks into ragged harmony whenever an anthem of heartbreaking personal relevance is played. Come here for a strong coffee or a rum.

Information

There are a couple of ATMs on the plaza.

Banco Agrario de Colombia (Carrera 7)

Bancolombia (Carrera 6)

Pretty much all the accommodations offer free wi-fi access.

Getting There & Away

Minibuses run to/from Armenia every 20 minutes (COP$4500, 45 minutes, 5:20am to 8pm). Armenia buses run along a route through the town and pass the plaza before leaving from the **Salento Transport Office** (Carrera 2 No 4-30) (though on weekends you'll have to go direct to the bus office). You can also take a taxi direct from Armenia (30 minutes, COP$85,000).

There is a direct bus service from the terminal in Pereira to Salento (COP$6500, 1½ hours) at 6:50am, 1:30pm and 4:30pm on weekdays, and 6:50am, 7:30am and then hourly until 5:30pm on weekends. Buses leave the Salento Transport Office for Pereira three times daily on weekdays and hourly on weekends. Coming from Pereira, you can also take an Armenia-bound bus to Las Flores and cross the road to grab a Salento-bound bus from Armenia.

Flota Occidental (☎310-449-4444; www.flotaoccidental.com; Carrera 2 No 4-40) runs four express vans per day direct between Medellín and Salento (COP$47,000, seven hours). Vans depart from the Terminal del Sur in Medelllín at 9am, 11am and 1pm. From Salento vans leave the transport office at 8am, 10am, noon and 4pm. Buy tickets in advance to be sure of getting a spot.

Filandia

☎6 / POP 13,520

A short distance from Salento, slow-paced Filandia is a traditional coffee town that is every bit as charming as its popular neighbor, but gets a fraction of the visitors. It has some of the best-preserved architecture in the region, a panoramic lookout, fine handicrafts and lush nature reserves full of wildlife.

Sights

Colina Iluminada VIEWPOINT
(Km 1 Via Quimbaya; COP$8000; ⏲9am-6pm Mon-Fri, to 9pm Sat & Sun) On a hill just outside town, this impressive 19m-tall wooden structure offers breathtaking views over three departments and, on a clear day, Parque Nacional Natural Los Nevados.

Centro de Interpretación de la Cestería de Bejucos MUSEUM

(☎310-380-8247; cesteriacafetera@hotmail.com; cnr Carrera 5 & Calle 6, Casa del Artesano; ⏰9am-6pm) FREE Filandia is famous for its woven baskets, an art that can be traced back to those once used by coffee pickers to collect the harvest, and this museum run by a cooperative of local artisans provides an in-depth look at the traditions of the craft. You'll learn about the raw materials as well as the weaving process, and there are some high-quality finished products for sale.

If you want to try your hand, weaving workshops (from COP$20,000) can be arranged with advance notice.

Tours

Turaco TOURS

(☎315-328-0558; turaco@hotmail.es; Calle 7 No 4-51; ⏰9am-noon & 2-5pm, closed Tue) An enthusiastic local tour operator that runs guided treks into Cañon del Río Barbas and Reserva Natural Bremen – La Popa, as well as trips to waterfalls and local coffee farms. Expect to pay around COP$100,000 for a group of up to five hikers. Add COP$20,000 for transportation in a jeep to the reserves.

Sleeping & Eating

Hostal Colina de Lluvia HOSTEL $

(☎321-715-6245; aguadelluvia@outlook.com; Calle 5 No 4-08; dm COP$25,000, s COP$40,000-60,000, d COP$60,000-80,000; 📶) This well-decorated small hostel a couple of blocks from the park has bright rooms with polished wooden floors and a nice courtyard social area. All prices include breakfast.

La Posada del Compadre GUESTHOUSE $$

(☎316-629-2804; info@laposadadelcompadre.com; Carrera 6 No 8-06; r/ste incl breakfast COP$90,000/180,000; 📶) Set in a lovingly restored colonial mansion surrounding an elegant internal garden, this tranquil hotel offers real value. The views from the back porch over the surrounding mountains are spectacular. For couples it's worth splashing out on the spacious suite on the 2nd floor, which has amazing panoramas right from the bed.

★ **Helena Adentro** COLOMBIAN $$

(Carrera 7 No 8-01; mains COP$23,000-34,000; ⏰noon-10pm Sun-Thu, to 11pm Fri & Sat) Run by a talented young local chef and his Kiwi partner, this hip restaurant serves up some of the best food in the Zona Cafetera, with innovative takes on traditional Colombian cuisine made with fresh ingredients from local farms. The menu is constantly changing but it's all delicious and very reasonable considering the quality.

Getting There & Away

Buses run to/from Armenia (COP$5400, 45 minutes) every 20 minutes until 8pm. There is also a direct service to Pereira (COP$6300, one hour) every hour until 7pm. Coming from Salento, you can pick up a bus at Las Flores where the Salento road joins the main highway.

Valle de Cocora

In a country full of beautiful landscapes, Cocora is one of the most striking. It stretches east of Salento into the lower reaches of PNN Los Nevados, with a broad green valley framed by sharp peaks. Everywhere you'll see the palma de cera (wax palm), the largest palm in the world (up to 60m tall): it's Colombia's national tree. Set amid the misty green hills, they are breathtaking to behold, and the valley is protected as part of Unesco's Coffee Cultural Landscape of Colombia Heritage Site.

The highlight of a trip here is hiking the **Valle de Cocora Loop** that takes in the spectacular valley of wax palms.

It's also possible to rent horses in Cocora for a guided ride through the **Reserva Natural Acaime** (☎321-636-2818; incl refreshment COP$5000) (around COP$25,000 per hour), up to Acaime and its hummingbirds.

Sleeping

★ **Reserva El Cairo** BOUTIQUE HOTEL $$$

(☎321-649-3439; www.reservaelcairo.com; Km 3, Via Cocora, Vereda La Playa; r/f from COP$222,000/400,000) Coffee-country accommodations don't get much better than this. The elegant and comfortable rooms here are set in a charming traditional farmhouse in lush gardens, and the surrounding nature reserve contains some of the last tracts of primary forest in the valley. It's great for both birdwatching and more adventurous pursuits, such as paragliding. It's 3km from Salento, towards Valle Cocora.

Getting There & Away

Willys jeeps leave Salento's main square for Cocora (COP$3800, 30 minutes) at 6:10am, 7:30am, 9:30am, 11:30am, 2pm and 4pm, coming back an hour later. There are sometimes additional services on weekends. You can also contract a jeep privately for COP$35,000.

AT A GLANCE

POPULATION
2.2 million

ELEVATION
1018m

BEST INDIGENOUS ARTIFACTS
Museo Etnográfico (p250)

BEST SALSA DANCING
Alto de San Andrés (p249)

BEST VOLCANO VIEWING
Popayán Tours (p239)

WHEN TO GO

Aug
Afro-Colombian rhythms take over Cali during the Festival Petronio Álvarez.

Jul–Sep
Thermal winds pack an extra punch for the best kitesurfing on Lago Calima.

Dec & Jan
Clear skies make for pleasant hiking in Parque Nacional Natural (PNN) Puracé.

Desierto de la Tatacoa (p251)
DALEJANDRRO/GETTY IMAGES

Cali & Southwest Colombia

Out of the way and with a reputation for security problems, southwest Colombia is often overlooked by travelers, but this fascinating region warrants an appearance on all itineraries. It's an authentic land of contrasts: Andean and African, modern and pre-Columbian.

Security has improved markedly and destinations that were once off-limits are being put back on the map by adventurous trailblazers. Here you will find the best archaeological sites in the country and some of its finest colonial architecture. It's a region of immense biodiversity where you can pass through desert, jungle and *páramo* (high-mountain plain) ecosystems in just one day. Nature lovers will find active volcanoes, thermal springs and spectacular mountain ranges all easily accessible from thriving metropolitan centers famed for their vibrant culture.

INCLUDES

Cali 229
Lago Calima 236
Popayán 238
Coconuco 243
San Agustín 243
Tierradentro 248
Desierto de la Tatacoa 251
Pasto 252
Laguna de la Cocha ... 255
Ipiales 256
Santuario de Las Lajas 257

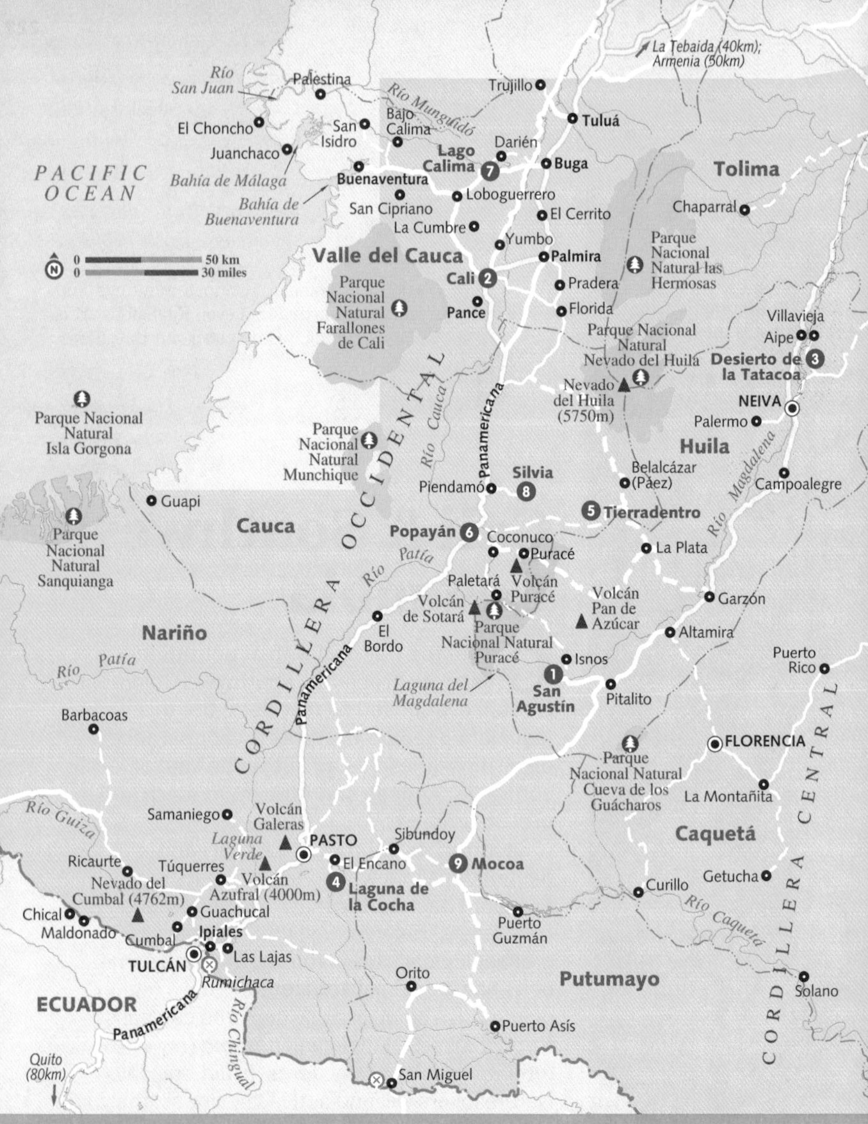

Cali & Southwest Colombia Highlights

1. **San Agustín** (p244) Gawking at giant pre-Columbian sculptures in phenomenal natural settings.

2. **Cali** (p229) Learning to swivel your hips and boogie in sweaty salsa joints.

3. **Desierto de la Tatacoa** (p251) Spending the night stargazing among the cacti in Colombia's tiniest desert.

4. **Laguna de la Cocha** (p255) Taking a boat ride to cloud-forest-clad Isla Corota.

5. **Tierradentro** (p248) Hiking the spectacular hills to visit ancient underground tombs.

6. **Popayán** (p238) Wandering along elegant streets and checking out imposing colonial mansions.

7. **Lago Calima** (p236) Picking up thermal winds rolling off the cloud-covered mountains while kitesurfing.

8. **Silvia** (p242) Getting up close to the indigenous Guambiano culture at the colorful market.

9. **Mocoa** (p247) Splashing through crystalline swimming holes flanked by rainforest.

CALI

2 / POP 2.4 MILLION / ELEV 969M

Cali is a hot, gritty city with a real zest for life that draws you in and stays with you long after you leave town. Beyond a handful of churches and museums, Cali is light on sights – but the city's main attraction is its beguiling, electrifying atmosphere. If you make the effort you will find great nightlife, good restaurants and plenty to do, especially in the evening, when a cool mountain breeze dissipates the heat of the day.

Cali is rich in Afro-Colombian heritage; nowhere is the nation's racial diversity and harmony more apparent. From the impoverished barrios to the big, slick clubs, everyone is moving to one beat, and that beat is salsa. Music in the world's salsa capital is more than entertainment: it is a unifying factor that ties the city together.

Sights

For a city of its size, Cali has very few top attractions but it compensates with atmosphere. *Caleños* are proud of their vibrant culture and have a rebellious attitude, reflected in the city's catchphrase: *'Cali es Cali y lo demás es loma, ¿oís?'* (Cali is Cali, and the rest [of Colombia] is just mountain, ya hear?).

Cerro de las Tres Cruces VIEWPOINT
(Av 10 Norte) The views are spectacular at these three crosses high in the mountains overlooking the city, and the hike up here is a popular outdoor activity among health-conscious *caleños* (residents of Cali). It's best to come early on weekends when there's a crowd and don't bring any valuables – the area is isolated and robberies are not uncommon.

Museo de Arte Moderno La Tertulia GALLERY
(2-893-2939; www.museolatertulia.com; Av Colombia No 5 Oeste-105; adult/student COP$10,000/7000; 10am-7pm Tue-Sat, 2-6pm Sun) Presents changing exhibitions of contemporary painting, sculpture and photography from both local and South American artists. Look out for works by contemporary Colombian artists such as Hugo Zapata and Beatriz Gonzáles. It's Cali's most important cultural space too, with regular art-house film screenings, poetry readings and music performances.

Iglesia de la Ermita CHURCH
(cnr Av Colombia & Calle 13; hours vary) Overlooking the Río Cali, this striking neo-Gothic church houses the 18th-century painting of *El señor de la caña* (Lord of the Sugarcane) that survived major earthquakes. Many miracles (including its own survival) are attributed to the image.

Museo de Arte Religoso La Merced MUSEUM
(2-888-0646; Carrera 4 No 6-60; adult/child COP$4000/2000; 9am-noon & 2-5pm Mon-Fri) Housed in La Merced convent, Cali's oldest building, this museum has an extensive collection of colonial religious paintings and relics. It's worth a visit even if religious art is not your thing, just to check out the charming 16th-century structure and its three internal courtyards. If you go on weekday mornings you can watch the nuns making *hostia* (Communion bread).

Cristo Rey MONUMENT
(Via a Cristo Rey) Resembling a scaled-down version of Rio's famous monument, this towering Christ statue atop Cerro las Cristales affords panoramic views of Cali. At the top you'll find a bunch of stands selling juices, snacks and ice creams. A round-trip taxi up here should cost around COP$50,000. Walking to the monument is not recommended as security along the remote road can be an issue.

Museo Arqueológico la Merced MUSEUM
(2-885-4665; Carrera 4 No 6-59; adult/child COP$4000/2000; 9am-6pm Mon-Sat, 10am-4pm Sun) Housed in an 18th-century annex to La Merced, this interesting museum contains a collection of pre-Columbian pottery by cultures such as the Tierradentro, Tolima and San Agustín. Among the highlights are figurines from the Tumaco culture and intricately painted Quimbaya vessels.

Activities

★**Sabor Manicero** DANCING
(315-289-4040; https://salsa-classes-in.cali-colombia.co; Calle 5 No 39-71, 3er Piso; salsa classes 4:30-6:30pm & 7-9pm Mon-Fri, 2-4pm Sat) One of Colombia's largest dance schools, offering cheap group salsa classes for all ability levels. You can also learn to shake your hips to the rhythms of bachata and merengue here.

Pacific Diving Company DIVING
(2-554-2619; www.pacificdivingcompany.co; Calle 4a No 36-41) Diving trips to Isla Gorgona, Isla Malpelo and parts of the Choco. The boat, *Sea Wolf*, sails from Buenaventura.

Eco Aventura Turismo Ecologico ADVENTURE SPORTS
(304-571-5693; www.facebook.com/ecoaventura.calicolombia; Carrera 12 No 1-31 Oeste)

Cali

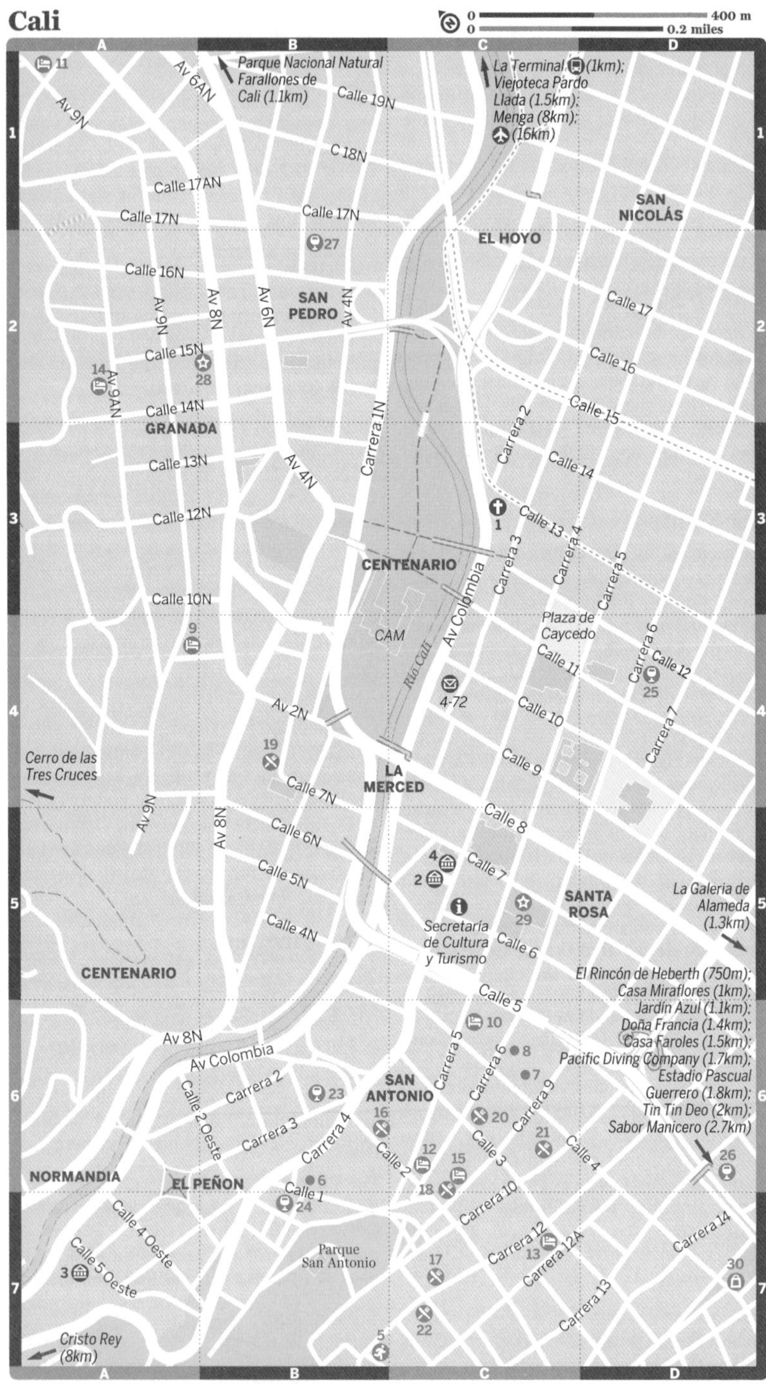
0 400 m
0 0.2 miles
Parque Nacional Natural Farallones de Cali (1.1km)
La Terminal (1km); Viejoteca Pardo Llada (1.5km); Menga (8km); (16km)
Av 6AN
Av 9N
Calle 19N
C 18N
Calle 17AN
Calle 17N
Calle 16N
Calle 15N
Calle 14N
Calle 13N
Calle 12N
Calle 10N
Calle 7N
Calle 6N
Calle 5N
Calle 4N
Av 9N
Av 8N
Av 6N
Av 4N
Av 9AN
Av 2N
Av 8N
Carrera 1N
SAN PEDRO
GRANADA
EL HOYO
SAN NICOLÁS
CENTENARIO
CAM
Río Cali
Av Colombia
LA MERCED
Plaza de Caycedo
Calle 17
Calle 16
Calle 15
Calle 14
Calle 13
Calle 12
Calle 11
Calle 10
Calle 9
Calle 8
Calle 7
Calle 6
Calle 5
Calle 4
Calle 3
Calle 2
Calle 1
Carrera 2
Carrera 3
Carrera 4
Carrera 5
Carrera 6
Carrera 7
Carrera 9
Carrera 10
Carrera 12
Carrera 12A
Carrera 13
Carrera 14
4-72
Cerro de las Tres Cruces
Secretaría de Cultura y Turismo
SANTA ROSA
La Galeria de Alameda (1.3km)
El Rincón de Heberth (750m); Casa Miraflores (1km); Jardín Azul (1.1km); Doña Francia (1.4km); Casa Faroles (1.5km); Pacific Diving Company (1.7km); Estadio Pascual Guerrero (1.8km); Tin Tin Deo (2km); Sabor Manicero (2.7km)
CENTENARIO
Av Colombia
Calle 2 Oeste
SAN ANTONIO
NORMANDIA
EL PEÑON
Calle 4 Oeste
Calle 5 Oeste
Parque San Antonio
Cristo Rey (8km)
A
B
C
D
1
2
3
4
5
6
7
1
2
3
4
5
6
7
8
9
10
11
12
13
14
15
16
17
18
19
20
21
22
23
24
25
26
27
28
29
30

Cali

Sights

1 Iglesia de la Ermita ... C3
2 Museo Arqueológico la Merced ... C5
3 Museo de Arte Moderno La Tertulia ... A7
4 Museo de Arte Religoso La Merced ... C5

Activities, Courses & Tours

5 Ecoaventura ... B7
6 Lingua Viva ... B6
7 Salsa Pura ... C6
8 Valley Adventours ... C6

Sleeping

9 Casa de Alférez ... A4
10 El Viajero ... C6
11 Guest House Iguana ... A1
12 La Casa Café ... C6
13 La Maison Violette ... C7
14 La Sucursal Hostel ... A2
15 Ruta Sur ... C6

Eating

16 El Buen Alimento ... B6
17 El Zaguán de San Antonio ... C7
18 Pargo Rojo ... C6
19 Platillos Voladores ... B4
20 Trilogia ... C6
21 Zahavi ... C6
22 Zea Maiz ... C7

Drinking & Nightlife

23 El Faro ... B6
24 La Colina ... B7
25 Pérgola Clandestina ... D4
26 Topa Tolondra ... D6
27 Zaperoco ... B2

Entertainment

Cinemateca La Tertulia ... (see 3)
28 Lugar a Dudas ... B2
29 Teatro Municipal ... C5

Shopping

30 Parque Artesanías ... D7

A nonprofit outfit that organizes interesting ecological-themed activities around Cali, including night hikes and abseiling trips.

Valley Adventours WALKING
(☎301-754-9188; www.valleyadventours.com; Carrera 6 No 4-26; tours COP$60,000-170,000) Offers city tours both on foot and with transportation in addition to organized visits to San Cipriano and Lago Calima. Other alternatives include hikes to Pico de Loro in PNN Farallones de Cali (p236) and horseback-riding trips in the countryside.

Hiking

No trip to Cali is complete without visiting Cerro de las Tres Cruces (p229), three crosses that tower over the city. The views here are spectacular. It's a hefty two- to three-hour walk (round trip) from Granada heading northwest – bring plenty of water. Security is an issue on the trail – especially on weekdays when it's more or less empty – so travel in a group and don't take any valuables. There are several trailheads; the easiest one to find is near Av 10 Oeste at Calle 12N.

Marker Km18 lies 18km west of the city. There are numerous bars and restaurants here. At 1800m it's pleasantly cool, and the nearby cloud forest is an Important Bird Area (IBA) with high biodiversity. The walk from here to the small town of Dapa (four hours) – off the Cali–Yumbo road – is a pleasant stroll. There are numerous crossroads – always take the left-hand fork.

There are regular bus services to Km18 from the bus terminal (COP$2500, 45 minutes). Buses and jeeps service Dapa every half hour (COP$4000, 30 minutes) from Sameco in the north of Cali.

Courses

Lingua Viva LANGUAGE
(☎323-587-1623, 316-442-8158; www.eslinguaviva.com; Calle 1 No 4B-46; private tuition per hour from COP$45,000) A Spanish school in San Antonio offering group classes and private tuition for foreign visitors. Teaching staff are experienced and enthusiastic.

Salsa Pura DANCING
(☎310-493-9660; www.facebook.com/salsapurabailesinfronteras; Calle 4 No 6-61; ⏲9am-8pm Mon-Fri, 10am-6pm Sat) This salsa school in the heart of San Antonio has experienced and enthusiastic instructors offering private and group classes for dancers of all levels. They're very responsive to inquiries, making them popular with travelers.

Festivals & Events

Festival Petronio Álvarez MUSIC
(https://petronio.cali.gov.co; Calle 9C, Canchas Panamericanas; ⏲Aug) A festival of Pacific music, heavily influenced by the African rhythms brought by the many slaves that originally populated the Pacific coast. *Caleños* turn up en masse for nonstop dancing, competitive

outdoor gigs and copious amounts of *arrechón* (a sweet artisanal alcohol).

Festival Mundial de Salsa DANCE
(www.mundialdesalsa.com; Sep) Amazing dancers of all ages from Cali and around the world take to the stage in colorful costumes during this hugely competitive salsa event. Finals take place in the Plaza de Toros.

Sleeping

For a taste of Cali's colonial origins and a plentitude of hostels, lay your head in laid-back San Antonio; nearby residential area Miraflores is calmer but still within walking distance of the action. If you're after high-end accommodations and nightlife head for Granada.

La Maison Violette HOSTEL $$
(2-371-9837; www.maisonviolettehostel.com; Carrera 12A No 2A-117; dm/s/d/f COP$30,000/70,000/80,000/150,000;) This colorful hostel on the edge of San Antonio has tastefully decorated rooms, spacious suites and a rooftop terrace with panoramic views of the city. It's in a great location, but the owner is not in the running for the 'Mr Congeniality' prize.

La Casa Café HOSTEL $
(2-893-7011; www.lacasacafecali.blogspot.com; Carrera 6 No 2-13; dm COP$25,000, s/d COP$50,000/80,000, without bathroom COP$40,000/60,000;) For an old-school, no-frills backpacking experience head to this cafe-bar, which rents good-value dorm beds and private rooms on the 2nd floor of its colonial building. Major bonus points for lovely owner Paola, who does a great job of looking after her guests. The cafe serves real coffee from small local farms around Valle de Cauca.

★ **Jardín Azul** BOUTIQUE HOTEL $$
(2-556-8380; www.jardinazul.com; Carrera 24A No 2A-59; r/tr from COP$96,000/150,000;) In a converted house on a hill near the colonial sector east of the center, this spotless small hotel has spacious, bright rooms with big beds and imported cotton sheets. Some rooms have private balconies and views of the city. Breakfast is served around a small pool set in an appealing garden.

Casa Faroles HOTEL $$
(2-376-5381; www.facebook.com/HotelFaroles; Carrera 24B No 2-48 Oeste; r COP$86,000-105,000;) You'll receive a warm welcome at this excellent-value little hotel run by an affable ex-NYC cop and his *caleña* wife. Rooms are spacious, spotless and well equipped and there's a fine terrace with sweeping views. Set on a hill in a quiet part of town, it's still within walking distance of San Antonio and Parque del Perro.

Ruta Sur HOSTEL $$
(2-893-6946; www.hostalrutasur.com; Carrera 9 No 2-41; s/d/tw/tr COP$88,000/118,000/130,000/150,000;) This homey, welcoming hostel in a converted colonial house in the heart of San Antonio is popular with travelers looking for a quiet base in a central location. Rooms are comfortable, tastefully decorated and arranged around several courtyards aflit with hummingbirds.

★ **La Sucursal Hostel** HOSTEL $$
(301-576-2474; www.facebook.com/lasucursalhostel; Av 9AN No 14-61; dm COP$23,000-25,000, s/d COP$80,000/160,000) Very sociable without being a party place, this large, colorful hostel is run by the awesome José, who goes above and beyond the call of duty for his guests. Expect free salsa lessons, a great open-air bar area with hammocks and lounges, lots of local tips and a variety of tidy, brightly painted rooms spread over several floors.

Some rooms don't have much natural light, so ask to see a few. The top-floor terrace is a good spot for enjoying the evening breeze with a view.

Casa Miraflores HOSTEL $$
(2-377-8177; www.casamirafrorescali.com; Carrera 24B No 2a-136; dm COP$25,000-32,000, r COP$95,000) On a quiet residential street a 15-minute walk from San Antonio, this supremely laid-back hostel has bright, comfortable rooms and fine common areas. Its peaceful atmosphere makes it a good base for working travelers.

El Viajero HOSTEL $$
(2-893-8342; www.facebook.com/ElViajeroHostelCali; Carrera 5 No 4-56; dm COP$33,000-34,500, s/d from COP$93,000/115,000, without bathroom from COP$68,000/96,000;) In a renovated colonial house, El Viajero is a popular choice among young travelers looking to hang out on the fairy-light-strung poolside patio or to take advantage of the free salsa classes and group outings. The private rooms are spacious, and bunks come with individual sockets and small fans, but the cleanliness of common facilities could be improved.

Prices are higher at weekends.

Casa de Alférez HOTEL $$$
(2-393-3030; www.movichhotels.com; Av 9N No 9-24; r COP$249,000-295,000;) This

ultraluxurious hotel offers elegant rooms with king-sized beds, spacious bathrooms and French windows that open onto small balconies on a lovely, tree-lined street. There are two restaurants on-site.

Eating

Zea Maiz COLOMBIAN $

(Arepas Cuadradas; 311-846-2774; Carrera 12 No 1-21 Oeste; arepas COP$2000-9000; 5:30-10:30pm Tue-Sun;) Is it just us, or do *arepas* (corn cakes) taste better when they come in a square shape? This colorful basement restaurant in San Antonio stuffs them with all kinds of goodness and serves them with four homemade sauces, the *mango picante* being particularly satisfying. Ardent anti-*arepa* crusaders have been known to change their tune after eating here.

La Galeria de Alameda MARKET $

(cnr Calle 8 & Carrera 26; meals from COP$7000; 7am-3pm) This working-class food market serves cheap, classic Colombian meals at a number of small stalls, including plenty of seafood dishes prepared in front of you. The streets surrounding the market are full of good-value seafood restaurants where you can fill your boots for a pittance.

Pargo Rojo SEAFOOD $$

(2-893-6949; www.facebook.com/elpargorojocali; Carrera 9 No 2-09; set meal COP$13,000, mains from COP$20,000; noon-3:30pm Mon-Sat, plus 5-10pm Fri & Sat) Excellent typical seafood dishes, such as a lightly grilled tilapia with crisp *patacones* (fried plantains) and a dollop of punchy, spicy salsa, are prepared at this simple corner restaurant with just six tables. Set lunches come with a tasty fish soup and a big jug of lemonade.

El Buen Alimento VEGETARIAN $$

(2-375-5738; www.facebook.com/elbuenalimentovegetariano; Calle 2 No 4-53; set meal COP$12,000, mains COP$15,000-25,000; 8am-5pm Sun & Mon, to 10pm Tue-Sat;) A busy vegetarian restaurant serving hearty meat-free versions of Colombian classics, as well as ambitious fusion dishes such as Mexican lasagna, which is interesting rather than lovely. While the falafel wraps and the like are prepared with more enthusiasm than culinary skill, the fresh juices are great and come in glasses the size of soup tureens. It's all good value.

Doña Francia ICE CREAM $

(www.facebook.com/DonaFranciaCali; Carrera 27 No 3-100; snacks COP$2200-5000; 8am-7pm Mon-Sat, 10am-7pm Sun) Sit on benches outside this Cali institution and enjoy sensational juices, sorbets that are the sweet, tangy, edible equivalent of crystal meth, and some of the best *salpicón* (fruit salad) in all of Colombia. It's one block east of Parque del Perro.

Zahavi BAKERY $

(2-893-8797; www.zahavigourmet.com; Carrera 10 No 3-81; breakfast COP$7400-13,000, sandwiches COP$10,500-23,000; 8am-7:30pm Mon-Sat, to 6pm Sun;) This posh bakery in San Antonio serves good coffee, rich gooey brownies and delicious gourmet sandwiches. It's also popular with ladies (and gentlemen) that brunch.

El Zaguán de San Antonio COLOMBIAN $$

(Carrera 12 No 1-29; mains COP$20,000-30,000; noon-11:30pm) This family-run San Antonio institution serves traditional *vallecaucana* food, with portions large enough to get you through a siege, and excellent (though pricey) fresh juices. Much of the food is fried and underwhelming, but the moreish empanadas really shine. The real reason to come here is for the amazing view from the rooftop – a great place for a drink.

★ **Platillos Voladores** FUSION $$$

(2-668-7750; www.platillosvoladores.com.co; Av 3N No 7-19; mains COP$30,000-55,000; noon-3pm & 7-11pm Mon-Fri, 1-4pm Sat;) Cali's best fine-dining experience, Platillos Voladores offers an interesting and varied menu of beautifully presented gourmet dishes that feature a glorious interplay of Asian, European and Afro-Colombian influences and largely local ingredients. Mains run the gamut from *ceviche mixto* to tofu in green curry and Mexican *sopa de tortilla*.

Meals are served either outside in the garden area or inside in one of several air-conditioned dining rooms. Wash your meal down with an offering from an admirably select wine list. Reservations are essential.

Trilogia INTERNATIONAL $$$

(2-379-9606; www.trilogia.net; Carrera 6 No 2-130; mains COP$26,000-69,000; noon-midnight) At this well-loved high-end restaurant, colorful hand-painted chairs surround tables in a covered atrium overlooking the open kitchen. The menu is diverse and includes plenty of cuts of beef and a wide selection of fish dishes, plus pasta and risotto, but there's not much for vegetarian diners. The extensive wine list is among the best in town.

Drinking & Nightlife

Many *caleños* don't really go out drinking, they go out to dance. For a low-key night out head to Parque del Perro, home to numerous small bars. Just north of Cali is Menga, with many large discos. Further afield, several large *salsatecas* (salsa dance clubs) cluster in legendary Juanchito, although the area no longer attracts crowds like it once did.

★ Zaperoco CLUB

(☎315-520-1370; www.facebook.com/zaperocobar; Av 5N No 16-46; cover charge COP$20,000; ⏱8pm-4am Thu-Sat) If you only visit one salsa bar in Cali, make sure it's Zaperoco. Here the veteran DJ spins *salsa con golpe* (salsa with punch) from old vinyl while industrial fans try in vain to keep the place cool. Somewhere under the mass of moving limbs there is a dance floor – but we've never worked out exactly where it is.

There are often live acts, with rumba and Cuban *son* vying for the top spot with salsa.

Pérgola Clandestina CLUB

(www.lapergola.co; Carrera 1 No 13-42; ⏱9pm-late Fri & Sat) Located on the top floor of a tower block in downtown, this open-air bar has DJs spinning quality crossover music, plus great cocktails made from high-quality ingredients. It's popular with young and well-heeled *caleños*, but unfortunately there are often lines and the door staff can be less than welcoming. Dress nicely.

Topa Tolondra BAR

(☎323-597-2646; www.facebook.com/Latopabar; Calle 5 No 13-27; cover charge COP$10,000; ⏱7pm-1am Mon-Wed, 8pm-4am Thu-Sat) Popular with locals and travelers alike, this large salsa bar near Loma de la Cruz is always buzzing. The tables are pushed right up against the walls, leaving plenty of floor space to get your groove on. There's frequent live music.

La Colina BAR

(Calle 2 Oeste No 4-83; ⏱6pm-midnight) This is a friendly neighborhood shop-bar hybrid in San Antonio that's been around for over 70 years. Cheap beer accompanies classic salsa and bolero and it's a favorite *caleño* gathering spot before heading off elsewhere to dance till the wee hours.

CALI'S CARROT LAW

Closing time in Cali is referred to as the *ley zanahoria* (carrot law), because it's said that you'd have to be boring as a carrot to go home that early (at present, 3am on weekends).

El Faro BAR

(☎318-514-8229; www.elfaropizzabar.com; Carrera 3 No 2-09; ⏱4pm-2am) Not big on dancing? Find a table at this buzzing rock bar in El Peñon that's popular with all kinds of locals for live bands, the friendly service and will-do-in-a-pinch gringo food.

Viejoteca Pardo Llada SALSA CLUB

(Av 2N No 32-05; cover COP$6000; ⏱2-7pm Sun) Hosted in a lovely open-air dance hall upstairs at the senior citizens association, this is Cali's original and best *viejoteca* (seniors disco), where the city's old-timers dress up in their best threads and show off their impressive salsa moves. It's great to come and watch over a beer even if you don't dance. It's near the Parque del Avión.

Men wearing shorts will be denied entry.

El Rincón de Heberth BAR

(☎310-409-7229; www.facebook.com/elrincon.deheberth; Carrera 24 No 5-32; ⏱8pm-4am Thu-Sat) In a shopfront in a strip mall, this local institution of a salsa bar attracts a lively *caleño* crowd who come for the great music and laid-back vibe. Most people sit outside and drink in the fenced-in sidewalk area where it's fresher, until a particular song inspires them to take to the steamy dance floor. There's usually no cover.

Tin Tin Deo CLUB

(☎315-594-4712; www.facebook.com/tintindeocali; Calle 5 No 38-71; cover charge COP$15,000; ⏱8pm-3am Thu-Sat) This large, iconic, unpretentious 2nd-floor *salsateca* features a large dance area overseen by posters of famous salsa singers. While it sometimes feels like an expat hangout (especially on Thursdays), it's an excellent place for novice dancers to get on the floor and learn to salsa, Cali-style. Saturday is *pachanguero* ('party till dawn') night.

☆ Entertainment

For the latest on what's on around town, check the entertainment columns of Cali's broadsheet, *El País* (www.elpais.com.co). Or just ask your lodgings.

Cinema

For thought-provoking films, check the program of the **Cinemateca La Tertulia** (☎2-893-2939; www.museolatertulia.com/cinemateca; Av Colombia No 5 Oeste-105; tickets COP$7000), which generally has two shows daily from Tuesday to Sunday. Also attracting crowds to its free arthouse screenings is **Lugar a Du-**

das (☎2-668-2335; www.lugaradudas.org; Calle 15N No 8N-41; ⊙2pm-8pm Tue-Sat).

Soccer

Cali has two *fútbol* (soccer) teams in the top league. Deportivo Cali (www.deportivocali.co; Via Cali-Palmira, Estadio Monumental Palmaseca) wear a green kit and play home games at Palmaseca stadium near the airport. America de Cali, (www.americadecali.co; Carrera 36, Estadio Pascual Guerrero) whose uniform is red and who were once infamous for their connections to local narcos, play matches in the city at Estadio Pascual Guerrero.

Theater

Teatro Municipal THEATER
(☎2-881-3131; www.teatromunicipal.gov.co; Carrera 5 No 6-64) Completed in 1918, the city's oldest existing theater is used for various artistic forms, including musical concerts, theater and ballet. If there's nothing going on, you can ask the security officer to show you around the richly decorated interior, which boasts a finely painted ceiling and five levels of elaborate boxes.

★**Delirio** PERFORMING ARTS
(☎2-893-7610; www.delirio.com.co; Carrera 26 No 12-328; tickets COP$115,000-240,000; ⊙every other Friday) You'll need to plan well in advance to see Cali's legendary salsa circus but it's well worth the effort. Think street circus meets flashy dance club and you'll have some idea of what to expect from this explosive celebration of *caleña* culture that takes place twice monthly in a big top on the Cali–Yumbo highway. Admission is restricted to adults.

Shopping

Parque Artesanal Loma de la Cruz MARKET
(Loma de la Cruz; ⊙10am-8pm) This is one of Colombia's better *artesanía* (local craft stall) markets. You'll find handmade goods from the Amazon, Pacific coast, southern Andes and even Los Llanos, but you have to know what you're looking for to pick them out among the tide of dream catchers and other mass-produced tat.

Information

SAFE TRAVEL

During the day, the city center is alive with street vendors and crowds, but after dark and on Sundays it can get dodgy. Avoid the area east of Calle 5 and along the Río Cali at night. Catch a taxi and take extra care with your belongings.

MEDICAL SERVICES

Centro Medico Imbanaco (☎2-682-1000, 2-382-1000; www.imbanaco.com; Carrera 38bis No 5B2-04; ⊙24hr) High-quality private medical care.

MONEY

Most of the major banks have offices around Plaza Caycedo in the center and on Av Sexta (Av 6N). Avoid banks in the center once crowds dissipate.

Banco de Bogotá (Calle 6N No 25N-47) ATM in the north of the city.

Banco de Bogotá (Carrera 5 No 10-39) ATM in the center.

Banco de Occidente (Av Colombia 2-72) ATM close to San Antonio.

Bancolombia (Av 6N No 20-72) ATM in the north.

POST

4-72 (www.4-72.com.co; Carrera 3 No 10-49; ⊙8am-noon & 2-6pm Mon-Fri, 9am-noon Sat) Main post office.

TOURIST INFORMATION

Secretaría de Cultura y Turísmo (☎2-885-6173; www.cali.gov.co/turista; cnr Calle 6 & Carrera 4; ⊙8am-noon & 2-5pm Mon-Fri, 10am-2pm Sat) Helpful information office.

VISA INFORMATION

Migración Colombia (☎2-397-3510; www.migracioncolombia.gov.co; Av 3N 50N-20, La Flora; ⊙8am-4pm Mon-Fri) For visa extensions.

Getting Around

Cali's air-conditioned bus network, the **MIO** (www.mio.com.co; per ride COP$1900;), will remind many of Bogotá's TransMilenio. The main route runs from north of the bus terminal along the river, through the center and down the entire length of Av Quinta (Av 5). Other routes spread out across the city. You need a MIO card (purchased at the main stations) to use the public-transit system and it's only useful if you're staying around the Granada neighborhood and visiting central sights.

Taxis are plentiful and fairly cheap in Cali. The minimum fare is COP$5000 and there is a COP$1100 surcharge at night. It's best to use an app such as Uber, Easy Taxi or Tappsi for safety reasons.

AROUND CALI

While Cali is a sprawling metropolis, you don't have to travel far to be surrounded by some serious nature. Just south of the city, Río Pance is a favorite place for *caleños* to escape the heat. Pance backs on to Parque Nacional Natural (PNN) Farallones – the closest large national park to any major city in the country.

Heading out of Cali in the other direction, Lago Calima is a peaceful mountain reservoir surrounded by farms and prized by adventure-sports enthusiasts for its thermal winds.

Pance

☎2 / POP 2000 / ELEV 1550M

Surrounded by imposing mountains on the eastern edge of PNN Farallones, this small holiday town is full of holiday *fincas* (farms) and is popular with *caleños* looking to cool off in the town's crystal-clear river. The weather is a pleasantly fresh change from the heat of Cali. At weekends its one street opens and all the bars and restaurants are in full flower. During the week it's empty and you'll struggle to even get a meal.

Sights

Parque Nacional Natural Farallones de Cali NATIONAL PARK

(www.parquesnacionales.gov.co) This 1500-sq-km national park protects the headlands around Cali. During the height of the armed conflict it was closed and it has yet to be officially reopened to visitors. Security remains an issue in some areas and ecological protection measures are also in place to conserve the delicate ecosystem, making the majority of the park off-limits. The only path that is currently accessible, by hiring a guide in Pance, is the full-day hike to Pico de Loro (p236).

Studies are underway in order to evaluate whether to reopen the five-day hike to Pico de Pance, PNN Farallones' iconic peak, so check the latest news at the park office in Cali before heading out.

At the time of research the park charged no entrance fees but this is likely to change when it officially reopens.

Activities

In addition to swimming in the river or one of the local streams, you can also take a day hike to some nearby waterfalls or organize a longer trek into PNN Farallones de Cali.

Pico de Loro is a seven-hour round-trip hike west from Pance. Expect to pay around COP$80,000 per group for a local guide to show you the way. In order to hike the trail, you must enter the park before 10am, so it's best to stay in Pance the night before.

To visit the waterfalls from Pueblo Pance, walk 1km downhill to the bridge and turn right. Follow the road 2km uphill to El Topacio, where you'll find a visitor center and be met by a guide. Admission is limited to 40 visitors per day – if you want to reserve a place in advance you can pay at the Corporación Autónoma Regional del Valle de Cauca office in Cali ahead of your trip.

There are two short trails to explore here: the Barranquero trail leads to a 40m waterfall while the Naturaleza trail ends at a 130m cataract. Also ask about visiting La Nevera ('the refrigerator'), a pristine swimming hole fed by fresh mountain waters.

Sleeping & Eating

Several small rural hotels line the roads into Pueblo Pance and from the village up to PNN Farallones.

While roadside restaurants serve typical food at weekends – mostly barbecued meat, trout and soup – during the week you'll need to organize meals with your hotel.

La Fonda Pance HOSTEL $

(☎317-664-3004, 2-558-1818; www.lafondapance.com; contiguo al Finca Nilo; campsite per person COP$10,000, dm COP$20,000, r with/without bathroom COP$80,000/50,000; P @ ≋) Hands down the best choice for travelers in the area, La Fonda is a relaxing spot with comfortable modern rooms, mountain views and a huge garden divided by a gurgling stream. There's also an outdoor Jacuzzi to soak in after a long hike and a refreshing natural pool fed by waters rushing down from the surrounding peaks.

Meals are served and the friendly management can organize guides for treks in the area. It's 200m before the Topacio turnoff.

Getting There & Away

Minibuses head to Pueblo Pance roughly every hour (COP$2300, 1½ hours) between 5am and 8pm from outside the bus terminal in Cali. They are marked 'Recreativo 1A' and 'Pueblo Pance'.

The MIO reaches some parts of the river but does not make it all the way to Pueblo Pance.

Lago Calima

This artificial reservoir attracts kitesurfers and windsurfers from around the world for its year-round winds. The lake covers the flooded Darién valley of Río Calima, and was built in 1965. Some 86km north of Cali, its temperate climate also attracts *caleños* looking to cool off on weekends. The green hills that surround the lake are populated with holiday *fincas*.

Most tourist activity stretches along the northern bank of the lake, from the small town of Darién at the eastern end to the dam to the west. There's no beach; launching points are from grassy slopes that lead down to the water.

Because transportation is infrequent in the area, Lago Calima makes a difficult day trip. You're better off coming for a day or two, especially on the weekend, when the many visitors give the place a party atmosphere.

Activities

Escuela Pescao Windsurf y Kitesurf WINDSURFING, KITESURFING
(☎300-230-6097, 311-352-3293; www.pescaokitesurf.com) A well-organized school in a big warehouse on the edge of the lake. It's owned by a wheelchair-bound former champion kitesurfer who gives classes on the shore before sending students out onto the water with an instructor. It offers accommodations (COP$30,000 to COP$60,000) in the warehouse in tents with mattresses and sleeping bags.

Sleeping & Eating

Hostería Los Veleros HOTEL **$$$**
(☎2-684-1000; www.comfandi.com.co; Complejo Comfandi, Via Madroñal; s/d/tr incl 2 meals COP$214,000/234,000/280,000;) The best hotel on the lake, Los Veleros is part of the Comfandi complex, and prices include two meals and admission to the recreation center and pools. Some of the rooms have balconies with spectacular views of the lake. Packed on the weekend; during the week you'll have the place to yourself.

Meson llama COLOMBIAN **$$**
(☎318-415-3681; www.mesonilama.com; mains COP$26,000-40,000, pizza COP$19,000-35,000; ⏰7:30am-7pm Mon-Fri, to 9pm Sat & Sun) About 10km from Darién is this large, exposed-timber restaurant with great views of the lake. It does all the basics very well – *sancocho* (typical Colombian soup), *churrasco* (grilled meat), baby beef and trout. It also prepares good pizzas and has a variety of comfortable accommodations (rooms from COP$130,000) on the lakeshore.

Getting There & Away

Minibuses shuttle between Darién and the dam at Lago Calima (COP$2200), past the kite schools, from 7am to 7pm on the hour. You can also jump on buses heading to Buga/Cali – but make sure they are taking the lake exit.

Darién

☎2 / POP 15,824 / ELEV 1800M

This small town has a few budget hotels and ATMs, a couple of supermarkets and internet cafes and, on the weekends, several lively discos. It's a perfectly pleasant place that's mostly clustered within two or three blocks of Parque Los Fundadores, the main plaza, but a trip to Lago Calima is the big drawcard.

Sights & Activities

Museo Arqueológico Calima MUSEUM
(☎2-253-3496, 321-831-4780; www.inciva.org; Calle 10 No 12-50; adult/child COP$4000/3000; ⏰8am-12:30pm &1:30pm-5pm Mon-Fri, 10am-6pm Sat & Sun) Set in spacious, well-manicured gardens up the hill from the plaza, this museum houses an impressive collection of pre-Columbian pottery and some replicas of original indigenous dwellings.

Cogua Kiteboarding KITESURFING
(☎318-608-3932, 2-253-3524; www.coguakiteboarding.com; Calle 10 No 4-51) In addition to offering kitesurfing classes, the young owner of this laid-back outfit also runs a kiteboard factory, where he makes custom boards from coconut fiber and *guadua* (a type of bamboo). Visitors are welcome to drop by the factory to find out about the process or even to design their own board.

Budget accommodations are available in town for clients and they also offer stand-up paddle (SUP) rentals.

Getting There & Around

There is a frequent direct bus service to/from Cali (COP$14,500, 2½ hours) during the day. The last bus back to Cali leaves Darién at 6:30pm.

If you're coming from destinations to the north, get off in Buga and grab the half-hourly service to Darién (COP$7500, 1½ hours). The last bus back to Cali leaves Darién at 6:30pm.

Note that there are two bus routes, costing the same, that travel out to Lago Calima and Darién. If you're going direct to Darién, ask for the bus via Jiguales; for the kitesurfing/windsurfing schools, ask for the bus that goes *'por el lago'* ('along the lakeshore').

There are no taxis in Darién. However, there's a fleet of tuk-tuks that will get you around for a decent price. Jeeps hang out on the main square, and can take you around town and along the lakeshore, but they can be expensive (around COP$15,000 to Comfandi).

CAUCA & HUILA

These two departments are home to Popayán, one of Colombia's most charming colonial cities, plus two of the country's most important archaeological sites – San Agustín and Tierradentro. Here you'll also find the peculiar Desierto de la Tatacoa, a striking anomaly near Neiva, halfway between Bogotá and San Agustín.

In the days of river travel in Colombia, both Cauca and Huila were major hubs of commerce. The introduction of the railroad and highways in the early 20th century stunted their growth, and these days a sleepy languor envelops the region.

Popayán

☎2 / POP 285,700 / ELEV 1760M

A small colonial city famous for its chalk-white facades (its nickname is La Ciudad Blanca, or 'the White City'), Popayán is second only to Cartagena as Colombia's most impressive colonial settlement. Perched beneath towering mountains in the Valle de Pubenza, it was the capital of southern Colombia for centuries, before Cali overtook it.

Founded in 1537 by Sebastián de Belalcázar, Popayán became an important stopping point on the road between Cartagena and Quito. Its mild climate attracted wealthy families from the sugar haciendas of the hot Valle de Cauca region. In the 17th century they began building mansions, schools, churches and monasteries. In March 1983, moments before the much-celebrated Maundy Thursday religious procession was set to depart, a violent earthquake shook the town, caving in the cathedral's roof and killing hundreds.

Popayán is now home to numerous universities, and the streets of its old center are filled with students in the daytime.

Sights

On the last Friday of the month Popayán hosts the Noche de Museos (Night of Museums), when food and handicrafts stands line the streets, and the historic center is closed to traffic. Many of the city's museums stay open late and are free to visit.

★Iglesia de San Francisco CHURCH

(cnr Carrera 9 & Calle 4; hours vary) Dating back to the late 18th century, Popayán's largest colonial church is also its most beautiful. Inside are a fine high altar and a collection of seven unique side altars. The 1983 earthquake cracked open the ossuary, revealing six unidentified mummies. Two are left; ask in the office to the right of the entrance to have a look at them.

Museo Arquidiocesano de Arte Religioso MUSEUM

(☎2-824-2759; Calle 4 No 4-56; COP$6000; 9am-12:30pm & 2-6pm Mon-Fri, 9am-2pm Sat) You don't have to be an expert on religious art to be impressed by this collection of paintings, statues, altar pieces, silverware and liturgical vessels, most of which date from the 17th to 19th centuries. There's also a vault of valuable relics that is only opened during Semana Santa.

Puente del Humilladero BRIDGE

(Carrera 6) Popayán's emblematic landmark, this 240m-long, 11-arch brick bridge was constructed in the mid-19th century to improve access to the center from the poor northern suburbs. It dwarfs the adjacent Puente de la Custodia, a pretty stone bridge constructed in 1713 to allow priests to cross the Río Molino to bring the holy orders to the sick.

Casa Museo Mosquera MUSEUM

(Calle 3 No 5-38; adult/child COP$2000/1000; 9am-noon & 2-6pm Tue-Sun) This interesting museum is housed in an 18th-century mansion that was once home to General Tomás Cipriano de Mosquera, who was Colombia's president on four occasions between 1845 and 1867. The original French crystal chandelier in the dining room was transported from the Caribbean to Popayán by mule. Note the urn in the wall: it contains Mosquera's heart. A short tour in English is possible.

Iglesia La Ermita CHURCH

(cnr Calle 5 & Carrera 2; hours vary) Constructed in 1546, Popayán's oldest church is well worth seeing for its fine main retable and the fragments of old frescoes, which were only discovered after the 1983 earthquake.

Museo Guillermo Valencia MUSEUM

(Carrera 6 No 2-69; 10am-noon & 2-5pm Tue-Sun) FREE This late 18th-century building is full of period furniture, paintings, old photos and documents that once belonged to the Popayán-born poet who lived here. It has been left more or less as it was when Valencia died in one of the upstairs bedrooms.

Museo de Historia Natural MUSEUM
(www.unicauca.edu.co/museonatural; Carrera 2 No 1A-25; adult/child under 12 yr COP$3000/2000; 9-11am & 2-4pm) One of the best of its kind in the country, this museum on the grounds of Universidad del Cauca is noted for its extensive collection of insects, butterflies, stuffed birds and other animal life in Colombia. There's a fascinating variety of endemic plant species, too. A guide can show you around.

Activities

Popayán Tours ADVENTURE SPORTS
(2-831-7871; www.popayantours.com) A professional outfit, run by Scots Kim and Tony, offering a variety of adventurous tours in the countryside, including a downhill mountain-bike run from the Coconuco thermal springs, coffee-farm tours, guided outings to the Silvia market, night visits to the nearby hot springs (COP$60,000), ascents of the volcano in PNN Puracé (COP$130,000) and multiday trips to Tierradentro.

Intrepid adventurers should ask about the hiking and cycling combo, which involves trekking to the summit of Volcan Puracé before pedaling all the way back to Popayán.

Get Up and Go Colombia WALKING
(301-701-6240; www.getupandgocolombia.org; Parque Caldas) A free walking tour through the historic center run by enthusiastic university students. It leaves from Parque Caldas in front of the tourist office at 10am and 4pm. Tips are appreciated. In the evenings they offer free salsa, merengue and bachata dancing lessons, as well as hikes on Sundays (10am) and mountain-biking tours (COP$60,000), the last by reservation only.

Festivals & Events

Semana Santa RELIGIOUS
(Holy Week; Easter) Popayán's Easter celebrations are world famous, especially the nighttime processions on Maundy Thursday and Good Friday. Thousands of the faithful and tourists from all over come to take part in this religious ceremony and the accompanying festival of religious music. Hotel prices soar at this time; book well in advance.

Sleeping

Parklife Hostel HOSTEL $
(300-249-6240; www.parklifehostel.com; Calle 5 No 6-19; dm/s/d COP$25,000/52,000/64,000, s/d without bathroom from COP$43,000/55,000; @) You'd be hard pressed to find a hostel with a better location than Parklife's – it's attached to the cathedral wall. The common areas are a blend of chandeliers, antique furniture and colorful cushions. It's a sociable place, but not without its drawbacks: some rooms only have internal windows (thus little ventilation) and the bathrooms and kitchen could be cleaner.

Hostel Caracol HOSTEL $
(2-820-7335; www.hostelcaracol.com; Calle 4 No 2-21; dm COP$27,000, s/d without bathroom COP$48,000/62,000; @) In a renovated colonial house, this homey hostel is popular with laid-back independent travelers. It has smallish but comfortable rooms set around a pleasant courtyard common area, and offers plenty of information about attractions and entertainment in town. Some of the rooms only have windows into the common area.

Hostel Trail HOSTEL $
(2-831-7871; www.hosteltrailpopayan.com; Carrera 11 No 4-16; dm COP$27,000, s/d COP$55,000/75,000, without bathroom COP$40,000/62,000; @) This popular budget choice is a friendly, modern place on the edge of the colonial center with everything weary travelers need. There's fast internet, express laundry, a fully equipped kitchen, staff with a wealth of local know-how and free coffee. There's no real common area, though.

Hotel Los Balcones HOTEL $$$
(2-824-2030; www.hotellosbalconespopayan.com; Carrera 7 No 2-75; s/d COP$130,000/207,000;) Climb 200-year-old stone stairs to your spacious room in this regal 18th-century abode. The place has an almost-medieval feel, with antique furniture, stuffed eagles and a maze of corridors. In the lobby, MC Escher sketches hang next to a case of ancient pottery and plush leather sofas. The rooms on the top floor are quieter. Wi-fi struggles.

Hotel La Plazuela HOTEL $$
(2-824-1084; www.hotellaplazuela.com.co; Calle 5 No 8-13; r incl breakfast COP$150,000;) In a beautiful, whitewashed mansion complete with a lovely courtyard, this classy hotel has been fully refurbished but still retains much of the original antique furniture. The front rooms have effective soundproof windows and provide views of Iglesia San José.

Hotel Dann Monasterio HOTEL $$$
(2-824 2191; www.hotelesdann.com; Calle 4 No 10-14; s/d COP$295,000/365,000, ste

Popayán

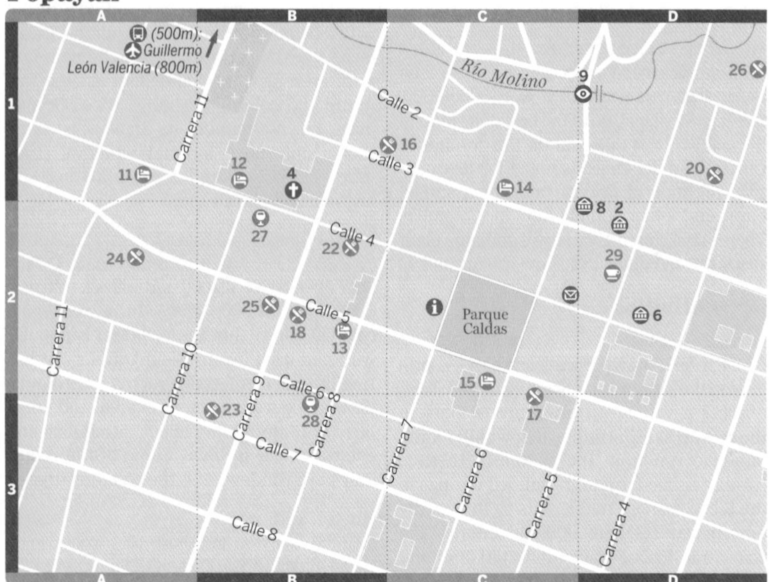

COP$400,000-540,000; @) A Franciscan monastery turned hotel offering elegant but not particularly luxurious rooms set around a vast arcaded courtyard. It's an impressive building full of character but rooms vary in quality so ask to see a few options. A new wi-fi system has been installed to penetrate the thick adobe walls.

The restaurant, at the rear of the building overlooking the garden, serves high-quality European and Latin American fare (COP$28,000 to COP$42,500).

Eating

Look out for typical local snacks and drinks such as *empanadas de pipián* (fried potato pastries served with a spicy satay-style peanut sauce), *champus* (a maize beverage with *lulo* and pineapple) and *salpicón payanese* (an icy blackberry concoction). Popayán's dining scene is a mix of local and international restaurants.

★Carmina MEDITERRANEAN $
(310-515-4934; Calle 3 No 8-58; mains COP$8000-20,000; noon-3pm & 6:45-10pm Mon-Sat;) A cute little Catalan-run cafe in a less busy part of the historic center, serving a fantastic spread of mostly Mediterranean dishes. Expect Spanish omelettes, pasta, lasagna, crepes filled with Nutella and other tasty treats. The desserts, such as the tiramisu, are top-notch.

★Mora Castilla CAFE $
(2-838-1979; www.moracastilla.com; Calle 2 No 4-44; snacks COP$2400-4000; 10am-7pm) This upstairs cafe is always busy with chatting locals and prepares excellent fresh juices and traditional snacks, including *salpicón payanese, champus, tamales* and *carantantas* (a kind of toasted corn chip). If you're still hungry, pop next door to sample some of Doña Chepa's famous *aplanchados* (flat pastries).

Pita LEBANESE $
(300-662-7867; www.facebook.com/pitartesanal; Carrera 2 No 3-58; snacks from COP$3500; 4:30-10pm Tue-Sat;) A friendly restaurant that stretches the definition of Lebanese cuisine almost to the point of no return. The pita bread and the variety of pre-fab toppings tend to be cold, and the straight-out-of-the-fridge falafel tastes as if it's been made by someone who either hasn't met chickpeas before or actively dislikes them. It makes a change from Colombian fare, though.

Tienda Regional del Macizo COLOMBIAN $
(Carrera 4 No 0-42; meals COP$6000; 8am-4pm) This small cafe is part of an organization that works to develop markets for

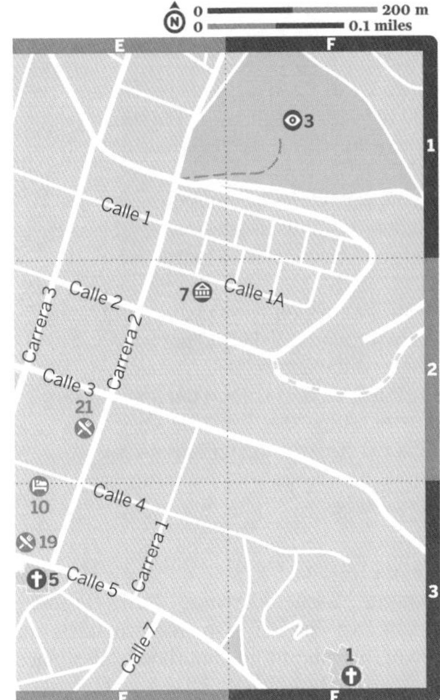

Popayán

Sights

1 Capilla de Belén ... F3
2 Casa Museo Mosquera ... D2
3 El Morro de Tulcán ... F1
4 Iglesia de San Francisco ... B1
5 Iglesia La Ermita ... E3
6 Museo Arquidiocesano de Arte Religioso ... D2
7 Museo de Historia Natural ... E2
8 Museo Guillermo Valencia ... D2
9 Puente del Humilladero ... D1

Sleeping

10 Hostel Caracol ... E3
11 Hosteltrail ... A1
12 Hotel Dann Monasterio ... B1
13 Hotel La Plazuela ... B2
14 Hotel Los Balcones ... C1
15 Parklife Hostel ... C2

Eating

16 Carmina ... C1
17 Hotel Camino Real ... C3
18 La Fresa ... B2
19 La Semilla Escondida ... E3
20 Mora Castilla ... D1
21 Pita ... E2
22 Restaurante Italiano ... B2
23 Restaurante Vegetariano Maná ... B3
24 Sabores del Mar ... A2
25 Tequila's ... B2
26 Tienda Regional del Macizo ... D1

Drinking & Nightlife

27 Bar La Iguana ... B2
28 El Sotareño ... B3
29 Oromo Café Ritual ... D2

farmers in the Macizo Colombiano. Needless to say the absurdly cheap lunches are made with the freshest ingredients. Buy your bags of coffee beans here, too.

Tequila's MEXICAN $$
(2-822-2150; Calle 5 No 9-25; mains COP$15,000-25,000; 3-10pm Mon-Sat;) Run by a Mexican expat and his local wife, this small restaurant in the center prepares good-value homestyle Mexican dishes. While some authentic ingredients are hard to find in small-town Colombia, their salsas pack real heat and their *enchiladas de mole poblano* are deeply satisfying.

Sabores del Mar SEAFOOD $
(Calle 5 No 5-9; set lunch COP$8000, mains COP$12,000-35,000; 7am-8pm) Run by a charismatic family from Tumaco, this tiny nautical-themed place serves a great-value seafood lunch. Try the *toyo* (a kind of shark).

La Fresa CAFE $
(Calle 5 No 8-89; snacks COP$400-3000; 7am-7pm) A grimy corner store with a few plastic tables, La Fresa is famed throughout Popayán for its delicious *empanadas de pipián* (potato empanadas with a spicy peanut sauce). Most locals wash them down with a *malta* (malt-based soda).

Restaurante Vegetariano Maná VEGETARIAN $
(310-890-5748; Calle 7 No 9-56; meals COP$4700; 8am-8pm;) Popular vegetarian place serving cheap and tasty meals featuring a variety of mains including soy protein, lentil dishes and tofu alongside many vegetable sides.

La Semilla Escondida FRENCH $$
(2-820-0857; Calle 9N No 10-29; crepes COP$7000-26,000, mains COP$12,000-36,000; 11:30am-10pm Mon-Wed, to 11pm Thu-Sat, noon-4pm Sun;) This bright bistro prepares great savory and sweet crepes, but beyond that, their ambition outstrips their culinary prowess and their pasta dishes and mains can occasionally be hit and miss. It's located a little northeast of the bus terminal.

Restaurante Italiano ITALIAN $$
(2-824-0607; Calle 4 No 8-83; mains COP$23,000-40,000; noon-10:30pm;)

WORTH A TRIP

SILVIA

A picturesque mountain town 53km northeast of Popayán, Silvia is the center of the Guambiano region. The Guambiano people don't live in Silvia itself, but in the small mountain villages of Pueblito, La Campana, Guambia and Caciques. The whole community numbers about 12,000.

The Guambiano are considered one of the most traditional indigenous groups in Colombia. They speak their own language, dress traditionally and still use long-established farming techniques. They're also excellent weavers and come to Silvia for the lively weekly market to sell their wares.

From the main plaza, walk uphill to the church for 360-degree views of the surrounding countryside. On the main plaza you can rent a horse (around COP$6000 per hour) with a guide to explore the surrounding Guambiano villages, with Pueblito being the closest.

Buses (COP$6000, 1½ hours) and *colectivos* (COP$7000, one hour) depart Popayán roughly every hour, with extra early-morning services on Tuesday. From Cali, take a Popayán-bound bus as far as Piendamó (COP$15,000, two hours), from where you can pick up an onward bus to Silvia (COP$3000, 30 minutes). Jeeps and *chivas* run from Silvia's main plaza for the surrounding Guambiano villages.

Swing open the saloon doors of this Swiss-owned Italian joint and you'll find great pizza and pasta as well as authentic fondue for those cool mountain nights. The steak is among the best in town and the lunch set meal (COP$12,000) is one of the best of its kind in Colombia.

Hotel Camino Real FRENCH, COLOMBIAN **$$**
(☎2-824-1254; Calle 5 No 5-59; mains COP$25,000-40,000; ⏱noon-3pm & 6-10pm) The owners of this hotel are key players in the Congreso Nacional Gastronómico and their passion for food is evident in the interesting menu, which combines both French and Colombian elements. Go for one of the set menus (COP$55,000), which include two appetizers, a main, cheeses and a fruit mousse. Reservations are recommended.

Drinking & Nightlife

There are several bars and clubs in central Popayán where you can alternately down a few beers and/or cocktails and shake your moneymaker. Students tend to congregate over cheap beers on the highway out of town, at the Campanario mall.

★ **Togoima Café Ancestral** COFFEE
(☎310-257-1219; Carrera 5 No 3-34; ⏱8am-7:30pm Mon-Fri, 9am-7pm Sat, 10am-6pm Sun) One of the best cafes in town, preparing a wide variety of hot and cold beverages using high-quality beans from around the country. There are so many combinations you'll never have to try the same drink twice.

New York SALSA CLUB
(contiguo Salon Communal, Barrio Pueblillo; ⏱9pm-3am Thu-Sun) On the outskirts of town, this vibrant neighborhood salsa place is as authentic as it gets. Take a seat in one of the vintage booths beneath the hundreds of old LPs, plastic toys and portaits of salsa heroes that are plastered all over the walls and ceiling. It's in a rough neighborhood; get a taxi (COP$8000) right to the door.

La Iguana Afro Video Bar BAR
(☎316-281-0576; www.facebook.com/LaIguanaAfroVideoBar; Calle 4 No 9-67; ⏱7pm-1am Mon-Wed, to 3am Thu-Sat) The place to go in the center to show off your salsa moves on the little dance floor. It sometimes has live bands, but can be hit or miss, depending on the night. 'Carousing not conversation' should be its motto.

El Sotareño BAR
(Calle 6 No 8-05; ⏱4pm-1am Mon-Thu, to 3am Fri & Sat) In a busy street in the center, this cozy Popayán classic plays tango, bolero and Ranchera on scratched old vinyls.

ℹ Information

There are many ATMs around Parque Caldas.

4-72 (www.4-72.com.co; Calle 4 No 5-74; ⏱8am-5pm Mon-Fri, to noon Sat) Post office.

Banco de Bogotá (Parque Caldas)

Banco de Occidente (Parque Caldas)

Clinica Salud Proteción (☎2-822-8800; www.saludproteccion.com.co; Carrera 11 No 5-41, Barrio Valencia; ⏱7am-6pm Mon-Sat) Non-emergency attention; for anything serious, head to Cali or Bogotá.

Migración Colombia (☎2-823-1027; www.migracioncolombia.gov.co; Calle 4N No 10B-66; ⏲8am-noon & 2-5pm) Arranges visa extensions.

Policía de Turismo (☎2-822-0916; Carrera 7 No 4-36; ⏲9am-6pm) Moderately helpful police officers who focus on tourist complaints.

Getting There & Around

AIR

Aeropuerto Guillermo León Valencia (Panamericana) is 1km north of the city center. There are up to four flights daily to Bogotá with Avianca (www.avianca.com) and EasyFly (www.easyfly.com.co).

BICYCLE

Bici Publica Popayán (Carrera 6 & Calle 3; ⏲8:30am-5pm) Free bike-rental program run by the local government.

BUS

The **Terminal de Transporte Popayán** (www.terminalpopayan.com; Panamericana) is 1km north of the city center. There are frequent services to Cali (COP$23,000, three to four hours). Direct buses to Bogotá (COP$110,000, 12 to 14 hours) and Medellín (COP$98,000, 11 hours) depart in the evenings.

There are regular minibuses to San Agustín (COP$37,000, five hours); most companies require a change of vehicle but **Sotracauca** (☎319-7170-503) offers a direct service four times daily.

Buses to Tierradentro (COP$26,000, five hours) leave at 5:30am, 8:30am, 10:30am, 1pm and 3pm. The 10:30am service takes you all the way to the Museo Arqueológico entrance.

Hourly buses connect to Pasto (COP$37,000, six hours) and Ipiales (COP$42,000, eight hours). It's best to travel during the day if possible, when you'll also be able to admire the amazing views.

Coconuco

There are two thermal springs near the town of Coconuco (2360m), in the mountains outside Popayán on the road to San Agustín. The weather here is decidedly cool, which makes the springs even more enjoyable.

On weekends the local thermal baths get packed with kids and rum-soaked parents; during the week they are all but empty.

Activities

Termales Aguatibia THERMAL BATHS
(☎315-578-6111; www.termalesaguatibia.com; Km 4 via Paletará; adult/child COP$18,000/8000; ⏲8am-6pm) These thermal baths are surrounded by splendid mountain scenery. Termales Aguatibia has six thermal pools, a mud spring and a 53m-long 'toboggan' – a butt-bruising concrete slide. Most of the pools here are warm rather than hot. There's also a pretty lake with rowing boats, a mud bath and a restaurant on-site (mains COP$14,000 to COP$20,000).

At the time of research, the owners were in dispute with the local indigenous community and access to the site was restricted. Check the latest in Popayán before heading out.

Agua Hirviendo THERMAL BATHS
(☎321-852-2694; COP$10,000; ⏲24hr) Run by the local indigenous community, this thermal spring has two large pools, several smaller ones and a sauna. There's too much concrete here for it to be a fully natural experience but the waters are piping hot. An adjacent restaurant serves meals until late. There are also very basic rooms for rent but staying in Coconuco is more comfortable.

Getting There & Away

During the week there is an hourly bus service from Popayán to Coconuco (COP$5000, one hour, 31km), with more buses on the weekends. From where the bus drops you, it's about a 45-minute walk to either of the thermal baths but note that the road to Agua Hirviendo is quite steep. Alternatively grab a jeep or a moto-taxi in town.

San Agustín

☎8 / POP 9500 / ELEV 1695M

This small, attractive colonial town basks in refreshing, springlike weather year-round and is the gateway to one of the most important pre-Columbian archaeological sites on the continent.

Five thousand years ago, two indigenous cultures lived in the adjacent river valleys of the Magdalena and the Cauca. Divided by uncrossable peaks, the rivers were their highways, and here, near San Agustín, those two civilizations met to trade, to worship and to bury their dead.

The volcanic rocks thrown great distances by the now-extinct nearby volcanoes proved irresistible to the local sculptors, who transformed them into more than 500 fantastic statues, scattered over the surrounding green hills.

Little else is known about the peoples of San Agustín. They didn't have a written language and had disappeared many centuries before the Europeans arrived. But their legacy is a mystical place in a spectacular landscape that is well worth making a detour for.

San Agustín

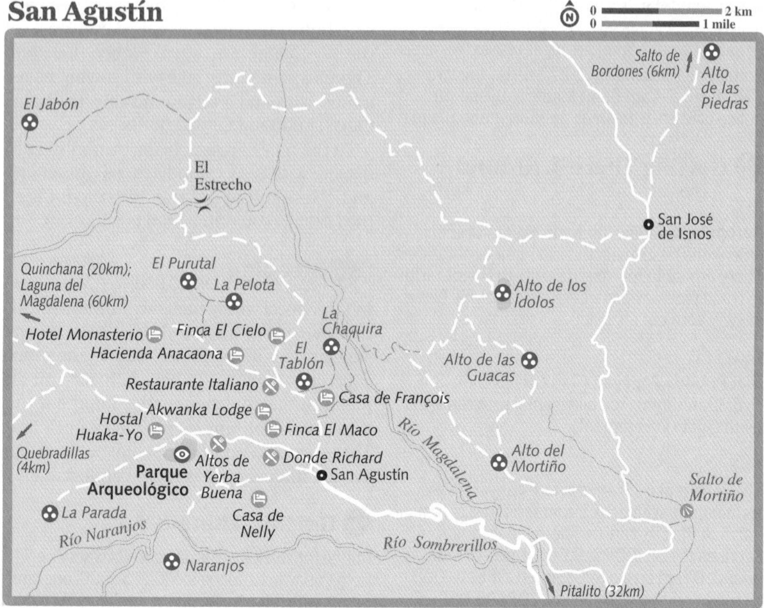

Sights

Upon paying your admission at either the Parque Arqueológico (p244) or Alto de Los Ídolos (p244) you'll be given a 'passport,' which is valid for entrance to both sites for two consecutive days.

★ **Parque Arqueológico** ARCHAEOLOGICAL SITE
(☎1-444-0544; www.icanh.gov.co; Via San Agustín; adult/student COP$25,000/10,000; ⌚8am-4pm) This 78-hectare archaeological park is 2.5km west of the town of San Agustín. There are over 130 statues in the park in total, either found in situ or collected from other areas, including some of the best examples of San Agustín statuary, with human or animal features, or a mixture of the two. Don't miss the carved tombs either. Reputable guides congregate around the museum.

At the entrance to the park is the **Museo Arqueológico**, which features smaller statues, pottery, utensils, jewelry and other objects, along with interesting background information about the San Agustín culture.

Beyond the entrance, you'll stroll along the statue-lined **Bosque de las Estatuas** before ascending the four funeral hills – *mesitas* A, B, C1 and C2 with their respective tombs and clusters of statues. Many of them are anthropomorphic figures, some realistic, others resembling masked monsters. There are also sculptures depicting sacred animals such as the eagle, jaguar and frog. Archaeologists have also uncovered a great deal of pottery. Mesita B's statues are the best known.

Besides the *mesitas* is the **Fuente de Lavapatas**. Carved in the rocky bed of the stream, it is a complex labyrinth of ducts and small, terraced pools decorated with images of serpents, lizards and human figures. Archaeologists believe the baths were used for ritual ablutions and the worship of aquatic deities.

From here, the path winds uphill to the **Alto de Lavapatas**, the oldest archaeological site in San Agustín. You'll find a few tombs guarded by statues, and get a panoramic view over the surrounding countryside.

Alto de los Ídolos ARCHAEOLOGICAL SITE
(Via a Isnos; adult/student COP$25,000/10,000; ⌚8am-5pm) Located across the Río Magdalena 4km southwest of San José de Isnos (26km northeast of the town of San Agustín), this is the second-most important archaeological park in the region after the Parque Arqueológico. Its stone carvings include the largest anthropomorphic statue in the San Agustín area, which is 7m tall but with only 4m visible above ground. Take an Isnos-bound bus (COP$2500) and ask to be let off at the entrance.

Alto de las Piedras ARCHAEOLOGICAL SITE
(Via a Bordones; adult/student COP$25,000/10,000; ⏲8am-5pm) This site is 7km north of Isnos and has tombs lined with stone slabs, some of which still show traces of red, black and yellow coloring. One of the most famous statues, known as Doble Yo, is here; look carefully as there are actually four figures carved in this statue. You'll also find an intriguing statue of a female figure in an advanced state of pregnancy.

El Tablón, La Chaquira, La Pelota & El Purutal ARCHAEOLOGICAL SITE
(entry COP$5000; ⏲8am-5pm) These four sites are relatively close to each other; most people visit them as part of a horseback-riding tour, although you can also hike up here from town. Don't miss La Chaquira, with divinities carved into the mountain face. It overlooks the stunning gorge of the Río Magdalena.

Activities

One of the best ways to explore the mountains surrounding San Agustín is on horseback. There's also decent rafting to be done on the Río Magdalena.

★**Francisco 'Pacho' Muñoz** HORSEBACK RIDING
(☎311-827-7972; Finca El Maco) A highly recommended horseback-riding guide who can take you around the archaeological sites and beyond. A day trip for one person costs around COP$70,000 and the horses are sweet-natured and suitable for beginners. You can usually find Pacho hanging around at Finca El Maco (p245); he's the resident guide there.

Pancho has been a horse guide for over 30 years and offers a multiday trip to Laguna del Magdalena, the birthplace of the mighty Río Magdalena high in the mountains above San Agustín, Tierradentro, and, if you are willing to purchase horses, even leads you all the way to Ecuador.

Laguna del Magdalena HORSEBACK RIDING
The journey to Laguna del Magdalena (3327m), the birthplace of the Río Magdalena, 60km from San Agustín in the Macizo Colombiano, makes an interesting horseback-riding trip, which can be organized with a local guide (p245). The region was historically infested by guerrillas but is now considered safe.

The trip takes three to five days depending on the route, and costs around COP$150,000 per person per day, fluctuating with group size.

Magdalena Rafting RAFTING
(☎ph & WhatsApp 311-271-5333; www.magdalenarafting.com; Calle 5 No 15-237) The Río Magdalena offers challenging white-water rafting through some phenomenal landscapes. Magdalena Rafting offers 1½-hour tours (COP$65,000 per person) with Classes II to III rapids for novices, and full-day, Class V tours for experienced pros. Minimum four people per group. It also offers kayaking classes.

Sleeping

You'll enjoy your time in San Agustín more if you stay outside the center of town in one of the many charming rural hostels, guesthouses or *fincas*. Accommodations are of a high standard and there's even a boutique hotel.

Casa de Nelly HOSTEL $
(☎310-215-9067; Vereda La Estrella; dm COP$25,000, s/d without bathroom COP$56,000/60,000, r COP$90,000; 📶) The original San Agustín hostel has a range of comfortable accommodations (including dorm with beds not bunks) set around the prettiest gardens in town. Its spacious social area is centered on an open fireplace and outdoor barbecue area. There's also a guest kitchen and the in-house chef prepares fresh meals each evening if you don't fancy the hike into town.

★**Finca El Maco** HOSTEL $$
(☎320-375-5982; www.elmaco.ch; Vereda El Tablón via Parque Arqueológico; dm COP$27,000, s/d/ste from COP$67,000/92,000/293,000; P@📶) This tranquil hostel has comfortable cabins set amid a pretty garden – all with piping-hot water and comfortable beds – while the dorm is inside a traditional *maloka* (earthen dwelling).

To reach the hostel, take the road to the Parque Arqueológico and turn right at the Hotel Yalconia. From here it's a 400m walk uphill (COP$7000 in a taxi).

The ecological suite is a winner, with two sleeping areas, a lounge with an open fireplace and a massive, bright bathroom. Homemade organic yogurt and excellent curry are served at the on-site restaurant. The helpful Swiss owner organizes trips throughout the region.

★**Casa de François** HOSTEL $$
(☎314-358-2930, 8-837-3847; www.lacasadefrancois.com; Via El Tablón; dm COP$30,000, r COP$80,000-85,000, cabaña COP$130,000-160,000; 📶) 🍃 Set in a lovely garden just above town overlooking the hills, this crea-

tive, ecological hostel is constructed of natural materials, with wood, stone and glass bottles embedded in rammed-mud walls. The breezy, elevated dormitory has fantastic views and there's a spacious shared kitchen. Excellent private cabañas with wooden floors, large bathrooms and porches affording mountain views are spread around the property.

The small restaurant serves a variety of quality meals and snacks made using fresh produce from the property, plus there's organic coffee.

Finca El Cielo HOTEL **$$**
(☎ 313-493-7446; www.facebook.com/fincaelcielo sanagustin; Via al Estrecho; incl breakfast s/d/tr/q COP$100,000/140,000/210,000/280,000;) This pretty posada built of *guadua* (bamboo) on the road to El Estrecho has tremendous views over misty green hills. Try to reserve one of the fantastic feature rooms: the spacious suite has two sofas, a bamboo balcony with rockers and a big bright bathroom, while the adjacent tree house is a cozy hideaway with twisting branches growing through the walls.

The friendly owners live on the ground floor and prepare good home-cooked meals with advance notice. No English is spoken, but the staff do their best to be accommodating.

Hacienda Anacaona HOTEL **$$**
(☎ 311-231-7128; www.anacaona-colombia.com; Via al Estrecho; s/d/tr COP$75,000/140,000/180,000;) This peaceful colonial-style hotel is a comfortable option set amid a well-maintained garden. Rooms are spacious and good value although bathrooms are a tad small. There are fine views from around the property and prices include a hearty breakfast.

Hostal Huaka-Yo HOTEL **$$**
(☎ 320-846-9763, 310-244-4841; www.huaka-yo.com; s/d/tr incl breakfast COP$60,000/150,000/180,000) Just a couple of hundred meters beyond the Parque Arqueológico, this large hotel is surrounded by forest and manicured lawns. Good-value rooms are modern, clean and spacious. It's usually a peaceful place but it can be popular with tour groups who can detract from the tranquility when they're around.

Prices rise during Colombian peak periods.

★ **Hotel Monasterio** BOUTIQUE HOTEL **$$$**
(☎ 311-277-5901; www.monasteriosanagustin.com; Vereda La Cuchilla; r/ste incl breakfast COP$290,000/485,000;) This German-owned monastery-themed boutique hotel outside town is San Agustín's plushest option. Rooms are characterful, with heavy wooden beams and superb bathrooms, plus porches with hammocks and views of the coffee plantations. All have their own fireplaces – an attendant will come and light your fire in the evenings. The restaurant serves Colombian-Mediterranean fusion and the breakfast buffet is excellent.

The common areas have been crafted with plenty of attention to detail, while candlelit staircases and a small chapel add to the classic ambience. The reception area and restaurant offer fantastic views across the valley to the mountains. It's a fair way down a dirt road off the El Estrecho road – take a taxi from town (COP$8000).

Akwanka Lodge HOTEL **$$$**
(☎ 321-450-1377, 320-392-9160; www.hotelakawankalodge.com; Vereda El Tablón via Parque Arqueológico; s/d from COP$220,000/270,000) Situated on a hill with sweeping views over town to the mountains beyond, this high-end hotel has plenty of character. Rooms are spacious with king-sized beds, exposed wooden beams, handwoven textiles and touches of art throughout. The best ones have big private balconies too. The lovely on-site restaurant is heated by an open fire.

Eating & Drinking

★ **Donde Richard** COLOMBIAN **$$**
(☎ 312-432-6399; Via Parque Arqueológico; mains COP$25,000; 8am-6pm Wed-Mon) This grill restaurant on the road to the Parque Arqueológico serves some of the best food in town, with the beguiling scent of roasting meat and the savory crunch of *patacones* luring in diners on their way back from the park.

Altos de Yerba Buena COLOMBIAN **$$**
(☎ 310-370-3777; www.altosdeyerbabuena.com; Km1 Via Parque Arqueológico; mains COP$28,000-40,000; 10am-8pm;) On a hillside on the way to the Parque Arqueológico, this cute little restaurant uses produce from its own organic garden to cook well-prepared Colombian and international dishes (mostly salmon, trout and pasta) with delicious sides. The diminutive dining room is beyond endearing.

El Fogón COLOMBIAN **$$**
(☎ 320-834-5860; Calle 5 No 14-30; mains COP$22,000-25,000; 7am-9pm) A local institution that's been overtaken by the town's other culinary offerings, El Fogón offers big portions of Colombian favorites and an excellent-value set lunch (COP$10,000), all prepared over a wood-fired grill in the open kitchen.

OFF THE BEATEN TRACK

MOCOA: JUNGLE ROUTE TO ECUADOR

If you are planning to travel from San Agustín to Ecuador, you don't need to return to Popayán. Just four hours from Pitalito by bus, the department of Putumayo is a land of rushing rivers, dense jungle and amazing wildlife. If you're not going to get to Leticia this trip, it is well worth making a detour (via the department's capital, Mocoa) to this accessible corner of the Amazon.

The departmental capital is Mocoa. The town itself is a fairly disorganized and unattractive agricultural center, but the surrounding area is a natural wonderland of crystal-clear rivers, swimming holes and waterfalls, including the towering **Fin del Mundo** (Km6 Via Mocoa-Villagarzón; COP$5000; ⏲7am-noon Wed-Mon) and the high-volume **Hornyaco** (Vereda Caliyaco, Via Mocoa-Villagarzón).

Mocoa hit the international headlines in early 2017 when a massive landslide flowed down several streams into the heart of the town destroying entire neighborhoods and killing 329 residents. The devastation was horrific and both the town and its residents are yet to fully recover. Despite this, the surrounding area's spectacular sights were unaffected by the disaster and tourism is vital to reinvigorating the shattered local economy.

Mocoa's **bus terminal** (cnr Carrera 5 & Calle 11) is on the banks of the Río Sangoyaco in an area badly affected by the landslide.

There are several companies running comfortable large-bus services direct to Bogotá (COP$75,000, 13 hours), with afternoon and evening departures. Transipiales has regular buses to Cali (COP$69,000, 11 hours) via Popayán (COP$50,000, nine hours). All of these services will drop off in Pitalito (COP$25,000) where there are regular connections to San Agustín.

Regular minivans run to San Miguel and on to the Ecuadorean border (COP$35,000, four hours) from 4am to 6pm; in San Miguel you change to a *colectivo* (included in the price) that takes you to the international bridge. At the bridge, another *colectivo* (COP$2000) takes you to the passport control building (with Colombian and Ecuadorian customs in the same location). After you've cleared those, there are buses on the Ecuadorian side, waiting to take you to Lago Agrio (US$1 or COP$3500, 30 minutes). From Nueva Loja (Lago Agrio) on the Ecuadorean side of the border there are flights and buses to Quito. Security remains unsettled in this area so it's worth checking on the latest news before setting out.

Pickups and small buses run between Mocoa and Pasto (COP$35,000, five to six hours) from 4am to 7pm along the Trampolín de la Muerte (Trampoline of Death), a frightening single-lane mountain road with sheer drops into deep ravines. It's one of the most spectacular – and most dangerous – roads on the continent. While traffic is light (this road is favored by some daredevil cyclists), when you meet oncoming traffic you often have to navigate this treacherous track in reverse! It is safer to travel in a pickup than by bus and to complete the trip while it's light.

Restaurante Italiano ITALIAN $$
(☎314-375-8086; Vereda el Tablón; mains COP$16,000-23,000; ⏲7-10pm) A little way out of town, this unpretentious restaurant serves authentic traditional Italian plates, including a selection of homemade pastas. A taxi here costs around COP$4000. The owner is sometimes away from San Agustín – call ahead to make sure it's open.

Macizo Coffee COFFEE
(Calle 2 No 13-17; ⏲8:30am-8pm) On San Agustín's central plaza, this popular cafe offers a wide variety of beverages (coffee COP$3500 to COP$6000) using certified coffee from local farms, as well as tasty light meals. There are another couple of branches in the Parque Arqueológico.

El Faro CAFE
(Ambrosia; Carrera 13 No 6-50; cocktails COP$10,000-17,000; ⏲5-11:30pm Tue-Sun) This laid-back cafe-bar has an arty vibe that's conducive to conversation over beers or cocktails. It also serves up San Agustín's best pizzas (COP$12,000 to COP$19,000) from the wood-burning oven in the courtyard.

Shopping

Farmers come to buy and sell at San Agustín's Monday market at **La Galería** (cnr Calle 2 & Carrera 11; ⏲5am-4pm). It's a raucous scene with few tourists. If you miss Monday, part of the marketplace is open the rest of the week, but it's a more subdued affair.

Information

Local touts pushing hotels and 'cheap' tours hang around in the center and often hustle passengers from arriving intercity buses. Arrange professional guides and jeeps through your hotel, at the tourism office or at the archaeological park.

Banco de Bogotá (Calle 3 No 10-61) A reliable ATM near the bus offices.

Tourist Office (320-486-3896; cnr Calle 3 & Carrera 12; 8am-noon & 2-5pm Mon-Fri) Official information point for visitors.

Getting There & Away

Bus company offices are located on the corner of Calle 3 and Carrera 11 (known as Cuatro Vientos). There are regular minibuses to Popayán (COP$37,000, five hours) and Cali (COP$42,000, eight hours). For Popayán the best service is provided by **Sotracauca** (314-721-2243; www.sotracauca.com; Cuatro Vientos; COP$30,000); it originates in San Agustín rather than Pitalito and doesn't require a transfer to the junction.

The road to Popayán passes through the spectacular *páramo* landscapes of Parque Nacional Puracé. Do not travel on this route at night as security remains an issue in remote mountainous areas.

Coomotor (315-885-8563; www.coomotor.com.co; Cuatro Vientos) and **Taxis Verdes** (314-330-0518; www.taxisverdes.net; Cuatro Vientos) have several early-morning and evening buses to Bogotá (COP$65,000 to COP$87,000, nine to 9½ hours), all of which will drop you in Neiva (COP$44,000 to COP$50,000, 4¼ hours). Coomotor also offers a direct service to Medellín (COP$120,000, 17½ hours) at 3pm in a large, comfortable bus.

For more frequent connections, travel to the large terminal in nearby Pitalito. Regular pickups (COP$5000, one hour) and buses (COP$10,000, one hour) ply the short distance between San Agustín and Pitalito.

For Tierradentro, go to Pitalito and change for La Plata (COP$25,000, 2½ hours), where you can get a bus or *colectivo* to San Andrés (COP$13,000, two hours). If you can't get a La Plata bus – they are somewhat unreliable – alternatively take a Neiva-bound bus from San Agustín or Pitalito to Garzon from where you can pick up a La Plata–bound service.

There's also a regular van service from Pitalito to Mocoa (COP22,000, three hours, six daily).

Arriving from Popayán, buses with few passengers will drop you at the crossroads 5km from town and pay your taxi fare to San Agustín. The taxi drivers often take you directly to a hotel they work with – be firm about where you want to go.

Getting Around

Around a dozen taxis service San Agustín. They can take you around town and, more importantly, to your lodging outside of town. The rates are fixed but confirm what you'll pay before you get in.

A bus runs the 2km to the archaeological park every 15 minutes (COP$1500) from the corner of Calle 5 and Carrera 14. Another service runs up the hill past El Tablón and La Chaquira to 'La Y.'

Colectivos ply the nearby country roads passing some of the rural hotels, although they are very infrequent and difficult to rely upon.

Tierradentro

2 / ELEV 1750M

Tierradentro is the second-most-important archaeological site in Colombia (after San Agustín) but gets surprisingly few visitors. Located well off the beaten track down some rough dirt roads, it is a peaceful place with friendly locals and awe-inspiring archaeological wonders. While San Agustín is noted for its statuary, the Unesco World Heritage Site of Tierradentro is remarkable for its elaborate underground tombs, created by those who lived here from AD 500 to AD 900. So far, archaeologists have discovered about 100 of these unusual funeral temples, the only examples of their kind in the Americas. There is a fabulous walk you can follow that takes in all the major tomb sites amid gorgeous mountain scenery.

Sights

Scattered across the hills around the little town of **San Andrés de Pisimbalá**, Tierradentro's **Parque Arqueológico** (Archaeological Park; 311-390-0324; www.icanh.gov.co; adult/student/child under 12yr COP$25,000/10,000/free; 8am-4pm, closed 1st Tue of month for maintenance) consists of five separate sites, four with tombs and one with an above-ground statuary, plus two museums.

Burial Sites & Statues

You can visit all the burial sites in Tierradentro on a full-day, 14km walk. Allow at least seven hours to complete the loop at a leisurely pace. The walk takes you through some spectacular scenery, and it's well worth doing the entire circuit. You can follow the loop in either direction, but it is recommended to head out counterclockwise, otherwise you will have a tough uphill climb at the be-

Tierradentro

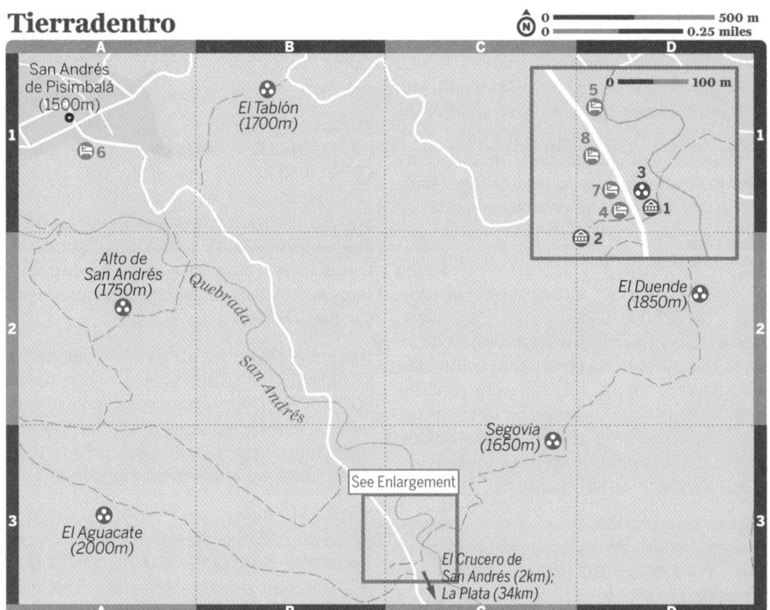

Tierradentro

Sights

1 Museo Arqueológico D1
2 Museo Etnográfico D2
3 Parque Arqueológico D1

Sleeping

4 Hospedaje Tierradentro D1
5 Hotel El Refugio D1
6 La Portada A1
7 Mi Casita D1
8 Residencias y Restaurante Pisimbalá D1

ginning of the hike. You'll need to pay your admission fee at the entrance to the Parque Arqueológico (p248) before setting out.

Only some of the tombs have electric lighting so bring a flashlight (torch) for better viewing. The tombs are open from 8am to 4pm.

Going counterclockwise, a 20-minute walk uphill from the museums is **Segovia** (8am-4pm) (1650m), the most important burial site. There are 28 tombs here, and it's believed that another 30-odd tombs remain buried nearby. Twelve of the tombs have electric lighting and are open to visitors; some with extremely well-preserved red, black and yellow geometric designs.

A 15-minute walk uphill from Segovia brings you to **El Duende** (8am-4pm) (1850m), where there are 12 tombs, five of which are open to visitors though their decoration hasn't been particularly well preserved. From here it's a 30-minute walk along the road to **El Tablón** (8am-4pm) (1700m), which has nine weather-worn stone statues of warriors, women and priests, similar to those of San Agustín, excavated in the area and now protected under a single roof. The site is poorly signposted; it is behind an adobe house with a tin roof perched on a hill on the left-hand side of the road. You can also get to El Tablón via the path off the main San Andrés road.

Continue into town. Next to the guesthouse and restaurant La Portada (p250) you'll find the path to **Alto de San Andrés** (8am-4pm) (1750m), with seven large tombs; Tomb 5 has remarkably well-preserved paintings, including depictions of human faces, and is considered one of the best in the park. Another of the tombs is closed because of structural instability and humidity, and another has caved in completely.

El Aguacate (8am-4pm) (2000m) is the most remote burial site, but has the best views. From Alto de San Andrés it's a steep 1½-hour walk up the mountainside, with superb countryside views en route, then downhill another 1½ hours back to the museums. There are 42 tombs, but most have been destroyed by *guaqueros* (tomb raiders). A total of 17 have been prepared for visitors, although only a few vaults still bear the remains of the original decoration. The best is Tomb 1, with its depictions of salamanders. Nearby, other overgrown tombs may appeal to those looking to discover their inner archaeologist.

Museums

Museo Arqueológico MUSEUM
(Parque Arqueológico; adult/student/child under 12yr COP$25,000/10,000/free; ⌚8am-4pm, closed 1st Tue of month for maintenance) Dedicated to the agricultural civilization behind the Tierradentro tombs, this museum contains pottery urns used to keep the ashes of the deceased. There are also miniature models of what the tombs may have looked like when they were freshly painted.

Museo Etnográfico MUSEUM
(Parque Arqueológico; adult/student/child under 12yr COP$25,000/10,000/free; ⌚8am-4pm, closed 1st Tue of month for maintenance) With a focus on post-Tierradentro indigenous communities, the Museo Etnográfico displays the utensils and artifacts of the Páez people alongside exhibits from colonial times, including a *trapiche* (sugarcane grinder), *bodoqueras* (blow-dart guns) and traditional clothing.

Sleeping

There are six basic lodgings clustered within the 500m stretch uphill from the Parque Arqueológico, many run by endearing senior citizens. The budget options charge around COP$18,000 to COP$25,000 per person.

For more creature comforts and better dining, you may prefer to stay in San Andrés de Pisimbalá, a 25-minute walk uphill from the Parque Arqueológico entrance.

★ **La Portada** GUESTHOUSE **$$**
(☎310-405-8560, 311-601-7884; http://laportadahotel.com; San Andrés de Pisimbalá; s/d COP$70,000/90,000, without bathroom COP$45,000/70,000; 📶) Right by where the bus stops in town, this simple, elegant lodge features plenty of bamboo and has spacious, clean rooms with hot-water bathrooms downstairs and cheaper rooms with shared cold-water bathrooms upstairs. Its breezy restaurant (meals COP$6000 to COP$11,000) also serves the best food in town, and it's the only local hotel with wi-fi.

Hosts Leo and Eva are a great source of information, and trekking and horseback-riding guides can be arranged (COP$60,000 per day).

Mi Casita GUESTHOUSE **$**
(☎312-764-1333; Tierradentro; r per person COP$20,000-22,000) One of the best options near the Museo Arqueológico, this basic but popular place has extremely friendly owners and a pleasant garden with mountain views. Some rooms have private bathrooms and there's a kitchen out the back that guests can use for COP$5000.

Hospedaje Tierradentro GUESTHOUSE **$**
(☎313-651-3713; Tierradentro; r per person COP$30,000) Offers clean, snug rooms located in a modern building at the back of the main house. It's a little more private than many of the other budget options here.

Hotel El Refugio HOTEL **$$**
(☎321-811-2395; hotelalbergueelrefugio@gmail.com; Tierradentro; s/d/tr COP$65,000/85,000/100,000; 🏊) The most comfortable option right near the Tierradentro museums, this community-run hotel has a big pool and tidy, if slightly generic, rooms with mountain views and cable TV. There's no wi-fi but you can watch horses roam free in the yard. Dining is limited.

Residencias y Restaurante Pisimbalá GUESTHOUSE **$**
(☎321-263-2334, 311-605-4835; Tierradentro; r per person with/without bathroom COP$22,000/17,000) The rooms here are set inside a family house and most have private bathrooms. The restaurant serves good, cheap meals (COP$7500 to COP$16,000) including vegetarian options.

Information

There is no bank near Tierradentro – bring sufficient funds.

Puerta Virtual (Via Sta Rosa, San Andrés de Pisimbalá; per hr COP$1500; ⌚9am-7pm Mon-Sat) offers a decent internet connection.

Getting There & Away

Arriving at Tierradentro, most buses will drop you at El Crucero de San Andrés, from where it's a 25-minute walk uphill to the Tierradentro museums and another 25-minute walk to San Andrés. Very irregular *colectivos* (COP$1500) make the trip. Moto-taxis are hard to find but the trip costs COP$3500 if you get lucky.

A direct bus from Popayán (COP$26,000, four hours) to San Andrés de Pisimbalá departs at

PARQUE NACIONAL NATURAL PURACÉ

Forty-five kilometers east of Popayán along the unpaved road to La Plata lies this 830-sq-km national park. The vast majority of the park lies within the *resguardo* (official territory) of the Puracé indigenous group.

At the time of research, the indigenous community had assumed control of the park following a dispute with the national government over its management. If you ask at any national parks or official government tourist office they will tell you that the park is closed, however the community is still accepting visitors and is dedicated to expanding its fledgling ecotourism program. In addition to your entrance fee, each group is required to hire an indigenous guide (COP$35,000 per group) to explore the park.

To get to the national park, take any La Plata–bound bus from Popayán to the Cruce de la Mina (COP$15,000, 1¼ hours). If you're visiting for the day, it's best to take the first bus at 4:30am or the 6:45am service at the latest.

From Cruce de la Mina it's a 1.5km walk uphill to the Cruce de Pilimbalá, where you turn left and walk another 1km to the visitor center (1km). There is usually a guide waiting at the bus stop to show you the way.

The last bus back to Popayán passes the Cruce de la Mina at around 4:30pm.

10:30am and passes in front of the museums, making the return journey at 6am. Alternatively, take a bus from Popayán to Inzá (departures at 5:30am, 8:30am, 10:30am, 1pm and 3pm) and get off at El Crucero de San Andrés. There are return buses to Popayán (typically at 8am, 1pm and 4pm). Timetables are subject to change due to the poor road conditions – landslides and breakdowns are not unheard of so taking the last bus is not recommended.

Buses and pickups typically leave San Andrés de Pisimbalá at 6am, 7am, 8am, 11:30am and 3pm for La Plata (COP$13,000, 2½ hours), where you can pick up connections to Bogotá, Neiva for the Desierto de la Tatacoa and Pitalito for San Agustín. Reserve a place in advance at the orange house in front of La Portada.

From San Augustín you can take the 6am Bogotá bus, get off in Garzón (two hours), transfer to a La Plata bus (arriving there around 10:30am), then take the 10:30am bus to San Andrés de Pisimbalá (2½ hours). To get to San Agustín around 1pm, take the 6am bus from San Andrés de Pisimbalá.

If you prefer a guided visit with your own 4WD transport, Popayán Tours (p239) in Popayán can make arrangements.

Desierto de la Tatacoa

Halfway between Bogotá and San Agustín lies the Tatacoa Desert, a striking landscape of eroded red cliffs and gullies, sculpted by the infrequent rain.

Tatacoa isn't really a desert, although the thermometer says otherwise – it sometimes hits 50°C (122°F). It's technically semi-arid dry tropical forest, averaging 1070mm of rain annually. Surrounded by mountains, the peaks around Nevado de Huila (5750m) grab most of the incoming precipitation, leaving 330-sq-km Tatacoa arid. The result is an ecosystem unlike anywhere else in Colombia – there are scorpions and weasels, fruit-bearing cacti, and at least 72 bird species.

To get to Tatacoa, you'll have to pass through **Neiva**, the capital of the Huíla department and a port on the Río Magdalena. From there take a *colectivo* one hour northwest to Villavieja. You can spend the night in Villavieja or in the desert.

Bring sturdy shoes (there are cactus spines on the ground) and a flashlight (torch).

★ Observatorio Astronómico Astrosur OBSERVATORY
(☎310-465-6765; www.tatacoa-astronomia.com; Tigre de Marte, Tatacoa; viewings adult/child under 10yr COP$5000/3000; ⏰7-9pm) Former Tatacoa Observatory resident astronomer Javier Rua Restrepo now runs his own observatory around 1km further away from town. He is a dynamic teacher who clearly loves his work and he has a number of high-quality telescopes for visitors to use. Talks at 6:30pm daily are in Spanish only.

Most desert accommodations are basically four concrete walls with a corrugated tin roof, worn bedding and no mosquito nets. There's also one high-end resort and a couple of places to pitch a tent. Accommodations in and near Villavieja eclipse those in the desert in terms of quality.

There are only a couple of basic dedicated eating places in the desert. However, all guesthouses prepare simple meals for their guests, usually consisting of meat, rice and salad.

Getting There & Away

Moto-taxis in Villavieja charge COP$16,000 to take up to three people to the Observatorio Astronómico de la Tatacoa and nearby guesthouses. One place in Villavieja, **Tatacoa Bicitour** (300-287-6696, 316-748-2213; www.tatacoa bicitour.com; Calle 7 No 2-59; rental per hour COP$10,000), rents bicycles, or you could walk the 4km, but take note that there's no shade, shelter or water on the way.

Villavieja

8 / POP 7560 / ELEV 430M

This small desert town is the portal to the Desierto de la Tatacoa. Founded in 1550, it has largely been forgotten about since. A few families continue to eke out a living herding goats, but many have turned to tourism.

On weekends and holidays it's often visited by *bogotanos* looking to warm up, but on other occasions you'll have the place to yourself.

Sights

You can see some of the region's rich paleontological findings at the **Museo Paleontológico** (8-879-7744, ext 10, 314-347-6812; Plaza Principal; COP$2500; 8am-noon & 2-5:30pm) on the main square.

Sleeping

There are several low-key hotels in town but most travelers prefer to spend the night in Desierto de la Tatacoa itself.

Hotel Boutique Yararaka BOUTIQUE HOTEL **$$**
(313-247-0165; www.facebook.com/HotelBoutique Yararaka; Carrera 4 No 4-43; r/f COP$170,000/ 350,000;) A good alternative to the rather generic hotel rooms on offer elsewhere in Villavieja, this colonial-style place has well-equipped rooms under a large thatched roof. All surround a courtyard swimming pool. The downside here is the lack of ceilings – while this keeps the rooms cool, it means privacy is at a minimum and noise can be an issue.

Villa Paraiso HOTEL **$$**
(321-234-5424; www.hotelvillaparaisovillavieja. com; Calle 4 No 7-69; s/d/tr/q COP$80,000/140, 000/180,000/240,000;) One of the most comfortable choices in Villavieja, Villa Paraiso offers smallish, whitewashed rooms with bright splashes of color, private bathrooms, air-con and cable TV along with a decent pool out the back. Staff can organise transfers to the desert.

Information

Banco Agrario (Calle 4 No 4-30) The only ATM in town.

Getting There & Away

Vans hop the 37km between Neiva and Villavieja (COP$8000, one hour) from 5am to 7pm and most continue on to the Cusco area of the Desierto de la Tatacoa (COP$16,000). Vans leave with a minimum of five passengers; there are frequent services in the early morning and late afternoon, but during the day you could be waiting an hour or two.

From Neiva there are frequent bus services to Bogotá (COP$30,000 to COP$45,000, six hours). There are several Coomotor buses a day direct to San Agustín (COP$30,000 to COP$45,000, four to five hours). For Tierradentro, change at La Plata (COP$25,000, two to 2½ hours).

NARIÑO

Welcome to Ecuador – almost. Nariño is Colombia's most southwesterly department, and the Ecuadorean influence is strong.

The Andes loom high and forbidding on their southerly march. The 'volcano alley' that runs the length of Ecuador begins here – pleasant Pasto, the departmental capital, sits a mere 8km from an active volcano covered in patchwork farmland.

Most people visit the region only to cross the border, but it's worth spending a few days here. Pasto has a compact center that's worth a stroll, Laguna de la Cocha is enchanting, and the towering Santuario de Las Lajas near Ipiales is an astonishing sight to behold.

Pasto

2 / POP 382,200 / ELEV 2527M

Just two hours from Ecuador, Pasto is a pleasant city nestling in a fertile valley, and the logical jumping-off point for the border. There are several fine colonial buildings and museums, and nature lovers might consider a longer stay, as Pasto is surrounded by some spectacular countryside and makes a good base for visiting Laguna de la Cocha, Laguna Verde and the restless Volcán Galeras.

The weather here is cool – so cool, in fact, you'll see *helado de paíla* being prepared fresh on the streets; it's traditional ice cream made in a copper tub sitting on a platform of ice.

Pasto

Pasto

Sights

1 Museo del Oro D4
2 Museo Taminango de Artes y Tradiciones A2

Sleeping

3 Hotel Casa Lopez C4
4 Hotel Casa Madrigal B2

Eating

5 Caffeto C2
6 Salón Guadalquivir C2

Drinking & Nightlife

7 Cafe La Catedral B2
8 Cola de Gallo C1

Shopping

9 Barniz de Pasto Obando A3

Sights

Museo del Oro MUSEUM
(2-721-3001; Calle 19 No 21-27; 10am-5pm Tue-Sat) FREE For insight into the pre-Columbian cultures of Nariño, check out this museum's small but interesting collection of indigenous gold and pottery. Among the most interesting pieces are the gold diadems worn by indigenous chieftains and the spinning discs used in ceremonies and events – a kind of pre-Columbian strobe.

Museo Taminango de Artes y Tradiciones MUSEUM
(2-723-5539; museotaminango@gmail.com; Calle 13 No 27-67; adult COP$3000; 8am-noon & 2-6pm Mon-Fri, 9am-1pm Sat) This museum has interesting displays on indigenous weaving techniques and *barniz de Pasto* alongside a hodgepodge of antiques. It's worth visiting since it's housed in a meticulously restored *casona* (large house) from 1623, reputedly the oldest surviving two-story house in Colombia.

Festivals & Events

Carnaval de Blancos y Negros CULTURAL
(www.carnavaldepasto.org; Jan) Pasto's major event is held on January 5 and 6. Its origins go back to the times of Spanish rule, when slaves were allowed to celebrate on January 5 and their masters showed approval by painting their faces black. On the following day, the slaves painted their faces white.

On these two days the city goes wild, with everybody painting or dusting one another with grease, chalk, talc, flour and any other available substance even vaguely black or white in tone. It's a serious affair – wear the worst clothes you have and buy an *antifaz*, a sort of mask to protect the face, widely sold for this occasion. Visitors with respiratory issues should not attend – you'll be coughing up talcum powder for days afterwards.

Sleeping

★**Hotel Casa Lopez** HOTEL $$$
(2-720-8172; hcasalopez@gmail.com; Calle 18 No 21B-07; r/tr/q from COP$214,000/249,000/284,000;) In a perfectly restored colonial home in the center, this family-run hotel is in a league of its own in terms of comfort, service and attention to detail. Set around a pretty, flower-festooned courtyard, the charming rooms have polished wooden floors and antique furnishings.

The affable owners are some of the most accommodating hosts around – don't be surprised if they pop around with a hot-water bottle or a cup of hot chocolate in the evening. There's a classy restaurant downstairs serving typical meals.

Hotel Casa Madrigal HOTEL $$$
(2-723-4592; www.hotelcasamadrigal.blogspot.com; Carrera 26 No 15-37; s/d/f incl breakfast COP$173,000/180,000/385,000;) Popular with business travelers, this well-equipped hotel has spacious rooms with king-size beds, work desks and all the mod-cons. The ample bathrooms have great showers and positively shine. There's a good restaurant downstairs.

Eating & Drinking

For fast food Nariño-style, visit a *picanteria* – diners that serve *llapingachos* (grilled potato cakes topped with cheese). Pasto is big on *cuy* (guinea pig): you will find it in barbecued form in many restaurants, especially on weekends.

The area around Palermo has many fine restaurants serving both local and international cuisine.

Guadalquivir Cafe COLOMBIAN $
(2-723-9504; Calle 19 No 24-84; snacks COP$1000-9000, mains COP$11,500-24,000; 7am-8:30pm Mon-Fri, to 8pm Sat, 8:30am-3:30pm Sun) This cozy cafe on the plaza serves classic *pastuso* snacks, including *empanadas de anejo* (small fried pastries), *quimbilitos* (sweet pastries of raisin, vanilla and sweetcorn) and *envueltas de chocolo* (sweetcorn cakes), in addition to traditional meals.

KRK Caffeto CAFE $$
(2-729-2720; www.krkcaffeto.com; Calle 19 No 25-62; mains COP12,000-26,000; 8am-10pm Mon-Sat) This fancy bakery-cafe does gourmet sandwiches, crepes, lasagna and salads. The cakes are stupendous, and it also serves enormous ice-cream sundaes and coffee

VOLCÁN GALERAS

Just 8km from the center of Pasto, Volcán Galeras (4267m), one of Colombia's most active volcanoes, continues to rumble and threaten. The upper part of the volcano is preserved as a national park, **Santuario de Flora y Fauna Volcán Galeras** (COP$2000; 8am-noon), while its lower slopes are a patchwork of farms and bright-green pastureland.

Much of the park has long been closed to the public due to the risk of eruption, however, the area around Telpis is open to visitors. Here you will find the Laguna de Telpis, a mystical lake surrounded by *páramo* (high-mountain plains) at more than 3000m, reachable via a 6km-long trail.

To visit from Pasto, take a taxi to Yacuanquer (COP$4000) from the parking lot in front of the bus terminal, then continue in either a moto-taxi or *colectivo* (both cost COP$2500) to the village of San Felipe. In San Felipe you will need to contract a guide (around COP$30,000 per group of up to 10 people) for the three-hour hike to the *mirador* (lookout).

You'll need to arrive at the park before noon or you won't be let in. Good shoes and cold-weather gear are essential for this hike.

hand-picked from *fincas* (farms) in the Nariño province.

Asadero de Cuyes Pinzón COLOMBIAN $$$
(☎321-570-6485; Carrera 40 No 19B-76, Palermo; cuy COP$42,000; ⏰noon-10pm Mon-Sat, to 2pm Sun) *Pastusos* get dressed up to eat at this place about 1.5km north of the center of town. There's only one thing on the menu: *asado de cuy* (grilled guinea pig). The best way to get the meat off the bone is to eat with your hands – you'll be given plastic gloves. One *cuy* is big enough for two.

Cafe La Catedral CAFE $
(☎2-729-8584; www.cafelacatedral.com; Carrera 26 No 16-37; cakes from COP$11,000; ⏰8:30am-12:30pm & 3:30-8:30pm Mon-Sat) Locals love sitting and chatting over a good cup of coffee at this cafe half a block from the cathedral, a popular place to hang out. There's a full selection of beverages but the real reason to swing by is for the amazing cakes and pastries.

Shopping

The city is known for *barniz de Pasto,* a traditional indigenous craft that uses processed vegetable resins from the Amazon region to decorate wooden objects in colorful patterns. Items can be bought at **Barniz de Pasto Obandos** (☎2-722-4045, 301-350-0030; Carrera 25 No 13-04; ⏰8:30am-12:30pm & 2:30-6:30pm Mon-Fri, 9am-12:30pm & 3-6:30pm Sat), where you can also arrange to watch the artisans work.

Information

Most of the major banks are around Plaza de Nariño.

4-72 (www.4-72.com.co; Calle 15 No 22-05; ⏰8am-6pm Mon-Fri, 9am-noon Sat) Post office.

Banco de Bogotá (Calle 19 No 24-68)

Banco Popular (Carrera 24 No 18-80; ⏰8am-5pm Mon-Fri, 9am-noon Sat)

Nariño Tourism Office (Oficina Departmental de Turismo; ☎2-723-4962; http://narino.gov.co/turismo; Calle 18 No 25-25; ⏰8am-noon & 2-6pm Mon-Fri) Useful tourism office covering the department of Nariño.

Pasto Tourism Office (Punto Información Turistica; ☎2-733-4765; www.turismopasto.gov.co; cnr Calle 19 & Carrera 25; ⏰8am-noon & 2-6pm) Offers advice about sights within the city.

Getting There & Away

Aeropuerto Antonio Nariño (Chachagüí, Panamericana), 33km north of the city on the road to Cali, has several daily flights to Bogotá and a single one to Cali. *Colectivos* (COP$11,000, 45 minutes) for the airport leave from Plaza de Nariño at the corner of Calle 18 and Carrera 25. A taxi will cost around COP$40,000.

The **bus terminal** (☎2-730-8955; www.terminaldepasto.com; Carrera 6) is 2km south of the city center. Frequent buses, minibuses and *colectivos* go to Ipiales (COP$9000, 1½ to two hours); sit on the left for better views. Pickups and *colectivos* also run to Mocoa via the spectacular and sometimes frightening Trampolín de la Muerte (COP$35,000, six hours); get an early morning ride. Plenty of buses ply the spectacular road to Cali (COP$32,000 to COP$40,000, nine hours). These buses will also drop you off in Popayán (COP$30,000, six hours). More than a dozen direct buses depart daily to Bogotá (COP$140,000, 20 hours).

Laguna de la Cocha

☎2 / ELEV 2800M

Set amid rolling green hills, and often shrouded in mist, this spectacular lake is a must-do day trip on your visit to Pasto. You can take a boat ride around the lake, stopping at Isla Corota along the way. This small **island** (Laguna de la Cocha; entry COP$2500) is a national park, and at an altitude of 2830m it offers a rare glimpse of a well-preserved, evergreen cloud forest. There's a small chapel and a biological research station here. A 550m-long boardwalk takes you the length of the island to a *mirador* (lookout). Boats to Isla Corota cost COP$30,000 for up to 10 people and leave from the hamlet of Puerto El Encano on the edge of the lake.

Sleeping

Hotel Sindamanoy HOTEL $$
(☎2-721-8222; www.hotelsindamanoy.gov.co; Vereda Santa Clara, Corregimiento el Encano; s/d/ste incl breakfast COP$109,000/160,000/198,000; 📶) An aging but elegant chalet boasting a spectacular location overlooking Isla Corota. While the views are impressive, some of the rooms are a little bit worn so ask to take a look around before choosing. The elegant restaurant (mains COP$23,000 COP$30,000) is a fine spot for a meal with a view.

Chalet Guamuez HOTEL $$$
(☎2-721-9308; www.chaletguamuez.com; Via Laguna de la Cocha, Puerto El Encano; r with fireplace/heater COP$264,000/189,000, 4-person cabaña from COP$265,000; 📶) This faux-Swiss resort has tidy rooms overlooking a flower-filled garden that runs down to the lake. The basic rooms are fine but the pricier options are a major step up and have a private fireplace

and small balconies. Ask for a room with a lake view – they're the same price as those looking toward the garden.

In fitting with the retreat vibe here, there are no TVs in the rooms, but there is a sauna, and horses are available for rent. The restaurant (mains COP$24,000 to COP$34,000) serves vegetarian dishes and fondue in addition to local favorites.

Getting There & Away

Shared taxis to Río Encano by the lake (COP$4500, 45 minutes) leave from the Plaza de Carnaval in central Pasto and from in front of the hospital along Av Colombia; double-check the best place to catch the bus with your lodgings. The taxis seat four people; if you're in a hurry, pay for all four seats.

It's possible to reach the lakeshore hotels by taxi from El Encano (around COP$10,000).

Ipiales

2 / POP 77,729 / ELEV 2898M

Ipiales is a commercial town only 7km from the Ecuador border. Driven by trade across the frontier, it's an uninspiring place with little to see or do, although there's a short side trip to the splendid Santuario de Las Lajas (p257), and riding the scenic Panamericana from Pasto is also thrilling.

GETTING TO ECUADOR

Getting to the border Frequent shared taxis (COP$3000, 15 minutes) travel the 2.5km from Ipiales to Rumichaca from around 5am to 8pm, leaving from the bus terminal and the market area near the corner of Calle 14 and Carrera 8. A private taxi is COP$10,000.

At the border Passport formalities are processed at the border in Rumichaca, situated 3km southwest of Ipiales and 8km east of Tulcán in Ecuador. The border is always open and the procedure is relatively straightforward. However, due to the current humanitarian crisis in Venezuela, and Venezuelan refugees fleeing to Ecuador, it may take 15 minutes to leave Colombia but five hours or so to enter Ecuador.

Moving on After crossing the border on foot, take another *colectivo* to Tulcán (COP$2000, 6km). Colombian and Ecuadorean currency is accepted. From Tulcán's Terminal Terrestre, long-distance buses run to numerous Ecuadorian destinations.

Sleeping & Eating

As a busy border town, Ipiales offers decent accommodations for all budgets, however, there are few good reasons to spend the night here; Pasto is a far nicer city and is not much further along the Panamericana.

For some typical grub head to the traditional Barrio El Charco, where there are a dozen or so places selling barbecued *cuy* – the guinea pigs are flattened out and cooked over an open fire on a mechanical spit. A few local restaurants dot the streets off the Plaza la Pola.

Gran Hotel HOTEL **$$**
(317-829-3982; Carrera 5 No 21-100; s/d COP$65,000/110,000;) Located in a commercial neighborhood a short walk from Ipiales' center, this friendly hotel has comfortable, tidy rooms with plasma TV screens and hot water. Some rooms can be a little noisy so ask to see all the options.

Information

There are numerous ATMs around Plaza la Pola.

Artesys Fast internet access.

Banco de Bogotá (Carrera 6 No 13-55) ATM in the center.

Ecuadorian Consulate (2-773-2292; www.ipiales.consulado.gob.ec; Carrera 7 No 14-10; 8:30am-5pm Mon-Fri)

Getting There & Away

Aeropuerto San Luis (Via Ipiales-Aldana) is 7km northwest of Ipiales, on the road to Cumbal, and is accessible by taxi (around COP$15,000). Satena (www.satena.com) has flights to Bogotá (1¼ hours) on Tuesday and Thursday.

Ipiales has a large colorfully painted **bus terminal** (Carrera 2) about 1km northeast of the center. Urban buses can take you into the center of town (COP$1300), or you can grab a taxi (around COP$4000).

There are several companies running buses to Bogotá (COP$129,000, 22 hours, six daily) and Cali (COP$36,000, 11 hours, seven daily). All will drop you in Popayán (COP$27,000, 8½ hours).

There are plenty of buses, minibuses and *colectivos* to Pasto (COP$8000 to COP$10,000, 1½ to two hours). They all depart from the bus terminal. Sit on the right for better views.

WORTH A TRIP

LAGUNA VERDE

You'll see photos of this striking emerald-green lake high in the Andes all over Nariño. It sits in the crater of the extinct Volcán Azufral (4000m), near **Túquerres** (3070m) – the highest major town in Colombia – and can be visited on a day trip from either Pasto or Ipiales, but you'll want to set out early.

At the park gate there are bathrooms and a little shop where you'll pay a small admission fee. From here it's a 6km hike taking 1½ to two hours up a gentle incline to the lookout at the crater's edge. If you want to get closer, a steep path leads 700m down into the crater to the lake's edge. It can be very muddy and the hike back up to the rim is tiring. While the hike is not particularly long, the high altitude makes it challenging, especially the climb back up from the lakeshore to the lookout. Allow around five hours for the round trip from La Cabaña. Bring good cold-weather gear and wear plenty of layers. It can get warm while hiking, but the weather changes very quickly and the wind can be extremely cold. It's also important to bring sunscreen even if it's overcast.

Buses to Túquerres depart from both Pasto (COP$6000, 1¾ hours) and Ipiales (COP$7000, 1½ hours).

Upon arrival in Túquerres, you'll need to hire a taxi (round trip COP$40,000 to COP$50,000) for the 30-minute trip to 'La Cabaña' (3600m) where the trail begins. It's advisable to arrange a time in advance with your driver for the return trip. Solo travelers could also take a motorcycle taxi (around COP$20,000 round trip). A more economic option is to take a bus from Túquerres to the hamlet of San Roque Alto from where you can hike up the road to La Cabaña, but this adds around three hours to the overall journey. Either way make sure you arrive before 1pm or the rangers may not let you onto the path.

Santuario de Las Lajas

ELEV 2600M

Built on a stone bridge spanning a deep gorge at the village of Las Lajas, the neo-Gothic **Santuario de Las Lajas** (⌚6am-6pm) is a strange but spectacular sight. On Sunday the place is full of pilgrims and vendors selling ice cream and souvenirs; during the week it gets hardly any visitors. The pilgrims place their faith in the Virgin Mary, whose image is believed to have emerged from an enormous vertical rock 45m above the river sometime in the mid-18th century. Plaques of thanksgiving line the walls of the canyon, many from prominent Colombian politicians.

The church is built directly against the rocky wall of the gorge where the miraculous image appeared. A gilded painting of the Virgin, accompanied by Santo Domingo and San Francisco, has been painted directly on the rocks just to be sure there is no confusion. The first chapel was built in 1803; today's church, designed by Nariño architect Lucindo Espinoza, was built between 1926 and 1944.

The best views of the church are found by the waterfall on the far side of the canyon.

Santuario de Las Lajas is easily accessible from Ipiales, but if you want to stay near the site there are several basic hotels lining the road down to the church.

ℹ Getting There & Away

The sanctuary is located 7km southeast of Ipiales. Shared taxis and vans run regularly from the corner of Carrera 6 and Calle 4 in Ipiales (COP$2500, 20 minutes) and from the town's bus station (p256) (COP$2500, 15 minutes). Pay for all four seats if you're in a hurry, or alternatively a regular taxi from anywhere in Ipiales will cost around COP$11,000. On Sundays there are direct shared taxis from Pasto if you prefer the greater creature comforts that the city offers.

AT A GLANCE

POPULATION
1.5 million

AREA
83,000 km²

BEST WHALE-WATCHING
Wildlife Pacific (p262)

BEST WATERFALL
Salto del Aeropuerto (p262)

BEST JUNGLE EXPLORING
Cascada del Tigre (p264)

WHEN TO GO

Jan–Mar
Lighter rains make for better hiking and other outdoor activities.

Jul–Oct
Humpback whales arrive in the region after an epic journey from Antarctica.

Sep–Dec
Watch giant marine turtles scramble up beaches to lay their eggs.

Coast of Choco (p260)
OSCAR GARCES/SHUTTERSTOCK

Pacific Coast

There are few destinations as ruggedly spectacular as the Pacific region of Colombia. This is where the jungle not so much meets the sea as comes crashing headlong into it. It is a place where waterfalls pour out of forest-covered bluffs onto spectacular gray-sand beaches, thermal pools lie hidden in dense jungle and tiny indigenous villages cling to the edge of wild rivers; where whales and dolphins frolic so close to shore you can admire them from your hammock and majestic sea turtles come even closer. There are plenty of comfortable ecoresorts throughout the region and you will find budget guesthouses in the many friendly Afro-descendant communities whose residents eke out a living from fishing and agriculture.

INCLUDES

Chocó 260
Bahía Solano 260
El Valle 264
Parque Nacional Natural Ensenada de Utría 265
Nuquí 266
South Coast 270
Parque Nacional Natural Isla Gorgona 271

National, State & Regional Parks

Parque Nacional Natural (PNN) Isla Gorgona (p271) and Santuario de Flora y Fauna Malpelo (p271) are both protected marine parks boasting interesting diving. Parque Nacional Natural (PNN) Ensenada de Utría (p265), halfway between El Valle and Nuquí, attracts whales in season that play in a narrow bay just a few hundred meters offshore.

Safe Travel

Security throughout the region remains an issue and while visitors are unlikely to have any problems, it's worth nothing that both paramilitary and dissident guerrilla groups remain active in remote areas, especially around Tumaco near the Ecuadorean border and in the northern reaches of El Chocó near Panama. Recently there has been an increase in paramilitary presence in more isolated areas around Nuquí and Bahía Solano, although a push by the Colombian military to reoccupy these areas has seen things calm down again.

When we visited, the areas covered were for the most part calm, but you may wish to check on the latest situation before planning your visit.

Getting There & Around

Only the Cali–Buenaventura highway links the Pacific coast to the rest of Colombia. From Buenaventura boats travel up and down the coast, although most travelers to the Chocó arrive by light plane via Medellín. It's also possible to reach here on very irregular boat services from Panama.

There is only one, very short road on the entire Pacific coast. Almost all local travel is in small boats that connect villages to transportation hubs. Wrap your luggage in plastic garbage bags to prevent a thorough soaking. Many villages and resorts don't have docks so you're likely to get a little wet when disembarking; wear shorts and sandals.

CHOCÓ

El Chocó is covered in dense jungle and is one of the wettest places on earth. On average, it receives 16m to 18m of rain per year. This defines the region, the people and its culture. When the sun shines, it's too hot to move too fast, and when it rains – almost every day – no one wants to go out and get wet. No wonder people joke about *hora chocoana* (Chocó time). Life here is slow.

It's not a cheap destination. Transportation is mostly in small boats that are much pricier than a comparable journey by bus. Furthermore, accommodations here are far more expensive than similar options elsewhere in Colombia. However, budget travelers should not be totally discouraged. With a bit of planning, a willingness to prepare your own meals and a flexible itinerary, it's possible to discover this amazing region without breaking the bank.

Bahía Solano

☎4 / POP 9375

Bahía Solano is the largest settlement on the Chocó coast. It is famous for its deep-sea sportfishing – some of the best in the world – and as a base to go whale-watching. It sits at the mouth of the Río Jella and faces north into the ocean. The town itself doesn't have a beach, although at low tide it's possible to walk around the bay to one and there are many nice stretches of sand a short boat ride away.

Sights & Activities

Near the town's south end close to the waterfront, an overgrown path leads upward to a small shrine to the Virgin Mary; it offers great views.

Specialist frog-spotting tours are becoming popular in the jungles around Bahía Solano, and birdwatching, diving (p260) and fishing (p260) are also good around here.

There is good scuba diving in 500ft-deep Bahía Solano. The warship *Sebastián de Belalcázar*, which survived the attack on Pearl Harbor, was sunk near Playa Huína to create an artificial reef (Buqué Hundido). Cave divers may like to explore the caves near Cabo Marzo. There are two dive operators in town but they are not always offering dives. Expect to pay around COP$280,000 for two immersions. **Posada del Mar** (☎314-630-6723; posadadelmarbahiasolano@yahoo.es; Barrio El Carmen) has enthusiastic management and offers packages with dives and accommodations; by the bridge over the river, **Cabo Marzo** (☎311-753-2880; blackmarlin19@hotmail.com; Donde Elvis) offers similar dives but is less organized.

Colombia's Pacific coast is one of the best places in South America to pull in record-breaking blue marlin and sailfish. Expect to pay around COP$1,800,000 per day for four to five anglers. A recommended skipper is **Vicente Gonzalez** (☎320-694-5256; Carrera 4).

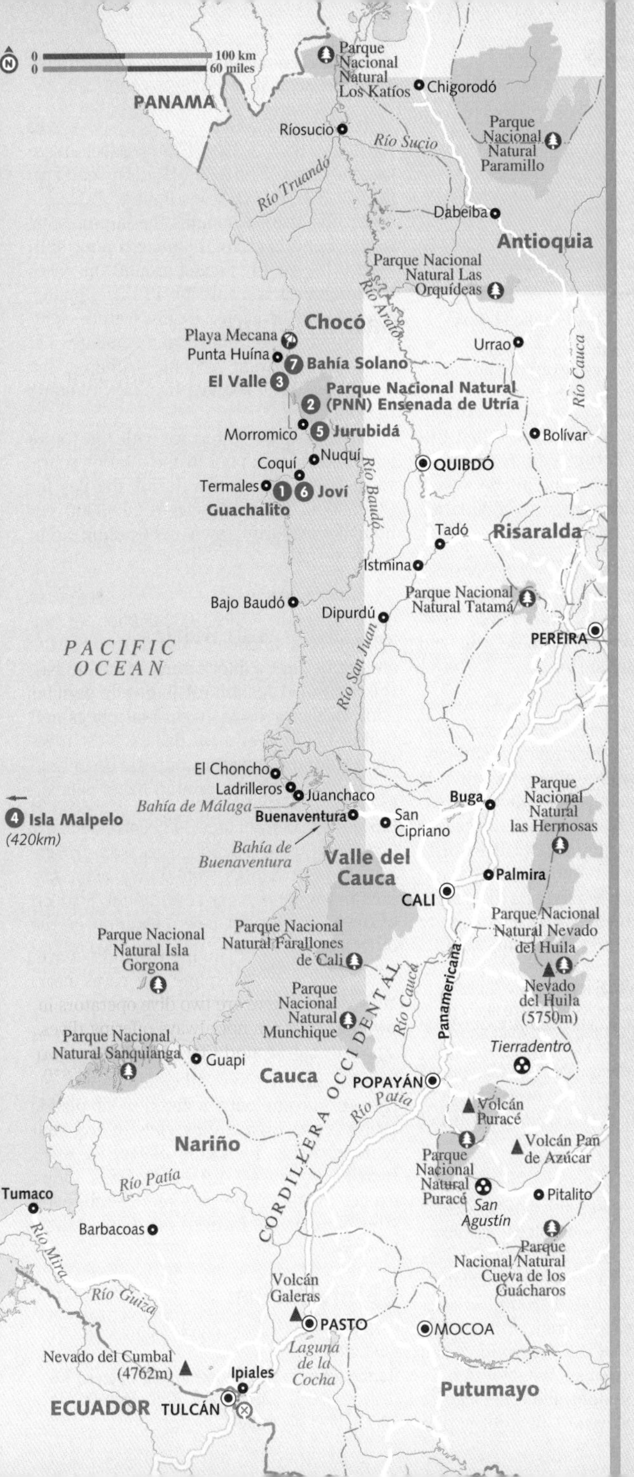

Pacific Coast Highlights

1 Guachalito (p268) Relaxing amid tropical gardens on gray-sand beaches in the Chocó's charming low-key resort district.

2 Parque Nacional Natural (PNN) Ensenada de Utría (p265) Spotting humpback whales playing with their young just offshore.

3 El Valle (p264) Surfing the Pacific's 2m waves with a dramatic jungle backdrop at Playa Almejal.

4 Isla Malpelo (p271) Diving with hundreds of hammerhead sharks at Colombia's most remote scuba destination.

5 Jurubidá (p267) Soaking in undeveloped thermal pools deep in the jungle beside this friendly little town.

6 Joví (p269) Traveling in a dugout canoe up a jungle-clad river to bathe in remote waterfalls.

7 Bahía Solano (p260) Hiking to swimming holes cloaked in virgin forest.

LOCAL KNOWLEDGE

BEST BREAKS

El Chocó has Colombia's best surf spots and the difficult access means you'll have them all to yourself:

- Pico de Loro, Cabo Corrientes near Arusí – left-hand reef
- Bananal, north of El Valle – left-hand reef
- Playa Almejal, El Valle – beach break
- Juna, north of Valle – right-hand reef

Cascada Chocolatal WATERFALL
Near the south end of town you'll find this impressive waterfall that empties into an icy-cold swimming hole. The jungle towers over you on both sides of the riverbank in a cascade of flowers and birdsong.

Salto del Aeropuerto WATERFALL
A short walk from the airport, this high-volume waterfall pours into deep, crystal-clear swimming holes where you can spot giant freshwater shrimp.

Wildlife Pacific WHALE WATCHING
(☎310-525-0023; www.wildlifepacific.com; half-/full-day trip COP$100,000/145,000; ⏱8:30am-6pm) Run by marine biologists, this is Bahía's most complete whale-watching tour. It's a full-day excursion that includes plenty of explanations and the use of underwater audio equipment to listen to the giant mammals. It also includes a meal in a local community and the chance to relax on an empty beach or at a fresh-water swimming hole.

Sleeping & Eating

All the hotels in the town itself are down by the waterfront in Barrio El Carmen.

If you're after a cheap, local meal, head to the no-name shacks near the hospital where you can get fried fish and *patacones* (fried plantains).

★ **Posada del Mar** GUESTHOUSE $$
(☎314-630-6723; posadadelmarbahiasolano@yahoo.es; r per person with/without bathroom COP$43,000/35,000; wifi) The best budget option in town has a number of brightly painted wooden huts dotted around a pleasant garden and cheaper rooms with shared bathrooms on top of the reception. The friendly owners organize whale-watching tours (COP$80,000) alongside other nature activities and are a wealth of information about attractions in the area. Good breakfasts are available for COP$10,000.

Hotel Balboa Plaza HOTEL $$
(☎310-422-3377, 323-318-4887; www.hotelbalboainn.com; Carrera 2 No 6-73; s/d incl breakfast from COP$91,000/115,000; wifi pool) Built by Pablo Escobar, the Balboa remains the largest hotel in town and is easily the most comfortable, even if it's slightly ragged around the edges (maintenance is a mission in this climate). The bright, spacious rooms feature split-system air-conditioning and satellite TV; many have private balconies although sea views have been blocked by a new building in front.

There's a rooftop terrace with fine views and a good large pool in the interior courtyard; visitors can swim during the day for COP$5000. Rents bicycles (COP$5000 per hour) for exploring town and heading out to the waterfalls.

La Casa Negra SEAFOOD $$
(Calle 2; mains COP$16,000-25,000; ⏱7am-8:30pm) In a wooden house in front of the children's park a block back from the bay, this unsigned restaurant is hugely popular with locals for its tasty seafood plates and typical Colombian meat dishes. Most reliable restaurant in town.

El Pailón Solaneño SEAFOOD $$
(Donde Doña Haydee; ☎320-736-9454; Carrera 5, Chocolatal; mains COP$16,000-22,000; ⏱8am-3pm) One of Bahía's well-known older residents prepares very traditional seafood dishes in this bright new restaurant on the other side of the river. It's a little hard to find – take a moto-taxi. Doña Haydee will open in the evening if you call ahead.

Restaurante Cazuela SEAFOOD $$
(Carrera 3; mains COP$20,000-30,000; ⏱8am-9pm) It doesn't look like much but this tiny restaurant with a handful of plastic tables serves up a wide variety of excellent seafood dishes including *ollitas en salsa* (whelks in sauce) and tuna steaks. Don't expect much in the way of vegetables on your plate. It's in front of the Banco Agrario (p262).

Information

4-72 (Calle 4; ⏱8am-noon & 2-6pm Mon-Fri) Post office agent.

Banco Agrario de Colombia (cnr Carrera 3 & Calle 2; ⏱8-11:30am & 2-4:30pm Mon-Fri) The only ATM in the region.

Internet Doña Olga (Carrera 3; per hour COP$2200; 8am-8pm) Slow internet access but the only option in town.

Super Giros (Calle 3; 7:30am-8pm Mon-Sat, 9am-noon Sun) Foreign exchange; domestic wire transfers.

Getting There & Away

AIR

Aeropuerto José Celestino Mutis is serviced by **Satena** (1-8000-912-034, 1-605-2222; www.satena.com) and **ADA** (www.ada-aero.com), although both companies have suspended services on occasion due to the poor condition of the runway. When the airlines pull out, a posse of charter pilots pick up the slack in their tiny prop planes.

The airport's nickname is 'Sal Si Puedes' (Get Out If You Can). Because of heavy rain, planes are sometimes unable to leave. It would be unwise to book international connections for the same day you leave Bahía Solano.

A moto-taxi to/from the airport costs COP$3000 per person.

BOAT

It's possible to travel to Buenaventura on the cargo boats that bring in supplies. The journey takes about 24 hours, generally leaving in the afternoon (both ways), depending on the tides. Check on the security situation in Buenaventura before heading out.

The most regular service is the *Bahía Cupica* run by **Transportes Renacer** (2-242-518, 315-402-1563; Muelle El Piñal, Buenaventura). It leaves Buenaventura on Tuesday in the afternoon and returns from Bahía Solano on Saturday around noon. It costs COP$150,000 for a *camarote* (bunk bed) including meals. Call in advance to confirm departures – you don't want to get stuck in Buenaventura.

From Bahía Solano you can travel by small boat to Jaqué, Panama (six to eight hours), although boats are very infrequent and usually only leave about once a month. Expect to pay around US$100 per person. Among the captains making the trip are **'Profesor' Justino** (313-789-0635; Barrio Nuevo), a veteran of the route who travels with a slow but steady philosophy that avoids unnecessary bumps. He is getting on a bit now and usually takes a younger captain with him to handle the boat.

Be sure to stamp out of Colombia at the **Migración Colombia** (321-271-7745; www.migracioncolombia.gov.co; Calle 3; 24hr) office in Bahía Solano before leaving town. To enter Panama you'll need a yellow-fever vaccination and enough cash to prove you can travel onward (a minimum of US$500). Once you reach Jaqué and stamp in to Panama, there are flights (US$90) twice a week to Panama City with Air Panama. There is also a boat service once a week for around US$20.

TAXI & MOTO-TAXI

For travel to/from El Valle, shared taxis (COP$10,000, one hour) leave opposite the school when full. An express trip in a moto-taxi costs COP$30,000.

Around Bahía Solano

You don't have to travel far from Bahía Solano to find the kind of jungle-backed beaches that grace the promotional material for the Chocó. Heading out of town a short distance by boat, there are wonderful solitary stretches of sand well suited to swimming, hiking and wildlife-watching.

Punta Huína

A 20-minute boat ride from Bahía Solano takes you to this pretty beach with a mixture of gold and black sand. It's lined with coconut palms and several modest resorts and is easily the best beach in the area for swimming.

A small indigenous community lives here along with Afrocolombian villagers. Punta Huína has no phone signal, but a **Vive Digital** (phone card COP$3000; 8am-8pm) kiosk offers satellite phone calls with the purchase of a prepaid phone card.

There are several jungle walks you can do in the vicinity, including to **Playa de los Deseos**, **Cascada El Tigre** and **Playa Cocalito**.

Sleeping

Los Guásimos RENTAL HOUSE $

(Donde Pambelé; 320-796-6664; r per person COP$35,000) One of the best deals on this stretch of the Pacific coast, this small house sits alone on a hill across the river at the end of the beach. It sleeps up to 10, but if you've six or more you get the entire place. It has a large deck with magnificent views and a small kitchen to prepare meals.

WARDING OFF THE EVIL EYE

Cabalonga, a hard nut grown in the Chocó, is worn on a necklace by indigenous children to ward off the *mal de ojo* (evil eye) that some elderly women are thought to possess.

Most locals don't know it by name – ask around for Pambelé, the owner who also runs a bar by the river.

Pacific Sailfish GUESTHOUSE **$$**
(☎322-442-0386; pacificsailfish@gmail.com; r per person incl breakfast COP$90,000; 📶) Under new ownership, this appealing lodge in the village has a variety of neat wooden rooms with small private bathrooms, and arranges sportfishing excursions throughout the region. Prices include transportation from Bahía Solano.

★**Choibana** LODGE **$$$**
(☎310-878-1214; www.choibana.com; r per person incl breakfast COP$110,000) Set on a hillside overlooking a private beach backed by thick jungle, this atmospheric wooden lodge is a great place to take it easy. It has just three rooms – all with private bathrooms – and a porch hung with hammocks offering views across the bay to Playa Mecana. Plenty of space, nature and tranquillity.

It is located on the other side of the headland at the far end of Playa Huína. During low tide it's possible to walk to the village. Transportation from Bahía Solano is COP$30,000 for up to three visitors.

GETTING THERE & AWAY

There is no public transportation to Punta Huína, but many hotels in the area offer transportation. Otherwise, if you hang around the Bahía Solano wharf at lunchtime you should be able to grab a ride with local villagers (COP$10,000). You can also hire an express boat (COP$100,000).

Playa Mecana

Playa Mecana, a lovely long beach strewn with coconut palms, lies a 25-minute boat ride away from Bahía Solano. A short distance upriver from the beach lies the small Afrocolombian/indigenous community of Mecana, which has a fine swimming hole with crystal-clear waters.

Jardín Botánico del Pacífico (☎321-759-9012; www.jardinbotanicodelpacifico.org; r per person incl meals & transportation COP$195,000-250,000) is a 170-hectare nature reserve running alongside the Río Mecana made up of mangroves, virgin tropical forest and a botanical garden of native plants and trees. Its staff includes members of the local Emberá indigenous tribe who can take you on fantastic treks through the property. They can also take you on boat rides up the river and organize whale-watching excursions. There is great birdwatching right by the lodge.

It is possible to walk here from Bahía Solano but you must leave at or before low tide *(mareada baja)*. It's an hour's walk each way. Alternatively if you hang around at Bahía Solano's Esso dock you may be able to get a ride with a local villager (COP$10,000). An express boat will cost around COP$60,000 for up to eight passengers.

El Valle

☎4 / POP 3500

On the southern side of the peninsula from Bahía Solano sits its smaller neighbor, El Valle. At the west end of town is the pleasant **Playa Almejal**, a wide black-sand beach with fine surf and decent accommodations. El Valle is a good jumping-off point to visit Parque Nacional Natural Ensenada de Utría. It's also a good place to observe sea turtles during nesting season (September to December) and to spot whales just off the coast.

Sights & Activities

Estación Septiembre WILDLIFE RESERVE
(☎314-677-2488; Playa Cuevita) 🌿 On Playa Cuevita, 5km south of El Valle along the coast, is the turtle-nesting sanctuary and research station of Estación Septiembre. From June to December sea turtles arrive to lay eggs. The best time to see them is at night. The conservation project is run by the community organization Caguama – visitors are essential to keep it running. Entry is by voluntary donation.

There are cabins (room per person with/without meals COP$80,000/40,000) you can stay in if you want to spend some time here.

You can walk to the sanctuary from El Valle (two hours), although a local guide is recommended to show you the way. Caguama staff can also organize nighttime turtle-watching tours departing from El Valle.

Cascada del Tigre OUTDOORS
(COP$5000) A tough four-hour walk north of El Valle through the jungle and along the shore takes you to Cascada del Tigre, an impressive waterfall with a swimming hole. Local guides charge around COP$50,000 per person. It's an exhausting full-day excursion if you travel both ways on foot – consider hiring a boat (COP$50,000 per passenger, 30 minutes) for the return leg.

You can get a typical lunch (COP$15,000) beside the waterfall and there is an open-air thatched hut where visitors can rent a hammock for the night (COP$20,000) or set up a tent. Guests can access a basic kitchen. The early mornings here are spectacular with the sound of the waterfall backed by a cacophony of birdsong. It's pure unadulterated nature.

Balmes BIRDWATCHING
(313-517-5691) A recommended local birdwatching guide who will take visitors to see both aquatic and jungle species. Ask for him at the Humpback Turtle (p265) hostel.

Sleeping

Posada El Nativo GUESTHOUSE $
(311-639-1015; r per person COP$40,000) For budget accommodations with a local flavor, head to this pair of thatched cabañas set in a lush garden about 100m back from the beach, run by tourism legend 'El Nativo' and his wife. To get here, cross the bridge on the left after the Telecom office and follow the road around.

Humpback Turtle HOSTEL $$
(314-538-9792; www.humpbackturtle.com; hammocks COP$20,000, dm COP$35,000, r per person COP$60,000) One of the most remote hostels in Colombia, this hip place at the end of Playa Almejal is right on the beach beside a pair of waterfalls. Accommodations are in a collection of wooden huts surrounded by a veggie garden; all have shared bathrooms. The thatched-roof bar area is a great place to chill when the rains come down.

El Almejal HOTEL $$$
(4-412-5050, 320-624-6023; www.almejal.com.co; cabañas per person COP$184,000-265,000) The most luxurious option in the Bahía Solano area, El Almejal is set on an 8-hectare nature reserve halfway down Playa Almejal. The cabañas here have the most ingenious design – the walls of the lounge area open completely, allowing a breeze to pass through. Meals are served in a spacious open-air dining area.

Eating & Drinking

Rosa del Mar COLOMBIAN $
(mains COP$13,000-15,000; 7am-8pm) On the street in front of the church, Doña Rosalia cooks up the best meals in town. Sit down and enjoy fresh seafood in her converted living room in front of the TV.

El Mirador BAR
(10am-6pm Fri-Sun) Built on top of a rocky outcropping in the middle of Playa Almejal is El Mirador, one of Colombia's most spectacular bars. You can sit at the makeshift tables and suck down rum while the stereo blasts vallenato and reggaeton at the crashing waves.

Information

There is no longer a tourist information office in town although the staff at the Parques Nacionales office may be able to answer questions about the area.

The closest ATM is in Bahía Solano.

Internet Martín Alonso (Salida Bahía Solano; per hour COP$2000; 8am-noon & 2:30-5pm) Offers computer rental and paid wi-fi access for phones and laptops.

Getting There & Around

Shared taxis to Bahía Solano (COP$10,000, one hour) leave when full from outside the billiards hall. Services are more frequent in the morning. An express moto-taxi between the towns costs COP$30,000.

Small boats leave for Nuquí (COP$70,000, 1½ hours) on Monday and Friday afternoons. The departure times depend on the tides.

Taxis and jeeps run from town to Playa Almejal – driving all over an important turtle-nesting beach. Do the turtles a favor and walk – it's not far.

Parque Nacional Natural Ensenada de Utría

This national park (Colombians/foreigners COP$17,000/44,500) is one of the best places to see whales close-up from land. If you have the budget and are not in a hurry, Utría is a magnificent place to get away from it all and contemplate some of Colombia's most phenomenal nature.

A visit here can be an expensive affair, however, and not all visitors feel that it offers real value. While it is an incredibly beautiful spot there is not actually that much visitors can do on their own and most organized activities involve additional costs.

This is especially true for day trips, which, once you add in transportation costs and the entry fee, make for an expensive meander through the mangroves. The best way to see the park is to get a group together to bring the prices down; some hotels and hostels in Nuquí and El Valle can arrange this.

The only place to spend the night in the park is at the **Centro de Visitantes Jaibaná** (s/d COP$179,000/299,000), on the eastern shore of the *ensenada* (inlet), which has refurbished cabins for up to 30 people.

For those spending the night in the park, meal packages cost a whopping COP$111,000 per visitor.

Getting There & Away

If they have space, the public boats from Nuquí to El Valle/Bahía Solano can drop you at the park for COP$70,000, but note that they only run twice a week so you'll need to spend several nights here.

If you have a group, a private transfer from Nuquí organized through the park costs COP$521,000 for one to four passengers and COP$600,000 for five to seven. Ask around town and you can probably organize your own transfer for less. From El Valle, official transfers run at around COP$302,000.

Alternatively, from El Valle you can organize a guide to take you on foot from town to Lachunga at the mouth of the Río Tundo at the northwestern corner of the *ensenada* (COP$50,000, four hours). From here you can be picked up in a boat and taken to the visitors center.

Nuquí

4 / POP 8000

Midway along the Chocó coast is the small town of Nuquí. It boasts a wide beach right in front of town and a long, rugged stretch of sand across the river. A short boat ride away, the secluded beach of Guachalito has some of the best resorts along this coast. A number of indigenous communities live up the Nuquí river but are not in the business of receiving visitors.

The town itself is paved with a mixture of concrete and gravel, but has no car traffic. It isn't a particularly attractive place but it's a convenient base from which to explore the gorgeous surrounding area.

Sights & Activities

Playa Olímpica BEACH

Just south of the mouth of the Río Nuquí, rugged Playa Olímpica stretches as far as the eye can see. A local named Señor Pastrana can paddle you across the river in his dugout canoe (COP$6000). To find him, walk south along the main beach road, past the church; he lives a block from the river in a wooden house.

Transporte Ecce Homo BOATING

(320-771-8865, 314-449-4446; Contiguo a Hospital) With an office near the park, Transporte Ecce Homo offers boat trips all around the region. Sample itineraries include PNN Ensenada de Utría via Playa Blanca and Morromico (COP$90,000), mangroves and thermal pools at Jurubidá (COP$50,000), and to Guachalito including Cascada de Amor and Las Termales (p270) (COP$60,000). In whale season all tours include whale-watching.

Prices are per person based on a group of six passengers (varying by group size and gasoline cost). The company also organizes express transportation and has some basic rooms with kitchen access for rent in the office.

Sleeping & Eating

Most hotels cluster at the northern end of town, near the beach where a nice breeze blows. There are a number of simple posadas in town.

There are just a couple of dedicated restaurants in town; fortunately they both prepare high-quality meals. Most hotels arrange meals for guests.

At the airport (p267) local women sometimes sell *mecocadas,* a tasty confection of coconut and guava paste.

Hotel Palmas del Pacifico GUESTHOUSE $

(314-753-4228; r per person COP$35,000) The best budget choice in town is a block back from the beach and offers simple, fan-cooled wooden rooms with cable TV and private bathrooms and a terrace with hammocks and glimpses of the sea. It's not luxurious – you're not guaranteed a shower head – but it's clean and tranquil.

Hotel Delfin Real HOTEL $$

(310-209-4699; Barrio La Union; s/d COP$65,000/80,000;) A new, good-value option in town, the Delfin Real has smallish but comfortable all-wood rooms with good sheets and modern bathrooms. Downstairs rooms can be a bit noisy, so go for one on the 2nd floor.

Hotel Nuquí Mar HOTEL $$$

(317-843-7354; www.hotelnuquimar.com; r per person incl 3 meals COP$145,000) On the beach just past the football field, this hotel has appealing all-wood rooms with screened windows and sparkling tiled bathrooms. The suite on the top floor has a large private balcony. It's a short walk to town but is far enough away to be peaceful. The staff fight to keep the beach in front clear of rubbish and flotsam.

Aqui es Chirringa COLOMBIAN $
(meals COP$13,000; ⏰7am-8pm) The entire family seems to work the kitchen at this simple open-air eatery around the corner from the airport (p267). It serves good-sized plates of tasty regional and Colombian cuisine complete with a bowl of fish soup.

Doña Pola COLOMBIAN $
(☎4-683-6254; meals COP$15,000; ⏰7am-9pm) Down a side street between the hospital and the football field, Doña Pola cooks up hearty home-style meals.

Shopping

Artesanías Margot ARTS & CRAFTS
(Contiguo aeropuerto; ⏰8am-5pm) Next to the airport (p267), this small *artesanías* shop has a great selection of wooden carvings and other local arts and crafts. You might even spot an authentic blow-dart gun.

Information

There's free wi-fi in the park in front of the police station, which has turned an almost abandoned public space into a hive of activity.

A Vive Digital kiosk was under construction when we last visited and should offer computers with internet access in the future.

There is no bank or ATM in Nuquí so bring sufficient funds.

Super Giros (☎4-683-6067; ⏰8am-noon & 2-6pm) Foreign exchange. You can receive domestic wire transfers here and buy credit for local phones.

Mano Cambiada (☎318-432-0163; www.manocambiada.org/en; Adentro oficina de Satena; ⏰hours vary) A community-based tourism organization that runs the accommodations and services in Parque Nacional Natural Ensenada de Utría. It also offers general tourism information about the region and can organize tours in many communities. It doesn't have its own office, instead working out of the Satena building.

Getting There & Away

Aeropuerto Reyes Murillo (☎4-683-6001) is serviced by **Satena** (☎1800 091 2034, 4-683-6550; www.satena.com) and a number of charter companies with direct flights to Medellín and Quibdó. Upon arrival at Nuquí, all visitors are required to pay a COP$9000 tourism tax.

Transporte Yiliana (Donde Sapi; ☎314-764-9308, 311-337-2839) offers boat services to El Valle (COP$70,000, 1½ hours) on Monday and Friday. Boats usually leave early in the morning. Make sure to book your place in advance. Depending on demand, this service will also drop off at Jurubidá and Utría.

Several cargo boats service Nuquí from Buenaventura. The most reliable is *Valois Mar,* which departs Nuquí every 10 days. Ask around town for **Gigo** (☎312-747-8374; incl meals COP$120,000), the owner. It's a 16-hour trip and costs COP$120,000 including meals. Investigate the security situation in Buenaventura before making plans.

Around Nuquí

Not many visitors come to Nuquí to hang out in Nuquí. The real attractions in the region are the unspoilt beaches a short boat ride to the north and south of the town.

Heading south from town there is a string of interesting Afrocolombian communities interspersed with delightful ecological hotels. The most popular beach in the area runs from Guachalito down to the town of Termales and is a true natural playground complete with lush gardens, waterfalls, thermal springs and rivers.

To the north of Nuquí lies the welcoming village of Jurubidá, set between two rivers and fronted by impressive rock formations, and nearby Morromico (p268), a calm, secluded bay backed by dense jungle.

Daily boat service (COP$30,000, one hour) from Nuquí to Arusí, west of Termales, can drop you anywhere along the way. It leaves Arusí at around 6am from Monday to Saturday and returns from the Muelle Turistíca dock in Nuquí just after 1pm.

Jurubidá

This colorful community of brightly painted houses, 45 minutes from Nuquí by boat, has plenty of attractions but doesn't receive many visitors. The bay in front of the village is dominated by the **Archipelago de Jurubidá** – a collection of spectacular rock formations covered in forest. When the tide drops, a natural pool forms in the rocks on one of the islands. Jurubidá is the closest village to Parque Nacional Natural Ensenada de Utría.

While the town and adjacent beach are not always that tidy, it's nevertheless a good place to get a taste of village life. It's also a good base from which to organize activities and explore the area.

WORTH A TRIP

JUNGLE LODGING

Located far from other properties on a rugged jungle-covered peninsula around the cape from Termales and Arusí, **Punta Brava** (☎310-296-8926, 313-768-0804; www.puntabravachoco.co; Cabo Corrientes, Arusí; r per person incl meals COP$230,000) is an ideal spot for nature lovers and those looking for total relaxation. Rooms in the wooden lodge aren't luxurious, but you'll spend most of your time on the spacious common deck with commanding sea views.

During whale season you can spot the playful mammals right from your hammock. Excellent communal meals are served at the large dining table and it's blissfully free of wi-fi and television (although staff have a connection in their quarters that they'll lend you if you really need to get online or make a call). A number of adventurous hikes and activities are offered to guests, or you can just chill on a good stretch of sand a short walk away. Arriving here is like being transported to the lost world – the little boat flies over the waves before pulling into a hidden little harbor where a crystal-clear river flows out from the wilderness into the sea.

Tours

Grupo Los Termales ADVENTURE

(Termales de Jurubidá COP$10,000, canoe trips COP$10,000-20,000, whale-watching/indigenous community visit per boat COP$120,000/150,000) A local cooperative that organizes guides to the Termales de Jurubidá, a pair of thermal pools surrounded by dense jungle. The cooperative can also organize canoe trips through the mangroves, whale-watching and boat trips to an indigenous community upriver. It doesn't have an office or phone number: ask at your hotel or around town.

The thermal-pool trip involves a short canoe ride and a beautiful walk alongside a crystal-clear river.

Sleeping

Cabaña Brisa del Mar HUT $

(Donde Tita; ☎312-688-7863, 314-684-9401; r per person with/without meals COP$75,000/35,000) Run by a hardworking local family, this tranquil spot near the river has six simple rooms in a homely thatched-roof cabaña. The owners know what budget travelers want; they prepare meals using produce from their farm and organize all kinds of trips in the area. There is a lovely small balcony with a hammock and beach views.

Ecohotel Yubarta GUESTHOUSE $$

(Donde Luciano; ☎316-779-5124, 316-242-8558; a lado de los termales; tent/r per person COP$25,000/50,000) Set on a hillside just outside Jurubidá with commanding views of the bay, this new budget travelers' lodge is a chilled spot to hang out while you explore the area. Accommodations are basic but it's breezy and you can spot whales right from the deck.

★ **Morromico** LODGE $$$

(☎312-795-6321; www.morromico.com; r per person incl meals COP$387,500) Situated on a magnificent private beach protected by forested headlands, family run Morromico is a beautiful, small ecoresort surrounded by thick jungle. The hotel is set in lush gardens framed by a pair of waterfalls where you can bathe in crystal-clear mountain waters. The comfortable new hardwood lodge building is both stylish and at peace with the surrounding nature.

The semi-open rooms, powered by a small hydroelectrico plan, have balconies overlooking the beach and big windows that let in the sounds of the jungle. The owners organize boat trips and some fantastic treks through the mountains to local indigenous communities. Rates include three very good meals. Reservations are essential.

Morromico is 15 minutes by boat from Jurubidá.

Getting There & Away

There is no scheduled public transportation here but there are usually villagers traveling most days to/from Nuquí. In Nuquí, most boats dock at the Almacén Wilmer Torres, a bar/grocery store in the center. The going rate is around COP$20,000 per person for the 45-minute trip. Alternatively you can hire an express boat for around COP$200,000.

Guachalito

A half-hour boat ride west of Nuquí is Guachalito. It's a long beach, clear of flotsam and debris. There are orchids and heliconias everywhere, the jungle encroaches on the beach, platter-sized mushrooms grow on the trees and coconut palms sway over the gray sand.

The Gonzalez family inhabits the beach's east end, which can feel just a little bit crowded when things are busy. Several more hotels are scattered along the remote 8km of the beach running down to Termales. On the way you'll pass **El Terco** and **El Terquito**, two almost-islands that serve as landmarks. You can walk the length of the beach (1½ hours). It's best to set out when the tide is low.

A 1km (20-minute) walk from the Gonzalez settlement, 200m inland from the beach, is **Cascada de Amor** – where a pretty waterfall surrounded by jungle empties into a natural rock pool. A 10-minute walk uphill takes you to an even bigger and more beautiful waterfall, which splits in two streams before filling a swimming hole below.

Activities

Paraisurf SURFING
(☎321-515-8362; board rental per hour COP$25,000) Located near the almost-island of El Terquito, this little sports shop rents surf boards and kayaks.

Sleeping & Eating

Originally Guachalito referred only to the Gonzalez family settlement at the eastern end of the beach. Four generations live here, and their four posadas (hotels) – run by competing siblings – offer a variety of accommodations ranging in price and comfort level.

To the west of the Guachalito settlement there are a number of ecohotels and resorts. Most offer packages including transportation from the airport, accommodations and food.

Brisas del Mar GUESTHOUSE **$$**
(☎311-602-3742, 314-431-2125; r per person with/without meals COP$130,000/70,000) The best option for budget travelers, Brisas del Mar has a handful of simple rooms in a new construction set just back from the water. Guests can use the kitchen downstairs so bring plenty of supplies from Nuquí. Rooms at the top are better – some open out onto a breezy balcony.

The owners run the tourist dock in Nuquí, where you can ask for information.

WORTH A TRIP

COQUÍ & JOVÍ

This pair of friendly villages, 25 minutes by boat from Nuquí, are typical small settlements in the region wedged between the jungle and the water. While the towns are not particularly interesting, both have good community tourism organizations. In Coquí, the **Grupo de Ecoguias** (☎310-544-8904; Coquí; per boat COP$70,000) can arrange boat trips through the mangroves. In Joví, **Grupo de Guias Pichinde** (☎321-731-1092; Joví) can take you up the Río Joví in dugout canoes. The latter can also arrange visits to the indigenous villages along the river.

Local villagers rent rooms in their homes for around COP$25,000 to COP$30,000. Accommodations are very basic; make sure you get a mosquito net.

★ **El Cantil Ecolodge** HOTEL **$$$**
(☎4-448-0767; www.elcantil.com; s/d incl meals COP$369,000/612,000) The most luxurious hotel on this beach, El Cantil has six duplex cabins surrounded by papaya plants and coconut palms. The restaurant (famous for its food) is perched atop a hill and has sweeping views. A small hydroelectric plant produces power for the restaurant; the cabins are lit by candles. Prices include meals and transportation to/from Nuquí.

Whale-watching expeditions can be organized and surfing guides can show you the best spots.

Pijibá Lodge HOTEL **$$$**
(☎311-762-3763; www.pijibalodge.com; r per person incl meals COP$235,000) Set among lush gardens, the three duplex cabins of Pijibá are constructed entirely of natural materials and let in plenty of fresh air. A tranquil low-key place to stay just steps from the sand; there's a little hut for yoga on-site. Food here has an excellent reputation.

Mar y Río GUESTHOUSE **$$$**
(☎316-426-1009; elmardeldiego@gmail.com; r per person from COP$130,000) A peaceful family-run affair, Mar y Río is on a quiet corner of beach with a stream flowing by and feels far removed from the tightly packed hotels around the corner. It has good views up the coast and a sweet swimming spot in front. There are two rooms above the restaurant and two self-contained cabañas in the yard.

La Cabaña de Beto y Marta HOTEL $$$
(311-775-9912; betoymarta@hotmail.com; r per person incl meals COP$250,000) This delightful hotel owned by two *paisas* (people from Antioquia) has four secluded cabins with hammocks and chairs on the deck from which to watch the sunset. The whole thing is set amid a spectacular garden, which includes lots of fruits and vegetables you'll find on your plate come dinnertime.

Getting There & Away

The Nuquí-Arusí boat calls at Guachalito on request – be sure to tell the driver where you plan to stay in order to be dropped in the right place. You'll be dropped on the beach and may have to wade a bit so wear appropriate attire.

Termales

The small village of Termales has a lovely wide stretch of gray-sand beach and a couple of places to stay for those who want to get close to the local culture and a set of relaxing thermal pools (p270) surrounded by jungle. As the sun sets children play games of football (soccer) on the beach, while chickens dart across the pitch and, in the distance, older youth take to the waves on boards donated by a nonprofit surf project.

There is no phone coverage in Termales, but business owners generally go elsewhere to check their phones if you want to leave a message.

Activities

From Termales you can hike the beach in both directions: north to Guachalito or south down to Arusí, but you'll need to head out as the tide is approaching its low point as there are several rivers to cross.

Surf House SURFING
(320-708-1421; classes per hour COP$35,000) Friendly instructor and minor local celebrity Nestor offers casual surf classes as well as full eight-hour courses for beginners (COP$250,000). He also organizes excursions to the best surf spots in the region and rents boards.

Las Termales THERMAL BATHS
(adult/child COP$12,000/5000, massage per hour COP$60,000; 8am-5pm) A gravel path leads 500m inland from the village's one road to Las Termales, a pair of thermal pools set by a rushing stream surrounded by jungle. The site has been tastefully developed by the community and features a restaurant and spa area. Buy your ticket at the office on the road in town before heading down to the complex.

Cocoter HIKING
(Oficina Corporación Comunitario) Local community organization that organizes hikes to **Cascada Cuatro Encantos** – a towering set of waterfalls with good swimming holes surrounded by lush jungle. Expect to pay COP$25,000 to COP$30,000 per hiker for the trip. The office is located next to Refugio Salomon (p270) – they don't use phones.

Sleeping & Eating

Refugio Salomon GUESTHOUSE $$$
(314-333-4411; r per person incl meals COP$120,000) This friendly place has a large balcony overlooking the beach and simple rooms with private bathrooms. It serves tasty home-style meals in the on-site restaurant, which is a good place to eat even if you're not staying here.

La Sazón de Yuli SEAFOOD $
(Arusí; mains COP$15,000; 7am-9pm) If you work up a hunger walking the beach from Termales down to Arusí, stop by this excellent little restaurant to enjoy good fresh seafood dishes made hot to order.

Getting There & Away

The passenger boat service from Nuquí to Arusí can drop and pick up travelers in Termales. There's no dock here so you might have to jump into knee-high water to disembark; wear shorts and sandals.

SOUTH COAST

Spanning the departments of Valle del Cauca, Cauca and Nariño, the little-visited southern Pacific coast boasts jungle-covered islands, traditional Afrocolombian villages and some of Colombia's most interesting diving.

However, security remains complicated in the area and great swathes of the region remain off-limits for tourism, although the recently reopened Parque Nacional Natural Isla Gorgona offers travelers a chance to get a taste of this fascinating region.

At the time of research, Buenaventura and its surrounds, along with Tumaco in the extreme south of the region, were considered unsafe for travelers.

OFF THE BEATEN TRACK

ISLA MALPELO

This tiny, remote Colombian island has some of the best diving in the world. A World Heritage site, it's a mere 1643m long and 727m wide, and is 378km from the mainland. It's the center of the vast **Santuario de Flora y Fauna Malpelo** (www.parquesnacionales.gov.co/portal/es/ecoturismo/region-pacifico/santuario-de-flora-y-fauna-malpelo; per day with diving Colombian/foreigner COP$103,000/193,500), the largest no-fishing zone in the Eastern Tropical Pacific, which provides a critical habitat for threatened marine species.

The diversity and, above all, the size of the marine life is eye-popping, and includes over 200 hammerhead sharks and 1000 silky sharks. It is also one of the few places where sightings of the short-nosed ragged-tooth shark, a deepwater shark, have been confirmed. The volcanic island has steep walls and impressive caves.

Dive conditions can be treacherous and accidents are not unheard of. Only advanced divers with experience should attempt this trip.

A contingent of soldiers guard Malpelo, and it's forbidden to set foot on the island.

With the introduction of new regulations, only boats operating out of Colombian ports may offer trips to Isla Malpelo. Basically that means boats operating out of Buenaventura. But be aware that many pack lots of divers onto each trip and most don't usually carry nitrox.

One well-run boat is the *Sea Wolf* operated by the Pacific Diving Company (p229) in Cali. Expect to pay around COP$7,000,000 per diver for three days of diving, and up to COP$9,200,000 for eight days in the water. Prices are slightly lower if you share a room.

Parque Nacional Natural Isla Gorgona

After being closed for more than two years following an unprecedented attack on the island by FARC, **Parque Nacional Natural (PNN) Isla Gorgona** (Colombian/foreigner COP$19,000/45,500) has recently reopened to visitors under new administration. Covering the entirety of remote Isla Gorgona, this rarely visited national park – 38km off the coast and 11km long by 2.3km wide – is a fine escape for nature lovers. Once a national prison, the island has now been converted into a high-end nature retreat. The two main reasons to visit the park are for scuba diving and whale-watching, preferably at the same time. Gorgona is not on any of the main shipping channels, so whales continue to come here every year to calve and raise their young. Apart from swimming and some short walks, activities on the island are limited; it's more a relaxation destination than an option for real adventure.

The island is covered in young, secondary rainforest (the convicts chopped down most of the trees for cooking fuel), which harbors an abundance of poisonous snakes. Gorgona is also noted for a large number of endemic species. You'll see many monkeys, lizards, bats and birds. Sea turtles come during breeding season and lay eggs on the beaches.

Gorgona's only hotel is set in renovated old prison barracks near the national park headquarters and can sleep up to 120 guests.

Most visitors come on a package deal organized through **Vive Gorgona** (☎321-768-0539; www.vivegorgona.com; r per person incl meals COP$280,000) that includes marine transportation from Guapi, accommodations, hikes and meals. Expect to pay around COP$750,000 to COP$815,000 per visitor for the basic two-night, three-day package. In whale season prices increase slightly and include whale-watching by boat.

For divers who don't want to stay on the island, boats out of Buenaventura offer weekend live-aboard diving trips, departing the *muelle turístico* on Friday night and returning Monday morning. The *Sea Wolf* run by the Pacific Diving Company (p229) in Cali offers two-day packages from COP$1,700,000 per diver. Nondivers are also welcome to visit the island on their boat; prices begin around COP$1,350,000 for the same trip.

Speedboats shuttle visitors with reservations to the island from the small town of Guapi (1¼ hours).

AT A GLANCE

ELEVATION
2615m

AREA
6200 km^2

BEST BIRDWATCHING
Cristales Macarena (p278)

BEST GEOGRAPHIC WONDER
Ciudad de Piedra (p276)

BEST BURGERS
Nomada (p277)

WHEN TO GO

Apr
The height of the dry season; very hot weather, but the best time to see wildlife.

Jun
The annual Torneo Internacional del Joropo dance comp happens in Villavicencio.

Jul–Nov
Caño Cristales takes on its famous red color as its unique plants roar to life.

Parque Nacional Natural Sierra de La Macarena (p277)
JULIO DUARTE/SHUTTERSTOCK

Los Llanos

As you head southeast away from Bogotá, the jagged Andean terrain soon flattens out as if a giant guillotine dropped down across the mountains, revealing an endless sea of green grasslands. This is Los Llanos (the Plains). Teeming with wildlife, Los Llanos harbors more than 100 species of mammals and more than 700 bird species, including some of the planet's most endangered species.

Until a decade ago much of this area was essentially off-limits to foreigners, but today, with the surrender of the FARC (Revolutionary Armed Forces of Colombia) and the retreat of drug traffickers and paramilitaries, the area is largely safe again and is quickly opening up to tourism. The biggest attraction here by far is Caño Cristales, the extraordinary multicolored rivers inside the Parque Nacional Natural Sierra de La Macarena (p277), but elsewhere in the region you'll find fascinating archaeological sites, natural wonders and the warmth and earthy humor of *llaneros* in abundance.

INCLUDES

Villavicencio............... 274

San José del Guaviare............... 276

Caño Cristales........... 277

Parque Nacional Natural El Tuparro...... 279

Safe Travel

Despite the great success of the peace process in Colombia, the security situation in Los Llanos remains very fluid and can change very quickly – always check current situations with authorities and/or travel agencies before embarking anywhere in this region. Getting detailed travel advice regarding trips into any remote areas is essential.

Getting There & Around

Villavicencio is the region's main transportation hub, just a three-hour journey down the highway from Bogotá or a short hop on several daily flights. The highway now extends all the way to San José del Guaviare too, after which things get decidedly more tricky. Villavicencio, as well as Bogotá and Medellín, have direct flight connections to La Macarena for access to Caño Cristales.

Villavicencio

☎8 / POP 495,000 / ELEV 467M

The heavily militarized highway heading south from Bogotá leads to Villavicencio – 'La Puerta al Llano,' the gateway to the plain – 75km southeast. It's a bustling though not particularly interesting city with a serious penchant for nightlife and grilled meat. The city is a good base for exploring the plains, and though it's no longer a requisite jumping-off point for trips to Caño Cristales, it does offer the most thrilling ride there: in an ancient and creaky, white-knuckle-inducing 1940s-era DC-3!

Festivals & Events

Torneo Internacional del Joropo DANCE

(late Jun) Every year in the last week of June the streets of Villavicencio become open-air dance floors for those who love joropo, a dance not dissimilar to the fandango that is much loved and practiced in Los Llanos. Dance enthusiasts from all over Colombia and Venezuela attend and compete for prizes.

Sleeping & Eating

As a busy commercial center, Villavicencio has a good provision of hotels. In general, budget and midrange options can be found downtown, while smarter top-end hotels are generally located on the outskirts.

Asaderos (restaurants serving roasted or grilled meats) dish up the regional specialty *mamona* (baby beef), and can be found all over town.

Hotel Sol Dorado HOTEL $$

(☎8-662-3671; hotelsoldorado@hotmail.com; Calle 37 No 29-66; s/d incl breakfast from COP$85,000/125,000;) This friendly place is one of the most comfortable and more salubrious of the downtown hotels. The 31 clean rooms are well looked after, if unremarkable, with mini-fridges and plenty of cupboard space. Those at the front are noisy but have balconies and natural light, while the ones at the back are a little dark and cell-like but quiet.

Estelar Villavicencio Hotel BUSINESS HOTEL $$$

(☎8-663-1000; www.hotelesestelar.com; cnr Av 40 & Calle 11, Costado Norte Metro Kia; r incl breakfast from COP$255,000;) Yes it may be out of the downtown area, but if you're looking for comfort, modernity and service, this is the splurge for you. Rooms are massive, spotless and have great bathrooms and comfortable beds. There's a huge lap pool and bar area, and the restaurant serves good meals.

Dulima COLOMBIAN $

(Carrera 30A No 38-46; set meals COP$10,000-15,000; 7am-8pm Mon-Sat, 8am-6pm Sun) A *comida corriente* staple since 1967, this popular downtown choice dishes up traditional set lunch plates served by friendly waiters (in cowgirl outfits on holidays). It does a great breakfast as well.

Information

Turismo Villavicencio (☎8-673-1313; www.turismovillavicencio.gov.co; Plazoleta Los Libertadores; 8am-noon & 2-6pm Mon-Sat)

Getting There & Away

The spectacular journey from Bogotá should not be missed as the magnificent highway pushes through the mountain valleys, first ascending and then descending towards Los Llanos. From the town's busy **Terminal de Transportes** (☎8-660-6535; www.terminalvillavicencio.gov.co; Av Los Maracos) numerous daily buses connect to Bogotá (COP$25,000, three hours) and San José del Guaviare (COP$49,500, six hours). Buses to La Macarena (p277) (COP$97,000, 24 hours) depart three times a week and take forever as the road circumnavigates the national park.

Villavicencio's **Aeropuerto de la Vanguardia** (☎321-762-2520; Carrera 19) has daily charter flights to La Macarena. There are also several flights a day to Bogotá (from COP$300,000) with Avianca.

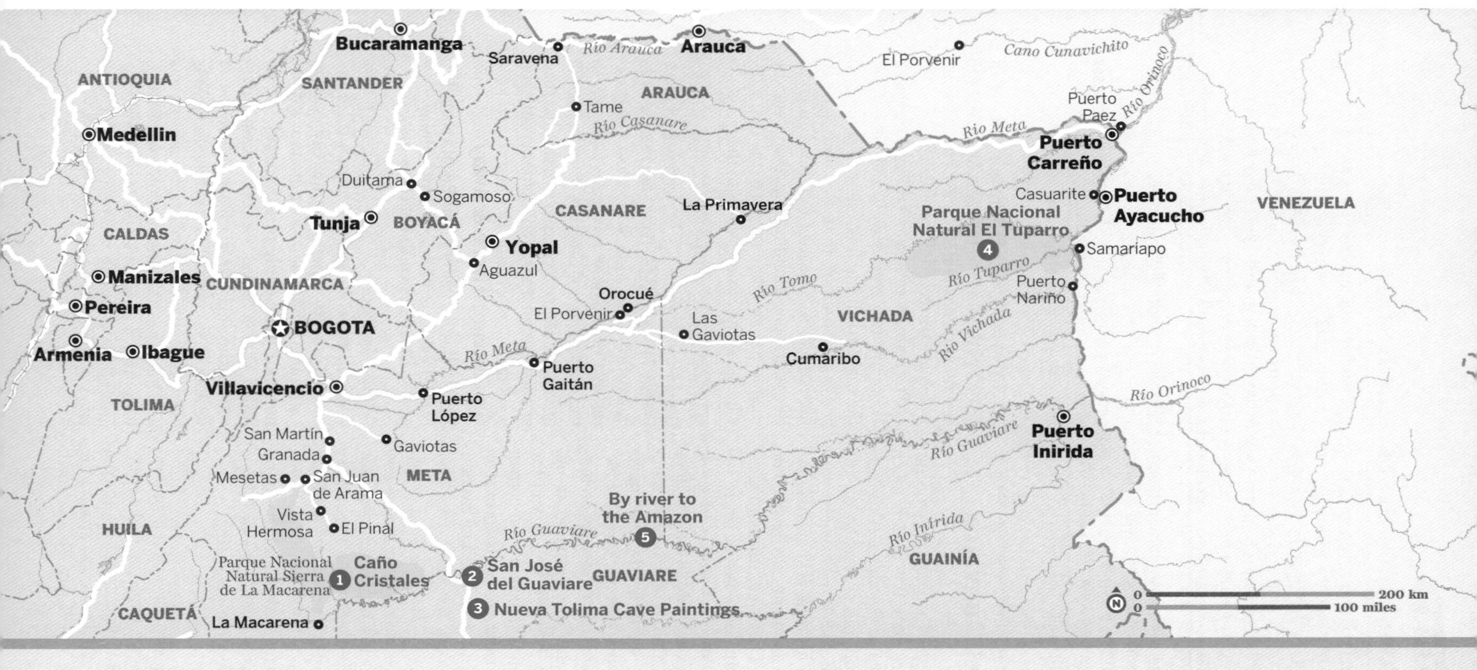

Los Llanos Highlights

1. **Caño Cristales** (p277) Witnessing the extraordinary combination of colors that explodes to life for a few months a year in these remote rivers.

2. **San José del Guaviare** (p276) Basing yourself in this lovable provincial town while exploring the surrounding countryside.

3. **Nueva Tolima Cave Paintings** (p276) Staring up in wonder at the fascinating messages left for posterity by long-vanished indigenous peoples.

4. **Parque Nacional Natural El Tuparro** (p279) Taking an adventurous trip to this truly remote slice of Los Llanos.

5. **Travelling by river to the Amazon** (p278) Undertaking the ultimate Colombian adventure: the two-week river journey through Los Llanos to the mighty Amazon River.

OFF THE BEATEN TRACK

A VILLAGE FOR SUSTAINABLE DEVELOPMENT

Off the beaten path, Gaviotas, about 100km southeast of Villavicencio, is a 'green' success story. The UN called the village a model of sustainable development, and Gabriel García Márquez called founder Paolo Lugari the 'inventor of the world.' The village of 200 people is operated on wind and solar power. Residents farm organically and have planted millions of trees. The town has become a world-class research and development center for green technologies and the commune-like society has no police, no mayor and no weapons. The village was profiled in journalist Alan Weisman's book *Gaviotas: A Village to Reinvent the World*.

Gaviotas is not set up for tourism, however, and with no hotels, restaurants, public transportation or methods to pay for services (money is not exchanged for goods or services), it would be tricky if you tried to engineer a visit on your own. Those who are curious to visit should contact Friends of Gaviotas (www.friendsofgaviotas.org) to see if there are any tours planned.

San José del Guaviare

☎8 / POP 65,600 / ELEV 185M

Likable San José del Guaviare may be the capital of Guaviare state but it feels much like any small town in Colombia. It's a mercantile and friendly place perched on the southern bank of the Río Guaviare with dusty roads and a bustling grid of shopping streets. San José's moment may have come as tourism to Los Llanos continues to grow and grow, with San José looking set to become its main center.

While the town may not have much obvious tourist appeal itself, it does boast a number of interesting sights nearby that make spending a day or two here very worthwhile. These include Guaviare's numerous archaeological sites, natural wonders and its all important position between Bogotá and the Amazon, which can be reached from here in two tough but exhilarating weeks of boat travel via the Guaviare, Orinoco and Yaví rivers.

Sights

There's not much to occupy you in San José itself, although there's a pleasant **mirador** (Calle 7 & Carrera 23) overlooking the mighty Guaviare River as it curves around the bend on which the town is built. The main sights outside the town can conveniently be found along the dusty road towards Nueva Tolima, making them perfect for a day trip.

Pozos Naturales NATURAL POOL
(COP$3000; ⏲9am-5pm) These lovely natural swimming holes hewn from the rocky riverbed are a wonderful place to relax and cool off once you've sweated your way around the other sights along the Nueva Tolima road. It's a five-minute walk through a series of signed paths down to the river, and there are several gorgeous pools, some as deep as 8m, which are perfect for a lazy bathe.

The setup is rather an odd one, however. There are two entrances to the pools from the main road: the first one you come to if you're approaching from San José is often unmanned, so you may well need to go to the second one a kilometer further along the road to pay and then return to the first gate, which has the easiest access to the pools.

Nueva Tolima Cave Paintings ARCHAEOLOGICAL SITE
(Nueva Tolima) FREE This fascinating site 22km from San José is the most easily accessible of the numerous cave paintings in the department of Guaviare, though it's still quite a challenge to find. Leave the dirt road at the sign for Finca Villa Nueva and then walk through farmland (it's best to greet the farmers and ask permission to cross) and climb up the hillside. At the top you'll find extraordinarily well preserved indigenous cave paintings open to the elements.

Ciudad de Piedra NATURAL FEATURE
(Via San José del Guaviare-El Capricho) FREE Located 17km from San José del Guaviare in La Pizarra subdivision along an unpaved but normally quite easily passable road, the so-called 'City of Stone' is a very unusual natural feature that attracts a steady stream of visitors. A number of large stone monoliths here give the sense of man-made streets and human-scale construction, even though it's purely a product of geology. Wandering around this site is enjoyably weird, and you'll usually be the only one here.

Sleeping & Eating

Hotel Colombia BOUTIQUE HOTEL $

(☎8-584-0823; Carrera 23 No 7-96; s/d COP $60,000/70,000;) Located above a popular *heladería* (ice-cream parlor) of the same name, this curiously designed place has some of the smartest and cleanest rooms in town. It's very comfortable, even if the Colombian folk art is at turns charming and awful. It's certainly the only place in town to offer chaise lounges as standard. The welcome is warm.

Hotel Yuruparí HOTEL $

(☎8-584-0096, 313-263-2695; www.hotelyurupari.com; Calle 8 No 22-87; s/d without air-con COP $50,000/70,000, with air-con COP$70,000/90,000;) This friendly and wonderfully central midrange hotel is our pick. The multigenerational family running the place is delightful, and while rooms are simple and unremarkable, they are spotless and great value.

Hotel El Jardín HOTEL $

(☎8-584-9158, 313-322-1120; Calle 9 No 24-34; s/d/tr COP$45,000/70,000/90,000;) Though there's little sign of the titular garden beyond a row of plants along a paved corridor, this is San José's best budget option. The rooms are clean and simple, and include fridges. You'll have to find breakfast elsewhere though.

Nomada BURGERS $

(☎310-581-7032; Carrera 23 No 9-131; mains COP$10,000-20,000; noon-11pm;) With its tables outside on the street sheltered by the market awning, Nomada looks at first glance to be just like any small *comida corriente,* but one look at the menu will tell you otherwise. There's a selection of burgers, meat grills, wraps and even crepes to choose from. Service is super-friendly and the entire place is rather stylish.

Cafeteria el Piel Roja CAFE $

(☎320-983-7715; Calle 8 No 23-96; 7am-7pm Mon-Sat;) This friendly family-run cafe serves up good coffee and pastries and is a convenient spot for breakfast.

Information

Tourist Information (☎314-281-8830; Calle 7 No 23-07; 8am-6pm Mon-Fri)

Getting There & Away

Flota La Macarena (☎321-205-5270; www.flotalamacarena.com; Carrera 20 No 12A-10) connects San José to Villavicencio (COP$49,500, six hours) and Bogotá (COP$69,500, nine hours) from its tiny bus terminal at the edge of downtown.

It's possible to take a 4x4 to La Macarena (COP$80,000, seven hours) from here too, with departures on Tuesday, Friday and Saturday. Ask at the tourist information (p277) office.

There's a small **airport** (Calle 10 & Carrera 25) just north of the town center with a few flights a week to Bogotá on **Satena** (☎311-236-2988; www.satena.com; Carrera 23 No 7-85).

Caño Cristales

☎8 / POP 33,000 / ELEV 233M

Caño Cristales, a series of remote rivers, waterfalls and streams inside the wilderness of **Parque Nacional Natural Sierra de La Macarena** (www.parquesnacionales.gov.co; foreigners/Colombians COP$92,000/60,000), has been called everything from 'The River of Five Colors' to 'The Liquid Rainbow.' This is due to a unique biological phenomenon that takes place for a couple of months between July and November when an eruption of algae forms an underwater blanket of bright red. This transforms the crystal-clear water into a river of cabernet that contrasts magically with the lunarscape of ancient, hollowed-out riverbed rock and the surrounding savannah landscape.

The main waterfalls and swimming holes are **Piscina del Turista**, **Piscina de Carol Cristal**, **Cascada del Aguila**, **Cascada de Piedra Negra** and **Caño la Virgen**. All access to the park is from the town of La Macarena, which sits just south of the park on the other side of the Río Guayabero. You will be guided throughout the park, and to keep tourism impact low, groups are divided up into different parts of Caño Cristales.

Coming here involves some expense, a lot of sweaty hiking and some fairly unexciting meals in the town of La Macarena, but the pay-off is immense. You'll no doubt agree when you dive into one of the numerous swimming holes, waterfalls or natural pools along the river, or come face-to-face with the impressive local wildlife.

Caño Cristales is no secret – Colombians swarm to it on long weekends (called *puentes*) when the maximum daily visitor count of 180 isn't always enforced. These holiday weekends are best avoided. Come midweek if you're able to.

Tours

You cannot visit Caño Cristales on your own – you are obligated to go into the national

OFF THE BEATEN TRACK

BY RIVER TO THE AMAZON

There's plenty of opportunity for great adventure in Colombia, be it mountain climbing, extreme sports or diving in the Caribbean, but if you're looking for the ultimate adventure then it's hard to imagine anything more challenging and exciting than the epic river journey from Los Llanos to the Amazon. This is a trip through almost total wilderness, where the largest settlements are remote indigenous villages set among hundreds of thousands of square kilometers of dense jungle, fast-flowing brown rivers and thick humidity. It's only become possible in recent years as guerrilla and paramilitary camps were gradually abandoned as part of the peace process.

While the journey is now possible, it's still a long way from easy or particularly comfortable, and you'll need at least two weeks to complete the trip from San José del Guaviare to Leticia, not to mention plenty of run-up time to arrange transportation through a travel agency. Attempting this without logistical support from an experienced operator would be extremely dangerous.

Contact travel agencies in Leticia to inquire about making the trip. Alternatively speak to staff at hotels in San José del Guaviare and ask if they know reliable guides. Either way ensure you begin the process several months before you want to undertake the journey and follow the travel agencies' advice regarding any changes in regional safety.

park with one of the official local guides. Most tours include air transportation to La Macarena, hotels, meals and guide services, and you'll normally be in a group of up to 12 people with a couple of local guides. You'll sleep in La Macarena and spend the days inside the national park.

★**Cristales Aventura Tours** OUTDOORS
(☎300-693-9988, 313-294-9452; www.cano-cristales.com; Calle 5 No 7-35, La Macarena) Friendly English-speaking experts Cristales Aventura Tours are very used to dealing with foreign visitors and offer a flexible range of packages to suit all interests. You can make your own way to La Macarena where they will meet you, or buy an all-inclusive package from Bogotá, Medellín, Calí or Villavicencio.

Cristales Macarena OUTDOORS
(☎313-499-6038; www.viajescristalesmacarena.com; Carrera 7 No 8-50, La Macarena) Doris Mora runs her own travel company offering tours to Caño Cristales. As well as organizing the usual Caño Cristales itineraries and travel from elsewhere in Colombia, Doris can arrange camping and birdwatching in the national park.

Doris has an office in Hotel La Fuente.

Ecoturismo Sierra de La Macarena OUTDOORS
(☎8-664-8400, 311-202-0044; www.ecoturismomacarena.com; Aeropuerto Vanguardia, Villavicencio; ⏲8am-6pm Mon-Fri, to 1pm Sat) This Villavicencio-based travel agency runs transportation and tours to Caño Cristales. Flights leave Bogotá Monday, Thursday and Saturday at 5am and Villavicencio daily at 7am.

Macarena Travels OUTDOORS
(☎312-884-9153; www.macarenatravels.com) This company doesn't have an office, but will arrange everything for you by phone or email. It offers a range of itineraries starting out from Bogotá, Villavicencio, Medellín and Calí, including land-only itineraries..

Sleeping & Eating

Hotel Antony's HOTEL $
(☎321-846-4402; Calle 8A No 3-71, La Macarena; r COP$45,000) You're right on the Parque Central here at this simple but clean place where some of the rooms even have natural light (quite a rarity here!). There's no restaurant on-site, but there are several nearby for breakfast.

Hotel Punto Verde HOTEL $$
(☎310-341-8899; Carrera 9 No 4-12, La Macarena; per person COP$90,000; ❄📶🏊) This is the best hotel in town, but you'll need to travel with Ecoturismo Sierra de La Macarena to stay here, as it leases the entire property between June and November. There's a large pool, gorgeous tropical garden and good cafe to boot.

Hotel La Fuente HOTEL $$
(☎313-496-7701, 312-365-5107; www.hotellafuentejn.com; Carrera 7 No 8-50, La Macarena; per person COP$80,000; ❄📶) This modern place is one of the most comfortable in town, with bright and airy rooms surrounding a garden where you'll find a pool, bar and restaurant. It has friendly staff and a few pleasing design touches.

Hotel Cascada HOTEL $$
(☎314-467-5256; hotellacascada19353@gmail.com; Calle 5 No 7-35, La Macarena; s/d with

fan COP$50,000/70,000 s/d with air-con COP$80,000/120,000; ❄ 📶) This deceptively large hotel (you enter through a long corridor from the street only to emerge into a crammed warren of rooms over several floors) is named after a temperamental water feature in the lobby. Its rooms are clean and practical, with fans or air-con in all, though very few enjoy natural light.

El Caporal GRILL $$
(Carrera 9 No 4-66, La Macarena; mains COP$12,000-25,000; ⏲6am-9pm) This is the only restaurant in town that really stands out, and even if it is a very big place aimed at groups, it's by far the smartest place in La Macarena. There's a big meaty menu (though vegetarians are well catered for too), a busy bar, a stage for live musical performances and a huge central fireplace.

Information

La Macarena has two ATMs and several money-changing offices, though it's always a good idea to bring cash with you instead of relying on being able to withdraw it in a remote small town.

Getting There & Away

Most package tours include transportation to **La Macarena Airport** by charter or scheduled flight from Bogotá, Medellín or Villavicencio, though it's perfectly possible to book your own transportation and arrange your tour to begin at the airport.

Easy Fly (☎ Bogotá 1-414-8111; www.easyfly.com.co) offers direct flights from Bogotá three times a week (COP$300,000) in high season (July to November). Alternatively, get yourself to Villavicencio (an easy bus ride from Bogotá) and then take one of the daily flights to La Macarena from there (COP$250,000).

Ecoturismo Sierra de La Macarena (p278) arranges daily flights from Villavicencio (COP$520,000 to COP$550,000), including rather adventurous Saturday outings in an aged 16-person DC-3.

Barely anyone tries to reach La Macarena by an overland route. However, there are several 4x4s that make the journey from San José del Guaviare several times a week (COP$80,000, seven hours). Ask around in San José del Guaviare.

Parque Nacional Natural El Tuparro

Parque Nacional Natural (PNN) El Tuparro (www.parquesnacionales.gov.co; Colombian/foreigner COP$12,500/37,000) is a 548,000-hectare nature reserve on the Venezuelan border. This biosphere of sandy river beaches and green grasslands is home to some 320 species of birds plus jaguars, tapirs and otters. Getting here is not easy, and there's almost no infrastructure for tourism, but those with plenty of time and cash on their hands may well find it very rewarding.

NATIONAL PARK RULES

Access to the Parque Nacional Natural (PNN) Sierra de La Macarena is closely controlled by the park authorities and there are several unusually strict rules that all visitors must follow. Most important of these is that sun cream and mosquito spray cannot be used on the body prior to entry into the park, as the introduction of chemical compounds to the water could pollute the otherwise-pristine waters and adversely affect the unique ecosystem that produces the rivers' extraordinary colors. Visitors are also banned from bringing in plastic bottles, from walking in sandals and from wearing shorts. There are checks by park rangers when you enter the park to ensure that these rules are not broken.

What to Bring

As you won't be able to wear sun cream or mosquito repellent, it's important to have a sun hat, long pants and long sleeves to avoid sun burn – bear in mind that shade is almost nonexistent inside the national park. Bring a large water thermos to supply yourself with plenty of water throughout the day, as it's unsafe to drink the river water. Sunglasses and good walking shoes are also advisable, as there is a lot of walking to be done, as well as several sections of scrambling over uneven rocks. As yellow fever is present in this area, it's important to have a vaccination card to present if you're asked for one.

Taxes & Fees

There are several local taxes and entry fees payable on arrival at La Macarena Airport (p279). These include a COP$39,100 town tax (COP$26,100 for Colombians), a COP$6000 airport tax and a COP$92,000 park entry tax (COP$60,000 for Colombians).

AT A GLANCE

POPULATION
960,000

AREA
483,000 km^2

BEST FOR NATURE
Lago Tarapoto (p290)

BEST INDIGENOUS CRAFTS
Galería Arte Uirapuru (p283)

BEST DONUTS
Donut Company (p287)

WHEN TO GO

Sep–Nov
Lower water levels afford excellent hiking and reveal white-sand beaches on the Río Yavarí.

Mar–May
Get closer to the canopy in wet season for peak birdwatching and wildlife spotting.

Jul & Aug
Loathe mosquitoes? They mostly retreat to the treetops during these months.

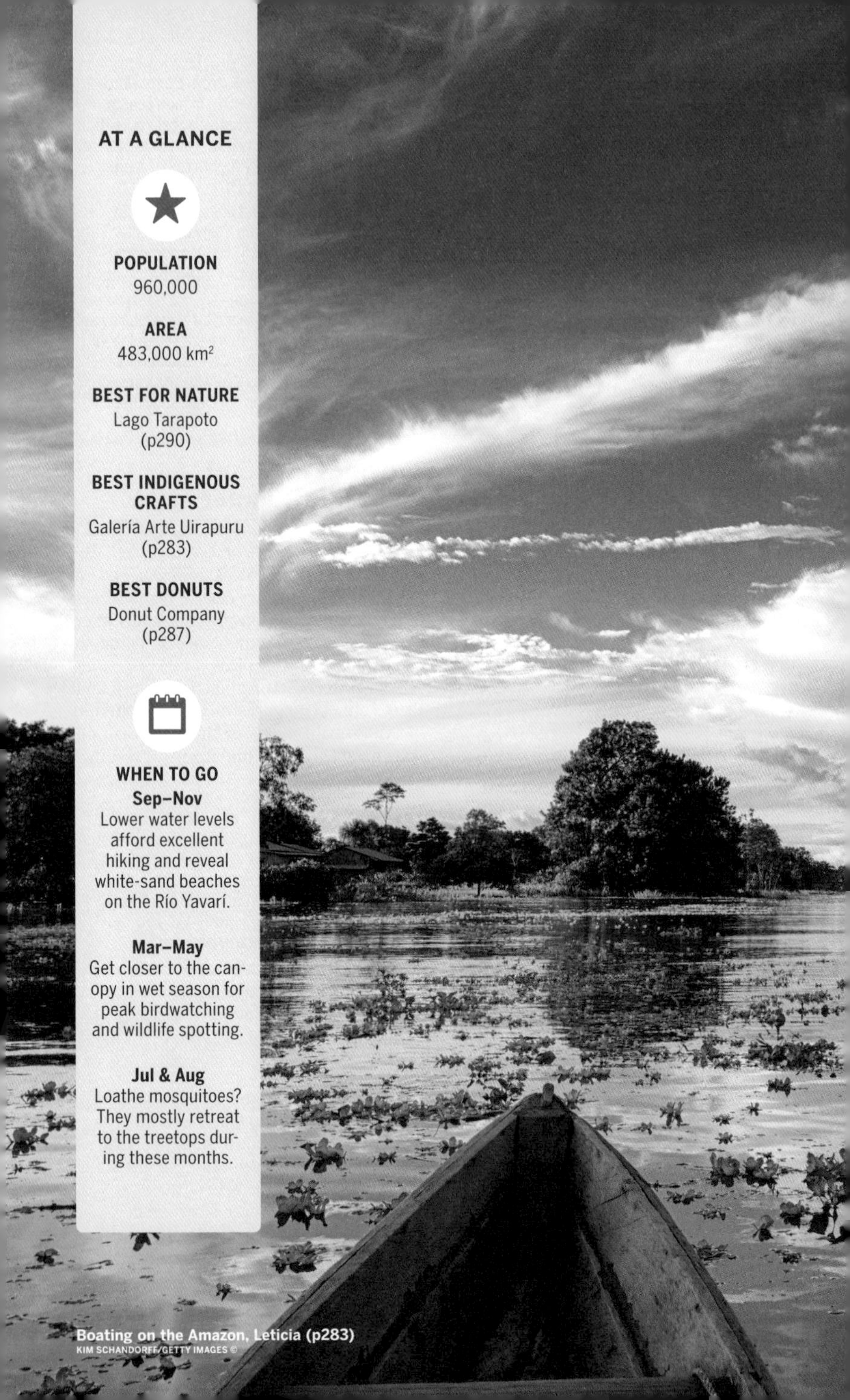

Boating on the Amazon, Leticia (p283)

Amazon Basin

Amazon. The very word evokes images of pristine jungle, incredible wildlife and, of course, one world-famous river. The region known to Colombians as Amazonia is a vast slice of rainforest accounting for a third of Colombia's total area – about the size of California – and spread over some eight of the country's departments. There are no roads here, just fast-flowing waterways and vast tracts of wilderness where, for now at least, humans have had relatively little impact on nature, and indigenous groups deep in the jungle have managed to keep their cultures intact.

Tourism is still relatively undeveloped here, and what little there is can be found in and around the towns of Leticia and Puerto Nariño. Yet precisely because of the lack of development, a visit here remains a transcendent experience, from thrilling rainforest treks to simple hammock siestas alongside the sounds of the jungle.

INCLUDES

Leticia. 282
Parque Nacional Natural Amacayacu 289
Puerto Nariño 289
Río Yavarí 291

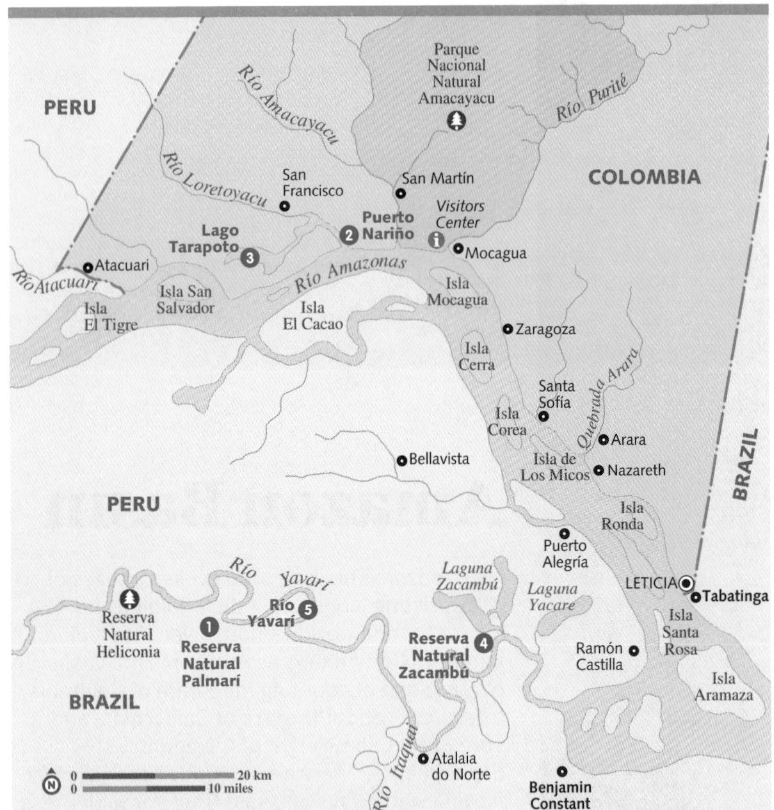

Amazon Basin Highlights

❶ **Reserva Natural Palmarí** (p291) Spending a few days observing the abundant wildlife at this wonderful reserve.

❷ **Puerto Nariño** (p289) Unwinding in this car-free, impressively sustainable and generally adorable village on the banks of the Amazon.

❸ **Lago Tarapoto** (p290) Spotting pink and gray dolphins in the warm waters of this jungle lake.

❹ **Reserva Natural Zacambú** (p292) Being serenaded by parrots and the calls of dozens of other animals in this rainforest reserve.

❺ **Río Yavarí** (p291) Canoeing silently into the jungle up the tributaries of this surging giant.

Leticia

☎8 / POP 29,700 / ELEV 95M

The capital city of the Amazonas province, Leticia is the largest settlement for hundreds of kilometers and yet still looks and feels very much like the small frontier town it is. Located on the Amazon River where Colombia, Brazil and Peru meet, Leticia is some 800km from the nearest Colombian highway. It's a bustling town abuzz with fleets of motorcycles, with a few minor sights to entertain you for a day or two.

Notwithstanding the oppressive heat, stultifying humidity and ferocious mosquitoes, Leticia is a pleasant enough town but not a destination in itself: it's a stepping stone for visiting the tropical rainforest that's right on your doorstep, with remote jungle lodges and indigenous communities just a short boat ride away along the Rio Amazonas.

History

Leticia was founded in 1867 as San Antonio. The origin of its current name has been lost to history. In any case, it was part of Peru until 1922, when both countries signed a controversial agreement that ceded the land to Colombia. In 1932 a war broke out between Colombia and Peru, ending in 1933 after the League of Nations negotiated a cease-fire, ultimately awarding Leticia to Colombia. In the 1970s Leticia became a lawless hub of narcotics trafficking until the Colombian army moved in and cleaned things up.

Sights & Activities

★Mundo Amazónico GARDENS

(8-592-6087, 321-472-4346; www.mundoamazonico.com; Km7.7, Via Tarapacá; tours COP$10,000; 8am-3pm Mon-Sat) This 29-hectare reserve works as a center for environmental education and makes for a great place to get to know something of the plants, trees and inhabitants of the jungle before you set out on an expedition. The extensive botanical gardens boast some 700 species of flora that can be visited on four differently themed tours (the botanical garden, sustainable processes, cultural presentations and the aquarium), each lasting between 30 and 45 minutes and leaving every hour until 2pm.

You can combine as many tours as you like, and they'll even serve lunch for COP$20,000 per person if you'd like to make a day of it. Call ahead to book the one English-speaking guide. To get here from Leticia, take any bus to Km7.7 and then follow the sign off the main road down the track for 10 minutes. Moto-taxis charge COP$15,000.

Museo Etnográfico Amazónico MUSEUM

(8-592-7783; Carrera 11 No 9-43; 8:30am-6pm Mon-Fri, 9am-1pm Sat) FREE This little museum has a small but thorough collection of indigenous artifacts. Learn about *malocas* (ancestral longhouses) and *chagras* (indigenous production systems) and peruse the musical instruments, textiles, tools, pottery, weapons and many ceremonial masks. Labeled in English, the exhibits make a good introduction to the indigenous cultures of the region, such as the Huitotos, Yukunas and Ticunas.

Galería Arte Uirapuru ARTS & CRAFTS

(Calle 8 No 10-35; 9am-noon & 3-7pm Mon-Sat, 9am-noon Sun) Leticia's largest craft shop sells artifacts from local indigenous groups, as well as traditional medicines from a natural Amazonian pharmacy. At the back is the rather dimly lit Museo Alfonso Galindo, which could be from the pages of a Graham Greene novel, featuring a collection of Ticuna crafts and cult objects along with other curios, such as a stuffed pink dolphin. None of the items are for sale, but it's quite compelling to look around.

Parque Santander PARK

A visit to Leticia's central square, which is filled with some fairly bizarre civic art and sculpture, is best made just before sunset when you can witness thousands of small screeching *pericos* (parrots) arriving for their nightly rest.

Tours

The real jungle begins well off the Amazon proper, along its small tributaries. The deeper you go, the more chance you have to observe wildlife in relatively undamaged habitats and to visit indigenous settlements. This involves time and money, but can be immensely rewarding, and there are numerous tour agencies and guides waiting to take you out here.

Amazon Jungle Trips TOURS

(321-426-7757; www.amazonjungletrips.com.co; Av Internacional No 6-25) With more than 25 years of experience catering to backpackers, Amazon Jungle is one of the oldest and most reliable tour companies in Leticia. Owner Antonio Cruz Pérez speaks fluent English and can arrange individually tailored tours, including trips to the two very different reserves the company runs: Zacambú (p292) and **Tupana Arü Ü** (321-426-7757; www.amazonjungletrips.com.co).

Zacambú is on the Río Yavarí in Peru, while Tupana Arü Ü is 60km upriver on the Amazon and deeper in the jungle. Both lodges are around an hour's boat ride from Leticia, though there's an extra 45-minute walk to Tupana Arü Ü from the river once you arrive at the Amazon settlement of La Libertad. A trip that includes a night or two at both reserves is optimal and surprisingly affordable at COP$330,000 per person per

Leticia

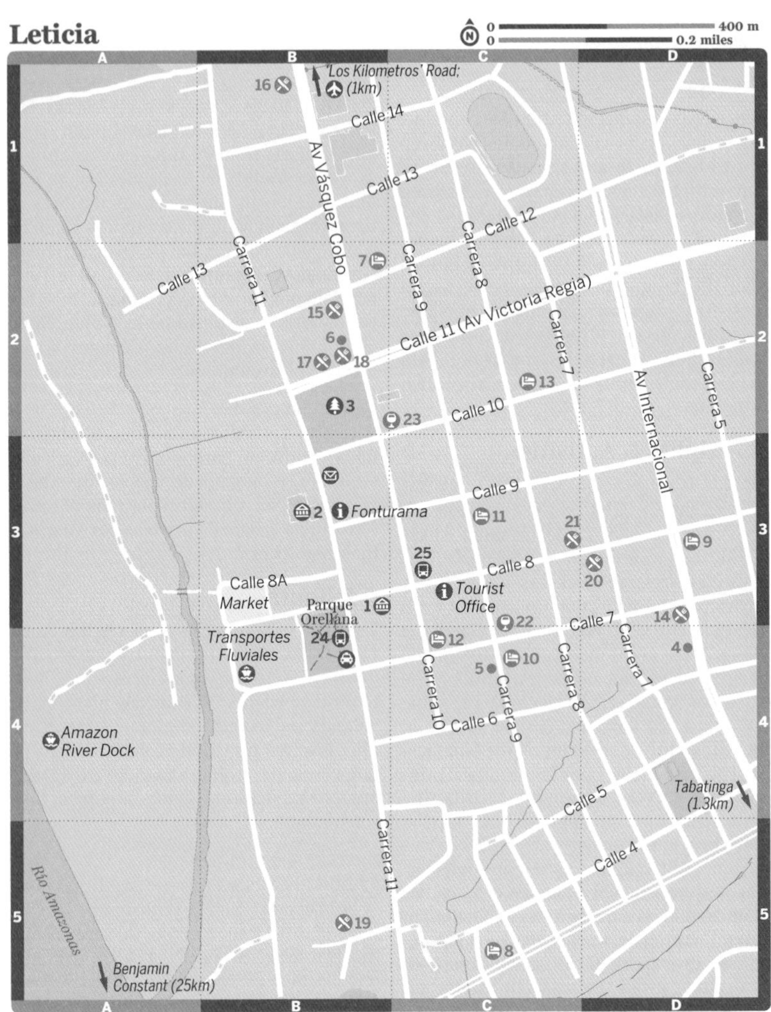

day, all-inclusive. Facilities are simple but include running water and mosquito nets, the food is good, guides are professional and the welcome is warm.

Colombia Remote Adventures WILDLIFE
(☎phone/WhatsApp 321-412-8372; www.colombiaremoteadventures.com) Veteran Amazon tour guide and fluent English speaker Eliceo Matapi Yucuna runs his own tour company offering all sorts of tailor-made Amazonian adventures combining cultural exchanges with Ticuna indigenous people and wildlife adventures in the rainforest. There's no office; everything is managed online and by telephone – talk to Eliceo directly and explain what you want.

Tanimboca Tours TOURS
(☎310-791-7470; www.tanimboca.org; Carrera 10 No 11-69) In addition to the activities on offer at Reserva Tanimboca to the north of Leticia, the friendly folks here can organize boat or hiking trips into the jungle outside Leticia, including trips to indigenous villages. The owner speaks German and English, and several of the guides speak English too.

Leticia

Sights
1 Galería Arte Uirapuru ... B3
2 Museo Etnográfico Amazónico ... B3
3 Parque Santander ... B2

Activities, Courses & Tours
4 Amazon Jungle Trips ... D4
5 Selvaventura ... C4
6 Tanimboca Tours ... B2

Sleeping
7 Amazon B&B ... B2
8 Ayahuasca Amazonas Hotel ... C5
9 Hotel Malokamazonas ... D3
10 La Casa del Kurupira ... C4
11 La Jangada ... C3
12 Waira Suites Hotel ... C4
13 Zuruma Hotel ... C2

Eating
14 El Cielo ... D3
15 El Santo Angel ... B2
16 Gael Pizzeria Gourmet ... B1
17 Govindas ... B2
18 La Casa del Pan ... B2
19 Numae Bistró ... B5
20 The Donut Company ... D3
21 Tierras Amazónicas ... C3

Drinking & Nightlife
22 Kawanna Bar ... C3
23 Mossh Bar ... C2

Transport
24 Colectivos to Leticia Airport ... B4
25 Minibuses to Tabatinga ... C3

Selvaventura TOURS
(8-592-3977, 311-287-1307; www.selvaventura.org; Carrera 9 No 6-85) Owner Felipe Ulloa speaks English, Spanish and Portuguese and can arrange a variety of trips into the jungle (including day trips on Río Amazonas) to both high-forest and *igapó* (flooded) ecosystems. He also sells tickets for various river trips into Peru and Brazil. The agency uses the Maloka jungle camp and the less remote Agape (at Km10).

Sleeping

Leticia is awash with accommodations, though quality is extremely variable and prices can skyrocket during high season, especially around Christmas and Easter. Note that many hotels are located on the airport road outside of town. While this makes them far less convenient for meals, they are essentially in the jungle canopy if you'd rather avoid the noise and traffic of downtown.

Omshanty Jungle Lodge LODGE $$
(311-489-8985; www.omshanty.com; Km11 Via Tarapaca; dm/s/d/tr/q COP$15,000/40,000/60,000/80,000/95,000) In a thick jungle setting and not strictly in Leticia itself, Omshanty is a clutch of simple cabins with kitchens and mosquito nets, with the restaurant next door serving terrific meals. Friendly English-speaking owner Kike organizes jungle excursions, and guests have been known to linger here for weeks, seduced by the jungle setting and excellent hospitality.

La Casa del Kurupira HOSTEL $
(313-468-0808, 8-592-6160; www.lacasadelkurupira.com; Carrera 9 No 6-100; dm/s/d COP$25,000/$60,000/70,000, s/d without bathroom COP$50,000/60,000;) Operated by the owners of Selvaventura (p285) across the street (whose offices also function as the hostel's bar and hangout), La Casa del Kurupira is very clean, bright and modern, with ceiling fans cooling the rooms and a large shared kitchen and roof terrace strewn with hammocks to chill out in. Laundry costs COP$10,000 and breakfast COP$8000.

La Jangada GUESTHOUSE $
(312-451-0758, 311-582-7158; www.lajangadamazonas.com; Carrera 9 No 8-106; dm COP$27,000, s/d COP$60,000/75,000, without bathroom COP$50,000/65,000;) This simple but good-value and popular central guesthouse arranges highly recommended river and jungle trips, including excursions on an ecologically sound bicycle-powered boat. There's a five-bed dorm with a breezy balcony and a hammock, and a few private rooms with fans. Breakfast is included in all categories.

Ayahuasca Amazonas Hotel HOTEL $$
(316-373-1359, 8-592-4356; ayahuascaamazonashotel@yahoo.es; Carrera 10 No 3-28; r/bungalow from COP$130,000/160,000;) Despite being named for the hallucinogenic indigenous brew, this is no retreat for self-discovery, just an immaculately clean and friendly family-run hotel in a bustling residential neighborhood by the Brazilian

GETTING INTO THE JUNGLE

Getting truly off the beaten path in the Colombian Amazon can be tricky, especially if you want to combine being in nature with experiencing the daily lives of the indigenous peoples of the region. The best solution is to visit one of the self-contained jungle lodges, which allow you to spend time close to nature while also having basic necessities such as electricity, meals and guides on hand.

With just six gorgeously designed rooms, the tiny **Calanoa Amazonas** (☎350-316-7210; www.calanoaamazonas.com; per person per night campsite/cabin US$135/165) jungle lodge truly is a slice of paradise, and one of the few in the Amazon Basin that allow visitors to relax in style. Two activities per day are included, ranging from long jungle hikes to night walks, canoe trips and visits to a nearby indigenous village that the lodge supports. For non–Spanish speakers, a translator costs an extra COP$200,000 per group per day, while the round-trip boat transfer from Leticia costs COP$90,000 per guest, including the pickup from Leticia's airport.

The small and very rustic family-run **Casa Gregorio** (☎310-279-8147; www.casagregoriolodge.com; San Martin de Amacayacu; full board per person from COP$180,000) in the Tikuna indigenous community of San Martin de Amacayacu is surrounded by majestic rivers and impressive rainforest. With just two double rooms in the main house and a separate cabin that sleeps five, the guesthouse is fully integrated into the community rather than feeling enclosed or apart. Rates include full board, rubber boots, rain gear, drinking water and all activities, workshops and river trips. You'll need to book ahead to stay here, as you have to be picked up by the Casa Gregorio staff on arrival at the Bocana Amacayacu dock on the Amazon (COP$30,000 per person).

border. While the owners speak no English, they look after their guests very well, and can arrange tours and expeditions into the rainforest. There's also a hot tub to relax in.

Hotel Malokamazonas BOUTIQUE HOTEL **$$**
(☎313-822-7527, 8-592-6642; www.hotel-malokamazonas.es.tl; Calle 8 No 5-49; s/d/tw/tr incl breakfast COP$85,000/150,000/165,000/225,000;) This charming place has been thoughtfully designed, with nine comfortable and attractive rooms set amid a garden overflowing with orchids and fruit trees. There's an abundance of natural wood furniture and indigenous handicrafts, and the welcome is warm and professional.

★ **Amazon B&B** B&B **$$$**
(☎8-592-4981; www.amazonbb.com; Calle 12 No 9-30; s/d incl breakfast COP$165,000/228,000, cabaña d/tr/f COP$280,000/350,000/420,000;) Leticia's most charming and stylish option, this hotel comprises six cabañas and four rooms surrounding a gorgeous tropical garden. The cabañas are spacious and come with high ceilings, well-stocked minibars and small, enclosed terraces with hammocks. Big discounts are available out of season, but note that only two rooms have air-con; the others are fan-cooled.

Zuruma Hotel HOTEL **$$$**
(☎311-262-5273, 8-592-6760; www.zurumahotel.com; Calle 10 No 7-62; s/d/tr incl breakfast COP$105,000/164,000/228,000;) With its rather modernist two-story blocks at the back of a large courtyard that boasts a very welcome pool to cool off in after a day in Leticia's relentless heat, the Zuruma has spacious, superclean if somewhat minimalist rooms. The owners may not be natural hoteliers (see: recycling bins next to the pool), but the welcome is warm.

Waira Suites Hotel HOTEL **$$$**
(☎8-592-4428; www.wairahotel.com.co; Carrera 10 No 7-36; s/d incl breakfast COP$192,000/296,000;) Its sleek white building and fittings set it apart from the usual dusty Amazon hotels here, but while it's definitely comfortable, some rooms are a little small and it's a little overpriced. That said, the pool is one of the best in town, set amid a blooming garden, and the staff is professional and polite.

Eating

There are a number of good restaurants in Leticia, although they mostly open only in the evenings. Leticia's specialty is fish, including the delicious *gamitana* and *pi-*

rarucú, which is best avoided out of season as some locals ignore bans on catching the species when spawning. Prices can be higher than in 'mainland' Colombia, but many restaurants serve cheap set meals.

Donut Company CAFE $
(☎321-318-3444; Calle 8 No 7-35; donuts COP$2200-3500; ⊙1-9pm Mon-Sat) This wonderful little cafe serves good, reliable coffee, and if you thought it was impossible to get freshly baked donuts in the Colombian jungle, 'donut' underestimate their baking skills! Run by an American evangelist couple, the cafe donates its profits to supporting an orphanage in Benjamin Constant.

Govindas VEGETARIAN $
(☎320-487-4066; Calle 11A No 10-56; set-price meal COP$10,000; ⊙noon–9pm;) A lifeline for vegetarians in these parts, Govindas serves set-price lunches and dinners from its yoga studio's terrace on one side of Parque Santander. The fare is unremarkable, but it's healthy and meat-free. Delivery is also available.

La Casa del Pan BAKERY $
(Calle 11 No 10-20; breakfast COP$5000-8000; ⊙7am-noon & 1-8pm) Facing Parque Santander, this friendly spot for a basic but filling breakfast of eggs, bread and coffee is a favorite with budget travelers.

★**El Santo Angel** INTERNATIONAL $$
(☎8-592-3866; www.facebook.com/elsantoangeld; Carrera 10 No 11-119; mains COP$15,000-37,000; ⊙4pm-midnight Tue-Sun;) With one of the most varied and interesting menus in town, Santo Angel is a popular place for an evening meal. Diners spill out all over the street, and there's often live (but not earsplitting) musical entertainment. On offer are wraps, nachos, salads, grills, pita bread, burgers and pizza, as well as German beers.

Gael Pizzeria Gourmet PIZZA $$
(☎313-359-1943; www.facebook.com/gaelpizzeriagourmet; Carrera 10 No 14-1; pizzas COP$14,000-33,000; ⊙6-10pm Wed-Mon;) At this roadside pizzeria the muted lighting and cute wooden tables alone tell you straightaway that it's unlike most other places in town. Gael prepares mouthwatering pizzas and calzones, as well as pasta dishes and lasagna – easily the best in Leticia!

★**El Cielo** AMAZONIAN $$
(☎320-454-4569; Av Internacional No 6-11; mains COP$17,000-33,000; ⊙4-11pm Mon & Wed-Sat, 11am-5pm Sun;) The pinnacle of culinary sophistication in Leticia, this cool, creative space serves *casabes* (mini-pizzas made from yuca instead of flour) with imaginative toppings, including *pirarucú* (a popular local fish) and *tucupi* (a cassava extract). Despite the busy location on the main road, its pleasantly lit gravel garden is a lovely place for a meal.

Tierras Amazónicas AMAZONIAN $$
(Calle 8 No 7-50; mains COP$17,000-32,000; ⊙7am-10pm Tue-Sun;) At first glance, this looks like an unapologetic tourist trap with walls covered in Amazonian knickknacks and folk art pieces all over the place. Nonetheless, it's a great place for a fun dinner, and one of the few good restaurants open for lunch. The specialty is fish – dorado, gamitana, piranha and tucanare – and that's what you should order.

Drinking & Nightlife

Leticia comes to life after sunset at 6pm. As the humidity and temperature drop (somewhat!), locals often find themselves sitting in the streets and the entire town takes on a fun and bawdy air. That bawdiness isn't always good, though – drugs and prostitution are ubiquitous and make it ill-advised to stray far from the center after dark.

Mossh Bar BAR
(Carrera 10 No 10-08; ⊙4pm-2am Tue-Thu, 4pm-4am Fri & Sat) This surprisingly modish joint facing Parque Santander has a red, white, black and chrome interior and attracts a classier crowd than most bars in town.

Kawanna Bar BAR
(cnr Carrera 9 & Calle 7; ⊙6pm-midnight Sun-Thu, 6pm-2am Fri & Sat) A good spot for a relaxed beer on the terrace once the sun is setting; there's also dancing inside later and on weekends.

Orientation

Leticia is an easy-to-navigate grid on the banks of the Amazon on the Colombia–Brazil border. Just across the frontier sits Tabatinga, a Brazilian town much the same size as Leticia, with its own airport and port that is the main gateway for boats downstream to Manaus. Visitors can freely move between the two cities as well as the Brazilian city of Benjamin Constant,

GETTING TO PERU

High-speed passenger boats between Tabatinga and Iquitos (Peru) are operated by **Transtur** (in Iquitos 51 6529-1324; www.transtursa.com; Jirón Raymondi 384) and **Transportes Golfinho** (in Iquitos 51 65-225-118; www.transportesgolfinho.com; Marechal Mallet 306, Tabatinga). Boats leave from Isla Santa Rosa daily at around 5am (Brazilian time!), arriving in Iquitos about 10 hours later. Don't forget to get your Colombian exit stamp at Leticia airport's office of Migración Colombia (p289) the day before departure. You can buy tickets through Selvaventura (p285) in Leticia, as neither company has an office in town.

The journey costs US$75 in either direction, including breakfast and lunch (mint-condition banknotes only; or COP$225,000). During dry season you can sometimes access Isla Santa Rosa only from Tabatinga's Porto da Feira, where water levels are always high. Check ahead. In fact, it's always easier in the middle of the night to go from Tabatinga, but taxi prices from Leticia can skyrocket to COP$30,000 for the ride.

Be warned: there are slower, cheaper boats to Iquitos, but they are not comfortable, often unsafe and best avoided.

Note there are no roads out of Iquitos into Peru. You have to fly or continue by river to Pucallpa (five to seven days), from where you can go overland to Lima.

If you need a Peruvian visa, there's a **Peruvian consulate** (8-592-7755; Calle 11 No 5-32; 8am-noon & 2-4pm Mon-Fri) in Leticia.

25km downstream, and the Peruvian island of Santa Rosa opposite Leticia/Tabatinga. Travelers wishing to venture further into either country must meet the immigration requirements (p289).

Information

SAFE TRAVEL

A long-standing military presence in the region has tried to keep Leticia/Tabatinga and the surrounding region safe, but there are issues. Former drug traffickers, guerrillas, paramilitaries and *raspachines* (coca-plant harvesters), reinserted into mainstream society and now living on the outskirts of Leticia and Puerto Nariño, run poker houses, brothels, dubious bars and the like. Don't wander outside these urban areas on your own at night, especially on Leticia's infamous 'Los Kilometros' road. In Peru, drug traffickers remain in business in this wayward corner of the country and have harassed tourists who've wandered off the beaten track. Tour operators and lodges in the region have been issued warnings about where they can and cannot bring tourists, so don't stray on your own beyond areas where local tourism guides normally operate.

EMERGENCY

Police (8-592-5060; Carrera 11 No 12-32) The main police station.

INTERNET ACCESS

Sluggish internet speeds plague Leticia, though nearly every hotel and most restaurants have free wi-fi. You can buy Claro and Movistar SIM cards on Carrera 11 near the Museo Etnográfico Amazónico (p283), though speeds are also very slow compared with elsewhere in the country. WhatsApp is heavily used.

MEDICAL SERVICES

San Rafael de Leticia Hospital (8-592-7826; www.esehospitalsanrafael-leticia-amazonas.gov.co; Carrera 10 No 13-78) Basic medical services; for anything serious, it's best to fly to Bogotá.

A yellow-fever vaccination is recommended 10 days before arrival; make sure to bring your yellow-fever certificate with you.

MONEY

There are ATMs in the town center, especially along Carrera 10 between Calles 7 and 10, and *casas de cambio* on Calle 8 between Carrera 11 and the market. Shop around; exchange rates vary.

POST

4-72 (Carrera 11 No 10-44; 8am-noon & 2-5pm Mon-Fri) Postal services.

TOURIST INFORMATION

Leticia's small **tourist office** (Secretaría de Turismo y Fronteras; 8-592-4162; Calle 8 No 9-75; 8am-noon & 2-5pm Mon-Fri, 8am-1pm Sat) is helpful and friendly.

Fonturama (Fondo de Promoción y Desarrollo Turístico del Amazonas; 8-592-4162; www.fonturamazonas.org; Carrera 11 No 9-04; 9am-noon & 2-7pm Mon-Sat) has info on sustainable tourism in the region.

VISA INFORMATION

Locals and foreigners may freely cross borders within an 80km radius of Leticia, but a passport is needed for points beyond.

If you plan on heading further afield, you must get your passport stamped at the Ministry of Foreign Relations office at Leticia's airport (p289). Importantly, you must get a second stamp (from either the Brazilian or Peruvian authorities) within 24 hours, so plan carefully. If you have an early departure from Leticia by boat, you'll need to get your stamp at the airport the day before. Citizens of some countries, including the USA, Canada, Australia and New Zealand, need a visa to enter Brazil and it may be costly. To avoid a lot of stress and heartache, it's strongly recommended to arrange your visa before arriving in the Amazon. But if you must, bring a passport photo and yellow fever vaccination certificate to the Brazilian Consulate (p321). Processing time is one to three days, depending on volume. If you're coming from or going to Iquitos, get your entry or exit stamp at the Policía Internacional Peruviano (PIP) office on Isla Santa Rosa, the Peruvian island facing Leticia. Travelers coming here from Brazil who need a Colombian visa may obtain one at the Colombian consulate in Tabatinga.

If you need a Colombian visa extension, there is no need to pay an extension fee. Simply stamp out and head to Brazil or Peru for one day and return for a fresh 60-day stamp.

Getting There & Away

The only way to get to Leticia is by boat or by air, as there are no roads connecting further into Colombia, Brazil or Peru from here.

AIR

All foreigners must pay a COP$32,000 tourist tax upon arrival at Leticia's airport, **Aeropuerto Internacional Alfredo Vásquez Cobo** (Carrera 10), to the north of town. Taxis into town cost around COP$10,000; if traveling light, hop on a moto-taxi.

Avianca (www.avianca.com) and Latam (www.latam.com) have several daily flights to Bogotá.

Tabatinga International Airport has flights to Manaus daily with Azul (www.voeazul.com.br). The airport is 4km south of Tabatinga; *colectivos* (shared taxis, minivans, or midsize buses) marked 'Comara' from Leticia will drop you nearby. Don't forget to get your Colombian exit stamp at Leticia's airport and, if needed, a Brazilian visa before departure.

When departing Leticia's airport, all foreigners must check in at **Migración Colombia** (☎8-592-7189; www.migracioncolombia.gov.co; Aeropuerto Internacional Alfredo Vásquez Cobo; ⏲7am-6pm Mon-Fri, 7am-4pm & 7-10pm Sat & Sun) before proceeding through airport security, regardless of whether they're leaving Colombia or not; you'll be directed there after check-in if you haven't done it already – it's a painless and free procedure that takes a matter of seconds.

BOAT

Buy tickets for Puerto Nariño and other points upriver from one of the three agencies at **Transportes Fluviales** (☎311-486-9464, 311-532-0633; Malecon Plaza, Carrera 12 No 7-36). Boats to Puerto Nariño depart from Leticia's **Muelle Turístico** at 7am, 9am, noon and 2pm daily (COP$31,000, two hours). Arrive in good time for your boat, as the dock can be hard to find. You'll need your passport when buying tickets.

If you're departing from Tabatinga, be aware that it is one hour ahead of Leticia. Don't miss your boat!

Getting Around

The main mode of public transportation is moto-taxis, with folks on motorcycles who zip around town with an extra helmet. The base rate is COP$2500. Frequent *colectivos* (COP$2500 to COP$7000) link Leticia with Tabatinga and the 'Kilometer' villages north of Leticia's airport. There are **minibuses to Tabatinga** (Cnr Carrera 10 & Calle 8) and **colectivos to Leticia airport** (Parque Orellana).

Standard **taxis** (Parque Orellana) are pricier than in the rest of Colombia; a short ride from the airport to town costs around COP$10,000, to Tabatinga's airport COP$15,000 and to the Porto Bras in Tabatinga COP$10,000.

Parque Nacional Natural Amacayacu

Sprawling across almost 300,000 hectares, **PNN Amacayacu** (☎8-520-8654; www.parquesnacionales.gov.co) is an ideal spot from which to observe the Amazonian rainforest up close, with extraordinary biodiversity and lots of wildlife. Sadly, however, following catastrophic flooding, the park facilities have been closed for some time and look likely to remain so in the near future, though it is still possible to enter the park and arrange tours with local indigenous people. Contact a tour operator in Leticia to arrange a visit.

Puerto Nariño

☎8 / POP 5500 / ELEV 110M

The Amazonian village of Puerto Nariño, 75km upriver from Leticia, is an inspiring example of human coexistence with nature. Here, cars are banned (the only two vehicles are an ambulance and a truck for collecting recyclables), rainwater is pooled in cisterns for washing and gardening, and electricity comes from the town's fuel-efficient generator, which runs only until midnight. Every morning, citizen brigades fan out to tidy up the town's landscaped sidewalks, and Puerto Nariño's ambitious recycling and organic-waste management programs would put most world cities to shame. As a contrast to dirty and polluted Leticia, it couldn't be more stark.

The majority of Puerto Nariño's residents are indigenous Ticuna, Cocoma and Yagua peoples. Their community experiment in ecological living has made ecotourism an important source of income, and this tranquil place is a great base from which to visit beautiful Lago Tarapoto and the Amazon in general.

Sights

Mirador Nai-pata VIEWPOINT
(Calle 4; adult/child COP$5000/3000; 7am-6pm Mon-Fri, 8am-5pm Sat & Sun) For a bird's-eye view of the village and the surrounding jungle and Amazon, climb this impressive wooden tower (*'nai-pata'* means 'tree-house' in the Ticuna tongue), on the top of a hill in the center of the village. Cool down afterwards with an ice cream next to the tower.

Centro de Interpretación Natütama MUSEUM
(313-410-1925; www.natutama.org; entry by donation; 8am-12:30pm & 2-5pm) The Centro de Interpretación Natütama has a fascinating museum with nearly 100 life-sized wood carvings of Amazonian flora and fauna and videos showcasing the plight of the pink river dolphin and the manatee. It's well worth purchasing handicrafts here, as the proceeds go toward conservation and community outreach efforts.

★ Lago Tarapoto LAKE
Lago Tarapoto, 10km west of Puerto Nariño, is a beautiful jungle lake fed by the Río Amazonas, and is home to pink dolphins, a tiny population of manatees and massive water lilies. A half-day trip to the lake in a *peque-peque* (a low-slung wooden boat) from Puerto Nariño (around COP$50,000 for up to four people for around four hours) is the main draw for visitors, who usually take a dip in the gorgeously clear water. Piranha fishing is also possible here.

Casa Museo Etnocultural MUSEUM
(cnr Carrera 6 & Calle 5; 8am-noon & 2-5pm Mon-Fri) FREE Located in the *Alcaldía* (town hall building), this mini museum has a small display of artifacts from the region's indigenous populations.

Sleeping

There are around two dozen hotels, guesthouses and hostels in town, so you'll never have trouble finding somewhere to sleep. Some hotel owners wait at the dock to meet the arriving boat from Leticia.

★ Maloca Napü GUESTHOUSE $
(314-437-6075, 315-607-4044; www.malocanapu.com; Calle 4 No 5-72; dm COP$20,000, r per person with/without balcony COP$30,000/25,000; @) Perhaps the most charming guesthouse in Puerto Nariño, Maloca Napü has the look and feel of a tree-house fort, surrounded as it is by a thickly forested garden. The rooms are simple but comfortable, with fans, shared bathroom with super-refreshing rain-style showers, and fully equipped kitchen. Everyone who works here is above-and-beyond friendly.

★ Alto de Aguila - Cabañas del Fraile CABAÑAS $
(314-201-3154, 311-502-8592; altodelaguila@hotmail.com; dm COP$20,000, r per person with/without bathroom COP$30,000/25,000) In the jungle outside the village, friar Hector José Rivera and his delightful monkeys run this hilltop oasis overlooking the Amazon. The complex includes several simple huts, shared facilities and a lookout tower. Between the monkeys, turkeys, dogs and macaws roaming about, there's a real menagerie to enjoy, along with utter isolation and free use of canoes on the Amazon.

To get here, take the main street (parallel to the Amazon, two blocks back) west out of Puerto Nariño across the big bridge; keep left at the cemetery and walk through the high-school campus, then turn right immediately after passing the soccer pitch.

Hotel Lomas del Paiyü HOTEL $$
(313-871-1743, 313-268-4400; hotellomasdelpaiyu@yahoo.com; Calle 7 No 2-26; s/d/tr/q COP$55,000/105,000/144,000/180,000) This tin-roofed 22-room hotel is a reliable choice

and has quite a bit of rough charm. Some bathrooms are almost as big as the fan-cooled rooms, the walls are framed screens, letting in the sounds of the rainforest, and the staff are super-helpful, setting you up with jungle guides and lending out rubber boots and life jackets. Breakfast costs COP$8000.

Waira Selva Hotel HOTEL **$$**
(8-592-4428; www.wairahotel.com.co; Carrera 5 No 6-72; s/d/t incl breakfast COP$90,000/132,000/180,000;) Smart but somewhat overpriced, the Waira Selva allows you to do the jungle in some comfort, with 13 spacious and comfortable rooms that feature lots of dark wood, have ceiling fans and balconies, and share access to a rather quirky tree-house-style viewing platform overlooking the village. Wi-fi supposedly works sometimes. Bookings are handled by its Leticia sister property, Waira Suites Hotel (p286).

The excellent restaurant is open to non-guests.

Eating & Drinking

Nightlife in Puerto Nariño involves drinking at one of the hole-in-the-wall bars fronting the basketball courts. It's quite safe to walk around after dark in this friendly and secure village.

Restaurante El Calvo COLOMBIAN **$**
(Carrera 6; meals COP$10,000-12,000; 7am-10pm;) Facing the sports grounds on Puerto Nariño's main street, this friendly place serves excellent grilled fish, as well as a vegetarian option. There's also a range of delicious fruit juices on offer.

Las Margaritas COLOMBIAN **$$**
(311-276-2407; Calle 6 No 6-80; set-price meals COP$15,000; noon-3pm) Under a huge *palapa* (thatched roof) just beyond the soccer pitch, lunch-only Las Margaritas is the best restaurant in Puerto Nariño, even if it's rather pricey by local standards and aimed almost entirely at visiting tour groups. The all-you-can-gobble buffet-style meals are delicious, though, and involve fish, chicken, *patacones* (fried plantains) and salad.

Information

There's a small **tourist office** (cnr Carrera 6 & Calle 5; 8am-noon & 2-5pm Mon-Fri) inside the town hall.

There's a small and basic **hospital** (cnr Carrera 4 & Calle 4) in Puerto Nariño, but for any serious medical problem, you'll need to return to Leticia.

Getting There & Away

High-speed boats to Puerto Nariño depart from Leticia's dock at 7am, 9am, noon and 2pm daily (COP$30,000, two hours); return-trip boats to Leticia depart at 7am, 10am, 1:30pm and 3:30pm.

You can purchase tickets at **Transportes Fluviales** (8-592-6752; Muelle Turistico). In Leticia boats can get very full, so buy your tickets early or the day before.

Río Yavarí

Within reach of large stretches of virgin forest, the meandering Río Yavarí offers some of the best opportunities to see the Amazon up close and undisturbed. Two privately owned reserves provide simple accommodations plus guided tours and activities, including kayaking, bird- and dolphin-watching, jungle treks and visits to indigenous communities. These make for some of the most accessible and relatively comfortable destinations in the rainforest and are highly recommended.

When planning a visit, bear in mind that costs take into account the number of people in the party, length of stay, season and number of guided tours; count on COP$180,000 to COP$350,000 per person per day, but as a rule, the more of you there are the better deal you'll get.

Reserva Natural Palmarí

About 105km by river from Leticia, **Reserva Natural Palmarí** (310-786-2770; www.palmari.org) sits on the high south (Brazilian) bank of the Río Yavarí, overlooking a wide bend where pink and gray dolphins often gather. It's the only lodge with access to all three Amazonian ecosystems: *terra firme* (dry), *várzea* (semi-flooded) and *igapó* (flooded).

The lodge itself is rustic, much of it rebuilt after arsonists set fire to it in 2010. It has helpful guides employed from the surrounding community (so no English, but *mucho* authenticity and expertise), and offers a wide choice of walking trips and night treks, boat excursions and kayaking trips. You'll find Palmarí offers the best walking options around the region, is the only option to encounter *terra firme* forest and is the best spot in the region to see animals, including tapirs, and for the supremely lucky, jaguars.

Access to the reserve is exclusively by private launch from Tabatinga (COP$100,000 per person). Journey time to the reserve is between 45 minutes and two hours depending on the water levels. To arrange the transfer, you'll need to speak with owner **Axel Antoine-Feill** (☎310-786-2770, 1-610-3514), who speaks fluent English. His representative in Leticia is Claudia Rodriguez.

Reserva Natural Zacambú

Reserva Natural Zacambú is one of the jungle reserves nearest to Leticia, about 70km by boat. Its **lodge** (☎321-426-7757; www.amazonjungletrips.com.co; COP$290,000 per person per day all inclusive) is on the Río Zacambú, a tributary of the Río Yavarí, on the Peruvian side of the river. Zacambú sits on a flooded forest that is a habitat for many species of butterflies, but unfortunately is also a popular hangout for mosquitoes. Its proximity to Peruvian communities also means it's not the best spot for wildlife, though it's still easy to see dolphins, piranhas and caiman in the river, as well as a rich variety of birdlife in the jungle. Both the lodge itself and tours are run from Leticia by Amazon Jungle Trips (p283), and it's one of the easier places to access in order to explore the natural world.

Understand Colombia

HISTORY 294
An uneasy peace? How Colombia shook off the Spanish, the narcos and the FARC.

LIFE IN COLOMBIA 304
Modern, progressive and life-affirmingly positive, Colombia is a society on the move.

THE ARTS 306
Colombia's cultural heritage is dominated by Márquez and Botero. But there is so much more...

THE NATURAL WORLD 309
Snowcapped mountains, deep blue seas, mystical jungle depths: Colombia will surprise you with its variety.

History

Colombia's history is one of war and bloodshed. Whether that's the cruelty of the colonial conquests, the fight with Spain for independence, the half a century of war between the Fuerzas Armadas Revolucionarias de Colombia (FARC; Revolutionary Armed Forces of Colombia) guerrillas and the paramilitaries, or the narco chaos of the 1980s and '90s, Colombia has sadly always been synonymous with violence. But things have changed dramatically in recent years, and Colombia today has its problems but is a safer place than it has been for decades.

Pre-Columbus Colombia

Set where South America meets Central America, present-day Colombia saw the continent's first inhabitants arrive between 12,500 and 70,000 years ago, having migrated from the north. Most – such as the ancestors of the Inca – just passed through. Little is known of the groups who did stick around (eg the Calima, Muisca, Nariño, Quimbaya, Tayrona, Tolima and Tumaco). By the time the Spaniards arrived, the first inhabitants were living in small, scattered communities, subsisting on agriculture or trade. They hardly rivaled the bigger civilizations flourishing in Mexico and Peru.

One of the best books on Colombia's history is David Bushnell's *The Making of Modern Colombia: A Nation in Spite of Itself* (1993), which follows colonization, partisan conflicts throughout independence and the emergence of cocaine politics in the 1980s.

The area's biggest pre-Columbian sites (San Agustín, Tierradentro and Ciudad Perdida) were already long abandoned when the Spaniards arrived in the 1500s. Ciudad Perdida, the Tayrona jungle city, was built around 700 CE, with hundreds of stone terraces linked with stairways. The Muisca, one of the country's larger indigenous groups, occupied present-day Boyacá and Cundinamarca, near Bogotá (itself named from a Muisca word), and numbered 600,000 when the Spanish arrived.

Spanish Conquest

Colombia is named after Christopher Columbus, even though he never set foot on Colombian soil. One of Columbus' companions on his second voyage, Alonso de Ojeda, was the first recorded European to arrive in 1499. He briefly explored the Sierra Nevada de Santa Marta and was astonished by the wealth of the local indigenous people. The shores of

TIMELINE

5500 BCE

Early groups of pre-Muisca begin moving to present-day Colombia. They continue to live in small, scattered, subsistence communities, while the Aztec and Inca established their empires.

700 CE

The Tayrona begin building their largest city, the legendary Ciudad Perdida (or Lost City), in lush rainforest, which would be 'discovered' only in 1972.

1499

On his second journey to the New World, Alonso de Ojeda lands at Cabo de la Vela – and a scientist onboard surprises the crew by discovering the place isn't actually Asia.

present-day Colombia became the target of numerous expeditions by the Spaniards. Several short-lived colonies were founded along the coast, but it was not until 1525 that Rodrigo de Bastidas laid the first stones of Santa Marta, the earliest surviving European settlement in mainland South America. In 1533 Pedro de Heredia founded Cartagena, the strategic position and far better harbor of which quickly allowed it to become the principal trade center on the Colombian coast.

In 1536 an advance toward the interior began independently from three directions: under Gonzalo Jiménez de Quesada (from Santa Marta), Sebastián de Belalcázar (aka Benalcázar; from present-day Ecuador) and Nikolaus Federmann (from Venezuela). All three managed to conquer much of the colony and establish a series of towns, before meeting in the Muisca territory in 1539.

Of the three, Quesada got there first, crossing the Valle del Magdalena and Cordillera Oriental in 1537. At the time, the Muisca were divided into two rival clans – one ruled by the Zipa from Bacatá (present-day Bogotá), the other by Zaque in Hunza (present-day Tunja) – whose rivalry helped Quesada conquer both clans with only 200 men. Belalcázar, a deserter from Francisco Pizarro's Inca-conquering army, gained control of the southern part of Colombia, founding Popayán and Cali. After crossing Los Llanos and the Andes, Federmann arrived in Bogotá shortly after Belalcázar. The three groups squabbled for supremacy until King Carlos V of Spain finally established a court of justice in Bogotá in 1550 and brought the colony under the control of the viceroyalty of Peru.

The largest indigenous group between the Maya and Inca at the time of the Spanish Conquest, the Muiscas inspired El Dorado myths with their gold *tujos* (offerings), while their *chicha* (fermented-corn beer) still intoxicates Colombians today.

The Colonial Era

In 1564 the Crown established a new authority, the Real Audiencia del Nuevo Reino de Granada, which had dual military and civil power and greater autonomy. The authority was run by a governor, appointed by the King of Spain. The Nuevo Reino at that time comprised present-day Panama, Venezuela (other than Caracas) and all of Colombia, except what is today Nariño, Cauca and Valle del Cauca, which were under the jurisdiction of the Presidencia de Quito (present-day Ecuador).

The population of the colony, initially consisting of indigenous communities and the Spanish invaders, diversified with the arrival of African slaves to Cartagena, South America's principal slave-trading port. During the 16th and 17th centuries the Spaniards shipped in so many Africans that they eventually surpassed the indigenous population in number. The emergence of *criollos* (locally born whites) added to the mix.

With the growth of the Spanish empire in the New World, a new territorial division was created in 1717, and Bogotá became the capital of its own viceroyalty, the Virreinato de la Nueva Granada. It comprised the territories of what are today Colombia, Panama, Ecuador and Venezuela.

The Spanish Crown rewarded the conquistador Sebastián de Belalcázar for killing thousands of indigenous people, but it sentenced him to death for ordering the assassination of rival conquistador Jorge Robledo in 1546.

1537–38

Conquistador Gonzalo Jiménez de Quesada twice finds a new settlement, Santa Fe de Bogotá, first without permission from the Crown, in 1537, then with approval in 1538.

1564

The Spanish Crown establishes the Real Audiencia del Nuevo Reino de Granada in Bogotá, subject to the viceroyalty of Peru in Lima.

1717

Bogotá becomes capital of the viceroyalty of Virreinato de la Nueva Granada, an area that encompasses present-day Colombia, Ecuador, Venezuela and Panama.

1808

Napoleon defeats Spanish King Ferdinand VII and installs his brother on the Spanish throne, sending a glimmer of possibility for independence-minded thinkers across South America.

GOLD!

From day one of their arrival, tales of gold overwhelmed the conquistador mind. Eventually glimpses of gold artifacts – and stories of much more inland – gave birth to the myth of El Dorado, a mysterious jungle kingdom abundant in gold and, in some versions, surrounded by mountains of gold and emeralds. Long into the colonial period, the struggling Nueva Granada viceroyalty's economy depended on only one thing: gold.

Eventually the legend became linked with the Muisca and their famous Laguna de Guatavita, which has suffered endless efforts to dig up enough wealth to change the world. Not much was ever found, however. Read more in John Hemming's fascinating book, *The Search for El Dorado* (1978).

In a neat little historical dovetail, during its last years in the jungle the FARC actually turned away from white gold – cocaine – to the more traditional yellow variety as it became more lucrative, with the price of gold rocketing following the global financial crisis.

Independence from Spain

As Spanish domination of the continent increased, so too did the discontent of the inhabitants – particularly over monopolies of commerce and new taxes. The first open rebellion against colonial rule was the Revolución Comunera in Socorro (Santander) in 1781, which broke out against tax rises levied by the Crown. It began taking on more pro-independence overtones (and nearly took over Bogotá) before its leaders were caught and executed. When Napoleon Bonaparte put his own brother on the Spanish throne in 1808, the colonies refused to recognize the new monarch. One by one, Colombian towns declared their independence.

In his magic-realism novel *One Hundred Years of Solitude*, Gabriel García Márquez depicts the back-and-forth brutality of Liberal and Conservative rivalries and vendettas in ongoing conflicts from 1885 to 1902 in the fictional village of Macondo.

In 1812 Simón Bolívar, who was to become the hero of the independence struggle, appeared on the scene. He won six battles against Spanish troops, but was defeated the following year. Spain recovered its throne from Napoleon and then set about reconquering the colonies, finally succeeding in 1817. Meanwhile, in 1815 Bolívar had retreated to Jamaica and taken up arms again. He went back to Venezuela, but Spanish forces were too strong in Caracas, so Bolívar headed south, with an army, and marched over the Andes into Colombia, claiming victory after victory.

The most decisive battle took place at Boyacá on August 7, 1819. Three days later Bolívar arrived triumphantly in Bogotá. Though some lesser battles were yet to come (including a victory at Cartagena in 1821), a congress met shortly after the Boyacá battle and pronounced the independent Republic of Colombia – comprising today's Venezuela, Colombia and Panama.

1819

Simón Bolívar – crossing Los Llanos with an army of Venezuelans and Nueva Granadans from present-day Colombia – defeats the Spanish army at Boyacá and the Republic of Gran Colombia is founded.

1830

Gran Colombia splits into Colombia (including modern-day Panama), Ecuador and Venezuela; Bolívar sends himself into exile; he dies in Santa Marta.

1880

Colombia elects Dr Rafael Núñez, who helps ease tension between state and church with new 'regeneration' policies outlined in a constitution that will stay in place for over a century.

1899

The three-year Thousand Days War between Liberals and Conservatives erupts around the country, providing a key backdrop for Gabriel García Márquez' *One Hundred Years of Solitude*.

The Formation of Political Parties

With Colombia independent, a revolutionary congress was held in Angostura (modern-day Ciudad Bolívar, in Venezuela) in 1819. Still euphoric with victory, the delegates proclaimed a new state, Gran Colombia, uniting Venezuela, Colombia, Panama and Ecuador (although Ecuador and parts of Venezuela were still technically under Spanish rule).

The Angostura congress was followed by another, held in Villa del Rosario, near Cúcuta, in 1821. It was there that the two opposing tendencies, centralist and federalist, first came to the fore. The two currents persisted throughout Bolívar's administration, which lasted to 1830. What followed after Bolívar's departure was a new (but not the last) inglorious page of Colombia's history. The split was formalized in 1849 when two political parties were established: the Conservatives (with centralist tendencies) and the Liberals (with federalist leanings). Fierce rivalry between these two forces resulted in a sequence of insurrections and civil wars, and throughout the 19th century Colombia experienced no fewer than eight civil wars. Between 1863 and 1885 alone there were more than 50 antigovernment insurrections.

For an excellent insight into life in contemporary Colombia, check out *Colombia Calling*, a weekly English-language podcast by British writer Richard McColl that discusses all aspects of life in the country.

In 1899 a Liberal revolt turned into the Thousand Days War, which resulted in a Conservative victory and left 100,000 dead. In 1903 the US took advantage of the country's internal strife and fomented a secessionist movement in Panama, then a Colombian province. By creating an independent republic there, the US was able to build and control a canal

THE FALL OF SIMÓN BOLÍVAR

Known as 'El Libertador,' Simón Bolívar led armies to battle the Spanish across northern South America, won the Colombian presidency, and ranks as one of the nation's great heroes. It's therefore surprising how it ended for him: humiliated, jobless, penniless and alone. He said, shortly before his death from tuberculosis in 1830, 'There have been three great fools in history: Jesus, Don Quixote and I.'

How did it happen? A proponent of a centralized republic, Bolívar was absent – off fighting back the Spanish in Peru and Bolivia – during much of his administration, leaving the running of the government to his vice president, and rival, the young federalist Francisco de Paula Santander, who smeared Bolívar and his ideas of being a lifetime president with the 'm' word: monarchist.

In 1828 Bolívar finally assumed dictatorship of a republic out of control, and restored a (hugely unpopular) colonial sales tax. Soon after, he narrowly escaped an assassination attempt (some believe Santander planned it) and a long-feisty Venezuela finally split from the republic. By 1830 Bolívar had had enough, abandoning the presidency – and then his savings, through gambling. He died a few months later in Santa Marta.

1903

Long cut off from the rest of Colombia, Panama secedes from the country.

1948

Likely Liberal presidential candidate, populist leader Jorge Eliécer Gaitán, is murdered leaving his office, setting off Bogotá and the country into bloody riots – the culprits are never identified.

1964

The Colombian military drops napalm on a guerrilla-held area, giving rise to the Fuerzas Armadas Revolucionarias de Colombia (FARC); the Ejército de Liberación Nacional (ELN) and M-19 follow.

1974

The National Front ends, and newly elected President Alfonso López Michelsen launches the first major counterinsurgency against all three main guerrilla groups.

across the Central American isthmus. It wasn't until 1921 that Colombia eventually recognized the sovereignty of Panama and settled its dispute with the US.

The 20th Century: Sowing the Seeds

The turn of the 20th century saw Panama seccede from Gran Colombia, but there was a welcome period of peace, as the economy started to boom (particularly due to the coffee trade) and the country's infrastructure expanded under the defused partisan politics of leader General Rafael Reyes. The brief lapse into a gentler world didn't last long, however. Labor tensions rose (following a 1928 banana strike) and the struggle between Liberals and Conservatives finally exploded in 1946 with La Violencia, the most destructive of Colombia's many civil wars to that point (with a death toll of some 200,000). Following the assassination of Jorge Eliécer Gaitán, a charismatic, self-made populist Liberal leader, more widespread riots broke out around the country (which came to be known as El Bogotazo in Bogotá – where Gaitán was killed – and El Nueve de Abril elsewhere). Liberals soon took up arms throughout the country.

There's little overt, official censorship in Colombia. But journalists, fearful of being targeted by bipartisan violence in the nation's ongoing civil conflict, routinely self-censor, says monitoring group Reporters Without Borders. It ranked Colombia 129th out of 179 countries in the NGO's 2017 survey of press freedom.

Generations of Colombians remained divided into the two political camps and each held a deep mistrust of the opposition. It's believed that 'hereditary hatreds' helped fuel revenge attacks and were the cause of countless atrocities (including rapes and murders) committed over the course of the next decade, particularly in rural areas.

The 1953 coup of General Gustavo Rojas Pinilla was the only military intervention the country experienced in the 20th century, but the coup was not to last. In 1957 the leaders of the two parties signed a pact to share power for the next 16 years. The agreement, later approved by pleb-

COLOMBIAN COFFEE

Colombia's coffee boom began in the early 20th century and found its exclamation point when the fictional Juan Valdez and his mule became the Colombian Coffee Federation's icon in 1959. (It was voted the world's top ad icon as recently as 2005.) In 2004 Juan Valdez opened more than 60 cafes in Colombia, the US and Spain, and is today by far the biggest coffee-shop chain in Colombia.

Despite competition from low-cost, lower-quality beans from Vietnam, Colombia's high-quality bean industry still supplies 12% of the world's arabica, employs around 600,000 people and earns the country billions of dollars in revenue a year. Yet in an irony that's simply puzzling, coffee in Colombia remains of generally poor quality – forget finding strong espresso outside big cities and content yourself with a watery *tinto* so beloved by locals instead.

1982

Gabriel García Márquez wins the Nobel Prize in Literature. In his acceptance speech he remarks that while Europeans value Latin America's art, they have no respect for its political movements.

1982

Pablo Escobar is elected to the Colombian Congress; President Belisario Betancur grants amnesty to guerrilla groups and frees hundreds of prisoners; Colombia abandons plans to hold the World Cup.

1990

The M-19 demilitarizes; the cartels declare war on the government and the extradition treaty, and a government building near the Paloquemao market in Bogotá is destroyed by a bomb.

1993

One-time Congress member – and more famous as a cocaine warlord – Pablo Escobar is killed a day after his 44th birthday on a Medellín rooftop by Colombian police aided by the US.

iscite (in which women were allowed to vote for the first time), became known as the Frente Nacional (National Front). During the life of the accord, the two parties alternated in the presidency every four years. In effect, despite the enormous loss of life, the same people were returned to power. Importantly, the agreement also disallowed political parties beyond the Liberals and the Conservatives, forcing any opposition outside of the normal political system underground and sowing the seeds for guerrilla insurrection.

The Birth of the FARC & Paramilitaries

While the National Front helped ease partisan tensions between Conservatives and Liberals, new conflicts were widening between wealthy landowners and the rural mestizo and indigenous underclass, two-thirds of whom lived in poverty by the end of La Violencia. Splinter leftist groups began emerging, calling for land reform and Colombian politics quickly became a brutal quagmire of violence, intimidation and kidnapping; Colombian society remains decimated by the events that followed. Much of what happened subsequently has been documented by international human rights groups such as Human Rights Watch.

New communist enclaves in the Sumapáz area, south of Bogotá, worried the Colombian government so much that its military bombed the area in May 1964. The attack led to the creation of the Fuerzas Armadas Revolucionarias de Colombia (FARC; Revolutionary Armed Forces of Colombia, led by Manuel Marulanda) and the more military-minded Jacobo Arenas. They vowed to overthrow the state and to redistribute land and wealth among the whole country, seizing it from Colombia's elites.

Other armed guerrilla groups included a fellow Marxist rival, the Ejército de Liberación Nacional (ELN; National Liberation Army), which built its popularity from a radical priest, Father Camilo Torres, who was killed in his first combat experience. The urban M-19 (Movimiento 19 de Abril, named for the contested 1970 presidential election) favored dramatic statements, such as the robbery of a Simón Bolívar's sword and seizing the Palace of Justice in Bogotá in 1985. When the military's recapture of the court led to 115 deaths, the M-19 group gradually disintegrated.

The FARC's fortunes continued to rise, though, particularly when President Belisario Betancur negotiated peace with the rebels in the 1980s. Wealthy landowners formed the AUC (Autodefensas Unidas de Colombia; United Self-Defense Forces of Colombia) or paramilitary groups, to defend their land in response to the FARC's advance. The roots of these groups – all generally offshoots of the military – began in the 1960s, but grew in the '80s.

The Explorers of South America (1972), by Edward J Goodman, brings to life some of the more incredible explorations of the continent, from those of Columbus to Humboldt, some of which refer to Colombia.

For a simple, independent and readable account of the FARC's origins, aims and ideology, try *The FARC: The Longest Insurgency* by Gary Leech (2011).

1995

The towns of San Agustín and Tierradentro in Colombia's southwest, with their many mysterious statues, carvings and burial tombs, are added to the Unesco World Heritage Sites list.

2000

Colombia and the USA agree on the expansive Plan Colombia to cut coca cultivation by 2005; the US spends over US$6 billion with no drop in cocaine production over its first decade.

2002

President Álvaro Uribe is elected on an uncompromising anti-FARC ticket; he launches an immediate and effective clampdown.

2004

Carlos 'El Pibe' Valderrama, the flamboyantly coiffured midfielder, is included in Pelé's FIFA 100 list of greatest living footballers, chosen by the soccer legend to celebrate the 100th anniversary of FIFA.

Cocaine & Cartels

Colombia is the world's biggest supplier of cocaine, despite exhaustive efforts to track down cartel leaders, drop devegetation chemicals on coca farms and step up military efforts. All for that little *erythroxylum coca* leaf – which you can buy in its unprocessed form in some Colombia markets. When the first Europeans arrived, they at first shook their heads over locals chewing coca leaves, but when (forced) work output started to decline, they allowed its usage. Eventually the Europeans (and the world) joined in, and in the centuries to follow, Andean cocaine eventually found its way worldwide for medicinal and recreational use.

Killing Pablo: The Hunt for the World's Greatest Outlaw (2002), by Mark Bowden, is an in-depth exploration of the life and times of Pablo Escobar and the operation that brought him down. While the book has some reputed small inaccuracies, it is a thrilling crime read.

The cocaine industry boomed in the early 1980s, when the Medellín Cartel, led by former car thief (and future *Narcos* star) Pablo Escobar, became the principal mafia. Its bosses eventually founded their own political party, established two newspapers and financed massive public works and public housing projects. At one point, Escobar even stirred up secession sentiments for the Medellín region. By 1983 Escobar's personal wealth was estimated to be over US$20 billion, making him one of the world's richest people (number seven according to *Forbes* magazine).

When the government launched a campaign against the drug trade, cartel bosses disappeared from public life and even proposed an unusual 'peace treaty' to President Betancur. The *New York Times* reported in 1988 that the cartels had offered to invest their capital in national de-

THE DISPLACED

Caught in the crossfire between paramilitaries and guerrilla forces, and sometimes outright targets in what the UN says is a 'strategy of war,' one in 20 Colombians (about 4 million, says the Internal Displacement Monitoring Centre) have become internally displaced since the 1980s, making Colombia at one point home to more displaced persons than any country except Sudan.

For decades hundreds of people were displaced daily, forced out of their homes at gunpoint – usually stolen for the land, livestock or its location on drug transportation routes – but sometimes not until after a loved one was murdered. Most of the dispossessed were left to fend for themselves, living in tarp-covered huts outside the main cities. Those who are able to obtain new land frequently find it in areas with no infrastructure, schools or hospitals. Often, displaced children fall into a world of drugs and crime.

The introduction of the 2011 Victims' Law, which aimed to compensate and return land to those who had it stolen, was the first step in a long process of restitution. Progress has been slow, inevitably, and priority is placed on the safety of returnees rather than huge numbers processed. There's still an enormous distance to go, but arguably the country is moving in the right direction on this front.

2006

Uribe is swept to power once more as his 'Democratic Security' policy brings stability and prosperity for many.

2006

Up to 20,000 AUC paramilitaries disarm in return for lenient sentences for their massacres and human rights abuses.

2006

Barranquilla-born Shakira's 'Hips Don't Lie' hits the number one spot in 25 countries – becoming the most successful song worldwide that year.

2008

FARC is duped into handing over its highest-value hostage, French-Colombian presidential candidate, Ingrid Betancourt, to the Colombian army.

velopment programs and pay off Colombia's entire foreign debt (some US$13 billion). The government declined the offer, and the violence escalated.

The cartel-government conflict heated up in August 1989, when Liberal presidential candidate Luis Carlos Galán was gunned down by drug lords. The government's response was to confiscate nearly 1000 cartel-owned properties and sign a new extradition treaty with the US, which led to a cartel-led campaign of terror resulting in bombed banks, homes and newspaper offices, and, in November 1989, the downing of an Avianca flight from Bogotá to Cali, which killed all 107 onboard.

After the 1990 election of Liberal César Gaviria as president, things calmed briefly, when extradition laws were sliced and Escobar led a surrender of many cartel bosses. However, Escobar soon escaped from his luxurious house arrest and it took an elite, US-funded 1500-strong special unit 499 days to track him down, finally shooting him dead atop a Medellín rooftop in 1993.

Amid the violence, the drug trade never slowed. New cartels learned to forsake the limelight, and by the mid-1990s, guerrillas and paramilitaries chipped in to help Colombia keep pace with the world's rising demand.

For a fantastically acted, high-budget and largely Spanish-language dramatization of the rise and fall of the Colombian drug cartels, watch *Narcos* on Netflix.

Paramilitaries & Guerillas

As communism collapsed around the globe in the late 1980s, the political landscape for the guerrillas shifted increasingly to drugs and kidnapping (kidnapping alone, by one account, brought FARC some US$200 million annually), and paramilitary groups aligned themselves with drug cartels and pursued the guerrillas with the cartels' blessing.

After September 11, terrorism became the new buzzword applied to guerrillas, and even some paramilitaries. One paramilitary group that made the US list of international terrorists, and which notoriously had been paid US$1.7 million by the Chiquita fruit company, were the infamous United Self-Defense Forces of Colombia (AUC). The firm paid a $25 million fine in US courts in 2007 for its repeated funding of the AUC.

Linked with cocaine since 1997, the AUC was inspired by paramilitary groups previously under the watch of the slain Medellín Cartel leader Rodríguez Gacha. The AUC was later run by brothers Fidel and Carlos Castaño, who set out to avenge their father, who was slain by guerrillas. The AUC, with a force of up to 10,000 troops, attacked *campesinos* (peasants) it alleged were guerrilla sympathizers. The guerrillas likewise attacked any *campesinos* they said were AUC supporters.

When the Álvaro Uribe administration offered lenient sentences for paramilitaries or guerrillas who demobilized, AUC handed over their guns in 2006.

2008

The FARC announces that its founder, Manuel 'Sureshot' Marulanda has died, aged 78, of a heart attack in the jungle.

2010

As President Uribe's security measures hit home, Colombia receives 1.4 million foreign visitors according to official statistics, shaking off its decades-long reputation as a danger zone.

2010

Uribe's former Defense Minister Juan Manuel Santos, of the influential Santos family is elected president in a landslide victory.

2011

Alfonso Cano, leader of the FARC and its chief ideologue, is killed in a bombing raid, raising hopes of an end to the conflict.

Uribe's Reign

Fed up with violence, kidnappings and highways deemed too dangerous to use, the nation turned to right-wing hardliner Álvaro Uribe – a politician from Medellín whose father had been killed by the FARC. Uribe ran on a full-on antiguerrilla ticket during the testy 2002 presidential election. While his predecessor Andrés Pastrana had tried negotiating with FARC and ELN, Uribe didn't bother, quickly unleashing two simultaneous programs: a military pushback of groups such as FARC, and a demobilization offer for both sides.

Even Uribe's harshest critics acknowledge much overdue progress was made under his watch. From 2002 to 2008, notably, murder rates fell 40% overall and highways cleared of FARC roadblocks became safe to use.

In March 2008, Uribe approved a tricky bombing mission across Ecuador's border, resulting in the successful killing of FARC leader Raúl Reyes. The bombing mission, however, nearly set the region into broader conflict, with Venezuelan president Hugo Chávez immediately moving tanks to the Colombian border, but things soon settled – and Uribe's approval levels hit 90%.

Uribe's presidency was ultimately tainted by scandal and by 2008, following his public feuds with the Colombian Supreme Court, 60 con-

PLAN COLOMBIA

In 2000 the US entered the war against the drug cartels, with the controversial 'Plan Colombia,' concocted by the Bill Clinton and Andrés Pastrana administrations to curb coca cultivation by 50% within five years. As the decade closed, and with US$6 billion spent, even the US International Trade Commission called the program's effectiveness 'small and mostly direct.' The worldwide street price for Colombian cocaine hadn't changed – indicating no lack of supply – and, after a few years of dipping coca cultivation, by 2007, a UN report concluded that cocaine production rose by 27% that year alone, rebounding to its 1998 level.

Emerging in the first decade of the century, new harder-to-track *cartelitos* (smaller-sized mafia groups) replaced the extinguished megacartels (capped with the 2008 extradition to the US of Medellín narco-king Don Berna). The *cartelitos* relocated to harder-to-reach valleys (particularly near the Pacific coast). Many were linked to FARC, who taxed coca farmers (earning FARC between US$200 to US$300 million annually, according to the *New York Times*); other *cartelitos*, however, were linked with paramilitary groups.

Despite all the money thrown at the problem, today Colombia still supplies about 90% of the USA's cocaine – usually transporting it there overland via Mexican cartels.

2011

A US-Colombia free trade deal is agreed to by US Congress after years of deliberation and delay over Democrats' concerns over human rights.

2012

Negotiations between the Colombian government and the FARC aimed at bringing lasting peace to Colombia begin in Havana, Cuba.

2014

Colombia's most famous writer, Nobel laureate Gabriel García Márquez, dies in Mexico City.

2014

The FARC announce an indefinite ceasefire against the Colombian army after two years of peace negotiations in Havana, Cuba.

gressmen had been arrested or questioned for alleged 'parapolitics' links with paramilitaries.

The *falsos positivos* (false positives) scandal, as documented by the UN in an in-depth 2010 report, showed how the Colombian military was incentivized to increase body count. From 2004, incidences of false positives – where army units killed innocent young men and claimed them as guerrillas killed in combat – soared. As the scandal grew, Uribe fired 27 officers in November 2008, and leading commander General Mario Montoya resigned.

FARC on the Defensive

After the constitutional court in 2010 refused to allow a referendum to let Uribe run for a third term, his defense minister Juan Manuel Santos was voted in by a landslide, and almost immediately claimed the single greatest victory ever won against the FARC: the killing of its new leader, Alfonso Cano.

Within days a new leader, Rodrigo Londoño Echeverri (alias Timochenko), on whose head the US had placed a US$5 million bounty, took control of the guerrilla organization. With a reputation as one of the organization's most bellicose minds, Timochenko stunned the nation by proposing peace talks with the government.

The Colombian government, war weary yet understandably suspicious, took a good deal of convincing that the offer of negotiations for a lasting peace were genuine. When negotiators from the administration finally sat down with representatives of the FARC in Havana in 2012, there was an outcry in the country, with many considering the move a betrayal of the victims of the conflict. This led to a polarizing presidential election and a country split down the middle as to whether the government should be pursuing the talks at all.

2016

The Colombian people narrowly reject the controversial peace agreement with the FARC during a national referendum.

2018

President Iván Duque Márquez from the Democratic Centre Party is voted into office as Colombia's youngest president, he stood against the Havana Accords with FARC.

2019

Bogotá-born Cyclist Egan Bernal won the Tour de France at 22-years-old, and becomes the first-ever Latin American, second from the Americas, to win the race.

2021

Rallies take place against the President's proposed expansion of a tax initiative. Protesters stand against increased taxes, corruption, police brutality and the government's overall handling of the pandemic.

Life in Colombia

Colombians are some of the warmest, most friendly and uncannily helpful people you'll encounter in South America. They handle life with good humor and a light-heartedness that is infectious. The country's geographical diversity – mountains and sea – has left discreet influences on the national psyche. While life is industrious and the Spanish crisp and formal in the Andean cities of Bogotá, Medellín and Cali, *costeños* (people from the coast) are more laid back and speak a heavier-accented, more drawling Spanish.

Lifestyle & Attitude

Wealthy urban Colombians live a very different life to their poorer counterparts. Their children go to private schools, they treat intercity planes like taxis and whiz through city streets glued to their smartphones in their 4x4s. They play golf in country clubs at weekends, and, more than likely, they own a small private *finca* (farm) where they occasionally indulge their rural fantasies.

Poorer Colombians buy their phone calls by the minute in the street, wait in interminable intercity and urban traffic jams, and dream of sending their children to any school at all. Indigenous people and those in isolated rural communities affected by the civil conflict are often focused on ensuring they have enough food to survive and in other senses often live totally outside mainstream society.

Between these extremes, Colombia boasts one of the largest middle-class populations in Latin America, where many of its neighbors suffer great disparity in wealth. The country's free-market policies and relatively low level of corruption have helped the middle class to flourish.

Same-sex marriages came into being in Colombia in 2013, though until 2016 there was no formal legal mechanism for it. Since 2016, however, same-sex marriage has been legal *and* simple.

All Colombians, though, are bound by strong family ties, not just to immediate blood relatives but also to their extended family, and childless visitors over 21 years of age will be quizzed endlessly on their plans to start a family. Although the dominant faith is Catholicism, very few people of any class attend Mass.

Women are the heart of a Colombian household. Machismo may be alive and well outside the home, where men are unquestionably in charge, but inside the Colombian home, women rule the roost. That's not the only place they rule. Women make up a significant number of the country's high-ranking politicians and diplomats, including cabinet ministers and ambassadors. In fact, a quota law passed in 2000 requires that at least 30% of appointed positions in the executive branch be filled by women.

Try not to get uptight if a Colombian is late – anything up to 45 minutes – and don't take it personally; instead, perhaps go with the flow and enjoy a culture that truly believes that most things aren't worth rushing for! Bus timetables, in particular, are a laughable fiction.

Most Colombians don't use drugs and you'll find a big taboo about cocaine use (and sometimes even discussing the subject) due to the drug's violent history. Younger people in urban areas do indulge in drug use, though drinking is far more popular – and how. The Carnaval de Barranquilla is a riot of licentiousness and rum-doused ribaldry and it is no exaggeration to call it Colombia's answer to Rio de Janeiro's carnival.

COLOMBIA'S INDIGENOUS PEOPLES

Colombia may be an ethnic mixing pot that can put most countries to shame, but its indigenous people – yet another part of the jigsaw for first-time visitors to explore and encounter – remain in many cases nations apart, often somewhat or totally removed from the mainstream of Colombian society. Comprising around 1.4 million people and divided into 87 different tribes, including some that remain uncontacted, this flipside to mainstream Colombian society is fascinating to explore.

Some indigenous groups you're likely to encounter include the Ticuna in the Amazon, the Wiwa, Kogui and Arhuaco in the Sierra Nevada, the Waayu in La Guajira and the Muisca around Bogotá. Indigenous reserves make up an extraordinary third of the area of Colombia, the land being collectively owned by the indigenous communities there. Yet despite legal protections, indigenous groups have often borne the brunt of the violence in recent decades, their vast reserves making perfect hiding places for guerrillas, paramilitary groups and coca plantations. As if to add insult to injury, the Plan Colombia spraying of many rural areas by the US Air Force to destroy coca farms has also destroyed or damaged perfectly innocent crops that have long been cultivated by Colombia's native peoples, leaving many traditional societies without food.

People & Place: A Cultural Sancocho

With a population of 48.6 million people, Colombia is the third-most populous country in Latin America after Brazil and Mexico, and the figure is rising fast. The rate of population growth in 2017 remained high at 1%.

Each city in Colombia has its own unique cultural mix, making traveling here as satisfyingly varied as a rich *sancocho* (soup). Many European immigrants populated Medellín, while much of the population of Cali is descended from former enslaved people. Bogotá and the surrounding areas saw much intermarriage between European colonists and indigenous people, while Cali and the Caribbean and Pacific coasts have a high proportion of African-Colombians.

Slavery was abolished in 1821, and the country has the largest black population in South America after Brazil. The last four centuries have seen plenty of intermarriage, meaning a great number of Colombians are of mixed race; indeed it's quite a challenge to picture a 'typical' looking Colombian!

James Rodríguez, known simply to most Colombians as James (pronounced *Ha-mes*), is currently the most famous footballer in the country and one of the most promising young players in the world, as the highest scorer of the 2014 World Cup tournament.

Balls & Bulls

Colombians love soccer. The national league has 18 teams across the country, and attracts rowdy and boisterous crowds during the two seasons (February to June and August to December). The standard of play is often poor, making for comical, error-prone matches.

After soccer, baseball is the second-most popular team sport in Colombia. Cycling is also hugely favored, with Bogotá's Ciclovía each Sunday bringing in thousands of cyclists and skaters to the city's roads, many of which are closed for the day.

Animal-lovers will be disappointed to witness the popularity of bullfighting in Colombia, whether at formal events or at *corralejas*, the wild-side variant that sees amateurs pitting their addled wits against a charging *toro* with predictably gory consequences. The formal bullfighting season peaks during the holiday period between mid-December and mid-January, and attracts some of the world's best matadors. The January Feria de Manizales is of great appeal to aficionados. Cock-fighting is also wildly popular in rural areas.

The Arts

Ask most people to name three famous Colombian artists, and you'll get Gabriel García Márquez, sculptor Fernando Botero and perhaps Shakira. But Colombia's artists have a lot more to offer than magic realism, fat-bottomed statues and hip-swinging pop.

Music

Colombia is famous for its music, and silence is a very rare commodity anywhere in the country. Indeed, once you've heard the volume at which music is played in a Colombian bar or nightclub, you'll find a new appreciation for both silence and earplugs.

Vallenato, born a century ago on the Caribbean coast, is based on the German accordion. Carlos Vives, one of the best-known modern Latin music artists, modernized the form and became a poster boy for the music. Vallenato's spiritual homeland is Valledupar. The style is not to everyone's taste, but if you leave Colombia without having danced to it a dozen times, you haven't really been there.

Cumbia, a lively 4/4 style with guitars, accordion, bass, drums and the occasional horn, is the most popular of the Colombian musical styles overseas. Groups such as Pernett and The Caribbean Ravers have modernized the sound, as have Bomba Estéreo. The funkiest group of recent years has been ChocQuibTown, a Pacific coast hip-hop band, who mix incisive social commentary with tough beats.

The Bogotá Festival Iberoamericano de Teatro, the world's largest such event, was set up in 1976 by Colombia's most influential actress, Fanny Mikey (1930–2008). See www.festivaldeteatro.com.co for more.

Salsa spread throughout the Caribbean and in the late 1960s it hit Colombia, where it's been adopted and made its own. Cali and Barranquilla are its heartland, but it's loved everywhere. The country went into mourning when Joe Arroyo, known locally as El Joe, died in 2011. The modern, tough urban salsa style is best typified by La 33 of Bogotá.

Joropo, the music of Los Llanos, is accompanied by a harp, a *cuatro* (a type of four-string guitar) and maracas. It has much in common with the music of the Venezuelan Llanos. Chief proponents Grupo Cimarrón will dazzle you with their virtuosity and rapid footwork, and any visitor to La Macarena or Villavicencio will have a chance to watch this music be performed.

Colombia has also generated many unique rhythms from the fusion of Afro-Caribbean and Spanish influences, including *porro, currulao, merecumbe, mapalé* and *gaita.* The Cartagena-born sound of *champeta,* meanwhile, mixes African rhythms with a bumping, rough-cut, block-party attitude: check it out in Cartagena's less touristy venues, such as Bazurto Social Club (p135). Reggaeton, with its thumping bass-snare loops, is popular as well, along with the rhythmically driven and heavy-on-the-downbeat merengue.

Colombian Andean music is strongly influenced by Spanish rhythms and instruments, and differs noticeably from the indigenous music of the Peruvian and Bolivian highlands. Among typical old genres are the *bambuco, pasillo* and *torbellino,* instrumental styles featuring predominantly string instruments.

In the cities, especially Bogotá and Medellín, many clubs play techno and house; big-name international DJs sometimes play both cities.

Colombian Literature

Colombia's long (if modest) literary tradition began to form shortly after independence from Spain in 1819 and gravitated towards European romanticism. Rafael Pombo (1833–1912) is generally acclaimed as the father of Colombian romantic poetry and Jorge Isaacs (1837–95), another notable author of the period, is particularly remembered for his romantic novel *María,* which can still be spotted in cafes and classrooms around the country.

José Asunción Silva (1865–96), one of Colombia's most remarkable poets, is considered the precursor of modernism in Latin America. He planted the seeds that were later developed by Nicaraguan poet Rubén Darío. Another literary talent, Porfirio Barba Jacob (1883–1942), known as 'the poet of death,' introduced the ideas of irrationalism and the language of the avant-garde.

Talented contemporaries of literary Nobel Laureate Gabriel García Márquez included poet, novelist and painter Héctor Rojas Herazo, and Álvaro Mutis, who was a close friend. Of the younger generation, seek out the works of Fernando Vallejo, a highly respected iconoclast who has claimed in interviews that García Márquez lacks originality and is a poor writer. Popular young expat Santiago Gamboa has written travel books and novels; Mario Mendoza writes gritty, modern urban fiction; and Laura Restrepo focuses on how violence affects the individual and society – they are prolific writers who have each produced major works in recent years.

Bogotá is Colombia's cultural capital. For a taste of what's on, check out www.culturarecreacionydeporte.gov.co.

GABRIEL GARCÍA MÁRQUEZ, COLOMBIA'S NOBEL LAUREATE

Gabriel García Márquez remains the titan of Colombian literature, despite his death in 2014. Born in 1928 in Aracataca, he wrote primarily about Colombia, despite actually living most of his life in Mexico and Europe.

García Márquez began as a journalist in the 1950s and worked as a foreign correspondent, criticizing the Colombian government and forcing himself into exile. His breakthrough novel came in 1967, with *One Hundred Years of Solitude*. It mixed myths, dreams and reality, and single-handedly invented the magic realism genre.

In 1982 García Márquez won the Nobel Prize in Literature. In the years following he created a wealth of fascinating work, including *Love in the Time of Cholera* (1985), a story based loosely on the courtship of his parents and *The General in his Labyrinth* (1989) recounts the tragic final months of Simón Bolívar's life. *Strange Pilgrims* (1992) is a collection of 12 stories written by the author over 18 years. *Of Love and Other Demons* (1994) is the story of a young girl raised by her parents' slaves, set amid the backdrop of Cartagena's inquisition.

In 2012, García Márquez' brother revealed that Gabo, as he was affectionately known to Colombians, was suffering from dementia, accelerated by his chemotherapy for lymphatic cancer. Following his death in 2014, García Márquez was buried in Mexico City, with the presidents of both Colombia and Mexico in attendance. His home town, Aracataca, inspiration for the fictional Macondo in *One Hundred Years of Solitude*, held a symbolic funeral for him as well.

You'll find editions of García Márquez' works on sale in English all over Colombia, and while there's a good reconstruction of his family home that serves as a museum in his hometown of Aracataca, the town itself will be a letdown for anyone wanting to get a geographic sense of García Márquez' books. For a better taste of Gabo's world, head to Cartagena or – better still – the isolated colonial town of Mompós, a modern-day Macondo that will delight any fan of *One Hundred Years of Solitude*.

FERNANDO BOTERO: LARGER THAN LIFE

Fernando Botero is the most widely recognized Colombian painter and sculptor. Born in Medellín in 1932, he had his first individual painting exhibition in Bogotá at the age of 19 and gradually developed his easily recognizable style – characterized by his figures' massive, almost obscene curvaceousness. In 1972 he settled in Paris and began experimenting with sculpture, which resulted in a collection of *gordas* and *gordos* (fat women and men), as Colombians call these creations.

Today, his paintings hang on the walls of world-class museums and his monumental public sculptures adorn squares and parks in cities around the globe, including Paris, Madrid, Lisbon, Florence and New York.

Moving from his typically safe subject matter in 2004, he shocked Colombia with a collection of works examining the country's civil war; and in 2005, he produced a controversial series of images that split critical opinion, featuring scenes from Iraq's Abu Ghraib prison, where US forces tortured and humiliated detainees. While some lauded Botero's move into more political matters, others regarded it as too little, too late, and still others thought this out-of-character development was inappropriate. He has since returned to his more recognizable still lifes.

Art & Abstraction

Fernando Botero is to Colombian painting what García Márquez is to the country's literature – the heavyweight name that overshadows all others. Two other famous Colombian painters, often overlooked, are Omar Rayo (1928–2010), known for his geometric drawings, and Alejandro Obregón (1920–92), a Cartagena painter famous for his abstract paintings.

Colombia is also home to a good deal of colonial religious art. Gregorio Vásquez de Arce y Ceballos (1638–1711) was the most remarkable painter of the colonial era. He lived and worked in Bogotá and left behind a collection of more than 500 works, now distributed among churches and museums across the country.

Telenovelas (soap operas) are Colombia's cultural barometer. Although they aren't high art, they reflect the country's concerns and passions as faithfully as any documentary. One of the most famous was *Chepe Fortuna* (Fishing for Fortune), a gloriously improbable tale of love, politics, environmentalism and, er, mermaids.

Since the end of WWII, the most distinguished artists have been Pedro Nel Gómez, known for his murals, watercolors, oils and sculptures; Luis Alberto Acuña, a painter and sculptor who used motifs from pre-Columbian art; Guillermo Wiedemann, a German painter who spent most of his creative period in Colombia and drew inspiration from local themes (though he later turned to abstract art); Édgar Negret, an abstract sculptor; Eduardo Ramírez Villamizar, who expressed himself mostly in geometric forms; and Rodrigo Arenas Betancourt, Colombia's most famous monument maker.

These masters were followed by a slightly younger generation, born mainly in the 1930s, including artists such as Armando Villegas, a Peruvian living in Colombia, whose influences ranged from pre-Columbian motifs to surrealism; Leonel Góngora, noted for his erotic drawings; and the most internationally renowned Colombian artist, Fernando Botero.

The recent period has been characterized by a proliferation of schools, trends and techniques. Artists to watch out for include Bernardo Salcedo (conceptual sculpture and photography), Miguel Ángel Rojas (painting and installations), Lorenzo Jaramillo (expressionist painting), María de la Paz Jaramillo (painting), María Fernanda Cardozo (installations), Catalina Mejía (abstract painting) and Doris Salcedo (sculpture and installations).

The Natural World

From snowcapped, craggy Andean mountains and the vast plains of Los Llanos, to the lush tropical forests of the Amazon basin and rolling green valleys full of coffee, Colombia is a mind-blowingly beautiful and varied country. What's more, it harbors astonishing biodiversity, being the second most biodiverse country on earth after neighboring Brazil.

The Land

Colombia covers 1,141,748 sq km, roughly equivalent to the combined area of California and Texas (or France, Spain and Portugal). It is the 26th-largest country in the world, and the fourth-largest in South America, after Brazil, Argentina and Peru.

While most people assume that Colombia is just a tropical land, the country's physical geography is amazingly varied. The country's environment is generally divided into five habitat categories: wet tropical forests, dry tropical forests, tropical grasslands, mountain grasslands, and deserts and scrublands.

The western part, almost half of the total territory, is mountainous, with three Andean chains – Cordillera Occidental, Cordillera Central and Cordillera Oriental – running roughly parallel north–south across most of the country. A number of the peaks are over 5000m, making them higher than anything in the USA. Two valleys, the Valle del Cauca and Valle del Magdalena, are sandwiched between the three cordilleras. Both valleys have their own eponymous rivers, which flow north, unite and eventually empty into the Caribbean near Barranquilla.

Apart from the three Andean chains, Colombia features an independent and relatively small range, the Sierra Nevada de Santa Marta, which rises from the Caribbean coastline to soaring, snowcapped peaks. It is the world's highest coastal mountain range, and its twin summits of Simón Bolívar and Cristóbal Colón (both 5775m) are the country's highest.

More than half of the territory east of the Andes is vast lowland, which is generally divided into two regions: Los Llanos to the north and the Amazon River basin to the south. Los Llanos, roughly 250,000 sq km in area, is a huge open swath of grassland that constitutes the Orinoco River basin. Colombians say it is like an internal, green sea. The Amazon region, stretching over some 400,000 sq km, occupies Colombia's entire southeast and lies in the Amazon basin. Most of this land is covered by a thick rainforest and crisscrossed by rivers, and remains totally cut off from the rest of the country by road, though sadly this doesn't stop illegal logging.

Colombia also has a number of islands. The major ones are the archipelago of San Andrés and Providencia (a long way off in the Caribbean Sea, 750km northwest of mainland Colombia), the Islas del Rosario and San Bernardo (near the Caribbean coast), and Gorgona and Malpelo (along the Pacific coast).

Gaviotas: A Village to Reinvent the World (1998), by Alan Weisman, tells the story of Colombian villagers who transformed their barren hamlet in Los Llanos into a global model for a sustainable community. See www.friendsofgaviotas.org for more information.

Wildlife

This huge variety of climatic and geographic zones and microclimates has spawned diverse ecosystems and allowed wildlife to evolve independently. And how. Colombia claims to have more plant and animal species per square kilometer than any other country in the world. Its variety of flora and fauna is second only to Brazil's, even though Colombia is seven times smaller than its neighbor.

Animals

From pink dolphins to colorful parrots, tiny cats to giant rats, Colombia has some of the most unusual animal life on the planet. It has nearly 1700 recorded species of birds – 74 of which are native to the country – representing about 19% of all the birds on the planet. Colombia also has about 450 species of mammal (including 15% of the world's primates), 600 species of amphibian, 500 species of reptile and 3200 species of fish.

Colombia is the only South American nation to have coastlines on both the Pacific Ocean and Caribbean Sea.

Some of the most interesting mammals include sleek cats such as the jaguar and the ocelot, red howler monkeys, spider monkeys, the three-toed sloth, giant anteaters, the goofy piglike peccary and tapir, and the hideous-looking capybara, or *chiguiro,* the world's largest living rodent that can grow to 48cm tall and weigh 55kg.

Colombia's Amazon waters are home to the famous rose-colored *boto* (Amazon River dolphin), the Amazonian manatee, and one of the most feared snakes, the anaconda *(Eunectes murinus),* which grows to 6m.

Colombia's famous aviary includes 132 species of hummingbirds, 24 species of toucans, 57 types of colorful parrots and macaws, plus kingfishers, trogons, warblers and six of the world's seven vultures, including the Andean condor – a national symbol of Colombia.

There is also abundant marine life in the country's extensive river systems and along its two coastlines. The islands of San Andrés and Providencia boast some of the largest and most productive coral reefs in the Americas, now Unesco listed as the Seaflower Biosphere Reserve in order to protect the ecosystem. The reefs are considered among the most intact in the Caribbean and play an important ecological role in the health of the sea. They provide feeding and nesting grounds for four species of endangered sea turtles and numerous types of fish and lobster. It has been determined that the health of certain fish stocks in the Florida Keys hinges directly on their ability to spawn in the Colombian reefs. The island of Providencia itself is home to the Providencia black crab *(Gecarcinus ruricola),* a unique species of crab that lives on the land, but completes an extraordinary annual migration to the sea to lay and fertilize eggs.

THE GREAT PROVIDENCIA CRAB MIGRATION

It truly is one of the most extraordinary sights you'll ever see: for a whole week in April the uniquely terrestrial Providencia black crab comes down from its habitat in the mountains and makes its way awkwardly towards the sea, where the females lay their eggs and the males then fertilize them, before returning inland shortly afterwards. During this time, the one road that rings this tiny Caribbean island is closed, and life for many becomes very static and even quieter than usual, with islanders only able to move around the island on foot.

A few months later, usually in July, the hatched juvenile crabs, still tiny, crawl out of the sea and head to the mountains. During this second migration the island shuts down again, and the sound of rustling is permanent day and night as the tiny crabs make their inelegant way up the hillside in their millions. If you're lucky enough to arrive on Providencia during either of these times, you're in for an unforgettable, if somewhat Hitchcockian, experience.

Top Macaw

Bottom Giant anteater

Endangered Species

The vast savanna of Los Llanos is home to some of the most endangered species in Colombia. Among them is the Orinoco crocodile, which can reach 7m in length. According to the Wildlife Conservation Society, only 200 of these crocs remain in the wild in Colombia, making it one of the most critically endangered reptiles in the world, mainly due to the creatures' valuable skin. The good news is that between 2015 and 2016, over 40 juvenile Orinoco crocodiles were released into Tuparro National Park as part of the Proyecto Vida Silvestre program, which promotes conservation efforts in Los Llanos. Other endangered creatures from the region include the Orinoco turtle, giant armadillo, giant otter and black-and-chestnut eagle.

The famous German geographer and botanist Alexander von Humboldt explored and studied regions of Colombia and described it all in amazing detail in *Personal Narrative of Travels to the Equinoctial Regions of America, During the Year 1799–1804.*

The cotton-top tamarin, a tiny monkey weighing just 500g, and its larger cousin, the brown spider monkey, are two of the most critically endangered primates in the world, according to the 2014 International Union for Conservation of Nature (IUCN) Red List of Threatened Species. Other critically endangered or endangered animals on the IUCN list include Handley's slender mouse opossum, mountain grackle and the mountain tapir. And two of the Amazon River's most famous residents, the pink river dolphin and the Amazonian manatee, are considered vulnerable.

Note that some remote restaurants and bars offer turtle eggs, iguanas and other endangered species on their menus. It's also worth noting that the *pirarucú* (a fish popular in the Amazon basin region around Leticia) has been subject to overfishing; locals routinely ignore regulations preventing fishing for this species when it's spawning. These animals are endangered and eating them may hasten their extinction, so think before you order: there are normally other fish available on menus in the Amazon.

Plants

Colombia's flora is equally as impressive as its fauna and includes more than 130,000 types of plant, a third of which are endemic species. This richness does not convey the whole picture: large areas of the country, such as the inaccessible parts of the Amazon, have undiscovered species. It is estimated that, at a minimum, 2000 plant species have yet to be identified and an even greater number have yet to be analyzed for potential medicinal purposes.

Birdwatching enthusiasts should pick up *A Guide to the Birds of Colombia* (1986) by Stephen L Hilty and William L Brown. Two great online resources for birdwatchers are www.colombiabirding.com and www.proaves.org.

Colombia has some 3500 species of orchids, more than any other country. Many of them are unique to the country, including *Cattleya trianae,* the national flower of Colombia. Orchids grow in virtually all regions and climate zones of the country, but are mostly found in altitudes between 1000m and 2000m, particularly in the northwest department of Antioquia.

Further up into the clouds you will find the *frailejón,* a unique, yellow-flowering, perennial shrub that only grows at altitudes above 3000m. There are some 88 species of *frailejón,* most native to Colombia. You'll find them in protected places such as Sierra Nevada de Santa Marta, Sierra Nevada del Cocuy and Santuario de Iguaque.

National Parks

Colombia has 59 national parks, flora and fauna sanctuaries and other natural reserve areas, all administered by the government's **Parques Nacionales Naturales (PNN) de Colombia** (353-2400 ext 138; www.parquesnacionales.gov.co; Calle 74 No 11-81; 8am-6pm Mon-Fri).

Unfortunately, simply declaring an area a national park has not stopped guerrilla activity, drug cultivation, illegal ranching, logging, mining or poaching. Most parks in the Amazon basin and along the Ecuadorian border should be considered off-limits. Other parks, such as Los Katios, a Unesco World Heritage Site near Darién Gap, are open but remain dodgy and access is limited; check the current security situation before proceeding.

On the bright side, many parks that were off-limits in recent years are now open for tourists and are included in our coverage. With the recent growth in tourism and ecotourism, the government is finally pumping pesos into its long-underfunded national parks system. New parks have recently opened and more are in the planning stages. Established parks are finally getting much-needed visitor amenities such as lodging and dining facilities, a rarity in Colombia.

This has not been without controversy. PNN has begun contracting with private companies to develop and operate tourist facilities inside some national parks, a move that some environmentalists fear will lead to overdevelopment. Some are concerned that prices will also increase and make the parks inaccessible to average Colombians. However, environmentalists have in recent years had some success checking such planned developments.

Colombia's most popular parks are situated along the country's pristine beaches. PNN Tayrona is by far Colombia's most popular national park, followed by Parque Nacional Natural (PNN) Corales del Rosario y San Bernardo and Parque Nacional Natural (PNN) Isla Gorgona.

Many other national parks offer just simple accommodations including basic cabins, dorms or campsites. Travelers wishing to stay overnight must book ahead with the PNN central office in Bogotá. There are also PNN regional offices in most large cities and at the parks. Most parks have an admission fee, payable at the entrance or at a regional PNN office.

It is always a good idea to check ahead of time with tour agencies and the parks department for up-to-date security and weather conditions for any park before visiting.

Colombia is the world's second-largest exporter of cut flowers, after the Netherlands. About US$1 billion worth of flowers are exported every year, mostly to the US. Americans buy 300 million Colombian roses on Valentine's Day, as the country's equatorial location means the roses grow perfectly straight.

GREEN FEVER

Colombia produces the largest percentage of the world's emeralds (50%; compared to Zambia's 20% and Brazil's 15%). Some estimate that the mines inside Colombia may actually contain up to 90% of the world's emerald deposits. This is good news for emerald prospectors but may not bode so well for the local environment – and perhaps Colombia as a whole. The fighting and destruction related to the production of these glamorous gems has had an impact on the country not so different from cocaine and heroin.

The main emerald-mining areas in Colombia include Muzo, Coscuez, La Pita and Chivor, all in the Boyacá department. Although the Muisca people mined emeralds in pre-Columbian times, the Spanish colonialists went crazy for the shiny green stones and greatly expanded the operations. They enslaved the indigenous locals to mine the gems and eventually replaced those workers with slave labor from Africa. Many of today's miners are the direct descendants of those slaves and live in only slightly better conditions.

The rich deposits in these areas have led to several environmental and social problems. Rampant digging has torn up the countryside and, in an attempt to find new digging sites or to improve their squalid living conditions, miners have continuously pushed further into the forest. Fierce battles have repeatedly been fought between rival gangs of miners, claiming lives and ravaging the mines. Between 1984 and 1990 alone, in one of the bloodiest 'emerald wars' in recent history, 3500 people were killed in Muzo. Yet 'green fever' continues to burn among fortune hunters and adventurers from all corners of the country and it may not stop until the last bewitching green gem is mined.

Private Parks & Reserves

In recent years the number of privately owned and operated nature reserves has increased. These are run by individual proprietors, rural communities, foundations and nongovernmental organizations. Many are just small, family reserves, sometimes offering accommodations and food. About 230 of these private parks are affiliated with the **Asociación Red Colombiana de Reservas Naturales de la Sociedad Civil** (http://resnatur.org.co).

Yet another new player in the park scene is the corporation. Future parks might look a lot more like the new Parque Nacional del Chicamocha (p108), near Bucaramanga. This for-profit, corporate-run resort opened in 2006, at a reported cost of US$20 million. In addition to hiking and trekking opportunities, this commercial theme park features dozens of restaurants, cafes, thrill rides, a zoo, cable cars and water park.

Conservación Internacional is one of Colombia's most influential environmental advocacy groups. To learn more about its positive work, check out www.conservation.org.co.

Environmental Issues

Many challenges remain, not least of which are the problems of climate change, habitat loss, and a loss of biodiversity through giant agribusiness megaplantations. The rapid push to develop a market-based economy and compete globally has put pressure on Colombia to build on its land and exploit its natural resources; these include farming, legal and illegal logging, mining and oil exploration. Such deforestation has increased the rate of extinction for many plant and animal species and destabilized soils, leading to the silting of rivers and devastation of marine species.

Even more troubling is the environmental impact of the illegal drug trade. Other illegal cash crops include marijuana and opium poppies. Attempts to stop farmers cultivating coca simply cause the producers to relocate. They move higher up the slopes and to the more remote, virgin forests of the Andes (aided by an increase in opium cultivation, which favors higher altitudes) and deeper into parks and the Amazon basin. In addition, antidrug efforts by the Colombian government (and, in large part, funded by the US war on drugs) have also taken some toll: the most common method of eradication has been aerial fumigation of coca fields; these hazardous herbicides destroy not just the coca plants, but surrounding vegetation as well, and no doubt seep into the watershed.

Sadly, the retreat of the FARC in many rural areas of Colombia has actually led to an acceleration in deforestation, as the rebels carefully controlled logging in order to keep their own locations covert. The FARC's surrender has left a power vacuum in many places and in 2016, deforestation jumped by an extraordinary 44% on the previous year to 178,597 hectares.

Survival Guide

SAFE TRAVEL 316
Safe Areas 316
Guerrilla & Paramilitary Activity 316
Theft & Robbery 317
Drugs 317
Interacting with the Police & Military 318
Overland Travel 318

DIRECTORY A–Z 319
Accommodations 319
Children 320
Customs Regulations . . . 320
Electricity 320
Embassies & Consulates 321
Food 322
LGBTI Travelers 322
Health 322
Insurance 323
Internet Access 323
Language Courses 323
Legal Matters 323
Maps 324
Money 324
Opening Hours 325
Post 325
Public Holidays 326
Telephone 327
Time 327
Toilets 327
Tourist Information 327
Travelers with Disabilities 327
Visas 327
Volunteering 328
Women Travelers 328
Work 328

TRANSPORTATION . 329
GETTING THERE & AWAY 329
Entering the Country 329
Air 329
Land 330
Sea 330
GETTING AROUND 331
Air 331
Bicycle 331
Boat 332
Bus 332
Car & Motorcycle 333
Hitchhiking 333
Local Transportation 333
Train 335

LANGUAGE 336

Safe Travel

Few countries in Latin America or elsewhere have done more to turn around their own image than Colombia, which spent most of the 1980s and '90s as a woefully feared tourism black hole, as an intertwined civil military conflict and international drug war wreaked havoc on daily life. Today, most travelers will find Colombia safer on average than all of the country's immediate neighbors – an astonishing turnaround. Problems remain, however. Street crime, like mugging and pickpocketing (sometimes with weapons) is still an issue, especially in bigger cities including Bogotá, Cali, Pereira and Medellín, so vigilance and common sense are always required. A fake police scam includes 'officers' asking to check your money to see if it is counterfeit. It's wise to be asked to be escorted to a local station (Centro de Atencion Inmediata). Guerrillas, paramilitaries and narco-traffickers still linger in some places, the latter at the Panama, Venezuela and Ecuador. Dozens of localised cases and violent clashes at protests have highlighted police brutality and criticised the managing of the pandemic in recent times, so avoid large gatherings. Keep up with local news reports and do forward planning, especially if you are going to get really off the beaten track. Road blockages and restrictions of movement could occur with little to no warning. Despite its record for crime, most visits to Colombia are trouble-free.

Safe Areas

The Colombian government's historic 2016 peace accord with the FARC – and a subsequent ceasefire with the ELN in 2020 – ended a five-decade civil war. As a result, the country is dramatically safer than it once was and many previously no-go areas are now safe for travel (though neo-paramilitary groups involved in drug trafficking are still present in many parts of the country and FARC dissidents remain in some jungle areas). There have been protests against police brutality, taxes and the handling of the coronavirus pandemic in 2020 and 2021, some turning violent and resulting in the death of protesters. These are localized, but it's wise for travelers to avoid large crowds and keep informed of the local news. All the areas covered by Lonely Planet are generally safe for travel, you aren't likely to run into any problems if you keep to the main tourist areas and book with recommended tours when going to more remote areas. Protests, however are localised, keep up to date with local news.

Guerrilla & Paramilitary Activity

Despite the peace deal between the government and the Fuerzas Armadas Revolucionarias de Colombia (Revolutionary Armed Forces of Colombia; FARC), there remain isolated pockets of guerrilla activity in remote

GOVERNMENT TRAVEL ADVICE

Government websites with useful travel advisories:

Australian Department of Foreign Affairs (www.smartraveller.gov.au)

British Foreign Office (www.fco.gov.uk)

Canadian Department of Foreign Affairs (www.travel.gc.ca)

German Federal Foreign Office (www.auswaertiges-amt.de)

New Zealand Ministry of Foreign Affairs (www.safetravel.govt.nz)

US State Department (www.travel.state.gov)

parts of Colombia, with dissident FARC soldiers operating in some areas. The Ejército de Liberación Nacional (National Liberation Army; ELN) has carried out terrorist attacks in Colombia in recent years, in 2019 it was responsible for a car bombing in Bogotá that killed 22 people. The ELN declared a ceasefire in March 2020 at the start of the pandemic, but the General Commander of the armed forces, General Luis Fernando Navarro, continued activities and stated that the ELN lost 700 members through targeted attacks by the country's armed forces in 2020, he estimated that the group still had 2,500 armed combatants.

Neo-paramilitary groups engaged in drug trafficking are also a concern, they extended their operations around the country following the withdrawal of the FARC, and whose areas of influence are more difficult to identify.

Going off the beaten track should be done with great caution, if at all. While most armed groups no longer specifically target tourists, most are very suspicious of unannounced visitors in their territory – and cases of mistaken identity have led to kidnapping and deaths.

Large swaths of Colombia are not currently covered by Lonely Planet, as the security situation remains dubious and tourist infrastructure simply does not exist: this is the case for much of the west of the country, remote areas bordering Venezuela and chunks of the Amazon region (though the area of the Amazon we cover is extremely safe).

PRACTICAL TIPS

Keep your wits about you, avoid dodgy parts of town and be extra vigilant after dark, and Colombia should offer you nothing but good times.

- Avoid wandering off the grid, especially without checking the security situation on the ground.
- Be cautious when using ATMs after dark; avoid doing so entirely on deserted streets.
- Carry a quickly accessible, rolled bundle of small notes in case of robbery.
- Avoid drug tourism.
- Be very wary of drinks or cigarettes offered by strangers or new 'friends.'
- Beware of criminals masquerading as plainclothes police.
- The border towns of Cúcuta and Maicao are best avoided at present due to the ongoing crisis in Venezuela.

Theft & Robbery

Theft is the most common travelers' danger. In general, the problem is more serious in the largest cities. The most common methods of theft are snatching your day pack, cell phone or camera, pick-pocketing, or taking advantage of a moment's inattention to pick up your gear and run away.

Distraction can often be part of the thieves' strategy. Thieves tend to work in pairs or groups, often on motorcycles; one or more will distract you while an accomplice does the deed. They may begin by making friends with you, or pretend to be the police and demand to check your possessions. Inside banks, pay special attention when withdrawing money from ATMs and be wary of criminals posing as bank employees and offering help – a common robbery tactic.

If you can, leave your money and valuables somewhere safe before walking the streets. In practice, it's good to carry a decoy bundle of small notes, a maximum of COP$50,000 to COP$100,000, ready to hand over in case of an assault; if you really don't have a peso, robbers can become frustrated and, as a consequence, unpredictable.

Armed holdups in the cities can occur even in some more upmarket suburbs. If you are accosted by robbers, it is best to give them what they are after, but try to play it cool and don't rush to hand them all your valuables at once – they may well be satisfied with just your decoy wad. Don't try to escape or struggle – your chances are slim, and people have been murdered for pocket change. Don't count on any help from passersby.

Drugs

Cocaine and marijuana are cheap and widely available in Colombia's major cities. Purchasing and consuming drugs, however, is not a good idea. Many Colombians find Colombian drug tourism very offensive, especially in smaller towns. It's important to note the majority of Colombians don't consume drugs and many believe the foreign drug trade is responsible for Colombia's decades of violent conflict. So, asking after drugs, or openly using drugs, could land you in a lot of trouble (note: it's illegal to buy or sell drugs in any quantity).

A recent rise in travelers coming to Colombia to use ayahuasca (or *yagé* as it's often known in Colombia) is another worrying trend. The hallucinogenic drug, derived from various rainforest plants and used by Colombia's indigenous peoples in ceremonies for centuries, causes

COCAINE HOLIDAY? CONSIDER THE CONSEQUENCES

Drug tourism is an unfortunate reality in Colombia. And why not? Cocaine is cheap, right? *Not exactly.*

What may appear a harmless diversion directly contributes to the violence and mayhem that play out in the Colombian countryside every day. People fight and die for control of the cocaine trade. Purchasing and consuming cocaine helps finance that conflict.

Worse still, the byproducts from the production of cocaine are extremely damaging to the environment. The production process requires toxic chemicals such as kerosene, sulfuric acid, acetone and carbide, which are simply dumped afterward on the ground or into streams and rivers. Further, it's estimated that between 500 and 3000 sq km of virgin rainforest are cut down every year for coca production.

Colombia is one of the most beautiful countries in the world. The people, the music, the dancing, the food – these are already enough stimulation to overwhelm the senses.

purging and vomiting alongside incredibly strong hallucinations. In 2014 a 19-year-old British backpacker died near Putumayo while trying the drug, and we strongly recommend that you avoid it.

Sometimes you may be offered drugs on the street, in a bar or at a disco, but never accept these offers. The vendors may well be setting you up for the police, or their accomplices will follow you and stop you later, show you false police documents and threaten you with jail unless you pay them off.

There have been reports of drugs being planted on travelers, so keep your eyes open. Always refuse if a stranger at an airport asks you to take their luggage on board as part of your luggage allowance.

Spiked Drinks

Burundanga is a drug obtained from a species of tree widespread in Colombia and is used by thieves to render a victim unconscious. It can be put into sweets, cigarettes, chewing gum, spirits, beer – virtually any kind of food or drink – and it doesn't have any noticeable taste or odor.

The main effect after a 'normal' dose is the loss of will, even though you remain conscious. The thief can then ask you to hand over your valuables and you will obey without resistance. Cases of rape under the effect of burundanga are known. Other effects are loss of memory and sleepiness, which can last from a few hours to several days. An overdose can be fatal.

Interacting with the Police & Military

While the Colombian military is highly trustworthy and the federal police have a decent reputation, local cops have more of a mixed reputation. They don't get paid a lot of money, and incidents of bribery and bullying of tourists have been reported.

Always carry a photocopy of your passport with you, including your entry stamp (you're more likely to avoid trouble if you keep your papers in order), and never carry drugs of any kind, either on the street or when traveling.

In some areas, there are specialized tourist police; many speak some English. They are uniformed and easily recognizable by the Policía de Turismo labels on their arm bands. At the first hint of trouble, go to them first if you can.

If your passport, valuables or other belongings are stolen, go to the police station and make a *denuncia* (report). The officers on duty will write a statement according to what you tell them. It should include a description of the events and the list of stolen articles. Pay attention to the wording you use, include every stolen item and document, and carefully check the statement before signing it. Your copy of the statement serves as a temporary identity document and you'll need to present it to your insurer to make a claim.

If you happen to get involved with the police, keep calm and be polite, and always use the formal '*usted*' (the word for 'you,' instead of '*tu*'). Keep a sharp eye out when they check your gear.

Overland Travel

Traveling overland in most parts of Colombia, especially during the day, will likely present no issues other than which Spotify playlist you choose to drown out the bus driver's loud and questionable musical taste. But you should still exercise caution when taking public transport in Colombia, there have been several recent incidents of armed robberies on buses, so keep valuable personal possessions (cameras, phones, laptops etc) out of sight. Night buses to most destinations are a comfortable way to avoid wasting a day in transit, plus you save the cost of a night's accommodation. Avoid traveling on your own at night.

Minor routes including the road from Popayán to San Agustín and from Ocaña to Cúcuta are best traveled when it's light.

Directory A–Z

Accommodations

Colombia offers choices for all budgets and traveling personalities, from excellent hostels and funky boutique hotels to occasional jaw-dropping accommodations clinging to cliffs or hanging over raging seas. Book ahead around major religious holidays and festivals like Semana Santa and Christmas.

Camping

➡ For ages camping was out of bounds in Colombia, but the 2016 peace accord ended the 52-year civil war, freeing up some remote regions of the country. As a result, more and more Colombians are strapping on a pack and getting reacquainted with their beautiful country via a small but growing list of campgrounds, as well as by pitching tents in the wild.

Hostels

➡ Backpacker tourism is booming in Colombia. All hostels have dorm beds for around COP$22,000 to COP$50,000, and most have a few private rooms for COP$65,000 to COP$120,000.

➡ Many of the most established hostels are members of the **Colombian Hostels Association** (www.colombianhostels.com.co). The most comprehensive listing of hostels is at www.hosteltrail.com.

Hotels

➡ Also sometimes called *residencias, hospedajes* or *posadas*, hotels generally suggest places of a higher standard, or at least higher prices. Cheaper accommodations are usually clustered around markets, bus terminals and in the backstreets of the city center. If you speak Spanish and wish to avoid the gringo trail, a budget private room with hot water, air-con and cable TV goes for between COP$35,000 and COP$45,000 – cheaper than a hostel.

➡ Midrange hotels are rare in Colombia. Prices tend to jump rapidly from budget cheapies to three- and four-star hotels, with little in between. Nevertheless, there are often a handful of hotels in the COP$80,000 to COP$190,000 range, usually in city centers, which cater primarily to Colombian business travelers, though a number of midrange boutique hotels have also popped up in recent times.

➡ All the major cities have top-end hotels charging from COP$190,000 per night. The best choices of top-end hotels are in Bogotá, Medellín and Cartagena.

Resorts

➡ There are a handful of package-style resorts on the Caribbean coast and on San Andrés. Most are frequented by Colombians, rather than foreign package tourists, and are usually excellent value.

➡ The Pacific coast also has several good all-inclusives, but they are definitely for the more adventurous type as the area is quite remote and is heavily patrolled by the army.

➡ For a selection of some of the best small resorts and rural accommodations, see www.colfincas.com (in Spanish only).

➡ If you are booking a package resort deal from outside the country, you are

SLEEPING PRICE RANGES

The following price ranges refer to a standard double room before discounts or taxes.

$ less than COP$75,000

$$ COP$75,000–COP$175,000

$$$ more than COP$175,000

PLAN YOUR STAY ONLINE

For more accommodation reviews by Lonely Planet authors, check out www.lonelyplanet.com. You'll find independent reviews, as well as recommendations on the best places to stay.

exempt from the 19% IVA hotel tax. Some hotels may not know this rule, so be sure to ask for the discount.

Taxes & Refunds

A law passed in 2016 technically exempts foreigners from taxes on some travel-oriented services (the 19% IVA tax on accommodations, for example). Theoretically speaking, if you're in Colombia for less than 60 days and show your lodgings the stamp in your passport, you shouldn't have to pay the accommodation tax. However, in practice this is patchy, and if you are charged the 19% IVA, getting the money back requires a bit of hoop-jumping. Receipts must be shown at an office of the **National Department of Taxes and Customs** (DIAN; www.dian.gov.co) before leaving the country; you'll also have to fill out a form and present your passport and a photocopy of a valid tourist visa.

Children

- Like most Latin Americans, Colombians adore children. Due to a high rate of population growth, children make up a significant proportion of the population, and they are omnipresent.
- Few foreigners travel with children in Colombia, but if you do plan on taking along your offspring, they will find plenty of local companions.
- Almost all attractions in Colombia offer discounted admission for children.
- Pick up a copy of Lonely Planet's *Travel with Children* for general tips.

Practicalities

- You can buy disposable diapers (nappies) and baby food in supermarkets and pharmacies.
- There are quite a few shops devoted to kids' clothes, shoes and toys; Pepeganga (www.pepeganga.com) in particular is recommended.
- Most restaurants with a menu, which excludes cheap set-lunch places, will have high chairs available for small children.
- Baby-changing facilities are not standard in public toilets and are rare in men's facilities.
- Breastfeeding in public remains controversial in some sectors of Colombian society although education programs are seeing attitudes slowly changing.

Customs Regulations

- Colombian customs looks for large sums of cash – over US$10,000 – (inbound), and drugs and exotic wildlife (outbound). If they have the slightest suspicion you are carrying any of these you can expect an exhaustive search of your belongings and your person.
- Expect to be questioned in Spanish or English by a well-trained police officer. The latest screening method is x-raying your intestines: if you look in any way out of the ordinary, or fail to give a convincing response to the officer's questions, they will x-ray you to see if you are a drug mule.
- You can bring in personal belongings and presents you intend to give to Colombian residents. The quantity, type and value of these items shouldn't arouse suspicion that they may have been imported for commercial purposes.
- You can bring in items for personal use such as cameras, camping equipment, sports accessories or laptops without any problems.
- When arriving by plane (but not overland), you'll be given a customs form, which you'll need to fill in and hand to the official after reclaiming your baggage. If you have a connecting domestic flight your bags may be sent right through from Bogotá to your final destination – which is unusual in the region – but you still need to fill out the form and pass customs before heading up to your domestic departure gate.

Electricity

Type A
120V/60Hz

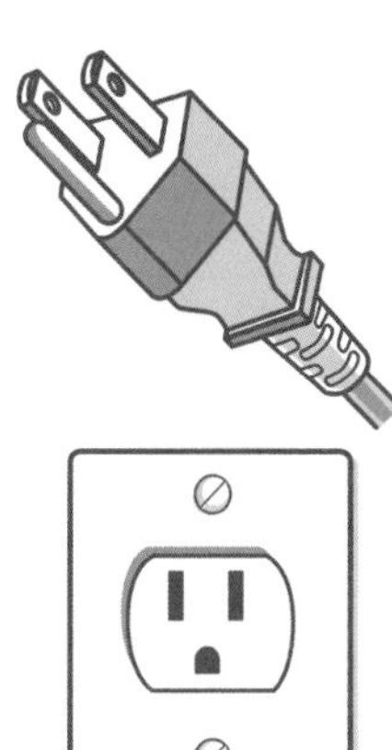

Type B
120V/60Hz

Embassies & Consulates

Most of the countries that maintain diplomatic relations with Colombia have their embassies and consulates in Bogotá. Some countries also have consulates in other Colombian cities.

In Barranquilla:

Panamanian Consulate (☎5-360-1870; Carrera 57 No 72-25, Edificio Fincar 207-208)

Venezuelan Consulate (☎5-368-2207; www.barranquilla.consulado.gob.ve; Carrera 52 No 69-96; ⌚8am-noon & 1:30-3:30pm Mon-Thu, 8am-noon Fri)

In Bogotá:

Australian Embassy (☎1-657-7800; www.colombia.embassy.gov.au; Av Carrera 9 No 115-06, edificio Tierra Firme, oficina 2002)

Brazilian Embassy (☎1-635-1694; http://bogota.itamaraty.gov.br; Calle 93 No 14-20, piso 8)

Canadian Embassy (☎1-657-9800; www.colombia.gc.ca; Carrera 7 No 114-33)

Ecuadorian Consulate (☎1-212-6512; www.colombia.embajada.gob.ec; Calle 89 No 13-07)

French Embassy (☎1-638-1400; www.ambafrance-co.org; Carrera 11 No 93-12)

German Embassy (☎1-423-2600; www.bogota.diplo.de; Calle 110 No 9-25, edificio Torre Empresarial Pacífic, piso 11)

Netherlands Embassy (☎1-638-4200; www.nederlandwereldwijd.nl; Carrera 13 No 93-40, piso 5)

Panamanian Embassy (☎1-257-5067; www.embajadadepanama.com.co; Calle 92 No 7A-40)

Peruvian Embassy (☎1-746-2360; www.embajadadelperu.org.co; Calle 80A No 6-50)

UK Embassy (☎1-326-8300; www.ukincolombia.fco.gov.uk; Carrera 9 No 76-49, piso 8)

US Embassy (☎1-275-2000; https://co.usembassy.gov/es; Carrera 45 No 24B-27)

Venezuelan Embassy (☎1-644-5555; http://colombia.embajada.gob.ve; Carrera 11 No 87-51, edificio Horizonte, piso 5)

In Cali:

Panamanian Consulate (☎2-486-1116; Av 6 No 25-58, Piso 3)

In Cartagena:

Panamanian Consulate (☎5-655-1055; Carrera 1 No 10-10)

Venezuelan Consulate (☎5-665-0382; Edificio Centro Executivo, Carrera 3 No 8-129, piso 14)

In Medellín:

Panamanian Consulate (☎4-312-4590; Calle 10 No 42-45, Oficina 266; ⌚9:30-11:30am Mon-Fri)

Venezuelan Consulate (☎4-444-0359; www.consulvenemedellin.org; Calle 32B No 69-59; ⌚8-11:30am Mon-Fri)

Argentine Embassy (☎1-288-0900; www.ecolo.mrecic.gov.ar; Carrera 12 No 97-80, piso 5)

Australian Embassy (☎1-657-7800; www.colombia.embassy.gov.au; Av Carrera 9 No 115-06, edificio Tierra Firme, oficina 2002)

Brazilian Embassy (☎1-635-1694; http://bogota.itamaraty.gov.br; Calle 93 No 14-20, piso 8) There's also a Brazilian consulate in Leticia (☎8-592-7530; Calle 9 No 9-73; ⌚8am-5pm Mon-Fri).

Canadian Embassy (☎1-657-9800; www.colombia.gc.ca; Carrera 7 No 114-33)

French Embassy (☎1-638-1400; www.ambafrance-co.org; Carrera 11 No 93-12)

German Embassy (☎1-423-2600; www.bogota.diplo.de; Calle 110 No 9-25, edificio Torre Empresarial Pacífic, piso 11)

Israeli Embassy (☎1-327-7500; http://embassies.gov.il; Calle 26 No 57-83, piso 7)

Italian Embassy (☎1-218-7206; www.ambbogota.esteri.it; Calle 93B No 9-92)

Japanese Embassy (☎1-317-5001; www.colombia.emb-japan.go.jp; Carrera 7 No 71-21, torre B, piso 11)

Netherlands Embassy (☎1-638-4200; www.nederlandwereldwijd.nl; Carrera 13 No 93-40, piso 5)

Panamanian Embassy (☎1-257-5067; www.embajadadepanama.com.co; Calle 92 No 7A-40) There are also consulates in **Barranquilla** (☎5-360-1870; Carrera 57 No 72-25, Edificio Fincar 207-208), **Cali** (☎2-486-1116; Av 6 No 25-58, Piso 3), **Cartagena** (☎5-655-1055; Carrera 1 No 10-10) and **Medellín** (☎4-312-4590; Calle 10 No 42-45, Oficina 266; ⌚9:30-11:30am Mon-Fri).

Peruvian Embassy (☎1-746-2360; www.embajadadelperu.org.co; Calle 80A No 6-50) There's also a consulate in **Leticia** (☎8-592-7755; Calle 11 No 5-32; ⌚8am-noon & 2-4pm Mon-Fri).

Spanish Embassy (☎1-622-00-90; www.exteriores.gob.es/embajadas/bogota; Calle 92 No 12-68)

UK Embassy (☎1-326-8300; www.ukincolombia.fco.gov.uk; Carrera 9 No 76-49, piso 8)

US Embassy (☎1-275-2000; https://co.usembassy.gov/es; Carrera 45 No 24B-27)

Venezuelan Embassy (☎1-644-5555; http://colombia.embajada.gob.ve; Carrera 11 No

87-51, edificio Horizonte, piso 5) There are also consulates in **Barranquilla** (☎5-368-2207; www.barranquilla.consulado.gob.ve; Carrera 52 No 69-96; ⏰8am-noon & 1:30-3:30pm Mon-Thu, 8am-noon Fri), **Cartagena** (☎5-665-0382; Edificio Centro Executivo, Carrera 3 No 8-129, piso 14), Cúcuta (☎7-579-1951; http://cucuta.consulado.gob.ve; cnr Av Camilo Daza & Calle 17; ⏰8-10am & 2-3pm Mon-Thu, 8-10am Fri) and **Medellín** (☎4-444-0359; www.consulveneme-dellin.org; Calle 32B No 69-59; ⏰8-11:30am Mon-Fri).

Food

Colombians are blessed with a fertile country: fish and plantain on the coast; legions of delectable tropical fruit; coffee, chocolate and dairy in the mountains; and cheap, fresh vegetables and meat everywhere. The collective cuisine is known as *comida criolla* (Creole food).

While Colombian cuisine can't boast the international recognition of Peru or the diversity of Brazil, it's a truly wonderful place to eat.

Colombia offers high-standard, stomach-filling food at great prices. There are plenty of budget places serving meals for COP$12,000 to COP$15,000. Lunch is the easiest: known as *comida corriente* (literally 'fast food' but used to mean a set lunch menu), this two-course meal will consist of soup followed by rice, beans, a choice of meat, a token salad and a glass of tropical fruit juice. Midrange restaurants (COP$25,000 to COP$45,000) tend to be a step up in quality and service, and meals in top-end restaurants generally cost more than COP$45,000.

Don't miss uniquely Colombian specialties *ajiaco* (an Andean chicken soup with corn, potato, cream and capers) and *bandeja paisa* (the '*paisa* platter'), a gut-busting mound of sausage, beans, rice, egg and *arepas* (ground corn cakes) – Colombia's de facto national dish despite controversy that its prevalence rarely strays from Antioquia. On the streets nationwide you'll find savory *arepas* of all ilk (with cheese, with ham and eggs, with chicken), *mazamorra* (a corn-based beverage), empanadas, and fresh-squeezed orange juice and fruit salads. Regional options include *llapingachos* (fried potato cakes with meat) and *helado de paila* (ice cream whipped in a copper tin) in Nariño, ceviche on the Caribbean coast, and tamales in Tolima and Huila. There's also plenty for your sweet tooth: *obleas con arequipe* are thin wafers doused in milk caramel, while *cuajada con melao* is fresh cheese with melted jaggery.

In terms of fruit, there's *zapote*, *nispero*, *lulo*, *uchuwa*, *borojo*, *curuba*, *mamoncillo*. Confused? You will be. Don't try and translate these fruits – they're native to Colombia and you won't find them in many other places in the world.

EATING PRICE RANGES

The following price ranges refer to the cost of main dishes for lunch and dinner.

$ less than COP$15,000

$$ COP$15,000–30,000

$$$ more than COP$30,000

LGBTI Travelers

- Compared to some Latin American countries, homosexuality is well tolerated in Colombia (it was declared legal by the government in 1981).
- There is a substantial gay undercurrent in the major cities and as long as you don't broadcast the fact in public you are unlikely to be harassed.
- With popular apps like Grindr for men, most contact is initiated online these days.
- In 2011 Colombia's Constitutional Court ordered Congress to pass legislation addressing same-sex marriage by June 2013; if they did not, the ruling dictated same-sex couples would automatically receive all marital rights from that date forward. Congress failed to act and Colombia's first gay wedding was performed on July 24, 2013. Full legal rights were confirmed in 2016 when the country's Constitutional Court ruled that the constitution required the state to process and recognize same-sex marriages.
- For LBGT-specific listings see the website www.guiagaycolombia.com.

Health

Most visitors travel to Colombia without incident, but there are certain medical conditions to be aware of and several things you can do to prevent sickness. Most illnesses are the result of Colombia's tropical-zone location. If traveling anywhere along the coast or jungle, you can bank on little tropical nuisances – infected bug bites, rashes or heat exhaustion. Other, more dangerous afflictions, including malaria and yellow fever, can strike travelers who get further off the beaten track or spend a lot of time trekking through national parks.

Dengue fever and the recent mosquito-borne threats, chikungunya, which arrived in 2014 on Colombian shores, and zika, which hit the country hard in 2016, are a risk in lowland population centers although the epidemic has passed and not many cases are being reported at present. Other problems can occur in the mountains, including *soroche* (altitude sickness).

The good news is that Colombia has some of the best medical care in South America.

Environmental Hazards

Altitude sickness may develop in travelers who ascend rapidly to altitudes greater than 2500m, including those flying directly to Bogotá.

Health Insurance

➡ While health care in Colombia is fairly affordable, bills can add up, making it worth having a comprehensive insurance policy that includes evacuation.

➡ Most hospitals and clinics will ask for proof of insurance or a cash/credit card deposit before treating patients for non-life-threatening conditions.

➡ Often you will have to pay the bill yourself before claiming reimbursement from the insurance company.

➡ If you plan on staying in the country Colombian health insurers offer monthly prepaid *'medicina prepaga'* plans that are more comprehensive than the basic private health care in the country.

Insurance

➡ Ideally, all travelers should have a travel insurance policy, which will provide some security in the case of a medical emergency, or the loss or theft of money or belongings. It may seem an expensive luxury, but if you can't afford a travel health insurance policy, you also probably can't afford medical emergency charges abroad if something goes wrong.

➡ If you need to make a claim on your travel insurance, you must produce a police report detailing loss or theft. You also need proof of the value of any items lost or stolen. Receipts are the best bet, so if you buy a camera for your trip, for example, hang on to the receipt.

➡ Colombian law stipulates that in emergency situations hospitals must treat you, whether or not you can pay. If you don't have the Spanish to insist on this right, you may have difficulty getting treatment.

GOVERNMENT TRAVEL ADVICE

Government websites with useful travel advisories:

Australian Department of Foreign Affairs (www.smartraveller.gov.au)

British Foreign Office (www.fco.gov.uk)

Canadian Department of Foreign Affairs (www.travel.gc.ca)

German Federal Foreign Office (www.auswaertiges-amt.de)

New Zealand Ministry of Foreign Affairs (www.safetravel.govt.nz)

US State Department (www.travel.state.gov)

Internet Access

➡ Colombia is a wired country. Internet is everywhere and while internet cafes have died out in large cities, some of the remoter places still retain one or two.

➡ In smaller towns and more remote destinations, the government's ambitious and heralded Plan Vive Digital has brought free wi-fi to almost everywhere. You can usually stop by the local library, park or cultural center to get online.

➡ Almost all hostels and hotels offer free wi-fi. Shopping centers often have free wi-fi and so do most restaurants and cafes. Major airports offer wi-fi although it's usually very poor.

Language Courses

Universities and language schools in the larger cities run Spanish-language courses. It is generally cheaper and better value to arrange a private one-on-one tutor. Popular backpacker hotels are the best places to ask about independent teachers. Enrolling in a university course is useful if you want to extend your stay beyond the six months a tourist visa permits you.

Legal Matters

If arrested you have the right to an attorney. If you don't have one, one will be appointed to you (and paid for by the government). There is a presumption of innocence and you can expect a speedy trial.

The most common legal situation that travelers find themselves in involves drugs. In 2012 Colombia's Constitutional Court decriminalized the possession of small amounts of cocaine (1g or less) and marijuana (20g or less) for personal use, and in 2016 it removed the cap on the legal amount of drugs for personal use, but that doesn't mean it's a good idea. Although you cannot be criminally prosecuted, police may still give you a hard time and you may be ordered to receive physical or psychological treatment depending on your level of intoxication.

ORIENTATION

Colombian cities, towns and villages have traditionally been laid out on a grid plan. The streets running north–south are called Carreras, often abbreviated on maps to Cra, Cr or K, whereas those running east–west are called Calles, often labeled on local maps as Cll, Cl or C. This simple pattern may be complicated by diagonal streets, called either Diagonales (more east–west and thus like Calles), or Transversales (more like Carreras).

All streets are numbered and the numerical system of addresses is used. Each address consists of a series of numbers, eg Calle 6 No 12-35 (which means that it's the building on Calle 6, 35m from the corner of Carrera 12 toward Carrera 13), or Carrera 11A No 7-17 (the house on Carrera 11A, 17m from the corner of Calle 7 toward Calle 8).

The system is very practical and you will soon become familiar with it. It is usually easy to find an address. It's actually one of the most precise address systems in the world; if you have an address you can determine the location of the place with pinpoint accuracy.

In the larger cities the main streets are called Avenidas or Autopistas. They each have their own names and numbers, but are commonly known just by their numbers.

Cartagena's old town is the only Colombian city where centuries-old street names have withstood the modern numbering system. Streets in some other cities (eg Medellín) have both names and numbers, but elsewhere only numbers are used.

Maps

- It's difficult to find detailed maps of Colombia outside the country itself. In the USA, Maps.com (www.maps.com) has an excellent supply of Colombian maps. A similarly extensive selection is available in the UK from Stanfords (www.stanfords.co.uk).
- Within Colombia, folded road maps of the country are produced by various publishers and are distributed through bookstores. Of special note is the Movistar *Guía de rutas*, a Spanish-language guidebook to Colombia with excellent maps. You can buy it at any tollbooth (ask the bus driver beforehand to buy it for you), or from a handful of better bookstores.
- The widest selection of maps of Colombia is produced and sold by the **Instituto Geográfico Agustín Codazzi** (IGAC; Map p42; ☎1-369-4000; www.igac.gov.co; Carrera 30 No 48-51), the government mapping body, which has its head office in Bogotá and branch offices in departmental capitals.

Money

- The Colombian peso (COP$) is the unit of currency in Colombia.
- There are paper notes of COP$1000, COP$2000, COP$5000, COP$10,000, COP$20,000, COP$50,000 and COP$100,000. The coins you will use are primarily the COP$100, COP$200, COP$500 and COP$1000; the COP$50 is rarely seen outside of supermarkets, and some people may refuse to accept it.
- Counterfeit pesos are a major problem in Colombia and you'll notice cashiers everywhere vigorously checking notes before completing transactions. While it is difficult for visitors to identify dud bills, if you are given one that is old, battered or just doesn't seem right, hand it back and ask for another.

ATMs

- Almost all major banks have ATMs, and they usually work fine with cards issued outside Colombia (Bancolombia being the ornery exception for some folks). Cash machines affiliated with Banco de Bogotá/ATH and BBVA are good bets.
- Most banks have a maximum cash withdrawal limit of COP$300,000 per transaction, but it varies. Bancolombia, Davivienda and Citibank allow double that from most branches. If you need more, just pull out twice, and be quick about it. The machines have very little tolerance for those that take their time navigating the menu – a second of hesitation and it cancels the transaction!
- If you must use an ATM after dark, always use one inside a gas station or shopping mall. Some ATMs can be fussy if you do not have a chip-and-pin ATM card.

Credit Cards

- Credit cards are common in Colombia and used extensively in the major cities and larger towns. When paying with a credit card, you will be asked, '*¿En cuantas cuotas?*' (How many payments?). Colombian customers can choose to divide the payment over 24 months. Foreign cardholders should just say 'one.'
- The most useful card for cash advances is Visa, as it's accepted by most banks. MasterCard is less common but still processed by many banks. Other cards are of limited use.

➡ You can get advance payments on cards from the cashier in the bank or from the bank's ATM. In either case you'll need your PIN.

International Transfers

➡ If you need money sent to you quickly, **MoneyGram** (☎1-800-269-4556; www.moneygram.com.co) and **Western Union** (www.colombia.westernunion.com) are your two principal options. MoneyGram is usually cheaper, and is what most overseas Colombians use to send remittances home to their families.

➡ Your sender pays the money, along with a fee, at their nearest MoneyGram or Western Union branch, and gives the details on who is to receive it and where. You can have the money within 15 minutes. When you pick it up, take along photo identification and the numbered password they'll give the sender.

➡ Both services have offices in all the major cities and most smaller towns.

Money Changers

➡ You are better off using your ATM card in Colombia, as you will get a much better exchange rate.

➡ The US dollar is the only foreign currency worth trying to change in Colombia; expect dismal rates for euros, pounds sterling, Australian dollars etc.

➡ Many but not all banks change money; in major cities and in border regions there are usually several *casas de cambio* (currency exchanges).

➡ Avoid changing money on the street; some informal changers have fast fingers and often dodgy calculators.

➡ Colombia is considered a leader in producing counterfeit banknotes, including US currency, which is worth noting if you are changing your pesos back at the end of a trip.

➡ Your passport is required for any banking transaction. You'll also have to provide a thumbprint.

➡ There's a fair amount of paperwork involved in changing money (to prevent money laundering).

Tipping

Restaurants A government regulation dictates that in midrange and top-end restaurants (anywhere there is a service charge), your waiter must ask you if they can add the 10% service charge to the bill. In midrange restaurants it's acceptable to decline to pay the service charge with a polite *'sin servicio, por favor'* if you are dissatisfied. In top-end restaurants refusing the pay the service charge is likely to bring a manager to your table to inquire what was wrong with your meal.

Taxis Tipping in taxis is not commonplace but rounding up to the nearest 500 or 1000 pesos is quite normal.

Opening Hours

Banks 9am–4pm Monday to Friday, 9am–noon Saturday

Bars 6pm to around 3am

Cafes 8am–10pm

Nightclubs 9pm until very late Thursday to Saturday

Restaurants Breakfast from 8am, lunch from noon, dinner until 9pm or 10pm

Shops 9am–5pm Monday to Friday, 9am to noon or 5pm Saturday; some shops close for lunch

Post

➡ Colombia's official postal service is the terribly named **4-72** (www.4-72.com.co), which has turned the debilitating pension liabilities and inefficiency of Colombia's former

PRACTICALITIES

Newspapers All major cities have daily newspapers. Bogotá's leading newspaper, *El Tiempo* (www.eltiempo.com), has reasonable coverage of national and international news, culture, sports and economics; *El Espectador* (www.elespectador.com) is also good. The leading newspapers in other large cities include *El Colombiano* (www.elcolombiano.com) in Medellín, and *El País* (www.elpais.com.co) in Cali. *Semana* (www.semana.com) is the biggest national weekly magazine.

TV Colombia has plenty of national and local TV stations. Each region has its own TV station; Bogotá TV is dominated by City TV (www.citytv.com.co). Nationwide channels include Caracol TV (www.canalcaracol.com.co), RCN TV (www.canalrcn.com), and government-run Señal Colombia (www.senalcolombia.tv).

Online For English-language coverage of Colombian news and current affairs check out Colombia Reports (www.colombiareports.com).

Smoking Forbidden in public transport, enclosed spaces, including bars and restaurants, and workplaces. Some hotels have ventilated smoking zones although many are completely smoke free.

Weights and measures Usually the metric system. Exceptions include petrol measured in US gallons, and fresh food often sold in *libras* (pounds).

government postal service, Adpostal (shut down in 2006), into a profitable and efficient business.

➡ There are also numerous private courier companies, including **Avianca** (www.puntosaviancaexpress.com), **Deprisa** (☎1-8000-519393; www.deprisa.com) and **Servientrega** (☎Bogotá 1-770-0200; www.servientrega.com).

➡ If you want to receive a package in Colombia, you have a choice. The sender can ship via a courier like DHL, which guarantees fast, dependable delivery, but also guarantees Colombian customs will open the box and charge often exorbitant duty. If you're not hurried, have the package sent via regular airmail (four to eight weeks).

➡ Identification is required to ship packages or letters from Colombia, so head to the post office with your passport.

Public Holidays

The following days are observed as public holidays in Colombia.

Año Nuevo (New Year's Day) January 1

Los Reyes Magos (Epiphany) January 6*

San José (St Joseph) March 19*

Jueves Santo & Viernes Santo (Maundy Thursday and Good Friday) March/April (Easter). The following Monday is also a holiday.

Día del Trabajo (Labor Day) May 1

La Ascensión del Señor (Ascension) May*

Corpus Cristi (Corpus Christi) May/June*

Sagrado Corazón de Jesús (Sacred Heart) June*

San Pedro y San Pablo (St Peter and St Paul) June 29*

Día de la Independencia (Independence Day) July 20

Batalla de Boyacá (Battle of Boyacá) August 7

La Asunción de Nuestra Señora (Assumption) August 15*

Día de la Raza (Discovery of America) October 12*

Todos los Santos (All Saints' Day) November 1*

Independencia de Cartagena (Independence of Cartagena) November 11*

Inmaculada Concepción (Immaculate Conception) December 8

Navidad (Christmas Day) December 25

SHOP TILL YOU DROP

Colombia is famous for everything from fat emeralds and colorful hammocks to beautiful La Chamba black-clay pottery cookware. Rich traditions and favorable prices mean you can pick up excellent, high-quality souvenirs that you won't find buried in your closet a few years down the road.

Emeralds Mined chiefly from the Muzo area, emeralds are sold in Bogotá at the flourishing emerald street market at the southwestern corner of Av Jiménez and Carrera 7 and nearby Plaza Rosario, where dozens of *negociantes* (traders) buy and sell stones – sometimes on the sidewalks.

Handicrafts Boyacá is the country's largest handicraft manufacturer, with excellent handwoven items, basketry and pottery. The Pacific coast also has an interesting selection of basketwork, plus the occasional blow-dart gun. Guapi is famous for its musical instruments, especially handmade drums. You may also find some good handwrought gold jewelry here. If you don't make it to the Pacific coast, the Parque Artesanal Loma de la Cruz (p235) in Cali is a good place to shop.

Woodwork Pasto is known for its woodwork – decorative items are covered with *barniz de Pasto*, a kind of vegetable resin. Ceramic miniatures of *chivas* (traditional buses) have become a popular souvenir.

Pottery La Chamba pottery and cookware, forged from black clay, is a specialty of Tolima and is as beautiful sitting on a fireplace mantel as a stove.

Hammocks These come in plenty of regional variations, from the simple, practical hammocks made in Los Llanos to the elaborate Wayuu-crafted *chinchorros*.

Ruanas Colombian woolen ponchos, known as ruanas, are found in the colder parts of the Andean zone. In many villages they are still made by hand with simple patterns and natural colors. Bogotá and Villa de Leyva are good places to buy them.

Mochilas The best and most fashionable *mochilas* (a kind of woven handbag) are the earthy-toned varieties of the Arhuaco from the Sierra Nevada de Santa Marta and the colorful offerings from the Wayuu in the Guajira. Authentic bags are not cheap, but are beautiful and usually of good quality.

When the dates marked with an asterisk do not fall on a Monday, the holiday is moved to the following Monday to make a three-day long weekend, referred to as the *puente* (bridge).

Telephone

The telephone system in Colombia is modern and works well for both domestic and international calls. Cell (mobile) phone coverage is extensive and inexpensive.

Cell Phones

Cell (mobile) phone and mobile data coverage is excellent. Most unlocked cell phones will work with a local SIM card.

Colombians love their cell phones, and in urban areas almost everyone has at least one. The three major providers are Claro (www.claro.com.co), Movistar (www.movistar.co) and Tigo (www.tigo.com.co). Claro has the best nationwide coverage, though all networks now have competitive data and call packages. Of the smaller providers, ETB is regarded as having the best internet speed. Cell phones are cheap, and many travelers end up purchasing one – a basic, no-frills handset will set you back around COP$130,000.

Alternatively you could bring your own cell phone from home and buy a Colombian SIM card, which usually costs between COP$2000 and COP$5000. You will need to take ID to buy a SIM from one of the phone companies; you can also buy them from third parties but eventually you'll need to register with the company or risk having your handset blocked.

Colombian cell-phone companies do not charge you to receive calls, only to make them.

Phone Codes

Many Colombian landlines are barred from making calls to cell phones.

Landline from cell (mobile) phone	☎03 + area code + 7-digit number
Colombian landline from abroad	☎57 + area code + 7-digit number
Colombian cell phone from abroad	☎57 + 10-digit number

Time

All of Colombia lies within the same time zone, five hours behind Greenwich Mean Time (GMT). There is no daylight saving time.

Toilets

➡ There are very few public toilets in Colombia. In their absence use a restaurant's toilet. Museums and large shopping malls usually have public toilets, as do bus and airport terminals and some supermarkets.

➡ You'll often (but not always) find toilet paper in toilets; it's wise to carry some with you. Never flush toilet paper. The pipes are narrow and the water pressure is weak, so toilets can't cope with paper. A wastebasket is normally provided.

➡ The most common word for toilet is *baño*. Men's toilets will usually bear a label saying *señores, hombres* or *caballeros*, while the women's toilets will be marked *señoras, mujeres* or *damas*.

➡ Bus-station restrooms will usually charge COP$800 to COP$1000 plus COP$200 to COP$300 for toilet paper.

Tourist Information

➡ Almost all towns and cities that are frequented by tourists have a Punto Información Turística (PIT) – an information kiosk or office identifiable by the red 'i' logo. They're often located near the central plaza as well as at transport terminals.

➡ Colombia has a number of good regional and national websites offering information (sometimes in English) about what to do and where to stay.

➡ The country's principal portal is the excellent www.colombia.travel.

Travelers with Disabilities

Colombia is taking strides toward improving accessibility but remains a somewhat-challenging destination for travelers with disabilities. Forward-thinking Medellín is perhaps the easiest place for travelers with reduced mobility, followed by other major cities like Bogotá, Bucaramanga and Cali.

Sidewalks are often uneven and while more and more ramps are being added they are far from being universal. Motorists also are used to flying around corners without stopping for those crossing the road.

Many restaurants and hotels do not have ramps for visitors with impaired mobility. Large chain hotels are more likely to have accessible rooms – usually just a couple – and public areas. Larger shopping malls also usually have ramps and elevators.

Most major integrated public-transport systems, including the TransMilenio in Bogotá and the metro in Medellín, have accessible stations and vehicles but overcrowding can make travel difficult and unpleasant. The majority of Colombia's taxis are small hatchback vehicles that are not particularly easy to get in or out of and often have little space for wheelchairs or other bulky items.

Visas

Nationals of many countries, including those from Western Europe and the Americas,

Japan, Australia, Israel and New Zealand don't need a visa. Otherwise, expect to apply in advance and pay a nominal fee.

Visa Extensions

Migración Colombia (Centro Facilitador de Servicios Migratorios; www.migracioncolombia.gov.co; Calle 100 No 11B-27; 7:30am-3:30pm Mon-Fri) usually handles visa extensions for tourists via Centros Facilitadores de Servicios Migratorios offices around the country, however, coronavirus has somewhat disrupted this process. Offices were closed at certain points of the pandemic and at the time of writing there was a gradual resumption of services. The option to extend a tourist visa is now available on the Migracion website (choose '*Permiso Temporal de Permanencia para Prorrogar Permanencia*'). Visitors on a tourist visa may extend up to an additional 90 days at the discretion of the officer. If you attend a visa office, you might be asked to submit your passport, two photocopies of your passport (picture page and arrival stamp) and two passport-sized photos, along with an air ticket out of the country in most cases. The fee of COP$103,000 can be paid by debit or credit card online and at Migración Colombia offices.

If you're paying in cash it must be deposited into the government bank account, which is often Banco de Occidente but depends on the city in which you are applying. Show up first to fill out forms, then they'll direct you to a nearby bank to pay the fee.

If you complete the process and pay online, once it's approved you may need to go into a Migración Colombia office to get the stamp.

If you apply for an extension in an office, expect the process to take an entire morning or afternoon. It can be done at any of the Centros Facilitadores de Servicios Migratorios offices in Colombia, which are present in all the main cities and some smaller towns (there's a list on the Migración Colombia website), but check they are open if coronavirus restrictions are in place before your visit. You may (but not always) get the extension on the spot.

Fines for overstaying range from half of to up to seven times the minimum salary (depending on the length of overstay): travelers in 2021 were charged around COP$700,000 for overstaying a few days.

Volunteering

Colombia offers a decent array of volunteering opportunities in education, the environment and social fields. Most major international volunteer boards have in-country listings.

One worthwhile local organization is Goals for Peace (www.goalsforpeace.com) in Bucaramanga where volunteers can help out giving English classes, sports training, arts and crafts workshops or with homework assistance.

While some hostels will offer travelers 'volunteer' positions in exchange for food and board, this is technically illegal as it takes jobs away from Colombians.

Let's Go Volunteer (301-600-6049, 310-884-8041; www.letsgovolunteer.info; Carrera 5 sur No 22-40, Ibagué) A small, Colombian-based NGO that offers opportunities working with underprivileged children, women who want to leave prostitution, children living with HIV and the elderly. Costs range from one week (US$250) to one month (US$500) to three months (US$3500).

Techo (in Chile +56-2-838-7300; www.techo.org) This Chilean-based, youth-led organization works to transform slums into empowered communities across 19 Latin American countries, including Colombia. Volunteers help build houses with families living in extreme poverty.

Globalteer (in UK 44-117-230-9998; www.globalteer.org) A registered UK charity which offers volunteer placements in Colombia working with children. Prices start from US$795.

Women Travelers

- Women traveling in Colombia are unlikely to encounter any problems.
- The usual caveats apply: bring your street smarts, don't wander alone in dodgy neighborhoods after dark, and keep an eye on your drink.
- Female travelers are also more likely to be victims of a bag-snatching or mugging attempt, as you will be perceived as less likely to fight back.
- Also be careful taking taxis alone after dark – while rare, there have been reports of taxi drivers raping single female passengers.

Work

- In order to take part in any paid employment in Colombia it's necessary to apply for the appropriate visa through Migración Colombia; your employer will need to sponsor the application, which is more likely if you have formal qualifications and are willing to commit to a longer contract.
- There is a growing demand for qualified English-language teachers in Colombia. Some schools may be willing to pay cash-in-hand for a short period of time, but for longer-term employment you will have to find a school willing to organize a work visa. Don't expect to get rich teaching English: you're unlikely to make more than a few million pesos a month, and usually much less.
- As a general rule, the more popular the city is among travelers, the harder it will be to find employment.

Transportation

GETTING THERE & AWAY

It's possible to arrive in Colombia by air, road, river and sea. The majority of visitors fly in through the major gateway airports of Bogotá, Medellín, Cartagena and Cali.

Colombia borders Panama, Venezuela, Brazil, Peru and Ecuador, but has road connections with Venezuela and Ecuador only. These are the easiest and most popular border crossings, although the political crisis in Venezuela has led to the borders operating irregularly.

You can also cross the border to Santa Rosa in Peru and Tabatinga in Brazil at the three corners near Leticia. There are privately run charter yachts to and from Panama and regular local boats running to Ecuador from Tumaco.

Flights, cars and tours can be booked online at lonelyplanet.com/bookings.

Entering the Country

Most travelers will arrive in Colombia by plane, or overland from Ecuador, Venezuela, and less often, Brazil. There are also numerous sailboats that bring travelers from Panama via the San Blas Islands.

You'll need a valid passport (with at least six more months of validity) and some nationalities will need a visa. Travelers receive a 90-day tourist visa, which can be extended another 90 days per calendar year.

When arriving by plane (but not overland), you'll be given a customs form which you'll need to fill in and hand to the official after reclaiming your baggage. If you have a connecting domestic flight your bags may be sent right through from Bogotá to your final destination – which is unusual in the region – but you still need to fill out the form and pass customs before heading up to your domestic departure gate.

Air

Airports & Airlines

Colombia's biggest international airport is Bogotá's newly renovated **Aeropuerto Internacional El Dorado** (Map p42; ☎1-266-2000; www.eldorado.aero; Av El Dorado). A second phase of the expansion project is underway.

Other major airports servicing international flights:

Aeropuerto José María Cordova (www.aeropuertorionegro.co) Serving Medellín.

Aeropuerto Rafael Núñez (www.sacsa.com.co) In Cartagena.

CLIMATE CHANGE & TRAVEL

Every form of transport that relies on carbon-based fuel generates CO_2, the main cause of human-induced climate change. Modern travel is dependent on airplanes, which might use less fuel per mile per person than most cars but travel much greater distances. The altitude at which aircraft emit gases (including CO_2) and particles also contributes to their climate change impact. Many websites offer 'carbon calculators' that allow people to estimate the carbon emissions generated by their journey and, for those who wish to do so, to offset the impact of the greenhouse gases emitted with contributions to portfolios of climate-friendly initiatives throughout the world. Lonely Planet offsets the carbon footprint of all staff and author travel.

DEPARTURE TAX

There is a COP$111,500 or US$38 departure tax on international flights. While previously it was paid at a separate window, it's now generally included in the price of the ticket.

In theory travelers visiting Colombia for less than 60 days are exempt from this charge; round-trip tickets for less than this period originating outside Colombia should not have the tax included.

Aeropuerto Alfonso Bonilla Aragón (www.aerocali.com.co) Serving Cali.

Colombia's national carrier is **Avianca** (☎1-8000-953434, 5-330-2030; www.avianca.com), which is one of the better airlines in the region both in terms of service and reliability.

Tickets

Colombia requires, technically at least, that visitors have an onward ticket before they're allowed into the country. Airlines and travel agents quite strictly enforce this, and no one will sell you a one-way ticket unless you already have an onward ticket. Upon arrival in Colombia, however, hardly any immigration officials will ask you to present your onward ticket.

The trick is to buy a fully refundable ticket with your credit card and request a refund upon arrival in Colombia. If arriving overland, a printout of an unpaid reservation may also be sufficient to get past the border guards. Scruffy-looking travelers are more likely to be asked to show an onward ticket than those who are neatly attired.

Onward Travel Within South America

Airline tickets in South America are often expensive. If you are traveling one way to Ecuador, Venezuela or Brazil, you will probably find it cheaper to fly domestically to the land border (Ipiales, Cúcuta or Leticia, respectively), cross the land border and take another domestic flight to your final destination.

That said, Bogotá is often the cheapest entry point to South America and there are plenty of intercontinental flights out of Bogotá, plus a few out of Cali and Medellín. You can fly Bogotá–Quito and Cali–Quito, for example. As a result of the political crisis in Venezuela, which has seen Avianca suspend service to that country, seats in and out of Caracas are becoming harder and harder to come by.

Land

Border Crossings

For information on visa requirements, see Visas (p327).

BRAZIL & PERU

The only viable border crossing from these two countries into Colombia is via Leticia in the far southeastern corner of the Colombian Amazon. Leticia is reached from Iquitos (Peru) and Manaus (Brazil) by riverboat. Flights are the only way to get from Leticia to other parts of Colombia.

ECUADOR

Virtually all travelers use the Carretera Panamericana border crossing through Tulcán (Ecuador) and Ipiales (Colombia). The part of the Panamericana between Pasto and Popayán has improved but to avoid problems altogether and enjoy fantastic views, it's best to travel this road during the day.

Another option is the crossing at San Miguel in Putumayo to Nueva Loja in the Ecuadorean Amazon. Backpackers have begun to safely use this route but check the situation on the ground with your hotel before proceeding as this area fluctuates often between acceptable and sketchy. Always travel by day on this route.

VENEZUELA

We do not recommend traveling to Venezuela at present. Most government-sanctioned travel advice is to avoid visiting the country due to civil unrest and violence. The border region with Colombia is particularly dangerous, and should be avoided.

Sea

There are marine crossings from Colombia to Panama and Ecuador.

Panama

Numerous sailboats operate between the Panamanian ports of Portobelo, Porvenir or Colón and Cartagena. This is a popular form of intercontinental travel, and generally passes through (and stops in) the beautiful San Blas Islands along the way. Some boats operating from Cartagena's yacht clubs work on a fixed schedule, others leave when full. The entire Cartagena–San Blas–El Porvenir trip by sailboat ranges between US$450 and US$650 all-inclusive, with the majority of boats charging US$550. From El Porvenir, you'll need to carry on by speedboat to Carti or Miramar, from where you can continue overland to Panama City; or fly from El Porvenir.

Boats have traditionally been unregulated and safety is an issue. Cartagena-based Blue Sailing (www.bluesailing.net), a Colombian-American agency, has begun to change that in recent years. At the time of research the company represented 25 boats, and it ensures they all have proper safety equipment for open sea navigation, monitor the boats' locations 24 hours a day and uses only licensed captains.

It is also possible to arrange transportation from Bahía Solano to Jaqué in Panama, although departures are very infrequent. From Jaqué you can continue along Panama's Pacific coast to Panama City or fly.

Ecuador

It is possible to cross the border via skiff along the Pacific coast near Tumaco, but security along the road to Tumaco and the security situation in the city itself make it a place for travelers to avoid.

GETTING AROUND

Air

- The easiest way to cover the huge distances between big cities in Colombia. Air travel has become more accessible lately with the advent of budget airlines, and booking in advance can make it a very reasonable way to travel. Nearly all cities have airports, as well as many smaller, remoter towns.
- While flights are normally always more expensive than a bus on the same route the difference is not always that great – especially on longer, high-volume routes. It's not worth taking a bus from Medellín to the Costa to save COP$30,000.
- Shop around among airlines as prices can vary greatly on the same route. Ticket prices to some destinations drop in the last week or two before the date; for some other destinations, they may rise significantly.
- It's cheaper to purchase online than in agencies and airline offices.
- Some airlines have different prices depending on which version of the website you are on – make sure to visit the Colombian page for the best prices.
- You can reserve and pay for some domestic flights online with a foreign credit card but for others you'll need to make a booking and then pay cash at an agent.
- Some airlines offer packages to major tourist destinations (for example, Cartagena and San Andrés), which can cost not much more than you'd pay for air tickets only. If purchasing these package deals from overseas you are exempt from the 16% IVA (sales tax) – be sure to ask for this discount, as many Colombians are unaware of it.

Bicycle

- Colombia is not the easiest of countries for cyclists, though the sport is wildly popular in certain regions (Boyacá, for example).
- Road rules favor drivers and you'll end up fighting traffic on main roadways. Never assume that a driver will give you right of way.
- On the plus side, most roads are paved and security is improving. Even the smallest towns will have a repair shop and you can get your bike fixed cheaply and easily.
- Bike rentals are uncommon outside main traveler areas but you can buy a bike almost anywhere.
- Colombian cities are becoming more bike-friendly, with new bike tracks and Ciclovía (the weekend closure of selected streets to cars and buses, making them tracks for cyclists and skaters instead).

AIRLINES IN COLOMBIA

Colombia has several main passenger airlines and many smaller carriers and charter airlines. Busy routes are operated on modern jet aircraft while flights in remote areas can be in anything from tiny single-propellor three-seaters to Soviet jets and even WWII-era DC-3s!

Avianca (www.avianca.com)

Easy Fly (www.easyfly.com.co)

LATAM (www.latam.com)

Satena (www.satena.com)

Viva Colombia (www.vivacolombia.co)

Wingo (www.wingo.com)

Boat

- Fast speedboats run between Turbo in northern Antioquia and the towns of Capurgana and Sapzurro in the Caribbean and in the Pacific between the towns of Bahía Solano to Nuquí.
- Cargo boats ply the Pacific coast, with the port of Buenaventura as their hub. Travelers with sufficient time can get a bunk for travel to points north and south including to Nuquí and Bahía Solano.
- Before railroads and highways were built, river transportation was the principal means of transportation in mountainous Colombia. These days river travel is not common but remains the only way to move in parts of the Amazon, such as from Leticia to Puerto Nariño.
- The Río Atrato and Río San Juan in the Chocó have passenger services but should both be avoided due to armed groups operating in the region.

Bus

The main way to get around Colombia, buses range from tightly packed *colectivos* (shared minibuses or taxis) to comfortable, air-conditioned, long-distance buses, and connect nearly every town in the country. Buses are the principal means of intercity travel, and go just about everywhere. Most long-distance intercity buses are more comfortable than your average coach-class airplane seat, and the overnight buses sometimes have business-class-sized seats. Wi-fi is now pretty much standard on nicer buses (though it's often patchy or doesn't work at all). A word of warning: many Colombian bus drivers turn the air-con up to arctic temperatures. Wear a sweater, a beanie and gloves, or better yet, bring a blanket. Bus drivers also tend to crank up the music and/or action movie (dubbed in Spanish) on the TV, even in the middle of the night. You may like to travel with earplugs.

It is common for buses to stop at *requisas* (military checkpoints), even in the dead of night. The soldiers at checkpoints will ask everyone to get off the bus, check everyone's identification, and then pat people down. They may look through your bags but often ignore foreigners altogether.

Long-distance buses stop for meals, but not necessarily at mealtimes; it depends on when the driver is hungry or when the bus gets to a restaurant that has an arrangement with the bus company.

All intercity buses depart from and arrive at a *terminal de pasajeros* (passenger terminal). Every city has such a terminal, usually outside the city center, but always linked to it by local transportation. Bogotá is the most important bus transportation hub in Colombia, handling buses to just about every area of the country.

The highway speed limit in Colombia is 80km/h, and bus companies are obliged to put a large speedometer at the front of the cabin, so passengers can see how fast the bus is going (although in practice they are often broken or disabled). Bus company offices are also

BUSING ABOUT, CHIVA-STYLE

The *chiva* is a Disneyland-style vehicle that was Colombia's principal means of road transportation several decades ago. Also called *bus de escalera* (which roughly translated means 'bus of stairs,' referring to the stairs along the side) in some regions, the *chiva* is a piece of popular art on wheels. The body is made almost entirely of wood and has wooden benches rather than seats, with each bench accessible from the outside. The body of the bus is painted with colorful decorative patterns, each different, with a main painting on the back. There are home-bred artists who specialize in painting *chivas*. Ceramic miniatures of *chivas* are found in just about every Colombian handicraft shop.

Today, *chivas* have almost disappeared from main roads, but they still play an important role on back roads between small towns and villages. There are still a few thousand of them and they are most common in Antioquia, Cauca, the Zona Cafetera, Huila, Nariño and on the Caribbean coast. *Chivas* take both passengers and any kind of cargo, animals included. If the interior is already completely packed, the roof is used for everything and everybody that doesn't fit inside.

Nighttime city tours in *chivas* are organized by travel agents in most large cities and have become a popular form of entertainment. There is normally a DJ, and sometimes even a band, on board playing loud music, and a large stock of *aguardiente* (anise-flavored liquor) to create the proper atmosphere. The tour usually includes some popular nightspots and can be great fun.

required by law to post their accident/fatality statistics at the ticket counter, which can give you a good idea of their safety record.

Types of Bus

Most intercity buses are air-conditioned and have good legroom. On shorter routes (less than four hours), smaller *busetas* ply their trade. There are sometimes also vans, which cost more but are faster although far from comfortable. In remote country areas, where the roads are bad, ancient *chivas* (a truck with a wooden carriage on the back with open rows of seats rather than a center isle) service smaller towns, picking up and dropping off passengers along the way. The fastest service is called Super Directo.

Costs

Bus travel is reasonably cheap in Colombia. Bus prices can be negotiable outside of peak holiday times although the agent often already quotes the discounted fare to ward off the competition – for this reason it's often cheaper to purchase tickets at the terminal than online. Try your luck with a polite '*Hay discuento?'* (Is there a discount?) or *'Cual es el minimo*?' (What is the minimum?), then work your way down the counters. You want to take the second-to-cheapest offer; there's usually something wrong with the cheapest bus.

When you get on a bus out on the road, you pay the fare to the *ayudante* (driver's sidekick). *Ayudantes* are usually honest, but it's worth knowing the actual fare beforehand to be sure you're not getting a gringo price.

Reservations

Outside of peak holiday periods (like Christmas and Easter), reservations are not needed. Just rock up to the bus station an hour before you want to leave and grab the first bus going. On some minor routes, where there are only a few departures a day, it's worth considering buying your ticket several hours before the scheduled departure.

A common trick, especially with smaller buses, is to say they only need one passenger to leave, then they lock your bag in the back and you end up waiting an hour for the bus to leave, watching other buses leave before you do. Don't get into the bus or pay until you see the driver start the engine and prepare to leave.

Car & Motorcycle

- Useful for traveling at your own pace, or for visiting regions with minimal public transport. Cars can be hired in major cities, but they're generally not cheap.
- What's more, the security situation remains dodgy in remote and rural parts of the country, increasing the risk of vehicle theft and pushing up insurance prices. Check government websites for warnings before setting out anywhere remote.
- In the cities, on the other hand, traffic is heavy, chaotic and mad. Driving 'manners' are wild and unpredictable. It takes some time to get used to the local style of driving. This goes without saying for motorcycle travel as well.
- Colombians drive on the right-hand side of the road and there are seatbelt requirements, so buckle up or risk a fine. The speed limit is 60km/h in the city and 80km/h on the highway. The nationwide highway police telephone number is 767.
- If you do plan to drive in Colombia, bring your driver's license. The driver's license from your country will normally do unless it's one of non-Latin-alphabet origin, in which case, you'll need an International Driving Permit as well.

Car Hire

Several international rental car companies, **Avis** (☎1-8000-12-2847; www.avis.com.co) and **Hertz** (www.hertz.com) for example, operate in Colombia. Expect to pay from COP$170,000 per day including Loss Damage Waiver, plus gasoline. You'll get better deals, as always, by booking online. Carefully check clauses pertaining to insurance and liability before you sign a rental contract. Pay close attention to any theft clause as it may load a large percentage of any loss onto the hirer. If you rent a car with tinted windows, you'll need a special document from the rental agency that police at checkpoints will ask for. Agencies don't generally volunteer the info so be sure to inquire.

Hitchhiking

- Hitchhiking in Colombia is uncommon and difficult. Given the complex internal situation, drivers don't want to take risks and simply don't stop on the road.
- Hitchhiking is never entirely safe, and we don't recommend it. Travelers who hitch should understand that they are taking a small but potentially serious risk.

Local Transportation

Bus

Almost every urban center of more than 100,000 inhabitants has a bus service, as do many smaller towns. The standard, speed and efficiency of local buses vary from place to place, but on the whole they are slow and crowded. City buses have a flat fare, so the distance of the ride makes no difference. You get on by the front door and pay the driver or the assistant. You never get a ticket.

In some cities or on some streets there are bus stops

(*paraderos* or *paradas*), while in most others you just wave down the bus. To let the driver know that you intend to get off you simply say, or shout, '*por aquí, por favor*' (here, please), '*en la esquina, por favor*' (at the corner, please) or '*la parada, por favor*' (at the coming bus stop, please).

There are lots of different types of local buses, ranging from old wrecks to modern air-conditioned vehicles. One common type is the *buseta* (small bus), a dominant means of urban transportation in cities such as Bogotá and Cartagena. The bus fare is usually somewhere between COP$800 and COP$2200, depending on the city and type of bus.

A bus or *buseta* trip, particularly in large cities such as Bogotá or Barranquilla, is not a smooth and silent ride but rather a sort of breathtaking adventure with a taste of local folklore thrown in. You'll have an opportunity to be saturated with loud tropical music, learn about the Colombian meaning of road rules, and observe your driver desperately trying to make his way through an ocean of vehicles.

COLECTIVO

Colectivo in Colombia can mean a midsized bus, a shared taxi, an overloaded jeep, and everything in between. They are most popular in short intercity hops of less than four hours. Because they are smaller than regular buses, they can travel quicker, and charge around 30% more as a result. They often depart only when full.

In some cities they depart from and arrive at the bus terminal, but in smaller towns they are usually found in the main square. The frequency of service varies greatly from place to place. At some places there may be a *colectivo* every five minutes, but elsewhere you can wait an hour or longer until the necessary number of passengers has been collected. If you're in a hurry you can pay for all the seats and the driver will depart immediately.

Mass Transit

Mass transit is growing increasingly popular in Colombia. Bogotá boasts the TransMilenio, and Cali and Bucaramanga have similar projects, called the Mio and Metrolínea, respectively. Medellín has its famous Metro, the only commuter rail line in the country. Pereira, too, offers the MegaBús system.

MAKING TRAVEL EASY: TOURS

A number of domestic agencies offer interesting specialty tours nationwide. Be on the lookout for operators affiliated with Acotur (www.acotur.co), Colombia's Association for Responsible Tourism. Some favorites:

Awake.travel (☎322-365-5135; www.awake.travel) Bogotá-based; offers good kayaking trips in the Amazon, on the Río Magdalena and other adventure opportunities.

Aventure Colombia (Map p48; ☎1-702-7069; www.aventurecolombia.com; Av Jiménez No 4-49, oficina 204; ⊙8am-5pm Mon-Sat) A good-time agency run by a charming French expat. It specializes in off-the-beaten-path destinations nationwide such as Punta Gallinas, indigenous homestays in the Sierra Nevada de Santa Marta, fascinating Caño Cristales in Meta, and adventure and ecotourism from the Caribbean coast to the Zona Cafetera and Parque Los Nevados to the Pacific coast.

Colombia 57 (☎6-886-8050; www.colombia57.com) This British-owned, Manizales-based tour operator specializes in custom-tailored tours.

Colombian Highlands (☎8-732-1201, 310-552-9079; www.colombianhighlands.com; Av Carrera 10 No 21-Finca Renacer) This highly regarded Villa de Leyva–based tour operator has gone national and now offers bespoke tours to Los Llanos, the Amazon (including Vapués) and La Guajira, among others.

Colombian Journeys (Map p54; ☎1-618-0027; www.colombianjourneys.com; Carrera 13 No 96- 67, edificio Akori, oficina 406-407) Bogotá-based company offering multilingual tours countrywide.

De Una Colombia Tours (Map p42; ☎1-368-1915; www.deunacolombia.com; Carrera 24 No 39B-25, oficina 501) This Dutch-owned company in Bogotá focuses on many far-flung destinations.

Mambe Travel (☎320-964-1846; www.mambe.org; Carrera 5 No 117-25; ⊙9am-5pm Mon-Fri, 10am-3pm Sat & Sun) Bogotá-based sustainable tourism NGO that digs deeper into six off-the-beaten-track destinations: the Amazon, the Chocó, La Guajira peninsula, Sierra Nevada de Santa Marta, Vichada and Caño Cristales.

Moto-Taxi

➡ Many smaller towns and some cities, especially in the north, use motorcycle-taxis, which are a quick way of getting around if you're on your own. These, however, are not the safest method of transportation and are even illegal in some places, including Cartagena (though no one seems to stop them).

➡ Helmet laws are enforced in built-up areas throughout the country – your driver will have an extra one for you although it may have a busted strap or other defect that renders it useless in a serious accident. Hopefully it won't be too sweaty from the previous client.

Taxi

Taxis are cheap, convenient and ubiquitous in the major cities and most midsized towns. In most big and medium-sized cities taxis have meters but in some parts of the Caribbean coast and in smaller towns prices are fixed according to the destination. While in theory these prices should be listed on a card hung from the passenger seat, this is in reality often missing, in which case you should agree a price before getting in.

When there are no displayed prices it's a case of haggle or pay extra, and many drivers are eager (especially in Cartagena) to see just how much they can take advantage of your naïveté. That said, a surprising proportion of taxi drivers are honest individuals; the better you speak Spanish, the more bargaining power you'll have, and the less likely you'll pay hyperinflated prices.

Although it is rare, there are occasionally deceptive, untrustworthy individuals masquerading as taxi drivers in fake taxis. Don't use taxis with a driver and somebody else inside. While taxi drivers sometimes have a friend along for company or for security reasons, such a situation may be unsafe for you; this is a common robbery tactic. If something doesn't seem right don't get in, hail another taxi. Better still call for a taxi, which costs a mere few hundred pesos extra.

Apps like like Tappsi (www.tappsi.co) and Easy Taxi (www.easytaxi.com) have drastically improved taxi security and should be used by all with a smartphone. They work in most of Colombia's major cities.

Taxi fares are always per taxi, never per number of passengers. Many taxis have somewhat flimsy doors – be kind, do not slam doors when getting into or out of the vehicle.

A taxi may also be chartered for longer distances. This is convenient if you want to visit places near major cities that are outside local transportation areas but too near to be covered by long-distance bus networks. You can also rent a taxi by the hour in the major cities – a good way to make your own impromptu tour.

Tricycle Moto-Taxi

Chinese-made *tuk-tuks* are becoming increasingly popular in smaller tourist towns. Moto-taxis seat three and have a covered roof, plus a tarp that can be lowered around the sides in case of rain. You'll see these in Barichara, Darién, Mompós, Santa Fe de Antioquia, the Desierto de la Tatacoa and some of the small towns on the Pacific coast.

Train

Colombia has a nationwide network of train track that is largely unused (or is overgrown or has been ripped up and sold off). The only train you're likely to board is **Turistren** (☎1-316-1300; www.turistren.com.co; Parque la Esperanza; round-trip adult/child COP$55,000/48,000), which runs on weekends from Bogotá to Zipaquirá.

Those visiting San Cipriano, just off the Cali–Buenaventura highway, can enjoy the novel sensation of traveling on a railroad handcart (trolley) powered by a motorcycle.

Language

Latin American Spanish pronunciation is easy, as most sounds have equivalents in English. Also, Spanish spelling is phonetically consistent, meaning that there's a clear and consistent relationship between what you see in writing and how it's pronounced. Read our coloured pronunciation guides as if they were English, and you'll be understood. Note that kh is a throaty sound (like the 'ch' in the Scottish *loch*), v and b are like a soft English 'v' (between a 'v' and a 'b'), and r is strongly rolled.

There are some variations in spoken Spanish across Latin America, the most notable being the pronunciation of the letters *ll* and *y* – depending on where you are on the continent, you'll hear them pronounced like the 'y' in 'yes', the 'lli' in 'million', the 's' in 'measure' or the 'sh' in 'shut', and in Colombia you'll also hear them pronounced like the 'dg' in 'judge'. In our pronunciation guides they are represented with y because you're most likely to hear them pronounced like the 'y' in 'yes'.

The stressed syllables are indicated with an acute accent in written Spanish (eg *días*) and with italics in our pronunciation guides.

The polite form is used in this chapter; where both polite and informal options are given, they are indicated by the abbreviations 'pol' and 'inf'. Where necessary, both masculine and feminine forms of words are included, separated by a slash and with the masculine form first, eg *perdido/a* (m/f).

BASICS

Hello.	*Hola.*	o·la
Goodbye.	*Adiós.*	a·*dyos*
How are you?	*¿Qué tal?*	ke tal
Fine, thanks.	*Bien, gracias.*	byen *gra*·syas
Excuse me.	*Perdón.*	per·*don*
Sorry.	*Lo siento.*	lo *syen*·to
Please.	*Por favor.*	por fa·*vor*
Thank you.	*Gracias.*	*gra*·syas
You're welcome.	*De nada.*	de *na*·da
Yes.	*Sí.*	see
No.	*No.*	no

My name is ...
Me llamo ... me *ya*·mo ...

What's your name?
¿Cómo se llama Usted? *ko*·mo se *ya*·ma oo·*ste* (pol)
¿Cómo te llamas? *ko*·mo te *ya*·mas (inf)

Do you speak English?
¿Habla inglés? *a*·bla een·*gles* (pol)
¿Hablas inglés? *a*·blas een·*gles* (inf)

I don't understand.
Yo no entiendo. yo no en·*tyen*·do

ACCOMMODATIONS

I'd like a ... room.	*Quisiera una habitación ...*	kee·*sye*·ra *oo*·na a·bee·ta·*syon* ...
single	*individual*	een·dee·vee·*dwal*
double	*doble*	*do*·ble

How much is it per night/person?
¿Cuánto cuesta por noche/persona? *kwan*·to *kwes*·ta por *no*·che/per·*so*·na

Does it include breakfast?
¿Incluye el desayuno? een·*kloo*·ye el de·sa·*yoo*·no

WANT MORE?

For in-depth language information and handy phrases, check out Lonely Planet's *Latin American Spanish Phrasebook*. You'll find it at **shop.lonelyplanet.com**.

KEY PATTERNS

To get by in Spanish, mix and match these simple patterns with words of your choice:

When's (the next flight)?
¿Cuándo sale (el próximo vuelo)? kwan·do sa·le (el prok·see·mo vwe·lo)

Where's (the station)?
¿Dónde está (la estación)? don·de es·ta (la es·ta·syon)

Where can I (buy a ticket)?
¿Dónde puedo (comprar un billete)? don·de pwe·do (kom·prar oon bee·ye·te)

Do you have (a map)?
¿Tiene (un mapa)? tye·ne (oon ma·pa)

Is there (a toilet)?
¿Hay (servicios)? ai (ser·vee·syos)

I'd like (a coffee).
Quisiera (un café). kee·sye·ra (oon ka·fe)

I'd like (to hire a car).
Quisiera (alquilar un coche). kee·sye·ra (al·kee·lar oon ko·che)

Can I (enter)?
¿Se puede (entrar)? se pwe·de (en·trar)

Could you please (help me)?
¿Puede (ayudarme), por favor? pwe·de (a·yoo·dar·me) por fa·vor

campsite	*terreno de cámping*	te·re·no de kam·peeng
cabin	*cabaña*	ka·ba·nya
hotel	*hotel*	o·tel
guesthouse	*pensión*	pen·syon
lodging/hostel	*hospedaje*	os·pe·da·khe
shelter	*refugio*	re·foo·khyo
youth hostel	*albergue juvenil*	al·ber·ge khoo·ve·neel
air-con	*aire acondicionado*	ai·re a·kon·dee·syo·na·do
bathroom	*baño*	ba·nyo
bed	*cama*	ka·ma
window	*ventana*	ven·ta·na

DIRECTIONS

Where's ...?
¿Dónde está ...? don·de es·ta ...

What's the address?
¿Cuál es la dirección? kwal es la dee·rek·syon

Could you please write it down?
¿Puede escribirlo, por favor? pwe·de es·kree·beer·lo por fa·vor

Can you show me (on the map)?
¿Me lo puede indicar (en el mapa)? me lo pwe·de een·dee·kar (en el ma·pa)

at the corner	*en la esquina*	en la es·kee·na
at the traffic lights	*en el semáforo*	en el se·ma·fo·ro
behind ...	*detrás de ...*	de·tras de ...
far	*lejos*	le·khos
in front of ...	*enfrente de ...*	en·fren·te de ...
left	*izquierda*	ees·kyer·da
near	*cerca*	ser·ka
next to ...	*al lado de ...*	al la·do de ...
opposite ...	*frente a ...*	fren·te a ...
right	*derecha*	de·re·cha
straight ahead	*todo recto*	to·do rek·to

EATING & DRINKING

Can I see the menu, please?
¿Puedo ver el menú, por favor? pwe·do ver el me·noo por fa·vor

What would you recommend?
¿Qué recomienda? ke re·ko·myen·da

Do you have vegetarian food?
¿Tienen comida vegetariana? tye·nen ko·mee·da ve·khe·ta·rya·na

I don't eat (red meat).
No como (carne roja). no ko·mo (kar·ne ro·kha)

That was delicious!
¡Estaba buenísimo! es·ta·ba bwe·nee·see·mo

Cheers!
¡Salud! sa·loo

The bill, please.
La cuenta, por favor. la kwen·ta por fa·vor

I'd like a table for ...	*Quisiera una mesa para ...*	kee·sye·ra oo·na me·sa pa·ra ...
(eight) o'clock	*las (ocho)*	las (o·cho)
(two) people	*(dos) personas*	(dos) per·so·nas

Key Words

appetisers	*aperitivos*	a·pe·ree·tee·vos
bottle	*botella*	bo·te·ya
bowl	*bol*	bol
breakfast	*desayuno*	de·sa·yoo·no
children's menu	*menú infantil*	me·noo een·fan·teel
(too) cold	*(muy) frío*	(mooy) free·o
dinner	*cena*	se·na

food	*comida*	ko·*mee*·da
fork	*tenedor*	te·ne·*dor*
glass	*vaso*	*va*·so
highchair	*trona*	*tro*·na
hot (warm)	*caliente*	kal·*yen*·te
knife	*cuchillo*	koo·*chee*·yo
lunch	*almuerzo*	al·*mwer*·so
main course	*plato principal*	*pla*·to preen·see·*pal*
plate	*plato*	*pla*·to
restaurant	*restaurante*	res·tow·*ran*·te
spoon	*cuchara*	koo·*cha*·ra
with	*con*	kon
without	*sin*	seen

Meat & Fish

beef	*carne de vaca*	*kar*·ne de *va*·ka
chicken	*pollo*	*po*·yo
duck	*pato*	*pa*·to
fish	*pescado*	pes·*ka*·do
lamb	*cordero*	kor·*de*·ro
pork	*cerdo*	*ser*·do
turkey	*pavo*	*pa*·vo
veal	*ternera*	ter·*ne*·ra

Fruit & Vegetables

apple	*manzana*	man·*sa*·na
apricot	*damasco*	da·*mas*·ko
artichoke	*alcaucil*	al·*kow*·seel
asparagus	*espárragos*	es·*pa*·ra·gos
banana	*banana*	ba·*na*·na
beans	*chauchas*	*chow*·chas
beetroot	*remolacha*	re·mo·*la*·cha
cabbage	*repollo*	re·*po*·yo
carrot	*zanahoria*	sa·na·*o*·rya
celery	*apio*	*a*·pyo
cherry	*cereza*	se·*re*·sa
corn	*choclo*	*cho*·klo
cucumber	*pepino*	pe·*pee*·no
fruit	*fruta*	*froo*·ta
grape	*uvas*	*oo*·vas
lemon	*limón*	lee·*mon*
lentils	*lentejas*	len·*te*·khas
lettuce	*lechuga*	le·*choo*·ga
mushroom	*champiñón*	cham·pee·*nyon*
nuts	*nueces*	*nwe*·ses
onion	*cebolla*	se·*bo*·ya
orange	*naranja*	na·*ran*·kha
peach	*melocotón*	me·lo·ko·*ton*
peas	*arvejas*	ar·*ve*·khas
(red/green) pepper	*pimiento (rojo/verde)*	pee·*myen*·to (*ro*·kho/*ver*·de)
pineapple	*ananá*	a·na·*na*
plum	*ciruela*	seer·*we*·la
potato	*papa*	*pa*·pa
pumpkin	*zapallo*	sa·*pa*·yo
spinach	*espinacas*	es·pee·*na*·kas
strawberry	*frutilla*	froo·*tee*·ya
tomato	*tomate*	to·*ma*·te
vegetable	*verdura*	ver·*doo*·ra
watermelon	*sandía*	san·*dee*·a

SIGNS

Abierto	Open
Cerrado	Closed
Entrada	Entrance
Hombres/Varones	Men
Mujeres/Damas	Women
Prohibido	Prohibited
Salida	Exit
Servicios/Baños	Toilets

Other

bread	*pan*	pan
butter	*manteca*	man·*te*·ka
cheese	*queso*	*ke*·so
egg	*huevo*	*we*·vo
honey	*miel*	myel
jam	*mermelada*	mer·me·*la*·da
oil	*aceite*	a·*sey*·te
pasta	*pasta*	*pas*·ta
pepper	*pimienta*	pee·*myen*·ta
rice	*arroz*	a·*ros*
salt	*sal*	sal
sugar	*azúcar*	a·*soo*·kar
vinegar	*vinagre*	vee·*na*·gre

Drinks

beer	*cerveza*	ser·*ve*·sa
coffee	*café*	ka·*fe*
(orange) juice	*jugo (de naranja)*	*khoo*·go (de na·*ran*·kha)
milk	*leche*	*le*·che
tea	*té*	te

(mineral) water	*agua (mineral)*	a·gwa (mee·ne·*ral*)
(red/white) wine	*vino (tinto/ blanco)*	*vee*·no (*teen*·to/ *blan*·ko)

EMERGENCIES

Help!	*¡Socorro!*	so·*ko*·ro
Go away!	*¡Vete!*	*ve*·te

Call ...!	*¡Llame a ...!*	*ya*·me a ...
a doctor	*un médico*	oon *me*·dee·ko
the police	*la policía*	la po·lee·*see*·a

I'm lost.
Estoy perdido/a. es·*toy* per·*dee*·do/a **(m/f)**

I'm ill.
Estoy enfermo/a. es·*toy* en·*fer*·mo/a **(m/f)**

It hurts here.
Me duele aquí. me *dwe*·le a·*kee*

I'm allergic to (antibiotics).
Soy alérgico/a a (los antibióticos). soy a·*ler*·khee·ko/a a (los an·tee·*byo*·tee·kos) **(m/f)**

Where are the toilets?
¿Dónde están los baños? *don*·de es·*tan* los *ba*·nyos

SHOPPING & SERVICES

I'd like to buy ...
Quisiera comprar ... kee·*sye*·ra kom·*prar* ...

I'm just looking.
Sólo estoy mirando. *so*·lo es·*toy* mee·*ran*·do

Can I look at it?
¿Puedo verlo? *pwe*·do *ver*·lo

I don't like it.
No me gusta. no me *goos*·ta

How much is it?
¿Cuánto cuesta? *kwan*·to *kwes*·ta

That's too expensive.
Es muy caro. es mooy *ka*·ro

Can you lower the price?
¿Podría bajar un poco el precio? po·*dree*·a ba·*khar* oon *po*·ko el *pre*·syo

There's a mistake in the bill.
Hay un error en la cuenta. ai oon e·*ror* en la *kwen*·ta

QUESTION WORDS

How?	*¿Cómo?*	*ko*·mo
What?	*¿Qué?*	ke
When?	*¿Cuándo?*	*kwan*·do
Where?	*¿Dónde?*	*don*·de
Who?	*¿Quién?*	kyen
Why?	*¿Por qué?*	por ke

ATM	*cajero automático*	ka·*khe*·ro ow·to·*ma*·tee·ko
credit card	*tarjeta de crédito*	tar·*khe*·ta de *kre*·dee·to
internet cafe	*cibercafé*	see·ber·ka·*fe*
market	*mercado*	mer·*ka*·do
post office	*correos*	ko·*re*·os
tourist office	*oficina de turismo*	o·fee·*see*·na de too·*rees*·mo

TIME & DATES

What time is it?	*¿Qué hora es?*	ke *o*·ra es
It's (10) o'clock.	*Son (las diez).*	son (las dyes)

morning	*mañana*	ma·*nya*·na
afternoon	*tarde*	*tar*·de
evening	*noche*	*no*·che
yesterday	*ayer*	a·*yer*
today	*hoy*	oy
tomorrow	*mañana*	ma·*nya*·na

Monday	*lunes*	*loo*·nes
Tuesday	*martes*	*mar*·tes
Wednesday	*miércoles*	*myer*·ko·les
Thursday	*jueves*	*khwe*·ves
Friday	*viernes*	*vyer*·nes
Saturday	*sábado*	*sa*·ba·do
Sunday	*domingo*	do·*meen*·go

January	*enero*	e·*ne*·ro
February	*febrero*	fe·*bre*·ro
March	*marzo*	*mar*·so
April	*abril*	a·*breel*
May	*mayo*	*ma*·yo
June	*junio*	*khoon*·yo
July	*julio*	*khool*·yo
August	*agosto*	a·*gos*·to
September	*septiembre*	sep·*tyem*·bre
October	*octubre*	ok·*too*·bre
November	*noviembre*	no·*vyem*·bre
December	*diciembre*	dee·*syem*·bre

TRANSPORTATION

boat	*barco*	*bar*·ko
bus	*autobús*	ow·to·*boos*
(small) bus/van	*buseta*	boo·*se*·ta
(traditional) bus	*chiva*	*chee*·va
plane	*avión*	a·*vyon*
(shared) taxi	*colectivo*	ko·lek·*tee*·vo
train	*tren*	tren

first	*primero*	pree·*me*·ro
last	*último*	*ool*·tee·mo
next	*próximo*	*prok*·see·mo
A ... ticket, please.	*Un boleto de ..., por favor.*	oon bo·*le*·to de ... por fa·*vor*
1st-class	*primera clase*	pree·*me*·ra *kla*·se
2nd-class	*segunda clase*	se·*goon*·da *kla*·se
one-way	*ida*	*ee*·da
return	*ida y vuelta*	*ee*·da ee *vwel*·ta

I want to go to ...
Quisiera ir a ... kee·*sye*·ra eer a ...

Does it stop at ...?
¿Para en ...? *pa*·ra en ...

What stop is this?
¿Cuál es esta parada? kwal es *es*·ta pa·*ra*·da

What time does it arrive/leave?
¿A qué hora llega/sale? a ke o·ra *ye*·ga/*sa*·le

Please tell me when we get to ...
¿Puede avisarme cuando lleguemos a ...? *pwe*·de a·vee·*sar*·me *kwan*·do ye·*ge*·mos a ...

I want to get off here.
Quiero bajarme aquí. *kye*·ro ba·*khar*·me a·*kee*

airport	*aeropuerto*	a·e·ro·*pwer*·to
aisle seat	*asiento de pasillo*	a·*syen*·to de pa·*see*·yo
bus station	*terminal terrestre*	ter·mee·*nal*/ te·*res*·tre
bus stop	*paradero/ parada*	pa·ra·*de*·ro/ pa·*ra*·da
cancelled	*cancelado*	kan·se·*la*·do
delayed	*retrasado*	re·tra·*sa*·do
platform	*plataforma*	pla·ta·*for*·ma
ticket office	*taquilla*	ta·*kee*·ya
timetable	*horario*	o·*ra*·ryo
train station	*estación de trenes*	es·ta·*syon* de *tre*·nes
window seat	*asiento junto a la ventana*	a·*syen*·to *khoon*·to a la ven·*ta*·na

I'd like to hire a ...	*Quisiera alquilar ...*	kee·*sye*·ra al·kee·*lar* ...
4WD	*un todo-terreno*	oon to·do·te·*re*·no
bicycle	*una bicicleta*	oo·na bee·see·*kle*·ta
car	*un coche*	oon *ko*·che
motorcycle	*una moto*	oo·na *mo*·to

NUMBERS

1	*uno*	*oo*·no
2	*dos*	dos
3	*tres*	tres
4	*cuatro*	*kwa*·tro
5	*cinco*	*seen*·ko
6	*seis*	seys
7	*siete*	*sye*·te
8	*ocho*	*o*·cho
9	*nueve*	*nwe*·ve
10	*diez*	dyes
20	*veinte*	*veyn*·te
30	*treinta*	*treyn*·ta
40	*cuarenta*	kwa·*ren*·ta
50	*cincuenta*	seen·*kwen*·ta
60	*sesenta*	se·*sen*·ta
70	*setenta*	se·*ten*·ta
80	*ochenta*	o·*chen*·ta
90	*noventa*	no·*ven*·ta
100	*cien*	syen
1000	*mil*	meel

child seat	*asiento de seguridad para niños*	a·*syen*·to de se·goo·ree·*da* *pa*·ra *nee*·nyos
diesel	*petróleo*	pet·*ro*·le·o
helmet	*casco*	*kas*·ko
hitchhike	*hacer botella*	a·ser bo·*te*·ya
mechanic	*mecánico*	me·*ka*·nee·ko
petrol/gas	*gasolina*	ga·so·*lee*·na
service station	*gasolinera*	ga·so·lee·*ne*·ra
truck	*camión*	ka·*myon*

Is this the road to ...?
¿Se va a ... por esta carretera? se va a ... por *es*·ta ka·re·*te*·ra

(How long) Can I park here?
¿(Cuánto tiempo) Puedo aparcar aquí? (*kwan*·to *tyem*·po) *pwe*·do a·par·*kar* a·*kee*

The car has broken down (at ...).
El coche se ha averiado (en ...). el *ko*·che se a a·ve·*rya*·do (en ...)

I had an accident.
He tenido un accidente. e te·*nee*·do oon ak·see·*den*·te

I've run out of petrol.
Me he quedado sin gasolina. me e ke·*da*·do seen ga·so·*lee*·na

I have a flat tyre.
Se me pinchó une rueda. se me peen·*cho* *oo*·na *rwe*·da

GLOSSARY

Spanish speakers wanting a complete reference to Colombian slang should pick up a copy of the *Diccionario de Colombiano Actual* (2005) by Francisco Celis Albán.

asadero – place serving roasted or grilled meats

AUC – Autodefensas Unidas de Colombia (United Self-Defense Forces of Colombia); a loose alliance of paramilitary squads known as *autodefensas*

autodefensas – right-wing squads created to defend large landowners against guerrillas, also called *paramilitares* or just *paras;* see also *AUC*

bogotano/a – person from Bogotá

buseta – small bus/van that is a popular means of city transport

cabaña – cabin, or simple shelter; usually found on beaches or up in the mountains

caleño/a – person from Cali

campesino/a – rural dweller, usually of modest economic means; peasant

casa de cambio – currency-exchange office

chalupa – small passenger boat powered by an outboard motor

chinchorro – hammock woven of cotton threads or palm fiber like a fishing net, typical of many indigenous groups; the best known are the decorative cotton hammocks of the Guajiros

chiva – traditional bus with its body made of timber and painted with colorful patterns; still widely used in the countryside

colectivo – shared taxi or minibus; a popular means of public transport

comida corriente – fast food; set lunch

costeño/a – inhabitant of the Caribbean coast

DAS – Departamento Administrativo de Seguridad; the security police, responsible for immigration (dissolved in 2011)

ELN – Ejército de Liberación Nacional (National Liberation Army); the second-largest guerrilla group after the FARC

FARC – Fuerzas Armadas Revolucionarias de Colombia; the largest guerrilla group in the country

finca – farm; anything from a country house with a small garden to a huge country estate

frailejón – *espeletia*, a species of plant; a yellow-flowering, perennial shrub that only grows at altitudes above 3000m, typical of the *páramo*

gringo/a – any white male/female foreigner; sometimes, (but not always) used in a derogatory sense

guadua – the largest variety of the bamboo family, common in many regions of moderate climate

hacienda – country estate

hospedaje – lodging (in general); sometimes, a cheap hotel or hostel

indígena – indigenous; also indigenous person

IVA – *impuesto de valor agregado*, a value-added tax (VAT)

merengue – musical rhythm originating in the Dominican Republic, today widespread throughout the Caribbean and beyond

meseta – plateau

mestizo/a – person of mixed European-indigenous blood

mirador – lookout, viewpoint

muelle – pier, wharf

mulato/a – mulatto; a person of mixed European-African blood

nevado – snowcapped mountain peak

paisa – a person from Antioquia

paradero – bus stop; in some areas called *parada*

páramo – high-mountain plains, at an elevation of between 3500m and 4500m, typical of Colombia, Venezuela and Ecuador

piso – story, floor

poporo – a vessel made from a small gourd, used by the Arhuacos and other indigenous groups to carry lime; while chewing coca leaves, *indígenas* add lime to help release the alkaloid from the leaves; a sacred ritual of the indigenous people of the Caribbean coast

puente – literally 'bridge'; also means a three-day-long weekend (including Monday)

refugio – rustic shelter in a remote area, mostly in the mountains

reggaetón – a mix of hip-hop and Latin rhythms, it has a distinctly urban flavor with fast-paced danceable beats

salsa – type of Caribbean dance music of Cuban origin, very popular in Colombia

salsateca – disco playing salsa music

Semana Santa – Holy Week, the week before Easter Sunday

tagua – hard ivory-colored nut of a species of palm; used in handicrafts, mainly on the Pacific coast

tejo – traditional game, popular mainly in the Andean region; played with a heavy metal disk, which is thrown to make a *mecha* (a sort of petard) explode

Telecom – the state telephone company

vallenato – music typical of the Caribbean region, based on the accordion; it's now widespread in Colombia

Behind the Scenes

SEND US YOUR FEEDBACK

We love to hear from travelers – your comments keep us on our toes and help make our books better. Our well-traveled team reads every word on what you loved or loathed about this book. Although we cannot reply individually to your submissions, we always guarantee that your feedback goes straight to the appropriate authors, in time for the next edition. Each person who sends us information is thanked in the next edition – the most useful submissions are rewarded with a selection of digital PDF chapters.

Visit **lonelyplanet.com/contact** to submit your updates and suggestions or to ask for help. Our award-winning website also features inspirational travel stories, news and discussions.

Note: We may edit, reproduce and incorporate your comments in Lonely Planet products such as guidebooks, websites and digital products, so let us know if you don't want your comments reproduced or your name acknowledged. For a copy of our privacy policy visit lonelyplanet.com/privacy.

WRITER THANKS

Alex Egerton

On the ground big thanks go out to Oscar 'El Chofer' Gilede, Carito, Jose, Rodrigo, Adriaan Alsema, Richard, Jorge, Nicolas Solorzano, Libertad, Jose Ivan, Alexa Juliana, Jose N, Melissa Montoya, Wilson, Tyler, Paty, Laura Cahnspeyer and all the generous Colombians that lent a hand with logistics. On the home front, thanks to Olga and Nick for their patience.

Anna Kaminski

Huge thanks to Bailey for entrusting me with half of this beguiling country, to my fellow scribe Brendan and to everyone who's helped me along the way. In particular: Jose and the Graffiti Tour folks in Medellin; Tony in Popayán, Soledad; and the mountain biking folk of Salento; Kolibri Hostel in Pereira; Gloria in Guatape; Finca El Maco and Pacho in San Agustín; plus the driver who successfully navigated the Trampolin de la Muerte.

Tom Masters

Thanks to the cast of characters who always make visiting Colombia so fun, but particularly this time to Andrés and Andrea in La Macarena, Ewa at Caño Cristales, Sandra Rodil in Santa Marta, David Salas at Expotur, Alejandro Dorante Zetans in Cartagena, Richard McColl in Mompós, Steeve Degroote at Aventure Colombia, fellow Colombia writers Kevin Raub and Alex Egerton and intrepid mother Rosemary Masters for her good company at various stages of research.

Kevin Raub

Thanks to my wife, Adriana Schmidt Raub. MaSovaida Morgan and my partners in crime, Tom Masters and Alex Egerton. On the road, Laura Cahnspeyer, Dipak Nayer, Camilo Rojas, Rodrigo Atuesta, Helena Davilá, German Escobar, Bogota&Beyond, Rodrigo Arais, Edgardo Areizaga, Diego Calderon and Lina Baldion.

Brendan Sainsbury

Muchas gracias to all the skilled bus drivers, helpful tourist information staff, generous hotel owners, expert *arepa* makers, and innocent passersby who helped me, unwittingly or otherwise, during my research trip. Special thanks to my wife, Liz for joining me on the road in Cartagena and Santa Marta.

ACKNOWLEDGEMENTS

Climate map data adapted from Peel MC, Finlayson BL & McMahon TA (2007) 'Updated World Map of the Köppen-Geiger Climate Classification', Hydrology and Earth System Sciences, 11, 163344.

Cover photograph: Fruit seller in Cartagena, andresr/Getty Images ©

THIS BOOK

This 9th edition of Lonely Planet's *Colombia* guidebook was researched and written by Jade Bremner, Alex Egerton, Anna Kaminski, Tom Masters, Kevin Raub and Brendan Sainsbury. The previous edition was also researched and written by Alex, Tom and Kevin and curated by Jade. This guidebook was produced by the following:

Senior Product Editor
Daniel Bolger

Product Editor
Amy Lynch

Cartographer
Corey Hutchison

Book Designer
Hannah Blackie

Assisting Editors Michelle Bennett, Katie Connolly, Lucy Cowie, Rebecca Dyer, Emma Gibbs, Jodie Martire, Lou McGregor, Monique Perrin, Benjamin Spier, Gabrielle Stefanos, Maja Vatric

Cover Researcher
Ania Bartoszek

Thanks to
Ronan Abayawickrema, Werner Bruyninx, Melanie Dankel, Michelle Gallant, Karen Henderson, Sandie Kestell, Sharon L Stern, Amy Lysen, Kirsten Rawlings, Raul R Rodriguez

Index

A

abseiling 30
accessible travel 327
accommodations 319-20, *see also individual locations*
  language 336-7
activities, 20-1, *see also individual activities*
air travel 19, 329-30, 331
Almond Bay 177
Amazon Basin 281-92, **282**
  climate 280
  highlights 282
  travel seasons 280
Amazon River 278
amusement parks 108
Andrés Carne de Res 64
animals 310-12, *see also individual animals*
Aracataca 144
archaeological sites
Alto de las Piedras 245
  Alto de los Ídolos 244
  El Fósil 90-1
  El Tablón, La Chaquira, La Pelota & El Purutal 245
  Nueva Tolima Cave Paintings 276
  Parque Arqueológico 244
  San Agustín 243-8
  Tierradentro 248-51, **249**
area codes 327
Armenia 219-20
Arrecifes 149
art galleries, *see* museums & galleries
arts 306-8, *see also individual arts*
ATMs 324
ayahuasca 317-18

B

Bahía Aguadulce 177
Bahía Manzanillo 177
Bahía Solano 260-3
Bahía Suroeste 177
Balneario Hurtado 160
Balneario La Mina 159
Barichara 104-7, **105**
Barranquilla 143
baseball 3075
Basílica de la Virgen de Chiquinquirá 91
bathrooms 327
beaches 14
  Almond Bay 177
  Bahía Aguadulce 177
  Bahía Manzanillo 177
  Bahía Suroeste 177
  Cabo San Juan del Guía 14, 148, **14**
  Cañaveral 149
  Cayo El Acuario 170
  Johnny Cay Natural Regional Park 170
  La Arenilla 149
  La Piscinita 170
  Playa Almejal 264
  Playa Blanca (Cartagena region) 138
  Playa Blanca (Tolú) 164
  Playa Cristal 14, 148-9, **14**
  Playa del Pilón 158
  Playa Mecana 264
  Playa Olímpica 266
  Playa Taroa 159
  Punta Bolívar 164
Belalcázar, Sebastián de 238, 295
Betancur, Belisario 299
Biblioteca Luis Ángel Arango 44
bicycle travel, *see* cycling
birds 310
birdwatching 31, 145, 265
boat travel 330-1, 332, *see also* canoeing, kayaking, white-water rafting
boat trips
  Coquí 268
  Guatapé 199
  Islas del Rosario 136-7
  Jurubidá 268
  Nuquí 266
  San Andrés 170-2
Bogotá 10-11, 39-79, **40**, **42**, **48-9**, **54-5**, **60**, **10-11**, **39-40**
  accommodations 56-9
  activities 50-1
  children, travel with 47
  climate 38
  courses 51
  drinking & nightlife 66-70
  entertainment 70-2
  festivals & events 53-6
  food 59-66
  highlights 40
  history 41
  itineraries 45
  LGBT travelers 68
  orientation 72-3
  planning 45
  Plaza de Bolívar 41
  safe travel 73
  shopping 72
  sights 41-50
  tourist information 73-4
  tours 51-3
  travel seasons 38
  travel to/from 74-5
  travel within 75-7
Bolívar, Simón 41, 46, 83, 87, 109, 122, 125, 139, 140, 161, 162, 296-7, 297
books 307, 312
border crossings 330
  Brazil 287, 330
  Ecuador 247, 256, 330
  Panama 166
  Peru 288, 330
  Venezuela 115, 330
Botero, Fernando 42-3, 190, 310
Boyacá 81-2, 83-100, **82**
  climate 80
  highlights 82
  history 83
  travel seasons 80
Bucaramanga 108-12, **110**
budget 18, 19, 319, 322
bullfighting 305
bus travel 332-3, 333-4
business hours 19, 325

C

Cabalonga 263
Cabo de la Vela 157-9
Cabo San Juan del Guía 14, 148, **14**
Cali 227-35, **228**, **230**
  accommodation 232-3
  activities 229-31
  climate 226
  courses 231
  drinking & nightlife 233-4
  entertainment 234-5
  festivals & events 231-2
  food 233
  highlights 228
  shopping 235
  sights 229
  tourist information 235
  travel seasons 226
  travel within 235
Cañaveral 149
Caño Cristales 13, 277-9, **13**
canoeing 30
Cañon del Chicamocha 108
canopying 30
canyoning 30
  Jardin 204
  Medellin 189
  Villa de Leyva 85
Capitolio Nacional 44
Capurganá 165-7
car travel 333
Caribbean Coast 119-67, **120-1**
  climate 118

Map Pages **000**
Photo Pages **000**

highlights 120-1
travel seasons 118
Carnaval de Barranquilla 20, 143
Carnaval de Blancos y Negros 20
Cartagena 12, 122-36, **124-5**, **12**
accommodation 129-31
activities 128
courses 129
drinking & nightlife 133-4
entertainment 134
festivals & events 129
food 131-3
history 122-3
orientation 134
shopping 134
sights 123-8
tourist information 134-5
travel to/from 135-6
travel within 136
Casa de Don Juan de Vargas 86
Casa de las Cajas Reales 115
Casa de Nariño 43
Casa del Fundador Suárez Rendón 86
Casona La Guaca 85
Castillo de San Felipe de Barajas 127-8
cathedrals, *see* churches & cathedrals
Cauca 238-52
caves
Caverna de los Guácharos 205
Cueva de la Vaca 100
Cueva del Esplendor 203-4
Cayo Cangrejo 177
cell phones 18, 327
Cerro Cristo Rey 203
Cerro de las Tres Cruces 229
Cerro de Monserrate 52
Cerro Nutibara 187
children, travel with 47, 320
Chiquinquirá 91
chivas 332
Chocó 260-70, **258**
churches & cathedrals
Basílica de la Virgen de Chiquinquirá 91
Basilica Menor de la Inmaculada Concepción 203
Basílica Menor de Nuestra Señora de Monguí 93
Capilla de las Nieves 112
Catedral (Cartagena) 127
Catedral de la Inmaculada Concepción 104
Catedral del Señor de los Milagros 112
Catedral Primada 44-5
Cerro de Monserrate 52
Convento de la Popa 128
Convento del Santo Ecce Homo 90
Iglesia de Inmaculada Concepción 207
Iglesia de la Ermita 229
Iglesia de San Francisco (Bogotá) 46, 238
Iglesia de San Francisco (Popayán) 238
Iglesia de Santa Bárbara (Mompós) 162
Iglesia de Santa Bárbara (Santa Fe de Antioquia) 201
Iglesia de Santo Domingo 125-6
Iglesia de Santo Toribio de Mogrovejo 127
Iglesia La Ermita 238
Iglesia Parroquial 85
Museo Santa Clara 43
Nuestra Señora de la Candelaria 97
Salt Cathedral 58
Santa Lucía Iglesia 107
Santuario de Las Lajas 257
Ciclovía 50-1
Ciudad de Piedra 276
Ciudad Perdida 16, 152-6, **16**
climate 18, 23-4
climate change 329
climbing 51
cocaine 300-1, 302, 317, 318, 323
Coconuco 243
coffee 17, 69, 209, 298, **17**
coffee plantations 17, **17**
Finca Don Manolo 215
Finca La Victoria 145
Hacienda Guayabal 210-11
Hacienda Venecia 211
Recuca 221
colectivo 334
Colina Iluminada 224
consulates 321-2
convents, *see* monasteries & convents
Coquí 269
costs 18, 19, 319, 322
courses
dancing 231
language 51, 102, 129, 190, 231, 323
crab migration 179, 310
credit cards 324-5
crocodiles 312
culture 304-5
cumbia 306
currency 18, *see also* money
customs regulations 320
cycling 9, 331, *see also* mountain biking
Bogotá 50, 52
Cartagena 128-9
Medellín 190
Villa de Leyva 85, 86

D
dance 15, *see also* salsa
dangers 316-18
Dapa 231
Darién 237-8
departure tax 330
Desierto de la Tatacoa 251-2, **226**
disabilities, travelers with 327
diving & snorkeling 29
Bahía Solano 260
Cali 229
Capurganá 165-6
Cartagena 128
Providencia 175, 177-9
San Andrés 172, 175
Sapzurro 165-6
Taganga 147
drinks
coffee 17, 69, 209, 298, **17**
language 338-9
driving, *see* car travel
drug cartels 300-1
drugs 300-1, 317-18

E
El Cerro de Moravia 187
El Cocuy 94-6
El Dorado 296
El Hayal 85
El Rodadero 139
El Valle 264-5
electricity 320-1
embassies 321-2
emeralds 71, 313
emergencies 19
language 339
endangered species 312
entry formalities 329
environmental issues 314
Escobar, Pablo 191
Estación Septiembre 264
ethnic groups 294, 307
Guambiano 242
Tayrona 153
events, *see* festivals & events
exchange rates 19

F
FARC 41, 296, 299, 301-3, 316-17
fauna 310-12
Feria de las Flores 24, 190, **2**
Festival de Música del Pacífico Petronio Álvarez 24, 231
festivals & events, 20-1
Alimentarte 53
Carnaval de Barranquilla 20, 143
Carnaval de Blancos y Negros 20
Crab Migration 179, 310
Expoartesanías 56
Feria de las Flores 21, 190, **2**
Feria de Manizales 208
Festival de Cine de Bogotá 53
Festival de Jazz 53
Festival de la Leyenda Vallenata 160
Festival de las Cometas 86
Festival de Luces 87
Festival de Música del Pacífico Petronio Álvarez 21, 231
Festival de Verano 53
Festival Iberoamericano de Teatro de Bogotá 20, 53
Festival Internacional de Jazz 190
Festival Internacional de Tango 190
Festival Internacional de Teatro 21, 208
Festival Mundial de Salsa 15, 21, 232
Festival of the Virgen Morenita 97
Fiesta de los Diablitos 201
Fiesta de Nuestra Señora de la Candelaria 129
Hay Festival Cartagena 129

Hip Hop al Parque 53
Mompox Jazz Festival 162
Providencia Cultural Festival 179
Rock al Parque 21, 53
Salsa al Parque 56
Torneo Internacional del Joropo 274
Filandia 224-5
flora 312
food 107, 322, *see also individual locations*
language 337-9
football 305
Fuerzas Armadas Revolucionarias de Colombia, *see* FARC

G
Gabriel García Márquez 296
gardens, *see* parks & gardens
Gaviotas 276
gay travelers, *see* LGBT travelers
geography 309
geology 309
Girón 112
glossary 341
Golfo de Urabá 165
government travel advice 323
Guachalito 268-70
Guadalupe 112-14
Guane 107-8
Guatapé 199-200
guerillas 301, 316-17
Güicán 96-8

H
Hacienda Guayabal 210-11
Hacienda Venecia 211
Haynes Cay 170
health 322-3
hiking 28-9
Bogotá 51
Cali 231
Capurganá 165-6
Ciudad Perdida 153-6
Guadalupe 113-14
Monguí 93-4
Pance 236
Providencia 179
Salento 222
Termales 270
Valle de Cocora 225
Villa de Leyva 85
historic buildings
Capitolio Nacional 44
Casa de Don Juan de Vargas 86
Casa de las Cajas Reales 115
Casa de Nariño 43
Casa del Fundador Suárez Rendón 86
Palacio de la Cultura Rafael Uribe Uribe 189
Palacio San Carlos 162
history 294-303
colonial era 295
drugs 300-1
FARC 41, 296, 299, 301-3, 316-17
gold 296
independence 296
Plan Colombia 302
Spanish Conquest 294-5
hitchhiking 333
holidays 326-7
horseback riding 30-2
Hoyo Soplador 170
Huila 238-52
hyperbaric chambers 29

I
indigenous peoples 305
insurance 323
international transfers 325
internet access 323
internet resources 19, 325
Ipiales 256
Isla Malpelo 271
Islas de San Bernardo 164-5
Islas del Rosario 136-8, **137**, **118**
itineraries 22-5
Bogotá to Bogotá 22, **22**
Complete Caribbean 24, **24**
See (Almost) Everything Route 23, **23**
Pacific Coast 25, **25**
Zona Cafetera 25, **25**

J
Jardín 203-5
Johnny Cay Natural Regional Park 170
joropo 306
Joví 269
Jurubidá 267-8

K
kayaking 30
Cartagena 128
Reserva Natural Palmarí 291
San Agustín 245
San Gil 102
kitesurfing 33
Cartagena 128
Darién 237
Lago Calima 237

L
La Comuna 13 186-7
La Guajira Peninsula 155-9
La Loma 170
Lago Calima 236-7
Lago de Tota 93
Lago Tarapoto 290
Laguna de Guatavita 78
Laguna de la Cocha 255-6
Laguna del Otún 213-15
Laguna Verde 257
language 18, 336-41
language 51, 102, 129, 190, 231, 323
legal matters 323
Leticia 282-9, **284**
LGBT travelers 322
Bogotá 68
literature 307
local transportation 333-5
Los Llanos 273-9, **275**
climate 272
highlights 275
travel seasons 272

M
Macondo 144
Manizales 205-10, **206**
maps 324
marijuana 317, 323
markets
Bogota 72
Cartagena 128
Villa de Leyva 89
Márquez, Gabriel García 307
measures 325
Medellín 183-225, 186-99, **184-5**, **188**, **192**, **196**, **182**
accommodations 190-3
activities 189
climate 182
courses 190
drinking & nightlife 195
entertainment 195-7
festivals & events 190
food 193-5
highlights 184-5
history 186
internet resources 195
shopping 197
sights 186-9
tours 190
toursit information 197-8
travel seasons 182
travel to/from 198
travel within 198-9
Mesa de Los Santos 113
Minca 144-7
Mirador Nai-pata 290
Mirador Torre Colpatria 46-71
mobile phones 18, 327
Mocoa 247
Mompós 160-3, **161**
monasteries & convents
Convento & Iglesia de San Pedro Claver 123-5, **2**
Convento de la Popa 128-53
Convento de los Franciscanos 93
money 18, 19, 324-5
money changers 325
Monguí 92-4
monkeys 312
monuments
Cristo Rey 229
Monumento a Los Colonizadores 207
motorcycle travel 333
moto-taxis 335
mountain biking 32-3
Minca 145
Salento 222
San Gil 102
museums & galleries
Casa Colonial 114-15
Casa de Moneda 44
Casa de Rafael Núñez 127
Casa Museo de Luis Alberto Acuña 85
Casa Museo Etnocultural 290
Casa Museo Mosquera 238
Casa Museo Pedro Nel Gómez 187
Casa Museo Quinta de Bolívar 46
Centro de Interpretación de la Cestería de Bejucos 225

Map Pages **000**
Photo Pages **000**

Centro de Interpretación Natütama 290
Centro de Investigaciones Paleontológicas 89
Colección de Arte 43-4
Convento & Iglesia de San Pedro Claver 123-5
Espacio KB 47-71
Lighthouse 177
Maloka 50-1
Museo Arqueológico 250
Museo Arqueológico Calima 237
Museo Arqueológico Eliécer Silva Célis 92
Museo Arqueológico la Merced 229
Museo Arquidiocesano de Arte Religioso 238
Museo Botero 11, 42-3, **11**
Museo Casa de Bolívar 109
Museo Casa de la Memoria 187
Museo Colonial 44
Museo de Antioquia 189
Museo de Arte Moderno 127
Museo de Arte Moderno de Medellín 187
Museo de Arte Moderno La Tertulia 229
Museo de Arte Moderno Ramírez Villamizar 114
Museo de Arte Religioso 201
Museo de Arte Religoso La Merced 229
Museo de Historia Natural 239
Museo de la Independencia – Casa del Florero 45
Museo del Arte Religioso 162
Museo del Carmen 84-5
Museo del Oro 10, 46, 140, 253, **10**
Museo del Oro Quimbaya 219
Museo del Oro Zenú 125
Museo Etnográfico 250
Museo Etnográfico Amazónico 283
Museo Guillermo Valencia 238-9
Museo Histórico Policial 44
Museo Juan del Corral 201
Museo Militar 45
Museo Nacional 47
Museo Naval del Caribe 127
Museo Taminango de Artes y Tradiciones 253-4
Palacio de la Inquisición 123
Quinta de San Pedro Alejandrino 139
music 23, 306-7

N

Nariño 252-7
national parks & reserves 260, 279, 312-13
Área Natural Única Los Estoraques 116
Ciénega la Caimanera 163-4
Estación Septiembre 264
Parque Nacional Natural Amacayacu 289
Parque Nacional Natural El Cocuy 98-100
Parque Nacional Natural El Tuparro 279
Parque Nacional Natural Ensenada de Utría 265-6
Parque Nacional Natural Farallones de Cali 236
Parque Nacional Natural Isla Gorgona 271
Parque Nacional Natural Los Nevados 16, 212-15, **214**, **16**
Parque Nacional Natural Puracé 251
Parque Nacional Natural Sierra de La Macarena 277, **272**
Parque Ucumarí 218-19
Reserva Ecológica Río Blanco 212
Reserva Natural Gallito de la Roca 203
Reserva Natural Palmarí 291-2
Reserva Natural Zacambú 292
Santuario de Fauna y Flora Los Flamencos 156
Santuario Otún Quimbaya 218
nature reserves 314, *see also* national parks & reserves
Nemocón 58
Nevado de Santa Isabel 213
Nevado del Ruiz 213
Nevado del Tolima 215
newspapers 325
Nuquí 266-7

O

Observatorio Astronómico 44
Observatorio Astronómico Astrosur 251-2
opening hours 19, 325
orientation 324
outdoor activities 8-9, 28-32

P

Pacific Coast 259-71, **261**
climate 258
highlights 261
travel seasons 258
painting 308
Palomino 150-2
Pamplona 114-15
Pance 236
paragliding 30
paramilitaries 299, 301, 316-17
parks & gardens
Jardín Botánico 189
Jardín Botánico del Quindío 219
Jardin Botánico Eloy Valenzuela 109
Los Yarumos 207
Mundo Amazónico 283
Parque El Gallineral 101
Parque Metropolitano Simón Bolívar 47-50
Parque Nacional del Chicamocha 108
Parque Nacional Natural Amacayacu 289
Parque Nacional Natural El Cocuy 16, 98-100, **16**
Parque Nacional Natural El Tuparro 279
Parque Nacional Natural Ensenada de Utría 265-6
Parque Nacional Natural Isla Gorgona 271
Parque Nacional Natural Los Nevados 16, 212-15, **214**, **16**
Parque Nacional Natural (PNN) Old Providence McBean Lagoon 177
Parque Nacional Natural Puracé 251
Parque Nacional Natural Tayrona 14, 148-50, **148-9**, **14**
Parque Para Las Artes 104
Parque Santander 283
Parque Ucumarí 218-19
Pasto 252-5, **253**
people 304-5
Pereira 215-17
Piedra del Peñol 200-1
Plan Colombia 302
planning 18-19, *see also individual regions*
budgeting 19
calendar of events 20-1
Colombia's regions 34-6
internet resources 19
itineraries 22-5
travel seasons 18-19, 20-1
plants 312
Playa Almejal 264
Playa Blanca (Cartagena region) 138
Playa Blanca (Tolú) 164
Playa de Belén 116-17
Playa Mecana 264
Playa Taroa 159
plazas
Plaza Central de Usaquén 47
Plaza de Bolívar 41, 125, **38**
Plaza de la Aduana 126
Plaza de los Coches 126
Plaza Mayor 83
Plazoleta de las Esculturas 187
Plazoleta del Chorro de Quevedo 44
Popayán 238-43, **240-1**
poporo 142
population 305
postal services 325-6
pottery 90
Pozos Naturales 276
Providencia 169-81, 176-81, 310, **171**, **178**
accommodation 179-80
activities 177-9
diving 175
drinking & nightlife 181
festivals & events 179
food 180-1
highlights 171
sights 177
tourist information 181
travel seasons 168
travel to/from 181
travel within 181
weather 168
public holidays 326-7
Pueblito 149
Puente de Boyacá 87

Puerto Nariño 289-91
Punta Gallinas 159
Punta Huína 263-4

R

rafting 30, *see also* white-water rafting
Ráquira 90
religion 306
Reserva Ecológica Río Blanco 212
Río Claro 205
Río Yavarí 291-2
Riohacha 156-7
rivers
  Las Gachas 113
robbery 317
rock climbing 30, 189

S

safe travel 316-18
  hitchhiking 333
Salento 222-4, **223**
salsa 15, 306
Salt Cathedral 58
San Agustín 243-8, **244**
San Andrés 169-81, 170-6, **171**, **172**, **174**
  activities 170-2
  climate 168
  diving 175
  drinking & nightlife 175
  food 173-5
  highlights 171
  sights 170
  tourist information 176
  travel seasons 168
  travel to/from 176
  travel within 176
San Gil 100-4, **101**
San José del Guaviare 276-7
Santa Fe de Antioquia 201-3, **202**
Santa Marta 139-44, **140**
Santander 81-117, 100-14, **82**
  climate 80
  highlights 82
  history 83
  travel seasons 80
Santuario de Iguaque 91-2
Santuario de Las Lajas 257
Santuario Otún Quimbaya 218
Sapzurro 165-7
scuba diving, *see* diving, snorkeling
sea travel 330-1
Semana Santa 23
shopping 326, *see also individual locations*
  language 339
Sierra Nevada del Cocuy 94-100, **95**
Silvia 242
smoking 325
snorkeling 31
  Providencia 177-9
  San Andrés 172
soccer 305
Sogamoso 92
Southwest Colombia 227-57, **228**
  climate 226
  highlights 228
  travel seasons 226
sports 72
Sugamuxi 93
surfing
  El Chocó 262
  Guachalito 269
  Termales 270
Sutamarchán 89
swimming
  Balneario Hurtado 160
  Balneario La Mina 159
  Minca 145
  Pozos Azules 91
  San Gil 102
  Valledupar 159-60
  Villa de Leyva 85

T

Taganga 147-8
taxis 335
Tayrona 14, 153, **14**
telephone services 327
Termales 270
Termales de Santa Rosa 217
Termales San Vicente 217-18
theft 317
thermal baths
  Agua Hirviendo 243
  Termales Aguatibia 243
  Termales de Santa Rosa 217
  Termales El Otoño 211
  Termales San Vicente 217-18
  Termales Tierra Viva 211-12
Tierradentro 248-51, **249**
time 327
time zones 18
tipping 325
toilets 327
Tolú 163-4
tourist information 327
tours 334
  Barichara 105-6
  Bogotá 51-3
  Caño Cristales 277-8
  Ciudad Perdida 152-5
  Filandia 225
  Guatapé 199
  Islas de San Bernardo 164
  Islas del Rosario 136-7
  Jurubidá 268
  Leticia 283-5
  Manizales 207-8
  Minca 145
  Parque Nacional Natural El Cocuy 98-9
  Parque Nacional Natural Los Nevados 213-15
  Pereira 215
  Riohacha 156
  Salento 222
  Santa Marta 140
  Taganga 147
  Tolú 164
  Villa de Leyva 85-6
train travel 335
transportation 329-35
  language 339-40
travel to/from Colombia 19, 329-31
travel within Colombia 19, 331-5
trekking, *see* hiking
Tunja 86
TV 325

U

Uribe 302-3

V

vacations 326-7
Valle de Cocora 225
Valledupar 159-60
vallenato 306
Valley of the Sun 93
Villa de Leyva 83-9, **84**
Villavicencio 274
Villavieja 252
Virgen Morenita de Güicán 97
visas 18, 327-8
Volcán de Lodo El Totumo 138
Volcán Galeras 254
volcanoes
  Nevado de Santa Isabel 213
  Nevado del Ruiz 213
  Nevado del Tolima 215
  Volcán de Lodo El Totumo 138
  Volcán Galeras 254
volunteering 328

W

waterfalls 9
  Cascada Chocolatal 262
  Cascada de Amor 269
  Cascada de Marinka 145
  Cascada Guatoque 91
  Cascada La Llanera 113
  Cascada Los Caballeros 113
  Cascadas de Juan Curi 100
  Salto del Aeropuerto 262
weather, *see* climate, *individual regions*
weights 325
whale-watching 32, 262
white-water rafting 30
wildlife 284, 310-12
wildlife reserves, *see* national parks & reserves
Willys Jeep 221
windsurfing 33, 237
women travelers 328
work 328

Y

Yipao 220

Z

Zipaquirá 58
ziplining, *see* canopying
Zona Cafetera 183-6, 205-25, **184-5**
  climate 182
  highlights 184-5
  travel seasons 182

Map Pages **000**
Photo Pages **000**

Map Legend

Sights

- Beach
- Bird Sanctuary
- Buddhist
- Castle/Palace
- Christian
- Confucian
- Hindu
- Islamic
- Jain
- Jewish
- Monument
- Museum/Gallery/Historic Building
- Ruin
- Shinto
- Sikh
- Taoist
- Winery/Vineyard
- Zoo/Wildlife Sanctuary
- Other Sight

Activities, Courses & Tours

- Bodysurfing
- Diving
- Canoeing/Kayaking
- Course/Tour
- Sento Hot Baths/Onsen
- Skiing
- Snorkeling
- Surfing
- Swimming/Pool
- Walking
- Windsurfing
- Other Activity

Sleeping

- Sleeping
- Camping
- Hut/Shelter

Eating

- Eating

Drinking & Nightlife

- Drinking & Nightlife
- Cafe

Entertainment

- Entertainment

Shopping

- Shopping

Information

- Bank
- Embassy/Consulate
- Hospital/Medical
- Internet
- Police
- Post Office
- Telephone
- Toilet
- Tourist Information
- Other Information

Geographic

- Beach
- Gate
- Hut/Shelter
- Lighthouse
- Lookout
- Mountain/Volcano
- Oasis
- Park
- Pass
- Picnic Area
- Waterfall

Population

- Capital (National)
- Capital (State/Province)
- City/Large Town
- Town/Village

Transport

- Airport
- Border crossing
- Bus
- Cable car/Funicular
- Cycling
- Ferry
- Metro station
- Monorail
- Parking
- Petrol station
- Subway/Subte station
- Taxi
- Train station/Railway
- Tram
- Underground station
- Other Transport

Routes

- Tollway
- Freeway
- Primary
- Secondary
- Tertiary
- Lane
- Unsealed road
- Road under construction
- Plaza/Mall
- Steps
- Tunnel
- Pedestrian overpass
- Walking Tour
- Walking Tour detour
- Path/Walking Trail

Boundaries

- International
- State/Province
- Disputed
- Regional/Suburb
- Marine Park
- Cliff
- Wall

Hydrography

- River, Creek
- Intermittent River
- Canal
- Water
- Dry/Salt/Intermittent Lake
- Reef

Areas

- Airport/Runway
- Beach/Desert
- Cemetery (Christian)
- Cemetery (Other)
- Glacier
- Mudflat
- Park/Forest
- Sight (Building)
- Sportsground
- Swamp/Mangrove

Note: Not all symbols displayed above appear on the maps in this book

Tom Masters
Tom has always had a taste for the remote, the unknown and the forbidden, dating from a childhood fascination with the Soviet Union. These interests have led to a writing career that has taken him to little visited spots all over the world, including North Korea, the Arctic, Congo and Siberia. Since escaping the English countryside at 16, Tom has made London and Berlin home. He currently lives in Berlin and can be found online at www.ambiguations.com.

After graduating with a degree in Russian literature from the University of London, Tom went to work in Russia as a journalist at *The St Petersburg Times*. This first writing job took him on to work at the BBC World Service in London, and as a freelance contributor to newspapers and magazines around the world. He has also spent several years working in documentary production for UK and US television companies.

Kevin Raub
Atlanta native Kevin Raub started his career as a music journalist in New York, working for *Men's Journal* and *Rolling Stone* magazines. He ditched the rock 'n' roll lifestyle for travel writing and has written over 95 Lonely Planet guides, focused mainly on Brazil, Chile, Colombia, USA, India, Italy and Portugal. Raub also contributes to a variety of travel magazines in both the USA and UK. Along the way, the self-confessed hophead is in constant search of wildly high IBUs in local beers. Find him at www.kevinraub.net or follow on Twitter and Instagram (@RaubOnTheRoad).

Raub has contributed to a variety of publications including *Travel+Leisure*, *Condé Nast Traveller* and *New York Times T Magazine*, among others.

Brendan Sainsbury
Born and raised in the UK in a town that never merits a mention in any guidebook (Andover, Hampshire), Brendan spent the holidays of his youth caravanning in the English Lake District and didn't leave Blighty until he was nineteen. Making up for lost time, he's since squeezed 70 countries into a sometimes precarious existence as a writer and professional vagabond. His rocking chair memories will probably include staging a performance of 'A Comedy of Errors' at a school in war-torn Angola, running 150 miles across the Sahara Desert in the Marathon des Sables, and hitchhiking from Cape Town to Kilimanjaro with an early, dog-eared copy of LP's Africa on a Shoestring. In the last eleven years, he has written over 40 books for Lonely Planet from Castro's Cuba to the canyons of Peru. When not scribbling research notes, Brendan likes partaking in ridiculous 'endurance' races, strumming old Clash songs on the guitar, and experiencing the pain and occasional pleasures of following Southampton Football Club.

OUR ST

A beat-up old car, a few dollars in the pocket and a sense of adventure. In 1972 that's all Tony and Maureen Wheeler needed for the trip of a lifetime – across Europe and Asia overland to Australia. It took several months, and at the end – broke but inspired – they sat at their kitchen table writing and stapling together their first travel guide, *Across Asia on the Cheap*. Within a week they'd sold 1500 copies. Lonely Planet was born.

Today, Lonely Planet has offices in Tennessee, Dublin and Beijing, with a network of over 2000 contributors in every corner of the globe. We share Tony's belief that 'a great guidebook should do three things: inform, educate and amuse'.

OUR WRITERS

Jade Bremner

Jade has been a journalist for more than 15 years. She has lived in and reported on four different regions. It's no coincidence many of her favourite places have some of the best waves in the world. Jade has edited travel magazines and sections for *Time Out* and *Radio Times* and has contributed to *The Times*, *CNN* and *The Independent*. She feels privileged to share tales from this wonderful planet we call home and is always looking for the next adventure.

Alex Egerton

A news journalist by trade, Alex has worked for magazines, newspapers and media outlets on five continents. Having had his fill of musty newsrooms and the insatiable corporate appetite for superficial news, Alex decided to leap into travel writing in order to escape the mundane. He spends most of his time on the road checking under mattresses, sampling suspicious street food and chatting with locals as part of the research process for travel articles and guidebooks. A keen adventurer, Alex has hiked through remote jungles in Colombia, explored isolated tributaries of the mighty Mekong and taken part in the first kayak descent of a number of remote waterways in Nicaragua. When not on the road, you'll find him at home amongst the colonial splendor of Popayán in southern Colombia.

Anna Kaminski

Originally from the Soviet Union, Anna grew up in Cambridge, UK. She graduated from the University of Warwick with a degree in Comparative American Studies, a background in the history, culture and literature of the Americas and the Caribbean, and an enduring love of Latin America. Her restless wanderings led her to settle briefly in Oaxaca and Bangkok and her flirtation with criminal law saw her volunteering as a lawyer's assistant in the courts, ghettos and prisons of Kingson, Jamaica. Anna has contributed to almost 30 Lonely Planet titles. When not on the road, Anna calls London home.

Published by Lonely Planet Global Limited
CRN 554153
9th edition – Nov 2021
ISBN 978 1 78701 680 4

10 9 8 7 6 5 4 3 2 1
Printed in Malaysia